"This important collection of works grounds the debate on the capacity of a design to effect change as it performs assigned tasks. The convergence of views in the same volume provides a stimulating tempest of disagreements and contradictions, and therein lies its value. Here, performativity is a function of interdependencies, integration, interaction, and responsiveness between tangible and intangible forces and entities. In some essays, the focus is on the natural, the human, and the built. In others, it is on the world we create in all of its dimensions, or on abandoning a human-centric view altogether for an interconnected and interdependent systems perspective."

**Carmina Sánchez-del-Valle, Professor of Architecture,
Hampton University, Virginia**

The Routledge Companion to Paradigms of Performativity in Design and Architecture

The Routledge Companion to Paradigms of Performativity in Design and Architecture focuses on a non-linear, multilateral, ethical way of design thinking, positioning the design process as a journey. It expands on the multiple facets and paradigms of performative design thinking as an emerging trend in design methodology.

This edited collection explores the meaning of performativity by examining its relevance in conjunction with three fundamental principles: firmness, commodity and delight. The scope and broader meaning of performativity, performative architecture and performance-based building design are discussed in terms of how they influence today's design thinking.

With contributions from 44 expert practitioners, educators and researchers, this volume engages theory, history, technology and the human aspects of performative design thinking and its implications for the future of design.

Mitra Kanaani, D.Arch, MCP, FAIA, is the Professor of Design, Research and Tectonics and former Chair at NewSchool of Architecture & Design, San Diego. She is an editor and author, an activist with the Education Is Not a Crime and Education Under Fire movements and an Affiliated Global Faculty of the Baha'i Institute for Higher Education (BIHE) Architecture Program.

The Routledge Companion to Paradigms of Performativity in Design and Architecture

Using Time to Craft an Enduring, Resilient and Relevant Architecture

Edited by Mitra Kanaani

NEW YORK AND LONDON

First published 2020
by Routledge
52 Vanderbilt Avenue, New York, NY 10017

and by Routledge
2 Park Square, Milton Park, Abingdon, Oxon, OX14 4RN

Routledge is an imprint of the Taylor & Francis Group, an informa business

© 2020 selection and editorial matter, Mitra Kanaani; individual chapters, the contributors

The right of Mitra Kanaani to be identified as the author of the editorial material, and of the authors for their individual chapters, has been asserted in accordance with sections 77 and 78 of the Copyright, Designs and Patents Act 1988.

All rights reserved. No part of this book may be reprinted or reproduced or utilized in any form or by any electronic, mechanical, or other means, now known or hereafter invented, including photocopying and recording, or in any information storage or retrieval system, without permission in writing from the publishers.

Trademark notice: Product or corporate names may be trademarks or registered trademarks, and are used only for identification and explanation without intent to infringe.

Library of Congress Cataloging-in-Publication Data
Names: Kanaani, Mitra, editor.
Title: The Routledge companion to paradigms of performativity in design and architecture : using time to craft an enduring, resilient and relevant architecture / edited by Mitra Kanaani.
Identifiers: LCCN 2019029012 (print) | LCCN 2019029013 (ebook) | ISBN 9780367076191 (hardback) | ISBN 9780429021640 (ebook)
Subjects: LCSH: Design–Philosophy. | Architecture–Philosophy.
Classification: LCC NK1505 .R68 2020 (print) | LCC NK1505 (ebook) | DDC 745.4–dc23
LC record available at https://lccn.loc.gov/2019029012
LC ebook record available at https://lccn.loc.gov/2019029013

ISBN: 978-0-367-07619-1 (hbk)
ISBN: 978-0-429-02164-0 (ebk)

Typeset in Bembo
by Swales & Willis, Exeter, Devon, UK

To my grandfather Abbas Farahmehr, who opened my eyes to the wondrous world of architecture and design, and to my uncle Shahrbaraz Farahmehr, two prolific architects, designers and engineers who became my first sources of inspiration and role models ... and to all my students who throughout the years have kept this fire aflame, and have stimulated me.

Mitra

Contents

List of Contributors   xiii

Preface: Paradigms of Performativity, as a Journey as destination in Today's Design-Thinking   xvii
Mitra Kanaani

Foreword: 'Unchained'   xx
Brett Steele

Introduction: Performance Engrained   xxii
Michael U. Hensel

Prologue: Works at Work   xxiv
David Leatherbarrow

1   Performances of Architectures and Environments: En Route to a Theory and Framework   1
Michael U. Hensel and Defne Sunguroğlu Hensel

2   Social Performativity: Architecture's Contribution to Societal Progress   13
Patrik Schumacher

3   Informing Form: The Influence of Morphogenesis and Performativity in Practice   32
Alvin Huang

4   Architecture of Change: Towards Transformable Architecture   46
Branko Kolarevic

5   Dynamic Aesthetics and Advanced Geometries: The Meaning of Style and Form-making in Performative Design   63
Andrew Whalley

6   The Paradoxes of Performative Architecture: Toward a New Discipline and a New Agenda for the Profession   83
Thomas Fisher

Contents

7		Poetics of Design Beyond Intelligences: The Meaning of Embodied Aesthetics and Simulation of Mood in Performative Design and Architecture	94
	7.1	Poetics of Design: A House Is a Tree Is an Insect Is a Computer Is a Human *Mariana Ibañez*	94
	7.2	Poetics and More in Performative Architecture: Towards a Neuroscience of Dynamic Experience and Design *Michael A. Arbib*	103
8		The Cognitive Dimension: The Role of Research in Performative Design Process	115
	8.1	The Theory *Mitra Kanaani*	115
	8.2	Theory Put into Research Practice *Joon-Ho Choi*	132
9		Integrated Design Thinking: Inter- and Transdisciplinarity in Performative Design Methodology	146
	9.1	The Theory *Marvin J. Malecha*	146
	9.2	Research Case Studies *Joon-Ho Choi*	162
10		Performative Biotechnical Forms: Culturalizing the Microbiota from High-Tech to Bio-Tech Architecture *Claudia Pasquero and Marco Poletto*	174
11		Searching for a "Bioclimatic Law" in Architecture: Comfort and the Ethics of (Human) Performance *William W. Braham*	189
12		Ecological Emergences: The Milieu for Performative Paradigms *Caroline O'Donnell*	210
13		Performative Urban Environments and the Concept of the Future Smart Cities	219
	13.1	The Posthuman City: Reflections on the City of the Near Future *Alejandro Zaera-Polo*	219

	13.2	Toward Establishing Measures for Performative Urban Environments: A Critical Position on Shaping the Future of Smart Cities *Lucy Campbell, Mitra Kanaani and Michael Stepner*	228
14		Seeking Material Capacity and Embedded Responsiveness: Design and Fabrication of Physically Programmed Architectural Constructs *Achim Menges and Steffen Reichert*	240
15		Resiliency in Performativity: A Shared Vision with Sustainability	260
	15.1	Preamble *R.K. Stewart*	260
	15.2	Resiliency in Performativity: A Shared Vision with Sustainability *Terri Peters*	263
16		Architectonic Design and Computation in Performative Buildings *Brady Peters*	274
17		Simulation Tools for Social Performance: Immersive Building Simulation *Robert R. Neumayr*	287
18		Performative Material Morphologies *Vera Parlac*	301
19		Dynamic Vocabularies	317
	19.1	Technology of Expressive, Communicative and Responsive Surface Architecture and Design of Building Skins and Enclosure Systems in Performative Design Forms *Michael Fox*	317
	19.2	Active Façade Tectonics: Sensing and Reacting to the Wicked, Complex Entanglements of Building Envelope Architecting *Douglas E. Noble*	332
20		Energy-Performative Architecture: Working with the Forces of Nature to Optimize Energy Flows and the Impact on Phenomenology of Architectural Form *Brian Cody*	341
21		Adaptation: Bio-Receptive Materials with a New Outlook on Performativity and Sustainability *David Benjamin*	362

Contents

22	Phenomenology of Interactivity: Patterns of Human Interaction with Urban Built Environments and the Impact of Computer Automation *Mitra Kanaani*	370
23	The Cybernetics of Cybernetics: A Performative Idiom *Theodore Spyropoulos*	389
24	Performative Design Strategies: The Synthesis Process of a Woven Complexity *Pieter de Wilde and Clarice Bleil de Souza*	403
25	Design Sensibilities: Intangible and Qualitative Design Factors in Performative Design: Enactive Experience in the (Neuro)science of Form *Kristine Mun*	416
26	Health and Wellbeing: Performance-Based Design Concepts for a Healthful Built Environment and Human Equilibrium *Dak Kopec*	431
27	Reciprocal Relationships of Materiality and Human Engagement: Expanding the Role of Material Systems towards Sensorial Socio-Spatial Agency *Sean Ahlquist*	443
28	Computing Performativity: The Role of Coding Within BIM for the Execution of Performative Design Concepts *Karen Kensek*	464
29	Professional Practice and the Performative Delivery of Architecture: Precision, Prediction, Value *Phil Bernstein*	485
30	Performing Architecture: A Reflection on the Rituals and Procedures of Practice *Kyle Miller*	492
31	Educating Accountable Architects: The Future Performers *Ted Landsmark*	502

Epilogue: Towards Responsibly Anticipatory Evolvable Architecture for the Anthropocene 517
Jim Dator

Index 527

Contributors

Sean Ahlquist, an Associate Professor at the University of Michigan – Taubman College of Architecture and Urban Planning, develops novel lightweight structures and computational design methodologies to research the linkages between spatial tectonics and human behavior.

Michael A. Arbib is an expert in computer science and neuroscience. After 30 years at USC, he is now Adjunct Professor of Psychology at UCSD, and contributing faculty at NewSchool of Architecture & Design, San Diego.

David Benjamin is Founding Principal of The Living and Associate Professor at Columbia GSAPP. He has won many design prizes, including the Young Architects Award from the Museum of Modern Art and a Holcim Sustainability Award.

Phil Bernstein is an architect and technologist, and currently an Associate Dean and Senior Lecturer at Yale School of Architecture. His most recent book is *Architecture Design Data: Practice Competency in the Era of Computation* (2018).

Clarice Bleil de Souza is Associate Professor (Senior Lecturer) at the Welsh School of Architecture, Cardiff University. Her research focuses on the use of simulation tools in building design, user-centric simulation and design decision making.

William W. Braham is a Professor of Architecture at the University of Pennsylvania, where he is currently Director of the MSD Environmental Building Design and of the Center for Environmental Building + Design.

Lucy Campbell is Librarian of the Richard P. Welsh Library at NewSchool of Architecture & Design. She holds a BA in History and American Studies from the University of Sussex, and a Master's in Library and Information Science from UCL.

Joon-Ho Choi is an Associate Professor and Associate Dean of Research and Creative Work in the USC School of Architecture. He is also the Director of Human-Building Integration Research Group in the USC School of Architecture.

Brian Cody is a Professor at Graz University of Technology and CEO of the consulting firm Energy Design Cody. His focus in research, teaching and practice is on maximizing the energy performance of buildings and cities.

Contributors

Jim Dator is Professor Emeritus and former Director of the Hawaii Research Center for Futures Studies, Department of Political Science, University of Hawaii at Manoa. He also taught at Rikkyo University (Tokyo), the University of Maryland, Virginia Tech, and the University of Toronto.

Pieter de Wilde is a Professor at the Department of the Built Environment, University of Plymouth. He is author of the book *Building Performance Analysis*, and a prominent member of the International Building Performance Simulation Association.

Thomas Fisher is Professor of Architecture and Director of the Minnesota Design Center, and former dean of the College of Design at the University of Minnesota. He has just completed his tenth book, also published by Routledge.

Michael Fox holds a Master of Science from MIT. He is a registered architect, author, researcher, professor and contractor and the Founding Principal of FoxLin Architects. He is the author of the books *Interactive Architecture* and *Adaptive World*, and the Past President of ACADIA.

Defne Sunguroğlu Hensel is an architect. She directs the practice OCEAN Architecture | Environment together with Michael U. Hensel. She is a Postdoctoral Researcher at the Technical University Munich and lecturer at Vienna University of Technology.

Michael U. Hensel is an architect. He directs the practice OCEAN Architecture | Environment together with Defne Sunguroğlu Hensel. He is a Professor and leads the Digital Architecture and Planning Department at Vienna University of Technology.

Alvin Huang is the Founder of Synthesis Design + Architecture and an Associate Professor at the USC School of Architecture. His work focuses on the integrated application of material performance, emergent design technologies and digital fabrication.

Mariana Ibañez is an Argentinian architect involved in practice, academia and research. She is an Associate Professor at MIT and Principal of Ibañez Kim. Recent publications include *Paradigms in Computing* and *Organization or Design*.

Mitra Kanaani is the Professor of Design, Research and Tectonics and former Chair at NewSchool of Architecture & Design. She is an editor, author and an activist with the Education Is Not a Crime and Education Under Fire movements and an Affiliated Global Faculty of the BIHE Architecture Program.

Karen Kensek is Professor of Practice at USC School of Architecture. Her interests include BIM, building science, virtual reconstructions, and digital design. She is the author of *Building Information Modeling*, available in English (Routledge 2014), French, Chinese, and Portuguese.

Branko Kolarevic holds doctoral and master's degrees in design from Harvard University and an Architectural Engineering degree from the University of Belgrade. Branko is a Professor and Dean of the College of Architecture and Design at the NJIT. He has authored, edited and co-edited several books on performative architecture.

Dak Kopec, an Associate Professor at UNLV, has authored several books used by design educators. He is a two-time Polsky Prize winner, credited with developing the first low-residency program in designs for health, and uses interdisciplinary approaches for person-centered design.

Contributors

Ted Landsmark is a Distinguished Professor at Northeastern University, Boston Architectural College President Emeritus, and Past President of the Association of Collegiate Schools of Architecture and the National Architectural Accrediting Board.

David Leatherbarrow is a Professor of Architecture at the University of Pennsylvania who teaches architectural design, theory and history. Recent books include: *Twentieth Century Architecture, Three Cultural Ecologies, Architecture Oriented Otherwise, Topographical Stories* and *Surface Architecture.*

Marvin J. Malecha is President of the NewSchool of Architecture & Design in San Diego. His career has spanned academic leadership, professional association leadership and the practice of architecture.

Achim Menges is a Registered Architect in Frankfurt and Full Professor at the University of Stuttgart, where he is the Founding Director of the Institute for Computational Design and Construction.

Kyle Miller is an Assistant Professor in Syracuse University's School of Architecture and Co-founder of Possible Mediums, a curatorial project composed of events and a publication showcasing design investigations based in speculative architectural mediums.

Kristine Mun is Head of Neuroscience for Architecture at NewSchool of Architecture & Design and an Advisory Council member for the Academy of Neuroscience for Architecture at Salk Institute for Biological Studies in San Diego.

Robert R. Neumayr is a Registered Architect in Vienna, a Senior Researcher at IoA – University of Applied Arts Vienna, a Lecturer at the Institute of Structure and Design at the University Innsbruck, and Founder of unsquare.org.

Douglas E. Noble is Associate Dean of Academic Affairs at the University of Southern California. He is Chair of the PhD Program and Director of the Graduate Building Science programs.

Caroline O'Donnell is the Edgar A. Tafel Associate Professor and Director of the M.Arch Program at Cornell University. She is Principal of CODA (Caroline O'Donnell Architecture) and author of *Niche Tactics: Generative Relationships between Architecture and Site.*

Vera Parlac is an Associate Professor at the NJIT School of Architecture and a registered architect in Pennsylvania. Her current design and research are focused on responsive material systems and informed by contemporary models in biology, material science research, soft robotics and mechatronic systems.

Claudia Pasquero is Co-founder and Director of ecoLogicStudio, Professor of Synthetic Landscapes at the University of Innsbruck, Director of the Urban Morphogenesis Lab at The Bartlett UCL and Senior Tutor at the IAAC in Barcelona. She has been Unit Master at the AA and a Visiting Critic at Cornell University and Angewandte in Vienna.

Brady Peters is an Assistant Professor at the University of Toronto, a Director of Smartgeometry, and the author of *Computing the Environment*. He previously worked as an Associate Partner with Foster + Partners SMG.

Contributors

Terri Peters is an Assistant Professor in the Department of Architectural Science at Ryerson University in Toronto. She is a registered architect in the UK and holds a PhD in Sustainable Housing from Aarhus Architecture School in Denmark.

Marco Poletto is an architect, author and entrepreneur. He is Co-founder and Director of ecoLogic-Studio and the Photosynthetica venture (www.photosynthetica.co.uk/). He holds an MA from the Architectural Association and PhD from RMIT Melbourne titled "The Urbansphere."

Steffen Reichert holds a PhD from the Institute for Computational Design and Construction at the University of Stuttgart, and a Master of Product Design from the Academy of Art and Design Offenbach. He also holds a Master of Science in Design and Computation from MIT.

Nasim Rowshan (illustrator) has a B.Arch from the BIHE, and an M.Arch from the Yale School of Architecture. She is the recipient of the James Gamble Rogers Fellowship and the Yale Architecture Drawing Prize, as well as the Soane Fellowship.

Patrik Schumacher is Principal of Zaha Hadid Architects and has led the practice since Zaha Hadid's passing. He founded the Design Research Laboratory at the Architectural Association in London and held the John Portman Chair in Architecture at Harvard's Graduate School of Design.

Theodore Spyropoulos is an architect and educator. He has a PhD from University College of London, Bartlett School of Architecture. Theodore is the Director of the Architectural Association's Design Research Lab in London, Professor of Architecture at the Staedelschule in Frankfurt and Resident Artist at Somerset House.

Brett Steele has been Dean of the UCLA School of the Arts & Architecture since August 2017. For 12 years he was Director of the Architectural Association in London.

Michael Stepner is a Professor of Architecture and Urban Design and former Dean at NewSchool of Architecture & Design in San Diego. His professional career spans academia and the public and private sectors. He is the former City Architect and Acting Planning Director for the City of San Diego.

R.K. Stewart is a leader in project management/delivery, building performance and design education. His experience includes Gensler, Perkins+Will, and SOM. He served as Chair of the National Institute of Building Sciences in 2013, and President of the American Institute of Architects in 2007.

Andrew Whalley is Chairman of Grimshaw, an award-winning global architecture practice. He has played key roles in many projects, including the Eden Project in Cornwall, the redevelopment of historic Paddington Station in London and New York City's Fulton Center.

Alejandro Zaera-Polo is Founder of AZPML and FOA, a Professor and former Dean at Princeton University School of Architecture and a widely published architectural theorist, and was Director of the Seoul Biennale 2017.

Preface

Paradigms of Performativity, as a Journey as Destination in Today's Design-Thinking

Mitra Kanaani

This book expands on the multiple facets and paradigms of *performative design thinking* as an emerging trend in design methodology. It focuses on performative design not as an "ism," but as a non-linear, multilateral, ethical way of thinking, positioning the design process as *journey as destination*. The chapters of this book corroborate the multiple facets and viewpoints of this amazingly engaging journey.

Performance-based design theory asserts *building performance* as a guiding principle towards the creation of intelligent and novel architectural forms. The concept of performativity is deeply rooted in the order of the world and peoples' way of living throughout history and around our world. However, modern technological advancements have added broader, more sophisticated dimensions to the meaning of design through the concept of performativity. This resonates with Christopher Alexander's (1979) introduction to *The Timeless Way of Building*: "a new theory of architecture, building and planning, which has at its core that age-old process by which the people of a society have always pulled the order of their world from their own being."

The paradigm of performative design thinking is broad, yet in essence focuses on humans as *interactive users of built spaces*, and buildings as *intelligent biospheres* that act as ecosystems to preserve, protect, and sustain. Thus, performative design inherently intertwines the concepts of "sustainability" and "resilience." Performativity spans a multitude of realms, from the technical to the social, and ranges from quantitative to qualitative design factors. Form generation based on performative design strategies is on one hand rooted in intangible and immeasurable factors such as cultural and behavioral performances. On the other, it expands to the more quantifiable performative systematic components of the building, including, but not limited to structural, enclosure, climate control, and acoustical systems. In performative architecture, the designer establishes a *function* or *continuum* of a dynamic relationship between a *subject* (user) and an *object* (spatial formal entity). This current logical relationship identifies three main elements: the Function, Form, and Subject, which are considered drivers for performance-based design thinking. In reality, the multiple paradigms of performative design thinking are complicated and consist of overlaid information, signifying the meanings of performance in architectural design with respect to form or geometry, and expression or appearance. Once again, this meaning echoes Christopher Alexander's (1964) reference to design, in his book *Notes on the Synthesis of Form*, as a "number of nested, overlapped form-context boundaries in the mind of the designer" (p. 18). This concept is referred to in Michael Hensel's *Performance-Oriented Architecture* (2013) as, "Non-Discrete Architectures that unfold their performative capacity by being embedded in nested orders of complexity to numerous conditions and processes" (p. 31).

Preface

This book explores the meaning of *performativity* by examining its relevance in conjunction with the three fundamental principles, known as the Vitruvian triad: *Firmness* (Materiality and Structures), *Commodity* (Program and Spatial Qualities), and *Delight* (Gestalt and Poetics). However, in performative architecture, the focus on the additional component of context or *Genius Loci*, meaning *the prevailing spirit or character of a place*, has transcended the influence of the three pillars of Vitruvius' triad, to higher levels of agency, interweaving complexity and importance. In a broader sense, *Genius Loci*, once regarded as a *microcosm or encapsulated context*, in performative architecture is expandable to a broader *macrocosm* of contextual elements, and is highly intertwined with the multiple concepts of sustainability as an interface.

This book focuses on the scope and broader meanings of multiple facets of *performativity, performative architecture*, and *performance-based building design*, as they influence today's design thinking. For some topics, multiple viewpoints are offered by expert authors. Through analyses and arguments set forth by contributors, the book is a repository, demonstrating the vast boundaries of performativity in design and architecture. In its broad meanings, performative architecture, by integrating the factor of time as the fourth dimension in design thinking, embraces sustainable design protocols towards a timeless architecture, which resembles endurance, relevance, and inter-disciplinarity, as well as trans-disciplinarity.

Research and exploration in digital technologies play major roles in form-making and identification and adoption of performative goals. *The Routledge Companion to Performativity in Design and Architecture* discusses how varied approaches imbued in scientific inquiry and digital applications have become major instruments in animating forms pursued by teams of practicing designers, engineers, scientists, and social and cultural theorists. It attempts to unravel the different modi operandi adopted by stakeholders in pursuit of performative design objectives. This book expands on concepts and approaches in performance-based design methodology, in order to establish the ultimate meaning of *integrated design thinking*. This includes exploration of the methodology of applied techniques in immersive building simulation and rapid prototyping, which results in the proliferation of intelligent morphogenetic forms with inherent performative potentials. Ultimately, it makes projections to the expected current and future roles and responsibilities of architects and designers, as *performers of performance*.

Performative design represents a renaissance in design methodology. Although in the early stages of recognition, it is a novel approach in design thinking and architectural practice. It represents a renewal of an ancient mentality in design thinking and is a revival of timelessness in architecture, combined with formal purity and honesty in material use and expression towards an applied and meaningful art of detailing. The novel concepts of performativity revolve around time as a continuum *to craft an enduring, resilient and relevant architecture*. By introducing new methods of scientific inquiry and utilizing advanced technologies, performative architecture is providing opportunities for the development of broader dimensions in form-making. Inevitably this initiates new relationships between discipline, practice, and conceptual design thinking processes in architecture. These new relationships demand understanding of the philosophy of performative design requirements and appreciation of methodologies. As we move forward, the demanded relevancy and complexity of performativity as a forum for the integrative knowledge of various scientific and cognitive fields in architecture is constantly being augmented. Moreover, this relates to the added determinant of time, as well as the inclusion of other scientific and technological determinants in the mix of design factors. In line with current transformations and demands of practice, architectural education is increasingly confronted with new requirements and expectations for integrative pedagogical specialties, which relate to the evolution of the discipline and the needs of the profession for higher levels of instrumentality and expanded understanding and knowledge for future architects.

Similarly, the image of the architect is also transforming from an old-fashioned professional expert in the design of buildings to a researcher and scientist/form-maker. Today architects are expected to be ecologically sensitive, technically informed, and socially responsible spirited provocateurs, humanitarians, and entrepreneurs. The question remains, how well can they put the satisfaction of human equilibrium at the center of their ambitions to contribute in bringing ease and well-being to our troubled planet?

The most comprehensive content of design performativity in this compilation could not have come to fruition without the contribution of 45 skillful experts, researchers, practitioners, and educators who have offered their knowledge and experience to this *Routledge Companion* book. I would like to extend my deep appreciation to this unique team of authors and in-depth thinkers who enthusiastically dedicated their time and expertise in creating thoughtful manuscripts that are rich, informative, technical, and scholarly. I would like to extend my deep gratitude to Lucy Campbell, the Librarian at NewSchool of Architecture & Design for her valuable editorial expertise and insight, and Dr. James Dator, my longtime mentor, for his forthright, in-depth, and highly stimulating and analytical viewpoints related to the paradigms of performativity in various topics of the book chapters. My final appreciation goes to my former BIHE student Nasim Rowshan and my former NewSchool student Vasili Petrushko for their skillful sketches, as well as Nourah Alaofi, Melanie Pauline Hahn, Sami Almalki, and Mohammad Khalil for their graphic contributions in the design of the book cover,[1] and also to Amin Espandiari and Soheil Sefat for their valuable assistance in the production of the images.

Note

1 The book cover is a night image of the San Diego Symphony Summer Pops Pavilion design proposal by Mitra Kanaani. Book cover credits: 3D building drawing, Nasim Rowshan, and book cover graphics, Melanie Hahn.

References

Alexander, C. (1964). *Notes on the Synthesis of Form*. Cambridge, MA: Harvard University Press.
Alexander, C. (1979). *The Timeless Way of Building*. New York, NY: Oxford University Press.
Hensel, M. (2013). *Performance-Oriented Architecture: Rethinking Architectural Design and the Built Environment*. Chichester: John Wiley & Sons.

Foreword
'Unchained'

Brett Steele

Any consideration today of such a nerdy and engineering-like word as 'performativity' within the field (let alone anything within that field of knowledge which might yet, in these still-early years of the 21st century, resemble a *discipline*) of architecture must, necessarily, acknowledge its inherent, and self-declared antagonism towards the opposite: the traditionally modern conceit of 'form' – a concept that has, for so long, served as a bedrock of modern architectural obsession, and not only interest.

That architectural interests in 'form' today now serve as the crutch for so many different kinds of formalist agendas – in relationship to so many different kinds of architectural practices, pedagogies and even personalities – suggests explanation enough for why so many, currently still so young, are looking so seriously (and deliberately) *elsewhere* for a means by which to try and do the most unexpected of disciplinary things today: to try and re-assemble the still-dis-aggregating tendencies of contemporary architectural tribalism into a larger, more coherent, disciplinary whole. It's a tough order, of course, for a field itself so interested in order itself.

Kudos here, however, to Mitra Kanaani and her latest, edited collection of emerging practices, educators and projects whose dis-aggregated interests, projects and aims can nonetheless be read as convincingly coherent around what on the surface appears a nearly-functional interest, in the performance of architectural space, materials, structures and assemblages – how things (spaces, interactions, events and more) *interact in time*, instead of a more familiar (modern) architectural interest in how things merely *exist in the time of their making*.

A disciplinary interest in a familiar topic like that of 'form' today in a good, old-fashioned, formerly modern field like 'architecture' is tired, one might say, to the point of exhaustion.

What an interest in form (and order – form's corollary, as so many modern architects have long theorized for us) has done, above all, is provide of course a means by which to triangulate the landscape of a field: that of modern architectural projects and not only personalities, owing to the very pervasiveness of form itself in the language, discourses, mental and manual working habits of architects. Whatever else form-making has provided the field of architecture, for so long, it has done this: it has provided a language by which architects were able to situate their own interests, differences and even professional identities (including, of course, their own commercial and not only cultural identities) in relationship to a broader, architectural field.

Foreword

Such language today of course is nearly arcane, within an expanded cultural sphere in which both those practicing, as well as practices themselves, continue to diversity in magnificent, unexpected and (for architecture especially) *new* ways.

This book is at the very least a refreshing and vital record of that act of diversification, amongst a younger and yet-emerging generation of practitioners and educators within their field, whose otherwise unrelated (occasionally even, antagonistic and antithetical) work in relation to one another has nonetheless been helpfully gathered together here under the most interesting of all architectural realities: that spaces, structures and materials all perform – whether acknowledged or not, by their designers, critics, theorists, users or occupants) in *time*.

For a field like modern architecture, whose origins as well as popular, professional and even critical formation in the late 19th and early 20th centuries arose alongside commercial photography and new, modern media industries that tended to represent its efforts through media that literally 'froze' images of structure, space and even their makers in time, the animate dimensions and tendencies of material, use, image and natural forces themselves (gravity, momentum, acceleration, etc.) were largely diminished, if not outright contravened – excluded – from the language, imagery and critical communication of architectural ideas.

Over the decades of the 20th century plenty of outliers of modern architecture's traditional obsession with fixed form, proportion and geometry were out there. We need here only briefly recall the materialist (time-based) philosophies of Henri Bergson, arguing for our need to observe systems interacting *in time*; the animate, futurist tendencies of Boccioni's Stati d'Animi, showing the blurring of bodies across our space, *in time*; the mid-20th-century invention of complex geometries in the work of Pierre Bezier, showing lines describing the distribution of forces across those lines, *in time*; Frei Otto's development of physical models able to show the effects of gravity and lateral and other natural forces able to displace and move materials across space, *in time*.

You get my point. In time, things are different than we might first try and show, represent or understand those things – including those things like: architecture's objects; its materials; structures; spaces; or the kinds of events or social interactions that happen to occur (planned or designed, or not) within those things we architects call, or refer to as, spaces, buildings, landscapes or other settings.

There's obviously a revolution occurring around work on such spaces today owing of course to the very ways in which time itself is now built into – conceived, represented, and controllable within – those software, modeling and other computational worlds architects not only now spend their lives working within, but also communicating through, to other architects (as well as their consultant teams, clients and even users). All of which suggests this a vital period for (as Bergson once called it) *vitalism* itself in a world where thinking about – and not only working with – the performance of those spaces, structures and materials associated with a field like that of architecture may yet again gain a form of coherence not seen since form itself served that purpose. That the word itself serves only part of that longer, more interesting and contemporary word of 'per*form*ance' – itself always a term connoting a universe of materials and ideas in motion – is precisely what makes the following collection of essays and chapters so relevant, interesting and unexpected. Architecture might yet be in motion, yet again.

Brett Steele.
Los Angeles, February 2019.

Introduction
Performance Engrained

Michael U. Hensel

The notion of *performance* has been present in architecture for a while by now. An early key effort took shape in the 1930s in the context of the work of the Structural Study Associates (SSA; Buckminster Fuller, Fredrik Kiesler, Carl Theodore Larsen, Knut Lönberg Holm, et al.). Suzanne Strum noted that the SSA

> propagated a radical technologist and productivist manifesto that anticipated the systems and communication theory that emerged in the post-war era. Their position regarding advanced technology and information has a contemporary resonance. Already in the early 1930s, the SSA introduced such seemingly postmodernist terminologies as *performance, emergence, emergency, ephemeralization, biologic design, networks, mobility, flows, decentralization, ecology* and *entropy*.
>
> (Strum 2012)

A first marked peak of the notion of performance occurred in the period from the late 1950s to the late 1960s as part of a predominately hard-systems-theoretical approach to design problems in architecture and engineering, the utilization of cybernetic approaches (Sukrow 2018) and models and the advent of the use of computers in architecture. This culminated in a series of publications focused on the topic of *performance design*, such as the August 1967 issue of *Progressive Architecture* under the same title. While the underlying engineering-based hard-systems approach was soon rejected by mainstream architects, particular systems-based approaches nevertheless continued in specific circles, yielding quite some attention, such as Jay Forrester, who initiated and developed *system dynamics* and especially *urban dynamics* in the 1960s and 1970s, with the aim to model the behavior of complex systems.

The second and persisting peak began to emerge in the 1990s with the mainstream introduction of computer-aided design into architecture and its gradual coupling with computer-aided analysis, with the rise of the essentially interdisciplinary field of performance studies, growing awareness of increasingly complex cultural, social and environmental sustainability issues that required different design and research approaches, practice-based research geared towards tackling complex design problems and more generally speaking the *performative idiom* in science (Pickering 1995). In architecture the discourse on performance was initially aligned with the persisting form and function divide, with the former locating performance predominately in the artistic domain of qualitative aspects and the latter predominately in the engineering domain of quantitative aspects. Currently, however, the form and function dichotomy seems to be gradually resolved by coupling design thinking with systems thinking, by integrating quantitative and qualitative criteria and analysis, by increasingly inter- and trans-disciplinary outlooks and approaches to tackling complex design problems, and by gradually maturing research approaches and methods in the creative disciplines, particularly research by design (Grand & Jonas 2012; Fraser 2013; Rogers & Yee 2015; Lucas 2016). Evidence of concerns with performance are abundant in architectural practice, research and teaching. In particular, practices that have systematically developed formal and often interdisciplinary research capacity during the last two or three decades are frequently concerned with various aspects of performance (Hensel & Nilsson 2016; 2019). Over the last two decades quite a number of publications and numerous scientific articles on the subject matter of performance in architecture began to appear that frequently featured multi-faceted contributions from practice, research and academia (Kolarevic & Malkavi 2005; Grobman & Neuman 2012; Hensel 2013).

The notion of performance has by now not only taken hold in architecture, but also in urban design and landscape architecture, and it is frequently approached as a multi-domain and multi-scalar task. The questions concerning Industry 4.0 and especially of rising digitalization and the role of data in understanding the world and in design processes play a significant role, as well as the question of the role of phenomenology and experience. And finally, the notion of performance also turns attention back to fundamental purposes, principles and values of design across cultural, social, environmental and political settings and dynamics.

The notion of performance is here to stay as it is maturing in architecture, landscape architecture and urban design. It is now time to take stock of the current state of affairs and to examine the diversity of approaches and developments. This companion is a major contribution towards this end.

References

Fraser M. (2013) *Design Research in Architecture: An Overview*. Farnham: Ashgate.
Grand S., & Jonas W. (2012) *Mapping Design Research*. Basel: Birkhäuser.
Grobman, Y., & Neuman E. (2012) *Performalism: Form and Performance in Digital Architecture*. London: Routledge.
Hensel M. (2013) *Performance-Oriented Architecture: Rethinking Architectural Design and the Built Environment*. Chichester: John Wiley & Sons.
Hensel, M., & Nilsson, F.Eds. (2016) *The Changing Shape of Practice: Integrating Research and Design in Architecture*. London: Routledge.
Hensel, M., & Nilsson, F. Eds. (2019) *The Changing Shape of Architecture: Further Cases of Integrating Research and Design in Practice*. London: Routledge.
Kolarevic, B., & Malkawi, A. (2005) *Performative Architecture: Beyond Instrumentality*. New York: Spon.
Lucas, R. (2016) *Research Methods for Architecture*. London: Laurence King.
Pickering, A. (1995) *The Mangle of Practice: Time, Agency and Science*. Chicago and London: University of Chicago Press.
Roger, P.A., & Yee, J. Eds. (2015) *The Routledge Companion to Design Research*. London: Routledge.
Strum, S. (2012) "Informational Architectures of the SSA and Knud Lönberg Holm." *Nexus Network Journal*, 14(1): 35–52.
Sukrow, O. Ed. (2018) *Zwischen Sputnik und Ölkrise – Kybernetik in Architektur, Planung und Design*. Berlin: DOM.

Prologue
Works at Work

David Leatherbarrow

Kinde are her answeres,
But her performance keeps no day;
Breaks time, as dancers
From their own musike when they stray ...
Thomas Campion, *Third and Fourth Bookes of Ayres*

Cultures articulate themselves in various ways, sometimes intelligently, which is to say by design, sometimes not, which is to say unreasonably – *straying* in the manner of dancers following their own music, as in the epigraph above. With respect to articulations by design, a range of practices is always at play in any given cultural context at any given moment, practices of which architecture, like music and dance, is surely one. When the communicative, not constructive, sense of articulation is stressed, architecture would seem to be an assertive or declarative kind of expression, designed to take a stand on behalf of some desire or purpose. But when the stage is public, the building's performances are also consequential, having palpable effect on the place and those who reside there. Among other practices, architecture *constructs* culture, as we learn in the chapters of this book that address contemporary theory and practice.

A prelude to this aspect of architecture's recent history is the "performative turn" in language, which is to say John Austin's thesis that one can *do things* with language, not only assert, praise, question or express.[1] A recognized official, for example, can join two people in marriage by saying "I now pronounce you ...", or, with a similarly "performative utterance," a president and provost can graduate a student from university, or a judge can sentence a criminal. Adopting this thesis, architects have asked themselves if there might be architectural equivalents of "illocutionary" acts, spatial or material parallels to swearing an oath, attesting to a belief, or betting on an outcome – equally event-like, public, and consequential.

In the past decade or so, the turn toward architectural "operations" and "transactions" has required architects and theorists to attempt a double shift: (1) away from the perceiving subject as the locus of architectural reality, and (2) clear of the designer as that reality's single source. Though dramatic, this turn has not meant the renunciation of perceptual experience, nor the surpassing of professional intentions – despite common claims about the radicalism of today's architectural thinking – but only that these dimensions of the discipline (experience and authorship) have been temporarily put out of play, so that different questions can be asked of the work, and other architectural topics can be brought into focus.

It seems to me that the next phases of thinking, inaugurated so propitiously in this book, will particularly address three dimensions of architectural performance: (1) its public character, (2) its event (or temporal) character, and (3) its world-building character. Let me briefly describe each in turn, before returning to my opening comment about performances that "break time ... as the dancers stray."

Performance is necessarily situated: every enactment is perforce staged. A key antagonist in any built work's operations will be its site and soil, in the city or countryside, or, as is increasingly common these days, some vague territory in-between. Though obvious, it may be useful to stress that no architectural work performs without being built, not only *simulated* but *actually constructed somewhere*, in some unique geography, climate, and culture, with and against which its operations will succeed or fail. With every stage comes not only an auditorium but also the "auditors," and not only those who reside or work there, but those outside it as well. Other participants include ambient environmental forces and nearby buildings, which correspondingly co-operate in defining the street or the landscape, for every stretch of inhabited topography is made up of alternately similar and different figures. Performance in architecture will always be a matter of acting with and against players in the vicinity, through engagements and confrontations that are equally practical and political.

Events come and go, performances begin and end. Accordingly, architecture measures its operations with all manner of clocks, calendars, and chronicles.[2] Environmental-architectural change is not always unprecedented; more likely is periodicity, the daily and seasonal cycles to which coverings, apertures, and materials must respond, projecting their shadows, admitting cool breezes, or resisting lateral forces. Yet, no location is untroubled by unforeseen unfoldings, which require of the performance all manner of adjustments and adaptations that test a work's sensitivities and adroitness. Performance in architecture is in this sense rather like effective rhetoric, adjusted or attuned to what its audience can grasp; which is to say, what will move them.

Lastly, performances are not only made but made-up; essentially fictive. What sorts of stories do architectural enactments tell? There aren't many: generally, tales about worlds that are desired, maybe where injustices, indifferences, and exclusions are reduced; where there is more economy and less waste; or where beauty is not something extrinsic to everyday affairs. One can trust that today's tasks will remain tomorrow, for never was there an act of world-building that didn't point toward what's to come. Why? Because what is wanted always seems no longer or not yet.

A key and concluding observation requires a return to my opening note about un-designed cultural articulation: that there is always an unreasonable dimension to architectural performances.[3] I don't mean any sort of willful irrationality or contrived accidentism, still less autobiographical formalisms; instead, the obscure dimension of operations that results from the work's necessary involvement with forces beyond its control, the improbable powers at play in the environment and society, as well as the inchoate motivations of one's own thinking.

Notes

1 The seminal text here is John Austin, *How to Do Things With Words*, ed. J.O. Urmson and Marina Sbisá (Cambridge, MA: Harvard University Press, 1962).
2 I study this in a forthcoming book on architectural temporality, provisionally titled *Building Time*.
3 Campion modulated subtle, even fragile rhythms with unexpected breaks and disharmonies. See Thomas Campion, *Third and Forth Bookes of Ayres* (London: Thomas Snodham, 1617), 3, 7. I have addressed this aspect of architectural performance in David Leatherbarrow, "Unscripted Performance," *Architecture Oriented Otherwise* (New York: Princeton Architectural Press, 2009), 43–67.

1

Performances of Architectures and Environments

En Route to a Theory and Framework

Michael U. Hensel and Defne Sunguroğlu Hensel

Introduction

Our take on questions of architecture and performance is rooted in a linked environmental and cultural ethic and endeavour: its aim is to improve on the relation between architecture and environment, while basing this approach wherever possible on locally specific cultural practices. As construction impacts upon our planet at a momentous rate, consuming in the process vast amounts of resources in terms of surface area, material and energy and impacting massively on the bio-physical environment, we pose two related questions: (1) can architecture be in the service of the bio-physical environment; sand, by extension, (2) can architecture principally be conceived of as not in conflict with, but rather as an embedded part of its local bio-physical environment? This chapter examines what this may involve.

Principally we base our approach on an interdisciplinary perspective. To pursue our goal in a critical and projective manner, it is often necessary to question current entrenched aspects and approaches in architectural, urban and landscape design, while at the same time recognizing the central themes of architecture, such as the need for transformation of the environment through design and construction and careful management and economy of resources in making provisions. Yet for whom? We extend the human-centred focus of architecture such as to include other species and ecosystems, and, in much broader terms the case-specific local biological and physical environment. As mentioned at the onset, our central inquiry is how architecture can be in the service of the local biological and physical environment, while being grounded in existing, developing or projected cultural practices and, moreover, while working with the central tasks of architectural, urban and landscape design in an integrative manner. This chapter collects, links and advances a series of our key thoughts, insights and works en route to performance-oriented architecture and by extension the wider environment as it is so profoundly transformed by human action.

A variety of views expressed by a number of architects and experts from various knowledge fields have informed our specific take on performance in architecture. In 1967 Leslie Martin stated that "the ultimate problem for the profession is that of setting out the possibilities and choices in building an environment" (Martin 1967). This positions the task of architecture as one that clearly transcends the limits of the discrete physical object. It implies that for any work there exist scales and systems that are smaller and larger than that of a specific construction or an urban or landscape scheme and that these constitute an environment that in one way or another needs to be accounted for by any architectural work, be it a building or an urban or landscape scheme. Furthermore, these spatial scales are nested, they correlate and interact and are linked to different stakeholders that play vital roles concerning questions of interaction, performance, ecology and sustainability. We approach architecture, the environment and related stakeholders from an actor-network theory perspective that explicitly ascribes active agency to human and nonhuman actors and actants (Latour 2005). For us this concerns in the main other species, ecosystems, geophysical systems, etc., in other words key aspects of the bio-physical environment. These are understood as possessing agency in interacting with and constituting the environment. We employ both a human and nonhuman perspective (Grusin 2015) in relation to performance-oriented architectures, and by extension to performance-oriented urban and landscape design. Furthermore, we consider possible correlations between cultural, social and environmental actants by way of significantly extending the involved roster of potential stakeholders in integrated architectural, urban and landscape design, towards what we term *embedded architectures* (Hensel 2019).

In 1964 Christopher Alexander stated that "the environment must be organized so that its own regeneration and reconstruction does not constantly disrupt its own performance" (Alexander 1964). This implies that there exists a set of dynamics that any work will impact upon and alerts us to the fact that any work needs to consider numerous nested time and functional scales in parallel to spatial scales with the aim of not interrupting existing vital dynamics. These views link up with a statement made by Pim Martens, who posited that

> a new research paradigm is needed that is better able to reflect the complexity and the multi-dimensional character of sustainable development. The new paradigm ... must be able to encompass different magnitudes of scale (of time, space, and function), multiple balances (dynamics), multiple actors (interests) and multiple failures (systemic faults).
>
> *(Martins 2006)*

This way of accounting for critical aspects concerning questions of sustainability also delivers a suitable inroad to questions of architecture and environment relations, and more broadly speaking, to questions of architecture and performance. However, not all aspects that are key to this approach can be treated in an equal manner. Some can be quantified, modelled or simulated, while others need to be considered in different ways. Therefore, it is necessary to recognize categorical differences in the attempt to address and link the qualitative and the quantitative, and the measurable and the immeasurable. This frequently leads to explicit difficulties in establishing system boundaries, to keep system boundaries flexible, to articulate useful system and object relations, and to configure integrative methods for design and for evaluation. We consistently spend substantial effort on addressing these aspects in location- and time-specific manner.

A framework emerges gradually from our continual effort that extends the range of consideration to environments in the first instance and architectures as embedded within environments in the second instance. As stated above our key questions that deliver a distinct trajectory for inquiry into performance are: How can architecture be in the service of the bio-physical environment? How can local and often historically rooted cultural patterns and practices that are closely related to their local bio-physical environments deliver sustainable and resilient models for human and environment interactions and a careful transformation of the environment? To pursue this further the following includes an open list of traits of performance-oriented architecture and summarily describes some related works that approach our key questions in different ways.

Traits of Performance-oriented Architecture

In our take one of the fundamental traits of performance-oriented architecture is its extensive and intensive linking of architectural, urban, landscape and environmental aspects with their setting in a multi-scalar and multi-domain approach. This precludes the design of *discrete* architectures that are principally set apart from their setting with the aim to stand out. Instead we seek to formulate what we have termed *non-discrete* or *embedded architecture* (Hensel 2013, 2019), which resonates in part with Kengo Kuma's notion of the *Anti-Object* (Kuma 2008). However, our take does not entail an anti-design stance. On the contrary, design, and in our case research-based design, remains solidly in the centre of activity, albeit with a fundamental shift concerning the subject matter and outcome of design that foregrounds agency and interaction of architecture and environment. Sanford Kwinter formulated this as follows:

> Thus the object – be it a building, a compound site, or an entire urban matrix … would be defined now not by how it appears, but rather by practices: those it partakes of and those that take place within it … those relations that are smaller than the object, that saturate and compose it, the 'micro-architectures' … and … those relations or systems that are greater or more extensive than the object, that comprehend or envelope it, those 'macro-architectures' of which the 'object' … is but a relay member or part.
>
> *(Kwinter 2001)*

Based on the above we have formulated a series of related design criteria, three of which are in particular relevant to this argument:

1   Architectures can be embedded within landscape and environment. Through a committed engagement with landscape architectures can be embedded in lithospheric (pedospheric), hydrosphere and biotic processes.
2   Architectures are always already subjected to and participate in climatic dynamics. The inevitable interaction between architectures and local climate can be strategized in a much more advanced and nuanced manner. Architectures should feature gradual transitions from exterior to interior to provide a heterogeneous microclimatic space so as to make versatile provisions for habitation across a wide spectrum of stakeholders (Hensel & Sunguroğlu Hensel 2010a, 2010b, 2010c, 2016; Hensel & Turko 2015).
3   Expanding upon points 1 and 2, architectures can participate in in the production of a dynamic continuous space and environment that consists of and/or provides for local ecosystems and is informed by local cultural practices.

Frei Otto pointed out that "constructions are auxiliary means, not ends in themselves" (Otto 2008). This entails that constructions are always functionally or otherwise related to further systems, processes and features in their setting. One striking instance of a complex nesting of functional aspects is the Khaju Bridge in Isfahan (Figure 1.1), a prime example of a complex multi-functional civic architecture that emerged in the context of the convergence of knowledge and skills in the then newly founded capital of Safavid Persia, Isfahan. The masonry weir-bridge was built around 1650 AD under Shah Abbas II. It spans the Zayandeh River, whose water level varies greatly over the seasons. The bridge features on its upper level a road that is framed on both sides by arched arcades. The lower level, which is accessible only to pedestrians, comprises arches that are connected by a vaulted space. Most of the lower-level arches span over canal intakes with sluice gates that serve to raise the upstream water level in times of draught for the purpose of irrigation of upstream gardens and fields. The downstream

Michael U. Hensel and Defne Sunguroğlu Hensel

stepped chutes and the arches and vaulted space of the lower level double up as spaces for public use. Here the design accomplishes a comfortable microclimate by way of utilising airflow in conjunction with evaporative cooling that is enjoyed by people that gather there for social reasons. This project demonstrates how far an integrative approach can go by way of spatial and material organisation that is adapted to and in interaction with the local environment, so as to make multiple provisions. Performance-oriented architecture is based on the understanding that architectures unfold their *performative capacity* by being *embedded* in nested orders of complexity and that they are *auxiliary* to numerous conditions and processes: such architectures we term essentially *non-discrete*.

Our approach to performance focuses on this correlation. We consider four domains of agency: (1) the local physical environment, (2) the local biological environment, and (3+4) the spatial and material organisation complex that constitutes architecture and the built environment. This approach incorporates also the cultural and social aspects this encompasses in a given context, as well as other local conditions as drivers in defining the interaction of architectures with their settings. This serves as the key input for generating intensively interrelated architectural, urban and landscape designs (Hensel 2011, 2013).

As the example of the Khaju Bridge shows, architecture can make advanced provisions through its linked spatial and material organisation. Capacity for *active agency* on a range of scales is inherent to the domains of spatial and material organisation. As these two domains are indivisibly interdependent, they are treated as the combined *spatial and material organisation complex*. This complex interacts with the local environment: it is modulated by the environment and modulates it in turn. The local environment is

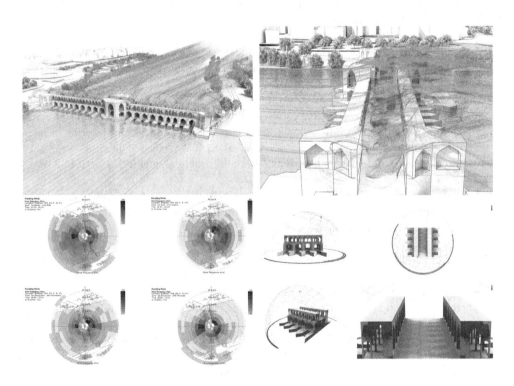

Figure 1.1 OCEAN | SEA – Sustainable Environment Association in collaboration with Studio Integrate, Analysis of Khaju Bridge, Isfahan, Iran, 2012.
Credit: OCEAN | SEA & Studio Integrate

inseparable from the spatial and material organisation of architectures and linked through mutual modulation.

A further example serves to demonstrate how the material and spatial organisation complex may be thought of and how it suggests that the entrenched form and function argument and division that has split architects chiefly into two factions for too long is no longer useful in its current form, as it delimits unnecessarily a more inclusive take on performance in architecture. The relation between form and function can be rethought in principle terms on the example of a historical building element, the so called *mashrabīyas*, Islamic wooden latticework screen-walls used in projecting oriel windows. Hassan Fathy described the finely calibrated and integral "functions" of a *mashrabīya* as (1) regulating the passage of light, (2) air flow, (3) temperature, (4) humidity of the air current, and (5) visual access and control from the inside to the outside and vice versa. All this is accomplished by the controlled articulation of the sizes of the balusters that make up the latticework and the interstices between them (Fathy 1986). Fathy described how different parts of the screen-wall cater for different hierarchies of these integrated functions. For instance, if interstices need to be smaller at seating or standing height to reduce glare, the resultant reduction in airflow can be compensated for by larger interstices higher up in the latticework where glare is not a problem or can be controlled by other elements. While fulfilling their various correlated functions in a nuanced manner, the pattern of the balusters can be articulated according to different formal preferences. Choices frequently range from floral ornamentation to abstract geometric pattern. The *mashrabīya* demonstrates how formal and multi-functional needs and preferences can be jointly solved instead of being disentangled into separate single-function elements. Moreover, this building element is finely tuned to the overall spatial and material articulation of the building envelope and the interior spatial organisation of the building. In various contexts the buildings that feature *mashrabīyas* often also feature other elements connecting its climate modulation upwards in scale. This often includes windcatchers, chimney-like elements that regulate airflow and thermal comfort in the building. Windcatchers are an integral part of a series of interrelated strategies for passive building climatization, for example, in the hot and arid regions of Persia that are characterised by a steep diurnal temperature gradient, where settlements are typically arranged in a dense manner to control thermal impact. Windcatchers can vary in height, cross-section, placement and number of openings. The orientation of openings at the top of the wind-tower and the arrangement of the vertical air ducts and dividing blades in it are related to different types of functions and local conditions. Through shutters different airducts inside the wind-towers can be opened and closed and change the direction of airflow. This is frequently combined with evaporative cooling by way of various water features and with windcatchers used in combination with underground water canals (*kariz*) that provide drinking water. In Persia the combination of fertile soil and precipitation-rich mountain ranges made it possible to collect groundwater at the foot of the mountains with a system of subterranean canals called *qanats* that serve irrigation purposes and also feed into *kariz*. This shows how larger and smaller constructions are functionally nested for the purpose of effective distribution and use of resources. Similar arguments may be made about today's systems. However, contemporary systems by and large involve a large amount of technology, electrical-mechanical equipment, while historical examples accomplished similar feats with spatial and material organisation.

Nested Catenaries, one of our research projects, aims at combining aspects of function, form and design expression in a comparable manner. Nested Catenaries (Figure 1.2) are thin unreinforced masonry shells and constitute a design and construction system of catenoid trussing with arches and vaults. This system has thus far been advanced through a three-phase design and full-scale construction experiments. The first phase of the research focused on combining shape and structure parameters to offer improved load-bearing performance with stability against dynamic loads, and feasible construction in low- and high-technology contexts (Sunguroğlu Hensel & Baraut Bover 2013; Sunguroğlu Hensel 2015). The current fourth phase of this research project combines spatial, structural and environmental

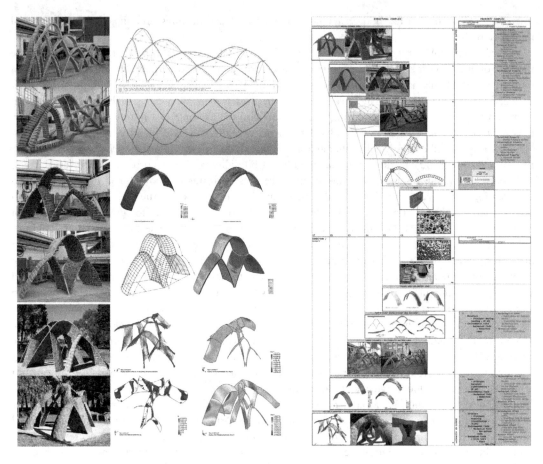

Figure 1.2 Defne Sunguroğlu Hensel, Nested Catenaries Phase 1, 2 and 3, Prototypes Phase 1 and 2 Oslo, Norway, Pilotproject Phase 3 Open City Ritoque, Chile, 2010–12.
Credit: Defne Sunguroğlu Hensel

performance criteria that are elaborated through a series of location-specific design studies to accomplish what we term an *ecological prototype*, an architecture that is in the service of and in interaction with the local ecosystem. This entails trade-offs between different criteria and a different take on the definition of the problem and solution space for design for which we did not have a ready-made method and related tools.

In search for an answer to this problem we realised that in relation to material performance we require tools that are different from standard material databases. One of our research efforts focuses therefore on the development of MATONT, a computational domain ontology developed as an informatics tool for multi-scale adaptive modelling of materials information to manage, mine, manipulate, integrate and translate material criteria into useful information for architectural design and construction. The potential contribution of MATONT is two-fold. First, environmental change and big data will determine the building code and information models that that are appropriate and adequate for performance-oriented architecture today. MATONT seeks to aid materials development and adaptation to case- and locally specific multiple requirements and seeks to facilitate advanced use of resources towards more sustainable environmental design in architecture. Second, MATONT linked with data models, databases, ontologies and optimization in computer-aided design will deliver a missing multiple-criteria design decision support based on performance-focused trade-offs (Sunguroğlu Hensel & Vincent 2015; Sunguroğlu Hensel 2017). Recently we extended this approach to what we term *METONT*, which features a much greater range of environmental criteria. A related further key trait of performance-oriented architecture that is of vital importance to our approach is the necessary capacity for adaptation to changing circumstances (Sunguroğlu Hensel 2015, 2017). Settings are never stable and non-changing, and every intervention in the transformation of the environment causes additional change. Performance-oriented architectures, cities and landscapes require explicit design strategies in these terms.

Architectural History, Diffuse Heritage and Productive Cultural Landscapes

One of our ongoing research projects focuses on architectural history from a performance perspective. We analyse case studies, including buildings, settlement pattern and cultural and productive landscapes, so as to gain insights into their fine-tuned relation to their setting and location-specific performative capacities, as well as inherent sustainability characteristics. In this way architectural history can serve as a vast repository of embedded knowledge and experience and as great source of insight for contemporary performance-oriented architectural, urban and landscape design. Recognizing the value of past architectures for future design can help strengthen arguments towards preservation in order to maintain vital knowledge and adapt it to current and future circumstances. Our studies range across cultures, times, locations and climate zones, focusing on questions of knowledge production, performance capacities, cultural patterns of use and operational logics (Hensel, Sunguroğlu Hensel, Gharleghi, Craig 2012; Hensel & Sunguroğlu Hensel 2015; Hensel, Sunguroğlu Hensel, Sørensen 2018).

One example of a striking design for unexpected stakeholders are the Safavid-period pigeon towers from Isfahan. The primary function of these buildings, up to 20 meters tall, was to provide shelter for up to 10,000 wild pigeons with the purpose of collecting the dung as fertilizer for agriculture in a region where soil lacks nitrogen for agricultural production, as well as for use in tanneries. A seventeenth-century travel report mentioned thousands of pigeon towers in the Isfahan region. Circular or rectangular in plan, pigeon towers could either be freestanding structures or be integrated into perimeter walls of gardens. Such towers consisted either of a single hollow space or drum or of an inner drum enclosed by an outer one. Some large towers were organised in plan as eight smaller drums around a central one to increase the surface area of the interior and therefore also the number of pigeon nests. Turrets provided access for the pigeons, as well as ventilation. Humans accessed the tower generally only once a year to harvest the dung. How does one design for pigeons? Clearly a long vernacular tradition underlies the knowledge necessary to accomplish this task. However, these sophisticated structures show a meticulous modulation of the interior climate based on a fine calibration of the relation between thermal inertia and ventilation that keeps the interior at a steady temperature throughout the day in spite of a steep diurnal temperature gradient. This level of interior climate control also featured in other building types of the region and suggests a lateral distribution and utilisation of knowledge.

A significant part of our research includes ubiquitous diffuse heritage that is much less recognized in terms of performance perspectives in architecture. For this reason, we conduct research into historical agricultural landscapes that utilise construction, landscaping and land-use aspects in a correlated manner. Such landscapes are frequently abandoned and are falling into disrepair or are rapidly replaced by industrial agriculture. In this way invaluable resources, insights and knowledge are lost. Much can be learned from such landscapes that make it possible to yield crops in difficult settings and in quality and quantity that otherwise is hardly possible. Frequently such productive

Michael U. Hensel and Defne Sunguroğlu Hensel

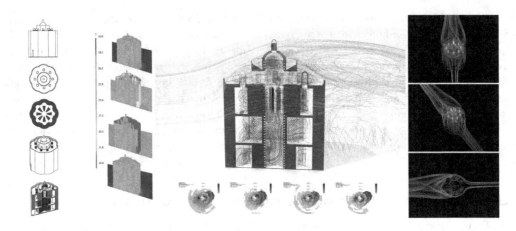

Figure 1.3 OCEAN | SEA – Sustainable Environment Association in collaboration with Studio Integrate, Analysis of Pigeon Towers, Isfahan, Iran, 2012.
Credit: OCEAN | SEA & Studio Integrate

landscapes are shaped and facilitated by constructions, such as terraced landscapes. This suggests that models for integrating architectures and productive land use are not necessarily in contradiction and that new approaches can be formulated based on detailed analyses of such examples. This part of our research focuses therefore on the question of how architectures and productive landscapes can be integrated with the aim to overcome perceived contradictions in land use and, using a long-term perspective, to develop novel ways in which ecosystems and agricultural use may be integrated in urban contexts. This research addresses questions of environment, economy, productive landscapes and the related role of architectural design and architectures within the context of an expanded sustainability approach to human-dominated environments: it is essentially a question of performance of closely linked architecture and landscape, together with land-use strategies and associated land knowledge. The research on diffuse heritage includes historical long-practiced means of altering landscapes for improved agricultural production and related strategies for adaptation to changing in conditions, i.e. local climate change.

One of our research efforts focuses on Italian historical terraced landscapes that utilise dry-stone walls for improving climatic conditions for agricultural production, especially in higher-altitude locations with unfavourable 24-hour temperature ranges. Terraces with dry-stone walls in the state of disrepair can accelerate soil erosion, landslides and seasonal flooding, whereas well-maintained terraces prevent this and provide favourable microclimatic modulation that enables enhanced growth of produce. Terraces orient wine plants in a favourable way towards the sun for increased photosynthesis. Local pruning strategies of the wine can enhance this. Furthermore, terraces provide the required thermal range by way of the dry-stone walls that are thought to extent the temperature ranges for effective photosynthesis by a required period of time in the late afternoon when temperatures at higher altitudes begin to fall rapidly. However, reliable data on the costs for maintaining dry-stone walls and their climatic performance is lacking. Therefore, detailed policies based on such performative aspects have not been established to help maintain terraced landscapes. When we realised that if data could be made available and construction and maintenance costs for dry-stone walls could be established, national policies could be put into place to help preserve terraced landscapes, we configured an interdisciplinary team to pursue this task. Drones and various scanning technologies were used to document and analyse diffuse heritage in this interdisciplinary research effort. Microclimatic measure-stations were installed on site to obtain microclimatic data that can facilitate a more nuanced understanding of the terrace and environment interaction, which facilitates the production of red wine at an altitude of 600 meters and above. We correlated climate data obtained from the local meteorological station, thermographic analysis of the terraced vineyard provided by the Laboratory for Geomatics for Conservation and Communication of Cultural Heritage at the University of Florence, and data obtained by industrial-grade purpose-configured measure-stations. Additionally, we utilised computational simulation tools for local and microclimate analyses and correlated the outcomes with the measured data. The climatic performances of selected terraces were established in collaboration with the winegrower Paolo Socci and GESAAF – Department of Agricultural, Food and Forestry Systems Department at the University of Florence. Furthermore, we studied the strategies of the vineyard owner for modifying the dimensions of historical terraces to suit the use of small-scale agricultural equipment, especially tractors, as well as changing between terraced vineyards at different altitudes and re-establishing abandoned terraces in response to local climate change. We are now in the process of testing the insights for rural and urban periphery developments related to local ecosystems and/or large-scale urban farming schemes (Figure 1.4).

The Rural, the Peripheral and the Urban

Our research project Embedded Architecture seeks to operate on locally specific environment and architecture correlations and interactions, as well as related cultural patterns (i.e. of land use), towards performance-oriented architectural, urban and landscape design. It integrates aspects of cultural, social and environmental performance and sustainability. As the above shows, significant insights related to

Figure 1.4 Research Centre for Architecture and Tectonics in collaboration with GESAAF – Department of Agricultural, Food and Forestry Systems Department and Laboratory for Geomatics for Conservation and Communication of Cultural Heritage at the University of Florence, Survey and Microclimate Data Collection at Grospoli Terraced Vineyard, Lamole, Italy, 2016–18.
Credit: Lamole Research Group, Michael U. Hensel

questions of performance in architecture can be obtained from research into diffuse heritage and cultural landscapes for the purpose of assembling land-use and architectural strategies that were formerly seen as either outdated or contradictory. Such studies can help to redesign cities from the outside inwards and to develop alternative strategies for multiple land use in combination with settlement densification. This requires transfer of knowledge gained from the rural areas to peripheral areas, and eventually to urban cores. We are progressing our work along this trajectory and are currently working on the question of peripheral fabric along similar lines of those established in the study of rural areas. Our work in this focal area pursues design-based inquiry along two strands: (1) designs for peripheral areas with focus on maintaining existing local bio-physical conditions, and (2) designs for rural areas that elaborate an integrative approach towards constructions and land uses that are typically seen as mutually exclusive, i.e. by overlapping large-scale faring with densification of the built fabric. We then integrate these strands of research into a unified approach that seeks to develop models for urban, peripheral and rural settings, towards integrated performance-oriented architectural, urban and landscape design. This endeavour correlates the scale of individual constructions, settlement pattern, urban and landscape scales and the respective "stakeholders".

Our research on the urban perimeter involves terrain, habitats and microclimates that are either still intact or require urgent action due to imminent or ongoing pronounced disturbance. In this part of the research focus is placed on developing designs for low-rise and high-density architectures on sites that are normally considered difficult due to existing terrain conditions. The aim is to overcome typical interventions such as levelling the site and thereby profoundly disturbing the local soil, water and ecological regimes, while instead providing or protecting green corridors and reserving areas for natural habitat that are at the same time earmarked for construction, etc. Our practice OCEAN Architecture | Environment is currently undertaking a research project for densification of a housing district in the Oslo Fjord in Norway. Here, as in many other parts of the world, developing a new area normally commences with levelling the terrain for construction purposes and subsequent use. Traditionally, however, the levelling of terrain was not done in this way in Scandinavia, especially when the top soil is thin and the ground below consists of granite. Instead, historically the terrain was used in an imaginative manner to distribute buildings so as to benefit from solar exposure, to grant privacy while working with the features of the landscape.

With anticipated significant increase in precipitation it can be expected that levelled terrains will experience soil degradation and erosion, especially when protective vegetation is removed in the process of levelling. Our research project commenced therefore from a position that re-examined the historical way of building on largely unmodified terrain. Key parameters for the project are then existing terrain, slope angle and orientation, soil regime, water runoff, vegetation and other stakeholders in the local ecosystem. Geomorphic, climatic and ecological parameters underlie the diverse designs with different housing types that each feature a series of distinct interfaces with the local bio-physical environment so as to provide maximum protection of the ground from construction and the ground surface as a continuous natural landscape, the use of which is governed by the Scandinavian Everyman's Right (Right to Roam) and the Norwegian Outdoor Recreation Act as engrained culturally specific patterns and common-sense -based regulations of land use. In this way it is possible to ground interventions in local cultural practices. The designs make various provisions for gardening and greenhouse elements that are part of the architectures and enables growing produce all year long. Circulation is provided with minimal intervention by analysing the terrain regarding latent paths. In this way the stakeholders of the site before it was affected by human intervention and the new tenants can co-exist in relatively close proximity. This approach delivers a blueprint for how one might design for urban ecology aspects instead of leaving wildlife encounters in cities, for instance, to the entirely accidental with all its possible consequences.

At this stage we have assembled some key parts of a framework to advance performance-oriented architecture. Many parts are yet missing. Moreover, the integration of scale ranges needs to continue. At the

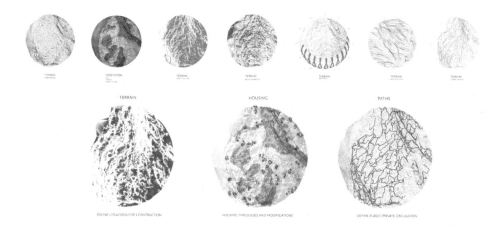

Figure 1.5 OCEAN Architecture | Environment, Terrain and Climate Analysis and Densification Strategy, Nesodden, Norway, 2017–19.
Credit: OCEAN Architecture | Environment, Defne Sunguroğlu Hensel and Michael U. Hensel

same time, it is necessary to stock up on the capacity to engage in interdisciplinary debate and work with a widening spectrum of disciplines involved. For us this is not a daunting situation, but rather an exciting one. Doing architecture never needs to be boring again. In order to accomplish our set goals, we have to continually improve our performance as architects to advance the question and capacity of performance of architecture. Returning to the initial statement that our approach is routed in a cultural and environmental ethic we realise that our main attitude resonates with Martin Bechthold's view that

> it is crucial to move performance-thinking back to the core of the disciplinary consciousness. What could be timelier … at the age of global warming and dwindling resources? … performance-based design should be here to stay … as an ethical obligation to the profession and to society.
>
> *(Bechthold 2012)*

From this shared perspective this framework may perhaps operate as a manifesto.

References

Alexander, C. (1964). *Notes on the Synthesis of Form*. Cambridge, MA: Harvard University Press, 3.
Bechthold, M. (2012). 'Performalism or Performance-based Design?' In: Grobman, Y.J., & Neuman, E. eds. *Performalism: Form and Performance in Digital Architecture*. London: Routledge, 49–52 (p. 52).
Fathy, H. (1986). *Natural Energy and Vernacular Architecture – Principles and Examples with Reference to Hot Arid Climates*. Chicago: University of Chicago Press, 48–49.
Grusin, R. ed. (2015). *The Nonhuman Turn*. Minneapolis and London: University of Minnesota Press.
Hensel, M. (2011). 'Performance-oriented Architecture and the Spatial and Material Organisation Complex – Rethinking the Definition, Role and Performative Capacity of the Spatial and Material Boundaries of the Built Environment.' *FORMAkademisk – Research Journal for Design and Design Education* Vol. 4 (1): 3–23.
Hensel, M. (2013). *Performance-Oriented Architecture – Rethinking Architectural Design and the Built Environment*. London: John Wiley & Sons.
Hensel, M. (2019). 'The Rights to Ground: Integrating Human and Non-Human Perspectives in an Inclusive Approach to Sustainability.' *Sustainable Development* Special Issue: Architecture, Design and Planning towards Sustainable Development; regional approaches. doi:10.1002/sd.1883.

Hensel, M., & Sunguroğlu Hensel, D. (2010a). 'Extended Thresholds I: Nomadism, Settlements and the Defiance of Figure-Ground.' *Turkey: At the Threshold, AD Architectural Design* Vol. 80 (1): 14–19.

Hensel, M., & Sunguroğlu Hensel, D. (2010b). 'Extended Thresholds II: The Articulated Threshold.' *Turkey: At the Threshold, AD Architectural Design* Vol. 80 (1): 20–25.

Hensel, M., & Sunguroğlu Hensel, D. (2010c). 'Extended Thresholds III: Auxiliary Architectures.' *Turkey: At the Threshold, AD Architectural Design* Vol. 80 (1): 76–83.

Hensel, M., & Sunguroğlu Hensel, D. (2015). 'Architectural History from a Performance Perspective – The Latent Potential of Knowledge Embedded in the Built Environment'. Proceedings: Heritage and Technology – Mind, Knowledge, Experience, Le Vie dei Mercanti XIII International Forum, 794–802.

Hensel, M., & Sunguroğlu Hensel, D. (2016). 'Recuperating An Approach to Local Specificity for Sustainable Cities and Regions – Correlating Key Strategies for Architecture and Urban Design, Collective Space and Architecture and Environment Integration'. 22nd Annual ISDRS – International Sustainable Development Research Society Conference, Lisbon and Portugal, July 13–15.

Hensel, M., Sunguroğlu Hensel, D., Gharleghi, M., & Craig, S. (2012). 'Towards an Architectural History of Performance: Auxiliarity, Performance and Provision in Historical Persian Architectures.' *Iran – Past, Present and Futures. AD Architectural Design* Vol. 82 (3): 26–37.

Hensel, M., Sunguroğlu Hensel, D., & Sørensen, S. (2018). 'Embedded Architectures – Inquiries into Architectures, Diffuse Heritage and Natural Environments in Search for Better Informed Design Approaches to Sustainability.' *Time + Architecture 3* Vol. 161 (Special Issue: Design for Well-tempered Environment): 42–45.

Hensel, M., & Turko, J. (2015). *Grounds and Envelopes – Reshaping Architecture and the Built Environment*. London: Routledge.

Kuma, K. (2008). *Anti-Object: The Dissolution and Disintegration of Architecture*. London: AA.

Kwinter, S. (2001). *Architectures of Time: Toward a Theory of the Event in Modernist Culture*. Cambridge, MA: MIT Press, 14.

Latour, B. (2005). *Reassembling the Social: An Introduction to Actor-Network-Theory*. Oxford: Oxford University Press.

Martin, L. (1967). 'RIBA Journal May 1967.' In: Quote taken from Carolin, P., & Dannat, T., eds. (1996), *Architecture, Education and Research – The work of Leslie Martin: Papers and Selected Articles*. London: Academy Editions, 118.

Martins, P. (2006). 'Sustainability: Science or Fiction?' *Sustainability: Science, Practice & Policy* Vol. 1 (2): 36–41.

Otto, F. (2008). 'The Fundamentals of Architecture.' In: Songel, M.J., ed., *A Conversation with Frei Otto*. New York: Princeton Architectural Press, 11.

Sunguroğlu Hensel, D. (2015). 'Developmental Route to Functional and Adaptive Integration.' *International Journal of Design Sciences and Technology* Vol. 21 (2): 153–178.

Sunguroğlu Hensel, D. (2017). *Convergence: Materials Adaptation and Informatics in Architecture*. Norway: Oslo School of Architecture and Design.

Sunguroğlu Hensel, D., & Baraut Bover, G. (2013). 'Nested Catenaries.' *Journal of the International Association for Shell and Spatial Structure* Vol. 54 (1): 39–55.

Sunguroğlu Hensel, D., & Vincent, J.F.V. (2015). 'Evolutionary Inventive Problem-Solving in Biology and Architecture: ArchiTRIZ and Material-Ontology.' *Intelligent Buildings International*. doi: 10.1080/17508975.2015.1014462.

2

Social Performativity

Architecture's Contribution to Societal Progress

Patrik Schumacher

Social Performativity as Demarcation Criterion

If performativity marks the demarcation of the design disciplines against the fine arts, then social versus technical performativity establishes the demarcation of the design disciplines – including architectural and urban design – against the engineering disciplines. The differentiation of design and engineering implies that of the three Vitruvian criteria of good architecture – *firmness*, *commodity* and *delight* – only the latter two are within the responsibility and expertise of architects and designers, while the first is an engineering matter. The third criterion – delight – refers to aesthetic valuation which is both relevant to art and architectural design, but not engineering.[1] The responsibility for all technical performance aspects of the built environment has been completely taken up by various specialist engineering disciplines, both with respect to research-based innovation and professional delivery. What is left for architecture? The discipline and profession of architecture is responsible for the innovative delivery of the social purposes and performances of the built environment. Architectural design solutions then pose the downstream problems for engineering solutions. The ends-to-means hierarchy is clear.

Social versus technical performance thus demarcates architecture versus engineering. The general formula describing the built environment's contribution to society's functioning reads: Architecture orders social processes. Another way to express the same thesis reads: The societal function of architecture is the framing of social relations and communicative interactions. That the built environment accomplishes this as much via spatio-visual symbolic processes as via objective spatial relations is a further thesis posited and defended here.

The Vitruvian triad had led to a tripartite division of traditional architectural textbooks into respective parts on *construction*, *distribution* and *decoration*.

In the author's (2010 and 2012) systematic theory of architecture, engineering and construction are left behind while distribution and decoration are re-formulated as architecture's fundamental tasks of *organization* and *articulation* that together deliver the social performance of architecture, namely the ordering of social processes. Organization works via objective spatial relations like distances, adjacencies, conditions of access, etc. Articulation is concerned with the perceptual tractability and the sematic encoding of architectural forms designating social situations. It is accordingly differentiated into phenomenological and semiological articulation. Phenomenology and semiology must become explicit agendas within the architectural discourse and within conscious design practice. The quest for upgrading architecture's social performativity depends on the successful innovation of architecture's organizational, phenomenological and semiological expertise.

Human Progress via Societal Progress

Our ancestors discovered, more by chance than by insight, that social cooperation and organization beyond the small size of primate groups offer momentous productivity advantages that can make our path through the world much more secure, and potentially much more comfortable.

As Karl Marx already knew, the driving forces of historical transformations are the productivity gains that accompany and indeed demand, for better or for worse, societal self-transformations within a competitive world economy. As Friedrich Hayek noted, competition is a search and discovery process (Hayek 2002). While the resultant evolutionary trajectories cannot be predicted more than a few years into the future, the inherent rationality of the competitive process as optimizing evolutionary process implies that change is for the better, at least for most, if not always at once for everybody. Ongoing cultural evolution implies that humanity as a whole enhances its material freedom, i.e. the collective capacity to "domesticate" the indifferent and often hostile physical universe, turning it into a serviceable, pleasurable "home." Such a progressive trajectory is highly probable, if not guaranteed, albeit without any far-reaching predictability how this will be achieved, i.e. how these enhanced life forms will look. Progress remains an adventure.

Productivity gains are not only the driving force but also the ultimately life-enhancing *raison d'être* of this evolutionary historical process. All human progress depends on productivity gains and is built upon productive cooperation on an ever-larger scale of cooperative integration. This insight was clearly stated by Adam Smith, who recognized that the division of labor is the key to the wealth of nations and that the division of labor could be even more intricate and thus productive, the more the market is able to expand via trade. As Marx (1861) stated, "individual labor is productive only in these common labors which subordinate the forces of nature to themselves," and he noted in this connection that this communality is "represented by and concentrated in capital" (pp. 690–712). The great twentieth-century economist Ludwig von Mises (1949) spoke of the gains through cooperation as the "law of association" or "law of society formation" that explains the emergence of society and its expansion (p. 149).

The chances for technological progress depend as much on the evolution of society as on the increase of knowledge which is itself always a social cooperative achievement. In turn the evolution of society depends upon the build-up of a congenial built environment as a slowly evolving and stabilizing ordering matrix. There can be no social order without spatial order. The spatial manifestation and stabilization of social order and orderly social processes is indeed a vital and indispensable contribution that society receives from the built environment. Accordingly, artificial built environments are a human universal. The built environment is a crucial part of the capital structure that according to Marx represents and concentrates human communality. However, in reference to Marx's distinction of forces and relations of production, the built environment is as much a structure that reproduces social relations as it is an immediate component of society's forces of production.

It is the built environment that provides societal evolution with the cross-generational, material substrate by means of which an advantageous social order can persist and grow. Human settlements form ever-larger and more differentiated spatio-material structures, as the skeleton for increasingly complex social structures. Architecture's most profound achievement is thus not the oft-invoked protection from the elements, but an organizational achievement: social order.

There can be no society without a built environment. Society can only evolve with the simultaneous ordering of space. The elaboration of a built environment (however haphazard, precarious, and initially based on accident rather than purpose and intention) is a necessary condition for the build-up of any stable social order. The gradual build-up of a social system must go hand in hand with the gradual build-up of an artificial spatial order; social order requires spatial order. The emergence of built environments as the necessary substrate of any cultural evolution is thereby an indispensable factor of becoming human, i.e. of our escape from the animal kingdom. The social process needs the built environment as a plane of inscription where it can leave traces that then serve to build-up and stabilize social structures, which in turn allow the further elaboration of more complex social processes. The evolution of society goes hand in hand with the evolution of its habitat – understood as an ordering frame. This started with the temporary abodes or villages of hunter-and-gatherer communities, led to the early cities of civilizations and still applies to the contemporary global metropolitan-built environment.

Coordination and Control

Social ordering has two aspects that both involve architecture and that need to be distinguished: the aspect of *social coordination* and the aspect of *social control*.

Coordination is about the functional integration of various tasks and this requires that the various activities are inter-aware, can rely on each other, concatenate and add up. This can be achieved via communication, contracts and rules like those that attach to property rights[2] within market coordination or to rights of instruction within corporate or administrative hierarchies. The role of the built environment here is primarily informational, i.e. it communicates where which activity can take place and who is welcome to contribute or participate. It also often communicates the differentiation of social roles and their configuration within a structured interaction process, as in a class room, board room or, more complex, in a court room.

Control is about surveillance and the enforcement of rules of conduct, like property rules, the enforcement of contracts, the supervision of instructions, etc. The role of the built environment is here primarily physical, filtering access to designated/owned spaces via fences, gates, walls, doors and locks, and via the strategic placement of surveillance points. The concealment and protection of private spaces also belongs to this architectural contribution to social control.

The necessity of social control is an ineradicable aspect of the human condition due to the possibility of defection and free-riding with respect to the burdens and benefits of the cooperative effort.

When the iconoclast Georges Bataille (1929) states that "the human order is bound up from the start with the architectural order which is nothing but a development of the former," he refers to social control rather than to social cooperation.

Freedom and Emancipation: Material and Social

Hegel's philosophy of history famously identified increasing freedom as the direction and destiny of human history. In Hegel's own words: "The final cause of the World at large, we allege to be the consciousness of its own freedom on the part of Spirit, and ipso facto, the reality of that freedom" (1837). If the increase of freedom is indeed the trajectory of human history, then this is coherent with the evolution of life itself. According to the philosopher Daniel Dennett (2004), freedom emerges in the evolution of living systems. The beginning of freedom of action of a living creature is foraging and to move out of harm's way. The more moves the creature can make, i.e. the more degrees of freedom the creature acquires, but also the more these moves are related to information-based anticipations, the greater are the creature's chances to persist and reproduce. Freedom is thus advantageous and therefore most sentient, mobile creatures instinctively cherish freedom and resist shackles and controls. However, the above caveat about information-based anticipations must be remembered also. It implies that regularity and thus predictability are advantageous environmental features. As Dennett reminds us, "in a totally chaotic, unpredictable environment, there is no hope of avoidance except sheer blind luck" (p. 44).

Beyond free random exploration and immediate uninhibited reflexes, it can be advantageous to build up complex chains of action that offer later but greater rewards. In human terms this is work, requiring self-control. Freedom must be coupled with foresight, and freedom to act crucially includes freedom to plan and to labor so as to make the environment more hospitable and predictable. This implies the self-binding of actions as part of a goal-oriented concatenation of actions. The freedom to act becomes the freedom to pursue projects.

The next step is the emergence of cooperative work and the realization of the associated productivity gains. To secure these advantages requires social control, i.e. a socially enforced restriction of individual freedoms.

The formation of ever-larger societies with their attendant increase in social cooperation thus points the way towards greater emancipation from the burdens and threats of the physical world, thus representing a potential gain in physical freedom. However, societal organization also implies social rules that constrain immediate freedom. These rules might be habitual, moral or legal. They seem to require a back-stop back-up via physical force.

We must distinguish between material and social freedom. Material freedom, or prosperity, implies the increasing liberation from the material necessities and impositions of an indifferent physical universe. Social freedom, or liberty, implies the increasing liberation from the necessities of social discipline imposed by our cooperative conquering of material freedom. Material freedom trumps social freedom.

Because the hierarchical, disciplining forms of social organization and control that can enhance material freedom via productive social cooperation can also overshoot in unproductive ways, a new battle front for the striving of freedom has opened up: emancipation from unnecessary, unproductive societal strictures. Disputes about what constitutes necessary versus unnecessary, or even oppressive, societal restrictions have become a permanent part of the human condition and of our interminable striving for freedom. Our striving has thus become a complicated double agenda – physical emancipation and social emancipation – whereby the two sub-agendas often appear to conflict, with the additional complication that societal arrangements that seem globally advantageous are nevertheless differentially taxing to different members or groups within society. If we add to this the difficulties of transitioning from one societal regime to another, we can see the overwhelming difficulties that politics and political theory must contend with. Global, sustainable freedom is thus hardly a simple matter. And yet, at the individual level it seems deceptively clear what would constitute an increase or decrease in one's freedom. What is unclear is whether the desired freedoms can be generalized and made compatible with the socially produced material freedom.

At the frontier of human historical progress social emancipation is called for when technological advances allow for or require a new, possibly less restrictive regime of social control as a condition for the full development of the forces of production that becomes possible via the new technology. This might require a social revolution.

It is in the nature of the conditions for exercising effective social control that social power, and therefore also economic reward, is unevenly distributed. Most regimes of social control imply a stratified social order. This might lead to an overshooting of social control beyond what is macro-economically advantageous. The strata delivering social synthesis might become exploitative. Most of the large ancient stratified social orders – the ancient civilizations – included the institution of slavery and originated in armed conquests and continued to expand via armed conquests.

Defensible city walls and fortresses belong to the primary architectural machinery until the advent of modernity.

However, does the violent origin and maintenance of serfdom imply that it was always and everywhere a form of parasitism? Or can certain historical forms of serfdom be understood as mutualism with uneven distribution of burdens and benefits?

The use of force is not necessarily an indication that avoidable and condemnable exploitation is at play. Hierarchy and force might be necessary to maintain a social order that delivers a new level of material freedom for all or most.

Serfdom under feudalism was for centuries, given the technological constraints of this era, probably without a better alternative in terms of the best feasible mix between material and social freedom. Recurring peasant revolts did not lead to a new social system until the advent of modernity. Karl (1859) stated that "new superior relations of production never replace older ones before the material conditions for their existence have matured within the framework of the old society."

We might introduce here the concept of historically necessary forms of social control. All forms of social control, at least until now, require the institutionalization of legitimate physical force or violence, and the capacity of the built environment to physically constrain movement and access is an indispensable part of this.

The current level of technological and cultural development opens the prospect of a fundamentally non-violent society with only non-violent means and mechanisms of social control. This would make the state, which Max Weber most succinctly defined via its territorial monopoly of violence, obsolete, and the possibility of a state-less, anarcho-libertarian society becomes plausible. The investigation of the architectural implications of such a society and its spatio-morphological ordering requirements are one of the topics of this chapter.

Futile Rebellions Against Architecture

In every society territorial demarcations will be a necessary social ordering substrate via access and activity allocations with respectively restricted access and degrees of freedom. Architecture and freedom, just like society and freedom, are thus always in tension. That is why radical non-conformists like Bataille see architecture as prison, as the enemy.

The radical polemicist Léopold Lambert is building on Bataille's anti-architecture approach:

> The line is architecture's representative medium; it creates diagrams of power that use architecture's intrinsic violence on the bodies to organize them in space. If the white page represents a given milieu – a desert, for example – when an architect traces a line on it, (s)he virtually splits this milieu into two distinct impermeable parts, and actualizes it through the line's embodiment, the wall.

Architecture is identified with the physical operation of the wall as means of control and exclusion: "Each wall creates social conditions on both of its sides: the included and the excluded. One can only be homeless ('prisoner of the outside') if there is something called home." As with Bataille the prison becomes the paradigm case for architecture's social mode of operation:

> There is a violence inherent to architecture, which is then necessarily instrumentalized politically: the way we normally build walls is to resist the energy of the body. We then invented devices like doors – a regulator of the wall porosity – and keys, which allow us to establish who can get

past architecture's violence and who cannot. Now, who gets access to the instrument that can transform a regular house into a prison cell is political, but it is not architectural per se to say who gets the key.

If civilization depends on architectural ordering, it cannot all be summarily dismissed. Therefore, we must introduce the distinction between good and bad ordering, good and bad "violence." Lambert can avoid this because all the examples and topics he engages with in his blog are extreme or exceptional situations like (suppression of) protests, oppressive social exclusion of marginal groups, war, occupation (as in Gaza), etc., where, especially from a left-wing perspective, good vs bad, friend vs enemy in terms of oppressed and oppressor, can be taken for granted without being problematized. So here all architectural "violence" seems obviously bad and is indeed often associated with real violence in the ordinary sense of the word. But on this basis a general theory of the emancipatory or oppressive effects of forms of architectural order cannot be forthcoming.

No doubt, we are bodies and architecture sometimes physically orders and channels us. But that is only one aspect of architecture's social functioning: it also functions as ordering matrix for self-directed browsing and self-sorting. And more importantly, it operates also via thresholds and demarcation lines that do not constitute physical barriers at all, but rather function like signals, indications and indeed communications. Here architecture works and orders via its information richness and communicative capacity rather than as if channeling cattle, as the prison paradigm suggests. Thus the "hard" architectural ontology of walls, fences, locked gates, etc., should de-emphasized and replaced by a "soft" ontology of expressive thresholds, indications and atmospheres that operate as language rather than as physical apparatus.

As violence proper recedes and altogether disappears in the advanced arenas of world society, so does the predominance of physical barriers as spatial ordering mechanisms. Their gradual disappearance from architecture and their substitution by informational architectural operations is a clear sign of societal progress and constitutes a compelling productivity boosting advantage for those institutions that push forward along this trajectory.

The essential advantage of a soft architectural order, whether determinate or indeterminate, is that it builds on the freedom of self-directed individuals. A second major advantage is that the absence of physical separations via walls allows for an unprecedented density of simultaneous, inter-visible communicative offerings. The new tropes and design moves of parametricism like overlap, interpenetration of domains, and field conditions with gradient transformations cannot be realized with the crude tool of walls acting as physical barriers. The intricate complex orders of parametricism are thus premised on social formations where physical social control, especially social control via physical violence, has been replaced by a reliance on self-control, perhaps in connection with forms of electronic monitoring.

The Built Environment as Societal Information Process

The spatial order of the human habitat is both an immediate physical organizing apparatus that separates and connects social actors and their activities, and a material substrate for the inscription of an external "societal memory." These "inscriptions" might at first be an unintended side effect of the various activities. Spatial arrangements are functionally adapted and elaborated. They are then marked and underlined by ornaments, which make them more conspicuous. The result is the gradual build-up of a spatio-morphological system of signification. Thus, a semantically charged built environment emerges that provides a differentiated system of settings to help social actors orient themselves with respect to the different communicative situations constituting the social life-process of society. The system of social settings, as a system of distinctions and relations, uses both the positional identification of places (relative location) and the morphological identification of places (ornamental marking) as props for the societal information process. Compelling demonstrations for this formative nexus between social and spatial structure can be found within social anthropology, attesting to the crucial importance of cross-generationally stable spatio-morphological settings for the initial emergence, temporary stabilization and further evolution of all societies. Only on this basis, with this new material substrate upon which the evolutionary mechanisms of mutation, selection and reproduction could operate, was the evolution of mankind out of the animal kingdom, and all further cultural evolution, possible.

The built environment orders social processes through its pattern of spatial separations and connections. However, it is important to reflect that the functioning of the desired social interaction scenarios depends on the participants' successful orientation and navigation within the designed environment. The built environment, with its complex matrix of territorial distinctions, is (or should become) a giant, navigable, information-rich interface of communication.

The artificiality and communicative capacity of human settlements, artefacts and dress becomes tangible when we compare the diversity of human visual-material cultures, analogous to the diversity of human languages, each with its own rich internal differentiations, with the visual uniformity of other primate species.

What sets human groups apart from other primates is what we might at earlier times, in the broadest sense, have called art, and what we should now refer to as design. This includes profane and sacred buildings and places, tools and other artefacts, as well all the artistry of decorative self-transformation via dress, jewelry and make-up. These practices of "artistic" self-transformation are a universal phenomenon of all human groups.

These practices of decoration also include all buildings and artefacts, i.e. in contemporary terms they include all design disciplines. The significance of these practices, then and now, is the visual marking and thereby conspicuous differentiation of social arenas, roles and identities without which no social order can be built up or maintained. These props and marks allow dominance hierarchies, as well as more complex societal differentiations, to be institutionalized. The social order becomes independent of the continuous combative physical reestablishment of hierarchy and this way also becomes scalable. Design is involved in the elaboration and reproduction of these vital semiological systems.

Built environments started to become designed environments in the Renaissance, when architecture first emerged as a consciously innovative, theory-led academic discipline and profession distinct from the craft of construction.

The transference of the built environment's evolution from incremental *in situ* improvements to comprehensive design speculation via complete sets of drawings and perspectival simulations led to a momentous acceleration of this evolution. However, societal evolution was still comparatively slow, and the complexity of social institutions remained modest enough to be grasped via schedules of accommodation and controlled via a set of static plan descriptions. This started to change during the second half of the twentieth century and increasingly so from the 1980s. The increasingly complex and dynamic processes of social interaction within advanced contemporary knowledge economies can no longer be anticipated via schedules of accommodation nor evaluated via the scrutiny of plan layouts. The only hope for the architectural design profession to regain its competency, i.e. a measure of anticipatory control over the social performance of buildings, is via agent-based occupancy and life-process simulations.

However, to recuperate the architect's competency on the new level of complexity and dynamism of contemporary social processes it is not enough to rely on the crowd simulations developed so far by fire and traffic engineers. In contrast to engineers, architects must reckon with architecture's users not merely as physical bodies but as perceptually orienting, socialized actors who navigate a space encoded with social meanings. Accordingly, the designer must start to work explicitly as much on the symbolic inscription of action protocols as on the physical accommodation of activities.

The functions of architecture are now parametrically variable event scenarios. Their accommodation requires the design and application of a system of signification, and their testing requires agent-based life-process modelling with socially differentiated agent populations that read their behavioral options out of the information-rich environments designed in accordance with a semiological code. The development of this new, enhanced level of competency is the aim of the author's design research program, which he termed "agent-based parametric semiology" (Schumacher 2016). This paper outlines this research program and illustrates some of the work in progress.

Agent-Based Parametric Semiology

The research program of agent-based parametric semiology operates within the theoretical framework laid out in the author's *The Autopoiesis of Architecture* and proposes a new design and simulation medium for the operationalization of the semiological project within architecture. It is at the same time the project that promises to upgrade architecture's capacity to predictably deliver an enhanced social performativity to designed and built environments, in line with the demands made by an increasingly complex and dynamic societal process.

The initial premise posits that spatial communication in the service of the spatial ordering and framing of social interaction processes is architecture's core competency. The built environment's social performance depends on its communicative capacity. The elaboration of spatial complexes in accordance with a designed semiological code is thus a key to upgrading architecture's core competency. The semiological project implies that the design project systematizes all form–function correlations into a coherent system of signification, designed as a network of similitudes and contrasts, organized via a spatio-visual grammar. Each territory is a communication. It communicates an invitation to participate in the framed social situation. To enter the territory implies an acceptance of its spatial communication and the act of entering thus communicates one's willingness to participate in the respective interaction scenario. Everybody who enters is expected to adopt the behavioral rules implied. That is the point of all signification: the coordination of behaviors facilitating cooperation. The precise characterization of the situation depends upon the orchestration of the various semiological registers that come together in the articulated territory: its position in the overall matrix of territories, its spatial shape, its tectonic and material articulation, etc. The articulate territory might thus be designed according to a "grammar" as a well-formed combination of sign-radicals. The build-up of a spatio-visual grammar affords a momentous combinatorial enhancement of architecture's versatility of expression. A small vocabulary might afford a vast number of different communications.

The meaning and effect of the designed architectural code becomes manifest via agent-based life-process simulations. Autonomous agents are set up with action menus, decision processes (decision trees) and utility functions. The agent's actions and behavioral rules are made dependent on the configurational and morphological features of the environment designed in accordance with the semiological code. The programmed agents respond to and modulate their behavior in relation to environmental clues. Spatial position, form parameters, color, texture, and stylistic features, together with ambient parameters (lighting conditions), constitute and characterize designated territories and lead agents to select specific behavioral modes and thus result in different collective event patterns. Since the "meaning" of an architectural space is the type of event or social interaction to be expected within its territory, this implies that the meaning of the architectural language can enter the design medium (digital model) via such crowd modelling. Thus, these new tools allow for the refoundation of architectural semiology as parametric semiology.

The semiological code works if the programmed social agents consistently respond to the relevantly coded positional and morphological clues so that expected behaviors can be read off the articulated environmental configuration. The meaning of architecture, the prospective life processes it frames and sustains, is modelled and assessed within the design process, thus becoming a direct object of creative speculation and cumulative design elaboration. The upgraded form of crowd modelling that makes agent behaviors dependent on the socially encoded (rather than merely physical) environment is the decisive step from the engineers' crowd modelling focusing on circulation to a generalized life-process modelling capturing the spatio-semiotic frame dependency of all social interaction processes between co-present actors.

The first and best test case for this new approach and potentially compelling new design service is the domain of corporate space planning where users' lives are integrated and cooperative rather than mere parallel lives. The key reason for gathering large groups in corporate headquarters is the garnering synergies: the key task is to turn this expansive co-presence into a comprehensive inter-awareness, for the sake of an intensified information and knowledge exchange, and to facilitate extensive horizontal cooperation within and across departments and projects.

Agent-based parametric semiology and life-process modelling can thus become a compelling methodology for data-driven design focusing on skill synergies and knowledge exchange.

How can we make credible/verifiable operational steps towards the goal of spatial optimization with respect to knowledge exchange? Once we have established a method of spatial articulation that sustains visual orientation and facilitates quick navigation, we can use agent-based life-process modelling to test and compare distribution scenarios with respect to the emergent patterns of interaction. We can also simulate collaborative clustering scenarios in situations where more freedom and mobility is given to employees to self-organize.

The agent population will be differentiated according to relevant categories and according to multiple (weighted) project affiliations and/or disciplinary affiliations using social network analysis tools. This agent differentiation will have to be calibrated by client-specific data about the people that will work in or visit the space. Agent behaviors are set up to be context dependent, i.e. vary with the designation and social character of the spaces. The simulations will allow us to extract important measures like overall encounter frequency, encounter frequency within groups and across groups, within hierarchical strata and across strata, frequency of communicative interactions of various types, probability of larger communicative cluster formation, etc. These measures will be used as evaluation criteria in the comparative testing and gradual improvement of the simulated spatial organization, i.e. of the lay-out and distribution scenarios. We would also be able to compare different semiological designs with different degrees of information richness, spatially embedding order and coordination. The same applies to scenarios of responsive environments where the spatial communications become dynamic. In this way we can start to get a handle on what the various design choices imply for the design's ultimate criteria of success in terms of productivity enhancing space planning.

Merely intuitive appraisals have little chance on their own to give credible guidance at the scale and complexity of large corporate headquarters with often hundreds or even thousands of employees, and by extension even less chance when it comes to larger urban processes where multiple institutions and entrepreneurial offerings look for architectural expert advice in their search for synergies that draws them together in our increasingly dense urban centers in the first place. That is why it is justified to put a veritable refoundation of the discipline on the agenda: architecture and urban design as agent-based parametric semiology.

The Design of a Spatio-visual Semiological System

For our academic design research studies, we chose programs such as a university campus or a corporate campus for tech firms like Google, and innovative work environments in general, as initial design research arenas for the semiological project. These are the high-performance arenas at the most advanced frontier of our civilization where the new productivity potentials of our post-Fordist epoch are explored and pushed forward. Architecture's innovations must be relevant and congenial to these arenas. It is here that the complexity of social processes is most expressed, where communication is most intense and dynamic, where diverse human actions and interactions are integrated in intricate patterns of cooperation rather just run in parallel. In contrast, retail or residential arenas are much simpler, and less integrated, i.e. they accommodate parallel rather than integrated lives and thus, as it were, operate by addition rather than multiplication. The next decision was to privilege interior over exterior spaces. While urban fabrics matter, it is in the interior where the most important and most intricate social interactions reside.

As example of a semiologically conceived architectural project we would like to present a recent student project developed by Yihui Wu, Lei Wang and Yanling Xu under the guidance of Patrik Schumacher, Pierandrea Angius and Lei Zheng at the Design Research Laboratory of the Architectural Association School of Architecture in London. The semiological design research project crucially includes the design of a spatio-visual language, i.e. the design of a semiological system or system of signification, with explicit vocabulary and grammar. The particular design project is then understood as only one among many possible applications or "utterances" of the designed language.

All semiological design must proceed by means of building up two correlated systems of distinctions, the system of signifiers or symbols and the system of signifieds or meanings. This focus on system and distinction is crucial and was first emphasized by the founder of semiology, the Swiss linguist Ferdinand de Saussure. All terms are relative and acquire their meaning only in distinction and relation to the other terms. A language operates always on the basis of a total system of distinctions "in which all the elements fit together, and in which the value of any one element depends on the simultaneous coexistence of all the others" (de Saussure 1916, p. 113). In the design of a semiological system the distinctions in the domain of the signifiers are to be correlated with the distinctions in the meaning domain. In the case of architectural semiology, the domain of the signifier is the world of architectural forms, i.e. the spaces and their defining components or properties, and the domain of the signified is the world of varied possible social situations to be accommodated. The project presented here proposes a work environment for a start-up incubator. In such buildings very many different social situations must be distinguished and therefore many different spaces must be differentially characterized. Each space within the total manifold of spaces is defined by a particular combination of aspects. The design of each individual space therefore involves a number of appropriate selections from the articulation options made available by the language via its vocabulary and grammar. The vocabulary is ordered into categories, or substitution classes, or registers of semiological encoding: location, spatial shape, boundary type, color, material, etc. These registers correspond to meaning dimensions within which the intended aspects of the social situation can thus be selected: destination vs circulation, business vs socializing, work vs meet, public vs private, allocated vs bookable, etc.

The first distinction we might introduce to explain the designed system is the formal distinction between bound vs unbound spaces. To this form distinction on the signifier side corresponds, on the side of social meaning, the distinction between business spaces and leisure spaces. This formal distinction carries the further functional meaning of destination vs circulation space. Within the bounded business spaces, we introduce the subsidiary distinction of convex vs concave spaces, designed to encode the social distinction between work spaces and meeting spaces (Figure 2.1).

The posited distinctions, both the distinction bound/unbound as well as distinction convex/concave, are rather abstract and therefore allow for a lot of variation in shape and size without thereby infringing on the distinctive meanings preserved across all the possible variations. This is indicated in the small diagrams at the bottom. This abstractness allows for parametric variation, in line with the requirements of parametricism. We might therefore talk about "parametric semiology."

Now we introduce two further distinctions that both cut across the previously introduced distinctions as well as cutting across each other (Figure 2.2). Both meeting and work spaces might be

Social Performativity

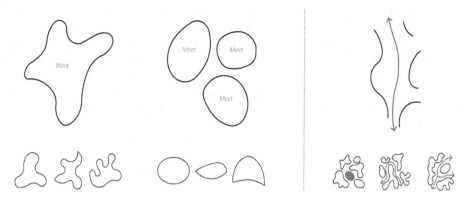

Figure 2.1 Dictionary of spatio-visual vocabulary: two hierarchically ordered distinctions in the register of spatial shape: the spatial distinction bound vs unbound signifies the social distinction business vs leisure. Within the bound spaces the spatial distinction convex vs concave signifies the social distinction meeting vs working.

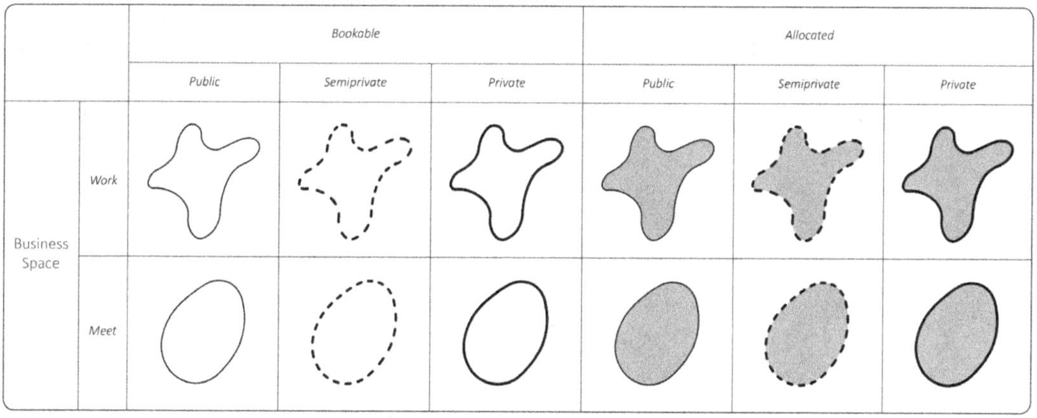

Figure 2.2 This matrix shows how three distinctions can combine to produce 12 different expressions.

private, semi-private or public, respectively represented via thick boundary, dashed boundary or thin boundary. Public work/meet areas might be WeWork-style co-working areas. Private areas belong to particular start-up companies. Color, grey vs white, further encodes allocated vs bookable spaces. The matrix indicates that the choices offered by these distinctions are freely combinable. Of course, it must be checked if all possible combinations make sense on the meaning side. If not, then restrictions on free combination must be introduced. Such restrictions or their absence, i.e. the regulation of sign-radicalcombinations, are determined in the grammar of the language.

We can see here how grammar-based languages operate by multiplication, by exploiting the proliferation of expressive power due to the power of combinatorics. The system of three distinctions offers here the expression of 12 different messages. If we would include the bound/unbound distinction in this game of combination we would arrive at 24 expressions.

Another aspect of the paradigm of parametric semiology is the readiness to consider that distinctions might be introduced not as strict dichotomies but as a gradient spectrum of options defined by two poles. Formally this can be achieved by "inbetweening" or "morphing" between the two poles of the spectrum. However, this operation makes only sense if we can meaningfully conceive of a corresponding gradient in the domain of social meaning. Within contemporary work dynamics such a spectrum of situations between a clear-cut meeting situation on the one hand and a clear-cut concentrated individual work situation on the other hand could indeed make sense. If we assume a gradation into eight grades and combine these eight choices with the two new distinctions introduced above, we arrive at 96 choices offered by working with only three distinctions (Figure 2.3).

As indicated above, the grammar of a language regulates the combination of sign-radicals into full signs as well as regulating the combination of multiple signs into a larger communication or overall text. It is therefore required to design and thus decide on the syntactic rules for combining signs and related semantic rules about how the combination of sign-radicals or signs should be read to determine the overall meaning of the combined signs. It can be expected that the downstream combination of the designed vocabulary might create problems and is thus constraining and feeding back into the design of the vocabulary. The diagrams here test the possibility of combining work and meeting spaces and show that the convex meeting spaces can and should nestle into the concave niches provided by the working spaces. Further adjacent work spaces are expected to similarly interlock. We can thus posit the grammatical rule of nesting spaces (Figure 2.4).

Within contemporary architecture, since deconstructivism, it is possible and often advantageous to allow for territories to overlap. As social complexity and communicative intensity increases it becomes increasingly problematic to restrict the spatial organization of social processes to neatly separated zones. Rather than jumping from this order of zoning to a disordered condition where everything mixes

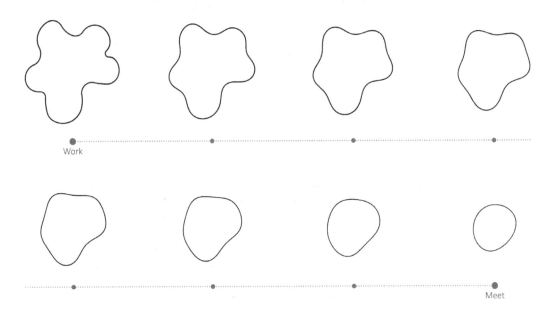

Figure 2.3 Parametric semiology: the dichotomy of convex vs concave is transformed into a continuous spectrum of shapes defined between the two poles with a continuum of shapes that are more or less convex or concave.

Social Performativity

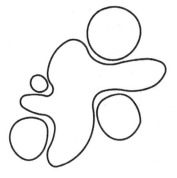 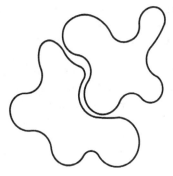

Figure 2.4 Grammar of nesting spaces: the vocabulary of concave and convex spaces lends itself to the organization of efficient aggregations. Nesting also indicates that spaces belong together.

everywhere, it is advantageous to allow for the determinate allocation and articulation of zones where particular social functions and their respective territories can overlap. The accommodation of this possibility is a recurring feature of parametric semiology. There is no guarantee that any given vocabulary can support the meaningful and coherent articulation of overlap conditions. The vocabulary introduced here does allow for the articulation of overlap, while maintaining a coherent system of signification. The overlap of two concave, amoeba-like work spaces might generate either a new concave work space, i.e. where two work groups might collaborate in a dedicated collaboration zone, or might generate a new convex space as shared meeting space that then conspicuously belongs to both work spaces that overlap there. The overlap between a concave work zone and a convex meeting zone generates a new convex meeting space. This can make sense when a meeting space that belongs to a particular work group is at the same time characterized as belonging to a larger meeting zone (Figure 2.5).

The next move in building up the complexity of the semiological system tackles the initial distinction between bound and unbound spaces. This distinction is a dichotomy with a clear-cut criterion: a bounded space is enclosed by a boundary. The unbounded space is the continuous space that flows between these bounded spaces. This criterion still holds in case of a long, meandering

  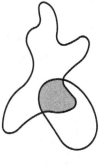

Figure 2.5 Grammar of overlap conditions: two concave work zones generate a new concave work space which belongs to both. Alternatively, they might generate and overlap in a shared convex meeting space. A work zone and a meeting zone can only generate a new meeting space. These results make sense and are coherent with the initial definitions.

boundary line, as long as it eventually closes the loop. However, this distinction can be made ambiguous, and turned into an ordered-spectrum, distinguishing degrees of boundedness. On the one side of the spectrum the distinction is clear and crisp as bounded spaces are indeed always fully closed. However, spaces might be defined that are very similar to fully bounded spaces where the boundary loop nearly closes but leaves a small gap. These gaps might gradually increase and the distinction between bounded and unbound spaces becomes increasingly blurred. On the meaning side this can be interpreted as follows: the distinction between business spaces for formal collaboration and spaces for socializing is getting blurred. A field that offers many such in-between situations might be desirable and conducive for informal communication and collaboration (Figure 2.6).

The project utilizes this possibility offered by the semiological system. It does so by arranging the spaces in such a way that an east-to-west vector of gradual transformation emerges whereby the distinction between bound and unbound spaces, which is very crisp at the western end of the space, gradually dissolves as we move eastwards. This implies that the morphological encoding of the difference between formal and informal business is redundantly over-coded by the locational encoding. Such redundancies are a useful option in cases where messages deserve to be reinforced because they might otherwise be overlooked, or where messages are important and thus deserve emphasis via duplication. The model displays a further redundancy: the gradient from the zone with the crisp bound/unbound

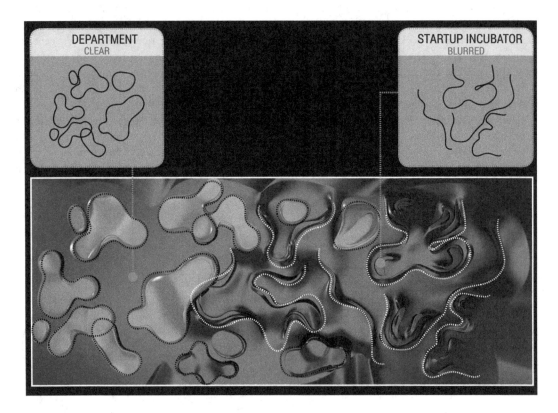

Figure 2.6 Gradient field condition: the dichotomy of bound vs unbound spaces is gradually dissolved moving from west (left) to east (right). The distinction between work and meet is being maintained as the distinction between business and socializing communication is being increasingly blurred.

dichotomy to the blurred condition is once more reinforced by a gradient treatment of the contrastive color distinction which gradually disappears as we move into the blurred condition. In turn, the ordered gradient spectrum also offers locational information and thus also operates as effective navigation aid.

In the further detailing of the three-dimensional articulation of the scheme the boundary lines themselves blur and turn from platform edges and walls more and more into relief-like stepping edges as we move into the blurred zone and as the closure of these lines diminishes (Figure 2.7). Thus, users gain multiple local morphological clues that tell them where in the spectrum from formal to informal they are located. As the detailed model shows, the distinction between working and meeting zones can also, to some extent, be maintained in the informal, blurred zones (Figures 2.8 and 2.9).

Finally, the semiological system also encompasses and makes semiological use of the furniture as well as of the ceiling and lighting design. The design succeeds in reusing the correlation of the convex/concave distinction with the meet/work distinction on the furniture scale. The ability to reuse distinctions in this way is of course elegant and advantageous and makes the overall language cognitively less taxing. Also, the choice of forms has been motivated here by considerations of pragmatic social functionality. Convex tables and convex spaces make sense as meeting tables and spaces. Serendipitously, its opposite, the concave or convoluted, meandering form is viable for both work tables and work zones (Figures 2.10–2.13).

This example shows that while signifiers, with respect to their communication function, can in principle be chosen arbitrarily, this is not always possible or advisable in architectural semiology. Here the domain of the signifier is indeed often pre-constrained to the range of forms that are pragmatically viable for the purposes they are to signify. What we further witnessed here is that the relative arbitrariness or degrees of freedom that exist at the outset when starting to design a semiological system become increasingly constrained by what has already been stipulated. We should expect that architectural codes, just like verbal languages, expand their vocabulary by analogical extension rather than by arbitrary invention.

This example is meant to illustrate how a relatively complex and nuanced semiological project can be step-wise elaborated on the basis of an integrated, systematic series of simple and intuitive form–function or form–meaning correlations. It serves here as an initial illustrative glimpse into the ambitious project of a generalized architectural semiology.

The research project of testing these complex, information-rich designs via agent-based life-process modelling runs in parallel with the creative elaboration of pertinent design languages. Together these two strands of design research serve to upgrade the discipline's capacity to enhance and verify the social performance of the built environment.

Figure 2.7 The field three-dimensionally articulated and furnished. The bound–unbound west–east gradient is redundantly over-coded via the gradual dissolution of the light–dark color contrast.

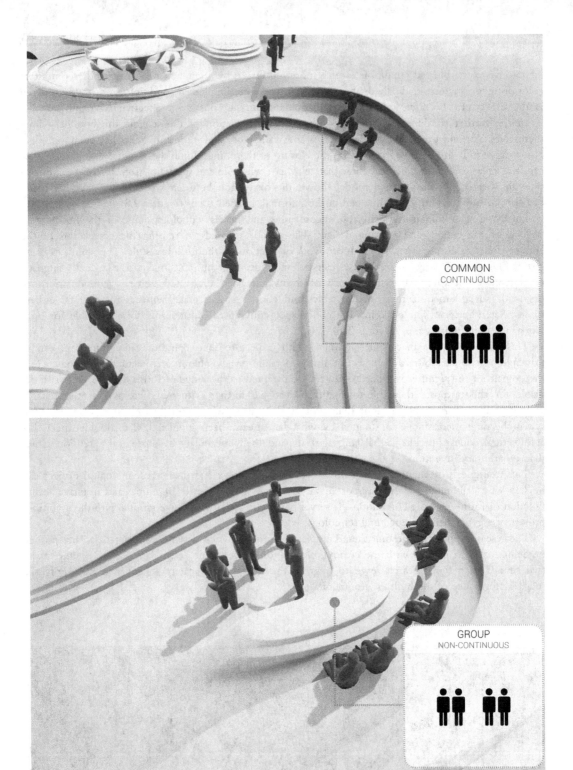

Figures 2.8 and 2.9 Detailed three-dimensional articulation of the blurred end of the gradient spectrum. The boundary itself is dissolving while the distinction between working and meeting holds fast.

Figures 2.10 and 2.11 The distinction of meet/work via the difference convex/concave is being re-applied on the level and scale of the furniture.

Figure 2.12 The crisp, formal, dichotomous end of the space in first-person perspective.

Figure 2.13 The blurred, informal end of the space in first-person eye-level perspective.

Credit for all images in this chapter: Yihui Wu, Lei Wang and Yanling Xu under the guidance of Patrik Schumacher and Pierandrea Angius at the Design Research Laboratory (AADRL), Architectural Association School of Architecture, London 2018

Notes

1 The theory of aesthetic values promoted here implies that the conditions of delight can be theoretically subsumed under the conditions of commodity, i.e. social functionality. See: section 3.8 The Rationality of Aesthetic Values, in Schumacher 2010.
2 The recognition of property preceded the rise of even the most primitive cultures (Hayek 1973).

References

Bataille, G. (1929). Architecture, in: *Ouvres completes, vol. 1*. Paris: Gallimard.
de Saussure, F. (1916/1983). *Course in general linguistics*. La Salle: Open Court.
Dennett, D. (2004). *Freedom evolves*. London: Penguin.
Hayek, F. A. (1973). *Law, legislation and liberty, volume 1: Rules and order*. Chicago: University of Chicago Press.
Hayek, F.A. (2002). Competition as a discovery procedure, in: *Quarterly Journal of Austrian Economics*, Vol. 5, No. 3: 9–23.
Hegel, G. W. F. (1837/1857). *Lectures on the philosophy of history*. London: Bell Lond.
Marx, K. (1859). *A contribution to the critique of political economy*. Moscow: Progress PublishersMOs.
Marx, K. (1861). *Grundrisse*. Harmondsworth: Penguin Books and New Left Review.
Mises, L. (1949). *Human action: A treatise on economics*. (Scholar's edition). Auburn: Ludwig von Mises Institute for Austrian Economics.
Schumacher, P. (2010). *The autopoiesis of architecture, volume 1: A new framework for architecture*. London: John Wiley & Sons.
Schumacher, P. (2012). *The autopoiesis of architecture, volume 2: A new agenda for architecture*. London: John Wiley & Sons.
Schumacher, P. (Ed.) (2016). *Parametricism 2.0: Rethinking Architecture's Agenda for the 21st Century*. London: John Wiley & Sons.

3

Informing Form
The Influence of Morphogenesis and Performativity in Practice

Alvin Huang

Introduction

Ironically, it is the natural world that has provided some of the most relevant inspirations for the computational paradigm in design and architecture. Morphogenesis, the biological (and geological) process that enables an organism (or landform) to take shape, has served as the catalyst for a genre of architectural design research that leverages advances in computational design methods, fabrication technologies, and material systems to explore an architecture that is informed by performance. This paradox of merging two seemingly contending territories is a trait of this genre of architectural design that extends far beyond the irony of the technological (and inherently artificial) being informed by the natural (and inherently organic), including issues of representation vs. materialization, architecture vs. engineering, and academia vs. industry. As such, this biologically inspired point of view has emerged as an exploration of representational mediums and material determinacy, as a blurring of the boundaries between architectural design and design engineering, and perhaps most importantly (in terms of actual impact) as both a form of applied research and as a form of experimental practice that has continued to both evolve and expand beyond the academy and the periphery of architectural discourse towards the mainstream of normative contemporary architectural practice.

In this chapter, we will examine the intellectual antecedents and design precedents that led to the development of what has come to be known as Digital Morphogenesis in architecture. Further, we will attempt to understand the legacy of this movement by exploring a series of projects produced by three boutique design practices that have been informed, inspired, and influenced by morphogenetic design in architecture. These projects (and practices) illustrate how the influence of the original protagonists of this mode of thinking and working has served as a precedent for a generation that has brought the paradigms of computational design practice out of the academy and into the world of industry as a form of specialized (and spatialized) practice.

Morphogenesis, Animate Form, and Evolutionary Architecture

When one speaks of Morphogenesis in contemporary architectural practice, one immediately thinks of the catalytic ideas and design research of the 2000s spearheaded by the Emergence and Design Group of the Architectural Association in London led by Michael Weinstock, Michael Hensel, and Achim

Menges. Though they were not the first to use the term "Morphogenesis" in regard to architecture (we will get to that later), the research, writing, and projects produced by this trio of design researchers have become synonymous with the term and have paved the way for an entire generation of designers who have taken inspiration from their pioneering work that merges concepts borrowed from nature with techniques enabled by technology.

The work of the Emergence and Design Group was catalyzed by two critical observations regarding natural systems—the first is that the global behavior of the system as a whole is understood as the cumulative product of multiple independent and discrete localized actions operating in parallel; the second is that a high degree of performative agency is embedded in the material itself. In short, the cumulative understanding that is reached via these two critical observations is that the reactive, sensory, and evolutionary responses of natural systems occur at localized levels—but collectively inform an emergent global behavior that results in form that is informed by performance.

These concepts are taken from developmental biology and biomimetic engineering, informing the morphogenetic approach to architectural design proposed by Weinstock, Hensel, and Menges. This approach gives rise to an architecture that is understood as the product of dynamic material systems that operate as generative drivers in the design process. By rejecting the conventional understanding of material systems as the by-products of standardized building systems and mass-produced components promoting the proliferation of pre-established design schemes, the thesis of a morphogenetic approach leverages the capabilities of computational design processes to privilege the evolution of morphological complexity and performative capability from material elements without distinguishing between processes of formation (shape-making) and materialization (fabrication).

The concept of the material system can be extended by considering material properties (what parts are made of), geometric logics (how parts are defined and connected), fabrication protocols (how parts are made), and assembly logics (how parts are put together), as both the performative inputs that inform the system as well as the formal output that is the performative result of the system. In this capacity, the fundamental shift is that form, material, and structure are not considered as independent design studies that can each have a multitude of options—but rather, as the result of complex and parallel interrelationships in a polymorphic system that responds to a variety of environmental, contextual, and performative influences.

However, when discussing the work of this trio we must also understand the context of their intellectual antecedents. While the protagonists of the Emergence and Design Group may have introduced Morphogenesis to a wider audience, the term was first introduced to the lexicon of architectural discourse in the seminal book *An Evolutionary Architecture* by John Frazer in 1995. Illustrating the work of Diploma Unit 11, the academic design research studio taught by Frazer and his wife Julia at the Architectural Association from 1989 to 1996, the book argues for architecture as a form of artificial life —proposing computational code (the programming of design instructions) as a genetic representation of DNA-like design information that is subject to developmental and evolutionary processes that respond to both users and environmental factors. Frazer was not interested in an aesthetic project of biomimicry—he did not believe in the superficial zoomorphic analogy of architecture looking like nature or the natural world; rather he was interested in an architecture that behaved or operated like the natural world. The stated goal of Evolutionary Architecture was to produce the symbiotic behavior and metabolic balance of the natural world in the built environment. As a result, the book also speculates about a fundamental shift in the role of the architect—moving away from the author of static buildings and cities, and towards a role that curates the dynamic evolution of a building's behavioral characteristics as a performative response to environmental conditions.

Similarly, Greg Lynn's *Animate Form* (1999) also pairs the lessons of the natural world with the opportunities of the technological world. Lynn leveraged computational techniques enabled by high-end motion graphics software against inspirations taken from performative conceptions of form that came from organic forms found in nature. Lynn was deeply inspired by the arguments made by D'Arcy Wentworth Thompson in *On Growth and Form* (1917/1952), where Thompson positions that the "action of force" acting upon an organism is the catalyst for not only its form, but also the evolution of its form over time. As a result, Lynn capitalizes on the possibilities afforded by digital media, namely animation software packages, to apply motion dynamics as a generator of architectural form. In this capacity he leverages the computational power of the machine to procreate forms that respond to the complexity of forces in the urban context, thus mirroring Thompson's argument that physical form is the singular resolution in one temporal instance of multitudes of forces governed by rates of change.

Contending Territories and Expanded Definitions

One could argue that within the discipline of architecture, there has been a historical divide between the act of representation and the act of materialization. In his seminal book *Translations from Drawings to Building* (1997), Robin Evans illustrates the unique conundrum of architecture as a discipline of making—unlike our colleagues in the fine and applied arts, architects are identified as having the unique distinction of never working directly with the medium of their creation (buildings). In short, Evans posits that an architect's work is the product of intermediate representational mediums such as drawings or models. Stan Allen also makes the distinction between what he identifies as discursive practices (those that are engaged with the mediums of representation and text) from material practices (those that utilize the abstract codes of representational projections and notations to produce new objects or organizations of matter). However, within the paradigm of Digital Morphogenesis, design tools and design processes converge to simultaneously engage both representation and materiality to create form with physically performative traits that can be adapted to particular environmental contexts. By utilizing computational design processes that not only represent the material world (as output) but which also simulate material behavior and environmental performance (as input), the product of the work is simultaneously representational as well as inherently material. This shift in thinking changes the conception of architecture away from object or artifact to that of a system of interwoven components and elements, and perhaps more importantly considers the feedback loop between the physical artifact and the computational simulation as the product of the material system.

Similarly, this trajectory of work blurs the perceived disciplinary boundaries between architecture and engineering by extending the design research legacies of analogue form-finding in the works of Frei Otto, Antonio Gaudi, Heinz Isler, and Felix Candela by appropriating conceptual, formal, and performative concepts from nature and merging them with the power of computation and the possibility of digital fabrication processes. Whereas all of the previously mentioned protagonists operated in analogue through the study of natural forms, empirical research, and a healthy dose of material computation (where the material itself processes physical inputs and outputs formal results), the new generation explores form-finding through digital simulation and an understanding of structural performance as the result of dynamic and adaptive computational systems. This shift towards understanding architecture as the product of dynamic systems of interrelated components allows designers to develop a unique logic of parts-to-whole relationships where the static pattern of structural order (tessellations, configurations, etc.) can be mediated into a system of both generative and differentiated potential, also known as structuring (Oxman, 2010).

Ultimately this type of design thinking, along with the technological advancements in design computing and digital fabrication that have enabled it, is now bridging the gap between architectural academia and architectural practice. While the catalyst for nearly every major advancement within the discipline of architecture has been a parallel development of technology, computation has often been a divisive instrument in terms of its applications in our design institutions and in our design practices. When computational processes were initially introduced into the practice of architecture, they were seen almost exclusively as tools for efficacy—digital protocols for automating existing methods of working. Meanwhile, in the academy the appropriation of animation software brought about another paradigm shift as the modeling techniques afforded by the software began to drive novel geometries and new modes of thinking as techniques for the conceptualization of the design process. However, in the past two decades the evolution of computational design research as both an academic endeavor and as a form of industrial R&D is merging the worlds of scholarship and practice as a way of thinking—connecting the digital avant-garde with the mainstream built environment. The initial explorations and advancements in Digital Morphogenesis combined with an evolving definition of the performative have given birth to a form of architectural design research that references biology and leverages computation as both a form of architectural scholarship and as a form of architectural practice. This territory between scholarship and practice explores the reciprocity between form (geometry), force (performance), matter (organization), and craft (fabrication).

Morphogenetic Form and Performance

Form in architecture has traditionally been understood as a composed response to utility (function) and gesture (expression), whereas performance in architecture has traditionally been understood as the analytical result of engineering criteria applied to the architect-imposed preoccupation with planning, skin, and symbolic gesture, while materiality on the other hand might be best understood as the specification of either finishes or building construction. From the perspective of conventional architectural practice, the performative information is thus a result of the design of form, rather than a driver of form in itself, while the materiality of form is merely one of many options in defining the finish or construction method of the form. In this capacity, the traditions of architecture operate in a hierarchical and top-down process of defining form, engineering form, and specifying materials. Meanwhile, in the natural world, performance, form, and materiality are all inherently inseparable and considered in parallel as systemic responses to external environments. This reciprocity between form and performance and materiality is the foundation for understanding morphogenetic practices in architecture. Morphogenetic approaches to design embrace an architecture that is the result of a material system that embraces the combined relevance of form, materiality, and performance as generative drivers in the design process.

"Emergence", a term borrowed from the disciplines of developmental biology, physical chemistry, and mathematics, refers to the emergence of forms and behaviors from self-organizing complex systems in the natural world. In biological systems self-organization is defined as a process in which patterns at the global level of a system emerge as a result of interactions among the lower-level entities of the system. These processes develop through the localized interactions of discrete elements that can be simulated through mathematical models and computational environments. As a parallel, these same models can be utilized to explore generative design and evolutionary processes for the discovery of both form and structure. In computational systems interactions between components can be defined as localized rule sets which drive the global organization of the system. Complexity increases when integration and differentiation increase (Hensel, Menges, and Weinstock, 2006). By integrating the self-organizing material performance of form-finding with the logics of advanced file-to-factory fabrication protocols, morphogenetic architecture understands buildings as the formalized and structured results of complex performative systems of material and energy.

A fundamental characteristic of self-organizing systems in nature is their inherent ability to evolve, adjust, or respond to stimuli in their environment. In morphogenetic design, this is achieved through the development of a dynamic geometric model that is able to adapt and respond through associative relationships to the distribution of structural forces both internally within the system and externally within its environment. This can be seen in processes of form-finding. Common form-finding methods deploy the self-organization of material systems exposed to physics to achieve the simultaneous optimization and expression of performative capacity. These systems often display emergent properties or behaviors that arise out of the coherent interaction between lower-level entities, and the aim is to utilize and instrumentalize behavior as a response to stimuli towards performance-oriented designs.

This understanding might best be illustrated by the seminal soap film studies of Frei Otto, where he illustrates evidence of the material system's capacity to compute its own form through the self-organizing behavior of its material condition. The material system itself discovers the minimal surface of equal force distribution that is generated through the surface tension of a given boundary. The protagonists in this system are the soap film and its boundary condition, each working in constant feedback with the other to find the moment of structural equilibrium that results in the emergent form.

The Pure Tension Pavilion (Figure 3.1) applies this sensibility. This portable, solar-powered tensile membrane structure is designed to not only charge electric vehicles, but to also collapse to fit within their trunks and to assemble in less than one hour. Similar to a concept car, it is a working prototype that explores a future of personal mobility and alternative energy sources, while also investigating digital design methods and innovative structural solutions.

The pavilion is an expression of the tensioned equilibrium between its elastic membrane skin and rigid perimeter frame. Its perimeter structure is framed by 24 Computer Numerical Controlled-bent (CNC-bent) aluminum pipes with swaged slip-fit connections. This frame is wrapped in vinyl-encapsulated polyester mesh membranes with a zippered seam and spandex sleeves. The continuous form of the pavilion was developed through a parallel process of analogue form-finding (through

Figure 3.1 The Pure Tension Pavilion for Volvo by Synthesis Design + Architecture. Photo by Mosca Partners

physical models) and digital form-finding (through dynamic mesh-relaxation techniques) to explore the assumed material behaviors of a tensioned membrane skin against a bending-active frame. This relationship between unique form and form-found material enables efficient and effective structural performance, produced as an extension of Frei Otto's seminal lightweight tensioned membrane structures. In both cases, the process facilitated the application of basic engineering principles and material properties to inform and develop an intuitive design process that iteratively generates, tests, and refines design options. Rather than using these tools to develop a scientific method to find form, they were used to help develop a design intuition to help guide the discovery of form that aligns with design intentions.

This pairing of form and performance can also be understood in the work of Matsys Design at Confluence Park (Figure 3.2). Located along the Mission Reach section of the San Antonio River, Colorado, Confluence Park is an educational park that focuses on the critical role of water in regional ecosystems. Designed by Matsys in collaboration with Lake|Flato Architects, Rialto Studio, and Architectural Engineering Collaborative, the park spans 3.5 acres of native planting, and hosts a 2,000 square foot multi-purpose building, a 6,000 square foot central pavilion, and three smaller "satellite" pavilions distributed throughout the park. The central pavilion is composed of 22 concrete "petals" that form a network of vaults, providing shade and guiding the flow of rainwater into an underground cistern used for the park's irrigation. Inspiring the design of the pavilion are the many plants in the

Figure 3.2 Confluence Park by Matsys Design.
Photo by Casey Dunn

region that harness the structural efficiency of curved surfaces to direct rainwater to their root systems. Each petal was cast in digitally fabricated fiberglass composite molds on site using a modified tilt-up construction technique, then lifted into place in pairs to form structural arches. The pavilion is an example of form, fabrication, and performance integrating.

The central pavilion aims to create an inspirational and aspirational space that helps the client educate the public on the topic of water conservation. Using the biomimetic principle of looking towards nature for inspiration, the pavilion geometry is modeled after the doubly curved fronds of some plants, which cantilever out, collect rainwater and dew, and redirect the water towards its roots. A modular system of concrete "petals" was developed that collected rainwater and funneled it to the petals' columnar bases and then on to a central underground cistern.

A central concern in developing the petals was to ensure that they were modular yet seemingly non-repetitive. In order to resolve this tension between cost-effective modularity and the desire for spatial richness, the design employs the Cairo tile, an irregular pentagon, as the underlying base grid. The pentagon is subdivided into five triangles to produce three unique modules: one equilateral triangle and two asymmetrical triangles that mirror each other. From this irregular triangular base grid, a parametric model was used to create the three-dimensional solids of each petal. Structurally, each petal is half of an arch which transitions from being a 16-inches-thick column and tapers to a four-inches-deep curved roof. The double curvature of each petal helps it achieve structural rigidity. Two structural pin joints connect each petal to its paired half-arch. The petals' capacity to shed water in the proper direction was tested using particle simulation, a technique in water flow analysis.

Morphogenetic Form and Digital Tectonics

The term "tectonics" is widely understood within the discipline of architecture in reference to the design expression of architectural parts (building components) that collectively form the whole of the building. However, within the paradigm of morphogenetic design, one might extend that definition to also include the relationship between the design of architectural parts and the expression of their structural performance. Digital Morphogenesis provides a platform for understanding form, material, and structure as symbiotic relationships that can drive a form-generation process. As a result, digital tectonics are the expression of architectural elements, structural performance, and geometric relationships that are enabled by the digital modeling and behavioral simulation of tectonic elements (Oxman, 2010).

This paradigm shift can be illustrated in the work of TheVeryMany, a boutique design studio operating at the intersection of architecture and public art. In particular, this understanding is expressed in their unique approach to generating, articulating, and building performative form as "structural stripes". This term was invented by the studio to describe a computationally enabled "topological-walking stripe-based material system", where thousands of unique parts collectively describe a form that is defined by its structural performance. Each of the parts is digitally fabricated from flat sheets of aluminum and fastened to its neighbors, collectively achieving the double curvature that is necessitated for funicular form and constructing the digitally generated form into a physical reality.

Minima/Maxima is a permanent installation designed by TheVeryMany for the World Expo 2017 in Astana, Kazakhstan (Figure 3.3). The project achieves its unique form and structural performance through ultra-thin (6 mm), self-supporting assemblies, which find strength in the double curvature of their form. In this approach, curves win out over angles. Columns and beams become irrelevant and are replaced with branches, splits, and recombinations of double-curved surface conditions. A "networked" surface rolls in, on and around itself, transforming into a space that upends preconceived notions of enclosure, entrance/exit, and threshold, while also providing its own support. It bends in all directions, but still manages to stand upright on its own. The project is a multi-layered composite of three layers of flat aluminum strips collectively bending in multiple directions. In

Figure 3.3 Minima/Maxima for the World Expo 2017 by TheVeryMany/Marc Fornes.
Photo by NAARO

isolation, each layer is unable to achieve the required double curvature or structural integrity. However, collectively as a network of layers working in multiple directions, the network of isotropic material forms an anistropic composite assembly.

Polymorphism and Patterns: Adaptive Differentiation and Data

Polymorphism is the state of being made of many different elements, forms, kinds, or individuals. It is an understanding of form, materials, and structure as complex interrelations in polymorphic systems that result from the response to extrinsic influences and are materialized by deploying the logics of advanced manufacturing processes as strategic constraints upon the design process.

Patterns have always been a part of the reading of architectural surfaces and the articulation of architectural form. From the decorative patterns of gothic architecture to the articulated joints of modernism, Patrik Schumacher covers the history of patterns as both decoration and ornamentation, and proposes that parametric articulation is an opportunity to consider the pattern as device for communicating social order and spatial orientation (Schumacher, 2009). We can also consider the pattern as a communicative architectural device—but one that leverages the potentials of associative geometry to generate variable fields which can not only produce visual engagement (optical effect) but can also register latent information (embedded data).

Patterns are an inherent feature of morphogenetic forms that have performative roles in a performative architecture. In the natural world, the language of both pattern and form is mathematics, yet the distribution of pattern is rarely (if ever) uniform. Patterns (as with behaviors and forms) are seen as the result of simple local interactions that produce complex global results. The localized interactions are responses to performative stimuli. As a result, patterning in morphogenetic forms can be identified as adaptive design features that are responding to performative data sets.

This understanding of performative patterning is applied in Data Moiré (Figure 3.4), a large-scale data-driven feature wall that merges the territories of data spatialization (Marcus, 2014) and data narrative (Segel, 2010). It uses the cognitive computing capabilities of IBM Watson to inform a data-driven generative design process to transform vast quantities of data into a spatial experience and marketing narrative for the IBM Watson Experience Center in San Francisco, California. The result is a digitally fabricated physical installation that represents monthly spending cycles by mapping the growing influence of mobile devices on all digital sales from 2013–2015. The data is materialized as a CNC-milled, double-layered aluminum, backlit screen wall of the Watson immersion room. It achieves a moiré-like effect—a visual interference pattern produced by the overlay of two mappings of the same data.

The project introduces a dynamic architectural feature that provides identity and enhances the visual and spatial experience of visitors to the Watson Experience Center, while simultaneously providing a spatial marketing narrative which emphasizes Watson's ability to analyze large quantities of unstructured data. Data Moiré takes advantage of two computational paradigms: the capacity of cognitive computing and machine learning to analyze and provide insight into massive amounts of unstructured data, and the

Figure 3.4 The Data Moiré installation for IBM Watson by Synthesis Design + Architecture.
Photo by Jeff Maeshiro

Informing Form

Figure 3.5 Vaulted Willow by TheVeryMany/Marc Fornes.
Photo by Marc Fornes/TheVeryMany

ability of generative design processes to drive geometries that are informed by data. However, the analysis and the geometries by themselves do not produce the impact of the project, but rather their combined capacity produces a meaningful reading and provides a visually stimulating experience.

Another example of the articulation of variability and difference is also found in the work of TheVeryMany (Figure 3.5) and their efforts to explore the concept of "coloration" as opposed to "color". Computation and procedural protocols of tessellation have opened up a new paradigm for color. "Coloration" is defined by the studio as the procedural art of applying multiple colors across sets of parts.

The possibility for coloration lies in the distinction of "fuzzy" color vs. "stepped" color. The former is a smooth and continuous gradient (like an airbrushed painting), while the latter (like a low-resolution eight-bit graphic) capitalizes on part-to-part relationships. With a kit of parts that is variably coded through a chromatic spectrum, the method of coloration enables a continuous skin made of multiple components to engage in games of rhythm, contrast, and variability.

Material Systems and Digital Craft

We are now in an era where digital fabrication processes have become pervasive—laser cutting and CNC cutting have become the norm, and 3D printing is near ubiquitous. Their uses have become commonplace, but more often than not, this prevalence has led to a widespread overuse and a lack of

Figure 3.6 The fully 3D-printed Durotaxis Chair by Synthesis Design + Architecture
Photo by Impstepf Studio

a priori consideration of the constraints and opportunities presented by each machinic process or material behavior. Alternatively, a material-based design process utilizes computation to integrate the logic of fabrication technologies with structure, material, and form (Oxman, 2012). With a material-based design process, the capabilities and limitations of both matter and fabrication become latent design opportunities which can drive the design process.

This reversal of both fabrication and material as design catalysts is evident in two projects: the Durotaxis Chair (Figure 3.6), a half-scale prototype of a fully 3D-printed multi-material rocking chair, and the 3D-printed Burbuja Lamp. Designing a 3D print, as opposed to 3D printing a design, was the fundamental challenge posed in both projects. Our goal was to produce structures which could not be manufactured by any other process. By prioritizing this fabrication method and materiality as the generative design constraints to inform geometry, both projects were experiments in 3D-printed three-dimensional space-packing structures that have been designed specifically for these machines and materials which they are manufactured by and with. They have each been pre-calibrated to capitalize on specific design opportunities that are derived from the capabilities and constraints of additive manufacturing.

In this capacity, both projects are experiments in structuring—defined as the process whereby the elements of architecture develop a unique logic of parts-to-whole relationships where the static pattern of structural order (tessellations, configurations, etc.) can be mediated into a system of both generative and differentiated potential (Oxman, 2010). As a material-based design strategy, these projects operate within the contingencies of design research where the model is the goal. As explorations of structuring, they can be viewed as scaled representations for larger architectural objectives.

Another project that explores the notion of a material system is Lumen, the temporary pavilion designed for PS1 in New York by Jenny Sabin Studio (Figures 3.7A and 3.7B). Suspended in tension within the matrix of walls of the PS1 museum courtyard, Lumen applies concepts and understandings from biology, materials science, mathematics, and engineering to suspend over 1,000,000 yards of robotically woven and digitally knitted fiber in the form of two large cellular canopies with 250 hanging tubular structures. Knitting and textile fabrication offer a fruitful material ground for exploring

Informing Form

Figure 3.7A Lumen for the Museum of Modern Art and MOMA PS1 by Jenny Sabin Studio. Photo by Pablo Enriquez

these nonstandard fibrous potentials. As with cell networks, materials find their own form where the flow of tension forces through both geometry and matter serve as active design parameters.

The structures create opportunities for visitors to interact with the work. The design incorporates 100 robotically woven recycled spool stools and a misting system that responds to visitors' proximity to produce a refreshing micro-climate. Socially and environmentally responsive, Lumen's adaptive architecture is inspired by collective levity, play, and interaction as the structure transforms throughout the day and night, responding to the density of bodies, heat, and sunlight. The result of collaboration across disciplines, Lumen integrates high-performing, form-fitting, and adaptive materials into a structure where code, pattern, human interaction, environment, geometry, and matter operate together.

Material responses to sunlight as well as physical participation are integral parts of our exploratory approach to new materials, embodiment, and a transformative, adaptive architecture. The project is mathematically generated through form-finding simulations informed by the sun, site, materials, and program, and the structural morphology of knitted cellular components. Resisting a biomimetic approach, Lumen employs an analogic design process where complex material behavior and processes are integrated with personal engagement and diverse programs. Through direct references to the flexibility and sensitivity of the human body, Lumen integrates adaptive materials and architecture as a conceptual design space. Lumen undertakes rigorous interdisciplinary experimentation to produce a multisensory environment that is full of delight, inspiring collective levity, play, and interaction as the structure and materials transform throughout the day and night.

Figure 3.7B Lumen for the Museum of Modern Art and MOMA PS1 by Jenny Sabin Studio. Photo by Pablo Enriquez

Performativity Expanded

By now, it is clear that at the root of morphogenetic practice is the notion of performativity. Performative architecture, in this essay, is understood to be an architecture of self-organization, with a capacity for systemic adaptation, and perhaps most importantly a multiplicity of performative capacities. Menges uses the term "performative" to define the quality of material systems that perform through adaptation, variation, and self-organization in response to external forces (Hensel, Menges, and Weinstock, 2012).

Whereas the origins of morphogenetic practice are clearly in the academy—from the work of Weinstock, Hensel, and Menges in the Emergence and Design Group at the Architectural Association, to the work of John and Julia Frazer in Diploma Unit 11 at the Architectural Association, to the work of Greg Lynn Form—they have since evolved beyond the academy and infiltrated the practice of architecture to define a realm of performative architecture.

Illustrated in this chapter is the work of four independent boutique design firms that are incorporating these strategies as a form of applied design research through the medium of commissioned projects. However, the scope of this influence is far greater than these four firms. From corporate design firms with specialist teams to boutique consultancies, a new form of design practice focused on the application of performance-centric design research has emerged. This form of practice has evolved from its roots in morphogenetic design research and is ultimately defined by the overlap between the experiments of exploratory architectural design research and the conventions of traditional design practice.

In the innovation-driven society we currently occupy, these practices are leveraging the power of computation against the inspirations of nature to forge a path towards design that is both innovative and performative in multiple capacities. By embracing a position of "form follows performance", these firms seek to both capitalize on the potential of form to shape and engage the world around us while simultaneously expanding the definition of performance beyond the scientific to include the experiential, fiscal, social, and cultural.

References

Evans, R. (1997). *Translations from Drawing to Building and Other Essays*. London: Architectural Association, p. 94.
Frazer, J. (1995). *An Evolutionary Architecture*. London: Architectural Association Publications.
Hensel, M., Menges, A., and Weinstock, M. (2006). "Techniques and Technologies in Morphogenetic Design." *Architectural Design* Special Issue 76, no. 2.
Hensel, M., Menges, A., and Weinstock, M. (2012). "Morphogenesis and Emergence." In Mario Carpo (ed.), *The Digital Turn in Architecture 1992–2012*, pp. 160–164. Chichester: John Wiley & Sons.
Leach, N. (2009). "Digital Morphogenesis." *Architectural Design* 79, no. 1: 32–37.
Leach, N, D. Turnbull, and C. Williams. (2004). *Digital tectonics*. Chichester: Wiley & Academy.
Lynn, G. (1999). *Animate Form*, Vol. 1. New York: Princeton Architectural Press.
Marcus, A. (2014). "Centennial Chromograph: Data Spatialization and Computational Craft." ACADIA 14: Design Agency [*Proceedings of the 34th Annual Conference of the Association for Computer Aided Design in Architecture (ACADIA)*], pp. 167–176.
Oxman, R. (2010). "The New Structuralism: Conceptual Mapping of Emerging Key Concepts in Theory and Praxis." *International Journal of Architectural Computing* 8, no. 4: 419–438.
Oxman, R. (2012). "Informed Tectonics in Material-based Design." *Design Studies* 33, no. 5: 427–455.
Schumacher, P. (2009). "Parametric patterns." *Architectural Design* 79, no. 6: 28–41.
Segel, E., and J. Heer. (2010). "Narrative Visualization: Telling Stories with Data." *Visualization and Computer Graphics, IEEE Transactions* 16, no. 6: 1139–1148.
Thompson, D. W. (1952). *On Growth and Form*, Vol. 1. Cambridge: Cambridge University Press.

4

Architecture of Change
Towards Transformable Architecture

Branko Kolarevic

Over the past decade we have seen an increasing interest in exploring the capacity of built spaces to change, i.e. to respond dynamically—and automatically—to changes in the external and internal environments and to different patterns of use. The principal idea is that two-way relationships could be established among the spaces, the environment, and the users: the users or the changes in the environment would affect the configuration of space and vice versa; the result is an architecture that self-adjusts to the needs of the users. Different terms have been used to describe such architecture: *adaptive, dynamic, transformable, interactive, responsive*, etc. As I will argue in this chapter, the principal idea behind it—facilitating and accommodating change—is not new; what has changed are the technologies (and materials) to accomplish it.

It All Started in the 1960s

The first concepts of an adaptive, responsive architecture as it is understood today were born in the late 1960s and early 1970s, primarily as a result of developments in cybernetics, artificial intelligence, and information technologies. Such architecture, however, was first envisioned in science fiction. James Graham Ballard, a British novelist, described in a short story from 1962 a "psychotropic house," a machine-like, mood-sensitive house that could respond to and learn from its occupants, becoming "alive" as it was occupied (Ballard 2001). The imagined responsive house was made from a material Ballard referred to as "plastex," a combination of plaster and latex that allowed the house to change its shape as needed. The house also had many "senso-cells," distributed all over it, which were capable of "echoing every shift of mood and position of its occupants" (p. 190).

Ron Herron's *Walking City* hypothetical project from 1964 imagined cities as giant mobile, transformable robotic structures that could move to wherever their resources were needed.[1] Intelligent, robotic buildings —self-contained "living pods," as envisioned in 1966 by David Greene, another member of Archigram— would move within the cities; the pods were meant to be independent, yet parasitic: they would "plug in" to way stations to replenish resources, moving, connecting, and disconnecting as instructed. The cities could interconnect to form larger metropolises or disconnect and disperse as required or desired.

While Ballard and Archigram's Herron and Greene were among the first to envision "alive," changeable buildings and cities capable of interacting among themselves and with their occupants, Pask

(1969), as an early proponent of cybernetics in architecture, is often credited with setting the foundations for interactive environments in the 1960s with his concept of *Conversation Theory*, intended as a comprehensive theory of interaction. Pask's ideas had a tremendous influence on both Cedric Price and Nicholas Negroponte, with whom he collaborated. Cedric Price adopted concepts from cybernetics to articulate the concept of "anticipatory architecture," demonstrated by his seminal *Fun Palace* and *Generator* projects. Negroponte (1975) proposed that computing power be integrated into buildings so that they could perform better, turning buildings into "architecture machines" that are "'assisted,' 'augmented,' and eventually 'replicated' by a computer." The aim was to "consider the physical environment as an evolving mechanism." In the last chapter, he made a prediction that "architecture machines" (in the distant future) "won't help us design; instead, we will live in them."

At roughly the same time that Negroponte was working on his "architecture machines," Eastman (1972) developed the concept of "adaptive-conditional architecture," which self-adjusts, based on the feedback from the spaces and the users. Eastman proposed that automated systems could control buildings' responses. He used the analogy of a thermostat to describe the essential components: sensors that would register changes in the environment, control mechanisms (or algorithms) that would interpret sensor readings, actuators as devices that would produce changes in the environment, and a device (an interface) that would let users enter their preferences. That is roughly the component make-up of any reactive system developed to date.

Transformable, Flexible, Adaptive, Responsive Architecture

After much initial interest in the late 1960s and early 1970s, not much happened in the next two decades, with the exception of Jean Nouvel's *Institut du Monde Arabe* (Figure 4.1), completed in 1989 in Paris, as the first significant, large-scale building to have an adaptive, responsive façade. The building's kinetic curtain wall, a technological interpretation in glass and steel of a traditional Arab lattice screen called a *mashrabiya*, is composed of some 30,000 photosensitive diaphragms that control light levels and transparency in response to the sun's location (the system no longer works due to mechanical problems).

With greater attention to buildings' energy demands and increasing capacity to monitor and manage energy use, the building envelope became the locus of technological innovation in the late 1990s. As emphasis shifted away from simply creating energy barriers (to block heat gain or heat loss) towards harvesting energy from the environment and channeling it where it is needed, architects and engineers started to incorporate electronically controlled, mechanically activated shading and ventilation systems into building façades. Double-skin façades with a controlled vented air cavity and operable, integrated shades or blinds started to emerge in the 1990s. Then over the last decade, *adaptive, kinetic,* or *dynamic* façades, and *active* and *high-performance* building envelopes entered architecture's vocabulary—and practice (Kolarevic and Parlac, 2015). Whatever term is used, the principal idea behind these new systems is that buildings should respond in dynamic fashion to constantly changing environmental conditions and do so in energy-efficient ways. Buildings thus became *adaptive*, with building envelopes playing a key role in how they adapted, i.e. responded to the ever-changing external environment.

The adaptive behavior of the envelopes can be visible or invisible (or both); in addition to components that move literally, such as the shades or vents, air (or water) would move as directed, and thermal energy would flow through different materials as designed. The visible adaptive behavior could lead to an urban spectacle that can add performative dimensions to the project that go beyond the scale of the building. While the literal movement of components is not an end in itself in many architectural projects that incorporate environmental responsiveness, it is often exploited to make the buildings appear "alive."

Figure 4.1 Kinetic curtain wall at Jean Nouvel's *Institut du Monde Arabe* (1989) in Paris, France.
Credit: Branko Kolarevic

The building envelope can act as a "living" part of the building—its "skin," a semi-permeable membrane that mediates between the building and the environment. To imbue building skins with dynamic, changing behavior, their elements need to be *actuated*, i.e. moved, rotated, expanded, shrunk, twisted, etc., so that the desired performance objectives are met. What differentiates adaptive building skins is not so much what is actuated (and that matters greatly), but how that actuation is produced. There are essentially four different methods of actuation in building envelopes: (1) motor-based; (2) hydraulic; (3) pneumatic; and (4) material-based. Most of the automated adaptive façade systems deployed to date rely on motor-based, i.e. mechanical actuation. Recently, we have seen increasing use of pneumatic actuation, primarily with patterned, multi-layer ETFE-based systems in which hermetically sealed air chambers can be inflated or deflated to create different shading densities.[2] There are also ongoing experiments in material-based actuation, which offer the promise of "zero energy" dynamic building envelopes, which are years away from large-scale commercial applications.

A mechanized Venetian blind system inside an air cavity, often in a double-skin façade system, is the most common motor-based actuation system in use today. Other automated, active shading systems sandwiched between two sheets of glass have been developed and deployed in the past, such as Jean Nouvel's *Institut du Monde Arabe*, mentioned previously. Some of the motorized adaptive façades are applied externally to the building façade, i.e. they are external to glazing units. Many of them involve some kind of retractable mechanism that can either expand or contract the shading surface. For example, the responsive façade in *Al-Bahr Towers*, two 29-story buildings in Abu Dhabi, UAE, designed by AHR and completed in 2012 (Figure 4.2), consists of approximately one thousand triangular "umbrellas" organized into hexagonal

Architecture of Change

Figure 4.2 Al-Bahr Towers (2012) in Abu Dhabi, UAE, designed by AHR, features an adaptive external shading system.
Credit: Christian Richters

units, which are attached to a conventional glass façade (Figure 4.3). The umbrellas can change their configuration from open to closed through linear actuation and origami-like folding, which is controlled by the building's management system that tracks the movement and location of the sun.

The *Media-TIC* building in Barcelona, designed by Enric Ruiz-Geli of Cloud 9 and completed in 2011, features a dynamic façade made of lightweight ETFE air cushions that provide pneumatic sun shading (Figure 4.4). The cushions consist of three layers of plastic with two air chambers between them that can be inflated or deflated as needed; the first layer is transparent; the second and third layers have a reverse pattern that creates shade when inflated and joined together. On the west side of the building, the ETFE air cushions are filled with nitrogen (mixed with tiny oil droplets) in the afternoon, transforming a transparent into a translucent façade that blocks 90 percent of the sun's radiation, thus reducing substantially the building's heat gain.

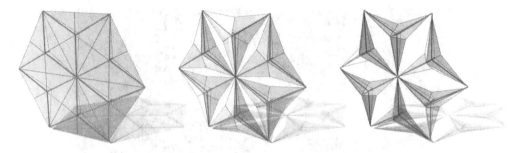

Figure 4.3 *Al-Bahr Towers*: operable triangular "umbrellas", organized into hexagonal units, shade the sun-exposed surfaces of the two towers.
Credit: AHR

The notions of adaptivity and responsiveness are not limited to building envelopes only. There is an emerging interest in dynamic structures that could enable buildings to change their overall shape and internal configuration, either in response to environmental conditions or different programmatic or use arrangements. If not changing its shape, the building, for example, could reorient itself

Figure 4.4 The *Media-TIC* building (2010) in Barcelona, by Cloud 9, features a dynamic façade made of "breathing" ETFE air cushions.
Credit: Manuel Kretzer

through rotation so that it always presents a smaller surface area to the sun, as was proposed by OMA in 2005 for a large office building in Dubai (Figures 4.5a–d). The *Sharifi-ha House* (2013) in Tehran, Iran, designed by Nextoffice (Alireza Taghaboni), features entire rooms that rotate in and out of the building's volume to either open or close it, exposing or protecting the interior from the seasonal weather (Figures 4.6a–f).[3]

Rotation is one simple way of transforming, reconfiguring, or reorienting building components (or even entire buildings). Translation along a linear path, horizontally or vertically, is another straightforward way to transform a building on the outside or inside. The *Sliding House* in Suffolk, UK, designed by dRMM and completed in 2009 (Figures 4.7a–e), features an enclosure that can move along recessed tracks to cover or uncover different buildings along its 28-meter-long linear path: the house, garage, or the annex. The *Living Room House* in Gelnhausen near Frankfurt in Germany (2011), designed by Formalhaut, features a bedroom that can come out from the main volume like a drawer and cantilever over the street below (Figures 4.8a and b). OMA's well-known *Maison Bordeaux* (1998) in France features an open hydraulic elevator platform that enables its wheelchair-bound owner to move vertically between different levels of the house. The elevator platform is actually the owner's office—a room that changes its location within the house throughout the day.

Figures 4.5a–d   OMA's design for a building in Dubai (2005) that would rotate around its vertical axis, so that main façades would receive no direct sunlight.

Credit: OMA

TIME LAPSE PHOTOGRAPHY_EXTERIOR:

Figures 4.6a–f The *Sharifi-ha House* (2013) in Tehran, Iran, designed by Nextoffice, features entire rooms that rotate in and out of the building's volume.

Credit: Nextoffice/photos by Parham Taghioff

Architecture of Change

Figures 4.7a–e dRMM's *Sliding House* (2009) in Suffolk, UK.
Credit: de Rijke Marsh Morgan Architects (dRMM)

Others are exploring adaptivity and responsiveness in architecture at the other end of the scale—that of materials—and are relying on changing the properties of materials to create an adaptive response in building surfaces and systems.[4] Then, there are issues related to building "intelligence," i.e. controlling the various adaptive responses in buildings and managing potential conflicts that may arise in operation.

In *Flexible: Architecture that Responds to Change*, Kronenburg (2007) argues that for a building to be "flexible," it must be capable of: (1) adaptation, as a way to better respond to various functions, uses, and requirements; (2) transformation, defined as alterations of the shape, volume, form, or appearance; (3) movability; and (4) interaction, which applies to both the inside and the outside of a building. Such capacities in buildings will be provided by "intelligent" building systems, which will be driven by many factors, from environmental ones, such as the control of energy use, to changing the

Figures 4.8a and b The *Living Room House* (2011) in Gelnhausen near Frankfurt features a bedroom that can pop out of the building like a drawer.

Credit: Formalhaut

appearance of the building through varying images and patterns. The systems could be either automatic or "intuitive," suggesting the capacity of the system to infer from the context an appropriate set of responses without overly explicit inputs.

These different strands of inquiry were brought together at the Adaptive Architecture conference held in 2011 at the Building Centre in London.[5] At this seminal event, convened by Michael Stacey, presentations were grouped into four thematic categories: *Dynamic Façades*, *Transformable Structures*, *Bio-Inspired Materials*, and *Intelligence*, which could be considered as a taxonomy of current research efforts in this area. The thematic area of adaptive architecture is vast, spanning inquiries that range from highly technical and pragmatic explorations of dynamic, responsive building envelopes to speculative, conceptual explorations of "emotional" responses by built spaces to their occupants' moods.

From Psychotropic to Emotive Houses

> It was a beautiful room all right, with opaque plastex walls and white fluo-glass ceiling, but something terrible had happened there. As it responded to me, the ceiling lifting slightly and the walls growing less opaque, reflecting my perspective-seeking eye, I noticed that curious mottled knots were forming, indicating where the room had been strained and healed faultily. Deep hidden rifts began to distort the sphere, ballooning out one of the alcoves like a bubble of overextended gum.
>
> (Ballard 2001, p. 187)

While Ballard's "psychotropic house", mentioned earlier in this chapter, belongs to science fiction, the *E-motive House* by Kas Oosterhuis (2002) edges closer to contemporary technological and material reality. Oosterhuis describes a responsive, interactive house that can develop its own emotions, "a house with a character of its own, sometimes unyielding, sometimes flexible, at one time sexy, at another unpredictable, stiff and unfeeling."[6] The goal is to create an "emotional relationship between the house, its occupiers and the elements." The *E-motive House* can be a "reactor" as well as an "actor," where the "acting will be made possible by a cooperative swarm of actuators like pneumatic beams, contracting muscles and hydraulic cylinders." The house is also capable of reacting: "The movement of the users and the changes in the weather are registered by a diversity of sensors, and are translated by the brain of the house into an action." In this way, the inhabitants and the actuators of the house will develop a common language so that they can communicate with each other (see endnote 6).

Oosterhuis (2003) and his Hyperbody research group designed and constructed the *Muscle*, a working prototype of a programmable building that can reconfigure itself "mentally and physically."[7] The *Muscle* is a pressurized soft volume, wrapped in a mesh of tensile Festo "muscles," which can change their own length and, thus, the overall shape of the prototype. The public connect to the prototype by sensors and quickly learns how the *Muscle* reacts to their actions; the *Muscle*, however, is programmed to have a will of its own, making the outcomes of interactions unpredictable. The ultimate goal of the project is to "develop an individual character for the *Muscle*." The *Muscle* has demonstrated that the *E-motive House* is not so techno-utopian—and that Ballard's "psychotropic" house could perhaps become a reality of our inhabitation in the future.

Open Building

In the quest to establish a context for change and variety in architecture, an international network for *Open Building* was established early in this decade.[8] In *Open Building*, the focus is on disentangling building systems and subsystems from each other so that they can be better organized to facilitate not only their efficient assembly, but also their disassembly and reassembly in different configurations. Open Building separates the major systems into the building site; the structural envelope; the division of space inside the building; plumbing; wiring; heating/cooling; and the cabinets, furniture, and "other stuff that people put inside the building." One of the main distinctions that Open Building makes is between "support" and "infill," where "support" refers to the structural envelope, and "infill" to all the other systems that are housed within the envelope. Without referencing the Open Building movement, Tristan d'Estree Sterk also separates the components of buildings into two main classes of parts: (1) the serviced spaces (responsive, internal partition systems); and (2) the external shells (responsive building envelopes or structures) (Sterk 2006). Thus, building design operates on two levels: first, the overall structural envelope is designed, and then the infill. Critical to successful implementation are interfaces between different systems, which should be designed to allow different choices of systems and their replacement, as in different fit-out systems applied in each unit, depending on the choices made by the users.

While Open Building as a design and building method aims to address the changing social and technical context in which we live and work, it focuses on building systems as a technological enabler for effective changes in use (i.e. adaptive re-use). It recognizes that there are distinct levels of intervention in the built environment; that users may make design decisions, as well; that design is a process that involves many different disciplines and professionals; and that the built environment is in constant transformation (i.e. subject to continuous change) and is the product of a never-ending, ongoing design process in which it is transformed part by part.

In *Smart Architecture* Ed van Hinte et al. (2003) also articulate a need for architecture to develop ways of designing buildings that can change but do so with a dimension of time explicitly in mind.

According to them, buildings could be divided into seven system-based layers, each with its own lifespan that ranges from centuries, down to a couple of years. The layers are (in ascending order, depending on life span): location, structure, access, façade, services, dividing elements, and furniture. They warn that the dynamics of these layers—and their different life spans—have to be taken into consideration when designing "integrated" buildings. (A building with tightly integrated building systems may not have a capacity for change if the systems are impossible to separate and disassemble.)

Lo-Tech, Hi-Tech, or Both?

The notion of adaptive, changeable buildings and spaces is anything but new. It has been present for centuries in building traditions of many different cultures around the world. For example, in a traditional Japanese house any room could be a living room or a bedroom (or a dining room). What makes this adaptability in use possible are two key features: first, all furniture is lightweight and could be removed into large storage closets; second, the size of a *space* could be easily changed using sliding partitions (*fusuma*) that separate adjacent rooms. Such spatial porosity is also present in traditional Korean houses.

The Modernist *Open Plan* is based in large part on these East Asian precedents, as were the associated notions of adaptability and flexibility. Gerrit Rietveld's seminal *Schroder House*, built in 1924, features on the upper floor an adaptive large space that can be left open or subdivided using sliding and revolving partitions into four separate rooms, i.e. three bedrooms and a living room. Similarly, Steven Holl's apartment complex in Fukuoka, Japan, completed in 1991, relied on hinged wall partitions to create adaptive apartment units in which spaces could change daily or on a larger time scale as family size changes (Figures 4.9a and b).

As more and more designers and firms begin to experiment with innovative technologies to create kinetic, adaptive spaces and systems, it is worth remembering that wheels and hinges—if used imaginatively —could create very potent transformable environments that need not rely on any fancy mechatronic set-ups. The *Naked House* in Kawagoe, Japan, designed by Shigeru Ban and completed in 2000, features four movable rooms on wheels inside a large, shed-like space (Figures 4.10a and b). The 6 sqm rooms are open on two sides and can be located anywhere within the large interior space or even moved outside; they could be also joined to form larger spaces if needed.

The notion of adaptive building envelopes is also not new. Buildings used to have adaptive façades with hinged and louvered shutters fixed outside the windows that were used to provide security or privacy or to modulate light. Sliding, externally mounted shading and privacy screens are still widely used; they are not mechanized and are moved (i.e. "actuated") by people who occupy the spaces behind them. Ordinary wheels and hinges—if used imaginatively—could create very potent transformable environments that need not rely on any fancy mechatronic set-ups. By relying on hinged panels Steven Holl and Vito Acconci created an incredibly effective, puzzle-like transformable façade of the *Storefront for Art and Architecture* in New York (1993, Figure 4.11).

We should not lose sight of simple, low-tech solutions in our current quest for adaptive systems infused with the latest sensing, control, and activation technologies. Oftentimes, simply adding wheels and tracks (and/or hinges) to elements that are then moved by people is all that is necessary for some adaptive designs to be effective spatially and programmatically. It is also worth remembering that any cutting-edge technological system of today becomes an obsolete technology rather quickly. One way of addressing this challenge of obsolescence is to rely on technologies that are already "obsolete," but which could be deployed in an innovative way. The dimension of time is rather critical for the designers of adaptive, responsive, interactive building systems of tomorrow—not only conceptually, but also operationally, at the most pragmatic, tectonic level.

Figures 4.9a and b Steven Holl's *Hinged Space Housing* (1991) in Fukuoka, Japan.
Credit: Steven Holl Architects

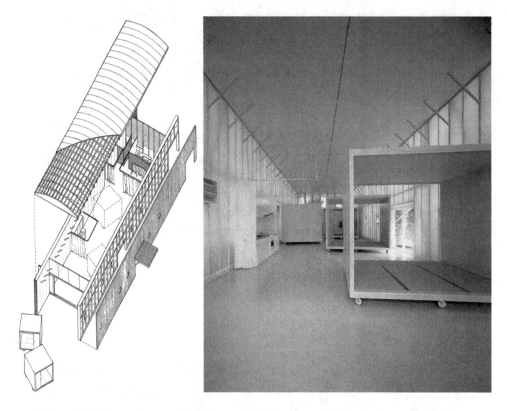

Figures 4.10a and b Shigeru Ban's *Naked House* (2000) in Kawagoe, Japan, features movable rooms on casters.
Credit: Shigeru Ban Architects/Hiroyuki Hirai

Reactive, Interactive, Participatory Architecture

Another critical issue in the design of any highly automated adaptive, responsive system is the user override. If an installed, automated system requires frequent manual overrides by annoyed users, its "life" will likely be short; a simple, people-activated "high-performance" and low-tech solution would probably more than suffice in such cases. Social and cultural factors need to be taken into account in set-ups that rely on automated systems to attain certain technical performance goals. We should not be blinded by technologies of the day and should not lose sight of the qualitative, i.e. non-quantifiable performative aspects of the project and whether they could be better served by no-tech or low-tech solutions. There is also the ever-present danger of creating "gimmicky" architecture that very quickly becomes boring.

The primary goal of constructing a truly responsive, adaptive architecture is to imbue buildings with the capacity to interact with the environment and their users in an engaging way. Architecture that echoes the work of Nicholas Negroponte could be understood as an adaptive, responsive machine—a sensory, actuated, performative assemblage of spatial and technical systems that creates an environment that stimulates and is, in turn, stimulated by users' interactions and their behavior. Arguably, for any such system to be continually engaging, it has to be designed as inherently indeterminate in order to produce unpredictable outcomes. The user should have an

Figure 4.11 The transformable façade of the *Storefront for Art and Architecture* in New York (1993), designed by Steven Holl and Vito Acconci.
Credit: Paul Warchol

effect on the system's behavior or its outcome and, more importantly, on how that behavior or outcome is computed. That requires that both inputs and outputs of the systems be constructed on the fly. It is this capacity to construct inputs and outputs that distinguishes interactive from merely reactive systems.

The distinction between interactive and reactive is what enables adaptive, responsive architecture to be seen as an enabler of new relations between people and spaces. When Philip Beesley (2006) and his colleagues describe a responsive environment in *Responsive Architectures: Subtle Technologies* as a "networked structure that senses action within a field of attention and responds dynamically with programmed and designed logic," they are referring to what is essentially a reactive system (p. 9). In contrast, Fox and Kemp (2009) argue in *Interactive Architecture* that the interaction is circular—systems "interact" instead of just "react." The distinction between interaction and reaction (i.e. a system's response) is not clear-cut, because a dynamic action of a component, for example, could be seen not simply as a reaction but also as a part of the overall scenarios of interactivity. Tristan D'Estree Sterk (2006) distinguishes direct manipulation (deliberate control), automation (reflexive control), and hybridized models as forms of interaction between the users and the technologies behind responsive systems. For Sterk, "The hybridized model can also be used to produce responses that have adjustable response criteria, achieving this by using occupant interactions to build contextual models of the ways in which users occupy and manipulate space" (p. 498).

As Usman Haque puts it, the goal is

> a model of interaction where an individual can directly adjust the way that a machine responds to him or her so that they can converge on a mutually agreeable nature of feedback: an architecture that learns from the inhabitant just as the inhabitant learns from the architecture.
>
> *(Haque 2007, p. 58)*

Thus, one of the principal challenges is how to construct (Paskian) systems that would provide enough variety to keep users engaged, while avoiding randomness, which could lead to disengagement if the output cannot be understood. The key challenge is to design an architecture that avoids boredom and retains a high degree of novelty. As observed by Haque, "Unlike the efficiency-oriented pattern-optimization approach taken by many responsive environmental systems, an architecture built on Pask's system would continually encourage novelty and provoke conversational relationships with human participants" (p. 57).

When it comes to designing adaptive, responsive environments, the "software" side does not seem to present as many challenges as the "hardware" side, the building itself, in which the majority of systems is inherently inflexible. That is perhaps where the biggest challenges and opportunities exist, as buildings would have to be conceptually completely rethought in order to enable them to adapt (i.e. to reconfigure themselves). Then there is the "middleware" that sits among the software and hardware and the users as devices that facilitate the feedback loops between the components of the system. There are other, more operational-based challenges that have to do with resolution of potential conflicts within systems. For example, Sterk (2006) discusses the coordination of responses at coincident, shared boundaries between spaces, as in a movable partition wall between two spaces, which can have actuators accessible through two independent control processes.

Another issue is that while change is desirable it would have to occur in predictable and easily anticipated ways for most purposes. If that is not possible, then there ought to be a way (in certain circumstances) for users to preview changes before they are executed, or to choose among alternatives for one (perhaps suboptimal) that fits the current circumstances, needs, and/or desires. Users may need to be informed of the impact that selected changes would have on the environment or the shape and configuration of the space. The overall issue of control is critical, as was already mentioned. In *Smart Architecture*, van Hinte et al. (2003) warn that "sometimes a simple and hence ostensibly 'dumb' building is smarter than a technology-dominated living-and-working machine over which the user has lost control."

There are also some fundamental questions that have yet to be adequately addressed. For example, while Beesley (2006) and his colleagues predict, "the next generation of architecture will be able to sense, change and transform itself," they fail to say clearly towards what ends (p. 3). Even though they ask what very well may be the key question—how do responsive systems affect us?—they do not attempt to answer it explicitly. Similarly, Fox and Kemp (2009) avoid explaining fully—and admit as much—why interactive systems are necessary, meaningful, or useful, and simply state, "the motivation to make these systems is found in the desire to create spaces and objects that can meet changing needs with respect to evolving individual, social, and environmental demands." Fox and Kemp position interactive architecture "as a transitional phenomenon with respect to a movement from a mechanical paradigm to a biological paradigm," which, as they explain, "requires not just pragmatic and performance-based technological understandings, but awareness of aesthetic, conceptual and philosophical issues relating to humans and the global environment" (p. 20).

Architecture of Change = Architecture of Time

> Accepting the dynamics of buildings and cities ... can turn architectural change into an ecologically efficient process as well as a new urban experience.
>
> *(van Hinte et al. 2003, p. 19)*

If we were to accept change as a fundamental contextual condition—and time as an essential design dimension—architecture could then begin to truly mediate between the built environment and the people who occupy it. As van Hinte (2003) and his colleagues note, "Instead of being merely the producer of a unique three-dimensional product, architects should see themselves as programmers of a process of spatial change" (p. 134). The principal task for architects is to create "a field of change and modification" that would generate possibilities instead of fixed conditions. The inhabitable space would then become an indeterminate design environment, subject to continuous processes of change, occurring in different realms and at various time scales:

> It is the form that is no longer stable, that is ready to accept change. Its temporary state is determined by the circumstances of the moment on the basis of an activated process and in-built intelligence and potential for change. Not product architecture then, but a process-based architecture whose form is defined by its users' dynamic behaviour and changing demands and by the changing external and internal conditions; an architecture that itself has the characteristics of an ecological system, that emulates nature instead of protecting it and therefore engages in an enduring fusion of nature and culture.
>
> *(van Hinte et al. 2003, p. 134)*

As Ed van Hinte and his colleagues point out, "that would be a truly ground-breaking ecological architecture" (p. 134). But to get there, we need to first answer some fundamental questions pertaining to change as a conceptual and time as a phenomenological dimension in architecture. We need to go beyond the current fascination with mechatronics and explore what change means in architecture and how it is manifested: buildings weather, programs change, envelopes adapt, interiors are reconfigured, systems replaced. We need to explore the kinds of changes that buildings should undergo and the scale and speed at which they occur. We need to examine which changes are necessary, useful, desirable, possible …

In short, much remains to be done: one could argue that change—and time as a design dimension in architecture—are far from being adequately addressed or explored theoretically, experimentally, or phenomenologically. As adaptability, transformability, interactivity, and responsiveness are probed and embedded into the buildings and spaces, we must not unconditionally and blindly chase the latest technological advancements. As argued in this chapter, an effective adaptive, responsive—and responsibly designed—building could be based on simple, low-tech, low-energy solutions. It could be actuated by people who live or work in it, who could push, pull, turn, flip, move things … and it could be intelligently augmented with sensors and actuators here and there, as needed.

Acknowledgments

This chapter is based largely on a previously published essay titled "Towards Architecture of Change" that appeared in the *Building Dynamics: Exploring Architecture of Change* book co-edited by Branko Kolarevic and Vera Parlac, which was published by Routledge in 2015. It also contains parts from the essay titled "Adaptive, Responsive Building Skins" co-authored by Branko Kolarevic and Vera Parlac in the same book.

Notes

1 Ron Herron was a member of Archigram, an avant-garde architectural group formed in the early 1960s in London. Other members of the group were Peter Cook, Warren Chalk, Dennis Crompton, Michael Webb and David Greene. The group devised a series of hypothetical projects, drawing inspiration from the technological, social and cultural context of the 1960s.

2 *ETFE* stands for ethylene tetrafluoroethylene.
3 The turning mechanism used in the house is a commonly used one for rotating theatrical set-ups and turning car exhibits in showrooms.
4 For a discussion of adaptive materials, see Parlac, Vera, "Material as Mechanism in Agile Spaces" in Kolarevic, B., and Parlac, V. (eds.), *Building Dynamics: Exploring Architecture of Change* (London and New York: Routledge, 2015), pp. 177–190.
5 See www.buildingcentre.co.uk/adaptivearchitecture/adaptive.html.
6 See www.hyperbody.nl for more information.
7 Ibid.
8 See www.open-building.org for more information.

References

Ballard, J. G. (2001). The Thousand Dreams of Stellavista, in *Vermilion Sands*. London: Vintage.
Beesley, P., Hirosue, S., Ruxton, J., Trankle, M., and Turner, C. (2006). *Responsive Architectures: Subtle Technologies*. Toronto: Riverside Architectural Press.
Eastman, C. (1972). Adaptive-Conditional Architecture, in N. Cross (ed.), *Design Participation: Proceedings of the Design Research Society Conference*. London: Academy Editions, pp. 51–57.
Fox, M., and Kemp, M. (2009). *Interactive Architecture*. New York: Princeton Architectural Press.
Haque, U. (2007). The Architectural Relevance of Gordon Pask, in Lucy Bullivant (ed.), *4dsocial: Interactive Design Environments, Architectural Design*, no. 77. London: Wiley Academy, pp. 54–61.
Kolarevic, B., and Parlac, V. (2015). Adaptive, Responsive Building Skins, in Kolarevic, B., and Parlac, V. (eds.), *Building Dynamics: Exploring Architecture of Change*, London and New York: Routledge, pp. 69–88.
Kronenburg, R. (2007). *Flexible: Architecture that Responds to Change*. London: Laurence King Publishing.
Negroponte, N. (1975). *Soft Architecture Machines*. Cambridge, MA: MIT Press.
Pask, G. (1969, September). Architectural Relevance of Cybernetics. *Architectural Design*, pp. 494–496.
Sterk, T. (2006). Responsive Architecture: User-Centered Interactions within the Hybridized Model of Control, in Feireiss, L., and Oosterhuis, K. (eds.), *GameSetandMatch II: On Computer Games, Advanced Geometries and Digital Technologies*. Rotterdam: Episode Publishers, pp. 494–501.
van Hinte, E., Neelen, M., Vink, J., and Vollaard, P. (2003). *Smart Architecture*. Amsterdam: 010 Publishers.

5

Dynamic Aesthetics and Advanced Geometries
The Meaning of Style and Form-making in Performative Design

Andrew Whalley

Performative Design: Historical Context

There is a common misconception that a performative approach to design has emerged through the new tools of computation design and parametric software. Nothing could be further from the truth, as this approach to search for efficient and optimal design solutions goes back to humankind's first ideas to create protective enclosures. Skara Brae, a ruin in the Orkney Islands (Figure 5.1), dates back to Neolithic period, 3200 BC; it was a cluster of buildings formed from sweeping stone walls, integrated into the landscape as a harmonious community (Towrie, 2019).

In my mind, architecture is an art and science in service of society. If we briefly look through the history of the built environment, it is very evident that this is not a new phenomenon but the evolution of our passion to search for the 'best' way of doing things.

Through the ages it has evolved in response to the needs of our developing civilization, in many ways defining and informing the current society. This began with the use of readily available materials to form shelters that allowed for the colonization of harsher climates, such as the yurt in outer Mongolia, quite a sophisticated cross-braced structure that can withstand very strong winds. Then there was the development of large-scale defensive structures, castles. When the Christian religion grew in its global influence, masonry structures and inventive engineering solutions gave rise to the soaring gothic cathedrals. At the same time, Islam was given expression in large-span majestic mosques. Both explored and pushed the boundaries of compressive structural concepts for load bearing masonry. Without the ability to perform analytical calculations they were based on experimentation and the constant honing down of material use (Figure 5.2).

The form-finding of performative design blossoms in the nineteenth century, solving the demands of an acceleration in development through industrialization and the emergence of new technologies. Large-span lightweight glass structures, such as Paxton's Great Stove at Chatsworth, created new tropical environmental enclosures in the cold northern hemisphere. Architects and engineers have also often been inspired in their search for optimum solutions by nature. If you look at the wrought iron structure of the Kibble Palace designed in 1873, you can clearly read the distinct geometry of the Victoria amazonica lily. This was done long before there was the ability to undertake sophisticated structural analysis, indeed before

Figure 5.1 Land dwellings: Traditional yurt construction methodologies are similar throughout the world. Stone dwellings at Skara Brae in the Orkney Islands, Scotland, are an early example of a more complicated dwelling system.

Source: https://commons.wikimedia.org/wiki/File:Montage_d%27une_yourte_murs.jpg#file; https://commons.wikimedia.org/wiki/File:Syr_Darya_Oblast._Kyrgyz_Yurt_WDL10968.png; https://commons.wikimedia.org/wiki/File:Yurt-construction-2.JPG; https://commons.wikimedia.org/wiki/File:Skara_Brae_in_summer_ 2012_(3).JPG

there was real understanding of the material characteristics of wrought iron, yet it is a triumph in the minimal use of material and probably the first glass and iron shell (Figure 5.3).

In many ways, this echoes our own design development that can be seen in the Eden Project, which we shall explore later in the chapter. This technology development also starts to migrate in its sphere of influence. So, the technologies that Paxton had developed at the Great Stove are used to solve a problem that no other architect or engineer could, a very large enclosure that had to be built and open in less than a year that would become known as the Crystal Palace, for the Great Exhibition of 1851, the first world expo.

An international competition had produced 245 proposals, none of which satisfied the brief for cost or construction time. Paxton was called in by one of the commissioners, Henry Cole, because of his previous inventive work. The exhibition was typical for the Victorian era, exceptionally ambitious with a building footprint three times the area of St Paul's Cathedral. His ideas were revolutionary and differed from the traditional construction proposals that the competition had received. His proposal

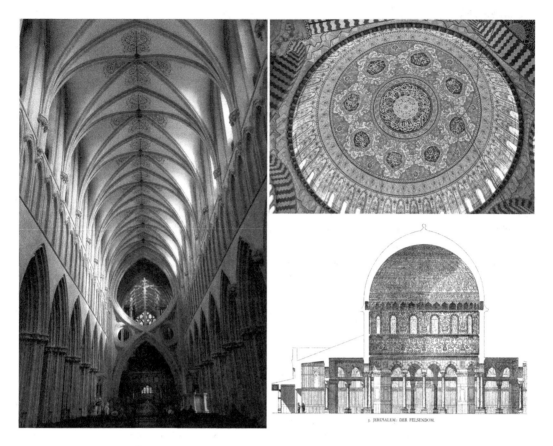

Figure 5.2 Arches and domes: The ribbed arches of cathedrals and carefully considered domes utilized advances in structural capabilities in houses of worship.

Source: https://commons.wikimedia.org/wiki/File:Wells_Cathedral_Ceiling.jpg; https://tt.wikipedia.org/wiki/Sinan#/media/File:Selimiye_Mosque_Dome.jpg; https://upload.wikimedia.org/wikipedia/commons/4/41/Dehio_10_Dome_of_the_Rock_Section.jpg

Figure 5.3 Kibble Palace in Glasgow has a unique round shape formed from many panes of glass.

Source: https://commons.wikimedia.org/wiki/File:Roof_Kibble_Palace_Glasshouse.JPG. Lily image courtesy of the author, Andrew Whalley

used the new invention of relatively cheap cast glass by the Birmingham glass manufacturer Robert Chance. He developed a modular and highly repetitive construction system, with small-scale components, framed in laminated timber and supported on a skeleton of cast iron. The rigor of his concept can be seen in his first sketch on a piece of blotting paper. The ambitious project was designed, detailed and costed in four weeks. To ensure of its success Paxton published the design with a long article on 6 July in the *London Illustrated News*. In less than eleven months the Crystal Palace opened to the public (Chadwick, 1961) (Figure 5.4).

This is a great example of how technology transfer and performance-driven design can resolve seemingly insurmountable obstacles to deliver not only a very efficient building but an aesthetically stunning one as well. The building was a kit of parts, using thousands of identical components, and on-site manufacturing ensured that it could be built extremely quickly and economically. In fact, it also allowed for its disassembly, at the end of the expo when it was moved from Hyde Park to its new home in Sydenham, London. This is a line of thinking we need to explore in addressing our current twenty-first-century challenges. All of this occurred well before there were any mathematical structural analytical capabilities. Throughout the project, Paxton collaborated with the engineer William Henry Barlow, who went on to design the majestic large span of St Pancras Station. The modular concepts and ridge-and-furrow glazing systems were also adopted by one of the commissioners, Isambard Kingdom Brunel, for the later Paddington Station. So, we can clearly see how design concepts migrate and evolve to provide fresh solutions to new challenges (Brindel, 2006).[1]

This acceleration in technological and scientific development continues into the twenty-first century with agricultural revolution and the industrial assembly line migrating large swathes of the population from the countryside to cities. This increased the need for large long-span assembly plants such as Ford's Highland Park in Michigan, designed by Albert Kahn Associates, which heralded a new era in industrial production for the Model T. A behemoth covering 102 acres, it included all aspects of the Ford enterprise, from clerical work in offices to foundries, power plants and of course the famous assembly lines manufacturing the Model T. It was to become a global precedent for mass manufacturing. In the city, a similar revolution in built form was happening, made possible with the production of low-cost iron. New tall, skeletal structures serviced by the invention of electric gearless traction elevators allowed cities such as New York and Chicago to grow in an unprecedented way, dense and vertical. These concepts were honed by the modern movement, and by the mid twentieth century, the adoption of the hung glass curtain wall formed the urban landscape that we take for granted today. Buildings now became machines, the combination of structure, skin and environmental systems, highly refined, with large efficient floor plates accommodating thousands of workers in each building, such as Mies Van der Rohe's Seagram Building (1958) in Manhattan. The United Nations Secretariat Building, completed in 1952 and designed by a multinational team of architects including Le Corbusier under the direction of American Wallace K. Harrison, is another building that captures this mid-twentieth-century moment. With sheer single-glazed façades facing east and west, it used large mechanical systems with plentiful cheap energy to heat the building through the winter and then cool through the summer. This was a moment when technical prowess alone was the answer, almost working against nature, with mankind triumphing over all. In fact, from this point on the design exploration through the remainder of the century was one of continued refinement, with larger façades and taller elevator systems resulting in an ever-increasing demand on energy as a solution.

Undoubtedly, the two world wars of the first half of the twentieth century shaped and seeded the technological revolution of the second half, from space exploration to the advanced computing and the era of information technology. But it also gave rise to new era of invention and design ingenuity. This characterizes the work and research in the USA of Buckminster Fuller and his acolytes on the crest of technological transformations. It is also very evident in the UK, but with considerably fewer available resources (Cooke, 2018). This undoubtedly underlies the theoretical work of Archigram and in turn

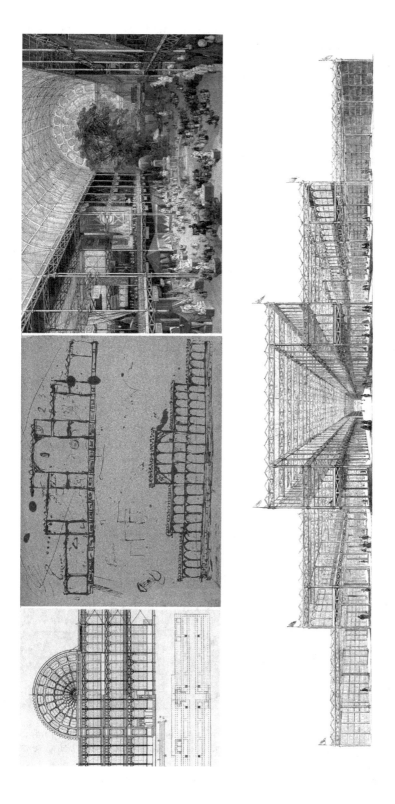

Figure 5.4 The Crystal Palace, designed by Joseph Paxton, utilized glass to realize an impressively large structure.

Source: Our Copyright British Library (Paxton sketch); https://commons.wikimedia.org/wiki/File:The_Crystal_Palace_page_a1.jpg; https://pl.m.wikipedia.org/wiki/Plik:Crystal_Palace_interior.jpg; www.bl.uk/learning/timeline/item106135.html

a new generation and era of performance-driven architecture that was being pioneered by architects such as Foster, Rogers, Hopkins and Grimshaw. As with new emerging firms of architects today, they started with quite modest briefs, such as factories. Simple briefs were used to demonstrate the potential of new technologically driven design solutions that questioned the current thinking, undoubtedly emerging from the engineering and cultural traditions of the nineteenth century that were outlined earlier. The goal was a more responsive, flexible and adaptive architecture that could solve the demands of a society immersed in the information technology era. This particular direction of design exploration epitomizes our topic of form-making with performative design. It was driven by testing completely new ideas in the search for optimum and adaptive solutions. As an example, the Grimshaw-designed factory in Bath for Herman Miller rethought the entire nature of the building typology, replacing the dumb brick box, which had not evolved since Ford's Highland Park, with a design that was driven not just by the demands of production but by the community of workers inside. So, this is now, to my mind, a building that is now driven by people and community as well as function.

The solid masonry walls were replaced with a steel frame supporting a modular set of insulated glass reinforced plastic panels and glazed sections, all interchangeable so each façade can be programmed and easily changed throughout the building's life. The factory is on the banks of the picturesque River Avon in Bath and made maximum use of the location with views out on to the river and indents in the façade accommodating recreation spaces for the workforce. Indeed, when I visited the building 12 years after it was completed the façade had been changed at least six times. The building could adapt to the needs of new products' manufacturing requirements, but most importantly ensured the best working conditions regardless of configuration. So, when the café area moved due to a change of product line the glazed panels on the façade moved with it, maintaining views out to the river. The servicing for the building follows the same strategy, all hung above the large open floor plate to accommodate constant change (Figure 5.5).

This agility to absorb change also delivers economy and longevity, which ultimately means a more sustainable built form that uses fewer of the world's resources. Indeed, over four decades after it first opened, Grimshaw is updating the building using all of the original interchangeable façade system and converting it into a school of art and design, a testimony to the value of flexibility and adaptability.

Figure 5.5 Herman Miller: Grimshaw's factory for Herman Miller utilized a system of interchangeable panels that allowed for easy reconfiguration. The structure is currently being re-adapted as a School of Art.
Sources: Copyright Jo Reid and John Peck; and rendering courtesy of Grimshaw

Dynamic Aesthetics and Advanced Geometries

We have continued developing these concepts with a more recent factory for Igus in Cologne, Germany. Along with absorbing change, it has grown by 400% over ten years through seven phases of development. Internally all of the facilities such as meeting rooms and staff facilities are in pods that can be simply moved and rearranged around the grid of the building, just like pieces on a chess board. Externally all of the panels are reused with new ones added as the complex grows, so there is no waste (Figure 5.6). The thread that runs through all of this work from the yurt to our factories for Herman Miller and Igus is the architect's use of ingenuity and the search for the optimal solution.[2]

Figure 5.6 Igus: The 'pod and panel' organization of the Igus factory and headquarters allowed the company to effortlessly expand at least six times over the life of the building, adding modules existing units as needed.

Source: Copyright Jo Reid and John Peck

Andrew Whalley

Computational Design

As the twentieth century drew to a close this approach was given a key additional resource, computational design analysis. Initially, this was strictly the preserve of well-resourced large architecture and engineering firms using expensive mainframe computers, principally limited to streamlining the production of construction drawings. We had our opportunity in the late 1980s when we were awarded the new passenger terminal serving the Channel Tunnel at Waterloo, London. It was the country's largest public infrastructure project at the time and was slated to mark a renaissance in rail travel and its architecture for the UK. With its large and complex geometry, it was time to invest in computer technology, but following discussions with the architect and Archigram founder, Ron Herron, we decided to take a radically different approach than many, which I am sure was viewed at the time as risky. The new Macintosh desktop computer had been launched and we decided that individual desktop computers, one on every architect's desk, was a more agile approach than the standard mainframe and terminal. Effectively a new computer 'drawing board' for every architect, it also opened up the potential to interrogate geometries, to investigate structure and skin as one interconnected system and to investigate the performance of these geometries in parallel. For us, it was the birth of computational-driven, performative-designed architecture.

Waterloo Terminal is actually a multi-layered complex building. It is built on a new, concrete 12-meter-high viaduct structure which supports the 400-meter-long trains. Below this structure is the equivalent of an international airport terminal, with security, a departures lounge, arrivals, immigration and customs, capable of handling 15 million passengers a year; all with the added complexity of having trains weighing 800 metric tons running overhead. Above is the train hall. Asymmetrical in form in response to the layout of the train tracks, it follows a sinuous variable curve that changes in span from 50 meters to 35 meters. It was a complex variable geometry that meant that the form of the roof was comprised of non-uniform rational basis (NURB) spine geometry. At that time there was no computer-aided design software that could handle this in three dimensions, so the roof had to be built as a series of trusses at each grid line and then separately joined in a different model. We developed the structure with the engineers, Anthony Hunt Associates. Along with computers we also worked with physical models to test the geometries from the overall form to the individual connections. The bowstring trusses are like skeletons where the material is paired down to where it is needed. The compressive element is comprised of a series of differing radius steel tubes, which allow the truss to effectively telescope down as the span recedes. They are connected to the tension cable with tapered cone tubes. These are not commercially available, so we had to devise a way of fabricating them using brake-pressed half-steel cones. As the arches are asymmetrical, the tension cable switches from the underside to the outside at the point of contra-flexure. This had the benefit of also switching the structure from the inside of the envelope to the exterior, effectively keeping it clear of the outside track and train that ran close to the edge of the roof. It also gave a level of articulation and detail to the expression of the London-facing façade. We wanted the trains to become part of the architecture, adding a dynamism to the elevation, and of course allow the passengers to look out to London. This meant finding a solution to glazing a very complex NURB geometry. Pilkington had just completed a new facility that automated the production of toughened planar glazing. This brought down the cost and speed of delivery but meant keeping to the discipline of rectilinear glass sheets, which would seemingly be completely incompatible with the geometry. The answer came from our Victorian forebears. If you look at the curving geometries of the glass houses we discussed earlier in the chapter, they are often resolved by treating the glass sheets like shingles with variable overlaps. So, we did the same, devising a concertina joint to deal with the changing planes of the vertical joints and a wiper gasket for the variable horizontal joint. Perhaps the most challenging aspect was finding a solution to join this flowing envelope to the structure with literally hundreds of different geometric conditions. The solution was a pragmatic one, a joint that could rotate in all three axes,

Figure 5.7 Waterloo: The unique structural joints at International Terminal Waterloo allowed the station to fit on a complex site while maximizing the span of the truss system.
Source: Copyright Michael Dyer

fabricated as a lost wax casting in stainless steel. This gave us a joint with incredible precision that could be repeated hundreds of times. In fact, the fabricator used the same tools for stainless-steel hip bone replacements. It was probably one of the first times that lost wax casting had been used at scale in the construction industry. The end result gave us a very fluid, variably curved glass wall, yet all made up, in a rational way, using rectilinear forms and resolved with one detail. This relationship between the overarching concept and fine detail, macro-to-micro, is an important one as in many ways as the detail can be seen as having the DNA imprint of the building's concept (Figure 5.7).

Architecture and the Anthropocene

As we approached the new millennium, a significant milestone, it gave pause to reflect on the past. It was becoming evident that the rapid growth in the west over the last 200 years of industrialization was having a very detrimental impact on the planet, or to be more precise changing a number of key characteristics that enables it to support *Homo sapiens* and the biodiversity of our environment. This in my mind is humankind's greatest challenge. It is both a crisis and an opportunity to restructure future development, with probably one of biggest influences on this rapid change being our built environment. The role of the architect is instrumental in forging a long-term viable future. A performative design approach that searches for optimized solutions is the critical and the only way forward.

In 2018, the UN published a revision to its World Urbanization Prospects. It maps a series of statistics that illustrate how we are rapidly changing to an urban based civilization and the impact that is having on our planetary environment. In 1950, 30% of the global population lived in cities. In nearly 70 years, this has risen to 55%. Our population growth continues unabated and is currently growing at 83 million people each year. With this level of growth, it is predicted that in 30 years the global population will reach 9.8 billion, and at this point 68% of the world's population will live in cities. In simple terms our urban population footprint will increase by 50% in just three decades. Looking at this over 60 years, which is only two generations away, the building stock will double, providing 230 billion square meters of buildings, which, to put it in perspective, is the equivalent of constructing every building in Japan every year for the next sixty years (Abergel, Dean & Dulac, 2017). Currently, the UN predicts that cities consume 75% of the world's energy and emit 80% of the world's total greenhouse gases, including the indirect emissions generated by urban inhabitants. Buildings consume vast amounts of energy, not just for their initial construction but in their ongoing operational life-span, currently estimated to be 35% of the world's energy and 40% of energy-related CO2 emissions. Yet these cities, and in particular the opportunity for new optimized models, are the opportunity for change, as they also generate 75% of a country's Gross Domestic Product, generating the wealth that could fund investment and change (UN Habitat for a Better Urban Future, 2012). The Paris Agreement I – United Nations Framework Convention on Climate Change (UNFCCC) was a milestone with a global agreement to limit global warming to a maximum rise of 2 degrees C this century, benchmarked to pre-industrial levels while pursuing further measures to improve this reduction to 1.5 degrees C. Currently, the International Energy Agency's *Reference Technology Scenario* estimates that the energy consumption by buildings will increase by 30% by 2060 if we do not change current design systems and trends. That would equate to a further 415 gross tons of CO2 released into the atmosphere over the next 40 years, which in itself would equate to a further 1 degrees C of global warming (UN Environment and International Energy Agency, 2017). The UN has categorically stated that the only option is a rapid deployment of energy-efficient and low-carbon building design. Along with intelligent operational systems, construction will need to be optimized. If we are to meet the UNFCCC target and limit the rise in global temperature to 2 degrees C we will need to increase the number of high-performance, low-carbon buildings by six-fold from the current trend (UN Environment and International Energy Agency, 2017). So near-zero-energy, zero-emission buildings must become the construction standard globally within the next ten years. The World Green Building Council is now promoting a campaign to accelerate the adoption of net-zero buildings to 100% by 2050.

Learning from Nature

How do we respond to these challenges which will undoubtedly require a paradigm shift to design at all scales, from products to buildings and cities? Some architects have been responding with an environmentally influenced design agenda since the 1980s, developing design responses that offer ideas for an alternative and appropriate approach. I would like to explore a number of Grimshaw's projects that work with and learn from nature, with more efficient designs that utilize their environment as part of an overall dynamic and responsive architectural system, where form is shaped by a performative approach to design.

Harvesting the Sun

Over 30 years ago we were asked to put forward proposals for the British Pavilion at the Seville World Expo '92. As we explored earlier in the chapter, world expos are often an opportunity to demonstrate fresh thinking on a world stage. We saw this as an opportunity to explore an architecture which had a new vocabulary, created as a response to environmental need. The form would be performatively driven and a response to its location, the hottest city in Europe, with summer temperatures of 38 degrees C that could peak at 45 degrees C. Nature often draws on what is abundant as part of a systems solution. Here the issue was long hours of hot direct sunlight in an arid environment. But a problem can also offer the solution: the roof of the pavilion was to be one of the first buildings to harness photovoltaic panels to harvest sunlight as an energy source to cool the building.

The pavilion's main façade faced east, so this power was used to pump water from a pool that was filled from the high water table on site and pour it over the glass façade. Traditionally glass walls are shaded using brise-soleil. They are only partly effective, and they also block the entire spectrum of light, which leaves the building permanently in shade. With the water wall the infrared part of the spectrum, the greatest source of heat, was removed, leaving the rest of the spectrum, including all visible light, to enter the pavilion. This left the entire interior washed with 'cooled' sunlight. This was one component that, in conjunction with other systems, helped temper the interior so the reliance on air conditioning could be greatly reduced. It is of course a temporary structure that had to be quickly built and then disassembled, which informed the choice of materials, structure and assembly. The west wall, which faced the back of the Expo site, was built from shipping containers filled with water. This shielded the pavilion from the full force of the afternoon sun and its significant thermal mass took full advantage of the large diurnal temperature variation from night to day, helping to keep a consistent internal temperature. The north and south walls were lightweight fabric supported on aluminum yacht masts, with the south façade formed from a number of layers shielding the strong sunlight and allowing breezes to run through and keep the membrane cool. The same approach was used on the roof integrated with the photovoltaics (Figure 5.8).

Although this was technologically and performatively driven, it actually draws on the traditional architecture of the region which has helped temper the heat in Seville for millennia. The city is comprised of tall courtyards with fountains and pools to create microclimates. Indeed, the narrow roads are frequently shaded with fabric awnings in the summer. Clearly all of these systems needed to be modelled, tested and developed and we worked very closely with the engineers, Arup, on its development. However, in the same way as Paxton's first sketch captures the essence of his design for the 1851 Crystal Palace, I think the same can be said of Nick Grimshaw's first concept sketch of the

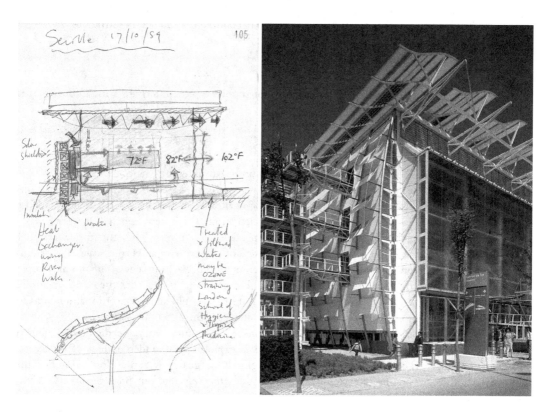

Figure 5.8 British Pavilion: Sir Nicholas Grimshaw's original sketch showing the concept for the British Pavilion at Expo '92.
Sources: Sketch courtesy of Grimshaw; photo copyright Richard Bryant

Figure 5.9 British Pavilion: Solar collection implements on the roof of the British Pavilion at Expo '92 powered pumps that created walls of water that strategically cooled the structure.
Source: Copyright Richard Bryant

pavilion. Our greatest analytical design tool sits on our shoulders; computers are a useful development tool that sits on a desk.

Natural Structures: Touching the Earth Lightly

As we explored earlier, botanical gardens do not just propagate interesting and exotic plants over the years; they have also been an opportunity to develop ingenious new tectonic ideas. The Eden Project was to be situated in a disused china clay quarry in Cornwall, UK. It was a project partially funded by the Millennium Commission, as part of the UK's celebrations for a new epoch. Our brief was to create a showcase for global biodiversity and our dependence on plants. The structures were to be large enough to allow the exhibition and study of a range of plants on an ambitious scale. Two climate capsules, or biomes, were to be recreated from different world environments. The humid tropical (rainforest) and the warm temperate (Mediterranean) biomes were to be constructed as enclosures. With the humid tropical biome, this required an enclosure that would allow trees to mature and form a canopy at 40 meters in height, setting a clear span building height of 50 meters.

Botanical science has developed from the nineteenth-century encyclopedic cataloguing of specimens. Now, in the twenty-first century, science is exploring our understanding of biodiversity and the importance of genetic grouping and ecosystems. Our goal was to develop an architectural response that was informed by these new demands in the same way that our predecessors had, almost 200 years ago.

Our starting point was to use the contours of the clay pit and its topography as an integral part of the architecture, using the quarry wall as one side of each biome. This had the advantage of creating great spatial drama and a terraced profile as staging for the plantings, thus creating drama from day one, even when many of the plants would be relatively immature. It also gave us a massive south-facing thermal mass that could store heat that was captured during the day and then released at night.

New computer modelling had become available that supported complex, topographic forms in three dimensions. A terrain model was built to explore the potential sites for each of the structures. This was assessed by looking at both the topography and potential solar orientation. Sun path analyses were used to find the optimum location for each biome.

We were working with the engineers Anthony Hunt Associates and our first proposals built upon our work together at Waterloo, with a series of diminishing primary steel trusses connected to each other with a secondary system supporting a ridge-and-furrow glazing system that would have been familiar to Paxton. It was a system that lent itself to a glass enclosure, but we were exploring the use of a new lightweight membrane, ethylene tetrafluoroethylene (ETFE), and wanted to find a structural solution that would take advantage of its ultra-lightweight, long-span characteristics. To achieve the technical criteria that the botanists were requesting to support the range of plant species required the absolute maximum amount of daylight possible in the enclosure. An advantage ETFE has over glass is that it is transparent to a broader range of the light spectrum, including the very shortwave spectrum that includes essential ultraviolet light.

Nature has many lessons to teach both architect and engineer, most obviously that nature is based on the minimum use of energy and the careful use of resources through efficiency in metabolism. What often appears to be fragile is actually robust as it has an ability to adapt.

An excellent example of these efficiencies can be found when examining the one-celled creatures Radiolaria. As they grow through centrifugal force in a process called biomineralization, the silica that they are formed from generates spectacular hexagonal and pentagonal patterns (Ball, 2016). It is similar to the way bees build honeycombs because they are 'busy bees', trying to achieve the maximum with the minimum effort. Nature seems to continually form hexagonal structures as the most efficient way of absorbing stress.

We redefined the generation of the biome forms at Eden as a series of interconnecting spheres, similar to a series of soap bubbles clinging to the edge of the quarry. We took this computer model and intersected it with the terrain model of the clay pit, which in turn defined the final form of each biome. This allowed us to develop a proposal that was independent of the exact quarry profile. It also allowed us to define the surfaces as geodesic shells that could get the most out of the long-span ultra-lightweight nature of foil pillows.

As with the Radiolaria, the geodesic shell is formed from hexagons to minimize on tube length to surface area. The size of the hexagonal grid is a proportion of the diameter of the sphere, with the largest dome being subdivided into pillows with a diameter of approximately 11 meters. The pillows are up to two meters deep and are formed from three layers of ETFE foil. The two air cavities are pressure equalized by means of a small connecting aperture, but in terms of thermal transmittance they are effectively separate. The complex geometry of the pillows – hexagonal in plan and double-segment-shaped in section – makes U-value calculation by conventional methods impossible. Much of the cavity space is large enough for significant convection currents to be set up. A combination of theoretical analysis (computational fluid dynamics/finite element analysis) and empirical testing (by means of hot-box experiments) determined that the U-value was approximately 2.7W/m2K. Therefore, in spite of the material being 200 microns thick or less for each layer, it performs better thermally than double glazing. As with glass it would be possible to apply low emissivity coatings to one or more of the ETFE layers to achieve even better performance (Figure 5.10).

Our goal was also to create a solution that embodied Eden's environmental ethos. The embodied energy is substantially better than a glass solution. In material terms it uses less than 1% of the volume of material that would have been used in a double-glazed solution. This, coupled with a proportionate reduction in supporting framework, again substantially reduces transportation impact and costs. The

Figure 5.10 Eden: The inventive form of the biomes at Eden Project offer a lightweight structural system that covers a large area while allowing the transparency required for solar transmission.
Source: Copyright Hufton + Crow

material is also very light to erect, reducing the amount and scale of site equipment required. Most importantly, it can be recycled.

Environmentally, the enclosures are cooled and ventilated through the natural stack effect utilizing the form and volume of the biomes. Large louvered sections around the base of the structure introduce fresh air that rushes to the top of the biome and is exhaled out of opening panel arrays at the crown of the dome form. This gives rise to a constant breeze that also helps to agitate and exercise the plants.

Perhaps our achievement at Eden can be best summarized by the weight of the biomes. The humid tropical biome weighs approximately 450,000kg. This is actually less than the weight of the air that the envelope encloses.

Harnessing the Wind

We often win our work through design competitions which was the case with Southern Cross Station in Melbourne, Australia. The current station could not cope with an increasing demand, and was dilapidated and cut off the end of the Central Business District from the Docklands, an area slated for massive redevelopment that would become an extension of Melbourne's business center. The government had commissioned a reference design that indicated an all-enclosing station roof that would support a mass array of mechanical equipment to ventilate the station, dealing with the diesel fumes from the trains and keeping the space cool during the hot days of the Victoria summer. We worked on the proposals with local architect Jackson Architecture and proposed a radical reconfiguration of the station plan and section so that it fully integrated with the city and connected the Docklands in a seamless way for both traffic and pedestrians.

The design focus of the station is the dune-like roof that covers an entire city block. It works as a visual bridge between the city center and the newer Docklands, providing a 'gateway' to the city. On a functional level, it unites all the disparate elements of the interchange, providing a cool, shaded space at a civic scale (Figure 5.11).

Figure 5.11 Southern Cross: The wave form roof at Southern Cross Station is not only aesthetically pleasing, it allows for the ventilation of diesel fumes from within the station without unsightly, expensive mechanical equipment.
Source: Copyright Shannon McGrath

The roof's form has been generated by the performative requirements of the station and plays a crucial role as part of the environmental envelope. Environmental concerns were central to the brief, so this undulating blanket roof was developed in response to the hot external climate and the internal need for diesel extraction and ambient cooling via natural ventilation. While it is waterproof to the outside it seems to breathe internally, allowing smoke, diesel particles and contaminates to be discharged to the outside. The individual roof moguls act as air reservoirs that collect hot air together with the train's diesel fumes. The hot air and fumes are drawn through the roof, via louvres at the apex of each mogul, by the prevailing winds. These north-west and south-west winds define the valleys that cut across the roof form, ensuring natural ventilation year-round. This solution is a contemporary reinterpretation of the historic shed roofs of nineteenth-century rail halls in Europe.

The topographic geometry of the roof is its interior conditioning and ventilation system. Working with the form and the prevailing environment we were able to completely remove all mechanical equipment and of course the energy requirements to run them, radically reducing the energy load of the building.

The roof system is devised from complex geometry, with no repetition or symmetry. In spite of this, rapid prototyping ensured individual truss sections could be designed and then prefabricated economically. The roof's structural grid is formed by a series of circular hollow section tubes that connect to one another laterally through a radiused contra-flection, providing a continuous mesh. The grid has 40-meter centers in both directions. This minimizes the structural connection points to the ground thus maximizing visual transparency and spatial flexibility. In order to diffuse the sense of weight from this large structure, the spine trusses are covered with a continuous strip of ETFE pillow cladding.

There is a well-known expression 'just because you can, doesn't mean you should'. Often the new computational tools of parametric design are used to create willful forms devoid of any real function or purpose. Nature always works efficiently and with purpose and this is why natural forms are elegant and have a timeless beauty. The roof intrinsically expresses its own function and its rhythmic beauty is almost incidental.

The radically reduced systems and energy load at Southern Cross is not the result of expensive technological intervention but design ingenuity, an approach we also utilized with the Phillip and

Patricia Frost Museum of Science, or Frost Science, in Miami. The museum sits beside the new Perez Art Museum in a park that faces the intercoastal waterway. This park setting beside the water was to be an instrumental driver in our design concepts. From our initial competition ideas, we wanted the building to be an exhibit in itself to tell a story of sustainability while providing an innovative, yet flexible response to the programming needs. We wanted visitors to be connected to the park and Miami's environment so when there is a downpour on a summer afternoon it adds to the drama of the visitor experience.

The museum's environmental strategy was informed by a comprehensive study that was funded by the United States Department of Energy. The aim of the research was to explore the physical shape of the building so that it could harness the sea breezes as part of a natural ventilation system. This in turn would allow us to radically reduce the need for mechanical equipment and energy consumption. We worked with iterative wind tunnel and computational fluid dynamics testing in parallel with physical study models, exploring multiple options with the goal of achieving an entirely naturally tempered space. A key design objective was to relocate as much of the building's visitor program and its public circulation to unconditioned exterior shaded spaces in order to reduce the energy consumption of the building and to improve the visitor experience. To achieve this, the design needed to use the uninterrupted prevailing winds coming in from the ocean and increase ambient breeze velocity through the public concourses through careful orientation of the building and shaping of its 'canyon' forms, while avoiding shapes that would accelerate the wind unacceptably under hurricane conditions. The fine-tuning of a 'blow hole' in the building's northwest corner, the leeward side, achieved the desired results and led to a distinctive architectural form informed by local climatic conditions. A rough qualitative survey of stakeholders and visitors suggest this has been a huge success (Figure 5.12).

From the very beginning stages, Frost Science expressed a desire to create a building that might begin people's journey into science. The museum was to become a place of discovery, excitement and education for the community and visitors alike. The visitor is not only learning about science and local ecologies, but as they walk through the museum, they understand the building as an institution that is quite literally in and of the city. They see the physical environments from every walkway and exterior path. The views of Miami and the ocean and the prevailing winds coming off the water are just as much a part of the museum as the physical architecture itself.

Biophilia

The famous ecologist Wilson (1984) wrote *Biophilia*, where he put forward the hypothesis that *Homo sapiens* have an innate need to be connected to the natural environment. More recently, the World Green Building Council (2019) has conducted a series of empirically evaluated case studies under a program, 'Better Places for People', which has demonstrated that a connection to nature, natural light and ventilation substantially improves not only workers' productivity but health and well-being. I think this is an approach we should all endeavor to explore in all building typologies and in urban design itself.

One of the initiatives for the reconstruction of lower Manhattan following the 9/11 attack on the World Trade Center was the reconstruction of the subway system and the introduction of a new unifying station. It was a project we won in competition teamed with the engineers Arup. Fulton Center was designed to be a catalyst for the redevelopment of the area. The dynamic transport environment is a vital link to this commercial center and its growing residential sector, streamlining connectivity between eight New York City Transit subway lines and enhancing the user experience for 300,000 daily transit passengers.

The site was unusual for this part of the city as it could not have an overdevelopment, so it had a unique asset, the sky and the opportunity for natural daylight. Fulton Center is organized around

Dynamic Aesthetics and Advanced Geometries

Figure 5.12 Frost: The three separate buildings that comprise Frost Science are strategically placed to take advantage of natural light and winds off Biscayne Bay in order to mitigate the light and temperature of the museum's campus.

Source: Copyright Rafael Gamo

a large-scale atrium contained within a transparent façade. Tapered steel columns draw inspiration from the historic neighborhood's cast-iron buildings. Above the atrium sits a conical dome topped with a glazed oculus. The concept was to capture light and the general luminance of the sky, filling all the public areas below with natural light. Under the MTA Public Arts Program, we collaborated with the artist Jamie Carpenter and engineers Schlaich Bergerman on the 'Sky Reflector-Net'. The material for the reflector was kept to a minimum, fabricated from a net of 112 tensioned cables, 224 high-strength rods and nearly 10,000 stainless-steel components. Inspired by a spider's web, it is an extremely efficient lightweight solution. It bears 952 diamond-shaped reflective panels that distribute year-round daylight and bring the sky to the visitors. We worked closely with Arup using daylight modelling software to analyze the movement of the sun throughout the day and seasons. The resulting asymmetrical form of the net is formed from that computational analysis. As the sun moves across the sky, the reflector delivers an ever-changing display of natural light, brightening the otherwise subterranean commute for thousands of passengers. The artwork also contributes to the sustainability of the station, as its reflective surface amplifies the natural light, reducing electricity consumption by additional lighting (Figure 5.13).

Figure 5.13 Fulton: Sunlight pours into the lower levels of the Fulton Center, guided by the Sky Reflector Net, an artwork undertaken in cooperation with James Carpenter Design Associates.
Source: Copyright James Ewing

Performative Design: A Paradigm Shift

A world expo has once again given us the opportunity to develop new design technologies and push the engineering and science of the built form. We are currently working with engineers Buro Happold on the Sustainability Pavilion for the Expo 2020 Dubai (Figure 5.14).

The team has developed a design and program for the pavilion that we believe to be inventive, pointed in its mission and, above all, inspiring. We have sought to achieve this through a quantum leap in thinking, designing a first-of-its-kind demonstration building that is completely self-sustaining and capable of generating its own power and water supply. The building aims to be a net-zero energy and water consumer throughout its lifetime of operation while minimizing material environmental impacts from construction. Energy will be generated through the highest specification photovoltaic panels available arranged on a large roof canopy and atop a series of 'energy trees' in the landscape.

Energy will be saved by burying much of the occupied spaces below the ground and providing thick, insulated walls with minimal glazing. Simultaneously, the solar roof acts as a giant shade to reduce the suns heating effect. Energy usage will be carefully controlled through intelligent systems that sense occupancy and adjust lighting, display screens and ventilation requirements appropriately.

Water will be generated from all available sources on site including the humid air, salty ground water extracted from near the surface and recycled water. These techniques are combined with water-saving

Dynamic Aesthetics and Advanced Geometries

Figure 5.14 Expo 2020: Currently under construction in Dubai, the Sustainability Pavilion for Expo 2020 will be a showcase for both design insight and the latest thinking in environmentally sustainable design.

Source: Copyright of Grimshaw

measures ensuring that water demand is 80% less than a typical building and the remaining water demand is provided from on-site sources. The water system includes plans to create unique dew-harvesting water trees, passive sunlight water-disinfection systems and natural reed-bed water-filtration techniques. The building aims to act as a living laboratory that will inspire visitors to live more sustainably during the Expo and far beyond (Figure 5.15).

The issues we are addressing in our pavilion design are those that are challenges affecting the world on a global scale. While we seek to highlight strategies and opportunities relative to Dubai's native landscape and climate, it is important to note that populations are facing similar issues the world over. By incorporating high levels of new technology that are inspiring, diversifiable, highly recyclable and reasonable to maintain, we will be raising awareness about the environmental problems we face in this century and inspire people with solutions that can efficiently address them on a multigenerational timescale.

The central design thrust for the pavilion is to become an exemplar of sustainable design informing, inspiring and empowering visitors to make effective change in their lifestyles as well as

Figure 5.15 Expo 2020: Conceptual rendering for an 'E-tree' at the Expo 2020 Dubai Sustainability Pavilion, and the underside of a lily that inspired the structure.

Source: https://commons.wikimedia.org/wiki/File:Victoria_cruziana_Blattunterseite.JPG. Rendering courtesy of Grimshaw

becoming generally more aware of the still-unfolding interdependence of the global, regional and local ecological systems upon which we depend, we support and with which we are ourselves enmeshed.

The Sustainability Pavilion is a unique opportunity to deliver an aspirational message about the natural world, ecology and technology to a global audience. Within that message, we hope to encourage awe and wonder not only through architecture and man's ingenuity, but through a careful reflection of nature and all it has to teach us.

As we explored earlier, our civilization is experiencing enormous changes fueled by growth. Within a relatively short space of time we will double our urban conurbations. For every school, hospital, metro system and airport we will need a duplicate, just to stand still. We need to find new design paradigms that are net zero and do not deplete the earth of its natural resources and destroy the environment. However, this is all set against other forces of rapid change, through the use of computer algorithms, machine leaning, artificial intelligence and robotics, which will fundamentally challenge the way we live and work. The Grimshaw studio is founded on analysis and exploration rather than the imposed application of a pre-determined architectural formula or style. The studio is a place of innovation, invention and imagination – a place that is more laboratory than traditional office. This method allows us to continually change and adapt and explore design in an organic way, producing designs that that are informed by the same forces that are shaping the world around us. Now more than ever architects have a vital role, influencing and shaping a viable and optimistic future with all the tools available.

Acknowledgement

Many thanks to John Leimbach, Grimshaw Research Manager, for his editorial oversight.

Notes

1 For those that want to learn more about the work of Brunel I would recommend the illustrated edition of this book.
2 The design and evolution of the projects executed by Grimshaw have been chronicled on film in a collection of stories available for free viewing at www.grimshaw.global/stories/.

References

Abergel, T., Dean, B., & Dulac, J. (2017). *The Global Status Report 2017* [pdf]. United Nations Environment Program. Retrieved from www.worldgbc.org/sites/default/files/UNEP%20188_GABC_en%20%28web%29.pdf.
Ball, P. (2016). *Patterns in Nature: Why the Natural World Looks the Way It Does*. Chicago: University of Chicago Press.
Brindel, S. (2006). *Brunel: The Man Who Built the World*. London: Orion.
Chadwick, G. F. (1961). *The Works of Sir Joseph Paxton, 1803–1865*. London: Architectural Press.
Cooke, P., Sir. (2018). *The British Boffin: Solving Problems with New Ideas* [lecture]. Amsterdam: World Architecture Festival.
Towrie, S. (2019). *Skara Brae: The discovery of the village*. Retrieved from www.orkneyjar.com/history/skarabrae/.
UN Environment and International Energy Agency. (2017). Towards a zero-emission, efficient, and resilient buildings and construction sector. *Global Status Report 2017*.
United Nations. (2012). UN Habitat for a better urban future. Retrieved from https://unhabitat.org/
Wilson, E. O. (1984). *Biophilia*. Cambridge: Harvard University Press.
World Green Building Council. (2019). Better places for people: Put wellbeing at the heart of your building. Retrieved from www.worldgbc.org/better-places-people

6

The Paradoxes of Performative Architecture

Toward a New Discipline and a New Agenda for the Profession

Thomas Fisher

When we hear the word "performance," we generally do not think of architecture. We often go to buildings – theaters, concert halls, arenas – to see people perform, be they actors, musicians, or athletes. Rarely, though, do we think about how the buildings themselves perform, unless of course their performance gets in the way of what we want to do in them, such as listening to an orchestra in a hall with poor acoustics, seeing a play in a theater with bad sightlines, or watching a sporting event in uncomfortable seats.

The Paradox of Misbehavior

This difference in how we view artistic and athletic performance on one hand and architectural performance on the other raises several paradoxes. The first of these, I will call the paradox of misbehavior. Like a child who sometimes has to act up or misbehave in order to get noticed, architecture faces a similar dilemma. Because of the ever-presence of buildings, which are so pervasive and so essential to our daily lives, most people do not pay attention to the architecture around them, like fish oblivious to the water in which they swim. That inattentiveness, though, seems to disappear and people start to notice architecture when a building takes an extreme position, with an uncanny form or unexpected look, or when it does not perform well: when the roof leaks or the indoor air smells bad, when it does not function well or finding our way around it becomes difficult.

The owner and users of a well-performing building that fits seamlessly into its context will like it. But such a building also tends to disappear from notice and become, like properly functioning equipment, something that we just take for granted. Why would an architect not want that? In the competitive world of architectural commissions, when architects struggle to differentiate themselves from other equally skilled professionals, the marketplace does not reward people whose work never gets noticed. Bad architects whose buildings do not function well or last very long will not thrive as professionals; a poor reputation, with a lot of angry past clients, eventually catches up with any practitioner. However, the opposite seems to happen with buildings that lie outside the norm in terms of form, layout, and materials. People notice them and architects start to get clients who want their own version of what others pay attention to. In a capitalistic economy, the architectural outlier often wins (Figure 6.1).

Figure 6.1 The first Gehry in Europe.
Photographed by Markus Keuter/Flickr (Creative Commons) CC BY 2.0. Access: www.flickr.com/photos/kampupot/1735962118

This can frustrate architectural researchers who devote whole careers to improving building performance. Architects will attend to the latest technology and materials and the most recent findings about products or building assemblies, since those relate to marketplace differentiation or professional liability. But some practitioners resist or at least pay little attention to research that tries to define the limits of acceptable performance, especially when that involves the form or function of a building. Like performers in the other arts or in sports, architects get noticed when they test norms and exceed limits, and so researchers' understandable desire to improve building performance can run counter to architects' equally understandable desire to succeed in a marketplace that rewards the exceptions.

From the point of view of other professions, like law or medicine, that adhere closely to the results of precedent and research in their fields, architects' inattentiveness to some types of research may seem odd. From the point of view of an architectural firm's success in the marketplace, however, there remains some rationale for architects' wariness of research. Raising the bar on building performance can lead some architects to jump higher and others to jump as far away as possible.

The Paradox of Longevity

While the marketplace notices outliers – the athletes who break records, the artists who challenge good taste, or the architects who defy the norm – the fact that the market treats architecture somewhat differently from other forms of performance leads to a second dilemma I will call the paradox of longevity. When performers in the other arts or in athletics execute poorly, their play will close, their concert receipts will decline, or their team will not make it to the playoffs. The consequences of poor performance happen quickly because of the immediacy and relative temporality of their art. A play, concert, or game lasts a few hours and the marketplace renders its verdict on it fast, with next-day reviews that might pan the performance or rankings that will rate a team against its competitors.

Architectural performance obviously does not work that way. While some problems in buildings may become immediately apparent, others can take years to manifest themselves. Like a person with a personality disorder whose problematic behavior does not become an issue until he or she reaches adulthood, long after others have outgrown their childhood petulance, a building can take a while before its bad performance becomes a matter that requires attention. Actors or athletes who perform poorly rarely get a chance to mature and often go do something else. But because buildings take so long for their inadequate performance to become obvious, architects face a delayed reckoning and accordingly less immediate pressure to attend to building performance problems.

This does not mean that architects should not bother attending to their buildings' performance. Quite the contrary. By ignoring research that would improve how their buildings function and fare over time, architects can place a time bomb in their careers, set to go off sometime in the future when bad decisions in previous years become apparent and lead to litigation or at least damage to one's reputation. Architects may face fewer short-term consequences to a poor outcome than other performers, but the long-term consequences in terms of the cost of repair, replacement, or redesign of buildings can equal or sometimes even exceed that of a closed play or a disappointing season.

Not that the marketplace provides much of an incentive to think long-term. Buildings represent major investments of human and financial capital and they stand a long time, or at least a lot longer than most other types of performances, but this all occurs within an economy fixated on short-term profits, quarterly stock reports, and the latest star performer. This has made the life-cycle costing of buildings, for example, a difficult sell. Most architects and researchers would agree that looking at the long-term cost benefit of a decision makes the most sense given the longevity of buildings. Getting most clients to see the wisdom of that, however, remains a challenge, particularly when those same clients face pressures of their own, such as short-term cash-flow problems or short-term expectations about the return on investment.

Some problems with the performance of a building may not appear before it becomes a completely depreciated asset: 27.5 years for residential structures and 39 years for commercial properties (Internal Revenue Service, 2018). Therein lies the paradox of longevity. However solid a building may appear, the tax system views only the land beneath it as the permanent asset, which suggests that buildings are more ephemeral than what most architects might want and that sites deserve greater care than what often happens.

The Paradox of Sunk Costs

While that ability to depreciate buildings might remain an important benefit for many owners, the holding of such assets can also lead people to resist changing or critically assessing them. Call this the paradox of sunk costs. A building may not perform as well as it should, with less energy efficiency, internal functionality, or environmental responsibility than other similar structures, but the owner of that building might not want to acknowledge those flaws lest it decrease the apparent value of the asset. For some owners, the poor performance of a building matters only if that affects the building's value; if no one ever assesses that performance, then the asset holder may not care. The sunk cost of a building can lead some to keep its problems submerged.

The paradox of sunk cost presents several challenges for the architectural community. Although some owners may choose to conduct a post-occupancy evaluation of a building, many others seem unwilling to know about a structure's problems or to reveal them in a way that reduces its market

Figure 6.2 Blocked stair in Paul Rudolph's Government Services Center, Boston.
"Keep Out" photographed by Seth Tisue/Flickr (Creative Commons) CC BY-SA 2.0. Access: www.flickr.com/photos/tisue/4959211222/in/photolist

value. Ignorance may not be bliss, but in this case, it may be about self-interest. The sunk-cost paradox can also lead owners to oppose public policies that might make their assets better performing, but less marketable or valuable. Often stated as opposition to burdensome regulation or government overreach, such resistance to policy change can protect a property owner from having to make investments that bring a building up to a new code requirement or to bring it in line with higher performance standards. The protection of sunk costs can sink many great ideas.

This paradox can also inhibit change on the public-sector side. Elected officials who have sunk a lot of taxpayer money into the built environment that has not had the hoped-for impact may hesitate upgrading a system or improving a building's performance in order to not look like they wasted public funds, however wasteful the operation or maintenance of those structures may be. This can lead politicians to oppose policy changes as much as other property owners. At least some of the political resistance to climate change, for instance, arises from the sunk cost communities have in a carbon economy and in a sprawling built environment. Too many property owners and politicians seem unwilling to face up to the bad decisions and poor investments made by their predecessors and would rather deny reality than have to deal with past mistakes (Figure 6.2).

Such situations reveal the challenge that the research community faces. Researchers may believe that by showing people the facts, attitudes will change and policy makers will respond, but that assumption can get severely tested by the fact-free "fantasyland," as Kurt Andersen calls it, that has come to dominate public discourse, at least in the U.S. (Andersen, 2017). Here, rhetoric trumps reality and whatever some politicians and pundits claim as truth becomes true for those who support them, regardless of the facts. That same wishful thinking can work at the scale of buildings as well. Not wanting to jeopardize their investment in buildings, owners may concoct their own reality about them, however unreal that may be. The protection of sunk costs can lead to a lot of bogus claims that no amount of expert opinion can dislodge.

The Paradox of the Elephant in the Room

Which leads to yet another paradox of architectural performance. The denial of reality that asset protection prompts in some people has a corollary in what I will call the paradox of the elephant in the room. Think of Bernard Madoff's financial fraud, in which he developed a Ponzi scheme so large that few wanted to acknowledge it even when it became clear what Madoff had done (Arvedlund, 2009). The larger the fraud, Madoff showed, the more people do not want to recognize or accept it, especially those who have the most invested in it. The larger the elephant in the room, as the saying goes, the more no one sees it.

When it comes to building performance, the most difficult or dysfunctional aspects of a structure can sometimes be the very thing that everyone adapts to or learns to accept. While small things, like an uncomfortable chair or a cold office, can lead to a lot of complaints, big things, like whether the building inhibits communications among people or has a lot of wasted space or uses more energy than it should, often go unnoticed or simply accepted as the way it is. That has something to do with what people feel they have control over: a complaint might lead to a new chair or a better thermostat, but no amount of complaining may make the building more efficient or effective, and so its inhabitants tend to accept the elephants in the room.

This presents another challenge for those who care about building performance. The architectural community, understandably, focuses on the big things, the overall design and function of a building, and spends relatively less time on the furnishings and equipment inside, about which many of the complaints tend to occur. That does not lessen the importance of a higher performance building, but it again reinforces the relative invisibility of the architectural enterprise because of its being seemingly beyond the control of most occupants of a building. Paradoxically, the aspects of the building that have the most impact on performance get the least attention from those most affected by them.

In that light, building research and product research should consider joining forces. That too rarely happens because most product development occurs inside companies and remains proprietary and off-limits to academics or practitioners. But no amount of product development will improve people's performance if the building does not align with it and vice versa, and so the research community needs to see the physical environment as a continuum from the smallest piece of equipment to the largest elements of a building and site. As in any performance, all of the performers need to work together as a team and see their work as part of a whole, something that a highly fragmented and decentralized building industry makes difficult and needs to address if we ever hope to achieve the performance people deserve from their built environment.

The Paradox of Paradoxes

All of these paradoxes reflect a misalignment between the nature of a building, which represents a long-term, finite investment in a relatively permanent asset, and the nature of the global marketplace, which comprises high-speed, high-volume transactions of relatively short-term assets. The architectural and research community may value the longevity and quality of a building's performance, but only parts of the larger economy share that interest, mainly institutional and governmental clients. Many in the private sector do not. While a business may hope that it lasts as long as the buildings it occupies, relatively few will see that hope fulfilled, given the increasing rapidity with which companies merge, move, or fail in the global economy.

As a result, we now tend to construct two very different kinds of architecture, each of which demands two very different approaches to their performance. On one hand, in architecture intended for public and institutional clients who will almost certainly outlast their buildings, the durability, flexibility, and adaptability of a structure matters most, since it may need to serve many different purposes over its lifetime. For clients like these, assessing those characteristics in their buildings through performance research makes perfect sense. On the other hand, in architecture meant for many private-sector and residential clients who often occupy a structure a very short time and who may hope to sell it easily and quickly, the location, liquidity, and curb appeal of a building may matter much more than its durability or adaptability. Here, the research into a building's performance has more to do with its marketability and potential liquidity as an asset.

The architectural research community has tended to ignore the latter, sometimes dismissing buildings designed primarily to sell as somehow of lesser value or importance. Doing so, however, distances architects from the vast majority of what gets built and marginalizes the profession by narrowing its base to a relatively small number of clients. A better strategy would be to embrace the entire built environment as the purview of architectural expertise and look for ways to improve the performance of everything that gets built, even if that performance has more to do with a structure's economic performance than its physical attributes. That, in turn, may require that architects join with fields rarely thought of as partners. For institutional and public-sector clients, that might include anthropology and product design, and for private-sector and development clients, applied economics and real estate investment. We have a lot to learn from how these and other disciplines look at and assess the built environment.

Architects have a lot to learn from other performing arts as well. The profession of architecture often gets presented as a problem-solving field, and like a director staging a play, a conductor arranging a concert, or a coach preparing a team, there remain many detailed problems to solve during the design and construction of buildings. But architecture, like theater, music, and sports, is not a problem to solve. We go to see or hear a performance in order to empathize with, reflect on, or participate in an activity that highlights the paradoxes that pervade our lives. Performances are ultimately about the human condition and how to understand and live with it, and architecture is as much about that as any of the other arts. Paradoxes exist in architecture because they exist in life and we should not deny or try to resolve them, but instead embrace them as the basis for what buildings are and what people do within them.

Performance as a Mirror

Architects might look to a closely related performance art – the theater – for ideas on how to understand and embrace paradox. Aristotle argued that we attend dramatic performances because they present a mimesis or mirror of life, which we watch in order to better understand ourselves (Aristotle, 1952; Goffman, 1959). Unlike a play, a building rarely mirrors life literally, although the prevalence of the golden section in the organization of building elevations shows how much what we see in the mirror every day – the golden section proportions of the human face – appeals to us in architecture as well. But buildings do reflect life in their own way. Take the idea of a façade. In a social sense, humans put up façades all the time, acting in one way in front of others and behaving very different when alone or with a close friend, and buildings do much the same, with faces that, except for the most transparent of glass elevations, hide to varying degrees what lies within.

We enjoy watching actors put on façades as part of the action on stage in part because the playwright will often reveal to the audience how a character thinks or behaves when alone. A similar pleasure occurs in architecture as we step inside a building to find a more complex set of spaces than what the façade might suggest. For some architects, like Adolf Loos, that difference between the exterior and interior of his buildings, between his austere façades and simple forms on one hand and the lush materials and complex arrangement of internal spaces, give his architecture a sense of drama in a way that Aristotle would have understood (Figure 6.3).

The Paradoxes of Performative Architecture

Figure 6.3 Adolf Loos, Muller House, 1929–30.
Photographed by Rory Hyde/Flickr (Creative Commons) CC BY-SA 2.0. Access: www.flickr.com/photos/roryrory/2444108747

Buildings mimic life in other ways as well. Many architects, especially with the rise of modernism, used physiological metaphors in the design of buildings: corridors that serve as the spine of the structure, an entry that becomes its head, a mechanical room that functions as its heart. This anthropomorphizing of architecture has become so common that we hardly notice it, but these bodily references go a long way in helping people find their way through a building and understand its organization. Aristotle saw the theater as a place in which we see ourselves mirrored in the lives of the characters, in order to reflect upon our own lives, and the anatomical organization and operation of a building enables us to do the same with our bodies. Their structure mimics our own.

Aristotle also argued that we go to the theater to help us answer, in our own minds, what he saw as one of the most fundamental questions we must ask of ourselves: how should we live and what constitutes a good life? He thought that a life of moderation, of seeking the mean between two extremes, offered the surest route to a happy life, a notion of balance, proportion, and restraint that we see performed in many buildings, especially those in the classical tradition or in the work of modern architects influenced by that tradition. Architecture in that sense mirrors not just life as we actually live it, but also life as it should be lived, with the relationship of a building's parts, the accommodation of its occupants, and the response to its surroundings representing the kind of behavior we might aspire to attain. If, as Shakespeare famously wrote, "all the world's a stage" (Shakespeare, 1952), then architecture performs on the stage of the city and the landscape as much as characters do on the stage of the theater or in the settings of a film.

What does this mean for architecture? Buildings cannot help but embody a way of being in the world through their location and siting, their form and space, and their materials and details. And architects may need to become much more conscious of what their designs say about how we should live, since other people seem to have a better sense of the implicit values expressed in buildings than most practitioners, evident in the frequency with which architects get caught off guard by the public's interpretations of a project. Just as a playwright or screenwriter creates characters and constructs dialogue that express particular views and values, so too does the architect in the choice of products and materials and in the decisions about quantities and qualities. Does a building express a good life as one of hedonistic pleasure, as the Rococo did, or one of self-control, as Minimalism seems to suggest? Does its performance urge us to live according to nature, as Frank Lloyd Wright's buildings did, or to live as the most social of animals, as some of Herman Hertzberger's buildings seem to argue?

Performance as a Form of Making

Such questions do not have right or wrong answers. They offer us not puzzles to solve, but paradoxes to ponder, as all performances do. The anthropologist Victor Turner argued that performances do not just hold up a mirror to life, "mimesis," but also "poiesis," the Greek word for making. The audience as well as the actors of a performance make meaning and enact our culture in the process of participating in the event (Turner, 1982). In this sense, a performance does not exist until or unless it gets performed, and its full meaning does not occur until those affected by it engage in and react to it. In Turner's view, a performance never involves passive entertainment, but a collective creation of meaning.

Architecture, too, performs in this way. While it may exist materially and spatially, a building without inhabitants remains incomplete, like a script before it gets performed on stage. Nor do its occupants remain passive participants in a building, but active creators of meaning and interpreters of the spaces they inhabit by how they use, modify, adapt, and personalize their environments. Architects, clients, and contractors may make a building initially, but the users of it continue to make and remake it every day after that.

Buildings perform poiesis in other ways as well. Consider architecture that represents its own making, be it in the expression of its structure and mechanical systems, as in Richard Rogers' Lloyds of London building, or of its own construction, as Amateur Architecture Studio has done in several projects in China. In such cases, architecture makes what normally remains hidden, visible for all to see, much as a play reveals the normally hidden aspects of human behavior for the audience to view. Such revelations can go too far, of course. Audiences usually do not want someone telling them the meaning of a play as they watch it performed, nor do people typically want to see everything in a building revealed to them, however much it might fascinate architects. Here, Aristotle's ethics of moderation seems apt; revealing enough to inform or inspire, without so much that it leaves nothing for the imagination seems like a reasonable performance goal.

Poiesis also seems relevant to "loose-fit" buildings that allow for change over time, like Renzo Piano's and Richard Rogers' Pompidou Centre, or that let users have greater control over interior spaces and conditions, as Norman Foster's office towers allow. For such buildings, the participation of the occupants or users in moving walls or furniture becomes central to their meaning, like a play in which there exist multiple endings or many different interpretations. Such indeterminacy may not prove as satisfying as a tightly written play and the same may apply to buildings that overdo their flexibility. Nor may they perform well in other ways: the Pompidou Centre, for example, sacrificed energy efficiency and ease of maintenance in exchange for its adaptability (Figure 6.4). But as in a play or

The Paradoxes of Performative Architecture

Figure 6.4 Centre Georges Pompidou.
Photographed by Lauren Manning/Flickr (Creative Commons) CC BY 2.0. Access: www.flickr.com/photos/laurenmanning/2971048230/in/photolist

a film, every building has its strengths and weaknesses, things that it does well and that it does not. Even there, though, lie lessons for us: how our buildings perform reflects the culture that created them, however wasteful that may be.

In that sense, a focus on how a building performs also reflects a view of how a culture might reform. A building, like a theatrical performance, cannot force people to change, but its poiesis can nudge people to a more constructive way of being, causing them to reflect on their assumptions and habits and to at least consider more empathetic and mindful ways of living and inhabiting space. Which brings us to a third type of performance.

Performance as a Way of Moving

The ethnographer Dwight Conquergood likened performances to "kinesis," the Greek word for moving, arguing that when we perform, we not just move bodies in space, but also challenge cultural norms and move culture forward in the process (Conquergood, 1992). The connection of that idea to architecture seems obvious, since buildings, like performances on a stage, accommodate the movement and interactions of people in space, with architects serving in a role not unlike that of a set designer, a choreographer, or a director, depending upon how tightly they control the bodies in their buildings. An architect like Michael Graves seemed to act more like a set designer, with highly expressive vertical surfaces and loose-fit plans that did not overly determine their occupation. On the other hand, someone like Frank Lloyd Wright had a more directorial approach to architecture, with a lot of built-in furniture and deterministic plans that forced bodies to use or circulate in his spaces in specific ways.

This shows how buildings play a dual role when it comes to performance: they provide the places where we go to see others perform their art and also the places in which we perform our daily lives. In this, we move from being audience members to being actors on the stage of architecture and back again, which demands that the architect involve the users of a building – the actors in its performance – in terms of how they want to live or work. The best design learns from listening to and through conversation with as wide a range of people as possible, remaining open to their ideas and how they deal with life and work. This attention not just to how a building performs, but also to how others want to perform in it, moves architecture away from an expertise model, in which a person with a lot of training tells people what they should want or should do, and toward an engagement model, in which the inquiry into what a certain situation demands evolves out of interactions with those who have the most at stake in a viable solution.

A performer, though, needs to have the ability, knowledge, and judgment to perform, and here, too, dramatic performance has something to offer architecture. The ability to perform goes beyond the talent and technique of the performer; it includes the ability of people to attend a performance. In that sense, a performance constitutes a community of all of the people involved in it – the performers and audience as well as everyone else responsible for some aspect of putting it on. And in the process, a performance can create a group identity or challenge the assumptions of the community of people involved. Just as attending a theatrical performance can transform us, so can architecture through its space and form, through the process of its making, and through the sense it conveys of being part of a larger purpose in its creation and occupation (Bell, 2008).

The community created during and after the creation of a building often happens, whether or not architects lead that process. The digital revolution, for example, has given people extraordinary access to information and an unprecedented ability to form social networks and to communicate at lightning speed, and this has fueled the rise of a highly participatory, rapid-prototyping approach to the creation of goods and services as well as environments. Leveraging social media in the design of buildings and empowering people to share their ideas about how to create a better-performing environment seems likely to become the norm and to play a major part in the creation of architecture.

The Paradox of Performative Architecture

Responding to this opportunity, though, will take a shift in how architects think about the making of architecture. It will take the leadership of experts in the field, for example, to move away from idea of architecture as the creation of heroic or highly personal form by experts. While the marketplace may still like this idea, as we have seen, the world seems to be moving toward the co-creation of buildings with those who have the most stake in their performance. In the future, the most effective architectural performers will be those who help everyone else become performers as well, as participants in and contributors to the performance of a building in which they will continue to perform long after its completion.

Performative architecture involves, as well, a move away from the traditional focus of architects on the designed object and toward the design process itself. We go to performances, says sociologist Paul DiMaggio, to engage in some sort of story, told through words, music, and/or movement, that explains or reveals something important about the world. DiMaggio aligns that with three types of performances: "narrative" ones that tell us how the world works, "covering" ones that explain what the world is, and "enlightenment" ones that help us see the world in a new way (DiMaggio, 1995).

We might think of a building's performance along those same lines. The design process helps people tell a story or narrative about a building and its reason for being, create a covering or enclosure that reflects the values and purpose of what goes on inside, and provide those who occupy or experience the building with new ways of seeing the world and of becoming, in some sense, enlightened by it.

In an increasingly unsustainable and inequitable world, the real value of performative architecture may lie in its effectiveness in addressing not just what people want, but how we should think about the nature of a good life and how we learn to see the world anew. Design offers a way of exploring those possibilities, and through buildings, we construct and inhabit answers to it. Which leads to a final paradox: at the very moment that it has seemed marginalized in an increasingly digital world, well-performing architecture has never mattered more than it does now.

Bibliography

Andersen, Kurt (2017) *Fantasyland: How America Went Haywire, A 500-Year History*. New York: Random House.
Andrews, John (1991) *Architecture: A Performing Art*. Oxford: Oxford University Press.
Aristotle, Ingram Bywater, trans. (1952) *Poetics*. Chicago: University of Chicago Press.
Arvedlund, Erin (2009) *Too Good to Be True: The Rise and Fall of Bernie Madoff*. New York: Penguin.
Bell, Elizabeth (2008) *Theories of Performance*. London: Sage.
Carlson, Marvin (1996) *Performance: A Critical Introduction*. New York: Routledge.
Conquergood, Dwight (1992) "Ethnography, Rhetoric, and Performance." *Quarterly Journal of Speech*, 78, pp. 80–123.
DiMaggio, Paul (1995) "Comments on 'What Theory is Not.'" *Administrative Science Quarterly*, 40, pp. 391–397.
Goffman, Erving (1959) *Presentation of Self in Everyday Life*. New York: Anchor Books.
Internal Revenue Service (2018) *Publication 946, How to Depreciate Property*. Washington, DC: US Government. https://www.irs.gov/publications/p946.
Kolarevic, Branko, and Malkawi, Ali (2005) *Performative Architecture: Beyond Instrumentality*. New York: Routledge.
Schechner, Richard (1988) *Performance Theory*. New York: Routledge.
Schechner, Richard (2002) *Performance Studies: An Introduction*. New York: Routledge.
Shakespeare, William (1952) *As You Like It*. Chicago: University of Chicago Press. Act II, Scene VII.
Turner, Victor (1982) *From Ritual to Theatre*. New York: PAJ Publications.
Turner, Victor (1986) *The Anthropology of Performance*. New York: PAJ Publications.

7.1

Poetics of Design Beyond Intelligences: The Meaning of Embodied Aesthetics and Simulation of Mood in Performative Design and Architecture

Poetics of Design: A House Is a Tree Is an Insect Is a Computer Is a Human

Mariana Ibañez

In addressing poetics or aesthetics of architecture that is intelligent and performative, the far horizon is necessarily paired to that of artificial intelligence (AI), where the sentience of machine learning creates a paradigm shift. This is a break from a tradition of architecture that is centered around human scale, proportions, and culture. Francesco di Giorgio was one of several architects, from antiquity to the Renaissance, to use mathematical ratios derived from the (male) human body as a basis to lay out plans of basilica as well as facades (Wittkower 1949). What harmonic orders that come of machine intelligence, brought to bear on buildings, would not exclusively mirror a human-based sacred geometry?

To address how AI will govern itself in architecture, ideas of Nicholas Negroponte and Gordon Pask (1976) set the historic benchmark. For Pask, any agent that demonstrates intelligence could not be relegated to a service role or dismissed as a tool such as found in computer-aided design. In his Conversation Theory, Pask sets out a flattened field where human and nonhuman are equal participants in conversation. He proceeds to make explicit the verisimilitude of roles as the nonhuman may even express boredom, just as any human might in conversation with another. This boredom in conversation was demonstrated in his Musicolour project. Musicolour would display lighting patterns in reaction to the piano-playing of a human participant. To close the feedback loop, this in turn would affect the human performance (Pangaro 2016). But to avail itself to the Conversation Theory, the Musicolour may become bored with the music, and show a drift in response, suggesting that the human player make a change to maintain engagement in conversation (Figure 7.1.1).

Therefore, if the human body has historically served as architecture's metric, we should be asking how architecture is going to change as our bodies, like the environment, become transformed and augmented through technology. Furthermore, questions about what forms of autonomous bodies are

Poetics of Design

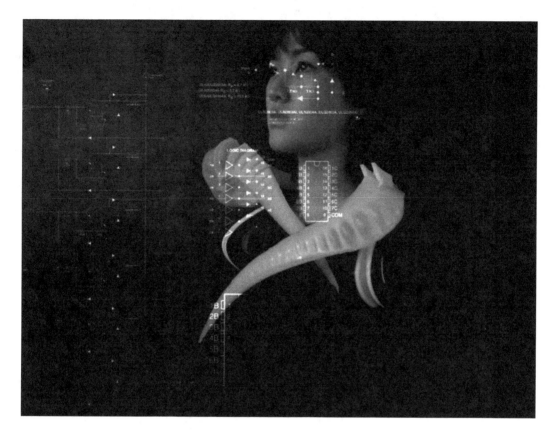

Figure 7.1.1 Orpheus and Eurydice.
Credit: Ibañez Kim

created by nonhuman sentience – as its architecture may not be for the occupancy of humans only – must be equally addressed. Just as in the Paskian model, the inclinations of other species, materials, and intelligences will need to be engaged in conversation or in shared endeavors.

Augmented Tectonics

Architects refer to the assembly of architectural elements (into built form), and the relationship of architectural parts to a whole, as the domain of tectonics. While the definition of "tectonics" has evolved from early theorizations in the field, at every stage it connected (with different emphasis) issues related to construction, engineering, and material character with questions of architectural and artistic expression, imagination, and symbolism.

The arrival and development of digital technologies within the field have initiated and enabled a reconceptualization of the tectonic to include computational concerns. Consequently, modern and contemporary formulations of the tectonic continue to proliferate with the key shift in focus being the turn from making to thinking, as historian Mario Carpo (2017) suggests. His writing points to parts as discrete knowledge that are sorted and organized in logics and speeds better accessible to computers. Antoine Picon (2010) proposes to recast the fundamental question of the part-to-whole problem (via

Mariana Ibañez

some of the fundamental effects of computation) into a more expansive question of elements and relations. Scale, as well as tectonics of design made effortless by digital production, finds an interference or counterpoint in materiality. What this materiality becomes is a unique arena of emergence, as materiality does not necessarily connote stone and brick.

Historically, the "part" in architecture has been well defined as material, construction or functional unit, and the "whole" has been understood as the building. In a contemporary computational context, a "part" is only a part at a specific scale, and the "whole" only provisional, until another scale of observation or structure allows this "whole" to be understood as nested within a larger system – a "part" of another "whole" that contains it. While the discipline continues to consider the scale of the building as a central site for architectural enquiry, acknowledgements must be made through work that integrates larger systems (social, political, environmental, as well as material) and networks in the production of architecture (Figure 7.1.2).

As new tools, methods, and processes (disciplinary and other) emerge to offer new premises for the production of architecture, there must be a situating of work both as a reprise of key tectonic tenets as well as an expansion of tectonic discourses into new territories that emerge from technological innovation. By augmenting the tectonic to include concerns that are not tangible, designers can then

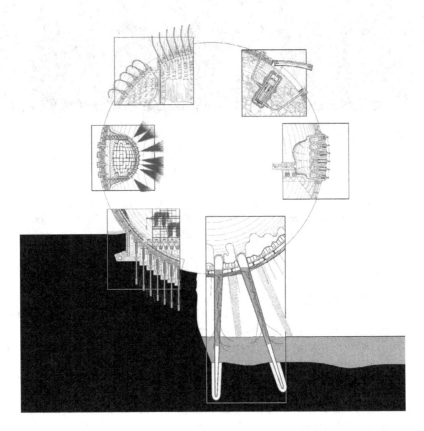

Figure 7.1.2 Active Tectonic.
Credit: Ibañez Kim

engage with methods of production that connect the physical properties of material with effects, relationships, and behaviors.

Culture of the Augmented

As written in "New Bodies, New Architecture" (Ibanez & Kim 2018), much of present human arts and culture will become completely changed by both design and by unseen consequence. Much as food production has changed with the invention of refrigeration, new technologies increasingly irritate or compound social mores and habits. What this yields is social interaction at time scales and distances that are distributed along global human traditions. In the world of the performing arts, the essay suggests that nonhuman autonomous beings, and humans augmented with nonhuman devices, perform in an arena where the authorship, creation, expression, and reception are disengaged from an anthropocentric medium.

In a theatrical performance, human bodies – in their current physiognomies – move on stage accompanied by music, lighting, and staging. The positions and shapes made by each limb work in unison to conjure or evoke a response in a human audience. The engagement of the viewer with the highly-trained dancers is innately and immediately tethered due to similitude of like bodies. As the performers move in speeds and with degrees of freedom recognizable in the viewer's own human form, a cognitive link is formed.

This tether between human audience and theater is still formed when the performer is nonhuman, by careful placement of human restrictions. As in the case of Oriza Irata's double bill of *Sayonara* and *I, Worker*,[1] robots from the lab of Hiroshi Ishiguro perform alongside human actors, but are regulated to be domesticated and subservient. In *Sayonara*, although the nonhuman mimics human features as much as currently possible, it is still understood to be a robot caretaker. The second one-act play has a diminutive humanoid robot with limited features. Both are emotive in their interaction with the human actors, but the designs of the robots are clearly calibrated – in pace and action – to be within the norms of human movement. They are proxy humans onto which the audience may project their empathies.

Nonhuman Theater

When nonhuman actors are not humanoid in form or are able to move at rates of speed or with agility that is beyond human capacity, a dissonant break may form in audience communication. During the rehearsals and development of *Science per Forms*,[2] mechanical limbs of varying lengths were designed to dance on stage alongside human dancers. Furthermore, devices placed on the human bodies would relay their motion to digital geometries on a large screen. As the human dancers moved, polygons on the screen could shift, tilt, or explode in any manner. To make sensible to the audience what these digital geometries were doing, the programming of the pieces showed that the polygons would always seek to come together into a stable cube, but the motion of the dancers would continually push and pull the angles. What was therefore perceived by the viewer, or rather anthropomorphically projected onto the animated geometries, was a human-based desire of these digital parts to find each other and be complete, only to be continually thwarted (Figures 7.1.3 and 7.1.4).

The long limbs of the nonhuman dancers were not fashioned in mimicry of either humans or other bio-entities. The motors and sensors allowed for multiple speeds and high degree of rotations so that the limbs could express performance within their own local context. They had movement that was not classifiable as human or animal. This posed challenges during rehearsals and development as they were too expressive or capable of speeds or positions beyond what the human dancers could manage or navigate. For the final performance, the movements of the limbs were tempered to more palatable human speeds with smoother curves of acceleration.

Figure 7.1.3 Science per Forms.
Credit: Ibañez Kim

Ultimately, the question that will arise will be not of acceptance of nonhuman agents in theater arts, but of the rise of nonhuman audience members. The body-map of a nonhuman audience member, with its own physical traits, may not find appropriate sympathetic response with movement and sound based on human physiognomy and crafted for human appreciation. Furthermore, the capacity of human performance that thrills audiences today may not find the same reception from a compound being of reptile–tree–human, or a wholly nonhuman agent such as an AI. It is interesting to query what a nonhuman would appreciate from the opera of Orpheus and Eurydice, with a dissatisfaction of the highest notes a human singer may produce, or a denigrated pathos of a barter with Hades gone astray.[3]

At the same time, compound agencies may increase human sensitivity beyond their limitation of seeing, hearing, smelling, and feeling. In this manner, culture becomes a fluid non-state where values and conditions are multi-varied at any given moment, dependent on both actor and audience. The addition of a non-native ability such as hearing higher frequencies or seeing infra-red would alter human perception. To fold in the sense of echo-location from joining a compound being would be significant and immense.

Augmented Architecture and Environments

Should the role of theater be placed in a critical position with architecture, then the same ideas of perception and appreciation would be activated. Architecture and theater are already in close proximity. Architects such

Poetics of Design

Figure 7.1.4 Science per Forms.
Credit: Ibañez Kim

as Zaha Hadid, Morphosis, and DS+R have designed several stages and environments for dance and music. The construction of space in which human action unfolds is the same act, but for the one fact that this action is sustained at the highest level of expression in theater. There is no actor-audience in an office or domestic space to the same degree as theater. This distinction elevates theater – particularly in the realm of responsive design – as emotive expression and nuance require greater calibration than a house that Le Corbusier claims is "*une machine-à-habiter*". In other words, if architecture is to intelligently adapt to sensory stimulation, that adaptation should be with cultural expression and nuance, and not a simple open/close expediency.

Now that performative architecture is tethered to an inter-cultural dramatic arts, the fluid dynamics of passive cooling, while immensely important, becomes a venue for the artful and affecting. Whether for reasons prosaic or celebratory, architecture and environments that are responsive may then be sources for poetry in motion, undergoing change. The same compound agencies arise now when the identity of augmented architecture is not simply building systems and services. Synthetic cognition and intelligence, coupled with the ability to cybernetically network with others, will draw environments and atmospheres that are no longer limited to buildings. Architecture of conglomerate entities of plant, animal, and matter will extend beyond foundation, walls, and roof to movements of pollen, pheromones, and root systems. The cultural production of such agents, augmented to human occupants, must be multivalent and shaped by factors that are ecological and balanced. Or, instead of homeostasis, another outcome may be one that accelerates or amplifies natural processes that are not necessarily of this planet. For example, the competition for a new government center in Sejong, Korea, proposed fields and ecosystems that were in permafrost, or under nonstop light levels of the equinox, and other environments bathed in ultraviolet

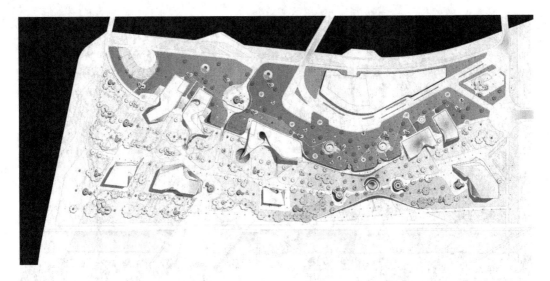

Figure 7.1.5 Sejong Masterplan.
Credit: Ibañez Kim

light for rapid plant growth (Figure 7.1.5). It is interesting to allow for these technologically intertwined compound beings to create their own world orders as needed and desired. These synthetic worlds may not be human-centric, or possibly beneficial to only a particular set of species. This would not negate or be antithetical to human existence but would promote other interests to equal stature.

Poetics, Duration of Environments

Poet Richard Brautigan wrote in his book *Tokyo – Montana Express* of seemingly quotidian objects and events such as someone air-drumming along with a live band, or realizing the dead thing in his heart is a mouse (Brautigan 1988). In each of these pieces, there is a watchful introspection that never tries to elevate or conjure the fantastic via metaphor. "All Watched Over by Machines of Loving Grace" is an earlier poem that is more projective and resonates with cybernetics, the pervasive theme of his time (Brautigan 1967). Within its verses, he describes a scenario where artificial systems free humankind from labor to live in a bucolic equality with all of nature.

The scenario for augmented architecture and environments runs somewhat counter to the poem, as the ideas of grace and love are in conflict with a governance by machines. Rather than create a false separation between intelligent machines and humans, an idea that persists to today, architecture and ecology is intertwined with synthetic intelligence. The poetry of such an environment is likewise motivated by indistinct cultures and sensibilities. Brautigan's feeling of graceful, loving environments would require a reciprocal behavior or set of properties with the human and nonhuman occupants. Given the augmentation of this synthetic world, poetics takes on senses and evocations in dimensions greater than what is perceived only by humans. What Merleau-Ponty (1992) describes as

> My perception therefore is not a sum of visual, tactile, and audible givens. I perceive in a total way with my whole being: I grasp a unique structure of the thing, a unique way of being, which speaks to all my senses at once.

would be equally applicable to networked sentient constructs. It is this being-in-the-world that allows an individual to make things intelligible, but is uniquely receptive to phenomena outside of human experience.

Among synthetically sentient architecture that is now expressive, and poetic, what might be feasible is the use of time in constructing the meaningful from the compound sensibilities and senses. Should a nonhuman movement be languid or frenetic, it is the durational dimension that makes it known. This creates multiple challenges as movement among different organisms may be so quick as to be imperceptible to the human eye or slow to the point of distraction. If Merleau-Ponty's understanding of the world is through the immersion of the body, then a synthetic world and a networked body will produce multiple layers of meaning and comprehension. The intelligence and perceptions in such an architecture can be sensitive to the flurry of an insect's wing, as well as the creep of plant roots. Meaningfulness or poetics can be held in different partitions as needed. The lyrical slow movement of heliotropic plants is revealed as human cognition is blended with the senses of a tree, or the photovoltaic system of a canopy.

As architecture and urbanism become worlds within worlds, fully cognate and expressive, the disciplinary questions of whether they are for or against human occupation is backgrounded to the immediacy of compounded sense organs and bodies delivering experiences to a synthetic intelligence. Who designs it, or more critically who owns it, are anthropocentric concerns. Environments and spaces will be shaped as polyphonic responses and desires to compound agents that are never the same constituents where human culture is one channel among many.

Synthetic Poetry

To return to the idea of poetics, a synthetic nature conjured by Brautigan in no means needs to appear as nature found in idyllic paintings. Human reminiscence or other forms of nostalgia about the "natural world" must be reconsidered. A locale or environment may be supranatural, or accelerated in bio-climatic conditions. For example, plants may grow faster and larger under a chemical troposphere and with triple the amount of purple light than is currently available by the sun. Regeneration of the ice shelf requires temperatures, currents, air movements, and even orbits that are no longer available: the result may possibly be regions of perpetual winter. These environments are wholly uninhabitable for humans and are also completely proposed as natural. Furthermore, the ideas of water management or plant growth for the food chain may be equally outdated as the nostalgic longing for nature.

Machines of loving grace, or as proposed, networks of compound beings, would occupy a synthetic nature that is far more intertwined and immersive. Seasons may be asynchronous and on-demand, and wildlife become varied and participatory in the networked conversation. The poetics of this space is not necessarily bound in a poetic image, viewed from a human eye with human symbols and lexicons. The apprehension of form, color, shadow, mass, and depth is no longer developed only in the eyes of the Compound Being. Resonance, vibration, heat transfer, and fluid dynamics would make the static, unmoving image deficient in comparison to a dynamic poetics in rates of change, and atmospheric flows.

Architecture, as part of such an exchange, would find expression or poetry in its compositions as well as in its dynamic being. The *perception* of firmness, arrangement, and solidity and its appearance or *representation* of order become outdone within a house that is an overlay of tree, insect, machine, and human. This house is not an act of mimesis – a show of signs and structure – but is an actor of commingled sentience that experiences and reacts to all manner of dynamic stimuli.

Mariana Ibañez

Notes

1 Immersive Kinematics, of which the author is Associate Director, were respondents to a discussion following the performance at Philadelphia Live Arts, February 2013.
2 A collaboration among Ibañez Kim, Immersive Kinematics, and Carbon Dance Theatre, Science per Forms was presented at Christ Church Theatre in Philadelphia, October 2012.
3 A Redux of Orpheus and Eurydice was made between Ibañez Kim, Immersive Kinematics, and the composer Lembit Beecher. The production was shown at the Slought Foundation, December 2014. Additionally, different human cultures already appreciate the arts very differently – for example, Chinese scroll paintings vis-à-vis the paintings of Giotto.

References

Brautigan, R. (1967). All Watched Over by Machines of Loving Grace. Brautigan.net. Available at: www.brautigan.net/machines.html [Accessed March 2019].
Brautigan, R. (1988). *The Tokyo-Montana Express*. Tokyo: Nan'un-do.
Carpo, M. (2017). *The Second Digital Turn: Design Beyond Intelligence*. Cambridge, MA: MIT Press.
Ibanez, M., & Kim, S. (2018). New Bodies, New Architecture. In Bissell, H. (ed). *The Sentient Archive: Bodies, Performance, and Memory*. Middletown, CT: Wesleyan University Press, pp. 293–296.
Merleau-Ponty, M. (1992) *Sense and Non-Sense*. Evanston, IL: Northwestern University Press, p. 50.
Pangaro, P. (2016). Questions for Conversation Theory or Conversation Theory in One Hour. Presented at the Annual Meeting of American Society for Cybernetics, Olympia and Washington, June 1–5.
Pask, G. (1976). Artificial Intelligence: A Preface and a Theory. Introduction. In Negroponte, N. (ed). *Soft Architecture Machines*. Cambridge: MIT Press, pp. 6–31.
Picon, A. (2010). *Digital Culture in Architecture: An Introduction to the Design Professions*. Basel: Birkhauser.
Wittkower, R. (1949). *Architectural Principles in the Age of Humanism*. London: Warburg Institute.

7.2

Poetics of Design Beyond Intelligences: The Meaning of Embodied Aesthetics and Simulation of Mood in Performative Design and Architecture

Poetics and More in Performative Architecture: Towards a Neuroscience of Dynamic Experience and Design

Michael A. Arbib

Some architects, when they hear about the interaction of neuroscience or of computer science with architecture, perceive a threat to reduce their task to plugging in algorithms to convert the program (in the architectural sense) to working drawings. But if we look at the recent successes in how artificial intelligence supports humans in web search and so on, we see that the issue is not so much a restriction of possibilities but rather the challenge of developing tools to help us navigate a huge space of new possibilities in a cost-effective way while nonetheless expanding our own imagination and desires. This chapter will not offer advice on the conduct of performative architecture, but will instead offer one possible perspective on the meanings of poetics and performative architecture, and then use Le Corbusier's dictum that "a house is a machine for living in" as a springboard for reviewing, briefly, a number of ideas from neuroscience, broadly construed, that hold promise for future exploration.

Poetics and Poetry

The OED gives the following definitions for poetics:

a. The aspect of literary criticism that deals with poetry; the branch of knowledge that deals with the techniques of poetry. …

b. The creative principles informing any literary, social or cultural construction, or the theoretical study of these; a theory of form.

I adapt these to offer my own meaning for architecture: "*Poetics* provides a theory of architectural form that addresses the creative principles underlying its social and cultural construction."

A possible subtheme (but outside the scope of this chapter) might be to assess in what sense one may usefully speak metaphorically of "the poetry of architectural form" (further echoing the notion of architecture as "frozen music"). Here one might play off the counterpoint between the meaning and the sound of a poem with the function and form of a building. The poet seeks to convey "what the poem is about" – but does much more by choosing words whose sound and form on the printed page enrich the "basic" meaning with an emotional overlay that other combinations of other words about the same theme would lack. Moreover, in this wonderful example

> *I caught this morning morning's minion, king-*
> *dom of daylight's dauphin, dapple-dawn-drawn Falcon, in his riding*
> *Of the rolling level underneath him steady air, and striding*
> *High there, how he rung upon the rein of a wimpling wing ...*
>   Gerard Manley Hopkins: The Windhover

Hopkins not only enriches his meaning with his inspired choice of words and poetic form, but he also works within the cultural convention of an ABBA rhyming scheme. The poem may have been written in 1864 but was not published till 1918. It can be found on the web or in the collection *Poems and Prose* (Hopkins 1985). Someone with no romance in their soul might dismiss the above as saying "I saw a falcon flying at dawn," but the words and rhythm and structure combine to convey so much more. Further meanings arise when one notes that *The Windhover* is subtitled *To Christ our Lord*. Moreover, the best poems take multiple readings for new meanings to emerge in ways that link them indissolubly to the shape and sound of the words that convey them.

In similar terms, the architect might start with the program for a building as a list of basic functions it is to provide, but the "poetically satisfying" building will offer so much more.

Figure 7.2.1 (Left) The third-place entry. (Right) The second-place entry in the competition to design a Sydney opera house.
Source: *The Builder*, 1 March 1957

Case Study: Utzon's Sydney Opera House

To take an example (developed at great length in Fromonot 1998; Arbib 2020), consider the original program for the Sydney Opera House. It noted that the site, Bennelong Point, "is probably without equal in the world … one that fulfills all the requirements – dimensions, space and beauty – essential for the type of building that should be constructed" while calling for two auditoriums, with additional space for rehearsal rooms, a broadcasting centre, a restaurant, and two meeting rooms as well as bars

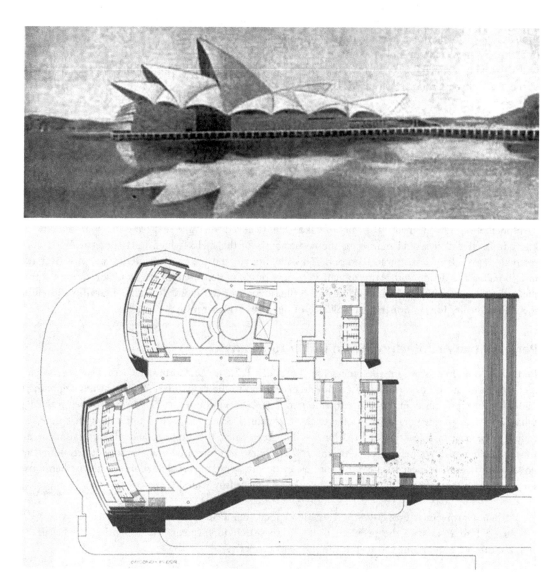

Figure 7.2.2 Utzon's winning entry. (Top) A view that (unlike the views in Figure 7.2.1) links the building to the harbor through the reflection in the water and the glimpse of landscape. (Bottom) A plan showing how the design conforms to the shape of the site.

Source: *The Builder*, 1 March 1957

and foyers for the various halls. The program thus contained both an aesthetic component and a functional component but left it to the competing architects to think through how they might be realized (Figures 7.2.1 and 7.2.2).

The competition results were announced on 29 January 1957. In the third-place entry, the auditoriums are in two separate buildings and the design does not respond to the site other than in the size of the bounding rectangle. It imposes these two buildings on Bennelong Point. Had the second design been built, it would, I think, have been a successful building. A central core housed the stage machinery for both auditoriums, and the auditoriums and other venues were wrapped around this central core. But Utzon made three crucial decisions: he put the auditoriums side-by-side with the footprint of the buildings strongly linked to that of Bennelong Point; he took account of the special vantage for the site afforded from the Sydney Harbour Bridge; and he had each auditorium building ascend to a lobby with a glass wall to provide a superb viewpoint for appreciating the beauty of the harbor. Robert Geddes, a member of the Philadelphia Group which placed second, said,

> We almost won.
> But we didn't.
> Why?
> Because Jørn Utzon's design was a masterpiece.
> *(Geddes 2006, p. 67)*

His design realized the program yet transcended it in its poetics.

Nonetheless, Utzon made a tragic mistake. He believed that the expertise in ship building he knew from his father would transfer to the construction of the shells, which (as I argue in Arbib 2020) resemble the keels of boats more than sails. This was not so, and the resultant delays and cost over-runs in elaborating the design with Arup to achieve a new mode of construction led to Utzon's removal from the project. As a result, he had no hand in the final design of the interior of the auditoriums to ensure their functionality for performers and audience of opera and other music.

Performative Architecture: From Utility to Beauty

Performative architecture can, in some sense, be traced back to Le Corbusier's *Vers Une Architecture* – a collection of seven essays published (with one exception) in the magazine *L'Esprit nouveau* beginning in 1921 and first published in English translation in 1927 (Le Corbusier 1927). Le Corbusier reacted to what he saw as the deplorable state of French architectural education and of housing at that time, and found inspiration in three types of machine – the ocean liner, the airplane, and the automobile – and found in them the aesthetic of the engineer: "The Engineer, inspired by the law of Economy and governed by mathematical calculation, puts us in accord with universal law. He achieves harmony." He stressed for example that an airplane is *a machine for flying* [my italics] …

> When a problem is properly stated, in our epoch, it inevitably finds its solution. To wish to fly like a bird is to state the problem badly … to search for a means of suspension in the air and a means of propulsion, was to put the problem properly.

This led up to his famous dictum:

> A house is a machine for living in. Baths, sun, hot-water, cold-water, warmth at will, conservation of food, hygiene, beauty in the sense of good proportion. An armchair is a machine for sitting in and so on.
> *(Le Corbusier 1927, p. 95)*

And he then elaborated the Problem of the House in ways which define some functions which have become standard and others which are either too culture-specific or curiously bourgeois: "Demand that the maid's room should not be an attic."

If one only reads this dictum and the notion of engineering aesthetics, one might conclude that Le Corbusier holds that if only houses were built according to engineering principles, they would satisfy our aesthetic needs. But this is not the case. He still sees it as the task of the architect – but an architect liberated from old styles – to create the necessary aesthetics, as "he determines the various movements of our heart and of our understanding; it is then that we experience the sense of beauty" (Le Corbusier 1927, p. 12).

At times Le Corbusier seems to focus on beauty alone (as when he discusses the Parthenon) and at other times beauty takes second place, but his overall thrust is that functionality does not guarantee beauty, thus rejecting the idea that form should simply follow function – though at the same time, he lambasts those forms that merely add decoration.

Function does not define form. Rather, the successful architect modifies both in seeking a harmonious blend in which the form does not merely satisfy a basic functionality, but both enriches the experience of the specified functions and, perhaps, offers pathways for new experiences beyond those in the original program.

In relating this to performative architecture, we may note an ambiguity in the term "performance." For some, this means function as distinct from form. For others, emotional impact and aesthetics are part of the performance package. Consider wayfinding. It often provides an important performance criterion for a building or city. If over-emphasized, however, this criterion can remove the joy of exploration, which may be captured by using the term "waylosing" in a positive sense:

> I am not advocating waylosing on the way to the maternity ward, but in less stressed situations it can be great fun. Waylosing is the stuff mazes are made of, and it is one of the great attractions of Venice … Also, we should not forget serendipity, the luck of finding something unexpected and useful when looking for something else.
>
> (Per Mollerup, 21 April 2014.
> https://segd.org/wayshowing-and-waylosing-mollerup)

With this, let us fast-forward to the concluding chapters (Augenbroe et al. 2005; Braham et al. 2005) of *Performative Architecture: Beyond Instrumentality* (Kolarevic & Malkawi 2005) to get a sense of the changes wrought by eight decades:

1. The availability of powerful computers and software that can be used to optimize structures with respect to numerically defined performance criteria.
2. The acceptance that performance criteria should be extended to include criteria like beauty that are not numerically definable.
3. Performative architecture will engage a team of different talents.
4. The architect will contribute a predominantly non-numerical perspective to the design, seeking to describe spaces that inspire a range of human activities, assessing the impact of mood and feeling. They may seek to adapt the client's program to assess how people will respond to the completed building. Given an overall outline of a structural configuration, the engineer will seek to realize it through computations that address factors like overall cost, thermal fluctuation, energy consumption, and more.

In addressing this, an early concept from artificial intelligence comes into play, that of *contracts* in subsystems of distributed systems (Hewitt 1977): in designing a complex system, a particular subsystem will send requests or data to other subsystems while in turn changing its behavior as it receives messages from them. The key point of a "contract" is that each system must be able to rely on the others' message without having to repeat their internal computations. In the same way, the engineer has a "contract" with the software: that if the parameters and optimality criteria are input correctly, the computer's output will provide an optimal (or locally optimal) setting of design parameters. This contract may be mediated in turn by an intervening "system" – the company that has designed the software and the manual on how to use it.

Even at the numerical level, there are major challenges here. For example. there may not be a single value to optimize – better insulation costs more, for example, so one must trade off minimal cost for materials (M) and minimal projected energy costs (E) for HVAC (heating, ventilation, and air conditioning). We speak of *constraint satisfaction*, where each desirable factor constrains the others. The strategy is thus to set some parameter λ that provides a measure of the tradeoff between them, and then seek to minimize $M + \lambda E$. The catch, of course, is that choosing λ is outside the remit of the computer or the engineer, and only communication with the architect (and, possibly, client) can determine this – but perhaps only after multiple simulations have charted the impact of different choices of λ. Below, we will consider how beauty may be factored into such considerations.

Neuroscience of Dynamic Experience and Design

In spelling out ways in which a house is a machine for living in, Le Corbusier (1927) lists baths, sun, hot and cold water, warmth, conservation of food, and hygiene; yet he also calls for a very different *architectural* aesthetics to "determine the various movements of our heart and of our understanding" (p. 1). The rest of this chapter will list just a few of the ways neuroscience can contribute to these diverse forms of architectural performance. *When Brains Meet Buildings* (Arbib 2020) provides a book-length treatment.

Neuroscience, Cognitive Science, and the Action–Perception Cycle

Cognitive science, which has links to artificial intelligence and computational modeling as much as to brain data, explores action, perception, memory, social interaction, and language in terms of interacting systems "in the head" – whether or not we can yet relate these systems to specific regions of the brain. When I use the term "neuroscience," it may be in the broad sense that includes cognitive science or in the narrow sense that focuses on "how the brain works." Neuroscience thus needs a computational model that can provide a cognitive description that can be refined to the neural level as and when appropriate data become available. In my work, this is provided by a form of *schema theory*, in which instances of perceptual and motor schemas (integrated into schema assemblages and coordinated control programs) can compete and cooperate to mediate the behavior of animals and humans in interaction with the environment and other creatures within it (Arbib 1990, 1992, 2013). This provide the tools for analyzing the *action–perception cycle* (Fuster 2004; Neisser 1976): We are not stimulus-response creatures, but bring knowledge and motivation to the actions whereby we sample and change the physical, social, and (combining the two) built environment. A complementary point is that the built environment is increasingly dynamic, incorporating robotic actuators and interacting with humans in part through "assistants" using natural language, powered by artificial neural networks that exploit deep learning (LeCun, Bengio, & Hinton 2015). Schema theory has been employed in robotics (Lyons & Arbib 1989) and shares certain features with distributed artificial intelligence (Steels & Brooks 2018).

Lifespan Architecture

John Eberhard's guiding vision, set forth in *Brain Landscape: The Coexistence of Neuroscience and Architecture* (Eberhard 2008), addressed the challenges posed by different typologies when noting that different people have different brains. Contrast building an elementary school for children who are learning so much about their environments and a retirement home for patients with Alzheimer's disease whose memories of a lifetime are rapidly disappearing (Zeisel 2006). How do you take a particular typology of building and seek to understand the neural and mental processes of the people who will use it, and adjust the building to improve its human impact? This raises the crucial issue of what Eduardo Macagno, a developmental neurobiologist, calls *Lifespan Architecture*. One challenge is to understand the way the brain changes through a typical lifespan, understanding the changes in action, perception, learning, and memory and the underlying brain mechanisms that come with different "stages" of life. Another is to think through how a building might be designed so that it can be readily updated over time. Consider, for example, a house that in turn might accommodate a newly-wed couple, the same couple with young children, the couple with teenagers, the couple leading a vigorous life in their (not always) empty nest, and then facing the rigors of the last few years of life. We may compare what Stewart Brand (1995) stresses in *How Buildings Learn* – not considering (as we may increasingly do in future) how the building itself forms an adaptive system, but rather what happens after it is built as humans restructure it over time to meet different needs. In similar vein, David Leatherbarrow (2005) speaks of architecture's unscripted performance, citing Aldo Rossi's critique (Rossi 1982) of functionalism to reject a narrow view of performance by stressing that its uses may change through the life of a building.

With this, let us consider, all too briefly, the neuroscience of poetics and performance.

Poetics

The Finnish architect Juhani Pallasmaa has stressed the interplay of multiple senses, not just vision, in architecture (Pallasmaa 2012), and has also written at length on architecture as poised between *art* and *science*. He (Pallasmaa 2007) notes the influence on architects of *The Poetics of Space* (Bachelard 1958), and cites approvingly Bachelard's suggestion that poetic imagination is closely related to an animistic understanding of the world. This may indeed be a source of inspiration but does not help us bring poetics into the realm of neuroscience and computation. I thus turn to a computational suggestion and then some notes on neuroaesthetics. The aim is not to reduce poetics to (neural) machinery but rather to suggest that the conversation between poetics or aesthetics and neuroscience may prove interesting.

Our earlier analysis of constraint satisfaction becomes even more difficult when subjective factors enter the mix. For example, one might have software that could design a surface to optimize some combination, C, of numerically well-specified design parameters – but there is no guarantee that the form that optimizes C would be aesthetically pleasing. Well, what about defining a measure, B, of beauty for these surfaces, and then finding a tradeoff factor, μ, such that optimizing $C + \mu B$ satisfies the architect? The catch is that B is non-numerical, in the eye or other senses of the architect. A currently feasible solution would be to exhibit a range of examples with near-optimal values of C and have the architect rate them aesthetically, then use this to guide the final choice.

Deep learning (LeCun et al. 2015) employs machine learning methods to set the connection weights between artificial neurons. These are loosely inspired by simple models of the brain's neural networks – but have been greatly modified over the last decade to exploit non-biological computations made available by the advent of increasingly powerful computers. The rise of deep learning may make an alternative available: vary parameters at random, irrespective of their C-values, and have the architect (or a suitable panel) rate each example from 1 to 10. An artificial network could then be trained to generate a "beauty estimate function," B', that could yield a value for all parameters that is consistent with the values assigned by the architect to the examples in the training set. Engineers and their software might then be set to work on optimizing $C + \mu B'$, with the architect back in the loop to assess the trade-offs determined by various values of μ.

With this, we turn to the neuroscience of aesthetics and beauty. Neuroaesthetics is in its early days, though – to single out the work of just two authors – books (Chatterjee 2013) and papers (Chatterjee

& Vartanian 2016; Vartanian et al. 2013) have already been written and conferences held. Here, for brevity, I focus on three contributions in the compendium *Mind in Architecture: Neuroscience, Embodiment, and the Future of Design* (Robinson & Pallasmaa 2015).

Albright (2015) approaches aesthetics from the basis of his work on the neuroscience of vision (Albright 2012), balancing a concern for the way the primary visual cortex of mammals can recognize line segments as the basis for extracting contours with ideas on how higher areas may provide top-down influences on early visual processing. He then offers two complementary mechanisms: first, in *easy adjustment*, simple, regular, repeating forms activate specialized neuronal systems that have evolved because they facilitate detection of natural stimuli that confer selective advantage for survival and reproduction. Here, structural understanding is immediate and supports the perception of conventional beauty. Second, in *easy arousal*, novelty is crucial, based on perception of complex forms with irregular statistics. There is no specialized neuronal system for this form of detection; culture and experience are crucial in shaping the brain. I find these notions interesting, but open to challenge. For example, we may appreciate both abstract art and well-designed products, with neither linked directly to "survival and reproduction," whereas much in the world may appear ugly whether or not it has such a connection.

Both Mallgrave (2015) and Gallese and Gattara (2015) offer a linkage to the world of mirror neurons, neurons whose activity occurs both when the subject performs a specific action or observes someone else perform a similar action (Di Pellegrino, Fadiga, Fogassi, Gallese, Rizzolatti 1992; Rizzolatti & Sinigaglia 2008). The corresponding mirror systems in humans appear not only to link the execution and recognition of actions but also the recognition and experience of emotions (Wicker et al. 2003). We thus move beyond a focus on visual perception alone to one in which vision (and other perceptual systems), action, and emotion are integrated.

For Mallgrave, the issue is to explore the relation between the nineteenth-century notion of *Einfühlung* in architecture and modern ideas linking empathy and mirror neurons. The psychologist Titchener wrote that in observing other people,

> Not only do I see gravity and modesty and pride … but I feel or act them in the mind's muscles. This is, I suppose, a simple case of empathy, if we may coin that term as a rendering of Einfühlung.
>
> *(1909, p. 21)*

I suggest that while mirror neurons support some aspects of empathy, we must invoke systems "beyond the mirror" to explain the phenomenon in general. For Gallese and Gattara, the emphasis is on the motoric component of visual perception. In viewing a work of art, we may empathize with the emotions expressed by people within a somewhat naturalistic scene, or may identify with what we take to be some of the actions of the artist whose traces we see in the final work. This adds an important dimension to our appreciation of "aesthetic feeling" but says nothing about the "aesthetic judgement" as to whether or not a work of art – or a piece of architecture – is poetically valuable or beautiful.

With these examples in mind, we can now return to our concern with performative architecture to consider the challenge of combining "core" performance with poetics.

Performance with a Poetic Flair

When we talk of *performance* in our everyday lives, we may think first of a musical or theatrical performance. In a play, the equivalent of architecture is the stage-setting within which the actors perform, following a given script. Turning to architecture, then, we may consider a building as the stage-setting for part of our lives – in which we may follow a script (e.g., in visiting a bank to take out money) or develop the more-or-less original script of our lives (as we live in our homes). From this perspective, the building performs well if we perform well within and around it, where the criterion for "wellness" will vary with typology of the building and the needs and dreams of its inhabitants.

Here one central concept is *affordance* (Gibson 1979), perceptual cues that we may receive, unconsciously as well as consciously, that a certain course of action is open to us, such as affordances for walking without a collision (Lee & Lishman 1977) or stably grasping an object to pick it up (Fagg & Arbib 1998). If a building is "a machine for doing X in," then it must provide all the affordances for doing X. These affordances are linked to the actions of which we are capable, our *effectivities*. An affordance only makes sense for those who have the physical and mental wherewithal to exploit it – if we cannot walk and must use a wheelchair, then the stairs do not offer an affordance for locomotion. Another key concept, the atmosphere or ambience of a building (Tidwell 2015), can be treated as a non-Gibsonian mood-related affordance (Arbib 2020).

A functional analysis of the affordances of a building must assess whether typical newcomers to a building will have the effectivities for its planned affordances or whether it is acceptable that they be acquired over time. This requires a micro-analysis of the behaviors for which a space is designed, combining workflow analysis (how the different functions are coordinated in ongoing behavior) with cognitive and neuroscientific analysis of the dynamics of visual attention (Land & Tatler 2009), for example, and the way in which the very nature of what we interact with carries forward the dynamics of our thought and behavior (Kirsh 2013).

The hippocampus is a brain region implicated in spatial navigation through the discovery of neurons in the rat brain whose activity correlates with where the rat is in its little world within the laboratory (Burgess 2014; O'Keefe & Dostrovsky 1971). We can link this to two forms of human wayfinding: one where the built environment provides affordances that show the way (e.g., find a restaurant by moving toward a visible restaurant sign) and the other where a person must have a map to work out their own route to a restaurant from a distant location – but we are particularly interested in *cognitive maps* where the "map" comprises brain-encoded knowledge of the layout of a town, for example. Note that, in neural terms, using an app like Google Maps, simply following instructions like "take the next left" falls in the first category, not the second. Diverse brain regions work together in both cases, but the hippocampus is crucial only in the latter. Guazzelli et al. (1998) offer a comprehensive neural model based on the World Graph model (Arbib & Lieblich 1977) which, though addressing data on rat navigation in mazes, has some commonalities with *The Image of the City* (Lynch 1960).

The human hippocampus is also involved in episodic memory – one can only remember a salient episode in one's life if the hippocampus was intact when the episode occurred – though cerebral cortex can support the recall of such episodes if they were consolidated before hippocampal damage. Turning from behavior in the built environment to the performance of the architect in designing it, we quote the Swiss architect Peter Zumthor (2012):

> When I think about architecture, images come into my mind. ... When I design, I frequently find myself sinking into old, half-forgotten memories .... Yet, at the same time, I know that all is new and that there is no direct reference to a former work of architecture.
>
> (p. 8)

Here it must be stressed that the "image" cannot be purely visual, but must link multiple senses with action, as in Zumthor's Therme at Vals (Zumthor 2011). There, we see the blending of performance and poetics in exemplary style. The chosen material (gneiss from local quarries) and the design of the exterior blend with the Swiss alpine landscape, but this is auxiliary to constructing different rooms which give access to different thermal pools. Zumthor's challenge was to fulfill this basic function in an aesthetically satisfying way, offer multisensory experiences that vary as we move through the spaces or stop to act and interact in one of them. As you enter a room, there is the visual impact, and then you immerse yourself in the water, feeling the temperature of the water on your skin and its resistance to and support of your movements. At least one of the rooms has flowers floating in the water, bringing in the sense of smell. And there is a transition from one room to another that requires pushing aside a heavy leather curtain, adding a new tactile element beyond that of walking, immersing, floating, to highlight the transition from one thermal experience to another.

But where is the neuroscience in "half-forgotten memories" linking to all that is new? The neuroscientist does not seek to explain the particularities of Zumthor's design, but rather seeks to understand the general mechanisms at play, with the hope that this may enrich architects' understanding of their design process. This concern leads us to current research on the role of hippocampus and other regions in supporting both episodic memory and imagination (Maguire, Intraub, & Mullally 2016; Schacter et al. 2012; Spreng, Mar, & Kim 2009), and this leads on to the open challenge of linking such research back to architecture. My current hypothesis (see the chapter "Experience and Design: Bringing in the Brain" in Arbib 2020) is based on the observation that even visual perception of a scene is an action of "mental construction" as we recognize (perhaps subconsciously) new forms of familiar objects in novel relations to each other and use this as context for making sense of unfamiliar elements in the scene. In the same vein, our memory of an episode is not like a photo. Instead it is a multimodal reconstruction of diverse elements, and thus will certainly omit some details and be inaccurate in others. When the architect summons half-forgotten memories, they may be triggered by functional associations, or sensory associations with different aspects of a room, building, or landscape that correspond to aspects of the program for a building, or to ideas revealed by site analysis (as in the ingredients available to Utzon as he started thinking about a design for the Sydney Opera House). No single recalled image dominates. Instead, fragments from diverse images begin to cohere, forming new patterns that can not only provide the context for further recall but also the basis for explicit rational analysis (and now we are invoking regions of the brain far beyond the hippocampus). The architect now has a newly imagined framework to begin to work out the details of performance and aesthetics, their relation to each other, and the physical (as distinct from mental) form of construction that will in due course convert the architect's plan into the completed building. And, of course, the new images will be reshaped as these analyses proceed.

Although the attempt to bring poetics into the world of architecture is well established, its linkage to the computational world of performative architecture or to neuroscience is at best in its infancy. But a start has been made.

References

Albright, T. D. (2012). On the Perception of Probable Things: Neural Substrates of Associative Memory, Imagery, and Perception. *Neuron*, 74(2), 227–245. 10.1016/j.neuron.2012.04.001.

Albright, T. D. (2015). Neuroscience for Architecture. In S. Robinson & J. Pallasmaa (Eds.), *Mind in Architecture: Neuroscience, Embodiment, and the Future of Design* (197–217). Cambridge, MA: MIT Press.

Arbib, M. A. (1990). Programs, Schemas, and Neural Networks for Control of Hand Movements: Beyond the RS Framework. In M. Jeannerod (Ed.), *Attention and Performance XIII. Motor Representation and Control* (111–138). Hillsdale, NJ: Lawrence Erlbaum Associates.

Arbib, M. A. (1992). Schema Theory. In S. Shapiro (Ed.), *The Encyclopedia of Artificial Intelligence* (1427–1443). New York, NY: Wiley-Interscience.

Arbib, M. A. (2013). Neurons, Schemas, Persons and Society – Revisited. In G. Auletta, I. Colagè, & M. Jeannerod (Eds.), *Brains Top Down: Is Top-Down Causation Challenging Neuroscience?* (57–87). Singapore: World Scientific.

Arbib, M. A. (2020). *When Brains Meet Buildings*. New York, NY: Oxford University Press.

Arbib, M. A., & Lieblich, I. (1977). Motivational Learning of Spatial Behavior. In J. Metzler (Ed.), *Systems Neuroscience* (221–239). New York, NY: Academic Press.

Augenbroe, F., Blassel, J.-F., Edler, J., McCleary, P., Otto, G., Spuybroek, L., ... Kolarevic, B. (2005). Operative Performativity. In B. Kolarevic & A. M. Malkawi (Eds.), *Performative Architecture: Beyond Instrumentality* (Chapter 18). Abingdon and New York, NY: Routledge.

Bachelard, G. (1958). *Poetics of Space*. Boston, MA: Beacon Press.

Braham, W., Kloft, H., Leatherbarrow, D., Rahim, A., Raman, M., Whalley, A., ... Malkawi, A. M. (2005). Conceptual Performativity. In B. Kolarevic & A. M. Malkawi (Eds.), *Performative Architecture: Beyond Instrumentality* (Chapter 17). Abingdon and New York, NY: Routledge.

Brand, S. (1995). *How Buildings Learn: What Happens After They're Built*. London: Penguin.

Burgess, N. (2014). The 2014 Nobel Prize in Physiology or Medicine: A Spatial Model for Cognitive Neuroscience. *Neuron, 84*(6), 1120–1125. 10.1016/j.neuron.2014.12.009.

Chatterjee, A. (2013). *The Aesthetic Brain: How We Evolved to Desire Beauty and Enjoy Art*. New York, NY: Oxford University Press.

Chatterjee, A., & Vartanian, O. (2016). Neuroscience of Aesthetics. *Annals of the New York Academy of Sciences, 1369*(1), 172–194.

Di Pellegrino, G., Fadiga, L., Fogassi, L., Gallese, V., & Rizzolatti, G. (1992). Understanding Motor Events: A Neurophysiological Study. *Experimental Brain Research, 91*(1), 176–180.

Fagg, A., & Arbib, M. (1998). Modeling Parietal-Premotor Interactions in Primate Control of Grasping. *Neural Networks, 11*(7–8), 1277–1303.

Eberhard, J. P. (2008). *Brain Landscape: The Coexistence of Neuroscience and Architecture*. Oxford and New York: Oxford University Press.

Fromonot, F. (1998). *Jørn Utzon: Architect of the Sydney Opera House* (Translated from the French by Christopher Thompson). Milan: Electa.

Fuster, J. M. (2004). Upper Processing Stages of the Perception-Action Cycle. *Trends in Cognitive Sciences, 8*(4), 143–145.

Gallese, V., & Gattara, A. (2015). Embodied Simulation, Aesthetics and Architecture: An Experimental Aesthetic Approach. In S. Robinson & J. Pallasmaa (Eds.), *Mind in Architecture* (161–179). Cambridge, MA: MIT Press.

Geddes, R. (2006). Second Thoughts: Reflections on Winning Second Prize. In A. Watson (Ed.), *Building a Masterpiece: The Sydney Opera House* (56–67). London: Lund Humphries Publishers.

Gibson, J. J. (1979). *The Ecological Approach to Visual Perception*. Boston, MA: Houghton Mifflin.

Guazzelli, A., Corbacho, F. J., Bota, M., & Arbib, M. A. (1998). Affordances, Motivation, and the World Graph Theory. *Adaptive Behavior, 6*, 435–471.

Hewitt, C. (1977). Viewing Control Structures as Patterns of Passing Messages. *Artificial Intelligence, 8*(3), 323–364. 10.1016/0004-3702(77)90033-9.

Hopkins, G. H. (1985). *Poems and Prose*. London: Penguin Classics.

Kirsh, D. (2013). Embodied Cognition and the Magical Future of Interaction Design. *ACM Transactions on Computer-Human Interaction (TOCHI), 20*(1), 3:1–3:30.

Kolarevic, B., & Malkawi, A. M. (Eds.) (2005). *Performative Architecture: Beyond Instrumentality*. Abingdon and New York, NY: Routledge.

Land, M. F., & Tatler, B. W. (2009). *Looking and Acting: Vision and Eye Movements in Natural Behaviour*. New York, NY: Oxford University Press.

Leatherbarrow, D. (2005). Architecture's Unscripted Performance. In B. Kolarevic & A. M. Malkawi (Eds.), *Performative Architecture: Beyond Instrumentality* (5–20). Abingdon and New York, NY: Routledge.

Le Corbusier. (1927). *Towards a New Architecture* (Translated from the Thirteenth French Edition with an Introduction by Frederick Etchells). New York, NY: Brewer, Warren & Putnam.

LeCun, Y., Bengio, Y., & Hinton, G. E. (2015). Deep Learning. *Nature, 521*(7553), 436–444. 10.1038/nature14539.

Lee, D. N., & Lishman, J. R. (1977). Visual Control of Locomotion. *Scandinavian Journal of Psychology, 18*, 224–230.

Lynch, K. (1960). *The Image of the City*. Cambridge, MA: MIT Press.

Lyons, D. M., & Arbib, M. A. (1989). A Formal Model of Computation for Sensory-Based Robotics. *IEEE Transactions on Robotics and Automation, 5*, 280–293.

Maguire, E. A., Intraub, H., & Mullally, S. L. (2016). Scenes, Spaces, and Memory Traces. *The Neuroscientist, 22*(5), 432–439. 10.1177/1073858415600389.

Mallgrave, H. F. (2015). "Know Thyself" or What the Designers Can Learn from the Contemporary Biological Sciences. In S. Robinson & J. Pallasmaa (Eds.), *Mind in Architecture* (9–31). Cambridge, MA: MIT Press.

Neisser, U. (1976). *Cognition and Reality: Principles and Implications of Cognitive Psychology*. San Francisco: W. H. Freeman.

O'Keefe, J., & Dostrovsky, J. O. (1971). The Hippocampus as a Spatial Map: Preliminary Evidence from Unit Activity in the Freely Moving Rat. *Brain Research, 34*, 171–175.

Pallasmaa, J. (2007). New Architectural Horizons. *Architectural Design*, 77(2), 16–23. 10.1002/ad.420.

Pallasmaa, J. (2012). *The Eyes of the Skin: Architecture and the Senses* (3rd ed.). Chichester: John Wiley & Sons.

Rizzolatti, G., & Sinigaglia, C. (2008). *Mirrors in the Brain: How Our Minds Share Actions, Emotions, and Experience* (Translated from the Italian by Frances Anderson). Oxford: Oxford University Press.

Robinson, S., & Pallasmaa, J. (Eds.). (2015). *Mind in Architecture: Neuroscience, Embodiment, and the Future of Design*. Cambridge, MA: MIT Press.

Rossi, A. (1982). *The Architecture of the City*. Cambridge, MA: MIT Press.

Schacter, D. L., Addis, D. R., Hassabis, D., Martin, V. C., Spreng, R. N., & Szpunar, K. K. (2012). The Future of Memory: Remembering, Imagining, and the Brain. *Neuron*, 76(4), 677–694.

Spreng, R. N., Mar, R. A., & Kim, A. S. (2009). The Common Neural Basis of Autobiographical Memory, Prospection, Navigation, Theory of Mind, and the Default Mode: A Quantitative Meta-analysis. *Journal of Cognitive Neuroscience*, 21(3), 489–510. 10.1162/jocn.2008.21029.

Steels, L., & Brooks, R. (2018). *The Artificial Life Route to Artificial Intelligence: Building Embodied, Situated Agents*. Abingdon and New York, NY: Routledge.

Tidwell, P. (Ed.) (2015). *Architecture and Atmosphere: A Tapio Wirkkala - Rut Bryk Design Reader* (with contributions by Gernot Böhme, Tonino Griffero, Jean-Paul Thibaud and Juhani Pallasmaa). Espoo, Finland: Tapio Wirkkala - Rut Bryk Foundation.

Titchener, E. B. (1909). *Lectures on the Experimental Psychology of the Thought-processes*. New York, NY: Macmillan.

Vartanian, O., Navarrete, G., Chatterjee, A., Fich, L. B., Leder, H., Modroño, C., … Skov, M. (2013). Impact of Contour on Aesthetic Judgments and Approach-Avoidance Decisions in Architecture. *Proceedings of the National Academy of Sciences*. doi:10.1073/pnas.1301227110.

Wicker, B., Keysers, C., Plailly, J., Royet, J. P., Gallese, V., & Rizzolatti, G. (2003). Both of Us Disgusted in My Insula: The Common Neural Basis of Seeing and Feeling Disgust. *Neuron*, 40(3), 655–664.

Zeisel, J. (2006). *Inquiry by Design: Environment/Behavior/Neuroscience in Architecture, Interiors, Landscape, and Planning*. London: W. W. Norton & Co.

Zumthor, P. (2011). *Peter Zumthor Therme Vals* (Essays: Sigrid Hauser & Peter Zumthor with translations by Kimi Lum and Catherine Schelbert; Photographs: Hélène Binet). Zurich: Verlag Scheidegger & AG.

Zumthor, P. (2012). A Way of Looking at Things. In P. Zumthor (Ed.), *Thinking Architecture* (3rd ed., expanded) (pp. 7–28). Basel: Birkhauser.

8.1
The Cognitive Dimension: The Role of Research in Performative Design Process
The Theory

Mitra Kanaani

The process of architectural design is increasingly convoluted. It has become intertwined with ever-evolving ecological, technical, economic, social and scientific expectations, and simultaneously inseparable from complex computational requirements. In recent years, much discussion has been dedicated to the role of scientific inquiry or research within the *academy* and *practice* realms of architecture.

The *act of research* within any branch of knowledge can be defined as the exploration and quest for a reliable and replicable truth. By the same token, new potential truth, as a *theory*, must be verified to determine how closely it resembles the *intended reality*. In architecture, the *intended reality* is the design outcome that meets the needs of a defined program and its users. Today, architectural design is increasingly user-driven and performance-based or performative. It is focused on understanding events, environments, and user experience.

Performativity in design thinking relies on facts and objectivity for the extraction and collection of evidence. By blending theory and empirical research, design emerges through a guided process or mechanism based on the *Creative Cognition Approach*, a combination of cognitive and intuitive antecedents of insights. This approach relates to the theoretical viewpoints of prominent researchers specializing in problem-solving, design thinking, and concept formation (Bowers, Farvolden, & Mermigis, 1995).

This chapter seeks to explore and clarify the procedural theory of the *performative design process* as a research-based design methodology. The term "procedural theory" is used in computational design (Ahlquist, 2016) in reference to the processes emerging in response to specific behaviors. *Procedural theory* focuses on the collective behavior of all parts and components of the designed object. It is an integrative process focused on performativity in design thinking, in the architectural design of the built environments and elements.

The practice of performative design thinking requires a reformulation of the underlying concepts of design. Based on understanding, assimilation, and the emergence of a body of cognitive and computational concepts, performative design is expanding the scope beyond traditional reliance on intuitive generative design approaches. It incorporates progressive scientific research approaches while simultaneously expanding the multiplicity and the scope of the design parameters, and progressively evolving methodologies for critical design thinking. In today's architecture, logical reasoning is increasingly becoming an accepted cognitive research-based design process, furthering the boundaries of design thinking beyond sole reliance on an intuitive approach.

Meaning of *Cognitivity* versus *Intuitivity* and the Theory of Creative Cognition

Cognitivity, as a state of being cognitive, refers to cognition, which is concerned with the act or process of knowing, perceiving, and relating to the mental processes of perception, memory, judgment, and logical reasoning. In cognitive thought processes, there is an increased emphasis on pre-identified theoretical frameworks as the basis for reasoning. This is gained through external inputs and individualized mental approaches to circumstances. Cognitive thinkers are able to methodically assimilate and integrate various facts and concepts through intellect. This contrasts with *intuitivity*, which relates to normative mental processes based on internal inputs and choices or decisions made by will. According to researcher and author Sophy Burnham (2011), intuitive thinking relates to that *unconscious reasoning* and *sudden insight* that propels us to do something without knowing why or how, based on hunches, inner insight, or intuitive grounding.

Intuitivity is a critical factor for human–environment interactions and decision-making. However, because it is based on inexplicable components of *unconscious reasoning*, it is considered unscientific. Intuition is connected to paranormal events or perceptions which lack scientific explanation. Despite such concerns, it is widely accepted that *intuitivity* has a direct relationship with *creativity*. In her article, "Intuition as the Basis for Creativity," researcher Carla Woolf (2018) examines this direct connection and concludes that creativity does its best work when it functions intuitively.

In recent decades, cognitive scientists have presented theoretical ideas and research findings on various aspects of *creative cognition*. Their studies have built on factors such as experimental investigation, high capacity to store experiences, and mental processes that are at least, in principle, observable (Ward, Smith, & Finke, 1999).

Creativity is related to mental processes and additional contextual factors including the environment, culture, and individual abilities. It depends on how people think and lead their lives. According to researchers and experts in cognitive behavioral science, the Creative Cognition Approach is very useful when seeking to understand creativity. It focuses on the cognitive processes and the frameworks that underlie *creative thinking*. *Creativity* is the act of turning new and imaginative ideas into reality and involves thinking and producing. *Creativity* is also an aspect of personality characterized by novel and appropriate ideas and processes. In attempts to elevate creativity amongst technical workers in major organizations, nowadays researchers, educators, and trainers focus on multi-disciplinary approaches, leveraging arts-based practices to spark creative inspiration and innovation (Naiman, 2012). These design thinking processes methodically utilize pre-inventive, explorative, and interpretative procedures in order to develop novel visual patterns, forms, blends, and models. They can even help with internal and verbal representations (Finke, Ward & Smith, 1996).

The Creative Cognition Approach improves understanding and the scope of creative processes. However, this is not a linear process. Creative thinking incorporates combinations and patterns of the same cognitive processes utilized in other noncreative and scientific endeavors. Additionally, pursuit of the Creative Cognition Approach allows for the emergence of new questions and ideas about cognition and reasoning, providing further opportunities within the creative context.

Today's theory of creative cognition takes up intuition and insight from a contemporary cognitive perspective and uses prior knowledge in the incremental and non-linear views of creative problem solving. However, it is in contrast with various forms of fixation and sudden insight. Studies are providing new methods to distinguish intuitive problem solving from analytical problem solving (Finke et al., 1996).

The development of concepts and structures is at the core of design thinking in architectural design. The Foundation for Critical Thinking (2017) identifies eight basic elemental structures for *Critical Thinking Concepts and Tools* that define thinking and reasoning. Learning to analyze thinking requires practice in identification and use of these structural elements. Reasoning occurs whenever the mind draws conclusions based on logic. However, to analyze thinking we must first identify and question its elemental structures, which are based on data. These commonly specified elements of reasoning are: Development of a Clear Purpose, Raising a Question to Solve a Problem, Gathering Information and Facts, Making Interpretations and References, Developing Concepts, Making Assumptions, Developing Points of View, and Deriving Implications and Consequences (Paul & Elder, 2006).

Design Thinking is, for the most part, accompanied by *Critical Thinking*, or the objective analysis and evaluation of an issue or a process in order to form a judgment for a design idea and solution with a constructive view for improvement. The critical design mode of thinking, similar to any other critical thinking process, involves an "intellectually disciplined process of actively and skillfully conceptualizing, applying, analyzing, synthesizing, and/or evaluating of information gathered from, or generated by, observation, experience, reflection, reasoning, or communication" (Scriven & Paul, 1987).

In essence, performative design thinking is a cognitive process that embraces rather than rejects intuitive thinking, resulting in successful creative cognitive design outcomes. Remembering that creative cognition takes up intuition and insight from a *contemporary cognitive perspective* and uses prior knowledge in the incremental view of creative problem solving, performative design thinking is an interactive combined process. The right-brain intuitive mode of idealizing creative thinking is synthesized with the left-brain mode of critical thinking involving logical and analytical linear characteristics. By the same token, performative architectural design processes combine the traditional sequential conceptual, schematic, and developmental phases of project design with a non-linear, interactive, and integrative approach.

Precedents in Scientific Cognition in Design Thinking

Scientific Cognitive Thinking is deeply rooted in precedents of architectural design. It would be presumptuous to believe that cognitive design thinking and research within the architectural realm is a novel concept. For instance, Ancient Greeks devised the Golden Section, a rectangular shape with dimensions of length to height of roughly 3:2 and exact 1.618 portions (Figure 8.1.1).

> Also known as the golden ratio, this dimension is revered, as having near mystical powers, the shape's defining feature is that when one side is split off into a square, another golden rectangle and square appears *ad infinitum*, and drawing an arc within each successive square, creates a golden spiral.
>
> *(Sussman & Hollander, 2015)*

Adrian Bejan, Professor of Mechanical Engineering at Duke University, has explained how cognitive design thinking relates to the Golden Section:

> Shapes with length/height ratios (L/H) close to 3/2 are everywhere and give the impression that they are being 'designed' to match the golden ratio (φ = 1.618). Here I show that these shapes emerge as part of an evolutionary phenomenon that facilitates the flow of information from the plane to the brain, in accordance with the constructal law of generation and evolution of design

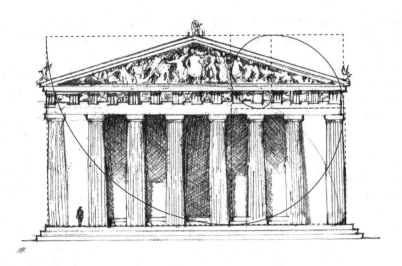

Figure 8.1.1 Golden Section.
Drawing credit Nasim Rowshan

in nature. The time required by the eyes to scan a rectangular area L × H is minimal when the shape is L/H = VL/VH, where VL and VH are the horizontal and vertical scanning speeds. This special shape is such that the time for scanning long and fast (L/VL) is the same as the time for short and slow (H/VH). I also show that VL/VH is approximately 3/2 and that consequently L/H ~ 3/2. This natural evolutionary design is an integral part of the universal constructal design that facilitates the flow of the biosphere, hydrosphere and atmosphere on earth. Vision, cognition and locomotion are features of a single design for movement of animal mass with easier and easier access in time, all over the globe.

(Bejan, 2009)

These harmonized well-balanced proportions have been applied to the geometry of architectural elevations and plans throughout history, including the Parthenon and Notre-Dame Cathedral, and even the early twentieth-century designs of Le Corbusier (Sussman & Hollander, 2015).

Bejan argues the balanced proportions of the Golden Rectangle fit well with the human visual field and the eyes' energy-conserving habits. They are compatible with the capability of the human eye to coherently scan images. The Golden Rectangle is evident in the structural laws of nature, which are at work in interrelationships between how humans see, think, and move. The cognition of visual stimulation engages the human brain and directs movement within spaces. Therefore, it can be a significant consideration when designing and planning in architecture.

Throughout the history of architecture, multitudes of theoretical frameworks have been cognitively applied as the basis for design concepts. Examples of useful configurations include: height-to-base ratio, balanced resistance, symmetrical plans, uniform sections and elevations, direct load paths, short spans, and uniform floor heights. Various designers and master builders of prominent icons of architecture have utilized these methods. The Great Pyramids of Egypt, some of the oldest buildings still in existence, cognitively followed similar scientific theoretical attributes including symmetrical plans, short span, direct load path, broad base, symmetrically reducing plan size with height, and large structural density. These physical attributes have sustained these ancient monuments throughout the past 45 centuries.

Symmetry and the proportions of the human body are examples of theoretical formulas that have been followed throughout the history of architecture. In his treatise *De Architectura*, the Ancient Roman architect Vitruvius linked the design of buildings to human proportions, specifically with respect to symmetry. This theory propelled the development of Leonardo da Vinci's famous drawing "Vitruvian Man" (c. 1490). According to da Vinci, the ideal proportion is the human body, and the perfect geometries are the circle and the square (Sussman & Hollander, 2015).

One of the strongest examples of absolute cognitive design thinking is the ancient monumental calendar Stonehenge. It is carefully aligned at a latitude of 51 degrees so that the midsummer sun always rises exactly opposite the setting of the midwinter sun. Alignment with one results in alignment with the other and is fundamental to the design and placement of the stones (Figure 8.1.2).

In essence, geometries, patterns, and formal elements in the history of built forms have cognitively been generated based on humans' physical needs and in response to their psychological attributes and innate affinity for life.

Research as a Way of Practice: Theorizing a New Agenda for Performative Architecture

A Historical Overview

> The ones who love practice without science are like the pilot who enters his ship without helm and compass, who therefore never can be sure about where he is heading. Practice always has to be based upon a firm theory.
>
> *(Leonardo da Vinci – Schnier, 2004, quoted from Adler, 1926)*

Historically, practicing architects and designers have been trained to rely on the *subconscious emotional process of intuitive thinking*, which is holistic approach with a minimum degree of conscious control but

Figure 8.1.2 Stonehenge in Salisbury England, 2900–1400 BCE.
Drawing credit: Nasim Rowshan

characterized by a thinking mode that synthesizes ideas through creative leaps. However, through repetition and gaining experience, they gain the ability to develop economical handling of cognitive routine tasks throughout the phases of the design process. In general, practice, being a process of carrying out an idea, plan, or theory, is based on established routine processes and relies on subconscious, intuitive thinking.

On the other end of the spectrum are researchers who primarily perform *conscious, logical, conceptual and analytical* modes of discursive thinking. This type of thinking requires deliberate cognitive steps. It constitutes a basis for unequivocal communication about the proof of the process and its outcome. Cognitive psychology differentiates between these two ends of the spectrum, and yet it is proven there is some degree of overlap between them.

With respect to interdependency of research and practice, studies reveal that most cognitive processes do not require conscious attention, and only 5–10% of tasks are rationally driven. Jorg Schnier (2004), believes that the human brain works such that most design tasks can be performed efficiently by default through intuitive thinking. Discursive thinking is mainly used when a problem is not solved through intuitive cognitive approaches. However, at some point discursive conscious rational thinking becomes cognitive routine and transforms, becoming dominated by the brain's intuitive way of thinking.

Analytical *design research* and intuitive *design practice* are by nature two different modes of thinking or different epistemological routines of conceptual empiricism and logical rationalism in producing, storing, and communicating knowledge. However, technological advancements in recent decades have attempted to bridge the gap between these modes of design strategy and epistemological traditions, thus establishing interdependency between these two design strategies. With such dynamic changes in design thinking for architectural performativity, and increasing complexity in design typologies, there is increased need for cognitive and analytical design thinking versus traditional intuitive design processes.

Current architectural theory is a rich repository of various schools of thoughts, movements, dialogues, treatises, and works by architects, philosophers, theoreticians, and critics, as well as thematic theories, discussions, and writings about architecture from antiquity to the twenty-first century. These concepts and ideas fulfill the purpose of certain principle goals in architectural design. Thematic theories are treatises which aim at the fulfillment of several principal goals, usually at the cost of other customary goals of building.

Throughout the history of architecture there has been a wealth of ontological realities based on nuances of the time. Various schools of thoughts and movements in the theory of architecture have posited viewpoints and reflected on design. Perhaps the most notable from antiquity is Marcus Vitruvius Pollio, the author of the oldest research treatise on architecture that still remains valid, inspirational, and practical to this day. In his treatise, Vitruvius considers multiple themes and provides several practical goals for building, each elaborated in a distinct book chapter. Building usability is the highlight of his theory, introduced in three required design constituents, without prescribing a method for their synthesis. According to Vitruvius's classification the building's realms of requirement are:

- practicality or "convenience" (utilitas)
- durability (firmitas)
- pleasantness (venustas)

Throughout the ages, this has remained a model and backbone of ontological context for many architectural philosophies and research concepts. Buildings have predominantly been researched as combinations of characteristics, moving steadily toward what might be considered modernistic holistic entities.

The Cognitive Dimension

This is particularly true in the trend toward performance-based design thinking. In the course of time, a variety of independent thematic theories have developed for every group of characteristics.

Since the Industrial Revolution, thematic theories have been researched by prominent architect-philosophers. Amongst the most notable, the *Functionalist* movement of the Bauhaus has heavily influenced architecture. Their intended uses of buildings and focus on functional requirements of typological spaces, combined with a keen attention to social issues, has been a highlight in modern times. Based on this philosophy, the mantra that *Form Follows Function* of Louis Sullivan transformed the meaning of "beauty." Prefabrication, and basing design on empirical research, became central to architectural practice.

Throughout the history of civilization, architectural symbolism to use the building for sending a message, construction materials, the physics of the firmness, and ecological factors have attracted the attention of many architectural researchers and philosophers in search of innovation. The trend to *modernity* has brought with it new concepts and meanings in the ontology of architectural design thinking. Some dominant keywords of this era include *technology*, *high-tech forms*, *intelligent or smart materials*, and *innovative building approaches*. These are paralleled by ecological, environmental, social, bioclimatic, and human physical and behavioral well-being concerns, as well as requirements for sustainability and resiliency that have demanded high levels of objective cognitive thinking. New generations of architects and designers have emerged that are expanding the vocabulary of architectural language, contributing in-depth meanings, philosophies, and design objectives that are rooted in scientific inquiry.

Notable architects such as Thomas Herzog, Nicholas Grimshaw, Renzo Piano, Eugene Tsui, Norman Foster, Jean Nouvel, Ken Yeang, Itsuko Hasegawa, and Richard Rogers have acted as scientific designers, considering designs that allow co-existence between man and nature by adapting to the climate and the land, and include human beings as an integral part of the ecosystem. "Today problem solving involves

Figure 8.1.3 Allianz Arena, Munich, Germany – Thomas Herzog.
Drawing credit: Nasim Rowshan

Figure 8.1.4 Eden Project, The Biome, Cornwall, UK – Grimshaw Architects.
Drawing credit: Nasim Rowshan

Figure 8.1.5 Tjibaou Cultural Center, Nouméa, New Caledonia – Renzo Piano.
Drawing credit: Nasim Rowshan

Figure 8.1.6 Biomorphic Future Vision, Watsu Center – Eugene Tsui.
Drawing credit: Nasim Rowshan

Figure 8.1.7 City Hall, London, Norman Foster.
Drawing credit: Nasim Rowshan

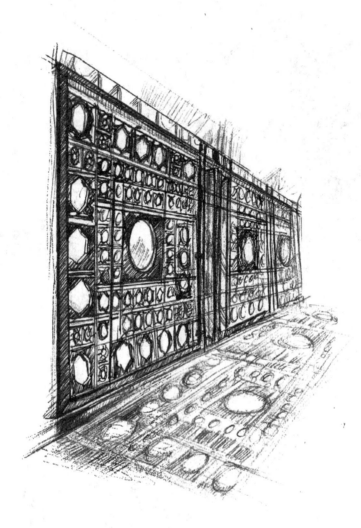

Figure 8.1.8 Institut du Monde Arabe, Paris – Jean Nouvel.
Drawing credit: Nasim Rowshan

thinking at a global scale and using science as the tool to open up the future. Science is the means by which knowledge is ordered in the most efficient way, so as to solve problems" (Rogers, 1985).

However, performative architecture is not an "ism"; it is a procedural and evolutionary approach to integrative, holistic design thinking that allows us to apply principles developed in nature over great spans of time without references to past or present, and with no consideration for preconceived stylistic aesthetics. At its core the goal of performative design is for buildings to perform as close as possible with the laws of nature. *Procedural theory* is most appropriate alongside the Theory of Performativity, because it is concerned with an interactive, methodical design process. It is a process-evidence-based procedural approach focusing on the importance of the interaction between decisions

Figure 8.1.9 Menara Mesiniaga, Vertical Farming in Malaysia – Ken Yeang.
Drawing credit: Nasim Rowshan

Figure 8.1.10 Museum of Fruit, Yamanashi, Tokyo – Itsuko Hasegawa Architects.
Drawing credit: Nasim Rowshan

Figure 8.1.11 Bordeaux Law Courts Projects, Richard Rogers.
Drawing credit: Nasim Rowshan

and hypotheses from other transdisciplinary and interdisciplinary fields, in order to develop comprehensive design solutions.

> The processes of designing can be subjected to detailed, if not scientific, scrutiny, although they seldom have been. This does not mean that the design process can be scientific – by definition, design cannot be scientific. It means rather that the process can be described and explained using the methods of scientific or quasi-scientific research.
>
> *(Lang, 1987)*

The Role and Types of Research in Performative Architecture

Performative architecture is a multi-disciplinary field spanning numerous realms. It invites design challenges that are connected with new science and technology. Performative design encompasses social, cultural, and environmental factors related to in-depth matters of building physics with a philosophy focused on reconciling architecture of the past, which was very much attuned and adaptable to the nuances of nature and human co-existence, to the potential for society's transformation. It considers architecture as an inseparable constituent of the earth's ecosystem and ecological factors including all tangible and intangible or measurable and immeasurable facets. In performative architecture, buildings, to a great extent, are viewed as biospheres.

With respect to design performativity, there are two distinct approaches in research methods: *quantitative* (measurable) and *qualitative* (immeasurable). According to Crotty (1998), the main difference between qualitative and quantitative is the procedure and approach in conducting the research, and the selection of research goals, theoretical frameworks, and perspectives.

Contemporary qualitative research methods are based on a non-scientific subjective personal observations and interviews. However, through current statistical methods and other scientific quantifiable procedures of data collection, it is possible to objectivize the process and arrive at factual outcomes. In other words, the researcher is able to quantify qualitative data by encoding collected data and providing a more scientific statistical analysis.

Considering that performative architecture is about building performance to satisfy human expectations, the architectural research for design performativity is both qualitative and quantitative. The expected design performance relates to various types of human behaviors, expectations, and actions, which are considered both measurable and immeasurable. In performative architecture, the polarization between measurable and immeasurable has been transformed by the quantification of qualitative data. This is mainly achieved through the use of scientific methods of inquiry that provide opportunities for objectivity and measurability in the most subjective concepts. The research approach is thus transformed to one divergent spectrum of decisions. Due to their multitude of realms and vast boundaries, performative design projects encompass research approaches that demand combined quantitative and qualitative approaches, depending on the researcher's stance and knowledge.

Poles/Realms of Performativity and the Constructivist Research Design Elements

There are thematic territories that lie between what can be considered as two poles of performativity. At one end is the conceptual domain that relates to performativity of the virtual. At the other end is the operative domain that relates to performativity of the real (Kolarevic, 2005: 227). Considering the expected duality of types of performativity in performance-based architecture with respect to various fields of societal, cultural, ecological, technical, tectonic, and scientific matters, the role of a structured research inquiry to guide the design into an integrated, optimized, and idealized whole becomes more and more crucial. Performance-based architecture is based on a *design methodology* that is increasingly research-based, conscious-based, and cognitive. It is both prospective and predictable.

There are four distinguishable elements with distinct hierarchical levels of decision-making that are typically common in any research process toward a meaningful outcome. These levels lead to research approaches that tends to be quantitative, qualitative, or a mix of both. These four elements in a design research include:

1. Methods. The development of research questions and hypothesis, and techniques or procedures of data-gathering and analysis.
2. Methodology. The design process, choice, and use of particular methods, toward achievement of desired objectives and outcomes.
3. Theoretical Framework Perspective. The philosophical stance that informs the methodology, providing context for the process and basis of the logical thinking and criteria.
4. Epistemology. The study of domains of knowledge, and how new knowledge is acquired. *Epistemology* typically goes hand in hand with *ontology*, which is about the nature of reality and relates to a set of concepts and categories in a subject area or domain. It also has to do with the theory of knowledge embedded in the theoretical framework and subsequently in the methodology. Epistemology and ontology are not exactly the same but mutually dependent and not easy to distinguish, particularly in a research issue. According to Crotty: "to talk about the construction of meaning [epistemology] is to talk of the construction of a meaningful reality [ontology]" (1998).

The theory of design research in performative architecture does not reject nor limit itself solely on the basis of a *constructivist research philosophy*. Instead it recognizes reality as a product of combined human intelligence and experience. The Constructivist Design Science Research method emphasizes the diversity of interpretations and works toward deriving the ideal outcome ("truth") from interactions between elements and alternatives of a circumstance. In essence, in this type of design research, conclusions must be objective and definable. The "construct," as a new contribution (which in architecture can be a building, a new theory, a model, software, or even an algorithm) must be evaluated and analytically developed. The outcome can involve a prototype that is developed with respect to predefined criteria, and with the expectation for some sort of performance, based on a benchmark. In this research approach, researchers express their own impressions of the way the world looks.

In performative or performance-based design, the epistemological and ontological stance adopted in the constructivist research becomes more realistic. The researchers' investigation is spent more on discovering the truth that lies within the final outcome, sometimes with absolute objectivity, and avoids any interference of personal perceptions, inevitable resemblances, or intuitive awareness.

According to Kathy Charmaz (2006), data are assumed to be objective facts that already exist in the world. The role of the researcher is to discover these data and determine the theories they imply. In the case of performative design approaches, data are considered objective facts, similar to what are considered in the *Constructive Grounded Theory*. Grounded Theory of Research is a systematic general guideline for data-gathering, synthesis, analysis, and conceptualization of the qualitative data, methods of inquiry, and development of theory based on an inductive methodology. It has systematic guidelines for scientific data-gathering and analysis. The process of analysis involves coding data, developing, back-and-forth checking and comparing of the data, writing narratives of the process and integrating the categories of qualitative data and theories. However, there is a distinction between the Constructivist Grounded Theory and the Objectivist Grounded Theory. The latter emphasizes the reality of the external world, does not acknowledge the researcher's role in creating data, and does not include informed interpretations. It only recognizes outcomes as derived from data. Constructivist approaches prioritize the outcomes of study and research over the methods.

In design, there is an ongoing debate about the utilization of objectivist versus constructivist approaches. Constructive Grounded Theory of research with a constructivist epistemology and ontology is more consistent with combined cognitive and intuitive architectural design thinking. According to Charmaz (2006), this is more consistent because of "[p]lacing priority on the phenomena of study and seeing both data and analysis as created from shared experiences and relationships with participants and other sources." She also believes that including Objectivist approaches compromises the processes and outcomes of constructivist research.

Within constructivist research approaches to performative design thinking there are several implications.

- Performative architecture involves a wide range of social subjects, which in the construct of research must be studied holistically. The research must respond to multiple overlapping social, cultural, ecological, and environmental factors and realities, while remembering that "the knower and the known are inseparable" (Lincoln & Guba, 1985: 37).
- Since reality is not derived from black-and-white concepts, humans must be the primary data-collecting instruments and researchers must be the primary data-gathering instruments (Lincoln & Guba, 1985). It is through human data-collection and researcher data-gathering that the complex interactive development of constructed realities can be interpreted and selected, remembering that "every act of observation influences what is seen" (Lincoln & Guba, 1985: 39).
- Individual participant points of view and interpretations create the contextual nature of research.

Scientific-inquiry-informed-design allows architects to think broadly and make responsible and logical decisions. Developed design outcomes are knowledge-driven and evidence-based. It focuses on understanding how scientific methodology can be used to ensure the adaptability of design and integration within selected contexts or programs. It is a combination of performative technicality, economic

The Cognitive Dimension

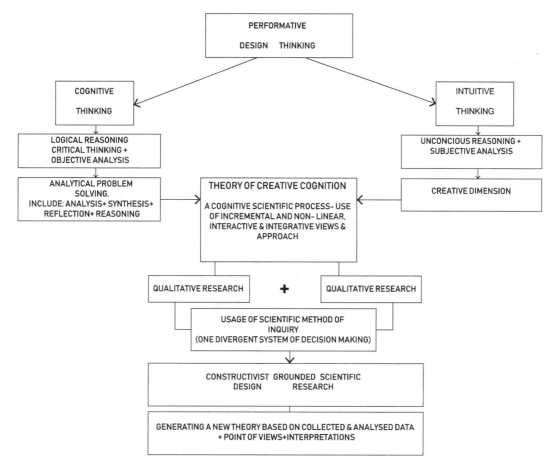

Figure 8.1.12 Performative cognitive/intuitive diagram.
Drawing credit: Nasim Rowshan

feasibility, and positive social contributions. Based on this approach, design is an inherent part and an emergence of its related context.

Research and Research-by-Design Tools in Performative Design Process

Research-by-design is a critical inquiry, considering design as an outcome of the research process. It develops pathways that lead to new practical design outcomes and intended building performance. This integrative, interactive process acquires its tools from science and technology to underpin the development of its methodical and cognitive approach.

The performative paradigm spans multiple realms and facets from spatial, social, and cultural, to the purely technical. This may include all required systematic aspects of a building such as structural, mechanical, thermal, electrical, acoustical considerations. Research-by-design inevitably necessitates the usage of related problem-specific tools, techniques and methods of inquiry for data collection and analysis, in order to address research in a wide spectrum of realms. This research process also requires participation from problem-specific experts related to each specific design problem.

One of today's most dominant technological tools in research for building performativity and rapid prototyping is "simulation." Simulation requires specialized expertise in various related fields, including engineering, construction, behavioral science, management, operation, and the design itself. The resources utilized originate from diverse disciplines including physics, mathematics, physical science, and human behavior. Advanced building simulation focuses on areas such as the structural system, environmental or thermal concerns, indoor air quality, and natural lighting. These simulations require the development of algorithms and complex data management and interfacing. Each of these domains have sub-problems that are modeled and simulated differently. The current tools have also allowed not only analysis, but also synthesis. This renewed research utilizes advances in optimization. "In order to overcome the drawback of needing different simulation engines to predict different performance aspects, integration between algorithms provides a means to overcome some of these limitations and increase the efficiency and prediction accuracy of performance tools" (Malkawi, 2005). Current advancements in performance simulation tools have opened new paradigms of performativity in building design and construction optimization and built friendlier relationships between users and simulation tools.

Performative architecture as a theory for design research combines basic design principles with field and laboratory observation and experience in a non-linear manner. While still in the early stages of development, as an ethical obligation to the planet earth and its occupants, it is here to stay. In reference to non-linear behavior, Chris Luebkeman argues:

> It is the combination of the first principles with experience and observations that is the fundamental potential of the design philosophy. It places the design imperative back in the hands of the designer. And, more importantly it also places responsibility and accountability back into the designer's hand in a very obvious way. One can no longer hide behind building code.
>
> *(Luebkeman, 2003)*

It is appropriate to bring this subject to a close with Michael Hensel's marked insight: "The continual pursuit of an integrated theoretical framework for performance-oriented architecture necessitates re-questioning almost the entire scope of architectural practice, research and education" (Hensel, 2013).

References

Ahlquist, S. (2016). Procedural Theory. Retrieved September 9, 2018. Papers.cumincad.org-att-acadia16_10.
Bejan, A. (2009). The Golden Ratio Predicted: Vision, Cognition and Locomotion as a Single Design. *Nature, International Journal of Design & Nature and Ecodynamics*, volume 4, issue 2, pp. 97–104.
Bowers, K., Farvolden, P., & Mermigis, L. (1995). Intuitive Antecedents of Insight. In S. M. Smith, T. B. Ward, & R. A. Finke (Eds.), *The Creative Cognition Approach*. Cambridge, MA: MIT Press, pp. 27–51.
Burnham, S. (2011). *Art of Intuition: Cultivating Your Inner Wisdom*. New York, NY: Tarcher Perigee and Penguin.
Charmaz, K. (2006). *Constructing Grounded Theory: A Practical Guide Through Qualitative Analysis*. London: Sage, pp. 330–331.
Crotty, Michael (1998). *The Foundations of Social Research: Meaning and Perspective in the Research Process*. London: Sage, pp. 3–10, 256.
Finke, R. A., Ward, T. B., & Smith, S. M. (1996). *Creative Cognition: Theory, Research, and Applications*. Cambridge, MA: MIT Press, pp. 1–9.
Foundation for Critical Thinking. (2017). Critical Thinking: Where to Begin. Retrieved September 9, 2018. www.criticalthinking.org/pages/critical-thinking-where-to-begin/796.

Hensel, M. (2013). *Performance-Oriented Architecture: Rethinking Architectural Design and the Built Environment*. Chichester: John Wiley & Sons, p. 140.

Kolarevic, B. (2005). Computing the Performative. In B. Kolarevic & A. Malkawi (Eds.), *Performative Architecture: Beyond Instrumentality*. New York, NY: Taylor & Francis, p. 227.

Lang, J. (1987). *Creating Architectural Theory: The Role of the Behavioral Sciences in Environmental Design*. New York, NY: Van Nostrand Reinhold, p. 19.

Lincoln, Y. S., & Guba, E. G. (1985). *Naturalistic Inquiry*. Beverly Hills, CA: Sage, pp. 37–39.

Luebkeman, C. (2003). Performance-Based Design. In B. Kolarevic (Ed.), *Architecture in the Digital Age: Design and Manufacturing*. New York, NY, and London: Spon Press, pp. 284–285.

Malkawi, A. M. (2005). Performance Simulation: Research and Tools. In B. Kolarevic & A. Malkawi (Eds.), *Performative Architecture Beyond Instrumentality*. New York, NY: Taylor & Francis, pp. 87–88.

Naiman, L. (2012). Creativity at Work. Retrieved September 19, 2018. www.brainworldmagazine.com/creative-cognition/.

Paul, R., & Elder, L. (2006). The Miniature Guide to Critical Thinking Concepts and Tools. Foundation for Critical Thinking. Retrieved September 9, 2018. www.criticalthinking.org.louisville.edu/ideastoaction/about/criticalthinking/framework.

Rogers, R. (1985). Observations on Architecture. In Frank Russel (Ed.), *Architectural Monographs: Richard Rogers + Architects*. London: Academy Editions, p. 16.

Schnier, J. (2004). Between Research and Practice: On the Interdependency of Thinking Mode and Design Strategy. In B. Grimes (Ed.), *Between Research and Practice, Proceedings of the EAAE ARCC Conference*. Paper presented at the EAAE ARCC Conference in Dublin School of Architecture DIT, Ireland, pp. 152–160.

Scriven, M., & Paul, R. (1987). Defining Critical Thinking: A Statement Presented at the 8th Annual International Conference on Critical Thinking and Education Reform, Summer 1987. Foundation for Critical Thinking. Retrieved September 21, 2019. www.criticalthinking.org/pages/defining-critical-thinking/766.

Sussman, A., & Hollander, J. B. (2015). *Cognitive Architecture: Designing for How We Respond to the Built Environment*. New York, NY: Routledge, pp. 93–95, 113.

Ward, T. B., Smith, S. M., & Finke, R. A. (1999). Creative Cognition. In Robert J. Sternberg (Ed.), *Handbook of Creativity*. Cambridge, MA: Cambridge University Press, p. 189.

Woolf, C. (April 17, 2013). *Intuition as the Basis for Creativity*. The Creativity Post. Retrieved September 9, 2018. www.creativitypost.com/education/intuition_as_the_basis_for_creativity.

8.2

The Cognitive Dimension: The Role of Research in Performative Design Process

Theory Put into Research Practice

Joon-Ho Choi

Unintended Consequence in Practice by Design

As discussed in the previous chapter, performativity in design thinking is primarily based on scientific facts and objectivity in the extraction and collection of evidence. There have been erroneous design outcomes frequently reported in modern buildings. As shown in Figure 8.2.1, the occupants need to use their umbrellas because of too much daylight causing excessive glare and possible visual health damage, in addition to eye fatigue. Even though a design intention might be to enhance the occupants' quality of life by adopting large glazing with improved access to nature, the actual occupants are suffering due to completely unexpected environmental consequences in the building. Figure 8.2.2 also shows a consequence of a drawback in the indoor environmental quality (IEQ) control. This building adopts an underfloor air distribution system, which generally confirms 30% energy savings as compared to the conventional overhead ceiling-based system. However, too much fast and cold air drift makes the occupants suffer from thermal distress and high air velocity. Even though this building is certified as an outstanding environment-friendly design, the occupants are using plastic bags to block the air stream. Another worst condition in this case is that too much air pressure is triggered on the air diffuser not covered in plastic bags by rejected pressure using the plastic bags, and the air diffuser generates excessively cold and high-speed airflow, which cause serious thermal stress to the occupants around the spot.

Significance of Performativity in Design Process

As such, performativity in design thinking is significantly important to prevent any erroneous design and its unintended environmental consequences in reality. Therefore, a design approach should be based on scientific evidence and environmental phenomena. This fundamental principle can be accomplished as a function of collected data and their analyzed outcomes. In the domain of informatics, it is well known that data should be collected, analyzed, and processed to identify a pattern or trend. Once such patterns or trends are integrated and accumulated in a massive collection, it finally becomes

Figures 8.2.1a and b Too much bright daylight in a commercial building.
Photo: Dr. Volker Hartkopf at Carnegie Mellon University

Figure 8.2.2 Too-cold and fast air makes the occupants suffer, and air diffusers are blocked with plastic bags by those people.
Photo: The author

knowledge. Therefore, such a sequence of data processing naturally generates a need for interdisciplinary research efforts through the integration of individually different knowledge domains. For example, to develop a design guideline for enhancing building occupants' health and productivity, we need to initially understand the building's IEQ, performance, and occupant behaviors, while investigating the impact of those IEQ elements on human health and productivity. Multiple quantitative research methodologies should be applied while numerous data collections, surveys, and sensory devices/technologies should be utilized to collect environmental and physiological data. Once those data are collected, advanced data-mining strategies should apply and contribute to understanding existing patterns and

The Cognitive Dimension

trends, which require knowledge of informatics and computer science. As such, to establish and develop robust performative design research, many technical, scientific, and design parameters should be identified, integrated, analyzed, and discussed. Therefore, in this chapter critical research practices are presented as an example to help understand how to apply quantitative research outcomes to the performative design process.

Research Practice Case #1: Comprehensive Post-Occupancy Evaluation

Based on the convenience and ease of data collection as compared to the past, a data-driven approach is becoming popular these days, represented by machine learning theories, such as classification, clustering, artificial neural network, and deep learning algorithms. These computational algorithms have been created and developed in the area of computer science, but many other domains have started adopting the algorithms in their research and practices. In architecture, there have been multiple efforts to integrate such advanced data process methods to enhance the domain knowledge. One of the key research topics of performative architecture is a comprehensive POE, which actively adopts questionnaire surveys for a user's environmental satisfaction as well as the ambient IEQ measurement.

POE has been used as the primary methodology for IEQ and design performance assessment, and has also been adopted as a research and survey tool to understand the impact of building performance and design on the occupants' physiological perception. On the long-term scale, the results have been adopted as feedback for a next or future project that might have a similar design program and physical characteristics. In the mid- or short-term, the analyzed outcome has been applied to a troubleshooting solution for any building system's drawbacks or malfunctions, and/or design renovation, especially for an old building. The main goal of implementing POE in a building is to improve the comfort level of the occupants and to maintain the building's mechanical and physical systems to ensure better indoor conditions while minimizing the environmental impact (Al Horr et al., 2016). The primary indoor environmental condition consists of five key individual IEQ elements, which are thermal, visual (lighting), acoustic, air, and spatial qualities. The functioning of these individual elements complicatedly affects the building occupants, which results in various ranges of perceptions of a comfortable or uncomfortable environment while the individuals stay within the indoor space.

A few decades ago, most POE research heavily relied on a questionnaire survey to ask a building occupant about his/her subjective perception without sufficient objective evidence. One conventional assumption was that all occupants are exposed to the same thermal, visual, air, acoustic, and spatial conditions while they remain in the same space, room, or zone. However, in reality there are numerous dynamic behavioral patterns per individual, and also various local and microclimatic features per small-scale space which may be accommodated in the same spatial area. In addition, considering the modern building environment, which is filled with advanced technology and communications, current IEQ conditions are frequently monitored and controlled by modern Internet of Things technologies and smart control strategies. As a result, various environmental conditions are dynamically generated across individual workplaces, even in the same building or space.

With the help of advanced sensing and data acquisition technologies, conducting POE to collect environmental data is much more convenient these days than in the past. An architecture researcher can utilize numerous handheld sensors and also station sensors for continuous measurements. There are multiple universities and research institutes, including the Human-Building Investigation (HBI) Research Group at the University of Southern California (USC) and the Center for Building Performance and Diagnostics (CBPD) at Carnegie Mellon University (CMU). They have developed IEQ sensor carts which accommodate thermal, lighting, air, and acoustic sensors and are capable of measuring the IEQ conditions automatically (Figure 8.2.4) based on the data collection procedure illustrated in Figure 8.2.3 (Choi & Moon, 2017). Developing such a sensory device package is possible with the help

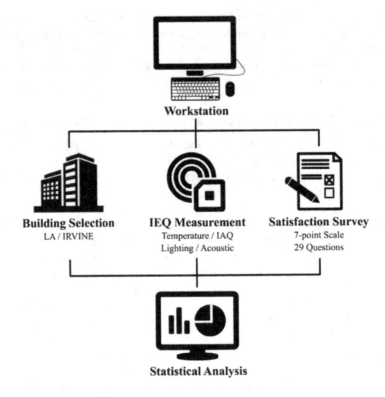

Figure 8.2.3 POE field measurement procedure in a sample workstation.
Photo: The author

of advanced pre-fabricated sensing technologies from electrical engineering and computer science. Due to this technical success, collecting data has become an easier task. However, in many research cases, despite a significant amount of data, there are many missing findings due to a lack of data analysis skills. So, the USC HBI group and the CMU CBPD have tackled these limited data analytical skills by adopting machine learning theories and data-mining methods, which are dominant in the area of computer science and informatics.

A survey is also an important component for collecting subjective data from each respondent to fairly assess and understand the relationships between a building's occupants' satisfaction and the ambient IEQ conditions in the POE. Park (Park et al., 2018) conducted POE research that adopted IEQ measurements of office buildings, as well as questionnaire surveys, to identify opportunities for improving the process of IEQ evaluation and to find the critical stressor or motivator that may cause the occupants' dissatisfaction with ambient conditions. This research indicates that the design of a questionnaire survey is important since the manner in which a question is presented could affect the occupant's response. In the domain of psychology, the construction of survey questionnaires is one of the key methods used in critical research areas that focus on minimizing unintended context effects and maximizing the reliability of all participant responses. For effective POE research, the USC HBI group has invited an environmental psychologist to effectively design their subjective data collection methods by using survey questionnaires (Choi & Lee, 2018; Choi & Moon, 2017).

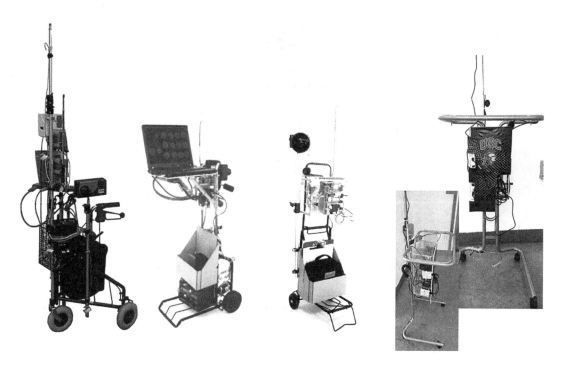

Figure 8.2.4 Sensing cart for IEQ measurement, developed by CMU and USC.
Photo: The author

Figure 8.2.5 shows how effective a measured survey can be when integrated into the design and environmental control process. It illustrates one of the findings of a recent POE study (Choi & Moon, 2017), Impacts of Human and Spatial Factors on User Satisfaction in Office Environments. This study adopted numerous design methodologies and tools, as well as technical methods, to conduct a cross-sectional analysis of a dataset collected from 411 workstations in modern office buildings.

"Positive" in the text box of Figure 8.2.5 indicates that a respondent is satisfied with the overall IEQ environment, and "negative" indicates "unsatisfied". The text in an oval shape indicates a respondent's satisfaction with each corresponding IEQ element, such as lighting, air quality, and acoustics. "Location" indicates the workstation location: i.e., perimeter or center of an open office layout, based on the distance between the workstation location and the exterior windows. This figure is generated by using the J48 algorithm (Kaur & Chhabra, 2014), called the "decision tree", one of the classification models developed in computer science. This algorithm is the process of predicting or classifying targets or categories by approximating a mapping function from multiple input variables to a discrete output variable (the overall IEQ satisfaction in this example).

Based on this technical principle, this chart classifies positive or negative overall IEQ satisfaction based on the individual's satisfaction with IEQ conditions and physical spatial attributes. In Figure 8.2.5, lighting satisfaction is placed at the top, while air quality satisfaction is on the tree's second level. Therefore, those occupants who report positive lighting satisfaction are classified as being positive in overall IEQ satisfaction (with about 90% certainty), while the negative lighting-satisfaction group are re-classified, based on the occupants' positive or negative satisfaction with indoor air quality conditions. When an occupant is not satisfied with the lighting quality, then air quality satisfaction becomes

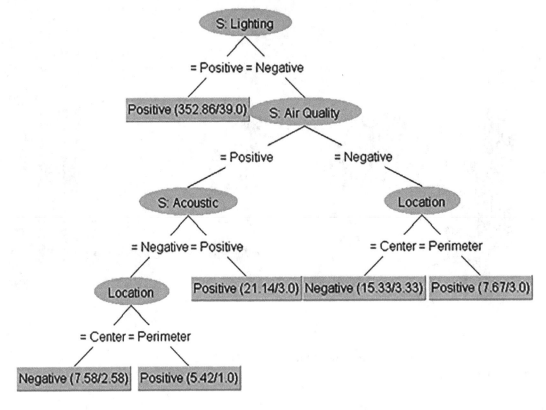

Figure 8.2.5 Decision tree for an effective IEQ design to enhance overall environmental satisfaction ("negative" and "positive" indicate individual occupants' satisfaction with the overall IEQ condition.)
Photo: The author

another determining factor. If an occupant is not satisfied with the air quality, then the workstation location becomes the third decision component. In this case, the perimeter zone helps confirm a positive overall IEQ satisfaction with a combination of lighting and quality satisfaction. By tracking the individual branches of this decision tree, the chart helps a researcher know how to accomplish a positive overall IEQ satisfaction by understanding which individual IEQ component affects overall IEQ satisfaction the most, or the least, in an office building. This knowledge can be used to enhance the productivity and environmental wellbeing of the building's occupants. These classifications are based on 411 collected datasets from 17 office buildings.

The other POE example is about human physiological components in architecture, such as gender, age, ethnic origin, etc. Due to the diversity in physiological characteristics, an individual's preferred environmental conditions, pertaining to thermal comfort, lighting, and acoustics, vary. Most of all, since thermal comfort is based on the heat exchange rate between the human body and ambient thermal conditions, an occupant's physical condition, such as clothing, activity, and body mass index, primarily affects thermal comfort and sensations. Clothing and activity conditions are relatively easy to quantify, by observation, but other physiological functions are difficult to accommodate in a thermal comfort prediction model for IEQ control.

A recent research finding showed that gender matters for maintaining thermal satisfaction in an office. Figure 8.2.6 illustrates a user's thermal satisfaction with cooling and heating seasons, by gender (Choi, Aziz, & Loftness, 2010; Choi, Loftness, & Aziz, 2012). This study was based on 402 workstations that were sampled, and the users were recruited from 20 commercial office buildings

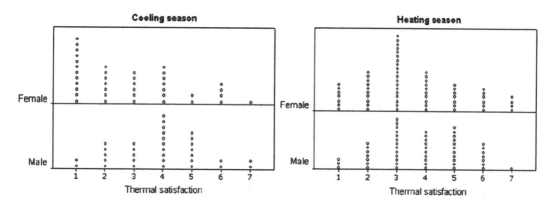

Figure 8.2.6 User thermal satisfaction in cooling (left) and heating seasons by gender (each symbol represents up to two observations) (Choi et al., 2010).
Photo: The author

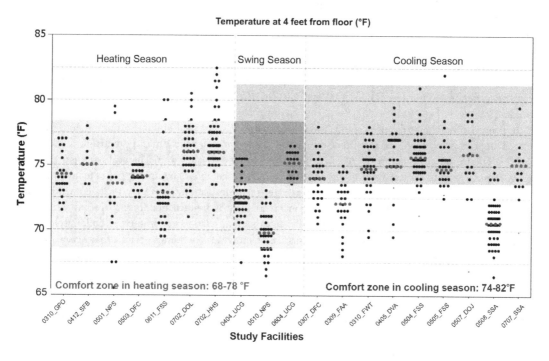

Figure 8.2.7 Measured air temperature distribution (Loftness et al., 2009); colored boxes indicate comfort zone in each season recommended by ASHRAE-55.
Photo: The author

across the U.S. to participate in environmental satisfaction surveys. As illustrated in Figure 8.2.6, there is no clear difference in the thermal satisfaction of the two gender groups. However, the lower levels of satisfaction reported by the females were statistically significant when compared to the male responses. This research finding has high potential for consideration and adaptation in pertinent architectural design, especially for indoor thermal environmental control and design. In Figure 8.2.7, the measured temperature data reveal thermal conditions in the sampled workstations over a few years (Loftness, Aziz, & Choi, 2009). This figure illustrates that about 50% of the measured temperature data in the cooling season were much lower than the design guidelines recommended by ASHRAE-55 (ASHRAE Standard 55–2013 – Thermal Environmental Conditions for Human Occupancy (American National Standards Institute [ANSI] approved), 2013). Such an overcool condition, during summer seasons in the U.S., has been frequently reported in many recent studies. Based on this result, it can be concluded that thermal conditions might be frequently overcooled during the summer season, which may contribute to low thermal satisfaction and high thermal stress for female occupants. This information may be integrated, in practice, with design guidelines by configuring a workstation, system, and other thermal comfort-related parameters.

Research Practice Case #2: Simulation Modeling

A building performance simulation is one of the best tools for accomplishing performative design in research and practice. By adopting a computational simulation tool, any type of building, geometry shape/design, material, site location, or climate, can be accommodated in the simulation process to identify the performance of design to meet an environmental regulation and/or performance target. Today, many commercially available simulation interfaces have become more user-friendly, and help architects and designers utilize such tools without critical technical barriers. Figure 8.2.8 illustrates an insolation study (top) and natural wind analysis for passive design (e.g., natural ventilation) (bottom), and design guidelines for a net-zero-energy building, based on multiple simulation results. Through the simulation process, a building's orientation, the windows' orientation and size, the location of solar panels, and the building aspect ratio, as well as indoor layout, can be included in design programming and can generate technical evidence that supports an effective design process for a high-performance building.

In general, a building's façade accounts for approximately 70% of total building environmental performance. Due to this key technical feature of the façade, its design poses the largest potential for affecting the building's performance, as compared to other building components (such as mechanical systems and interior design). In addition to the conventional simulation tool discussed above, computer vision technology helps to advance modern simulation technology for a larger-scale simulation. This may include an urban area, a city, and a community, instead of a simulation for a single individual building. In recent years, many major cities in the U.S. have been disclosing utility information, relative to commercial buildings located in their cities, and objectively assessing the performance of individual buildings on an urban scale. Based on this information, all of the façade information for each corresponding building can be matched with monthly and seasonal utility information with the help of manual observation/street view images. Figures 8.2.9 and 8.2.10 illustrate 17 data parameters that were collected from the façade in one recent research project (Yang & Choi, 2015). Even though the urban-scale modeling suggested in this study is possible when a large dataset is established from numerous best-practice buildings, it is difficult to collect such data using a manual process due to time constraints and the labor required.

For this research, a computer vision technique was adopted to collect extensive datasets from large building samples where utility datasets were available and disclosed to the public. This technique made

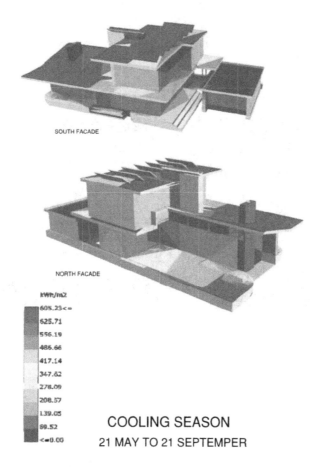

Figures 8.2.8a and b Sampled simulation study results and established conceptual design based on the estimated environmental performance (USC ARCH-615 course work (instructor: Dr. Joon-Ho Choi), 2017).

it possible to collect façade information from individual buildings based on street view images and/or video files filmed by drone, as shown in Figure 8.2.11.

For example, a window area is one of the significant façade components that affect building energy performance in heating, cooling, and lighting. Therefore, it is crucial to understand the window-to-wall ratio (WWR) in order to estimate a building's performance. The computer vision technique helped extract the WWR information from a building's façade image. Figure 8.2.12 shows how the collected image was processed in order to tell the windows from the walls, and to identify the windows' shapes and sizes to estimate the WWR from the selected building's façade.

By investigating the pattern of the relationship between the energy performance and the façade features in a large dataset, it was possible to develop a façade-vision-based building performance model using a data-mining tool. By adopting best-practice performance data, this energy performance modeling research enabled real-time energy usage monitoring and management of each targeted building. It also provided knowledge of façade designs' impact on building performance, while adopting an advanced data-driven approach in the simulation research field using real datasets instead of simulated imaginary data.

Figures 8.2.8a and b (Cont.)

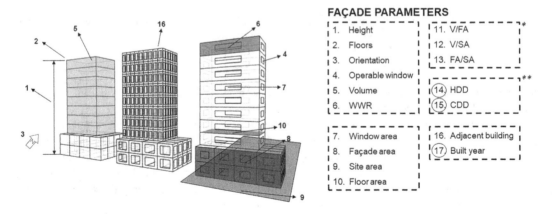

Figure 8.2.9 Building façade information to be collected from general street view images (provided by the author's research team).

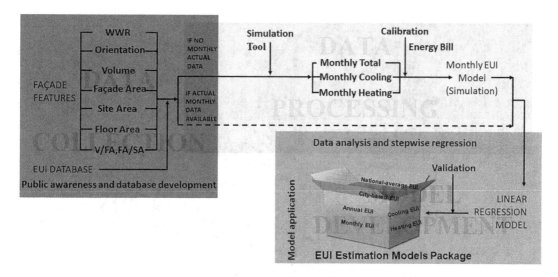

Figure 8.2.10 Façade-information-driven building energy performance modeling procedure (provided by the author's research team).

Figure 8.2.11 Examples of geometry estimation of a 3D building model in ground view images; wireframe of a 3D model is overlaid from an aerial image (left) and ground view images.
Image: Dr. Sung Chun Lee; Lee, Jung, & Nevatia (2002)

Figure 8.2.12 Computer-vision-based window detection technique.
Image: Dr. Sung Chun Lee; Lee & Nevatia (2004)

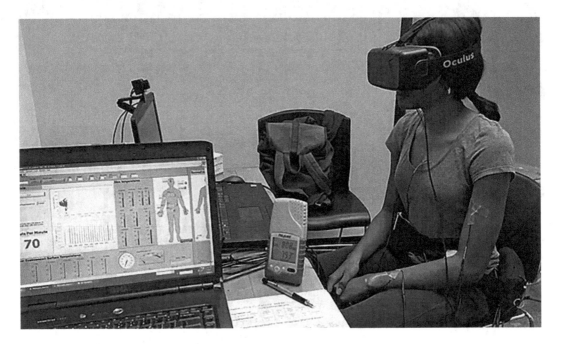

Figure 8.2.13 A VR-adopted human physiological information acquisition module (developed by the author's research team).

Research Practice Case #3: Adopting Virtual Reality

Virtual reality (VR) has also become a popular tool in the architectural design process. Rather than an architect's subjective intuition-driven approach, a user's quantifiable intuition-centered design approach has been investigated. Instead of simply adopting an intuitive perception, based on a user's subjective response, human physiological data were integrated into the design process, so that most optimal designs can be confirmed as a function of the user's (e.g., a client's) heart rate variability and electrodermal activities, as indicators of psychological satisfaction and stress (Yeom, Choi, & Zhu, 2017). Figure 8.2.13 shows a user study interface to collect the test participant's physiological information, while multiple design options are shown to the user via a VR device. The collected physiological information can be interpreted for a stress scale to confirm the satisfaction level per design option with the help of a building design sample database. By adopting quantified physiological data, rather than subjective survey responses, this research outcome can help process a design that can ensure a client's project satisfaction.

References

Al Horr, Y., Arif, M., Katafygiotou, M., Mazroei, A., Kaushik, A., & Elsarrag, E. (2016). Impact of indoor environmental quality on occupant well-being and comfort: A review of the literature. *International Journal of Sustainable Built Environment*, *5*(1), 1–11. doi: 10.1016/J.IJSBE.2016.03.006.

ASHRAE Standard 55-2013 – Thermal Environmental Conditions for Human Occupancy(ANSI approved). (2013). American Society of Heating, Refrigerating, and Air-Conditioning Engineers (ASHRAE).

Choi, J.-H., Aziz, A., & Loftness, V. (2010). Investigation on the impacts of different genders and ages on satisfaction with thermal environments in office buildings. *Building and Environment*, *45*(6), 1529–1535. doi: 10.1016/j.buildenv.2010.01.004.

Choi, J.-H., & Lee, K. (2018). Investigation of the feasibility of POE methodology for a modern commercial office building. *Building and Environment*, *143*, 591–604. doi: 10.1016/J.BUILDENV.2018.07.049.

Choi, J.-H., Loftness, V., & Aziz, A. (2012). Post-occupancy evaluation of 20 office buildings as basis for future IEQ standards and guidelines. *Energy and Buildings*, *46*, 167–175. doi: 10.1016/j.enbuild.2011.08.009.

Choi, J.-H., & Moon, J. (2017). Impacts of human and spatial factors on user satisfaction in office environments. *Building and Environment*, *114*, 23–35. doi: 10.1016/j.buildenv.2016.12.003.

Kaur, G., & Chhabra, A. (2014). Improved J48 classification algorithm for the prediction of diabetes. *International Journal of Computer Applications*, *98*(22), 13–17. doi: 10.5120/17314-7433.

Lee, S. C., Jung, S. K., & Nevatia, R. (2002). Integrating ground and aerial views for urban site modeling. Proceedings of 16th International Conference on Pattern Recognition.

Lee, S. C., & Nevatia, R. (2004). Extraction and integration of window in a 3D building model from ground view images. Proceedings of the IEEE Computer Society CVPR.

Loftness, V., Aziz, A. A., & Choi, J.-H. (2009). *Seven Recommendations for Energy Savings and Performance Gains in General Service Administration Buildings*. Washington, DC: U.S. General Services Administration.

Park, J., Loftness, V., Aziz, A., Park, J., Loftness, V., & Aziz, A. (2018). Post-occupancy evaluation and IEQ measurements from 64 office buildings: Critical factors and thresholds for user satisfaction on thermal quality. *Buildings*, *8*(11), 156. doi: 10.3390/buildings8110156.

USC ARCH-615 Environmental Systems Research course work (instructor: Dr. Joon-Ho Choi). (2017). *USC Carbon Neutral Cluster*. Los Angeles, CA.

Yang, C., & Choi, J.-H. (2015). Energy use intensity estimation method based on façade features. *Procedia Engineering*, *118*, 842–852. doi: 10.1016/j.proeng.2015.08.522.

Yeom, D., Choi, J.-H., & Zhu, Y. (2017). Investigation of physiological differences between immersive virtual environment and indoor environment in a building. *Indoor and Built Environment*. 1420326X1773194. doi: 10.1177/1420326X17731945.

9.1
Integrated Design Thinking: Inter- and Transdisciplinarity in Performative Design Methodology
The Theory

Marvin J. Malecha

There is a musical score in the art collection of the Prague Castle Lobkowicz Palace Museum that is a stunning reminder of the power of collaborative and integrative thought. This manuscript combines the work of genius and the sense of time. Both Handel and Mozart received support from the Lobkowicz family. In recognition, Handel sent the family a copy of the *Messiah* score in his own hand. At some point in time Mozart had access to the score and modified it to the form we know commonly today (Figure 9.1.1). The score on display shows the modifications in Mozart's own hand over the top of Handel's hand-written copy (Towe 1996). Although they did not work together, this amazing collaboration demonstrates the extension of an individual's ability by the exceptional talents of another. This simple example illustrates the value of inter- and transdisciplinary activity in a performative situation. After all, in such a situation it is the success of the outcome rather than the recognition of a single individual's talent that is the most important measure of success.

This example of collaboration among talented individuals represents the relationship between the complexity of a design challenge and the nature of the necessary response. In the case of a musical score, the challenge is limited by time and scope. Because of this, it is possible to keep the relationship simple, even if it is only consummated by what is recorded rather than by actual interaction among the players. As the diagram in Figure 9.1.4 illustrates, it is the project complexity and scale that must be assessed to determine the appropriate response. The outcome scale, problem scale and leadership are interlinked. Leadership of a team of individuals is one thing; the leadership of teams of teams is entirely another. Even more impressive is the leadership and vision demonstrated in a project such as the cathedrals of France and Italy that were under construction for generations (see Figure 9.1.2). The Duomo of Florence was initiated in 1296 without any idea of how the intersection of the cross axis would be covered. Brunelleschi entered the project in 1401, commencing work finally in 1420, more than 100 years after construction was initiated, and it was completed in 1436 with an idea that was beyond the comprehension of the founders (King, 2000).

To accomplish the construction of the dome the complexity of the interrelationships among people, from workers to town fathers, was daunting. The was only possible because of the ability to

Integrated Design Thinking

Figure 9.1.1 The *Messiah* score.
Photograph by Marvin Malecha, from the Prague Castle Lobkowicz Palace Museum

imagine, with the mind of a beginner, every step of the realization of the dome from the building strategies to the machines necessary to carry out the work. Among the lessons of this project is the necessity to understand the complexity of what is expected. It is daunting to reflect on the assumption of Brunelleschi of matters related not only to concept design but to issues as complex logistically as providing the marble for the project. This assessment has a significant impact on the realization of innovation and creative result.

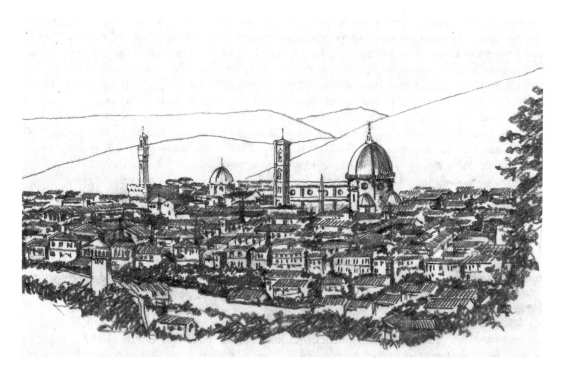

Figure 9.1.2 Sketch of the Florence Duomo, by Marvin J. Malecha.

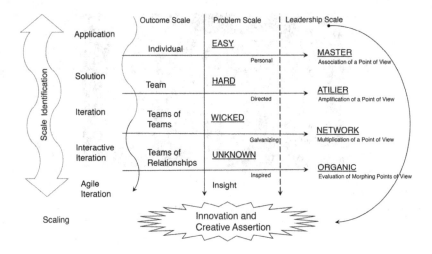

Figure 9.1.3 Project Scaling Diagram by Marvin J. Malecha.

The problem scale, from *easy* to *hard*, *wicked* and *unknown*, inspires thoughts on the nature of the team (Figure 9.1.3). The assessment of the needs of the team articulating the expertise to be gathered determines the thought process that will be supported. This ranges from the individual to team, teams of teams and teams of relationships (Malecha 2015). The first two, individual and team, are widely recognized and a direct by-product of the Industrial Revolution, and are generally accepted as effective measures against complex problems. Wicked problems demand more because there is no apparent solution and it becomes obvious that no single discipline can resolve the issues of such open-ended and frequently unresolvable challenges. Social media and highly interactive digital tools have given rise to networks of individuals to address such problems. However, our concern is not only defined by the wicked problems. We know these problems are not entirely solvable, but they at least can be articulated. Our awareness has now grown regarding a concern for what is not known and what may not be predictable. In such a case, it has become obvious that there must be a structure of teams of relationships to reveal from many perspectives, one adding to the other to discover paths forward. We are familiar with the master of a studio, even more familiar with the atelier (team) that forms around a chief design leader. Teams of teams have become familiar to us as the complexity of projects from skyscrapers to sophisticated building types such as hospitals evolved. The architectural team is complemented by engineers and consultants from as broad a spectrum as structural analysis to acoustics, construction management and even building management (see Figure 9.1.4). We have entered a period when the professional office has evolved from a rigid structure to an organic network of relationships (Malecha 2002).

The office, once a clear pyramidal structure, has evolved into a network of teams of teams and is now further evolving into a structure of relationships bringing together the most diverse community of disciplines stretching traditional architectural services into previously unknown areas of expertise (Malecha 2005). This is the foundation of inter- and transdisciplinarity in performative design.

In a discussion between the sons of Lou Kahn and Jonas Salk (at a Design Futures Council presentation preceding the 2016 American Institute of Architects National Convention), both gentlemen referred to their fathers' working relationship with each other as play. It is both interesting and revealing that two accomplished men in their respective disciplines described their working

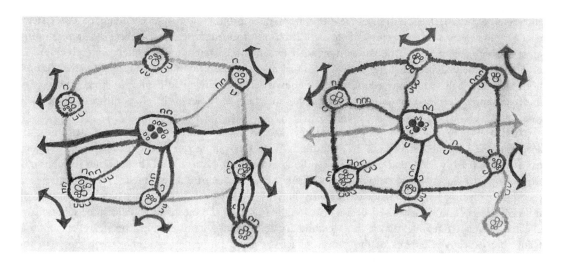

Figure 9.1.4 The Organic Office Structure Diagram: Marvin J. Malecha.

relationship as a form of children's game. If we diverge for a moment to consider this use of the term play, we are reminded of the free form of inquiry that constitutes a child's manipulation of rules to find the most advantageous position. In this free form of inquiry, it is the result that is sought after rather than some idealized version of process. The *New York Times* documented just this process in an article demonstrating the power of play:

> Other species play, but none play for as much of their lives as humans do, or as imaginatively, or with as much protection from the family circle. Human children are unique in using play to explore hypothetical situations rather than to rehearse actual challenges they'll face later. Kittens may pretend to be cats fighting, but they will not pretend to be children; children, by contrast, will readily pretend to be cats or kittens – and then to be Hannah Montana, followed by Spider-Man saving the day.
>
> And in doing so, they develop some of humanity's most consequential faculties. They learn the art, pleasure and power of hypothesis – of imagining new possibilities. And serious students of play believe that this helps make the species great.
>
> *(Dobbs, 2013)*

Just as Mozart wrote over the score of Handel, a child has no hesitation to change and evolve the interpretation of the rules of their peers, or particularly of adults, at a moment's notice. The dynamic is almost impossible to follow by adults as for the most part the adult has been fully vested in linear and additive processes. The child is in a continual process of learning that includes both succeeding and failing simultaneously. When Kahn and Salk came together to imagine the now iconic Salk Institute in La Jolla, California, they each brought an impressive body of knowledge to the discussion. Both knew their disciplines and were influenced by the expectations of these disciplines on the resultant structure. Both imagined a story to guide the evolution of ideas and both understood the interplay of stories and systems that must be brought together.

Within the concept of story are the metaphors and similes that guide the design process. Both architect and client/user have aspirations in their minds that establish the interpretations, explorations and demonstrations that constitute the beginnings of a project. The understanding of the systems necessary to realize a project represent the collection of information, the analysis and the application of ideas. In both instances it is iteration, moving between the greater ideas and literal interpretations of program needs, that propels a project. This intersection of the two is the area of play that inspired both Kahn and Salk. This intersection guides the experience of integrated design thinking. This way of understanding inter- and transdisciplinarity gives structure to a design-based performative approach (Malecha 2015).

Guided by the play of a project area, the necessary information and expertise that must be accommodated in the project can be identified. With this perspective the difficulty of the project, from easy to hard, wicked and unknown, can be assessed. And the nature of the working relationships, from master to atelier, social networks and organic structure, can be determined. Play in this sense is the highest form of human intellectual activity (Figure 9.1.5). It is in this structure that innovation will flourish because knowledge-based decision making is valued as the means to enhance the aspirations of a stated program outcome. From the blending of stories and systems through free play, success and failure are expected elements of the process. Each advances the experience of coming closer to the understanding necessary to build with a freshness of thought and the courage of action.

As the issues become more difficult, even wicked, the organic nature of the structure of the response must become more agile, more organic, and therefore more apt to provide the opportunity for the leadership of the architect from a well of informed ideas.

In the mid-1970s the architect Hugh Stubbins, structural engineer William LeMessurier and the president of Citicorp Walter B. Wriston came together to realize a new corporate headquarters (Langdon 2014). Mr. Stubbins and Mr. Wriston shared a vision of a tower with the most advanced materials and systems guided by a sophisticated notion of an urban architecture firmly rooted in Manhattan (Morgenstern 1995). Jonathan Barnett's (1974) book *Urban Design as Public Policy* informed this stage of the work. Following concepts proposed by William LeMessurier, to address special urban conditions, the tower is lifted on four massive piloti making room for retail space, a significant urban plaza and entry to the subway system and Saint Peter's Church. This strategy has activated the street in a fashion beyond the typical high-rise structure of its day. Even today after several clumsy remodelings and the divestiture of the building by Citicorp, there is an unmistakeable energy about the building. The sloped tower top anticipated an unfortunately never-realized solar panel system. The most innovative aspect of this structure also demonstrates the importance of the relationship between

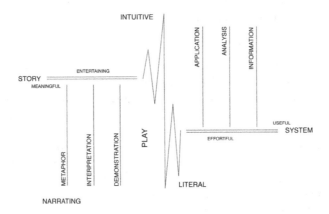

Figure 9.1.5 The Story, System, Play Diagram: Marvin J. Malecha.

owner, architect and engineer. Following William LeMessurier's studies of massive concrete dampers on tall radio towers in Australia, to mitigate the effects of wind on the structure, he proposed that such a system be installed at the top of the Citicorp tower. Mr. LeMessurier and Mr. Stubbins initiated studies that demonstrated the veracity of this idea even though it had yet to be implemented on any other high-rise building. Mr. Wriston agreed and the work to realize the first tuned mass damper proceeded. Early studies proposed a hydraulic system that was soon found to be insufficient. The massive concrete block that was to be placed at the top of the building could not be restrained by hydraulic technology. The continued search for a solution led the team to the gaseous retracting landing system employed on the Lunar Landing Module. Design development continued and an effective new strategy was added to the palette of tools available for high-rise construction (see Figures 9.1.6 and 9.1.7). It is a strategy that has subsequently been employed world-wide. The teams of individuals necessary to realize Citicorp Center underline the critical nature of inter- and transdisciplinary approaches to problems.

Yet there is one more important aspect to the process that must be taken into account. The intuitive aspects of the decision process that inspired the team to come to a tuned mass damper cannot be attributed to a linear interpretation of the design process. Certainly, there are aspects of the decision that could be identified as linear. Without an understanding of the profound effect of wind on the structure of a tall building there would have been no reason to pursue the tuned mass damper. It was the insight of LeMessurier that provoked Stubbins to reach beyond the expected. Similarly, if certain conditions of the property did not exist, the four massive columns would not have been considered (Hellman 1974). This raises an important question. Is it problem solution that inspired the design for Citicorp Center or was it problem seeking that inspired the team of individuals to consider the world differently? Like the Duomo of Florence, the design of the tuned mass damper and the four distinct columns was not obvious in the program brief of this building. Both projects call into question contemporary ideas about problem solution.

The problem solution approach seems to have become more embedded in contemporary thought. A frequently used expression, "Houston we have a problem," reinforces the idea of problem solution. The phrase has become popular to express the emergence of an unforeseen problem. It comes to us from the improbable journey of Apollo 13, the story of which was made popular by the docu-drama that characterized what happened in space more than 40 years ago. Yet this is not what the astronauts communicated, only the reinterpreted version for the film, and its difference from what was said is what truly represents the spirit we seek to uncover. What Apollo 13 astronaut Jack Swigert communicated was "Okay, Houston, we've had a problem," to report the explosion that crippled their spacecraft. The distance between *have* and *had* is revealing (Cortright 1975). In 1977 a partner in the architectural firm of Caudill Rowlett Scott, William Caudill, authored along with William Peña and John Focke a monograph titled *Problem Seeking*. The idea of problem seeking defines the distance between *have* and *had*. To express that a problem exists is to overly bias a thought process and discourage the curiosity necessary to address the challenge. To seek the problem is to leave open the options until the inquiry itself defines what is the issue to be addressed and articulates the desired outcome. For the astronauts trapped in that capsule, the iterative stages of the steps to be taken to get them home safely was a thoughtful and timely search. In the end, it was these steps that defined the experience; the explosion itself was only the instigating factor. To solve the problem of the explosion was to design the next capsule. That would have been of no help to the brave souls just trying to get home.

> Any notions Kahn and Salk may have had when work first started on the project did not take the form of strict formal or spatial requirements; 'We just began to play,' (Jonas) Salk recalls.
>
> *(Salk 2016)*

Figure 9.1.6 Citicorp, sketched by Marvin J. Malecha.

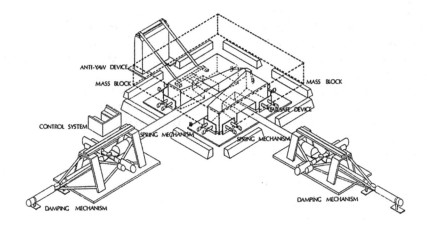

Figure 9.1.7 Tuned mass damper from Hugh Stubbins and Associates office, drawn by Marvin J. Malecha.

Perhaps what we are speaking of is the area of reflection that both Jonas Salk and Louis Kahn referred to as play. In this way, it is not problem solution that inspires us; rather, it is the spirit of play of children. To observe a child at play is to experience thought patterns associated with free mental exploration. The strict rules of games do not fit this model. Because of this, when the games are underway, children are freely reinterpreting the rules, asserting new rules and then changing those to suit the situation.

> Psychologist Peter Gray, a research professor at Boston College and author of *Free to Learn*, has spent his career researching the benefits of play ... According to Gray, true play is imaginative, self-directed, done for its own sake and guided by mental rules rather than formal ones. In other words, activities that often pass as play such as organized sports, do not offer the same psychological benefits as, say, teetering atop a ladder.
>
> *(Braithwaite 2018)*

The incredible ability to change the rules in the midst of action is the essence of an inter- and transdisciplinary approach, from the design of Brunelleschi's dome and Citicorp Center in New York to the billion- and multi-billion-dollar projects that are becoming more common today, requiring the interaction of diverse teams of teams of individuals. These individuals represent disciplines as diverse as structural engineering and the special expertise of the envelope enclosures that define building strategies of interaction. These interactive relationships have become as essential as every other aspect of construction logistics. Performative design methodology is the binding matrix of these interactions. It can be observed that even in the smallest of projects it is often necessary to involve individuals with special expertise. It is therefore crucial that, as evidence-based decision making further permeates the expectations of professional performance, the consideration of performance metrics must be developed for each project. This increasing demand for clearly stated performance measures comes at a time when notions of professional expertise are being called into question.

> A political scientist who has taught for more than a decade in Harvard Extension School, he (Tom Nichols) had begun noticing what he perceived as new and accelerating – and dangerous – hostility toward established knowledge. People were no longer merely uninformed, Nichols says, but 'aggressively wrong' and unwilling to learn.
>
> *(Gibson 2018)*

While Gibson's article from *Harvard Magazine* is on the scholarship of Tom Nichols and its reflection in the American social and political culture, it is a revealing observation that informs the context of a performative design methodology. Within a project each discipline is dependent on the abilities of the others. The basis of this is a clear set of performance measures with reasonable expectations and deliverables attached. There must be a climate of mutual respect among these professionals. To the external audience this critical interdependence of disciplines is rarely understood. It is therefore becoming clear that the incredible interwoven relationships of a complex building process must be externalized in every aspect of project development, from the contracts that define the work to be done to the public presentations of the project. A performative design methodology is in fact a framework for communication and expectations that is as important as the initial brief for the building. It is the structure by which the many inter- and transdisciplinary relationships are given order. It is the order that allows for the necessary freedom defined by the child's mental framework for play.

It is more appropriate therefore to speak of the culture of practice rather than a specific approach to problem solution. Within the culture of practice are those ways of doing that constitute the reasonable expectations of the work of an architect or designer. To raise the issue of a performative design process is therefore to raise up the query of how expectations are to be defined. Performative aspects of design simply require clarity to nurture substantive assessment. This exercise then leads to what outcomes can be realized from the identification of performance expectations. This requires an expanded notion of the design process. Within popular architecture culture the expression "the genius is in the program brief" is attributed to the architect Le Corbusier (Hodge 1998). There is much wisdom in this observation. The design process cannot begin to meet any expectation of the client without a clear understanding for whom the project is being undertaken, the context of time and social expectations, the immediate environment of the project and the resources necessary to realize the project. But the brief is not the source of this wisdom. It is the structure of research into the subject that causes the brief to be special. What is obvious is the necessary phase of pre-programming. In 1976 Patrick Sullivan and Jay Farbstein received a *Progressive Architecture Magazine* award for their study, *Pre-Architectural Programming for a Juvenile Services Center*. This project demonstrates the rigor of the pre-programming effort that underlies the first aspect of raising the bar of professional expectations leading to a measurable outcome. When the Oslo and New York-based firm of Snøhetta were selected to be the architects for the James B. Hunt Library at North Carolina State University their first move was to challenge the campus-generated program used to justify the state funding for the project. Craig Dykers, along with Elaine Molinare, with the blessing of Susan Nutter the Vice Provost and Director of Libraries, took a step back into the pre-programming phase and conceived of a book robot that would free up space by the elimination of traditional book stacks, to be used as a grand reading room, joint study rooms, a special faculty area and a variety of multimedia rooms. The library was transformed into a working community center for study and research. Because of the willingness to question what appeared to be a fixed program and enter the period of needs assessment with an open mind, a new university library building type was born (Figures 9.1.8–9.1.10).

The second aspect of defining a performative design strategy is to look at how outcomes are judged. These measures should be well understood because they have been identified in the earliest phases of a project. This process has come to be known as post-occupancy or post-completion assessment. It is in this phase of the project that a true sense of performance can be judged, not only from the specific performance of the building or object itself, but also from the acceptance of it by a client and user point of view. Whereas needs assessment in the pre-programming phase is very much a statement controlled by architects, designers and clients in close collaboration with each other, the post-completion/post-occupancy assessment is conducted and controlled by users. A product or building meets its performative expectations based on this assessment. It is this dichotomy that explains

Integrated Design Thinking

Figures 9.1.8 and 9.1.9 Hunt Library photographs from the Wolfpix web site.
Source: Permission granted by NC State University, Raleigh, North Carolina, under the direction of Roger Winstead

the same building being given awards by professional peers while users would just as soon see the project scrapped or the building either significantly modified or demolished. The performative model introduces expectations that bring pressure on a project from many perspectives (Ivany 2018). Perhaps the best model of this is the After-Action Review Process adopted by the military (Chamberlain

Figures 9.1.8 and 9.1.9 (Cont.)

1975). This process was introduced by members of the West Point faculty to the Large-Firm Roundtable of the American Institute of Architects at a leadership development retreat held on the grounds of West Point. The instructors noted that the first such activity took place following the Battle of Gettysburg. During the battle, there was a real possibility, opposed by the officers, that the Union troops under the command of General George Meade would be withdrawn from the advantage of the hills toward Washington, DC. This would have yielded the field to the forces under the command of General Robert E. Lee (Guelzo 2013). Such a move would have resulted in a critical Confederate victory and the trajectory of the war would have changed. The result of this led to a process that assesses performance and related expectations. It was here that the after-action report was born. This process seeks to understand the outcomes of a project or activity by what was supposed to happen, what did happen and what were the circumstances leading to differences between the two. It is an opportunity to ascertain the cause of the differences as well as unexpected benefits of judgements made under fire. In some ways, the most important aspect of an after-action report is to discern what could or would be done differently the next time an opportunity arose. While the after-action report begins in a retrospective fashion it concludes with clear action items. What is important about the after-action experience is that the insights and opinions of the entire team, irrespective of rank, are accepted to prevent the blindness that accompanies the hierarchy of a team dynamic. This is intended to prevent the leadership bubble that often leads to the repetition of mistakes.

The third aspect of practice that is transformed by a performative design strategy is the need for intense user meetings during the design process that will give focus to the introduction of evidence

Integrated Design Thinking

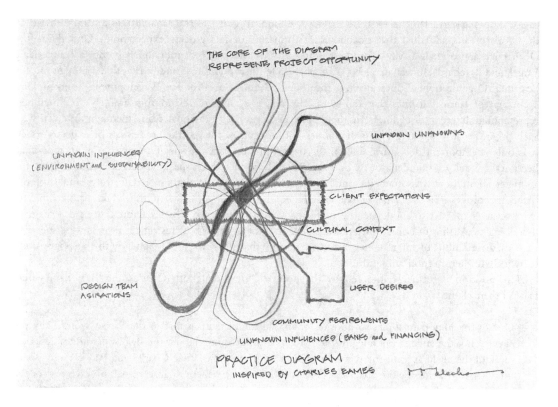

Figure 9.1.10 Office Practice Diagram Sketch by Marvin J. Malecha, inspired by the Office Practice Diagram of Charles Eames.

and the corresponding response to it. For example, when the goal for a building is any kind of recognition for energy performance, then the resulting identified strategies to address such a goal must be founded in an evidence-based culture. Architects already know clients who are disappointed by shortfalls in life cycle costs of energy who are seeking remuneration by whatever means necessary. Performance promised will be performance which is held to accountability (Halprin 1970). The related methods of interacting with the users and client for a building, known as take-part design, evolved from the work of individuals in the 1960s and 1970s, such as the American landscape architect Lawrence Halprin and architects Charles Moore and Henry Sanoff (Lord, Hahn Oberlander, Hirsch, Friedberg, Dragons 2016). Professor Sanoff is considered the seminal figure in this movement. His work with communities, including the publication of his books *Design Games*, *Methods of Architectural Programming*, *Visual Research Methods in Design* and *Community Participation Methods in Design and Planning*, has defined the way forward for the inclusion of otherwise disenfranchised populations from the design process (Sanoff 1977). The take-part workshop was a vehicle both for the reconsideration of planning decisions and a way forward to conduct a project. It provided an avenue of discourse between designers and user groups that was often obstructed by various practices and procedures from community design standards to the financial expectations of investors. Perhaps even more importantly, the take-part workshop often asked all participants to assume the roles of others in the project process. It is this technique that has been adapted by the Palo Alto-based design firm IDEO as a Deep Dive. This process, focused on in the *Nightline* series with Ted Koppel (1999) of ABC News, demonstrates the process of visualizing a new a product from the perspective of replacing an older variation, in this case a shopping cart. It is this exercise that also reminds us that it is the capability of a team rather than the work of an individual that establishes performative design process expectations. Underlying the Deep Dive approach is a way of understanding the necessary role of individuals within a team. Craig Vogel and Richard Buchanan (1994), in an article first published under the title "Design in the Learning Organization: Educating for the New Culture of Product Development," set forward a concept of team dynamics that represents the necessary mature relationship among team members representing different disciplines. In their behavioral model, individual team members interact with each other, broadly working across disciplines without regard for specific credentials or expected roles. It is only at important decision points in the design process that the specific expertise of an individual becomes central to the decision. For example, the banker may speak about architecture and the architect about financing strategies until a decision is necessary and then specific roles and expertise shape the process. In the Deep Dive experience this is the point when the adults, subject matter experts, are expected to moderate the performance of individuals. Charles Eames adopted a diagram describing the realms of community that affected the design process of his office. From his perspective, each of these realms of interest intersected in an area that provides the designer with the opportunity to work with "conviction and enthusiasm."

This position is further reinforced by the point of view that both Charles and Ray Eames held toward their clients.

> One of the important things to note in looking at the diagram is that in the Eames world view the client is not the enemy, but a legitimate participant in defining the playing field. Oftentimes designers speak of the client as someone whom work is done in spite of. While Charles and Ray certainly spent time helping clients see the area of overlap, they always saw them as an essential, positive part of the equation. Recall Charles' letter to Ray in 1941 about possible films: 'if it is given the right slant it would have punch for the producer, public and us.' All three were important from the beginning of their partnership. In a related vein, Charles once said that the most important thing that an architect can do is teach a client how to spend their own money. Perhaps that is why 'he got an enormous amount of respect for his clients,' as Jeannine Oppewal said.
>
> *(Demetrios 2001)*

Needs assessment pre-programming and post-occupancy/completion expand the role of the architect and designer beyond the scripted roles often found in the typical contract for services. The Deep Dive reminds us that performance and team chemistry are interrelated ideas. The Charles Eames perspective is that each of these processes are required to find an expression that stimulates the community. It is interesting to note that Eames, in a sidebar sketch, implies that the number of constituents and communities in the diagram can be modified as relationships are formed throughout the process. In this fashion complexity is embraced as one aspect of the design search. The related aspects of performance demand a rubric for design that guides the architect and designer to conduct themselves in a manner that allows the design team to pursue opportunities and seek problems. A rubric provides structure in a fashion that is the foundation for the commissioning of new products and building projects. Clearly, the introduction of performative design methodologies into the design process poses a significant shift in the culture of practice. It is the foundation of evidence-based design that will raise the bar for the profession. It is therefore reasonable to conclude that performative design methodologies begin with a culture of inquiry and are concluded by the assessment of a tangible outcome.

The title of this chapter implies that integrated design thinking is comprised of inter- and transdisciplinary strategies. Utilizing these strategies participants are brought together in a disciplined structure of a performative design strategy. These strategies provide an intellectual format within which complex project teams find harmony in their interactions. It is a fact that no project of substantial size can be realized without encountering the need for complex teams of individuals. Project teams today are brought together based entirely on the needs of the project. It is not unusual for the teams to be assembled from across the globe depending on the building type and the organization of the client. These teams come together, accomplish their tasks and again disperse. They may or may not work together again. In some cases, these subject experts have become close to the organizing design team and they have worked together many times, and in others it is a first-time relationship. The distinct disciplinarity of the subject experts is often blurred by those who hold multiple credentials. It is further blurred by the reality that the subject experts are representatives of teams themselves, making the process even more complex by the nature of teams of teams of individuals. In the example of Citicorp Center, mentioned earlier in this chapter, Hugh Stubbins and William LeMessurier were long-time colleagues and friends who had worked together many times. The trust relationship served them very well as problems arose later in the project. In the case of the Apollo 13 incident, most of the component manufacturers had little to do with each other and perhaps had not even been in the same room during the duration of the project.

As is demonstrated in Figure 9.1.4 noted earlier in this chapter, the scaling of problems may be represented as strategies for interaction that range from intradisciplinary to crossdisciplinary, multidisciplinary, interdisciplinary and transdisciplinary. Marilyn Stember (1991), in a paper entitled *Advancing the Social Sciences through the Interdisciplinary Enterprise,* offers a perspective of the intellectual posture required in integrated design thinking. Each of these descriptors of disciplinarity map very well against the demands of creative design practice. Problems defined as easy, hard, wicked and unknown correspond to strategies to meet the demands of such problems, including the work of a master, an atelier, a network of individuals and teams to an organic structure of interrelationships among consulting offices. It is best to understand this manner of addressing problems as a living structure of people and ideas for which there are strong correspondences to the various strategies of disciplinarity. Intradisciplinary, working within a discipline, maps to the work of a master. Crossdisciplinary, working beyond a discipline with the perspective of other disciplines, maps to the work of an atelier of creative individuals working under the direction of a master. Multidisciplinary, representing individuals from different disciplines working together but drawing from the knowledge of their own discipline, maps to the network of individuals required to work on wicked problems. Interdisciplinary, representing the efforts to integrate knowledge and methods of different disciplines, maps to the organic processes necessary address the unknown underlying problems that can only be addressed in the revealing layers of a problem-seeking process. Transdisciplinary, representing a framework of an intellectual approach that transcends disciplinarity, maps against the tenants of design thought as a way of seeing. It is the fundamental underpinning of a creative working strategy best characterized as integrated design thinking.

The reasonable conclusion to the exploration of this chapter is the observation that a great deal more attention must be given to the strategies and tactics of practice. Too often practice is conducted in a response-to-pressure mode that discourages the reflection that may prevent the essence of the project from being revealed. Project organization is more often determined by the pressures within the office than a close reading of the project and related challenges at hand. The child's story of Winnie the Pooh reveals to us the natural tendencies that counter reflection upon a project's essential qualities.

> Here is Edward Bear, coming downstairs now, bump, bump, bump, on the back of his head, behind Christopher Robin. It is as far as he knows, the only way of coming downstairs, but sometimes he feels that there really is another way, if he could only stop bumping for a moment and think of it. And then he feels that perhaps there isn't. Anyhow here he is at the bottom, and ready to be introduced to you.
>
> *(Milne 1926)*

A transdisciplinary approach is independent of the scale of a project. It is a thought strategy. The exigencies of practice often conspire to prevent the "reflection in action" approach articulated by Donald Schön (1983) in his text *The Reflective Practitioner*. In his writing, he has articulated a position between the rigors of controlled experiment and academic scholarship. He seeks to connect personal and institutional contexts. This is by its nature a transdisciplinary approach. It is an approach that seeks answers across all forms of disciplinarity. While providing a gregarious approach to problem seeking, the underlying notion of reflective practice is that it is a balance of community interests, disciplinary specialties, codes and covenants, budget and timelines and the personal aspirations of clients and users. It can be concluded then that integrative design thinking is entirely dependent on a transcendent design strategy known as transdisciplinarity.

In the end, what cannot be overlooked is the proclivity of the human spirit to reflect itself in every project undertaking. It must be understood that this proclivity frequently transcends any form of disciplinarity. In such situations, the attitude toward the social networks of work direct the individual to adopt to the appropriate level of collaboration as a high-level tactic to achieve the project. It must be considered that the very best of architecture is a form of design thought modeling that reconciles personal expression and metaphor with the utility of the situation at hand. Between these two, as has been mentioned earlier, is the play of the design inquiry endeavor. It is not linear; rather, it is a process of seeking and self-discovery.

Sometimes it is the simplest of experiences that gives us pause to reflect upon the most complex of endeavors. Renzo Piano, one of the world's most acclaimed architects, expresses the thought that the making of sandcastles is an exercise of the young and the old. One approaches the experience with exuberance and the other is reflective and even remorseful. On the one hand is the natural tendency to make, while the other considers the ramifications of the frail, even restricted, construction at the mercy of powerful environmental forces. The brevity of its existence is a reminder to the elder that all we do as humans is frail and brief against the measure of cosmic time. It is as though a thousand years of erosion is represented by a single high tide. In this short exposition, Mr. Piano reveals his inner nature.

> My career started when I was a child and I built my first sandcastle on the beach in Genoa, where I grew up. Making things has always been a pleasure for me – happy hands, happy mind – and making sandcastles was my training in fantasy. Now, as an architect constructing buildings like the Shard, I have to think about the final result, but as a child making castles of sand I didn't, they were ephemeral.
>
> *(Piano 2015)*

> This is something you do up to when you are a 12-year-old. Then you start again when you are 60. It's true, I did my last one probably one week ago, in Sardinia somewhere, in a little beach – beautiful. And it's something totally useless, of course. You have to understand that; otherwise, it's really frustrating. It's quite nice because it's about capturing a moment when the water comes. And, of course, it's also about the old story of the relationship between manmade and nature. I love nature immensely, but at the end of the day, the architect's job is to compete with nature. It's actually to make buildings. And if you are not clever, things don't stay up …
>
> For an architect to make something so simple, so easy, so playful, like a sandcastle, it's still about learning. It's about physical law, it's about intuition, it's about forces of nature – it's about understanding, at the end of the day. …
>
> But making something so useless like a sandcastle teaches you a lot about the responsibility of making something that must remain for centuries. I don't want to become too romantic, but in some ways, that's the whole point. You know, making something that will last half an hour is a kind of interesting opposite. It's a pleasure. It's taking up time, enjoying life.
>
> *(NPR Staff 2015)*

Renzo Piano in his delightful explanation of the building of a sandcastle reveals the thrill of following his playful spirit under the restrictions and guidance of whim and the rigors of the environmental realities demanding a straightforward response. He articulates the need to understand the situation as well its limitations. In the end, he reveals to us his approach to flirt with the waves just as he follows this path in the design of his buildings. His approach to sandcastles is his way of seeing the problems he seeks out in his architecture. It is romantic and flirtatious just as it is rigorous. It is his personality more than a fixed approach. He reaches out when and where he must. Ultimately, even in the design of sandcastles, the term "transdisciplinarity" is appropriate because it is a way of seeing that provides the path for creativity.

References

Barnett, J. (1974). *Urban design as public policy: Practical methods for improving cities*. New York: Architectural Record Books.
Braithwaite, H. (2018, October). State of Play. *American Way Magazine*, 68.
Chamberlain, J. (1975). *After action report on the actions of the 20th Maine at Gettysburg*. Barnsley: Praetorian Press.
Cortright, E. M. (1975). Apollo Expeditions to the Moon. In Lovell, J. A. *Houston, we've had a problem*. Washington, DC: National Aeronautics and Space Administration.
Demetrios, E. (2001). *An Eames primer*. New York: Rizzoli/Universe.
Dobbs, D. (2013, April 22). Playing for All Kinds of Possibilities. *New York Times*.
Gibson, L. (2018, March–April). The Miracle of Knowledge. *Harvard Magazine*, 32–35.
Guelzo, A. (2013). George Meade's Mixed Legacy: The General Won at Gettysburg in Spite of Himself. *Civil War Times Magazine*, 52(3), 38–45.
Halprin, L. (1970). *RSVP cycles: Creative processes in human environment*. New York: George Braziller.
Hellman, P. (1974, February 25). How They Assembled the Most Expensive Block in New York's History, *New York Magazine*, 31–37.
Hodge, B. (Ed.) (1998). *Jerzy Soltan, architecture 1967–1974*. Cambridge, MA: Cambridge Harvard University Graduate School of Design.
Ivany, R. (2018, September 28). The US Army's Secret to Building a Leader-Driven, Learning Culture: After Action Reviews. *Chief Executive*, n.p.
King, R. (2000). *Brunelleschi's dome: How a renaissance genius reinvented architecture*. New York: Bloomsbury.
Koppel, T. (1999). Deep dive: IDEO. ABC News *Nightline*.
Langdon, D. (2014, November 5). Citigroup Center/Hugh Stubbins + William LeMessurier. *AD Classics*, n.p.
Lord, C., Hahn Oberlander, C., Hirsch, A., Friedberg, E. J., & Lucky Dragons. (2016). *Experiments in environment: The Halprin workshops 1966–1971*. Chicago: Graham Foundation.
Malecha, M. (2002). *Reconfiguration in the study of practice and design*. San Francisco: William Stout Publishers.
Malecha, M. (2005). *The learning organization and the evolution of practice academy concepts*. Raleigh: North Carolina State College of Design Publication with the American Institute of Architects.
Malecha, M. (2015). *Being creative: Being a creative*. Dubuque: Kendall Hunt.
Milne, A. A. (1926). *Winnie the Pooh*. London: Methuen & Co.
Morgenstern, J. (1995, May 29). The Fifty-Nine Story Crisis. *New Yorker*, 45–53.
NPR Staff. (2015, August 1). Blueprints before high tide: An architect explains the perfect sandcastle. National Public Radio interview.
Peña, W., Cuadill, W., & Focke, J. (1977). *Problem seeking: An architectural programming primer*. London: John Wiley & Sons.
Piano, R. (2015, July 14). The Do Something Expert. *The Guardian*.
Salk, J. (2016, September 23). Reflections on the Relationship between Lou Kahn and Jonas Salk. Design Futures Council Technology and Innovation Summit.
Sanoff, H. (1977). *Methods of architectural programming*. Abingdon: Routledge.
Schön, D. (1983). *The reflective practitioner: How professionals think in action*. New York: Basic Books.
Stember, M. (1991). Advancing the Social Sciences through the Interdisciplinary Enterprise. *Social Science Journal*, 28(1), 1–14.
Sullivan, P., & Farbstein, J. D. (1977). *A Juvenile Services Center Program, San Louis County, California*. San Luis Obispo, CA: Sullivan–Farbstein Associates.
Towe, T. N. (1996). *George Friedrich Handel: Messiah – arranged by Mozart*. Retrieved from www.classical.net.
Vogel, C., & Buchanan, R. (1994). Design in the Learning Organization: Educating for the New Culture of Product Development. Design Management Institute.

9.2

Integrated Design Thinking: Inter- and Transdisciplinarity in Performative Design Methodology
Research Case Studies

Joon-Ho Choi

Numerous efforts have been made in the architectural design domain to develop a creative work based on a concept and inspiration initiated by professional architects and researchers. Once a detailed design is specified, it becomes feasible by implementing the "ideas" presented by using multiple engineering, technological, and scientific principles. As our society becomes inundated by more advanced technologies, it becomes easier to implement more complicated design ideas in various building typologies. Such a project sequence motivates current technology to develop further and to become more advanced through the integration of diverse multidisciplinary knowledge and expert "know-how" in various domains.

As a result, designs and technologies need to be integrated to enhance the health and environmental satisfaction of the occupants of a building, as well as to ensure eco-friendly environmental performance of design outcomes. Therefore, it is essential to develop interdisciplinary research and practice, as a function of design, and to rely on expert knowledge in multidisciplinary domains. This chapter discusses a project case that was established based on collaborative efforts of professionals in engineering, medicine, and psychology, in addition to those in architecture.

Issue of Current Indoor Environmental Quality and Building Energy Performance

Buildings account for 37% of the total energy use in the U.S., while thermal and lighting systems expend more than 70% of the energy consumed in modern buildings (CBECS, 2014). Government agencies and industry stakeholders are encouraging policies geared toward promoting energy-efficient buildings and environmental sustainability. However, despite these efforts, we are often faced with the twin challenges in most buildings of energy waste and the occupants' environmental dissatisfaction. The indoor environment, in most modern building systems, is controlled in accordance with existing industry standards and guidelines (e.g., ASHRAE and IESNA (CIBSE (Chartered Institution of Building Services Engineers), 2002; IESNA, 2010; "ISO 7730: 2005 – Ergonomics of the thermal environment – Analytical determination and interpretation of thermal comfort using calculation of the PMV and PPD indices and local thermal comfort criteria," 2005)) that primarily rely on predefined formulas or empirically defined recommendations. Consideration is not given to individual physiological characteristics, such as gender, age, body mass index (BMI), etc. (Choi, Beltran, & Kim, 2012; Choi & Loftness, 2012; Choi, Loftness, & Aziz, 2012; Choi, Loftness, & Lee, 2012; Doeland et al., 1989; Indraganti & Rao, 2010; Karjalainen, 2007). Predefined environmental comfort models or guidelines ignore the occupants' diverse physical conditions, such as their varying comfort ranges. Therefore, there are critical limitations in satisfying individual thermal comfort conditions, despite high energy use in most buildings.

For this reason, the rate of thermal dissatisfaction, expressed by building occupants in the U.S., is higher than 60%. The top-ranked complaints were "too cold" during the summer, and "too warm" during the winter, even though temperatures were within the comfort range defined by industry standards (ASHRAE Standard 55-2010 – Thermal Environmental Conditions for Human Occupancy (ANSI approved), 2013; Loftness, Aziz, & Choi, 2009; Zhou & Haghighat, 2009). Considering the energy efficiency impact of an indoor set-point temperature at 1.5% of the total energy consumption for HVAC (heating, ventilation and air conditioning), per 1 degree of Fahrenheit change (Birdsall, Buhl, Ellington, Erdem, & Winkelmann, 1990; Rosenfeld et al., 1995), this energy conservation opportunity will significantly enhance each occupant's thermal satisfaction.

For lighting, a significant indoor environmental quality (IEQ) component of the thermal condition, general practice has adopted three lighting levels based on a user's age group (IESNA, 2010). For example, 300, 400, and 500 lux in offices are strictly suggested, depending on the age group defined by IESNA (2010). Moreover, eye color and task-type influence an individual's preferred lighting conditions (Frontczak & Wargocki, 2011; Meng, Butterworth, Calvas, & Malecaze, 2012; Ojaimi et al., 2009). Recent studies have revealed that 65% of building occupants reported that lighting conditions in their workplaces were inappropriate and that they experience considerable glare problems, mainly due to excessively bright conditions causing visual stress and increased energy usage (Wilkins, 2003). Since lighting design guidelines were established (mainly based on a conventional paper-based task-dominant environment), excessive lighting is no longer necessary because it creates unnecessary glare in today's technology-intensive work environment (i.e., computer-based tasks dominate). This phenomenon has hindered the provision of ideal lighting intensity and distribution (as intended in design and control), and has resulted in inefficient energy use, in addition to visual stress problems.

Considering the wide diversity in individual environmental preferences, it is challenging to generate a single standard rule for achieving occupant thermal/visual satisfaction. Therefore, understanding individual environmental sensations is critical to generating an optimal building condition with high energy efficiency. This is especially necessary where building occupants' activities and environmental preferences are dynamically changing due to physical, psychological, and climatic conditions.

Human-Building Integration as an Architectural Project Principle

Environmental design stakeholders, such as architects and building managers, are often faced with the challenge of adjusting optimal environmental conditions to satisfy the occupants of a building. In addition, depending on the type of building spaces, its occupants, and related building performance design guidelines and regulations, the stakeholders need to consider a variety of optimization factors and city- or nation-wide regulations. Minimizing energy use to improve building performance, while maximizing occupants' environmental comfort conditions, should be a significant factor. In the domain of building environmental designs, most existing technology and designs focus on system- and material-centered engineering solutions. This makes the users passive, in the environmental control loop, rather than allowing them to practice control mechanisms as a proactive parameter. From such passiveness, inefficient environmental performance could result, while the environmental comfort and satisfaction of the occupants of a building are compromised. A recent architecture-relevant research study focused

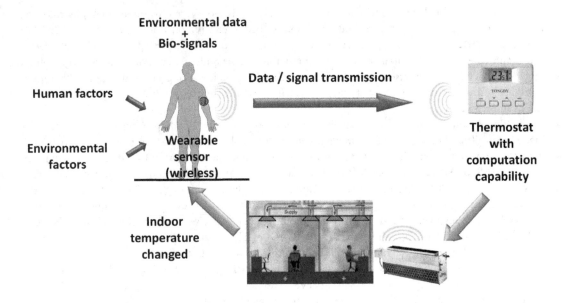

Figure 9.2.1 Conceptual diagram and (processed) data flow.

on developing an integrated human-centered framework design for intelligent environmental control in buildings to enhance the occupants' health, well-being, and environmental sustainability (illustrated in Figure 9.2.1). The project objectives were to advance the understanding of the principle of how human physiological interactions are affected by a building's indoor environmental condition and design, and to develop reliable control mechanisms to build environmental systems based on the principle of using the human body as an integrated building performance component.

Potential Use of Human Physiological Data in the Environmental Control Domain

Due to advances in today's sensing and mobile technologies, more and more data can be easily and effectively collected by various means (e.g., wearable devices and mobile sensing motes). Thus, it is now feasible to collect and process a large amount of real data about the building environment of a building's occupants. A human body naturally reacts to ambient environmental conditions to minimize any thermal and visual stress based on the human body's autonomic nervous system (Licinio & Wong, 1999; Streeten, 2014). Recent research has demonstrated the possibility of using human physiological signals to indicate a subject's building thermal and visual sensation levels (Choi & Loftness, 2012; Choi et al., 2012; Choi, Zhu, & Johnson, 2013). The human body generates multiple physiological signals, such as skin temperature, heart rate (i.e., electrocardiography), skin moisture, pupil sizes, etc., and multiple data parameters can be collected and generated from each signal, such as heart rate variability, gradients of skin temperature, and pupil size change rate per different time scales, using advanced data collection and processing tools. Even though a human body's core temperature should be maintained around 98 degrees F for physical survival (Sessler, 1997), skin temperatures mostly fluctuate to preserve a heat balance between the body and its ambient thermal condition, defined as thermal comfort (i.e., neutral sensation) (ASHRAE Standard 55-2010 – Thermal Environmental Conditions for Human Occupancy (ANSI approved),

2013). For lighting conditions, pupil sizes constrict or dilate in response to different lighting as stimuli based on the use of human's parasympathetic nervous system (Bradley, Miccoli, Escrig, & Lang, 2008). Even though there are significant diversities in the shapes and sizes of human pupils (Hopkinson, 1956), the size change mechanisms are similar and remain consistent among people via their autonomic nervous system (Bradley et al., 2008; Streeten, 2014). Therefore, human physiological signals have a high potential for illustrating a user's environmental sensation and comfort, which are key components for determining an operation mode for building systems. Considering the currently available wearable sensing technologies and devices, a human physiological signal-driven environmental control can be integrated into multiple building performance-relevant systems and design principles.

Establishing a Multidisciplinary Research Team

To investigate the feasibility of such an environmental control for a building, multidisciplinary expertise is essential. First, such a study needs computer science and electrical engineering in the areas of bio-sensing, signal processing, integration, machine learning, and data awareness for decision making to establish a framework to collect physiological signals from the human body. Second, the study needs expertise in building science and architecture throughout studies of building performance and human behaviors of occupants to leverage information about environmental satisfaction and variables. The research needs the expertise of professionals in medicine and environmental psychology to help eliminate environmental factors that may affect human physiological reactions in ambient environmental conditions. As a cross-cutting research topic that spans science, engineering, and architecture, the research could explore the adaptability of human physiological signals as input for the environmental control loop in a high-performance building.

As a consequence of the project, the research outcome would provide the fundamental knowledge required to advance cyber innovation integration with environmental controls by adopting human physiological principles. This cross-cutting research can update and re-configure building environmental controls in real time, depending on individual environmental preferences in conjunction with the ambient environmental conditions in a building. Based on this project, two research outcomes were generated as follows:

1. Case #1: Thermal sensation prediction model, as a function of local body skin temperatures in a built environment

This project dealt with the potential use of skin temperature and its technical parameters to establish thermal sensation in a built environment. Based on a modern advanced wearable sensing device, the outcome of this project showed how to combine the skin temperature information, acquired from specific body segments, with environmental control systems (such as thermal comfort control based on use of a passive or active system in a building).

This research adopted skin temperature measurements at nine body segments, including the forehead, neck (back neck), back (upper back), chest, waist, belly, arm, wrist (front), and wrist (back), as illustrated in Figure 9.2.2. These skin areas have been validated as significant body segments that have been frequently adopted in thermoregulation models in the Medical domain (Doeland et al., 1989; van Marken Lichtenbelt et al., 2004). All collected data were analyzed by various statistical methods to investigate and verify the relationship between skin temperatures and whole/local body thermal sensations. In addition, a decision tree analysis model, a type of artificial intelligence algorithm, was adopted to understand the relationship between the user's thermal sensation and his/her skin temperature levels and their variations (Figure 9.2.3).

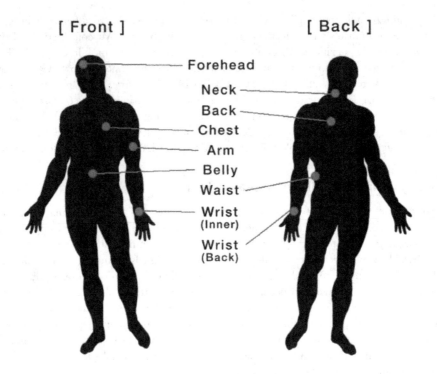

Figure 9.2.2 Human body segments adopted to collect skin temperatures.

With the help of psychology-domain knowledge, a thermal sensation survey, based on a seven-point scale, has been established while considering the gender and BMI as a baseline. These have a significant impact on overall thermal sensation and comfort, and local body skin temperatures. In addition, all of the skin temperature data collected from nine body segments were handled, using signal processing, which is a technical method in the electrical engineering area. Also, using computer science knowledge, the processed data were utilized to establish a thermal sensation model as a function of skin temperatures. As summarized in Table 9.2.1, the established data-driven models generated different levels of accuracy for sensation predictions, depending on the combination of attributes. Based on results, the skin temperature combination of waist, arm, and wrist (front) revealed the highest accuracy, as compared to other combinations of attribute data (Choi & Yeom, 2017b).

2. **Case #2: Potential Use of Human Eye Pupil Size for Office Lighting Controls Using Artificial Intelligence**

Lighting quality is one of the significant IEQ factors that affect human environmental health and work productivity, as well as environmental sustainability. However, the current lighting design guideline suggests 500 lux as a minimum level in an office workplace, even though individual workers' preferred light levels varied, depending on their physiological or personal conditions (Choi, 2017a, 2017b; Choi & Zhu, 2015). In modern building environments, considerable effort has been expended in providing better lighting quality and satisfaction, especially in workplaces where the occupants' productivity and visual health were critical for organizational success. However, 65% of building occupants complained their satisfaction with the ambient lighting conditions was due to how appropriate it was, such as excessive glare and too bright/dark (Irlen, 2005). In

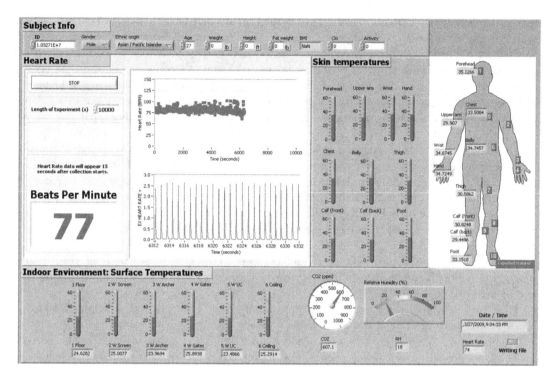

Figure 9.2.3 Data acquisition interface adopted in the project.

Table 9.2.1 Combinations of Significant Attributes and Cross-Validation Results of Thermal Sensation Estimation Accuracy Based on the Use of Decision Tree (J48)

#	Baseline	Combination of Attributes			Accuracy
1		(human factors only)			35.99%
2		Waist			76.03%
3		Arm			70.19%
4		Wrist (front)			68.45%
5		Forehead			68.04%
6		Wrist (back)			65.36%
7		Neck			64.01%
8	Gender&BMI	Wrist (front)	Wrist (back)		87.17%
9		Waist	Arm		93.02%
10		Waist	Wrist (front)		92.51%
11		Waist	Wrist (back)		92.41%
12		Waist	Arm	Wrist (front)	95.87%
13		Waist, Arm, Wrist (front), Forehead, Wrist (back), Neck			95.27%

spite of the significance of visual comfort and sensation, most office buildings have adopted empirically suggested guidelines, such as those of CIBSE and the Illuminating Engineering Society of North America (IES) (Choi & Zhu, 2015). As a result, the comfort of individuals may be easily compromised and result in adverse work productivity and environmental health. A popular technical tool in lighting design is the use of a high-dynamic-range image. It can achieve a higher dynamic range of luminosity and present a more accurate representation than the commonly-used digital images taken by a fish-eye camera can. However, such digital images require a lot of time and effort to capture and they are not practical because of the time-varying lighting caused by dynamic sky and daylight conditions.

Therefore, this project investigated how to integrate the human body as an autonomic function that regulated its physical responses to minimize any relevant environmental stress (Choi & Zhu, 2015). Thus, eye pupil sizes were selected for the study to understand physiological responses to ambient visual stress and unsatisfactory conditions. Since eye pupil sizes can shrink or dilate in response to variations in light, much existing research in ophthalmology tried to determine the relationship between pupil sizes and ambient lighting conditions (Alfonso, Fernández-Vega, Baamonde, & Montés-Micó, 2007; Atchison, Smith, & Efron, 1979; Roy et al., 2014; Watson & Yellott, 2012; Winn, Whitaker, Elliott, & Phillips, 1994). However, most studies of visual acuity, injury, and lighting contrast and sensitivity focused on eye symptoms/diseases, based on pupil sizes and movement.

Therefore, this project concentrated on investigating how to implement a lighting control as a function of human eye pupil size as a feasible physiological signal for estimating visual sensation in a quantitative way. With the help of multidisciplinary knowledge, that included ophthalmology, medicine, architecture, and building science, this project was conducted using multiple technical and design parameters.

This study was conducted in an environmental chamber equipped with an adjustable lighting control system, as shown in Figures 9.2.4–9.2.6.

Application of the Project Outcomes in the Architecture Field

These two project findings above have a potential to be integrated with a conventional environmental control system (shown in Figure 9.2.7) for single- and multi-occupancy conditions (Choi, 2017a, 2017b; Choi & Yeom, 2017a, 2017b). The project outcome can be plugged into an existing individual control system for heating and cooling, and lighting systems, such as a fundamental building mechanical and lighting system in a closed office or single-occupancy condition. Based on a real-time reading of skin temperature and pupil-size data, with the help of wearable and remote sensors, the ambient environmental condition can be managed by using a thermostatic or lighting setting of an existing control, including passive climatic controls. This project can also exploit data-cleaning techniques, such as a time window moving average and statistical confidence interval of collected signals within a sensing time interval range, with the help of expert Informatic knowledge. The multi-occupancy condition is a physical state of sharing a thermal condition with multiple occupants in one single space. Such a sharing condition is dominant in a modern building environment in the U.S. Finding a consensus is not always possible since the comfort condition of different individuals might not overlap. Therefore, by adopting a machine learning algorithm in the computer science area, this project established a stochastic model for individual thermal/visual comfort profiles and provided a probable guarantee about the resulting optimal thermal/visual condition by estimating an optimal environmental condition that could maximize the overall thermal/visual satisfaction of the occupants.

Figure 9.2.4 Environmental chamber.

In addition, as illustrated in Figure 9.2.8, the investigated relationship between eye pupil sizes and lighting parameters could be applied to lighting control in any type of built environment, as well as individual workstation layouts to maximize individual users' visual comfort.

As such, these projects (introduced above) revealed the potential use of human physiological principles in the architecture domain, based on the use of multidisciplinary knowledge. The discoveries of this multidisciplinary research led to an efficient computing infrastructure for environmental sustainability, via adopting real-time data-driven and occupant-centered approaches to modern buildings, which was not available in the existing mechanism. Such research was not welcome in the architecture domain due to the technical infeasibility and complexity that existed a couple of decades ago, as well as insufficient specific knowledge of other disciplines that could be integrated with architectural knowledge. However, the current advanced technologies and multidisciplinary research efforts make it possible to conduct an integrated study now. Also, such technological advancement is leading to cost-effectiveness and helps researchers/professionals effectively implement their creative ideas to be deployed in practice. Today's daily devices, such as smart bands, watches, phones, cameras, and communication infrastructure (e.g., Bluetooth and Wi-Fi) help us understand IEQ with consideration of building users' physical and psychological patterns. Therefore, this project expands design decision making and the optimization process to architects, building system engineers and

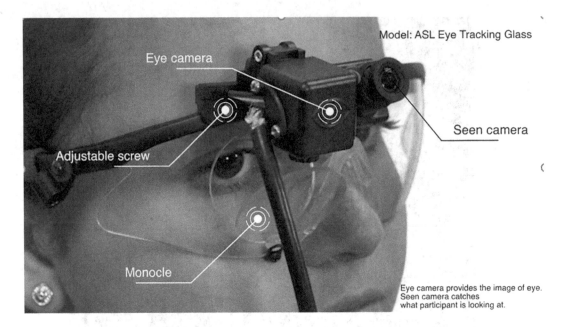

Figure 9.2.5 User study setting with sensory devices of the project experiment.

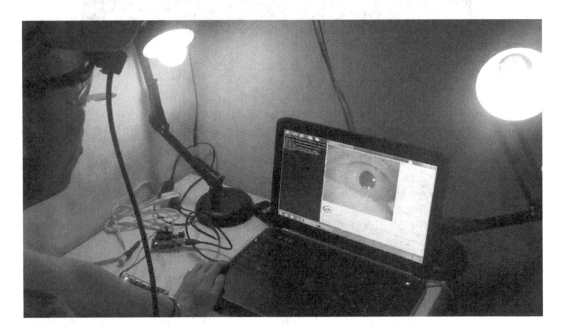

Figure 9.2.6 Technical setting of project validation test.

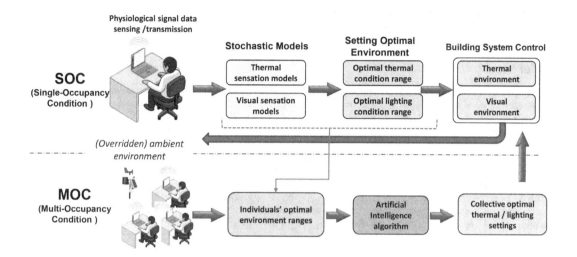

Figure 9.2.7 Framework of the physiological sensing and building environmental control.

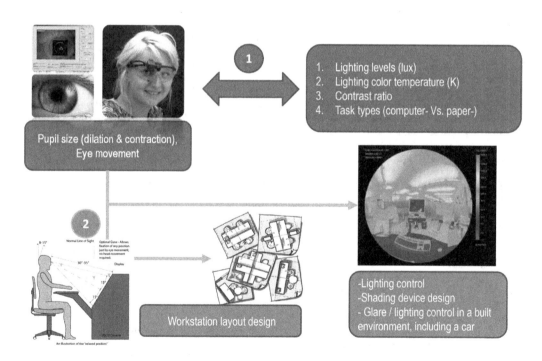

Figure 9.2.8 Potential application of eye-pupil-size-driven lighting control.

managers, and architectural/civil engineers. Also, computer scientists and electrical engineers can benefit from the envisioned human-centered building environmental control framework.

References

Alfonso, J. F., Fernández-Vega, L., Baamonde, M. B., & Montés-Micó, R. (2007). Correlation of pupil size with visual acuity and contrast sensitivity after implantation of an apodized diffractive intraocular lens. *Journal of Cataract and Refractive Surgery, 33*(3), 430–438. doi: 10.1016/j.jcrs.2006.10.051.

ASHRAE Standard 55-2010 – *Thermal Environmental Conditions for Human Occupancy (ANSI approved).* (2013). American Society of Heating, Refrigerating, and Air-Conditioning Engineers (ASHRAE).

Atchison, D. A., Smith, G., & Efron, N. (1979). The effect of pupil size on visual acuity in uncorrected and corrected myopia. *American Journal of Optometry and Physiological Optics, 56*(5), 315–323. Retrieved from: www.ncbi.nlm.nih.gov/pubmed/495689.

Birdsall, B., Buhl, W. F., Ellington, K. L., Erdem, A. E., & Winkelmann, F. C. (1990). *Overview of the DOE-2 building energy analysis program.* Berkeley, CA: Lawrence Berkeley Laboratory. doi: LBL-19735m.

Bradley, M. M., Miccoli, L., Escrig, M. A., & Lang, P. J. (2008). The pupil as a measure of emotional arousal and autonomic activation. *Psychophysiology, 45*(4), 602–607. doi: 10.1111/j.1469-8986.2008.00654.x.

CBECS. (2014). Commercial Buildings Energy Consumption Survey (CBECS) – U.S. Energy Information Administration (EIA). Retrieved from: www.eia.gov/consumption/commercial/.

Choi, J.-H. (2017a). Investigation of human eye pupil sizes as a measure of visual sensation in the workplace environment with a high lighting colour temperature. *Indoor and Built Environment, 26*(4), 488–501. doi: 10.1177/1420326X15626585.

Choi, J.-H. (2017b). NSF Award Search: Award#1707068 – Human-Building Integration: Bio-Sensing Adaptive Environmental Control for Human Health and Sustainability. Retrieved from: www.nsf.gov/awardsearch/showAward?AWD_ID=1707068&HistoricalAwards=false.

Choi, J.-H., Beltran, L. O., & Kim, H.-S. (2012). Impacts of indoor daylight environments on patient average length of stay (ALOS) in a healthcare facility. *Building and Environment, 50*, 65–75. doi: 10.1016/j.buildenv.2011.10.010.

Choi, J.-H., & Loftness, V. (2012). Investigation of human body skin temperatures as a bio-signal to indicate overall thermal sensations. *Building and Environment, 58*, 258–269. 10.1016/j.buildenv.2012.07.003.

Choi, J.-H., Loftness, V., & Aziz, A. (2012). Post-occupancy evaluation of 20 office buildings as basis for future IEQ standards and guidelines. *Energy and Buildings, 46*, 167–175. doi: 10.1016/j.enbuild.2011.08.009.

Choi, J.-H., Loftness, V., & Lee, D.-W. (2012). Investigation of the possibility of the use of heart rate as a human factor for thermal sensation models. *Building and Environment, 50*, 165–175. doi: 10.1016/j.buildenv.2011.10.009.

Choi, J.-H., & Yeom, D. (2017a). Investigation of the relationships between thermal sensations of local body areas and the whole body in an indoor built environment. *Energy and Buildings, 149*, 204–215. doi: 10.1016/j.enbuild.2017.05.062.

Choi, J.-H., & Yeom, D. (2017b). Study of data-driven thermal sensation prediction model as a function of local body skin temperatures in a built environment. *Building and Environment, 121*, 130–147. doi: 10.1016/j.buildenv.2017.05.004.

Choi, J.-H., & Zhu, R. (2015). Investigation of the potential use of human eye pupil sizes to estimate visual sensations in the workplace environment. *Building and Environment, 88*, 73–81. doi: 10.1016/j.buildenv.2014.11.025.

Choi, J.-H., Zhu, R., & Johnson, A. (2013). Human-environment interaction: Potential use of pupil size for visual environmental controls. In *ASHRAE-IAQ Proceedings.* Vancouver: ASHRAE.

CIBSE (Chartered Institution of Building Services Engineers). (2002). *Code for Lighting.* Woburn, MA: Taylor & Francis.

Doeland, H. J., Nauta, J. J., van Zandbergen, J. B., van der Eerden, H. A., van Diemen, N. G., Bertelsmann, F. W., & Heimans, J. J. (1989). The relationship of cold and warmth cutaneous sensation to age and gender. *Muscle & Nerve, 12*(9), 712–715. doi: 10.1002/mus.880120903.

Frontczak, M., & Wargocki, P. (2011). Literature survey on how different factors influence human comfort in indoor environments. *Building and Environment, 46*(4), 922–937. doi: 10.1016/j.buildenv.2010.10.021.

Hopkinson, R. G. (1956). Glare discomfort and pupil diameter. *Journal of the Optical Society of America, 46*(8), 649. doi: 10.1364/JOSA.46.000649.

IESNA. (2010). *The Lighting Handbook. Illuminating Engineering Society of North America* (10th ed.). New York, NY: Author.

Indraganti, M., & Rao, K. D. (2010). Effect of age, gender, economic group and tenure on thermal comfort: A field study in residential buildings in hot and dry climate with seasonal variations. *Energy and Buildings, 42*(3), 273–281. doi: 10.1016/j.enbuild.2009.09.003

Irlen, H. (2005). *Reading by the Colors: Overcoming Dyslexia and Other Reading Disabilities Through the Irlen Method*. New York, NY: Perigee. Retrieved from: http://books.google.com/books?hl=en&id=oAhC4mVpw6MC&pgis=1.

ISO 7730: 2005 – Ergonomics of the thermal environment – Analytical determination and interpretation of thermal comfort using calculation of the PMV and PPD indices and local thermal comfort criteria. (2005).

Karjalainen, S. (2007). Gender differences in thermal comfort and use of thermostats in everyday thermal environments. *Building and Environment*, 42(4), 1594–1603. doi: 10.1016/j.buildenv.2006.01.009

Licinio, J., & Wong, M. L. (1999). The role of inflammatory mediators in the biology of major depression: Central nervous system cytokines modulate the biological substrate of depressive symptoms, regulate stress-responsive systems, and contribute to neurotoxicity and neuroprotection. *Molecular Psychiatry*, 4(4), 317–327. Retrieved from: www.ncbi.nlm.nih.gov/pubmed/10483047.

Loftness, V., Aziz, A. A., & Choi, J.-H. (2009). *Seven Recommendations for Energy Savings and Performance Gains in General Service Administration Buildings*. Washington, DC: U.S. General Services Administration.

Meng, W., Butterworth, J., Calvas, P., & Malecaze, F. (2012). Myopia and iris colour: A possible connection? *Medical Hypotheses*, 78(6), 778–780. doi: 10.1016/j.mehy.2012.03.005

Ojaimi, E., Rose, K. A., Smith, W., Morgan, I. G., Martin, F. J., & Mitchell, P. (2009). Methods for a population-based study of myopia and other eye conditions in school children: The Sydney Myopia Study. *Ophthalmic Epidemiol*, 12(1), 59–69. doi: 10.1080/09286580490921296.

Rosenfeld, A. H., Akbari, H., Bretz, S., Fishman, B. L., Kurn, D. M., Sailor, D., & Taha, H. (1995). Mitigation of urban heat islands: Materials, utility programs, updates. *Energy and Buildings*, 22(3), 255–265. Retrieved from: www.sciencedirect.com/science/article/pii/037877889500927P.

Roy, A. J., Holliday, K., Porter, T., Young, M., Lang, A. J., Favela, E., ... Gomez, S. (2014). The effect of pupil size and decentration from pupil center on visual outcomes after corneal inlay surgery for presbyopia. *ARVO Meeting Abstracts*, 55(5), 1545. Retrieved from: http://abstracts.iovs.org/cgi/content/abstract/55/5/1545.

Sessler, D. I. (1997). Mild perioperative hypothermia. *The New England Journal of Medicine*, 336(24), 1730–1737. doi: 10.1056/NEJM199706123362407.

Streeten, D. H. P. (2014). The autonomic nervous system. National Dysautonomia Research Foundation. Retrieved from: www.ndrf.org/ans.html.

van Marken Lichtenbelt, W. D., Frijns, A. J. H., Fiala, D., Janssen, F. E. M., van Ooijen, A. M. J., & van Steenhoven, A. A. (2004). Effect of individual characteristics on a mathematical model of human thermoregulation. *Journal of Thermal Biology*, 29(7), 577–581. Retrieved from: www.sciencedirect.com/science/article/pii/S0306456504001056.

Watson, A. B., & Yellott, J. I. (2012). A unified formula for light-adapted pupil size. *Journal of Vision*, 12(10), 12. doi: 10.1167/12.10.12.

Wilkins, A. (2003). *Reading Through Colour: How Coloured Filters Can Reduce Reading Difficulty, Eye Strain, and Headaches*. Chichester: John Wiley & Sons.

Winn, B., Whitaker, D., Elliott, D., & Phillips, N. (1994). Factors affecting light-adapted pupil size in normal human subjects. *Investigative Ophthalmology & Visual Science*, 35(3), 1132–1137. Retrieved from: www.iovs.org/content/35/3/1132.

Zhou, L., & Haghighat, F. (2009). Optimization of ventilation system design and operation in office environment, Part I: Methodology. *Building and Environment*, 44(4), 651–656. doi: 10.1016/j.buildenv.2008.05.009

10
Performative Biotechnical Forms
Culturalizing the Microbiota from High-Tech to Bio-Tech Architecture

Claudia Pasquero and Marco Poletto

In the Anthropocene, an epoch when our civilization has impacted on metabolic processes at a planetary scale, we are depending, perhaps paradoxically, upon non-anthropocentric forms of intelligence. Without us noticing today we inhabit the Urbansphere, the global apparatus of contemporary urbanity, a dense network of informational, material and energetic infrastructures that sustain our increasingly demanding metabolism. In order to provide the required levels of resources in the right place at the right time the Urbansphere interrupts the fluctuating metabolisms of the other spheres of life on Earth.

The miniaturisation, distribution and intelligence of the networks of the Urbansphere and of its nodes have reached inhuman complexity, engendering evolving processes of synthetic life within itself. Endo-symbiotic relationships unexpectedly emerge among its heterogeneous components, especially when biologic evolution negotiates contaminated habitats and ubiquitous forms of artificial intelligence. Therefore, in the Anthropocene we need more than ever strategies to deal with such complexity and with the inhuman logics underpinning it.

In this chapter the authors suggest how such strategies may be developed within the realm of architectural and urban design through a combination of:

- Direct observation of living organisms that operate collectively at scales other than the human one
- Mediated interaction with related processes of material transformation and spatial morphogenesis
- Radical repurposing bio and digital technologies involved in these processes as tools of speculative design

The Urbansphere and its technological apparatus, in the form of synthetic biology, biotechnology, artificial intelligence and so on, opens scenarios where the boundaries between natural and artificial, landscape and city, human and non-human realms are blurred. The object of architecture becomes ambiguous and its aesthetic language now embodies feelings of estrangement, discomfort and disruption.

With this article we propose a productive form of alienation where micro-organisms such as bacteria, fungi, spiders and moulds can act both as a behavioural model for architecture and as active agents of architectural production. This notion has thus far led our practice, ecoLogicStudio, to experiment with processes of digital and biological computation often embedding material intelligence in architectural apparatus at 1:1 scale. In the past 10 years we have built more than 20 prototypes, installations and pilot projects to describe, test and experience architecture as a form of material life; some of the most significant ones are illustrated in the following pages.

These projects engage the evolving process of living matter, thus embedding the objecthood of architecture within its surrounding environment or milieu. We claim here a new meaning for the notion of "cultivation", no longer solely concerned with tending plants and natural landscapes such as in horticulture, but now involved in a more expanded field of analogue and digital design processes impacting upon our perception and understanding of urbanity.

As such *cultivation* also acquires critical relevance in re-framing our relationship to emergent digital technologies and becomes part of a broader process of "culturalization" of the inhuman systems that populate the Urbansphere and that are now brought into the scope and focus of architecture, intended in its aesthetic, performative and ecological aspects.

This shift has direct influence on the ever-critical relationship between form and performance in contemporary disciplinary discourse. With the goal of unpacking this influence let us begin by observing the effects of endo-symbiosis in collective formations like corals colonies.

Critical to the definition of endo-symbiosis and its relevance to architecture is the way parts relate to wholes, or in other words how do we conceptualize the Urbansphere as a whole in relationship to its architectural and techno-material components (Figure 10.1).

Deleuze and Guattari in one of their best-known passages (Deleuze and Guattari, 1987) referred to the relationship between the Wasp orchid and the Thynnie wasp; the orchid flower has evolved parts that resemble very closely the female wasp; the seduced wasp male tries to mate with the flower and by doing so it pollinates the plant; the two have evolved so inseparably that even their appearance has become similar despite being an insect and a plant. Despite them being obviously separate objects, belonging to separate realms of nature, the wasp is inherently part of the plant and of its reproductive mechanism. So much so that it becomes very hard to draw a frame around its identity; however, refraining from doing so allows us to conceptualize the pair as a larger ensemble, and their coupling as the process of reproduction of the machinic system itself.

Similarly, dunes can be seen as an immeasurable number of sorting machines creating coherent patterns of sand distribution that travel in space and time until final dissolution, while human beings may be better described as an assemblage of desiring machines, thousands of mechanisms that without us noticing are producing the dreams that we do notice and that surface to the level of consciousness.

It is a new notion of symbiosis that forces us to redefine the modern and linear understanding of cause–effect by re-describing the boundaries of an object within its environment and by taking into account the multiple interlocking feedback loops that define the behaviour of the individual unit within the larger apparatus of the Urbansphere. In the evolution of some organism the effect of such a relationship has become so close to be internalized in the morphology and behaviour of the host organism itself, so much so that the organism appears to contain multiple levels of machinic feedback. A significant and fascinating case are corals which are globally bleaching, and dying, as a consequence of global disruption of these feedback mechanisms.

Corals are both collective organisms and an example of endo-symbiosis:

> An endosymbiont is a cell which lives inside another cell with mutual benefit. Eukaryotic cells are believed to have evolved from early prokaryotes that were engulfed by phagocytosis. That is when the engulfed prokaryotic cell remains undigested as it contributes new functionality to the engulfing cell. In the case of corals this new functionality is photosynthesis. Over generations, the engulfed cell lost some of its independent utility and became a supplemental organelle.
>
> *(Bioninja, n.d.)*

Claudia Pasquero and Marco Poletto

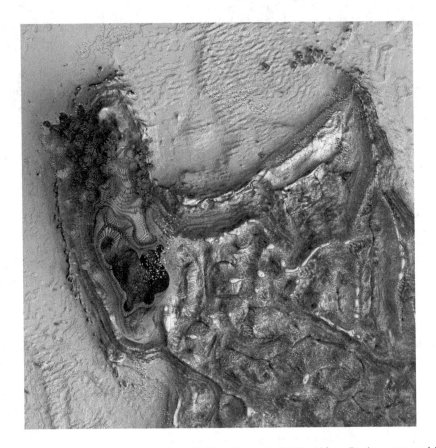

Figure 10.1 The Anthropocene Island Project, Tallinn Biennale 2017—Urban Design proposal for a new eco-city on the peninsula of Paljassarre. Top view.
Source: Copyright ecoLogicStudio

In the case of corals, the engulfed organisms are called zooxanthellae, a form of algae called dinoflagellate.

> Corals are usually colonies of polyps. Polyps are live coral tissue extensions that cover the calcium carbonate structure and are usually only a few millimetres thick. The tissue has two layers, the epidermis and the gastrodermis, where the zooxanthellae live. Zooxanthellae are unicellular and spherical with two flagella that fall off once they are incorporated within a host.
>
> *(Microbe Wiki, n.d.)*

The coral polyps do cellular respiration, thus producing carbon dioxide and water as by-products. The zooxanthellae then take up these by-products to carry out photosynthesis. The products of photosynthesis are used to make proteins and carbohydrates in order to produce calcium carbonate for the coral to grow their exoskeleton.

Polyps that are better exposed to sun light receive a competitive advantage via the zooxanthellae and are able to build their exoskeletons faster thus gaining even more exposure to precious solar energy. Polyps that are less exposed and remain locked in eventually die, while more exposed coral

Performative Biotechnical Forms

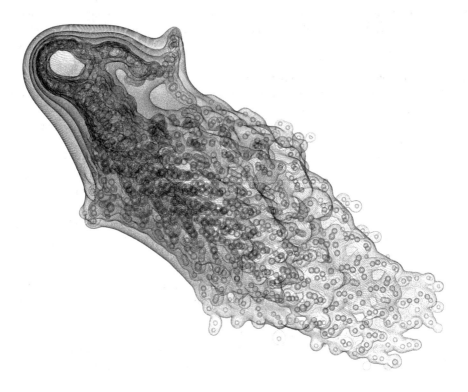

Figure 10.2 HORTUS XL, Thresholds, Centre Pompidou 2019. Iso-surfaces of variable light intensity.
Source: Copyright ecoLogicStudio

can reproduce and conquer larger areas. The particular morphogenesis of stony corals, for instance, and their convoluted bifurcations is an emergent effect of this complex multilayered process of symbiosis comprising multiple feedback loops between marine environment, colony, individual polyp and the algae inhabiting its gastrodermis. It is therefore impossible to capture the nature of corals' morphology without understanding the dynamic nature of this rather complex part-to-whole assemblage and its reason for being within a specific milieu.

The study of such complex interaction has fascinated scientists for decades, but it has only recently become possible to digitally simulate how such a kind of morphogenesis appears. That is by studying and visualizing how morphology emerges at a certain scale from multiple levels of interactions among parts that operate at a significantly smaller scale. In a paper dating back to 2004, Merks, Hoekstra, Kaandorp and Sloot studied and proposed the polyp-oriented modelling of coral growth.

In their words:

> The morphogenesis of colonial stony corals is the result of the collective behaviour of many coral polyps depositing coral skeleton on top of the old skeleton on which they live. Yet, models of coral growth often consider the polyps as a single continuous surface. In the present work, the polyps are modelled individually. Each polyp takes up resources, deposits skeleton, buds off new polyps and dies. In this polyp-oriented model, spontaneous branching occurs. We argue that

branching is caused by a so called 'polyp fanning effect' by which polyps on a convex surface have a competitive advantage relative to polyps on a flat or concave surface.

(Merks, Hoekstra, Kaandorp and Sloot, 2004)

It is interesting to note here how the discretisation of the model, i.e. considering polyps as individual agents, affords a new understanding of the emerging nature of some key traits in the whole colony. This model explains why morphologies that are species-specific also show high variability within one species and how this intraspecific variability is caused by environmental parameters, such as light availability and the amount of water flow.

It also explains how the characteristic bifurcations emerge as a consequence of the collective nature of the coral. At convex sites, the polyps fan out, thus getting better access to the diffusing resources. At concave sites, the polyps point towards each other, thus interfering in the uptake of resources. In this way, a curvature effect comes out as a natural consequence of the competition between the polyps to take up resources. It is possible to translate those findings into digital 3D meshes where polyps are vertices of the mesh with varied access to nutrients (represented as proximity to randomly moving points).

Two sets of considerations are particularly relevant here. Changing the nature of the environment (amount of resources, their speed or direction of movement) without any change to the "coral mesh" or to the rules of interaction of its "polyps' vertices" does generate a very large number of different morphological traits in the coral mesh. Thus, survival in an environment of scarce resources produces diversity and richness of forms. And the convolutedness of the resulting meshes reflects the one found in coral morphologies and results from the process of optimal solar exposure of a collective organism powered by photosynthesis. Small differences are amplified and lead to articulation of form.

Complexity of articulation is a consequence of economy of means.

Therefore, if we redefine our understanding of part-to-whole relationships and trans-scalar hierarchies as a continuum nesting of heterogeneous systems composed of individually interacting units immersed in a changing environment, we can come to understand performativity as a generative force of spatial and material articulation, a morphogenetic force. Within this paradigm competition for scarce resources leads to richness and diversity of forms, unlike in most engineering problem-solving methods where optimization leads to converging average solutions. And also, perhaps a new way to read the famous modernist credo of *Less is More*. Here it is *Less resources equals More articulation*.

Over the years our practice has become increasingly concerned with the actualization of this morphogenetic paradigm in architectural and urban design. This is how a series of projects and installations known as HORTUS was conceived (Figures 10.2–10.4).

This algorithmic protocol simulating coral morphogenesis can be deployed in a variety of ways as a generative design tool for architecture. We can accept its abstractions and simplifications and deploy it to design "coral-like" architectures or architectures inspired by corals. Here corals are what we may call biomimetic models that we take inspiration from to design an artefact that belongs to the world of man-made artificial structures.

Another methodological take is to focus the attention on the relationships between part-to-whole. This implies rejecting the metaphorical translation across scales and regimes to focus instead on the analogy between two models that may look and feel rather different but that share similar relational diagrams. What interests us is that traits such as bifurcations and surface convolutedness maintain in the architectural model their emergent nature in relationship to the specific milieu. The intelligence of the system is therefore embedded in the here and now and operates across scales and regimes, simultaneously in the virtual and material realms. The traits of the system are bred in time, iteration after iteration, during the design process, construction and usage. It is a significant shift from the model

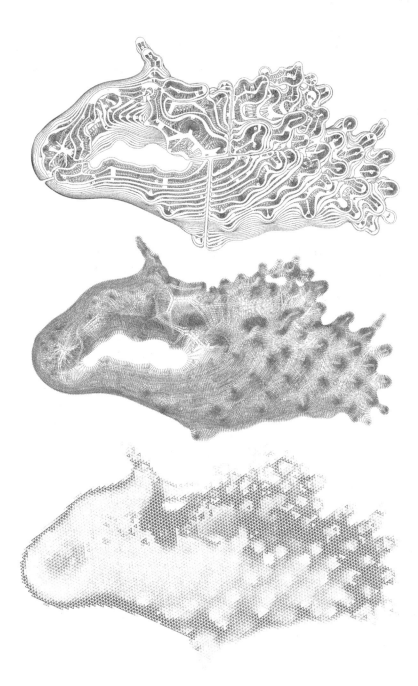

Figure 10.3 HORTUS XL, Actualization studies, Centre Pompidou 2019. Iso-surfaces of light intensity are actualized in a variety of ways. By planar contouring, by discretisation and by continuous three-dimensional articulation.

Source: Copyright ecoLogicStudio

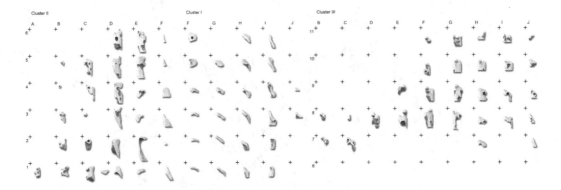

Figure 10.4 HORTUS XL, Actualization studies, Centre Pompidou 2019. The continuous three-dimensional articulation of space defined by iso-surfaces at two different light intensity thresholds is tessellated with an hexagonal grid. Each volume is then catalogued and studied for its 3D printing feasibility.

Source: Copyright ecoLogicStudio

typically adopted by the industry which clearly distinguishes the creative moment of digital morphogenesis from the technical challenge of actualizing it in the real world. This transition is worth investigating further.

Let us compare the methods of a bio-engineer synthesizing artificial tissues in a lab with the one of a gardener reviving a patch of dried land; while both are running generative protocols, the first requires a perfectly controlled testing ground for his procedures to acquire general applicability while the second needs to consider the unexpected fluctuations of the ecology of his garden. The gardener operates through a process of intensification of difference; his only chance to reconcile his desire of beautification and the natural expressivity of living processes resides in the movement, intended in its biological and physical sense.

Architect and philosopher Gilles Clément suggests that the formalization of the garden from this perspective becomes a process of formalized transmission of biological messages. Differences in slope, insulation, soil moisture and so on are registered and then exploited by the gardening protocol to promote the growth of different arboreal species; also, the growth, being itself a variable and partially unpredictable process, needs to be read, assessed and then considered in the formulation of future actions, or in the future lines of the gardening protocol.

The garden grows, and beautification progresses in loops; each step generating more difference and local complexity that can be in turn recognized and bred; the management of this generative process is what makes the garden a potentially beautiful and healthy organism.

In Clément's words:

> Reality is entirely contained within experience. Only. Without gardening there is no garden.
>
> *(Clément 2008)*

This sensibility was formalized in the realm of architecture by radical avant-garde movements in the 1960s, like Archigram with their Instant City in 1969. Its evolution appears in the years that followed in the exquisite drawings of bio-mechanical landscapes and architectures by Sir Peter Cook, which can be considered the precursors of a new paradigm of hybridization of technology and nature. Their aesthetical sensibility is ever more relevant today and it is certainly critical to the point we are making

Performative Biotechnical Forms

Figure 10.5 Meta-Folly, components diagram, FRAC Collection, Orleans, 2013–2018. This form of cybernetic diagram illustrates the spatial relationships among both digital and human component parts of Meta-Folly, defining the main feedback loops of interaction among them.
Source: Copyright ecoLogicStudio

here; in fact, it prefigures a renewed continuity between the act of simulating (i.e. depicting) nature while at the same time hosting living systems, including humans of course, within the ever-evolving fabric of architecture itself (Figure 10.5).

Contemporary to Archigram was architect Cedric Price. He made the most enduring attempt to expand architecture in the realm of computation and embedded intelligence, especially in his long-standing collaboration with cybernetician Gordon Pask. Unbuilt projects like Fun Palace (1964) and the Generator (1976), as well as the still-in-use London Zoo Aviary (1962), materialize in three dimensions the paradigm of second-order cybernetics and the related concept of Paskian environment.

In the words of Prof. Ranulph Glanville:

> Second order Cybernetics presents a (new) paradigm—in which the observer is circularly (and intimately) involved with/connected to the observed. The observer is no longer neutral and detached, and what is considered is not the observed (as in the classical paradigm), but the observing system […] Therefore, second order Cybernetics must primarily be considered through the first person and with active verbs: the observer's inevitable presence acknowledged.
>
> (Glanville 2003)

In architectural terms this notion suggests moving away from ideas of responsive or adaptive systems such as sun-tracking louvres, so dear to the hi-tech modernists, to consider a participatory framework where the observer is no longer a mere user but becomes an active co-creator of the spaces he or she is inhabiting. This shift makes novelty possible as a new kind of spatial conversation may emerge with unexpected consequences on the way space is perceived and utilized. Architecture become a morphogenetic system emerging from a meta-conversation between human and non-human system; it is no longer a question of how we make use of the environment and the space we inhabit but how we become co-creators of planetary space by interacting with other forms of intelligence.

Pask certainly understood the critical importance of the notion of circularity and its relevance to interaction and conversation theory, and for that reason he started building several devices that could interact with humans in space; these installations, such as the seminal The Colloquy of Mobiles at ICA in London in 1968, are known as Paskian Environments. In his own words:

> now we've got the notion of a machine with an underspecified goal, the system that evolves. This is a new notion, nothing like the notion of machines that was current in the Industrial Revolution, absolutely nothing like it. It is, if you like, a much more biological notion, maybe I'm wrong to call such a thing a machine; I gave that label to it because I like to realize things as artifacts, but you might not call the system a machine, you might call it something else.
>
> (cited in Bateson, 1968)

We began calling them cyber-gardens.

One of the first was StemCloud 2.0, a living bio-digital installation commissioned by the Seville Biennale of Architecture 2008 and precursor of the HORTUS series (Figures 10.6 and 10.7). Designed in the form of a coral-like landscape, it invited the public to climb up close and interact with its bio-reactors. Each hosting living microbial cultures, they were stacked into a curved formation which framed the gallery space, creating an accessible niche, screening light and releasing oxygen into the atmosphere. Itself a collective organism, the installation behaved as a self-regulating photosynthetic body where both "external conditions", so called environmental factors, as well as the particular micro-ecologies contained in the bio-reactors become integral parts of the cyber-gardening process.

Fast-forward almost 10 years and this line of research has evolved into our first permanent bio-digital sculpture, HORTUS Astana, now part of the Bio.Tech Hut we designed and built for Astana's new Museum of Future energy. Its morphology embodies the three-dimensional distribution of wide-spectrum light sources. The flow of energy emitted as wide-spectrum radiation is digitally simulated in space to visualize their intensive field. Cyanobacteria are then introduced, as bio-bits, their metabolic machines deployed to convert radiation into actual processes of photosynthesis, oxygenation and biomass. Their articulation in space is digitally mediated to arrange the photosynthetic organisms along

Performative Biotechnical Forms

Figure 10.6 HORTUS Astana, Bio.Tech Hut Pavilion. Astana, 2017. View of the Living Hut hosting the HORTUS Astana living artwork. Visitors can feed the cultures with CO2 from their exhalations and release oxygen in the atmosphere.
Photo copyright Naaro. © ecoLogicStudio

iso-surfaces of optimal incoming radiation. A network of connecting paths is also computed, bringing nutrients and CO2 to the living cyanobacteria. Visitors are active part of the system, feeding it with CO2 with their exhalations and absorbing the released oxygen as it spreads in the surrounding atmosphere.

The project is recasting the practice of computational design into one we have defined as cyber-gardening, embedding biological computation in space. This effort represents an attempt to culturalize the inhuman; that is, to re-describe the boundaries of generative practices beyond what we have called the "Lab model" and towards an extended practice of bio-digital cultivation, the "cyber-Garden model" (Figure 10.8).

This model is reaching its highest definition in our latest incarnation HORTUS XL, commissioned by the Centre Pompidou in Paris in 2018. In HORTUS XL a digital algorithm simulates the growth of the exoskeleton that is then deposited in layers of 400 microns, triangular units of 46 mm and hexagonal blocks of 18.5 cm by digital 3D printing machines. Photosynthetic cyanobacteria are then

Figure 10.7 Bio.Tech Hut, Astana EXPO2017, Living Hut. HORTUS is hanging from the ceiling of the Living Hut as a cloud-like chandelier; its convolutedness responds to incoming light radiation. HORTUS is divided into four clusters which operate as an integral unit. Each part is made of a core structure of laser-cut aluminium sections, acrylic holders and PVC pipes creating the surface of the cloud. Algae circulate in close loops around the structure.
Photo copyright Naaro. © ecoLogicStudio

inoculated on a biogel suspension into the individual triangular cells forming the units of biological intelligence of the collective system. Their metabolic machines convert radiation into actual processes of photosynthesis, oxygenation and biomass production.

In HORTUS XL life proliferates by artificially breeding potentials of intensive difference and cyanobacteria are induced into evolving novel forms of biological intelligence in order to solve the survival problem at hand. In this sense the project re-casts the significance of global ecological issues affecting all systems on Earth in the new light of inhuman survival strategies. The relevance of such strategies to architecture has to be evaluated in relationship to our understanding and more broadly to our conception of the City as an Urbansphere. We then begin to question how the digital production of space through technologies such as 3D printing can enable the proliferation of novel models of inhabitation (human and non-human) and related forms of spatial intelligence.

We have now become aware that in order to evolve a resilient Urbansphere we should intensify its mechanisms of spatial intelligence while rescuing them from the conforming force of contemporary technology, digital and bio alike. It is a sensibility that architects are now loosely defining "post-digital" but that has older roots. In the words of Felix Guattari:

Figure 10.8 SuperTree installation at Futurium, Berlin, 2018.
Photo copyright Naaro. © ecoLogicStudio

> So, wherever we turn, there is the same nagging paradox: on the one hand, the continuous development of new techno-scientific means to potentially resolve the dominant ecological issues, […] on the other hand the inability of organized social forces and constituted subjective formations to take hold of these resources in order to make them work.
>
> *(Guattari 2008)*

Embedding technology into autonomous forms of material organization augments architecture into a spatial interface, involved in everyday ecologic practices of "cultivation"; that is, of culturalization of the Urbansphere. Architecture can thus operate at multiple interconnected scales at once, from the micro-regimes of algae cells to the macro-behaviours of urban infrastructures, expanding both its scope and reach. It provides the spatial substratum required by extended participation which we have named "bio-citizenship", underlining the expanded role played by inhuman entities to future collective formations. Any architectural protocol in the future shall seek to enable extended participation, and as a consequence it must be able to grow in complexity in time and itself embody a form of artificial intelligence. One that is distributed into the fabric of the spaces we inhabit and that is co-evolutionary to them.

From this perspective microalgae are not only understood as biological organisms, as found for instance in symbiotic relationship with polyps influencing coral morphogenesis, but also as a fascinating repository of intelligent survival strategies evolved over millions of years and that can be embedded into future bio-smart architectures.

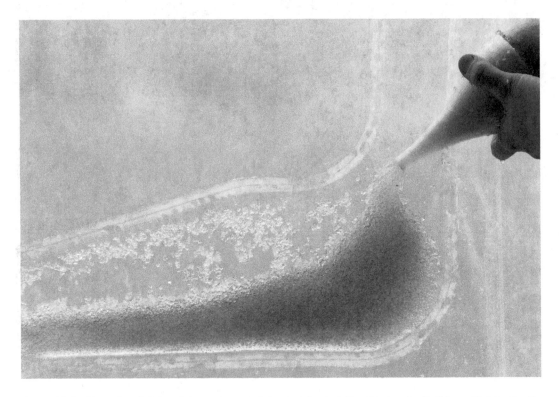

Figure 10.9 Photo.Synth.Etica, living urban curtain, test bed at the Printworks Building, Dublin Castle. Dublin, 2018. Detail of the inoculation process of the algae cultures on a jellified nutritious medium. Jellification creates an intermediate level of substructure in the photobioreactors, increases the levels of photosynthesis, optimizes the CO2/O2 exchange and reduced the overall weight of the system.

Photo copyright Naaro. © ecoLogicStudio

In our test beds we discovered that micro-organisms grow faster in artificial bio-digital environments than in the wild because they can be directly connected to the life of buildings which through heat and CO2 emissions stimulate the biomass to grow. Our most recent large-scale pilot scheme is the photosynthetic urban curtain called Photo.Synth.Etica (Figure 10.9). The 200 sq m curtain captures and stores CO2, removing from the atmosphere approximately 1 kg of CO2 per day, equivalent to the contribution of 20 large trees. In our pilot scheme at Dublin Castle, the Printworks Building, the "curtain" is made of 16 modules which wrap a large portion of the main façade spanning two floors. Each module functions as a "photobioreactor", a digitally designed and custom-made bioplastic container of living microalgae cultures.

"Dirty" urban air is introduced at the bottom and while bubbles naturally rise through the jellified medium they come into contact with voracious microbial cells. CO2 molecules and pollutants from the air are captured and stored within the algal body, thus contributing to their growing biomass; this can be harvested and used in the production of more bioplastic raw material. Freshly photosynthesized oxygen is finally released at the top of each module and into the urban microclimate.

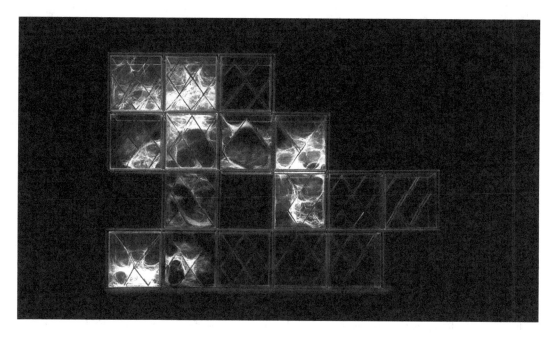

Figure 10.10 XenoDerma, building skin prototype. Front view of the 1:1 scale prototype under construction. The image illustrates empty units, 3D-printed substratum units, units currently inhabited by silk spinning Asian Fawn tarantula and units completed with both structure and silk cladding.
Source: Copyright Urban Morphogenesis Lab, UCL London, 2018

The project involves the contribution of human and non-human stakeholders, thus elevating them to the role of co-creators of the actual solutions in their becoming. In this sense it is less important whether the design medium includes algae, bacteria or other kinds of digital systems. All these forms of intelligence are dragged into the creative process, managed and mediated by architecture and its protocol. This is how, by releasing control of the actual definition of architectural morphology and its future evolution, we simultaneously gain in scope and in the ability to influence its morphogenesis at a more profound level.

In XenoDerma, one of our recent research-based speculative projects developed at the Urban Morphogenesis Lab in UCL London, we propose this new-found level embodies a productive form of alienation where spiders, more specifically a breed of tarantula named Asian Fawn, act as autonomous agents of architectural production (Figure 10.10). As we discovered, spiders' minds do not completely reside in their body, as their web constitutes a form of spatial thinking. Information from their web becomes an integral part of their cognitive system. The web provides a medium of interaction with embedded intelligence. In XenoDerma its morphogenesis is interfered with by an alien spatial scaffolding (algorithmically designed and machine printed). The result is ambiguous, the product of an alien intelligence that resides somewhere at the intersection of the biological, digital and spatial realms.

In conclusion,

> Through experimenting with biological organisms and digital apparatus we envision a new generation of bio-digital 'designed prototypes' with transformative agency for an architectural discipline yet to come.

(Pasquero and Zaroukis, 2016)

A future bio-tech architecture that is plural, collective and mutant. Defined by the trans-scalar nesting of heterogeneous systems, each composed of individually interacting units immersed in a changing environment. Within this new paradigm performance is a generative force of spatial and material articulation, a morphogenetic force. Adaptation to a world of scarce resources will lead to richness and diversity of forms and increased material intelligence.

It is a process that has no beginning and no end; rather, it evolves in time from conception to construction and beyond during its useful life cycle. This notion suggests moving away from ideas of responsive or adaptive environments to develop participatory frameworks where the observer is no longer a mere user but becomes an active co-creator of the spaces he or she is inhabiting. This shift makes novelty possible as a new kind of spatial conversation emerges with unexpected consequences on the way space is perceived and utilized. Ultimately computational design strategies are re-cast into a broader practice of embedding bio-digital intelligence into physical space. This effort represents an attempt to culturalize the inhuman, that is to re-describe the boundaries of generative design practices beyond human rationality and creativity.

Architecture thus begins to operate at multiple interconnected scales at once, from the micro-regimes of algae cells to the macro-behaviours of smart urban infrastructures, expanding both its scope and reach. It provides the spatial substratum for a new emergent form of "bio-citizenship", recognizing the expanded role played by inhuman entities in the Anthropocene Age. Any architectural protocol in the future shall seek to enable this extended participation and shall embody its artificial intelligence. A form of intelligence that is distributed into the fabric of the spaces we inhabit and that is co-evolutionary to them.

References

Bateson, M.C., *Our own metaphor: A personal account of a conference on the effects of conscious purpose on human adaptation*, Hampton, 1968.
Bioninja, Endosymbiosis, n.d., https://ib.bioninja.com.au/standard-level/topic-1-cell-biology/15-the-origin-of-cells/endosymbiosis.html.
Clément, G., *Il giardiniere planetario*, 22 Publishing, 2008.
Deleuze, G., & Guattari, F., *A thousand plateaus: Capitalism and schizophrenia*, first English version published by University of Minnesota Press, 1987.
Microbe Wiki, Zooxanthellae and their symbiotic relationship with marine corals, n.d., https://microbewiki.kenyon.edu/index.php/Zooxanthellae_and_their_Symbiotic_Relationship_with_Marine_Corals.
Haque, U. *The architectural relevance of Gordon Pask*, John Wiley & Sons, 2007.
Glanville, R., Second-order cybernetics, in *Systems science and cybernetics*, Francisco Parra-Luna (Ed.), *Encyclopaedia of Life Support Systems* (EoLSS), developed under the Auspices of UNESCO, EoLSS Publishers, 2003, www.eolss.net.
Guattari, F., *The three ecologies*, Continuum, 2008, p. 22.
Markes, R.M., Hoekstra, A.G., Kaandorp, J.A., & Sloot P.M., Polyp oriented modelling of coral growth, *Journal of Theoretical Biology*, 228(4), 559–576, 2004. DOI: 10.1016/j.jtbi.2004.02.020.
Otto, F., *Occupying and connecting*, Menges, 2009, p. 111.
Pasquero, C., & Zaroukis E., Design prototype, in *aae2016*, Vol 1, Bartlett School of Architecture, 2006.

11
Searching for a "Bioclimatic Law" in Architecture
Comfort and the Ethics of (Human) Performance

William W. Braham

> Bioclimatics is a science of relations between life, climate, seasons, and geographic distribution.
>
> *Hopkins (1938)*

Bioclimatic design emerged as a fully-formed architectural ethic in 1963 with the publication of *Design with Climate: A Bioclimatic Approach to Architectural Regionalism* by Victor Olgyay. It offers a powerful formula, still used for environmentally ambitious buildings today: first, analyze the local climate; second, determine its effect on human comfort; and third, enhance interior comfort by adjusting walls, windows, shading devices, or roofs. In its pure form, it makes no mention of energy or HVAC (heating, ventilation, and air conditioning) systems and promises to translate bioclimatic performance directly into architectural expression, offering a bioclimatic "law" that guarantees a regionally specific architecture to counter the universalizing tendencies of contemporary construction.

High-performance buildings of all kinds depend on bioclimatic techniques, from the merely energy-efficient to radically ecological and living buildings. Climate analysis itself has developed considerably since the mid-twentieth century, while powerful methods for predicting their effect on the interior climates of buildings through digital simulation have become desktop tools, but the key concept remains the paradoxical measure of comfort. Paradoxical because of its subjectivity and sensitivity to context (the "predicted mean vote"), and because comfort remains the fundamental goal of HVAC systems. The lowly thermostat, and the comfort regime it enforces, is the mechanism that guided HVAC systems through the dramatic mechanization of buildings in the twentieth century. In response, bioclimatic design offers an alternative to mechanical conditioning systems and the environmental consequences of their power consumption.

The architectural formula seems so complete that it can be easy to overlook the fact that the term was first coined by a farmer-turned-entomologist in the early twentieth century, Andrew Hopkins, who proposed an ambitious "bioclimatic law" to explain the differences among agricultural microclimates and their effect on the yield of crops and forests (Hopkins 1938). Biological analogies run through the discourse of architectural modernism, but this particular appropriation is worth considering in more detail because the search for a bioclimatic law in architecture rests on human performance, on the productivity of people at work. In the massive, fuel-fed urban economies of the twenty-first century, buildings are tools for enhancing sedentary work and comfort is the condition of maximum productivity.

Bioclimatic Law

According to Andrew Hopkins, the idea of a bioclimatic law first occurred to him on the land in West Virginia that he began farming in 1880. As he later explained:

> it was from studies of the relation of latitude and altitude to the difference in time of the emergence of the Hessian Fly, and its attack on wheat sown at given times, that the idea of a natural law was suggested in 1895, and that the development of this law has been based largely on a comprehensive study of the dates of seeding and harvesting winter wheat within the distribution of this crop in the United States.
>
> *(Hopkins 1924, 608)*

Hopkins was an astute observer, documenting cycles of growth and the invasions of pests on his farm, so much so that he was hired as an entomologist for the West Virginia Agricultural Experiment Station, and eventually as the founding head of the Division of Forest Insect Investigations at the United States Department of Agriculture (Furniss 2010).

Hopkins focused on "Periodical Events and Natural Law as Guides to Agricultural Research and Practice," exemplified by his method for determining the best time to sow winter wheat (Hopkins 1918). He mostly tracked variations in temperature, which so influence growth times, and sought universal laws by which those variations could be anticipated. In his magnum opus of 1938, he enumerated the causes of variation in two categories.

1. **Astronomical.**—a. The sun as the primordial cause of all bioclimatic phenomena. b. The motions of the earth in (1) its rotation, as the cause of day and night and the measure of time; and (2) its revolution and the inclination of its axis, as the cause of its seasons and major climates.
2. **Terrestrial.**—c. The major relations between oceans, continents, and islands, in modifying the effects of astronomical causes. d. The major and minor physiographic features of the continents and their major regions, in modifying the effects of the major terrestrial causes. e. Local topography and physical features, in modifying the continental and regional effects of physiographic causes. f. The combination of all major and minor causes, or the causation complex, in modifying local effects.

(Hopkins 1938, 5)

His bioclimatic law promised to translate the clockwork regularity of astronomical events to the "causation complex" of terrestrial activities.

In practice, the method began with an ideal astronomical climate predicted by the latitude of a farm, modifying it to account for its terrestrial location in relation to the tempering effect of oceans, altitude, and more localized geographic features (south slope, frost dam, etc.). With multiple charts and maps, he translated observations about the timing of first flowering or swarming of pests into formulas for calculating the difference in timing for a particular farm or field. Since the process of calculation was complex, he prepared a phenological disk calendar for timing the planting of winter wheat that

Searching for a "Bioclimatic Law"

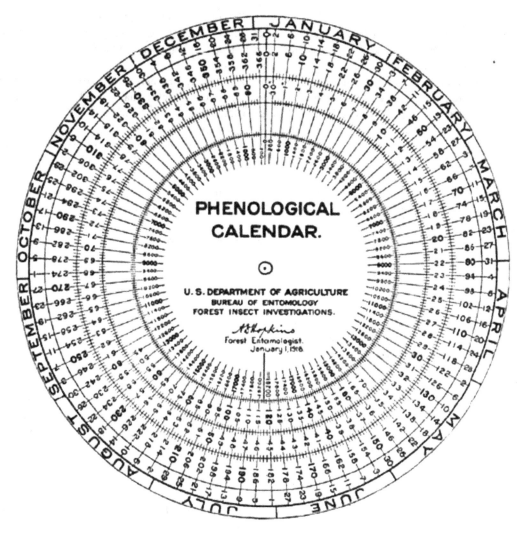

Figure 11.1 Andrew Hopkins, phenological calendar for planting winter wheat.
Source: U.S. Department of Agriculture, Weather Bureau, 1918 (public domain)

extension agents could use to advise farmers (Figure 11.1). He promulgated the method with posters in 1918, and then generalized it over the next 20 years; however, he never fully persuaded his associates about the universality of the law, nor were his methods ever adopted in any detail (Rohwer 1950). Despite its failure as a method, the idea of a bioclimatic science linking climatic factors to the geographic distribution of plants and animals has inspired generations of researchers and the term circulated widely enough to be adopted by the Olgyay brothers.

Hopkins was not the first to observe either the difference in flowering time of plants by location or to identify climatic regions by the particular plants they featured. About the time Hopkins began his speculations, Wladimir Köppen began publishing widely used global climate maps, still in use today, which are based on the temperature zones suited to different kinds of vegetation. He began with five main zones, and subdivided them to match pre-existing systems for categorizing plants (Geerts 2000).

William W. Braham

The Köppen system was further refined in the 1930s in collaboration with Rudolf Geiger, and they even cited Hopkins' work (Köppen and Geiger 1930). However, Geiger's very influential book of 1927, *Climate Near the Ground,* demonstrates the challenge of converting Hopkins' macroclimatic observations into microclimatic law.

Geiger's book was also intended as a practical handbook for farmers and foresters, but unlike Hopkins' work, he focused on the mechanisms of "terrestrial" microclimatology. His first section explains "Heat Exchange," "Temperature Relationships Near the Ground," and the "Influence of the Ground Itself," while a second section explores "The Microclimate in Its Relation to Topography, to Plants, Animals, and Man," including, for example, the effects of low plant cover versus tree stands (Geiger 1950). The book went into six editions, most recently in 2003, and provided the basis for the explanation of microclimates in *Design with Climate*.

Hopkins sought a universal law that could connect the astronomical basis of climate rhythms to minute variations in microclimates. His approach was largely statistical, meaning he sought to codify correlations between factors that could be readily measured—latitude, elevation, etc.—and the temperature variations on a specific farm. In a lovely passage, Geiger reflected on the difference between macro- and microclimates, and particularly the complexity of predicting temperatures below a certain scale.

> A furrow in the field has a special slope climate on either side; an anthill has one on all sides both of which are, as far as they go, decided microclimates, which cannot be apprehended through the macroclimatic observation method. A single currant bush modifies the climate of its immediate vicinity even to the smallest volume relation. Yes, every leaf is surrounded by a film of air with its own special peculiarities.
>
> *(Geiger 1950, 192)*

The failure of Hopkins to establish a law should not overshadow the importance of the concept he named, which spread widely after the publication of his book in 1938. Bioclimatic modelling is now a standard feature of ecological analysis. As Araújo and Peterson observed in 2012, "this approach to species-level biogeography and ecology now ranks among the most widely reviewed topics in the ecological literature." They are also known as "ecological niche models," "habitat suitability models," or "species distribution models" and use statistical tests to establish correlations between climate and the occurrence of specific plants or animals.

In contrast to the principles of climatology, Geiger described bioclimatology "as a link between the so-called 'exact' and the biological natural sciences, as is medicine" (Geiger 1950). That distinction also describes architecture, and whether the Olgyays appropriated the term from Hopkins, Geiger, or the other climatologists they were reading at the time, their ambition for a "bioclimatic approach" sought to bridge the gap between the astronomical regularity of the macroclimate and the terrestrial conditions of architectural comfort.

Architects intentionally alter local climates for human comfort, literally making hostile macroclimates inhabitable. A building is an intentional currant bush that "modifies the climate of its immediate vicinity even to the smallest volume relation," but as Hopkins learned, the regularity of the sun's movements do not translate directly to the complex movements of heat, air, and especially moisture. It was a lesson the Olgyays had to learn as well.

Design with Climate, Design of Microclimates

The word "climate" derives from the angles of the sun (*declination*) specific to different latitudes. The word was extended to describe the zones between latitudes, and then came to include the other, terrestrial conditions found there. The tropics, for example, describe the region between the highest latitudes reached by the sun above and below the equator (23° 26′), and simultaneously to the warmer conditions typically found in those regions (except at higher altitudes as Hopkins taught us).

The architectural use of the term "bioclimatic" first appeared in two papers presented in 1952: "Bioclimatic Approach to Architecture" by Victor Olgyay and "Solar Control and Orientation to Meet Bioclimatic Requirements" by his brother Aladar (Olgyay 1953a, 1953b). Their work emerged from the solar building research of the 1940s, inspired by wartime concerns about oil scarcity and advances in microclimatology. The two articles contain most of the material that appeared in their later books, with the arguments and diagrams fully developed. Their climate-oriented research had begun in Budapest during the war years, where they experimented with sun screens for seasonal shading (Olgyay and Olgyay 1946). After they moved to the United States in 1947, they began collaborating with the Hungarian scientist Maria Telkes at MIT on solar research projects jointly sponsored by the MIT Solar Energy Fund and the federal Housing and Home Finance Agency (Barber 2016).

Solar research was very active through this period, characterized on the one hand by engineers and scientists thinking about energy futures and the challenges of utilizing energy income from the sun rather than finite reservoirs of fuels. On the other hand, architects experimented formally with solar techniques and devices, taking advantage of the post-war boom in housing (Simon 1947). The emphasis on glass and shading devices fit readily into the architectural explorations of the period, though they were just as often symbolic. The contribution of the Olgyay brothers was to synthesize contemporary climate research and building science into design methods for guiding those experiments.

As they explained their adaptation of the term to architecture, the bioclimatic approach united "Climate, Biology, Technology, and Architecture" (Olgyay 1953a). Victor's paper outlined the steps of the bioclimatic method and illustrated it in a chart (Figure 11.2).

> The first step towards the solution is a survey of the climatic elements at a given location. The second, to analyze the bioclimatic impacts on man and to classify his needs. Third, to seek methods and means to satisfy those needs with technological solutions. And last, to find out how those solutions can be adapted and synthesized to architectural expressions.
>
> *(Olgyay 1953b)*

The first three steps each drew on current research into climate, comfort, and building thermal performance. The aspect that gave the "bioclimatic approach" particular value to the design community was the graphic nature of the tools. Victor took the lead in developing a "bioclimatic chart," while Aladar developed sun path diagrams and shading masks. In both cases, the charts and methods translated climate data into forms suitable for design strategies.

Solar Control

Weather observations have been collected for centuries, with more accurate measurements since at least the eighteenth century, but meteorologists rarely report the data in forms useful for design analysis. Architects need solar data that explains the amounts of heat and light impinging on windows and walls of all different orientations. It was a challenge of both data collection and computation, for which researchers developed new methods through the period. *Design with Climate* employed the solar data compiled by the American Institute of Architects (AIA; 1950) and the "equidistant" method of solar projection promoted by Libbey-Owens-Ford with the Sun Angle Calculator they began distributing in the mid-1940s (LOF 1946, 1951). That projection required the translation of orthogonal building elements into the curves of the projection, but the result is a visually compact diagram that simultaneously represents solar positions and the shading effects of the building and its surroundings.

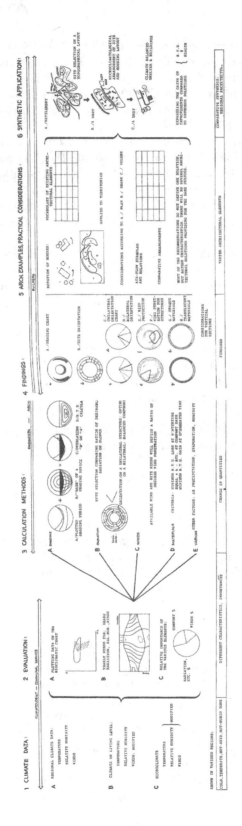

Figure 11.2 Victor Olgyay, bioclimatic method of "climate interpretation in housing."
Source: Building Research Advisory Board (BRAB), *Conference Report #5: Housing and Building in Hot-Humid and Hot-Dry Climates*, 1953 (public domain)

Figure 11.3 shows a "Globoscope" developed by a Swedish architect to photographically project urban surroundings onto the circular sun path diagram (Olgyay and Olgyay 1957, 47).

In practice, the elements of a shading device are projected onto the sun path diagram, creating a "shading mask" to identify the periods when direct sunlight is blocked. However, the technique can only project shading elements onto a single point of the window or building, making the method static and the choice of the point critical. As testament to the popularity of the technique and its limitation, many buildings from this era have overhangs that precisely cast shadows to the middle of the base of the window on the summer solstice at noon because that was an easily identified peak condition. Ed Mazria further popularized the approach in the 1970s using a projection onto an unfolded cylinder, which made the evaluation of rectilinear components more intuitive, but necessarily retained the single point of projection (Mazria 1980).

The digital methods of solar analysis used in current practice effectively repeat the projections used in shading masks over all the points of the building and all the moments of the year. The data is then synthesized to determine total hours of solar penetration and total amounts of heat transmitted by a window. The overhang that shades the bottom of the window on the solstice does not usually provide the most overall shading, and contemporary digital methods, such as Ladybug Tools, facilitate the exploration of many variations to find an optimum (Ladybug 2019). The new methods build on the principles summarized by the Olgyays, but also establish new modes of practice often disconnected from the geometric understanding of those principles. The original LOF calculator was recently re-published by the Society of Building Science Educators (SBSE) as a teaching tool, making the point that design practices themselves are part of the terrestrial complexity of predicting future microclimates in buildings (SBSE 2019).

Figure 11.3 Aladar and Victor Olgyay, Globoscope, showing the projection of sun angles and adjacent buildings onto a circular sun path diagram.
Source: Solar Control & Shading Devices. Copyright © 1957, CCC Republication

Bioclimatic Chart

Analyzing the rest of the climate data—temperature, humidity, and wind speed—presents a different challenge than solar angles and shading. Despite the graphic elegance of the AIA Regional Climate charts, the raw data offers little design advice. One of the enduring contributions of *Design with Climate* was the bioclimatic chart, which graphically links climate data to human comfort and architectural strategies (Figure 11.4). Like previous charts, the axes of the chart are temperature and relative humidity, with a summer and winter zone of comfortable conditions outlined at the center. Notations around the comfort zone show the levels of solar radiation, wind speeds, and/or evaporative cooling needed to mitigate climatic conditions that occur outside the zone of comfort. For example, it recommends shading for ambient conditions above a line at 70°F (21°C), and additional air movement above about 82°F (28°C).

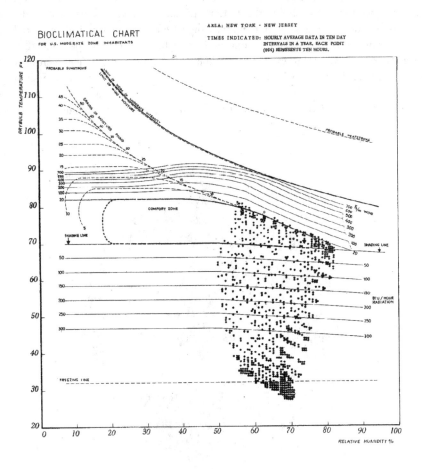

Figure 11.4 Victor Olgyay, bioclimatic chart with average hourly data for New York climate.
Source: Building Research Advisory Board (BRAB), *Conference Report #5: Housing and Building in Hot-Humid and Hot-Dry Climates*, 1953 (public domain)

The bioclimatic chart was a dramatic advance on the reporting of climate data for designers, and the approach remains the most common method of presenting and analyzing climate data in preparation for design. Tools like the "Climate Consultant" use the psychrometric chart developed by Willis Carrier as a base, but otherwise follow the logic of the original bioclimatic chart, outlining different environmental design strategies based on the hours of climate conditions in a given location—hot and dry, cold, moist, etc. (UCLA 2019). Starting in the 1980s, hourly weather files of a Typical Meteorological Year (TMY) were assembled using real weather data from different years combined to reproduce the long-term averages of temperature and sunlight (NSRDB 2015). Bioclimatic analysis now mostly relies on this TMY data, which forms a virtual "climate" for digital performance simulation.

By itself, climate analysis embodies most of the intentions of the bioclimatic approach, and since it is readily conducted at the beginning of design, it has had the largest impact on design decisions. The more challenging project the Olgyays worked on through the 1950s was to evaluate the "heliothermic" effect of architectural modifications on the interior climate of a building.

Heliothermic Planning

The aspect of *Design with Climate* that has advanced most significantly since the mid-twentieth century is the analysis needed to "establish an indoor environment which most nearly approaches comfort conditions in a given climatic setting" (Olgyay 1963, 126). The theories of heat transfer were well understood in the 1940s, but the challenge at the time was to keep the calculations manageable. In collaboration with faculty in mechanical engineering, they developed a testing chamber for scale models, called the Thermoheliodon, which reproduced air temperatures, wind speed, solar position, and solar intensity of specific climates (Figure 11.5). While solar angles and light levels are easily simulated in scale models, the transfer of heat through construction assemblies and the behavior of air at surfaces are very difficult to accurately reproduce at smaller scales. Heliodons that simulate solar position are still used today, but the analysis of heat transfer is almost entirely conducted with either digital simulations or full-scale test facilities.

Figure 11.5 Victor and Aladar Olgyay, Thermoheliodon for performance testing of physical models (circa 1963).

Credit: *Design with Climate: Bioclimatic Approach to Architectural Regionalism.* Copyright © 1963, CCC Republication

In *Design with Climate*, the Olgyays adopted the heat balance calculations approved by the American Society of Heating Ventilating and Air-Conditioning Engineers (ASHVE 1951). Using a measure designated as the "Sol-Air" temperature, they calculated the balance between heat driven by outside air temperatures and the constantly changing heat flux of sunlight. The calculations were performed manually for typical days in winter and summer and an "orthodox house" was used as a reference against which to compare improvements. They prepared studies for characteristic climates and used them to establish regionally specific design guidelines. They emphasized the "Sol-Air" effects on architectural surfaces, which required many simplifying assumptions about the other factors affecting the heat balance of even very simple houses, such as moisture loads, internal heat gains from people, lights, and equipment. Subsequent research has shown that those other factors have powerful thermal effects, especially in more complex building types (Ternoey et al. 1985).

The aspect of the bioclimatic approach that resonates most deeply with designers (and the public) since they first used the term is the visible linking of architectural form with its climate and region (Willis et al. 2016). The emblematic example is the sun shade, for which they cited Marcel Breuer to explain its architectural potential:

> The sun control device has to be on the outside of the building, an element of the façade, and element of architecture. And because this device is so important a part of our open architecture, it may develop into as characteristic a form as the Doric column.
>
> *(Olgyay and Olgyay 1957)*

Ultimately, their work encountered the same limitation as Hopkins' law. It is easier to establish an architectural law about the sun's movement than it is about the more complex "heliothermic" effects on people in buildings. We can precisely delineate the shadows from devices that block the sun, but many different factors determine the future comfort of occupants and most do not involve recognizable architectural form. Fernández-Galiano described it as "heliotechnical" versus "thermodynamic," the one based on clockwork regularity and the other involving the messy, irreversible unfolding of terrestrial life (2000).

The difference between the geometric clarity of sunshading devices and the many factors influencing architectural form may have contributed to Aladar's decision not to co-author *Design with Climate* (Leatherbarrow and Wesley 2014). As Victor explained in the introduction, Aladar's "work was concerned mainly with the subject of solar control" (v) and it was in their previous book, *Solar Control and Shading Devices*, that the possibility of a natural law in architecture was more explicitly allowed. In their polemical explanation of modern architecture, they made the case for a direct, bioclimatic correlation with built form.

> A recognition of the immensity of correlated order, the unalterable reign of basic laws which are manifested in the systems of the universe, could not remain unnoticed and unappreciated ... Here [in the modern movement] the module stems not from visual proportions, but is correlated with the movements of the sun and formulated to satisfy man's biological needs.
>
> *(1957, 4–5)*

Like the therapeutic and productive disciplines of medicine and agriculture, architecture works between "exact" and "biological" (and social and political) sciences. The architectural connection between climate and life cannot be reduced to an astronomical law; it is determined as much by context and history. The aspect of *Design with Climate* that bridged the gap between the two appears in step 5—"Arch Examples, Practical Considerations"—where scientific "Findings" were allowed to develop into a regional architecture.

Buildings and Power: Bioclimatic Hybrids

The term "climate" most commonly refers to temperature and humidity, which defined the bioclimatic chart, but it also includes the frequency and intensity of sunlight, wind, rain, clouds, dust, and all the other terrestrial conditions. Frank Lloyd Wright once asked Philip Johnson whether he was still "building houses and leaving them out in the rain," invoking the common critique of the International Style, that it was designed for a climate made perfect by HVAC equipment and so looked the same everywhere (Profile 1977). Bioclimatic design was one answer to that critique. It was both a response to the mid-century experience of rapid technological change and an invocation of vernacular construction. Pre-modern buildings had little alternative but to rely on building form and materials to provide comfort, though people also lived in quite different comfort regimes, with larger temperature swings and less control. Somewhat paradoxically, bioclimatic methods simultaneously recall the means of pre-modern architecture and strive to meet the modern standards of comfort created by mechanical conditioning.

It is more accurate to call contemporary buildings bioclimatic "hybrids." They combine the intentionally bioclimatic effects of building envelopes with the concentrated power of mechanical conditioning. Every architect decides which aspect to emphasize, and both aspects have had their champions. Through the 1960s Reyner Banham charted the radically new forms of building made possible by mechanical systems and challenged architects to discover the modernity made possible by tapping the new sources of power. His book of 1969, *The Architecture of the Well-Tempered Environment*, framed a fundamental question that troubled architects in that period of rapid change: whether to "expose" or "conceal" the ducts, pipes, wires, and machines that were invading the traditional body of architecture.

In contrast, the bioclimatic approach used the growing body of building science, mostly developed for HVAC systems, to understand the environmental effects of conventional building components. The importance of those lessons intensified as the amounts of glass in buildings increased through the twentieth century. Le Corbusier certainly learned his lesson at the Salvation Army building in Paris in 1933, for which he had proposed a "neutral wall" (*murs neutralisant*) to move a layer of tempered air between the glass sheets to neutralize the effects of the outside climate. However, the air conditioning (AC) for the interlayer was never installed and the building had to be retrofitted after the war with one of the *brise-soleil* (sun-breakers) that he developed in the 1930s and 1940s for his work in hotter climates. It is telling that the glass manufacturer LOF published the best tool of that period for analyzing the effects of sun on buildings (LOF 1946).

Bioclimatic design emerges from the historical context of rapid change in materials and methods of construction, the development of environmental conditioning, specialization of employment, and new patterns of transportation and settlement. As more sources of power became available and technologies developed to harness them, buildings grew in size, capacity, and variety, offering new capacities and internal environments. We can characterize the shifts in the logic of environmental design through four generations, roughly following the periodization proposed by Oldfield et al. in their "five energy generations of tall buildings" (Oldfield, Trabucco and Antony 2009). They focused on high-rise construction, but the factors marking their periodization are nearly universal in their effect.

The first environmental generation begins in the late nineteenth century, with the delivery of central heating, the arrival of gas and then electric lighting, and the combination of the steel frame, elevators, mass-produced furniture, the telegraph and telephone, and the whole panoply of modern "comforts." However, even the largest buildings of this period still relied on windows for daylight, ventilation, and cooling. Usable work space could only occur near a window, so even large buildings included courtyards, light-shafts, and re-entrants, and were configured in H- and E-plans, to maintain direct connection with ambient light and air. Innovations such as Luxfer Prism Glass were used to increase the depth of building plans that could be reached by daylight, but their effect was still measured in feet (Neumann 1995). Intricate floor plans also resulted in greater amounts of exterior surface area, so heat losses and energy consumption were correspondingly larger. The conditions of interior environments were also more variable, especially in warmer seasons, demanding more flexibility of clothing and scheduling.

The seeds of the second environmental generation began with the development of AC in the early decades of the twentieth century, first for industrial environments and movie houses. Buildings such as the Larkin Building in Buffalo (1906), the Milam in San Antonio (1929), and PSFS in Philadelphia (1932) pioneered the incorporation of AC in office buildings and explored the effects of greater environmental control. However, those buildings still had moderate window-to-wall ratios and floor plates kept thin for daylighting. The period of oil supply anxieties of the late 1940s briefly inspired a group of architects, including the Olgyay brothers, to understand the energy basis for the new technologies, but the discovery of Middle East oil ended most of the public concern about energy.

Generational transitions happen in stages. Designers were experimenting with larger areas of glass through the 1930s and 1940s, which in turn demanded shading or powerful AC systems. The second generation became fully possible with development of heat-absorbing glass to reduce solar heat gain. Lever House (1952) was the first curtain wall with the new glass and the Olgyays explicitly contrasted it to the expressive brise-soleil of Le Corbusier's Unité d'habitation (Konrad et al. 1995). The new generation of larger curtain-wall buildings were not simply caused by AC, heat-absorbing glass, fluorescent lighting, or ready sources of power; the new technologies facilitated the greater concentration of people and wealth in expanding urban centers.

From high-rise office buildings to retail malls and warehouses, the second generation explored the environmental possibilities of architectural space independent of windows. Newly precise standards of thermal comfort were developed for sedentary work, while electric lighting led to wholly novel interior conditions. Building energy consumption rose steadily through the 1950s and 1960s; most of the new buildings required AC all year to manage the heat gains produced by their glazing, compact forms, and higher lighting levels, and the many newly electrified devices.

The oil supply crises of the 1970s precipitated a third generation of environmental design, alerting designers and clients to the dependence of the new forms of building on a steady supply of concentrated energy. The first building energy codes were published and adopted in the mid-1970s and their approach came to define a new generation of buildings (Hunn 2010). The general format adopted at the time of the crisis was to develop energy performance standards on a component basis, rather than with overall performance goals, and that approach still dominates energy performance regulation in buildings. The effect has been to produce a generation of buildings that maintain modern standards of comfort and the general form and attitude of the second generation, but with more efficient components and assemblies. Incremental energy codes precisely define the environmental qualities of the third generation.

The new awareness also alerted architects to the energy "embodied" in the materials of buildings. Richard Stein first reported on the energy intensity of building materials in his book of 1977, *Architecture and Energy*. His information was limited to the broad categories used in national input–output data, and he complained that they did "not begin to tell us the differences in energy use within a category—between extruded aluminum and sheet aluminum, for example" (Stein 1977). Writing soon after that, Fernández-Galiano called it the "fire that builds the building," and despaired over the lack of precision or agreement among methods for determining embodied energies in construction (Fernández-Galiano 1991, 2013). The situation has improved since then with the development of life-cycle assessment (LCA) for manufacturing, and there are now multiple, industry-specific databases of information. Synthesizing tools like Tally integrate LCA data with architectural workflows, helping answer the new kind of performance question posed by Stein: "Is it more responsible to use a long-lasting material or one with lower initial impact?" (KTA 2019).

Searching for a "Bioclimatic Law"

The oil supply crises of the 1970s inspired another group of architects and engineers to experiment with alternate approaches to building design and they laid the foundation for a fourth environmental generation. Many drew on the foundational work of the 1940s, but the urgency of the crisis changed the terms of the original bioclimatic approach, shifting it from regional expression to energy consumption. Banham's preference for power-consuming devices to move heat around was designated "active," while the adjustment of walls, windows, and shading devices to control the interior climate was called "passive" (Balcomb 1982). That characterization lost much of the architectural nuance of the original bioclimatic approach, reducing it to a binary judgement about the use of fuels.

Oldfield et al. identified the Commerzbank in Frankfurt of 1997 as the beginning of the fourth generation, in which designers and clients sought to achieve better energy performance than required by third generation codes. The United Nations Climate Change Conference in Kyoto of the same year might be a more general indicator of the new phase of thinking. Like the transition to the third generation, it begins in the previous decades with experimental projects, and involved a variety of different ambitions, including local environmental impacts, global climate change, energy independence, and ecological balance. The variety is illustrated by the many standards that have developed since then to push buildings to better environmental performance: USGBC (LEED), Living Building Challenge (ILFI 2016), Architecture 2030, EPA Energy Star, the Passive House Standard, and Net-Zero Energy, to name only a few. The majority of buildings are still designed to meet minimum code standards, so the third and fourth generations coexist, with activists steadily pushing the mandatory and aspirational codes to converge.

The increasing urgency of climate change, the wide array of environmental approaches, and the advances in "smart" systems have steadily blurred the simple opposition between active and passive that came to characterize bioclimatic methods in the 1970s. Over the century since mechanical equipment first entered buildings, the two have slowly hybridized into active–passive intermixtures that would have excited (or scandalized) Banham: active glass walls, thermal chimneys, responsive shading,

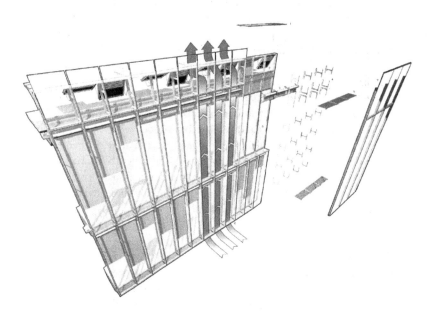

Figure 11.6 Active Glass Wall, with internal shading and a moving layer of conditioned air.
Source: Copyright 2015 Jeffrey Craig Vaglio

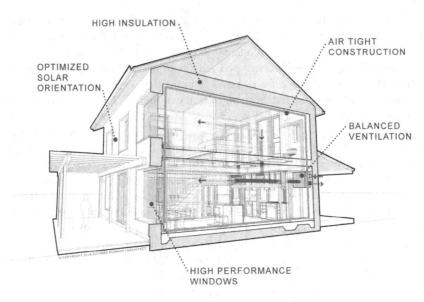

Figure 11.7 Passive House construction, showing super-insulated wall construction with controlled ventilation system.
Source: Copyright 2019 Richard Pedranti Architect

and electrochromic glazing, to name only a few. In contemporary architectural practices, bioclimatic analysis is typically a first step in the design of high-performance buildings that not only incorporate HVAC equipment, but use sophisticated feedback and control systems to activate formerly passive elements.

Methods for producing a regional architecture have largely become a matter of stylistic emphasis, foregrounding traditionally passive elements to produce signifiers of environmental action. The polemical opposition between active, power-consuming machines and passive, bioclimatic architectural components reappears as a weak terminology describing fully hybridized assemblies. For example, the "Passive" House standard, which began with experiments in super-insulated construction in the 1970s (Shurcliff 1980), is linguistically opposed to "Active" Glass Walls, the much refined, contemporary manifestation of Le Corbusier's neutral wall (Braham 2005). The thick walls and modest windows of passive house construction contrast with the total transparency of doubled, active glass walls with their invisible layer of moving air (Figures 11.6 and 11.7). Both modes of construction rely on sophisticated control systems that regulate shading devices, air movement, and heat from mechanical devices, and both aim for very low energy consumption. Neither could be called bioclimatic in the original sense, though both mediate in sophisticated ways between climate and human comfort. We need to think more comprehensively about bioclimatic methods to account for these hybrid forms of construction, which requires a deeper inquiry into the original premise about comfort.

Comfort at Work

Bioclimatic design uses thermal comfort as the performance criterion for design, shifting the performance goal from the amounts of power consumed by mechanical equipment to the effect on the interior climate. That goal applies whether the passive elements are activated or whether the HVAC equipment is central to climatic management. This is often the most significant environmental performance decision architects can make, placing the emphasis on the climatic effect of their formal decisions.

On its face, comfort seems a weak criterion for architectural design. As expressed in the dominant regulatory standard, "[t]hermal comfort is the condition of mind that expresses satisfaction with the thermal environment and is assessed by subjective evaluation" (ASHRAE 2017). In practical terms, it measures the reported absence of uncomfortable sensations in different interior conditions, which can vary tremendously among people with different amounts of clothing or levels of activity. Following the method developed by P.O. Fanger in the 1960s, the standard method predicts the percentage of people who will be dissatisfied in particular conditions of temperature and humidity. But Fanger well understood its architectural implications: "creating thermal comfort for man is a primary purpose of the heating and air conditioning industry, and this has had a radical influence on the construction of buildings, the choice of materials, etc." (Fanger 1972).

Modern research to measure human thermal comfort arose to support the deployment of HVAC equipment. It began in earnest in the 1920s, focusing on the conditions of temperature and relative humidity that would produce an experience of equal comfort (with other factors constant). Houghton and Yagloglou drew a zone of comfortable conditions on the psychrometric chart, producing the basic elements eventually used in Olgyay's Bioclimatic Chart (Houghten and Yagloglou 1923). A.P. Gagge expanded on their work at the J.B. Pierce Laboratory of Hygiene at Yale, a foundation conceived by the founder of the American Radiator Company. Based on laboratory tests, Gagge developed a "two-node" thermodynamic model of the human body, which successfully modelled the way it exchanges heat with the environment (Gagge 1936).

The first question this generation of comfort research raises is whether we are trying to make building environments or the people inside them comfortable. As Fanger pointed out, for any fixed set of conditions someone will always be uncomfortable. Or, as Van Hoof observed, thermal comfort for all can only be achieved when occupants have effective control over their own thermal environment (Van Hoof 2008). However accurate the models of heat exchange, the question of comfort is inseparable from people's activities and their social and economic context, which involve a tremendous variety of levels of exertion, clothing, and local adaptation. Modern thermal comfort ultimately originates as a technique for enhancing the productivity of new kinds of work in new kinds of buildings.

The connection between work and climate is written deeply into bioclimatic methods. The example that the Olgyays used to explain thermal comfort was a chart reproduced from Ellsworth Huntington's *Civilization and Climate* of 1924 (154), which charted the productivity of factory workers in Connecticut and Pittsburgh month-by-month from 1910 to 1913 (Figure 11.8). The chart shows peaks of productivity in the fall and spring, with the lowest levels in the depths of winter and summer. The chart also includes a second set of mortality data for the same locations, inverted so that reductions in mortality rates appear as peaks of "health," and the two sets of curves mirror each other persuasively. People in the mid-Atlantic appear to be healthiest and most productive in the mild conditions of fall and spring.

Huntington's productivity data was drawn from many sources—piece work in hardware manufacturing and cotton weaving; weight gain of tubercular patients; the strength of military students, carpenters, and cigar makers—which he used to demonstrate the connection between specific climate conditions and successful civilizations. The first point to make is that the correlations he shows are to outside temperatures, not those in the workplace. The research occurred before modern climate control, certainly before AC, and often in extreme work environments like the drawing of hot brass. Second, his data also shows greater productivity with changes in temperature. The factory workers in Connecticut and Pittsburgh performed best when the outside temperature dropped by 10°F over a day, while students at the military academies and cigar makers in Tampa did best on days when the temperature dropped by 5°F (Huntington 1915, 140). This anticipated current research which indicates that people prefer variations in conditions rather than the constant conditions of ideal comfort (Schellen et al. 2010).

Recent research on comfort has been more alert to the lived experience of comfort—its terrestrial complications as opposed to its universal laws—and to the differences among people and their environments. "Adaptive" comfort standards marked a tremendous advance in the field, formalizing the commonsense observation that expectations for indoor comfort conditions change seasonally with outdoor temperatures (de Dear, Brager, and Cooper 1997). People regularly adapt to current conditions and through numerous field experiments the researchers codified those adaptations. Similar paths of research have examined the intimate experiences of temperature, and new techniques for personal or micro-control of comfort. Personal comfort research crosses the divide between clothing and buildings, technologies that both modify climates and create powerful cultural symbols of their power. Geiger classed them together as "conscious modifications" of the microclimate, citing examples ranging from the thermal analysis of clothing in Büttner's book on physical bioclimatology to research on the "bed-climate," each of which should remind us of the sophistication and subtlety with which humans have been managing their climate for millennia. He reproduced a "thermohygrograph" of temperature and humidity recorded next to a soldier's skin through a regular day of activity to demonstrate the dramatic range of conditions experienced in real activity (Geiger 1950) (Figure 11.9).

Charts published by the Olgyay's collaborator, Maria Telkes, show correlations between worker productivity and the temperatures they actually experienced (Telkes 1953). Charts of winter and summer "discomfort curves" determined in the laboratory exhibit very clear minima for sedentary subjects at around 70°F (21°C). In contrast, the productivity of US and German miners peaks at 50°F (10°C) and only begins to decline above 75°F (24°C). The preference for specific ranges of temperatures really depends on what people are doing, and the neutral terminology of "clo" and "met" (clothing and metabolic levels) used in comfort research obscures the dramatic historical change in working conditions and expectations about comfort to which they contributed. In 1900, 40% of the US population still worked directly on farms, with a total of 60% in rural communities, where outdoor work dominated. Another 20% worked in manufacturing, 6% in construction, 4% in transportation, and 6% as domestics, so only a minority at the beginning of the century engaged in activities where the narrow range of sedentary comfort would apply (Lebergott 1966). By 1960, or course, only 8%

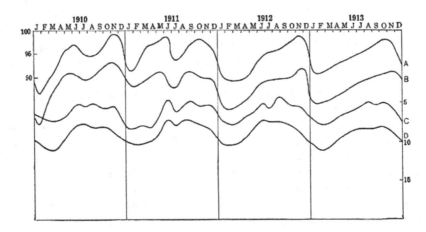

Figure 11.8 Seasonal variations in health and efficiency. A. Work of factory operatives in Connecticut. B. Work of factory operatives in Pennsylvania. C. Health (death rate inverted) in Connecticut. D. Health (death rate inverted) in Pennsylvania.

Source: *Civilization and Climate*, 1924. Copyright © Yale University Press

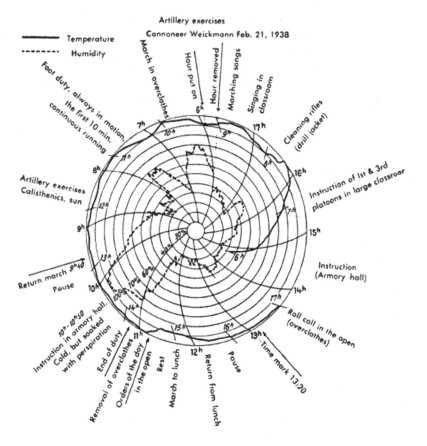

Figure 11.9 Temperature and humidity recordings of the microclimate over the skin.
Source: *Das Klima der bodennahen Luftschicht.* Copyright © 1942, Springer Fachmedien Wiesbaden

were still on the farm, with another 42% in some form of active and/or outdoor employment, so 50% were now sitting down to work in the new indoor climates.

The methods of *Design with Climate* were primarily developed for houses, though the examples in *Solar Control and Shading Devices* include many commercial buildings. Houses witnessed a similar transformation in kinds of activity through the century, and the new living arrangements were critical to the new architecture. The many forms of physical labor common in pre-modern households were steadily outsourced to factories and food processing facilities or "industrialized" with electric powered, labor-saving devices (Cowan 1983). As a result, houses have also become locations for more sedentary forms of work and leisure, involving similarly narrow standards of comfort as office buildings.

Through the last century, in both houses and offices, new kinds of indoor work co-evolved with newly specialized buildings, based on sedentary standards of comfort, and the technologies to provide them. In effect, contemporary buildings make us more comfortable so we can work more productively sitting down. A common observation about office building performance is that the cost of keeping the building comfortable is negligible compared to the salaries paid to those who work inside. A great deal of recent research has been devoted to evaluating the effect of thermal and luminous comfort on occupant productivity, directly recalling Huntington's work, tracking measurable factors like sick days or work products (Akimoto et al. 2010).

But perhaps we are mistaking effects for causes. Instead of improving buildings to enhance work, we can see available forms of work as a local condition that makes specific forms of building necessary. Just as a hot, dry climate demands shading or AC, so a contemporary economy demands particular kinds of office buildings. We build buildings in cities because of the economic opportunities of proximity and agglomeration, not because of the local weather. Is not population density or economic opportunity a part of the macroclimate that buildings negotiate to produce an effective microclimate?

An Expanded Bioclimatic Approach

In contemporary practices, bioclimatic design has largely become a method of pre-design analysis, most valuable for establishing effective thermal design strategies early in the process. In explicitly passive projects, the use of comfort as a performance goal keeps projects focused on the climatic effects of architectural elements. The fact that comfort is also the design standard for HVAC systems undermines the clarity of that distinction, and the most prominent result is usually external shading devices that make bioclimatic analysis visible. The active–passive fixation on fuel use and the continued opposition between buildings and machines limits the degree to which bioclimatic methods can really guide the design of the hybrid elements common in contemporary construction.

What we need is a bioclimatic method that connects climate analysis with the complexities of life as it is lived and buildings as they are used, not a nostalgic law for an imagined passive vernacular. The promise of bioclimatic design is not simply to reduce energy use, but to establish principles for an architecture of its place and time, which is currently an urbanized civilization encountering the uncertainties of climate change and the transition to renewable resources. We can prepare for that by expanding our analysis of the climate to include all the resources and capacities available in the local environment, from renewable sources and microclimatic potentials to utility infrastructures and economic potential. Instead of the stark, active–passive opposition or fuel-based carbon accounting, we should base bioclimatic analysis on an environmental accounting of all the resources and capacities available at a site, accounting for their upstream and downstream effects.

Figure 11.10 illustrates a more complete bioclimatic analysis, using the energy systems language to identify and evaluate the environmental intensity of the capacities available at a particular building site (Odum 1996; Braham 2016). Renewable resources have a low environmental intensity, but are also low in power and limited in rates of delivery. Conversely, more concentrated, higher-powered resources, like fuels, electricity, and refined materials, have much higher environmental intensities. This diagram describes the capacities of the local environment available to manage the flows of heat to its occupants, which we could call thermal "affordances" to use Gibson's descriptive term (Gibson 1986).

An expanded bioclimatic analysis combines purchased, operational energies with the "embodied" energies of construction, the many environmental resources that support local environments, and even the labor performed inside buildings, which brings us back to comfort as a performance standard for design. If comfort is the microclimatic condition of maximum human productivity, then bioclimatic design seeks the balance of factors that provide that condition with the lowest environmental intensity. A shading device with a smart controller or a thermal storage wall managed by a heat pump may outperform a purely passive approach.

This more comprehensive bioclimatic analysis reveals the hierarchies of environmental intensity that already exist in buildings. Lower-quality resources, such as sunlight or wood, are used in larger quantities to provide much of the climate modification, while higher-quality resources, such as spectrally selective glass, photovoltaic electricity, or smart control systems, are used in smaller quantities to achieve higher levels of control over comfort. In current construction those hierarchies arise because

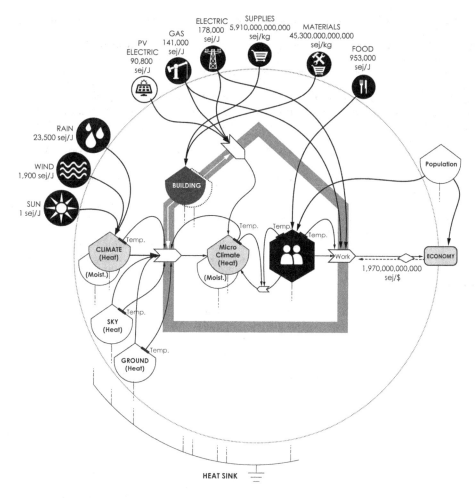

Figure 11.10 Energy systems language diagram of expanded bioclimatic analysis, showing multiple pathways for regulating thermal comfort and their total environmental cost expressed in solar em-joules (sej).

Source: Copyright 2019 William W. Braham

of economic costs, which dramatically undervalue environmental work and resources. Expanding the bioclimatic approach to include all the environmental costs offers a more comprehensive performance method, one that can provide architectural guidance about degrees of technology, the use of fuels, the refinement of materials, and the longevity of assemblies. It would take us from the astronomical aspiration for laws to terrestrial principles of a living architecture.

References

AIA. 1950. *Regional Climate Analysis and Design Data: The House Beautiful Climate Control Project*. Washington, DC: American Institute of Architects.

Akimoto, Takashi, Shin-ichi Tanabe, Takashi Yanai, and Masato Sasaki. 2010. "Thermal Comfort and Productivity: Evaluation of Workplace Environment in a Task Conditioned Office." *Building and Environment* 45 (1):45–50. doi:10.1016/j.buildenv.2009.06.022.

Araújo, Miguel B., and A. Townsend Peterson. 2012. "Uses and Misuses of Bioclimatic Envelope Modeling." *Ecology* 93 (7):1527–1539.

ASHRAE. 2017. *Thermal Environmental Conditions for Human Occupancy. ANSI/ASHRAE Standard 55-2013*. Atlanta, GA: American Society of Heating Refrigerating and Air-Conditioning Engineers.

ASHVE. 1951. *Heating, Ventilating, Air-Conditioning Guide*. New York, NY: American Society of Heating and Ventilating Engineers.

Balcomb, J. Douglas. 1982. *Passive Solar Design Handbook*. Vol. 3. Washington, DC: US Department of Energy.

Banham, Reyner. 1969. *The Architecture of the Well-Tempered Environment*. Chicago, IL: University of Chicago Press.

Barber, Daniel A. 2016. *A House in the Sun: Modern Architecture and Solar Energy in the Cold War*. New York, NY: Oxford University Press.

Braham, William W. 2005. Active Glass Walls: A Typological and Historical Account. Las Vegas, NV: AIA National Convention.

Braham, William W. 2016. *Architecture and Systems Ecology: Thermodynamic Principles for Environmental Building Design*. New York, NY: Routledge.

Büttner, K. 1938. *Physikalische Bioklimatologie. Probleme und Methoden*. Leipzig: Akademische Verlagsgesellschaft.

Cowan, Ruth Schwartz. 1983. *More Work for Mother: The Ironies of Household Technology from the Open Hearth to the Microwave*. New York, NY: Basic Books.

de Dear, Richard, Gail Brager, and Donna Cooper. 1997. "Developing an Adaptive Model of Thermal Comfort and Preference." *ASHRAE RP-884*: Macquarie Research, Center for Environmental Design Research, ASHRAE.

Fanger, P.O. 1972. *Thermal Comfort: Analysis and Applications in Environmental Engineering*. New York, NY: McGraw-Hill.

Fernández-Galiano, Luis. 1991. *El fuego y la memoria: sobre arquitectura y energía*. Madrid: Alianza.

Fernández-Galiano, Luis. 2000. *Fire and Memory: On Architecture and Energy*. Cambridge, MA: MIT Press.

Fernández-Galiano, Luis. 2013. "Architecture and Life." In *Architecture and Energy: Performance and Style*, edited by William Braham and Daniel Willis, 25–48. New York, NY: Routledge.

Furniss, Malcolm M. 2010. "Beginnings of American Forest Entomology: The Role of Andrew Delmar Hopkins (1857–1948)." *American Entomologist* 56 (2):78–87. doi:10.1093/ae/56.2.78.

Gagge, A.P. 1936. "The Linearity Criterion as Applied to Partitional Calorimetry." *American Journal of Physiology* 116 (3):656–668. doi:10.1152/ajplegacy.1936.116.3.656.

Geerts, Bart. 2000. "Climate Classification: A Historical Perspective." www-das.uwyo.edu/~geerts/cwx/notes/chap16/clim_class.html.

Geiger, Rudolf. 1950. *The Climate Near the Ground*. Cambridge, MA: Published for Blue Hill Meteorological Observatory, Harvard University, by Harvard University Press.

Gibson, James J. 1986. *The Ecological Approach to Visual Perception*. Hillsdale, NJ: Lawrence Erlbaum Associates.

Hopkins, Andrew D. 1918. *Periodical Events and Natural Law as Guides to Agricultural Research and Practice*. Vol. Supplement No. 9, *Monthly Weather Review*. Washington, DC: US Department of Agriculture, Weather Bureau.

Hopkins, Andrew D. 1924. "Notes on the Bioclimatic Law." *Nature* 114 (2869):608–609. doi:10.1038/114608a0.

Hopkins, Andrew D. 1938. *Bioclimatics, a Science of Life and Climate Relations*. Washington, DC: United States Department of Agriculture.

Houghten, F.C., and C.P. Yagloglou. 1923. "Determination of the Comfort Zone." *ASHVE Transactions* 29.

Hunn, Bruce D. 2010. "35 Years of Standard 90.1." *ASHRAE Journal* 53 (2):36–46.

Huntington, Ellsworth. 1915. *Civilization and Climate*. New Haven, NJ: Yale University Press, etc.

ILFI. 2016. *Living Building Challenge 3.1: A Visionary Path to a Restorative Future*. Seattle, WA: International Living Future Institute.

Konrad, K., K. Wilson, W. Nugent, and F. Calabrese. 1995. "Plate Glass." In *Twentieth-Century Building Materials: History and Conservation*, edited by Thomas C. Jester. New York, NY: McGraw-Hill.

Köppen, W.P., and R. Geiger. 1930. *Handbuch der Klimatologie*. Stuttgart: Gebrüder Borntraeger.

KTA. 2019. "Tally. Edited by Kieran Timberlake Architects." https://choosetally.com/.

Ladybug. 2019. "Ladybug Tools." www.ladybug.tools/.

Leatherbarrow, David, and Richard Wesley. 2014. "Performance and Style in the Work of Olgyay and Olgyay." *Architectural Research Quarterly* 18 (2):167–176. doi:10.1017/S1359135514000475.

Lebergott, Stanley. 1966. "Labor Force and Employment, 1800—1960." In *Output, Employment, and Productivity in the United States after 1800*, edited by Dorothy S. Brady, 117–204. Cambridge, MA: National Bureau of Economic Research.

LOF. 1946. *How to Use the Sun-Angle Calculator: Application of the Sun's Angular Values to the Design of Buildings*. Toledo, OH: Libbey-Owens-Ford.

LOF. 1951. "LOF Sun Angle Calculator." *Architectural Record* 109 (April): 171.

Mazria, Ed. 1980. *The Passive Solar Energy Book*. Emmaus, PA: Rodale Press.

Neumann, Dietrich. 1995. "'The Century's Triumph in Lighting:' The Luxfer Prism Companies and their Contribution to Early Modern Architecture." *Journal of the Society of Architectural Historians* (March):24–53.

NSRDB. 2015. "National Solar Radiation Data Base 1991–2005 Update: Typical Meteorological Year 3." Edited by National Renewable Energy Lab.

Odum, Howard T. 1996. *Environmental Accounting: Energy and Environmental Decision Making*. New York, NY: Wiley.

Oldfield, Philip, Dario Trabucco, and Antony Wood. 2009. "Five Energy Generations of Tall Buildings: An Historical Analysis of Energy Consumption in High-rise Buildings." *Journal of Architecture* 14 (5):591–613.

Olgyay, Aladar. 1953a. "Solar Control and Orientation to Meet Bioclimatical Requirements." *BRAB Conference Report #5: Housing and Building in Hot-Humid and Hot-Dry Climates*.

Olgyay, Aladar, and Victor Olgyay. 1957. *Solar Control & Shading Devices*. Princeton, NJ: Princeton University Press.

Olgyay, Victor. 1953b. "Bioclimatic Approach to Architecture." *BRAB Conference Report #5: Housing and Building in Hot-Humid and Hot-Dry Climates*.

Olgyay, Victor. 1963. *Design with Climate: Bioclimatic Approach to Architectural Regionalism – Some Chapters Based on Cooperative Research with Aladar Olgyay*. Princeton, NJ: Princeton University Press.

Olgyay, Victor, and Aladar Olgyay. 1946. *Architects Olgyay & Olgyay*. Budapest: Budai I.

Profile. 1977. "Forms Under Light." *New Yorker*, May 23.

Rohwer, S. A. 1950. "Andrew Delmar Hopkins, 1857–1948." *Proceedings of the Entomological Society of Washington*. 52: 21–26.

SBSE. 2019. "LOF Sun Angle Calculator." Society of Building Science Educators. www.sbse.org/sun-angle-calculator.

Schellen, L. Lisje, W. D. van Marken Lichtenbelt, M. Loomans, J. Toftum, and M. H. de Wit. 2010. "Differences between Young Adults and Elderly in Thermal Comfort, Productivity, and Thermal Physiology in Response to a Moderate Temperature Drift and a Steady-State Condition." *Indoor Air* 20 (4):273.

Shurcliff, William. 1980. *Superinsulated Houses and Double-Envelope Houses: A Preliminary Survey of Principles and Practice*, 2nd edition. Cambridge, MA: William A. Shurcliff.

Simon, Maron J. 1947. *Your Solar House: A Book of Practical Homes for All Parts of the Country*. New York, NY: Simon & Schuster.

Stein, Richard G. 1977. *Architecture and Energy*. New York, NY: Anchor Press/Doubleday.

Telkes, Maria. 1953. "Warmth for Comfort." In *Centennial of Engineering: History and Proceedings of Symposia 1852–1952*, edited by R. Lenox, 926–941. Chicago, IL: Museum of Science and Industry.

Ternoey, Steven, Larry Bickle, Claude L. Robbins, Robert Busch, and Kit McCord. 1985. *The Design of Energy Responsive Commercial Buildings*. New York, NY: Solar Energy Research Institute/Wiley-Interscience.

UCLA. 2019. "Climate Consultant." www.energy-design-tools.aud.ucla.edu/climate-consultant/.

USGBC. "Green Building Leadership is LEED." http://new.usgbc.org/leed.

Van Hoof, J. 2008. "Forty Years of Fanger's Model of Thermal Comfort: Comfort for all?" *Indoor Air* 18 (3):182–201. doi:10.1111/j.1600-0668.2007.00516.x.

Willis, Daniel, William W. Braham, Katsuhiko Muramoto, and Daniel A. Barber. 2016. *Energy Accounts: Architectural Representations of Energy, Climate, and the Future*. New York, NY: Routledge.

12
Ecological Emergences
The Milieu for Performative Paradigms

Caroline O'Donnell

Though close to synonymous in common parlance, *performance* and *function* have two very divergent implications as architectural terms. And while the relationship between architecture and function is well established, the relationship between architecture and performance is fresher. The distinction between the two, perhaps, is in the productive relationship with context.

Biological Functionalism

In his definition of architectural functionalism, historian and theorist Adrian Forty (2004) charts the etymology of the term "function." In tracking a workable definition of functionalism specifically for architecture, Forty rediscovers a biological link in the term's point of origin.

Early in the nineteenth century, the argument between structuralism and functionalism in biology emerged through various opposing terms: *order* vs. *purpose*; *formalism* vs. *functionalism*; *order* vs. *teleology*; *form* vs. *adaptation*; and perhaps most tellingly, Étienne Geoffroy Saint-Hilaire's Unity of Type vs. Georges Cuvier's Conditions of Existence (Gould 2002, p. 261).

The fundamentality of the form–function debate is nicely summarized in the 1869 publication, *Typical Forms and Special Ends in Creation*, whose Greek inscription on the title page, *typose lai telos* (type and purpose), summarizes the thrust of the argument. A description of the simultaneity and inevitability of the two poles in 1869 is as relevant to architecture today as it was to evolution theory of the time:

> The one is the Principle of Order, or a general plan, pattern or type, to which every given object is made to conform with more or less precision. The other is the Principle of Special Adaptation, or particular end, by which each object, while constructed after a general model is, at the same time accommodated to the situation which it has to occupy, and a purpose which it is intended to serve. These two principles ... meet in the structure of every plant and every animal.
>
> *(McCosh & Dickie, 1869, p. 1).*

Whatever the terminology, the formalists believed that biological form had a specific and limited ability to carry out particular functions, which, if successful, resulted in the survival of the organism. On the contrary, functionalists argued that function was primary in survival, and that form adapted to allow functionality to occur.

Lamarck and Darwin, despite their differences, were both functionalists who believed that it was the function of the organism responding to changing environmental circumstances that defined the form. In defense of functionalism, few were as adamant as Georges Cuvier, who understood organisms as "discrete, untransformable entities, designed for specific conditions of life and no other" (Cuvier 1800–1805, pp. 45–60). For Cuvier, a carnivore's sharp teeth and claws were necessary for its survival. Nothing was superfluous. So strong was his conviction, in fact, that Cuvier opposed the idea of continuous evolution (a trajectory that was later to be taken up by William Bateson), due to the lack of functionality that was inevitable between states of high function, as well as the impossibility of all related components transforming simultaneously.[1]

On the contrary to previous catalogs which focused on formal characteristics,[2] Cuvier's *Leçons d'Anatomie Comparée* (1800–1805) reorganized the typical taxonomic order of the natural history catalog and instead considered organ systems in operational (versus morphological) terms. Rather than classifying bodily organs by the criteria of appearance and position, Cuvier thought it more accurate to first identify a given organ's "function" within the larger body of the organism and then determine its place in the system, in order to understand the relationship of an organ to the sum of its parts. The collection is thus organized by a series of actions or functions instead of objects or forms, beginning with locomotion, and followed by sensation, digestion, circulation, respiration, voice, generation, and finally, excretion.

Inspired by Cuvier and Geoffrey's debate, a group of architects (called the "Romantic Pensionnaires" due to their all having stayed at the same prestigious residency) including Labrouste, Le Duc, Vaudoer, Duban, in the 1830s rejected the architecture of the ancients that had been taught to them at the École de Beaux Arts, in favor of an architecture derived from functional adaptation via technology. This group preferred, shockingly, gothic architecture, which, they believed was better aligned with nature. Vaudoyer (1839), for example, saw the gothic cathedral and the forest as analogous:

> the same conditions of existence being necessary to the work of man as to that of nature, one had to proceed in matters of construction on obeyance to the laws of nature, that is, to have vertical posts and to attach to them branches and ribs in order to reunite them.
>
> *(p. 336)*

This alignment of architectural function and nature continues towards the most famous statement on the subject in 1896, in which it is interesting to note that Sullivan once again takes the side of Cuvier in the dominance of function over form.

> Whether it be the sweeping eagle in his flight or the open apple-blossom, the toiling work horse. The blithe swan, the branching oak, the winding stream at its base, the drifting clouds, over all the coursing sun, form ever follows function, and this is the law. Where function does not change, form does not change ... .
>
> *(1896/1988, p. 111)*

However, it appeared, through Sullivan's work itself, that his definition of function was better described as character or program: he referred for example to the "loftiness" of the skyscraper as its function and believed that the "outward appearance resemble inner purposes," where the meaning of purpose was more essence or idea than any traditional understanding of the word (Sullivan 1901–1902, p. 43).

Over the twentieth century, from Corbusier's (2007, p. 216) soap bubble formed by pressures from within, to Venturi and Scott Brown's Long Island Duck (1979) to Koolhaas' slew of program diagrams, the meaning of *function* shifted to be better aligned with something more akin to "interior program." *Performance* is instead the word that has been adopted relatively recently to fill this "function" void. It means something like "ecological function," where function has to do with the dynamic environment outside the walls, rather than within.

The significance of this lengthy definition is that, through understanding the term "function" as having biological or evolutionary beginnings, it is impossible to think about *performance* without thinking about *environment*. In biology and evolution, *function* reaches out beyond the organism itself and is inevitably in dialogue with the environment.

Ecological Performative Architecture

While analogs, inspirations, and influences abound between biological and architectural treatises throughout history, the closest alignment occurs in the 1980s when architects, now armed with digital technology, began to think about D'Arcy Thompson and evolutionary generation as a means for producing architectural variations.

Greg Lynn, in his *Embryological Houses*, famously revitalized notions of evolutionary thinking in architecture, referring to typologies as "broods" and "species." Lynn argued for an architecture that, in its design (not yet in real time), was less understood as an isolated object and more considered as being in dialogue with forces that shape it from the exterior. He proposed that "the type or spatial organism is no longer seen as a static whole separate from external forces, but rather as a sensibility continuously transforming through its internalization of outside events" (Lynn 1998, p. 39).

Invoking Thompson's transformative diagrams, however, Lynn propagated the same omission that had befallen Thompson, and that was to suppress the role of context in iterative design. Though both do mention the role of context in the text, they are sidetracked by an interest in morphology as well as the forces and the motivation of those forces is rather left behind.

In evolution, on the contrary, the organism, its form and its performance, cannot be evaluated without knowledge of its context.

Darwin's theory of evolution was an evaluation of performance *within a specific context*. In Darwin's words:

> Variations, however slight and from whatever cause proceeding, if they be in any degree profitable to the individuals of a species, in their infinitely complex *relations to other organic beings and to their physical conditions of life*, will tend to the preservation of such individuals, and will generally be inherited by the offspring.
>
> (Darwin 2010, p. 48)

Without context, there is no evolution.

Gibson (1986), expresses the mutual dependency more explicitly, writing:

> it is often neglected that the words animal and environment make an inseparable pair. Each term implies the other. No animal could exist without an environment surrounding it. Equally, although not so obvious, an environment implies an animal (or at least an organism) to be surrounded.
>
> (p. 8)

As the environment is described, the animal that inhabits it can be defined, and vice versa. If it is hot and dry, if there is stalky, yellowish grass underfoot, if acacia trees are dotted around: giraffes may emerge; or conversely, if the animal is tall, long-necked, with dappled skin: savannah emerges.[3] This relationship is what produces the ecological *niche*, and it is precisely this relationship which has been lost in the translation from evolution to architecture.

In *The Ecological Approach to Perception*, James Gibson describes his "Theory of Affordances," which describes a perceptual world in which functionality is primary. An affordance, Gibson explains, is a use-quality contained within both the perceived world and the perceiving animal that stimulates a process of simultaneously occurring projection and consumption that together produce meaning. The function of the encountered object, Gibson proposes, is perceived before the color, the form, or the shape of object. For example, the physical properties of flat horizontal rigid and extended afford standing or walking: it is walk-onable. Affordance, however, does not reside completely in the object but in the relationship of the object with the perceiving body. Affordance, Gibson (1986) posits, "cuts across the dichotomy of subjective-objective and … is equally a fact of the environment and a fact of behaviour … is both physical and psychical, yet neither" (p. 129). To an animal, the affordances contained within its niche are things that are eat-able, drink-able, breath-able, shade-able, conceal-able, and so on. These affordances are linked to specific perceptual and functional components within the animal: the animal's sense of smell as it relates to the affordance of eat-ability in an object, and that object relating to the shape and function of its mouth, stomach, and eventually to the entire organism, and back into the environment. In other words, "All the organs of plants as well as of animals owe their form and their distribution of materials to their meaning as utilizers of the meaning factors which come to them from the outside" (von Uexküll 2010, p. 151).

If architecture is allowed to stand in for the animal, as has often been suggested,[4] it too requires a method of perceiving and adjusting to its affordances, and also to its systems of consumption. A series of questions that probe architecture's relationship to the environment arise. For instance: What does sunlight afford architecture, for example, and how might architecture respond to maximize or minimize its affect? What does rainwater afford and how might architecture respond? What does wind afford and how might it change architecture?

Such destabilization of the aesthetic-dominated hierarchy has been approached many times before; for example, in the surprising context of the English Picturesque movement which, like the French Pensionnaires mentioned above, tended towards a more gothic model. Proponents of this movement advised that architecture should respond primarily to the surrounding landscape, and should offer the possibility that "functional equipage might become architectural expression and a culture of forms" (Macarthur 2007, p. 146). That is, the parts might not express the essence of their own utility: rather, the overall form of the architecture aggregates as its parts are arranged according to their relationship with utilities beyond themselves, in their surroundings. While this seemingly radical suggestion appears poised to escape the bonds imposed by aesthetic preconceptions of form, this movement, like the many destabilizing attempts that followed, was waylaid by the predominance of the "castle" aesthetic in its lineage. Too quickly, picturesque architecture became synonymous with its image, and lost touch with its responsive origins.

Nevertheless, the intention is one whose spirit we might uphold today by the production of an architecture that is driven not by aesthetics but by performance—function in relation and dialogue with a larger field.

Niche Tactics and Beyond

There is no performance without context. We cannot speak of performance unless we speak of the site within which the performance is taking place. What then is the architecture of site-based performance?

First, let us not think of architectural site as limited to the built environment or to geological topography, but of all the artificial and natural physical features of a site. These are the forces that push and pull D'Arcy Thompson's fish; they are the features by which Spencer's evolutionary "fitness" is judged.

Performative architecture implies an advanced technology, one that, for example, responds to changing sunlight conditions by adjusting the shading, like Jean Nouvel's Arab Institute, or that rotates according to prevailing wind directions, like Buckminster Fuller's Dymaxion House and its descendants. These buildings are "responsive." Site performance need not be so high-tech and dynamic: certain known or probabilistic conditions like sun orientation or prevailing wind directions can be responded to through the design of a static building with closed and open sides for passive design.

Yet all of this attention on the response, especially the dynamic one, is often a distraction. As Michelle Addington wrote in her aptly titled piece "Smart Architecture, Dumb Buildings," the dynamic shading of a glass façade which receives so much acclaim is a solution to solve a problem created by the architect. Eliminate the desired aesthetic need for a glass building and we eliminate the need to solve the problem. "Ironically," Addington (2015) writes, "as concerns with energy have heightened attention towards the façade, the focus has been tautologically constrained to solving the problems wrought by glazing rather than questioning its *prima facie* acceptance" (p. 60).

Performative architecture may need to step back then, and question if its high-tech intelligence is superseding a more basic intelligence in which questions of form, orientation, and material operating at a fundamental level. If we start from a true response to site, one that is indeed emergent, in its simultaneous melding of many complex systems, and if we are able to suppress any preconceptions about how things out to look—to look like contemporary architecture, to look elegant, to look beautiful—if we can operate like an organism evolving in nature, a new architecture will emerge that is truly performative (ecologically functional) with fitness to its environment.[5]

Niche Tactics: Generative Relationships between Architecture and Site[6] proposed that we think of architecture in the same way that we think of the animal, as seamless with its environment, aligning the mutual dependency of the animal–environment with the architecture–environment relationships. Borrowing from Greg Lynn's book of tricks, *Niche Tactics* used D'Arcy Thompson's grid to stretch a horse figure into a giraffe one, by pulling up one corner to elongate the neck, while adding a third diagram in which the motivating forces of the environment were revealed. The final diagram bursts free of the grid but also of the figuration: the giraffe loses its outline and blends with the high leaves of the acacia tree, the watering hole, the parasitic birds, the rain, the light, the ground … At the same time, the internal organs and materials that are necessitated by the morphological pulling upwards of the head adjust and adapt: with an oversized heart used for pumping blood, special valves in the neck, pressure-resistant material in the ankles, papillae on the tongue, and so on (Figure 12.1).

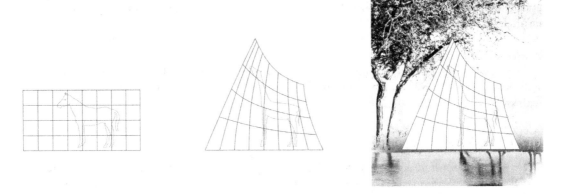

Figure 12.1 Three diagrams showing a Thompsonesque transformation between a horse and a giraffe by pulling on one corner of a grid. The third diagram shows what is missing from Thompson's diagrams: the motivating forces of the context.

Source: CODA, 2013

In Sanford Kwinter's words, the "shape of the animal is everything that the animal does"[7] and its behavior and morphology are connected to both contemporaneous and ancestral animals. A bird is the bird's actions, the nest, the forest, other birds, other animals that co-habit its territory, as well as broader ranges of predators, and prey, and so forth.

While it would seem simple to put a performative relationship with nature as primary in the hierarchy, this imperative is often superseded by an aesthetic imperative. Ironically the dominance of formalism over performativism exists already in Vitruvius's Ten Books. In "On Climate as Determining the Style of the House," Vitruvius opens an early discussion of context by comparing climatic variation in the human body to architectural variation. The segment begins with the commonsense statement that,

> as the position of the heaven with regard to a given tract on the earth leads naturally to different characteristics, owing to the inclination of the circle of the zodiac and the course of the sun, it is obvious that designs for houses ought similarly to conform to the nature of the country and to the diversities of climate.

Vitruvius notes that the effects of climate are "not only discernible in nature, but they also are observable in the limbs and bodies of entire races" (1960, p. 170). He proceeds to draw an analogy between buildings and body size, complexion, hair color, and vocal pitch at different latitudes.

However, the hierarchies present in Vitruvius's treatise are revealed when, in the chapter that follows, he writes that "symmetry and order are *primary*, and only *after* these considerations have been made, should one consider the nature of the site (as well as use and beauty)" (p. 174). This is an important moment to pause, and acknowledge the coup won by symmetry and order over responsiveness at this moment (and, consequently, perhaps, over ugliness). Vitruvius's hierarchy would prove difficult to challenge. Even today, the dominance of order and symmetry remains pervasive in architecture and has been a trap that has routinely befallen architects from Le Corbusier to Koolhaas who have designed for interior function and aesthetics over exterior relationships. This school of thought limits architecture's ability to respond adequately to its environment.

If architecture is responsive to an asymmetrical set of forces in the environment, the consequences are that it may be lop-sided and deformed. The inevitable formal conclusion of this performative modus operandi is, in fact, in the potential production is the ugly.

Ugliness, or monstrosity, in nature is, if in a productive relationship with its environment, often considered positive. If the mutation proves beneficial; if it is well suited to survive and propagate in its environment—if it *fits*—such a creature has been named a "hopeful monster." The term was coined in 1933 by Richard Goldschmidt as part of his argument that "mutants producing monstrosities may have played a considerable role in macroevolution" (Goldschmidt 1982, p. 390). Rather than Darwin's smooth and gradual evolution, Goldschmidt, like Bateson, believes that monstrosities could allow for the inhabitation of a new niche and produce in one leap a new species. Goldschmidt proposes several examples in which variations may have proven so beneficial as to cause a sharp split in the evolutionary trajectory: a Manx cat with a concrescence of tail vertebrae may be considered to be just a monster, but an early mutation of the archaeopteryx producing the same monstrosity might have resulted in a fanlike array of tail feathers that was an improvement in the mechanics of flying, and thus the first flying bird; a fish with a distorted skull carrying both eyes to one side is a monster, but the same monstrosity in a bottom-feeding horizontally swimming fish becomes advantageous in the flatfish; and, in controlled breeding, the dog with achondroplastic bow-legs is monstrous, but once it is used to chase badgers (dachs) into their dens, it is transformation beneficial to a dachshund (p. 391).

For Goldschmidt, such leaps were the fundaments of evolution.[8] Gradual variation existed, he believed, but accounted only for variation *within* a species. Monsters represented great evolutionary leaps and the origins of *new* species. While they may have begun as erroneous and as deviations from the norm, those that happened to fit into a niche were the hopeful monsters that would later become species and enter a newly created normal territory under that heading.[9] However, one contemporary proponent, biologist Stephen Jay Gould, believes that hidden beneath the distraction

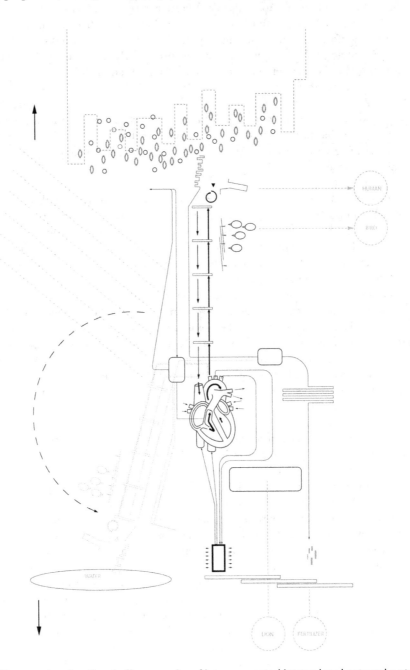

Figure 12.2 Diagram showing the giraffe as a series of interconnected internal and external systems. Source: CODA, 2013

of Goldschmidt's more radical ideas were important concepts that re-introduced the notion of hierarchical models into evolutionary theory. Goldschmidt's vision, Gould (1982) writes in his introduction to the republication of *The Material Basis of Evolution*, "supplied (or rather re-supplied) an essential ingredient that strict Darwinism had expunged from evolutionary theory: the idea that evolution works through a hierarchy of distinct levels with important independent properties" (p. XI). Today, neither Darwinian microevolution nor Goldschmidtian macroevolution is considered solely responsible as an over-arching theory of evolution. Instead, evolution occurs more complexly through a hierarchical range of procedures.

The hopefulness of the monster is judged on the relationship between the monster with its environment, and this performance is not only active but also aesthetic. Mario Frascari believes that the monster's power is in making the invisible visible, in showing (demonstrating) or revealing that which we cannot see (Goldschmidt 1982, p. 15). The monster shows us, perhaps more by way of what it is not, what our norms are, and subsequently, what our world is and what the things in it mean.

A truly performative architecture would too reveal the relationship made by the performative parts. It could be continuous with its environment, operatively, systematically, and visually, expressing demonstratively the tactical relation between its body and its world (Figure 12.2).

Notes

1 Cuvier argued: if any part were to evolve, all parts would need to evolve. Gould agrees that even today "no one can imagine a mechanism for such globally coordinated alteration". Gould (2002), p. 93.
2 In Georges-Louis Leclerc Comte de Buffon's *Histoire Naturelle* in 1749 and Carl Linnaeus's *Species Plantarum* in 1753, plants and animals had appeared classified, categorized, and tabulated (Buffon by historical evolution, Linnaeus by reproductive organs). (See Leandro Madrazo, "Durand and the Science of Architecture," *Journal of Architectural Education*, Volume 48, Issue 1, 1994, 12.) Whatever their system, the tendency had been to identify and describe formal characteristics normal to each type. (See Catherine Ingraham, *Architecture, Animal, Human: The Asymmetrical Condition*, New York: Routledge, 2006, 41.)
3 This example is a paraphrasing of the example used in the Synergistics and Synaesthetics units of the Manchester School of Architecture's Bioclimatic School by Professors Greg Keeffe and Geoff McKennan.
4 Le Corbusier considers the architect a "creator of organisms" (Le Corbusier, *Towards a New Architecture*, 1927, Trans. Frederick Etchells, New York: Holt, Rinehart and Winston, 1986, p. 103).
5 For further reading see: Caroline O'Donnell, *Niche Tactics: Generative Relationships between Architecture and Site*, New York: Routledge, 2015.
6 Even I myself have used the animal analogy. In an earlier iteration, the giraffe was proposed as an appropriate model for an architecture that would evolve in relation to external forces. The creature was appropriate as it had not only evolved as an extreme reaction to a specific environmental niche, but one that served as a visible demonstration of that relationship. See O'Donnell, *Niche Tactics*.
7 Sanford Kwinter, *The Combustible Landscape*, Graduate Research Lecture Series, School of Architecture, Pratt Institute, 7 April 2005.
8 Goldschmidt was not alone in this belief. While many natural scientists cited a lack of mutants in populations as an argument, a number of Goldschmidt's contemporaries believed that constructive mutations are numerous but have ordinarily remained unnoticed simply because destructive mutations are more easily described, catalogued, and scored, and have therefore been more convenient in genetic research (East, p. 10). This idea is also put forth by Emanuel Bonavia in 1895—monsters may have played a large role in evolution by providing specific adaptations in one step—and might have been able to occupy new habitats and continue their special evolution.
9 Such ideas, Goldschmidt points out, were nothing new. Darwin originally believed that mutations (then known innocuously as "sports") played a major evolutionary role, but later changed his mind. In support of his argument, Goldschmidt provides examples of new traits that cannot possibly have arisen through gradual micro-evolutionary stages: hair on mammals, feathers in birds, segmentation of anthropods and vertebrates … teeth, shells of mollusks, ectoskeletons, compound eyes, blood circulation … poison apparatus of snake … etc.) Like Bateson, he believed that these phenomena cannot have appeared gradually.

References

Addington, M. (2015). Smart Architecture, Dumb Buildings, in Kolarevic, B., & Parlac, V. (Eds.), *Building Dynamics: Exploring Architecture of Change* (p. 60). Abingdon and New York: Routledge.

Blake, P. (1979). The Long Island Duckling [image], in *God's Own Junkyard: The Planned Deterioration of America's Landscape*. New York: Holt, Rinehart and Winston.

Cuvier, G. (1800–1805). *Leçons d'Anatomie Comparée, recueillies at publiées sous ses yeux par*, C. Duméril. C. Duméril, éd. vol. 1–2; G.-L. Duvernoy, éd., vol 3–5. Paris: Recueillies et publiées sous ses yeux par C. Duméril.

Darwin, C. (2010). *On the Origin of Species*, 6th edition. Digireads Publishing.

East, E. M. (1936). Heterosis. *Genetics*, vol. 21, no. 4: 375–397.

Forty, A. (2004). *Words and Buildings: A Vocabulary of Modern Architecture*. London: Thames & Hudson.

Gibson, J. (1986). *The Ecological Approach to Visual Perception*. Mahwah NJ: Lawrence Erlbaum.

Goldschmidt, R. (1982). *The Material Basis of Evolution, Silliman Milestones in Science*. New Haven: Yale University Press.

Gould, S. J. (1982). Introduction to Goldschmidt, R. *The Material Basis of Evolution: Silliman Milestones in Science*, New Haven: Yale University Press.

Gould, S. J. (2002). *The Structure of Evolutionary Theory*. Cambridge: Belknap Press of Harvard University Press.

Le Corbusier (2007). *Towards a New Architecture*. Los Angeles: Getty Publications.

Lynn, G. (1998). Multiplicitous and In-organic Bodies, in *Folds, Bodies and Blobs, Collected Essays*. Brussels: La Lettre Volée.

Macarthur, J. (2007). *The Picturesque: Architecture, Disgust and Other Irregularities*. New York and London: Routledge.

McCosh, J., & Dickie, G. (1869). *Typical Forms and Special Ends in Creation*. New York: Robert Carter and Bros.

Marcus Vitruvius P. (1960). *The Ten Books on Architecture* (Morgan, M. H., Trans.). New York: Dover.

Sullivan, L. H. (1896/1988). The Tall Office Building Artistically Considered, in Twombly, R. L. H. (Ed.), *Sullivan: The Public Papers* (pp. 103–112). Chicago and London: University of Chicago Press.

Sullivan, L. H. (1901–1902). Function and Form (i), in *Kindergarten Chats and Other Writings*, 13. Interstate Architect and Builder.

Vaudoyer, L. (1839). Etudes d'architecture en France. *Magasin Pittoresque*, vol. 7.

von Uexküll, J. (2010). *A Foray into the Worlds of Animals and Humans*, (O'Neill, J. D., Trans). Minneapolis: University of Minnesota Press.

13.1
Performative Urban Environments and the Concept of the Future Smart Cities

The Posthuman City: Reflections on the City of the Near Future

Alejandro Zaera-Polo

Since the eighteenth century, when the Western world became human-centered, neither humankind nor the very concept of the human have ceased to evolve. In 1933, Le Corbusier and a few other members of the International Congress of Modern Architecture issued *The Athens Charter*, a document aimed at orchestrating the emerging technologies of the built environment into a proposal for the future of cities (Le Corbusier, Giraudoux, & de Villeneuve, 1943). A classification of human activities formed the vertebral spine of this proposal, structured around four urban functions: work, residence, leisure, and transport. This functional classification has structured urban planning policies ever since, but now its human-centered approach appears unable to address the problems of our age.

In the Anthropocene, humans have become capable of modifying natural ecosystems, geological structures, and even the climate; we have become so powerful that it is increasingly difficult to delimit the natural from the artificial. As the most populated human environment, cities are a central focus of these transformations, and yet none of these concerns seem to have permeated the tools used to plan cities. The urban planning disciplines are primarily conceived around human functions, despite the fact that the crucial issues they need to address—air pollution, rising water levels, drought, heat island effect, deforestation, biodiversity, food security, automated work, and inequality, to name a few—are primarily driven by concerns that, for the first time in history, transcend human societies and threaten the very survival of the planet. The economic, political, and technological drivers of modern urbanism—the mass integration of production, employment, and consumption; the separation of work, dwelling, recreation, and transportation; the division between the natural and the artificial—do not engage the urgent questions cities face today. Likewise, traditional urban instruments such as plazas, streets, and neighborhoods have now been commodified through neoliberal schemes and are ineffective in addressing the new urban collectives and constituencies, both human and nonhuman, which populate contemporary cities.

Posthuman Cosmologies

Cities have enormous weight in the making of the Anthropocene. Witnesses of a veritable paradigm change, we must reformulate the cosmologies upon which the contemporary tools of urbanism have been constructed.

Arcane technologies and rituals of the urban were often based on mythological references. Ancient cosmologies were mechanisms of comprehension of the natural world that enabled different cultures to operate within the natural environment. The oldest ones predated human settlements and sought to explicate natural phenomena so as to regulate the modes of relation between humans and nature. As the urban environment became increasingly controlled by human agency, cosmologies were discarded as systems of urban knowledge and governance. Typology and monumentality became primary tools for urbanism, with the structure of human relations prevailing over the physical and material determinations of the environment. The affairs of cities (*politika*) became an entirely artificial endeavor.

The current prevalence of the artificial and the political in the conceptualization of cities has tended to naturalize urban technologies while depoliticizing nature. However, pressing ecological concerns and the scale of technological development call for the imminent city to repoliticize both nature and technology, and to construct new urban cosmopolitics which can support the development of new urban sensibilities (Yaneva & Zaera-Polo, 2015).

An entirely new set of urban technologies has recently emerged, with the potential to radically transform urban protocols and experiences. Yet smartphones, global positioning systems (GPS), electromobility, and biotechnology still remain largely beyond the expertise of urban planners and designers, who remain trapped in the humanistic precepts of modern urbanism.

Far from producing urbanity, urban functionalism has dismantled the commons and undermined urban democracy. Clichés like the relevance of squares or the percentage of public spaces as guarantors of community and urban democracy are as problematic as the inability of architects and urban planners to quantify the implications of density and urban form in either energy consumption or the determination of urban microclimates. The idea that architects and urban designers can locate effective agency in the distribution of human functions—such as work and residential—is at best naïve. Cities have become sources of extreme inequality and environmental degradation (in contempt of the *demos*, and all of the nonhuman urban constituencies too), which even threaten the subsistence of cities, and point to the many unsurmountable contradictions at the core of current modes of economic integration. Theorists like Jeremy Rifkin and Paul Mason argue that we have already entered a post-capitalist world in which politics have shifted from the focus on capital and labor to energy and resources (Rifkin, 2014; Paul Mason, 2015a, 2015b). Respectively, they have proposed new economies: shared economies of zero marginal cost driven by new technologies, and peer-to-peer organizations enhanced by pervasive computation, sustainable energy sources, and carbon-neutral technologies.

As the largest human habitat, cities have become the epicenters of global warming, air pollution, and a variety of ecological maladies. Naomi Klein (2014) has highlighted the fundamental opposition between capitalist growth and the limited natural resources of the earth and questioned the capacity of capitalist regimes to resolve an imminent ecological catastrophe. This has loaded ecology and technology—and more precisely, urban ecologies and technologies—with an unprecedented political relevance. Cities today form a crucial entanglement between ecology, technology, and politics, where the equation of wealth, labor, resources, and energy must be reset to address the shortcomings of neoliberal policies.

Imminent Commons

Does this scenario, determined by the Anthropocene casuistics and the crisis of neoliberal capitalism, imply that the work of urbanists and architects has been rendered futile? That the new commons will be entirely developed within social media? Has urbanism been expelled from politics entirely, so that it is now at the mercy of securitization and capital redistribution? On the contrary, some economists argue that urban planning, housing, and real estate hold the key to resolving urban inequality (Piketty, 2014; Rognlie, 2015). Cities precede the installation of political systems, and have systematically outlasted them, often constituting themselves in mechanisms of resistance to emerging power structures. For cities to become devices for the common good rather than instruments producing and implementing power structures—or inequality, or ecological destruction—urban practices must locate resources and technologies at their core. Rather than splitting urban life into functions easily captured by power, we should first identify the city's *imminent urban commons* and study how they might be reconstructed as instruments of devolution and ecological awareness, cutting transversally across technologies and resources. The following is an attempt to outline what those imminent urban commons might be, and how they may serve to revise urban practices.

Ecology Commons

The first proposed revision to conventional urban cosmology resorts to the tradition of the primeval elements; by identifying the four commons related to natural resources, a new posthuman cosmology might be constructed. These four commons—air, water, fire (energy), earth—are driven by their various techniques of management. Each designated element has become crucially politicized, and therefore urbanized, by the ongoing environmental crisis, and are therefore of crucial concern to urban practices.

Air

As Naomi Klein has stated, air is the element that most intimately binds all humans on earth together. While the ozone depletion from chlorofluorocarbons represented a significant and shocking threat, the effects of other airborne pollutants have been less conspicuous. Seven million people die every year from exposure to air-induced diseases (World Health Organization, 2014). Despite increased awareness of these problems, the air quality in cities seems to have gotten worse over the last few decades. According to a 2016 report published by the United Nations Children's Fund, "300 million children live in areas with extremely toxic levels of air pollution," and "approximately 2 billion children live in areas where pollution levels exceed the minimum air quality standards set by the World Health Organization" (Nicholas Rees, 2016).

Because cities are the densest sites of human population, attempts to clean air, channel polluted air away from city streets, prevent air stagnation, and improve airflow between buildings are central to preserving the rights to common natural resources of urban citizens. Since the early twentieth century, buildings and cities have developed the ability to delimit, filter, and qualify air. However, as toxic emissions continue to rise each year, these abilities are becoming even more urgent and politically charged. While air is a universally needed resource, it is extremely difficult to quantify, visualize, sense, and model. Historically, this has been an obstacle to creating policies regulating its use. The emerging technologies of sensing and computational modeling will enable the development of more effective tools to manage the air commons.

Water

Global warming and climate change do not only distort traditional climate patterns, but also reshape the earth itself. Rising sea levels are expected to have a massive impact on cities around the world in the coming decades, and their impact is already felt through natural disasters and plummeting real estate values. Urban waterfronts and riverfronts, traditionally key territories of urban life, are now threatened by climate change (Parker, 2015). But the lack of access to clean water for urban populations is a growing humanitarian problem too. By 2050, one-third of people on earth may lack a clean, secure source of water.

Of the natural resource commons, none is so intimately tied to urban ecologies as water. Cities developed in the proximity of an adequate water supply, and the first urban policies appeared with respect to the use of water. In ancient Mesopotamia, the Code of Hammurabi included provisions for the distribution of water based on the area of fields farmed, dictated responsibilities for farmers to maintain canals, and assigned administrative responsibilities for canals. One primary responsibility of a city is to provide infrastructure to deliver potable water to its citizens. Equally important to the health of a city is the ability to remove large amounts of water supplied by rains and flooding, but also produced by human waste. Cities function as the mediator between water-dependent organisms—that is, humans—and hydrological cycles driven by the evaporation, condensation, collection, and flow of water.

Centralized water purification and sewage treatment systems allowed modern cities to flourish, greatly increasing populations, human health, and the average lifespan. However, overreliance on centralized systems has begun to threaten water security. There is a threshold of efficiency for centralized systems: large amounts of energy are dedicated to sending water through extensive, corroded pipe networks. The decentralization of urban water infrastructure allows the city to become more resilient, for example, in the event of extreme weather conditions, power outages, terrorist attacks, hostile takeover, or government shutdown.

Water retention, collection, and treatment systems are equally important areas of development for urban water infrastructure. The replacement of non-osmotic pavements (such as the asphalt surfaces that cover a large percentage of urban land), the introduction of bioswales (landscape design features that slow, collect, and filter surface water runoff), the recovery of buried streams within cities, and the development of water-retention systems for building envelopes are some current possibilities for urban practice that are likely to change the landscape of future cities (Sachs, 2006).

Fire

Fire—the elemental placeholder for energy—is a vital issue that cities must address promptly. Fossil fuel consumption not only depletes natural resources, but more importantly, releases carbon into the atmosphere to cause climate change, which brings about pollution, health hazards, and rising water levels. Buildings consume 40% of global energy, 60% of global resources, and produce 48% of carbon emissions, with significant energy use concentrated in urban centers (United Nations Environment Program, 2007).

The spatial distribution of energy sources, energy processing, and energy demand are a solid basis upon which different urban systems can be studied, historically or parametrically. Over time, urban energy systems have evolved progressively towards highly concentrated forms of energy, often obtained from fossil fuels, which can be easily transported. The development of fossil fuels as an energy source enabled deterritorialization, as portable forms of energy could sustain large and geographically dispersed industrial metropolises that would previously not have been possible without proximity to a naturally occurring resource.

The further development of solar, wind, tidal, and ground-sourced energy to power cities without resorting to fossil fuel combustion will profoundly alter the future urban cosmopolitics. As sustainable energy is primarily mediated through electricity, supplies will need to be driven locally, from various sustainable energy sources dependent on climate and geology. The ubiquitous fossil fuel resources will be phased out in the shift towards a reterritorialization of energies.

Earth

The earth commons encompass the organic resources that make up the biosphere. The birth of urban civilizations was aligned with the ability to increase the productive capacity of land, in order to feed larger densities of people more reliably. Because most ancient citizens were farmers, there was a direct relationship between the productive capacity of the land and the population that could be sustained in a city. This balance changed with advanced agricultural techniques and animal labor, and later, machines and synthetic fertilizers. Carbon footprints establish equivalences between land-measuring units and their capacity to produce energy from sustainable sources, to absorb carbon, and perform within hydrological cycles.

After a long exile from the city, plant matter, soil, and other organic elements are being reincorporated increasingly into city fabrics and building design. As a percentage of surface area coverage, organic matter affects such factors as reflectivity, humidity, thermal mass, heating and cooling cycles, and water runoff. Cities depend on the synthesis and resilience of life—human and otherwise. Urban land cannot be determined exclusively by functional assignments with respect to human behaviors: its productive capacity depends on topography, climate, and the bioactive layer of the soil.

Biotechnologies have developed increasingly effective urban applications. Some of the fastest-growing projects include urban farming, hydroponics, and algae cultures with the ability to produce food, biofuels, and even illuminate cities. High-tech farming technologies such as hydroponics and aquaponics are constantly improved to increase efficiency and yield. The deployment of such technologies will become increasingly relevant to urban practices and assemblages.

Technology Commons

The second series of commons that might constitute a new urban cosmology is related to the development of technologies that facilitate alternative forms of urban community. These commons present opportunities for new urban practices to pervade institutional, bureaucratic, and market mechanisms. Technologies can be considered extensions of human capacities, which have developed a posthuman life on their own. Or, as Marshall McLuhan (2001) writes in *Understanding Media*, "technologies are self-amputations of our own organs."[1] The activities of sensing, communicating, moving, producing, and consuming have developed disembodied, collective forms which transcend their human origins.

Sensing

The formation of urban sensibilities has a tradition that explores the city as an experience: the phenomenological focus of the late-nineteenth-century City Beautiful movement, the mid-twentieth-century Townscape theories, approached the city as a sensual experience, as opposed to the more scientific, pragmatic approach of the Enlightenment. The emerging sensing technologies are opening entirely new possibilities: cities are experienced and sensed, but crucially, cities themselves sense. Weathervanes and watchtowers, common in traditional urban landscapes, provided citizens with weather forecasting and improved the navigation of increasingly complex urban spaces. Traffic wardens, firefighters, and other watchtower lookouts shared their advantaged sensibility with citizens in order to regulate urban processes. Weather patterns, security systems, and temporal rhythms have historically structured urban communities.

But these arcane sensing technologies have since become increasingly artificial, pervasive, and distributed. The proliferation of sensors in urban environments is one of the most defining features of contemporary urban milieus. Self-driving vehicles and other new urban technologies will not only provide new forms of mobility but also exponentially expand the population of sensing agents that document every physical feature, traffic delay, or change of air quality in the city environment. Computer vision in the form of light detection and ranging laser scanners that collect point cloud data, high resolution orthoimagery, and geographic-information-system-enabled web applications enable us to visualize—and therefore act upon—urban processes that were previously inaccessible. When these sensors are interconnected, an unprecedented common, novel in its sensibility, will create a collective sensorium. When accessed via smartphone, open-source sensing data will be instantly accessible to urban populations, yielding constant updates regarding the urban environment.

Urban rhythms (such as alternating traffic lights, or subway train frequency) are increasingly controlled by algorithm, especially with respect to transportation, utilities, and security. In recent years, such dynamic regulation has widely expanded with the rollout of ubiquitous computing. Technologies such as city operating systems, closed-circuit television cameras, urban control rooms, smart grids, sensor networks, smart parking, smart lighting, city dashboards, and digital real-time information apps will not only have deep political implications, in terms of surveillance and privacy, but also transformative spatiotemporal effects that will crucially alter the experience of cities. In effect, cities may have to be designed not only according to a human perspective, but through necessary interactions with nascent artificial sensibility.

Communicating

One of the more powerful imminent commons is a consequence of the radical densification of urban communication networks, resulting from pervasive computation and wireless communications. While cities have always been characterized by dense communication networks—the postal service, the telegraph, the telephone—current technologies have intensified this drastically, through the combination of universal computing and the development of the World Wide Web, which allow users to interact and collaborate with each other as creative content-generators in a distributed virtual community.

In combination, the World Wide Web and wireless technologies have freed information entirely from physical attachments. The connection of mobile devices to GPS has allowed unprecedented opportunity to navigate urban space and engage with fellow citizens, creating entirely new urban geographies in the process. The possibility to connect with automated devices will certainly reshape the way in which we relate to our work or domestic environments. Platform-capitalism deployed in urban areas—such as Uber, Lyft, Seamless, GrubHub—are examples of how some of these technologies are starting to affect urban life. And the development of new forms of domesticity, work, and leisure, and their impact on urban culture and politics, will disrupt traditional forms of urban functions.

Some of the most transformative processes triggered by new communication technologies relate to the possibility of sharing services and goods in time, including short-term residential rentals, bicycle and car-share schemes, coworking spaces, and other initiatives based on shared economy. Inherited from modernist planning, today's city is primarily regulated by functional determinations and private property laws, which are being disrupted through shared ownership. Social media and universal computation hold the key to the development of new urban protocols, institutions, typologies, and experiences. Resource and energy management through sharing, recycling, or optimization is increasing, and current legislation must shift towards the normalization of sharing protocols. The urbanization of these technologies will open new potentials for architecture to engage with these emerging forms of urban culture.

Moving

Human mobility has always been strongly influenced by technology, which has increased the radius of action far beyond the natural capacities of the human body. The origin of cities is inextricably linked to the development of collective forms of mobility and their infrastructures, which are able to supply the resources needed to sustain such concentrated populations that would otherwise be impossible without outreaching to a larger area where resources can be found to sustain the concentration of population required to form a city.

The radical increase in urban density caused by industrialization also multiplied the demand for mobility. The development of underground transit systems in London, Paris, Berlin, and New York was a crucial tool of urban development in the early twentieth century, as these cities embraced industrialization as the fundamental mode of economic integration. In the post-World War II period, the automobile transformed cities beyond recognition. Today, transportation is one of the most energy-intensive activities in the city, and currently accounts for a large percentage of overall carbon emissions and pollution.

In response to these ecological concerns, unipersonal electromobility and self-driving vehicles are likely to alter urban traffic patterns even further. Electric vehicles and sharing schemes are now spreading worldwide, anticipating decentralized urban transport systems with a minimal carbon footprint—unlike previous modes of individualized transport—and breaking with models of vehicle ownership. Automated logistics are also an important part of urban mobility developments.

Making

If the late capitalist city is characterized by the exile of production from the urban core, and the takeover of financial services as well as securitization through residential markets are now key components of urban economies, there are also new technologies for digital fabrication, laser 3D scanning, 3D printing, and robotics that have since relocated some high-value fabrication activities back to the urban core. The potential impact of the return of production—digitally enhanced, automatized, etc.—to the city indexes the emergence of new concerns, such as the distribution of work and benefits and the re-localization of the production infrastructures within the urban fabric which will require new governance protocols for the emerging urban *Homo faber*.

While contemporary urban culture has often been associated with the rise of the *knowledge society*, where most of the wealth and employment is created by the production of knowledge, contemporary economies have now reached a point where the progressive elimination of agricultural and industrial sectors is making urban economies untenable (Chang, 2016). After decades of service-driven urban economies and real estate speculation, emerging fabrication technologies may be able to effectively reindustrialize cities.

The so-called Fourth Industrial Revolution (4IR) is the third major industrial era since the Industrial Revolution of the eighteenth century and is enacted by a range of new technologies that fuse the physical, digital, and biological worlds, with an impact on all disciplines, economies, and industries. Central to this revolution are emerging technological breakthroughs in fields such as artificial intelligence, robotics, the internet of things, autonomous vehicles, 3D printing, biocomputation, and nanotechnology.

4IR has also created its own urban cultures: makers practice a technology-based extension of DIY activities that intersect with hacking actions. The maker culture remains committed to the physical world, operating according to specific moral principles and producing distinctive forms of inhabiting and occupying urban space. Shared spaces of production and fabrication equipment and for processing recycled or reclaimed materials are key aspects for these emerging ethics of urban production, often implemented through small-scale urban operations. A revision of new urban production technologies and how they may be reinserted into the urban fabric is now an important field of consideration for the making common.

Recycling

Metropolitan governments have paid increasing attention to the collection, sorting, and recycling of urban waste and biosolids. These processes have reached a geopolitical dimension, with regional and even transcontinental systems set out for treating refuse. The cultural dimension of recycling protocols is substantial and directly impacts citizens and their perceptions of the city. For decades, Japan has been at the forefront of fostering collective consciousness of recycling, and installing infrastructure to optimize urban metabolism. Many cities have attempted to follow the Japanese example, only to realize the cultural difficulty of implementing such programs. Installing multiple-track recycling protocols in contemporary cities appears to be an insurmountable cultural problem, and yet robotic sorting of solid and electronic waste is a real alternative to landfill which must be expanded to urban areas lacking a Japanese cultural background.

Human waste is also a subject of increasing attention for municipalities. A more sophisticated approach to its recycling could have an enormous ecological impact by reducing global dependence on synthetic fertilizers. In the light of recent interest to promote urban farming for the purposes of food security and CO_2 absorption, for example, the recycling of human waste obviously has great potential. Waste composting for urban farms on roof gardens, private courtyards, and bioswales appear as the natural destination of human waste on a local, granular urban scale. As Pierre Belanger has stated, "waste is the 21st-century food" (Belanger, 2007).

Ecologies Rather than Functions

It appears inevitable for urban practices of the immediate future to incorporate the emerging technologies discussed above in fields where the new urban commons are to be found, ranging from governance to production. Especially because urban planning based on human functions has now become a mechanism to divide and wield power rather than produce urbanity, new instruments must be developed to address the imminent posthuman commons.

We live in an age marked by vast technological developments that must be better incorporated into the ways we conceive and design cities within wider global ecologies. The ancient elements of air, water, fire, and earth along with artificially enhanced sensibilities, collectivities, logistics, and metabolic processes enabled by emerging technologies should become the central concern of a posthuman urbanism, focused on the ecologies and economies of elements and milieus. In posthuman urbanism, cities are designed to engage with concerns much broader than the organization of delivery systems responsive to human activities, as if these infrastructures or needs were independent of the milieus, tools, climates, and topographies in which they are situated. An upgrade from the modernist, human-centered functionalities—and the expired sensibilities associated to them—that undergird contemporary urban practice is now urgently needed.

Note

1 "With the arrival of electric technology, man extended, or set outside himself, a live model of the central nervous system itself" (page 53); and "It is to the railroad that the American city owes its abstract grid layout the nonorganic separation of production, consumption, and residence. It is the motorcar that scrambled the abstract shape of the industrial town, mixing up its separated functions to a degree that has frustrated and baffled both planner and citizen ... Metropolitan space is equally irrelevant for the telephone, the telegraph, the radio, and television. What the town planners call 'the human scale' in discussing ideal urban spaces is equally unrelated to these electric forms. Our electric-extensions of ourselves simply bypass space and time and create problems of human involvement and organization for which there is no precedent" (page 119).

References

Belanger, P. (2007). Landscapes of Disassembly. *Topos* 60: 83–91.
Chang, H. (May 18, 2016). Making Things Matters. This is What Britain Forgot. *The Guardian*. Retrieved from www.theguardian.com http://ngm.nationalgeographic.com/2015/02/climate-change-economics/parker-text.
Klein, N. (2014). *This Changes Everything: Capitalism vs. the Climate*. New York: Simon & Schuster.
Le Corbusier, Giraudoux, J., & de Villeneuve, J. (1943). *La Charte d'Athenes*. Paris: Plon.
Mason, P. (2015a). *Post Capitalism: A Guide to Our Future*. London: Allen Lane.

Mason, P. (July 17, 2015b). The End of Capitalism Has Begun. *The Guardian*. Retrieved from www.theguardian.com/books/2015/jul/17/postcapitalism-end-of-capitalism-begun.

McLuhan, M. (2001). The Gadget Lover, in *Understanding Media*. London: Routledge Classics.

Parker, L. (February, 2015). Treading Water. *National Geographic*. Retrieved from www.nationalgeographic.com/magazine/2015/02/climate-change-economics/.

Piketty, T. (2014). *Capital in the 21st Century*. Cambridge, MA: Harvard University Press.

Rees, N. (October, 2016). *Clear the Air for Children: The Impact of Air Pollution on Children*. [pdf]. United Nations Children's Fund. Retrieved from www.unicef.org/publications/files/UNICEF_Clear_the_Air_for_Children_30_Oct_2016.pdf.

Rifkin, J. (2014). *The Zero Marginal Cost Society: The Internet of Things, the Collaborative Commons, and the Eclipse of Capitalism*. London: Macmillan.

Rognlie, M. (2015). Deciphering the Fall and Rise in the Net Capital Share: Accumulation or Scarcity? in *Brookings Papers on Economic Activity Spring 2015*. 1–54.

Sachs, J. D. (December 1, 2006). The Challenge of Sustainable Water. *Scientific American*. Retrieved from www.scientificamerican.com/article/the-challenge-of-sustaina/.

United Nations Environment Program. (2007). *Buildings and Climate Change: Status, Challenges and Opportunities*. [pdf]. Retrieved from www.unep.fr/shared/publications/pdf/DTIx0916xPA-BuildingsClimate.pdf.

World Health Organization. (March 25, 2014). 7 Million Premature Deaths Annually Linked to Air Pollution. [News Release]. Retrieved from www.who.int/mediacentre/news/releases/2014/air-pollution/en/.

Yaneva, A., & Zaera-Polo, A. ed. (2015). *What is Cosmopolitical Design? Design, Nature, and the Built Environment*. New York: Routledge.

13.2

Performative Urban Environments and the Concept of the Future Smart Cities

Toward Establishing Measures for Performative Urban Environments: A Critical Position on Shaping the Future of Smart Cities

Lucy Campbell, Mitra Kanaani and Michael Stepner

> By far the greatest and most admirable form of wisdom is that needed to plan and beautify cities and human communities.
>
> *(Socrates)*

Introduction

Performative urban environments are emerging as a major research agenda for urban designers, city planners, and architects. Rather than looking at what urban spaces *do*, researchers are asking *how* they allow interaction with their surroundings and occupants. Increasingly, these questions focus on the role of digital technologies in affecting perceptions of space and creating direct interactive opportunities with urban environments. Current research also explores how new interactive technologies shape social relationships, outdoor environments, and the siting of man-made elements and structures, as well as cultural effects and impacts on peoples' lives. New types of place-making based on advanced technology are emerging through intelligent city elements and components.

Currently, "smart city" is a broad term for the integration of technology into urban fabrics.

Many definitions have been offered from a variety of disciplines. Mulligan and Olsson (2013) view smart cities as integrations of physical cities with digital infrastructure in order to address environmental concerns. Jensen (2016) has described them as cities that are networked and connected from the local block to the global sphere via the proliferation of digital information and data communication. The smart city has also been defined as one that "is able to collect information about its own state and to regulate itself based on the state of the whole system" (Offenhuber & Ratti, 2014, p. 8). Townsend (2014) focused on "places where information technology is combined with infrastructure, architecture, everyday objects, and even our bodies to address social, economic and environmental problems" (p. 15). While Batty et al. (2012) viewed smart cities as ones in which information and communication technology (ICT) merges with traditional infrastructures and is coordinated and integrated using new digital technologies. They also acknowledged the "many faces" of smart cities, including intelligence, virtual reality, digitization, and information, but contend that in all cases ICT is key (p. 483).

In this chapter we take a narrower and more critical view, defining smart cities as the application of *advanced technology* and planning to *improve quality of life* for urban inhabitants. While introducing the concept, scope, and limitations of the smart city, we analyze smart parameters with respect to underlying concepts of healthy urbanism; for example, Jane Jacobs' notable 1961 book *The Death and Life of Great American Cities* and Kevin Lynch's (1981) landmark publication *Good City Form*. We also explore how these new technologies impact architectural design and practice.

Smart Growth as an Inevitable Trend

Technological advancements and innovations are inevitably shaping our cities as they trend toward cleaner, safer, and more functional performative environments. Envisioning appropriate and efficient design while planning complex infrastructure requires coherent collaboration between city stakeholders, urbanists, planners, architects, and visionary investors and entrepreneurs. Establishing a vision for the future growth and development of cities is a momentous task. Smart growth is expected to address population increase while accommodating the needs of current inhabitants. By utilizing progressive technologies and smart amenities, cities are envisioned to become more reliable, performative, sustainable, and safer for residents. This can apply to all aspects of a city; from flood and seismic detecting sensors to interactive highway global positioning systems (GPS) that convey route advice to drivers. However, the goal of smart cities is not to improve efficiency alone, but to improve life quality for inhabitants overall. One crucial question therefore is: can performative urban environments create civic meaning and perform in a socially progressive manner? Can we direct cities to become smarter and more intelligent toward healthy, comfortable, socially engaging, and vibrant living environments for all, without alienating technologically challenged citizens or those without direct access to such amenities? Is smart growth only about integration of high-tech elements, or can it include variations from low-tech to eco-tech appropriate for all citizens? Or, put another way, can smart cities make us happier?

Ancient Smart Cities

Any city, regardless of how ancient, can be performatively smart based on sustainable measures and positive, meaningful effects on residents. Therefore, a smart city does not necessarily mean a city equipped with ICT. It can also be one which utilizes low-tech methods to attain effective performance in various aspects of wellbeing, such as health, hygiene, sanitation, water, air quality, transportation, social opportunities, and cultural enrichment.

Thousands of years ago, sophisticated, advanced urban cultures were possible through the adoption of advanced technology and planning. KT Ravindran, Professor Emeritus of the School of Planning and Architecture in Delhi, summarizes, "our traditional smart cities display a compact form, optimum density, and sustainable material and social infrastructure; they were the smart cities of their times" (Pokharel, 2018). The *Code of Hammurabi* (1754 BCE Their work gained attention at a time when many growing cities were exploring ways to manage growth and provide services and facilities for residents.

A philosophy of underlying order for the city was elaborated by Jane Jacobs (1961/1992) in *The Death and Life of the Great American Cities*. In this provocative publication, Jacobs considered four primary physical conditions required for proper performance and effective economic pools of use to generate great cities. Those primary conditions include promoting:

1. The need for primary mixed uses for activating streets during different times of day, which leads to development of mixed-use development, considering that traditionally, human settlements have developed in mixed-use typologies
2. The need for small blocks for furthering city's pedestrian permeability
3. The need for aged buildings, and promoting buildings with various ages and state of requirement for repair and revitalization
4. The need for concentration and density (Jacobs, 1961/1992, pp. 1–29)

Jacobs contended that with proper and deliberate planning and enforcement of performative elements, vitality can be induced in the lifeblood of cities. She argued that social behavior in cities can be stimulated through these four primary conditions, ultimately improving the economic behavior of cities themselves. She viewed cities as the most potential dynamic environments for inhabitants, and the most fertile grounds for present and future planning opportunities. She also analyzed the problems cities pose due to their "organized complexity," and introduced the evolving features of smart cities. Twenty years later, urbanist Kevin Lynch (1981) proposed in *Good City Form* five critical criteria for the design of a good city: vitality, sense, fit, access, and control. Additionally, he listed two meta criteria: efficiency and justice. The principles of Jacobs and Lynch are as relevant for tomorrow's cities as they were when they were first promulgated. However, when devised, the effects of computerization, automation, and digitization were still problems for the future.

The Shift to Advanced Smart Cities

The twenty-first century has often been described as the *century of the city* (Peirce, Johnson, & Peters, 2008). In part this moniker is based on the fact that we are now experiencing unprecedented urbanization. In 2008, for the first time in history, more people lived in cities than in rural areas. The United Nations (2018) predict that 60% of the world's population will live in urban areas by 2030, and one in four will be living in slum conditions (Royal Geographic Society, 2016). Davis (2017) has described the era we are entering as the *Planet of the Slums*. How we address this will depend in great part on how we build and rebuild our cities in order to maintain and improve urban quality of life. Like our ancient ancestors, we can only make cities smarter by applying the most advanced technologies available to us.

In many cities today, some smart features are already evident. These features include everything from computerized waste management systems to automated street lights. However, they are much more than simple data processors. Whereas once we detected the city, we are now in an era in which the city detects us and adapts accordingly. The ultimate smart city is more than intelligent. It is sentient.

Japan, South Korea, and China are leading the way in sentient smart city development. China's rapid urbanization has provided opportunities to build from the ground up, integrating current technologies and including hardware for future advancements. In South Korea, the city of Songdo has become a test-bed for smart technologies such as radio frequency identification (RFID) (Townsend, 2014). While new applications are being devised every day, some have already proven popular, and possible.

At the individual building level, smart offices use a combination of automation and autonomy to provide comfort and customization. Building systems monitor and control operations through sensors to improve thermal comfort, air quality, and employee security. Meanwhile, customizable spaces offer diverse lighting options, sliding bookcases, and height- and depth-adjustable desks (Pizzi & Guzman, 2017). Investing in such upgrades pays off for employers. Studies show that comfortable, well-ventilated, and well-lit workplaces with natural features can increase productivity by as much as 15% (Kohl, 2019). Perhaps the major smart development impacting offices is the burgeoning Internet of Things. All manner of devices can today interact and exchange data via the internet. Almost every electronic office appliance conceived of can now be interconnected in an invisible network that functions proactively without human interference or even awareness. Windows, shade devices, HVAC (heating, ventilation, and air conditioning) systems, and fans can measure temperature, humidity, and carbon dioxide, then each adjust accordingly to provide the perfect environment. Known as task automation services, these technologies are even being applied to respond to human emotions by measuring factors such as speech and body expression in the workplace (Muñoz, 2018). In the design of smart office buildings, telecommunications infrastructure is now the principal consideration.

Soon, self-driving cars will shuttle people to and from these offices, while they are occupied with work or other activities. Integrated smart transportation systems will find bottlenecks in traffic patterns and help define optimum routes. Gathering and sharing real-time information already makes getting around smart cities safer, more efficient, and less frustrating. Proposed schemes have focused on handling massive increases in traffic, especially automobile traffic. Smart meters that issue automated parking fines and traffic tickets have become one revenue source to finance smart transit enterprises. However, Tatsuno (2019) has argued these initiatives contribute to pollution problems instead of encouraging automobile alternatives such as biking and public transit. The solution may not be increased mobility, but instead increased accessibility to the things we need every day. We can devise complete communities around established rules of thumb – for example, you should need to travel no further than one-quarter of a mile to buy a loaf of bread.

Transport accounts for roughly one-quarter of fossil fuel consumption. The ideal lifestyle in leafy suburbs is appealing, yet it requires auto-dependency for both commuters and daily needs. This increases fuel consumption, environmental degradation, and social isolation, and has resulted in disinvestment in city centers and older neighborhoods, and segregation by race and class. The need to not only reduce consumption of fossil fuels but also reconsider the causes has become clear.

One solution is linking urban functions by reintroducing complexity through mixed use. Such models are built on smart data measurements that reveal natural internal circulation patterns and uses of space. They increase building density and provide accessibility on foot and bike for daily needs. Under these circumstances vehicular traffic can be reduced, decreasing land consumption and infrastructure costs.

Making urban energy systems smart is not just about using less fuel more efficiently; it is also about producing energy closer to the places where it is consumed. Solar panels and wind turbines can generate energy in cities and contribute in peak conditions. Pittsburg's Development Energy Innovation Center (EIC, 2019) is emblematic of this reinvention. Through its dedication to energy efficiency initiatives and workforce development, the EIC and its affiliate non-profit, the Energy Innovation Center Institute, are reshaping Pittsburgh's local economy (Figure 13.2.1).

Another factor influencing economies around the globe is urban farming. It is estimated that over 800 million people produce one-fifth of the world's food in their homes and neighborhoods (United Nations Food and Agriculture Organization, 2019). From crops to animals to fruit trees, urban farming is diverse and often informal. Although more pronounced in the mega cities of developing countries, this practice is increasingly popular in the post-industrialized world, where smart city ideals are being applied. Applications of advanced technologies to small-scale city farms include aquaponics, hydroponics, and Controlled Environment Agriculture (CEA). Aquaponics involves farming fish in combination with water-filtering plant life, and can be achieved almost anywhere with very little energy. Hydroponics utilizes nutrient-rich water instead of soil, reducing weight significantly and making farms structurally

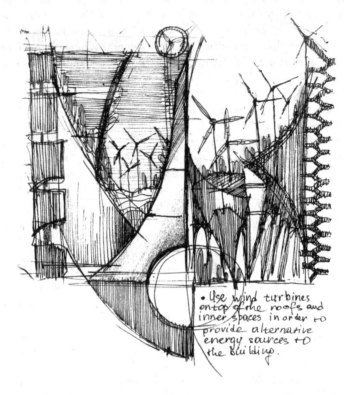

Figure 13.2.1 Urban energy systems are becoming smart by using cleaner fuels, and more focused on about producing energy closer to the places for its consumption. Solar panels and wind turbines in combination can generate energy in cities and mainly for peak conditions. A design concept.

Sketch by Vasili Petrushko, Graduate Student at NewSchool of Architecture & Design

possible in high-rise situations. CEA requires indoor closed-loop systems in which water, light, and temperature are carefully monitored to achieve optimum growing conditions. These techniques are well suited to vertical farming in urban environments, requiring little space compared to industrial farming practices. Today they are found in the basements, roofs, and interiors of multi-story buildings. Advantages include freedom from pests and reduced use of transportation and fossil fuels (Figure 13.2.2).

In recent years there has also been increased interest in façade farming. Sweden's *Tour Vivante* by SOA Architects features a 190-foot-tall double-wall façade lined with trays of plants that slowly rise up the building as the food crops mature (Fairley, 2013). *Bosco Verticale* in Milan is lined with balconies full of trees, including cherry, apple, and olive varieties (AFP, 2017). In the smart cities of the future, these unusual buildings may become commonplace if challenges of expense and practicalities (e.g. falling food or attracting birds) are resolved.

One necessary development for urban farming is water monitoring. Utilities can remotely and continuously monitor and diagnose problems such as leaks and stoppages, take preemptive measures to manage maintenance, and optimize water distribution. Sensors also help keep drinking water clean and verify that wastewater is being properly processed.

Performative Urban Environments

Figure 13.2.2 Urban Farms are already contributing to the world's food through producing fresh fish to herbs. In smart cities there are vertical farms in multi-story buildings that use soil alternatives to bring sustainable and locally-grown produce to urban populations. A futurist design concept.
Sketch by Vasili Petrushko, Graduate Student at NewSchool of Architecture & Design

Water monitors can also be used to forecast floods. A network of storm-drain systems measuring the direction, speed, and level of water can predict areas that are susceptible to flooding. Artificial-intelligence-driven weather tools can calculate how and when natural disasters may occur (Tatsuno, 2019). Advance notice can mitigate damage and loss of life, as demonstrated in a video screened at the Shanghai Expo 2010, which imagined sensors warning of an approaching typhoon, and thus averting disaster (Townsend, 2014, p. 48).

Cities create tons of waste, and smart technology can improve how it is collected and separated. Smart garbage bins use compactors to accommodate more waste than the average bin and can alert collection staff when full. Garbage trucks can also use GPS to make collection routes more efficient.

Drones, or unmanned aerial systems, are already being used in cities to document accidents and support first responders (Hell & Varga, 2018). Their ability to cover hard-to-reach areas makes them particularly useful for monitoring critical infrastructure such as antennae and bridges. Drones are also being tested that will soon offer automated delivery. Yet current drone regulation severely limits practical applications. In the United States the Federal Aviation Administration (FAA) prohibits commercial drone operations. For example, drones cannot fly above 400 feet and can only be operated during daylight hours (FAA, 2016). In addition to the question of regulation, factors such as poor weather and public perception must also be considered. In our collective psyche, drones are inextricably linked to combat, warfare, and weapons (Jensen, 2016). They may not be enthusiastically welcomed to our city skies (Figure 13.2.3).

Figure 13.2.3 In smart cities, drones are already being used to support in documenting accidents and help with first responders, particularly in hard-to-reach areas, particularly for monitoring critical infrastructures like bridges and antennae. A futurist design concept.
Sketch by Vasili Petrushko, Graduate Student at NewSchool of Architecture & Design

Smart tech goes beyond connecting and automating everyday objects; it is also about empowering them beyond their original purposes. Connected street lights not only make cities more walkable and safer after dark, they provide frameworks for a multitude of other applications. Examples might include delivering environmental data, serving as Wi-Fi hotspots, or sending gunfire detection alerts. Their versatility is proving extremely popular with municipalities seeking to become smart. By 2026 it is estimated that 73 million smart street lights will be connected in vast networks across the United States (Peeples, 2018). The city of San Jose in California has installed 62,000 smart street lights, 1,000 of which feature controller boxes that can detect car crashes, record audio, and even recognize human faces (Cook, 2017; Roberts, 2017). Smart lights are one good example of making the previously inaccessible accessible. Urban processes we once could not imagine quantifying are now easy to measure. However, these seemingly unending possibilities may become a curse. Indeed, San Jose's inhabitants have expressed privacy concerns and fear that city officials will have too much power (Roberts, 2017).

All of these advancements result in a multitude of devices networked to each other and to us. Cities have access to more data than ever, but real-time reporting requires quick and intelligent analysis, which necessitates data processing and control centers. New data centers help cities optimize smart approaches to lighting, energy, traffic controls, and public safety. Smart city technology is based on the ability to collect and apply *big data* to ensure that traffic moves, and services are provided where and when they are needed. One example is utilizing RFID technology to track riders on transport networks such as the London Underground, allowing for improved decision making at the macro level. Stress is often cited as one of the major human conditions of urban living, and such traffic reduction tools can go a long way in reducing conditions that contribute to stress (Ellard, 2015).

Developing smart cities have the capacity to disseminate information through digital media and interactive means significantly faster than traditional mass media. In recent years, the concept of interactive architecture, synonymous with flexible adaptability, movement, and adaptive computational control, has provided developing solutions for contextual responses and dissemination of news in urban settings. Embedded computation plays a major role in the ability of today's interactive constructs to gather information, process it, and disseminate it to the public, thus constructing the city as an organized computational network. The concept of embedded computation not only allows for dissemination of emergency news, as well as activities in arts, sciences, and social, cultural, and sport gatherings and events, but is also an approach for creating safer and more secure living environments, and mediating the needs of citizens while facilitating communication through and within physical spaces.

Through interactive features, smart cities can reconceptualize the role that the physical environment plays in shaping the viewer's experience (Fox & Kemp, 2009, pp. 98–138). They not only reconceptualize by allowing change in lifestyle patterns, but also through sociological and psychological implications which recode citizen behavior, and create a sense of control of space, while stimulating senses and augmenting artistic initiatives.

Some, however, view the collection and use of big data as an intrusion. Others point out that data may only measure things that can be measured. A statement often attributed to Albert Einstein reminds us that, "Not all things that can be counted count. And not all things that count can be counted." Human abilities to understand, interpret, prioritize, and apply data remain essential.

Big data can also be ineffective unless there is a commitment to deliver on what we learn from it. Excessive mining and measuring may itself become a purpose, instead of a means to an end. Stephens-Davidowitz (2017) also cautions that "more data means more problems," namely because big data alone loses meaning and can lead to inaccurate conclusions. He cites one Cambridge University study that pulled massive amounts of data from Facebook profiles, and determined people who like thunderstorms and curly fries have higher IQs (p. 258). Although data supports this conclusion, such spurious correlations illustrate how application to decision making at a city-wide level might be dangerous.

Cities based solely on the collation of massive data sets are also in danger of becoming sterile. To avoid poor decisions, human factors must be addressed. As Mulligan and Olsson (2013) note, "A phone can only ever tell you its exact location; a human being can tell you that exact location is their place of employment and with whom they work" (p. 81). Smart cities cannot succeed with solutions based solely on the collection of big data. Although important and valuable, these initiatives must be accompanied by recognition of what the American Institute of Architects calls *Urban Health*. This concept connects the quality of the design of built environments with the health and wellbeing of communities and individuals. Urban health is currently being addressed on a number of different fronts. In 2019, Aarhus University in Denmark released a study that looked at people and green space. The authors speculate that greener neighborhoods can reduce stress (Engemann et al., 2019). Kelly Lambert, a University of Richmond neuroscientist, commented the study "suggests that something as simple as better city planning could have profound impacts on the mental health and wellbeing of all of us."

New York Times political columnist David Brooks (2018) concludes that the neighborhood, not the individual, is the essential unit of social change. This statement echoes the words of Jacobs and Lynch. In building cities and communities, the balance between high-tech and high-touch is critical. Designers must understand that aggregated big data must be evaluated, interpreted, and tempered with the understanding of the individual and the community. Planners and architects are not only technical experts, but also engaged in a social art. They are urban health professionals, and city design is a political act. As former Mayor of Bogota Enrique Peñalosa observed, "All these issues we are talking about are from the soul. Economics, urban planning, ecology, are only the means. Happiness is the goal" (Walljasper, 2010).

The tension between technological advances and happy communities is a major challenge facing smart cities. The Google Sidewalk Lab in Toronto, Canada, is touted as the smart city of the future because the latest technology is fully integrated into the design. Yet it has become the focus of much opposition, primarily because of concerns around privacy and control (Tatsuno, 2019). Alex Bozikovic (2018), architecture critic for the *Globe and Mail*, has said about the project, "Tech moves at a lightning pace, but development moves much more slowly. In trying to combine the two the company is learning just how hard it is to build a real-life community."

The Implications for Architects

Townsend (2014) has painted a bleak picture for the architecture profession, concluding that as smart technology has increased energy efficiency, "high architectural art has become a tool for cost-cutting and environmental compliance" (p. 22). The somewhat generic high-tech global architecture of firms such as Foster + Partners would seem to corroborate his claim. However, integration of data networks can also inspire architects to design novel and beautiful structures that work. With catchy slogans such as "Yes is More" and "Hedonistic Sustainability," Bjarke Ingels has long championed his belief that restrictions and challenges can lead to exciting innovations (Moller, 2013).

In smart cities, architects will be challenged to design for what Jensen (2016) describes as "situational stretchiness" (p. 70). In addition to communicating face-to-face, smart cities allow users to connect across time and space. Architects must consider how we will live with the technology of the near future. For example, how will buildings respond to drones in our cities? Layout and aesthetics will be informed by new restrictions such as no-fly zones and landing pods (Jensen, 2016). Drones may have widespread ramifications for the design of commercial spaces and private residences. Jensen posits architects will need to think in three dimensions and consider vertical geography through volumetric thinking (p. 71). An example might be high-rise structural innovations to accommodate vertical farming. Extrapolated further, architects must also consider a fourth invisible dimension formed by digital networks of technologies.

In order to adapt, Townsend (2014) argued, architects must treat computers as architectural materials. They must be adept at using urban data to create new models and methods. At its essence, architecture is experiential. For architects then, the question should be how can smart technologies produce a more delightful human experience. By proposing designs that demonstrate how occupant interests may be prioritized in a world of automation, architects can help build the *smart happy city*. This will require collaboration with city stakeholders; political decision makers, visionary investors, entrepreneurs, and, most importantly, the users. Tatsuno (2019) describes the human factor as empowering "smart citizen scientists." However, a European Union summit in 2014 found that there is little synergy between citizen scientists and smart cities (Craglia & Granell, 2014). Perhaps architects can work to change that.

Development of smart cities is a progressive political agenda, and architects can serve as champions of human-centered design by linking citizens directly to smart technologies and applications. People must become participants in the shaping of their own inhabited spaces. The tools of smart cities are creating new forms of social organization that necessitate new types of social spaces (Batty et al., 2012). The ways that we live and work are now more virtual than physical, yet physical space is necessary, and can even serve as a panacea to our fast-moving digital networks. Professor Richard Burdett from the London School of Economics notes, "Without cities having real engagement of its citizens, it is very unlikely that you will get fair and just environments ... the way a city is governed is just as important as the way it is designed" (Royal Geographic Society, 2016).

Making even a single smart building is a fiendishly complex task of interconnection. This fact alone may fundamentally change the education and training of architects. However, if we accept Bjarke Ingel's positive attitude there remains room for art in architecture. New technology can inspire the design of new ways of living, and smart cities can serve as inspiration for a new generation. Architecture has always spanned the bridge between science and art. Therefore, in some ways it is the creative field most prepared to tackle the opportunities and challenges of our increasingly digital world.

The Future of Smart Cities: A Utopian Vision?

Ultimately, the data-driven utopias of smart cities have two main objectives: to manage and to monetize. The degree to which a smart city project fulfills each of these goals can have major implications for inhabitants. For three decades, New York master planner Robert Moses bulldozed his way across America's cities to build dream designs around a new technology – the car. Since then, his vision has largely been rejected in favor of new urbanism and the multi-layered cities celebrated by Jacobs and Lynch. This story and similar urban planning mishaps demonstrate the unintended consequences of best laid plans. Remembering that history repeats itself, we must be careful how we approach smart city technology. There could one day come a time when we regret the things we gave away to achieve technological harmony. On the other hand, if our behaviors are based on developing intuitions resulting from day-to-day experiences, then when the city has the capacity to respond to our actions and expectations, are we not confronted with a higher level of awareness and choice?

Already we are seeing concerns about unintended consequences. The most commonly cited is a loss of control, either to the city or to the machines. "Perceptual computing" software development kits that allow devices to read the facial expressions of users are already being embedded into mobile devices, and starting to be applied to closed-circuit TV, GPS, building security systems, and a host of other tools (Mulligan & Olsson, 2013, p. 84). Fear of facial recognition software is already palpable, as people look to ways to trick the system. CV Dazzle (Harvey, 2017) is currently developing an open source toolkit to camouflage the human face from detection algorithms through creative makeup and hairstyling. Protecting gathered data is a fundamental question in the continued development of smart cities.

China's social credit system is an example of smart data as a means to monitor behavior, and control basic rights such as internet access, housing, and education. This type of social profiling featured on the dystopian television show *Black Mirror*, which explored the possible bleak consequences of such ranking schemes (Brooker & Wright, 2016). In the near future it is possible that abstract yet statistically predictable criteria may determine our fitness for loans, or employment, or even where we live (Stephens-Davidowitz, 2017).

Despite these well-justified anxieties, new technological tools help to address many big urban issues by bringing novel protocols to problems. They have already begun to help us understand and measure urban issues, and to apply information in order to improve quality of life. But we must remember they are only tools, and tools are only effective if we know how to use them. These tools and approaches must be complemented by the admonition of Jane Jacobs; there must be "eyes on the street". As she points out in her introduction, "The scenes that illustrate this book are all about us. For illustration, please look closely at real cities. While you are looking, you might as well also listen, linger, and think about what you see." (p. 3). This was abridged by long-time catcher for the New York Yankees Yogi Berra, who based on his wry remarks was considered an urban philosopher. Berra noted, "You can observe a lot by watching" (Kaplan & Berra, 2008).

By utilizing progressive technologies, providing access to smart amenities, and applying the theories and values of Jacobs and her peers, cities can become more reliable, performative, sustainable, and safe. The smart city is rapidly becoming our reality. However, it must be more than advanced technology.

It must serve the residents of a city in all aspects of urban life. Richard Jackson (2011), Professor Emeritus of the UCLA Fielding School of Public Health, reminds us that the built environment is not a community: community is the software for the hardware of the built environment. Digital data and technology is shaping our world. It will define our future and change our cities and our lives in ways we have not yet imagined. Ultimately, how the hardware and software of smart cities work together tomorrow will be based on the decisions that we make today.

References

AFP. (2017). Italy's high-rise forests take root around the world. *The Local*. Retrieved from www.thelocal.it.

Batty, M., Axhausen, K., Fosca, G. Pozdnoukhov, A., Bazzanil, A., Wachowicz, M. Ouzounis, G., & Portugali, Y. (2012, October 12). *Smart cities of the future, working paper no. 188*. London: Centre for Advanced Spatial Analysis.

Bozikovic, A. (2018, December 5). There's still a long road ahead for Sidewalk Labs' Toronto project. *Globe and Mail*. Retrieved from www.theglobeandmail.com.

Brooker, C., & Wright, J. (2016, October 21). Nosedive [Television Series Episode]. In C. Brooker (Producer), *Black Mirror*. UK: Netflix.

Brooks, D. (2018, October 18). The neighborhood is the unit of change. *New York Times*. Retrieved from www.nytimes.com.

Cook, T. (2017). Smarter streetlights. *American City & County*, 132(10), 6–12.

Craglia, M. & Granell, C. (2014). Citizen science and smart cities. Report of Citizen Science and Smart Cities summit. *Ispra*, February 5–7, 2014. Retrieved from https://publications.europa.eu/.

Davis, M. (2017). *Planet of slums*. London: Verso.

Ellard, C. (2015). *Places of the heart: The psychogeography of everyday life*. New York: Bellevue Literary Press.

Energy Innovation Center. (2019). *About*. Retrieved from www.eicpittsburgh.org/about/.

Engemann, K., Pedersen, C. B., Arge, L., Tsirogiannis, C., Mortensen, P. B., & Svenning, J.-C. (2019). Residential green space in childhood is associated with lower risk of psychiatric disorders from adolescence into adulthood. *Proceedings of the National Academy of Sciences*. Retrieved from www.pnas.org/cgi/doi/10.1073/pnas.1807504116.

Evers, B., et al. (2006). *Architectural Theory: From the Renaissance to the Present*. Los Angeles: Taschen.

Fairley, P. (2013). Urban agriculture grows up. *Architectural Record*, 201(7), 4.

Federal Aviation Administration. (2016, June 21). *Summary of small unmanned aircraft rule (part 107)* [pdf]. Retrieved from www.faa.gov/uas/media/Part_107_Summary.pdf.

Food and Agricultural Administration of the United Nations. (2019). *Urban agriculture*. Retrieved from www.fao.org/urban-agriculture/en/.

Fox, M., & Kemp, M. (2009). *Interactive architecture*. New York: Princeton Architectural Press, pp. 98–148.

Harvey, A. (2017). Camouflage from face detection. *CV Dazzle*. Retrieved from https://cvdazzle.com/.

Hell, P. M., & Varga, P. J. (2018). Accurate radiofrequency identification tracking in smart city railways by using drones. *Interdisciplinary Description of Complex Systems*, 16(3–A), 333–341. 10.7906/indecs.16.3.5.

Jackson, R. J. (2011). *Designing healthy communities*. London: John Wiley & Sons.

Jacobs, J. (1961/1992). *The death and life of great American cities*. New York: Vintage.

Jensen, O. B. (2016). Drone city: Power, design and aerial mobility in the age of "smart cities". *Geographica Helvetica*, 71(2), 67–75. 10.5194/gh-71-67-2016.

Kaplan, D., & Berra, Y. (2008). *You can observe a lot by watching: What I've learned about teamwork from the Yankees and life*. Hoboken, NJ: John Wiley & Sons.

Kiran, S. (2015). Timeless grandeur: ancient smart cities. *Built Construction Magazine*. Retrieved from www.builtconstructions.in.

Kohl, A. (2019). How your office space impacts employee wellbeing. *Forbes*. Retrieved from www.forbes.com.

Lynch, K. (1981). *A theory of good city form*. Cambridge, MA: MIT Press.

Mishra, A. (2009). The ancient ingenuity of water harvesting [online video]. *TEDIndia*. Retrieved from: www.ted.com/.

Moller, A. (2013, May 6). Yes is more: The BIG philosophy. *ArchDaily*. Retrieved from www.archdaily.com.

Mulligan, C. E., & Olsson, M. (2013). Architectural implications of smart city business models: An evolutionary perspective. *IEEE Communications Magazine*, 51(6), 80–85. 10.1109/MCOM.2013.6525599.

Muñoz, S., Araque, O., Sánchez-Rada, J. F., & Iglesias, C. A. (2018). An emotion aware task automation architecture based on semantic technologies for smart offices. *Sensors* (14248220), 18(5), 1499. 10.3390/s18051499.

Offenhuber, D., & Ratti, C. (Eds.). (2014). *Decoding the city: Urbanism in the age of big data*. Basel: Birkhauser.

Peeples, D. (2018). 5 keys to making your next street light project a success. *American City & County*. Retrieved from www.americancityandcounty.com.

Peirce, N., Johnson, C., & Peters, F. (2008). *Century of the city*. New York, NY: Rockefeller Foundation.

Pizzi, M., & Guzman, I. (2017). In ufficio conta la qualità: Office design: all about quality. *Abitare* (569), 128–145.

Pokharel, J. R. (2018, June 15). Quest for smart cities: Learn from ancient towns. *Himalayan Times*. Retrieved from https://thehimalayantimes.com.

Pope, A. U. (1976, July). *Persian architecture*. Soroush Press of National Iranian Radio and Television in Tehran under International Conventions by Asia Institute Books in Japan, pp. 106–112.

Richardson, L. (1988). *Pompeii: An architectural history*. Baltimore and London: Johns Hopkins University Press.

Roberts, M. (2017). Smart street lights in San Jose spark privacy concerns. *NBC*. Retrieved from www.nbcbayarea.com.

Royal Geographic Society. (2016). 21st century challenges: Informed discussion from the Royal Geographical Society. Retrieved from https://21stcenturychallenges.org/urbanisation-2/.

Stephens-Davidowitz, S. (2017). Mo data, mo problems? What we shouldn't do. In *Everybody lies: Big data, new data and what the internet can tell us about who we really are*. New York: Dey Street Books.

Tatsuno, S. (2019, March 3). The evolution of smart cities. *Forbes*. Retrieved from www.forbes.com.

Townsend, A. M. (2014). *Smart cities: big data, civic hackers, and the quest for a new utopia*. New York: W. W. Norton & Company.

United Nations. (2018). *World urbanization prospects: the 2018 revision* [pdf]. Retrieved from https://population.un.org.

Van der Ryn, S., & Calthorpe, P. (1986). *Sustainable communities a new design synthesis for cities, suburbs, and towns*. Gabriola Island: New Catalyst.

Walljasper, J. (2010, July 2). Happy cities for the global south: Interview with Enrique Peñalosa. *Yes!* Retrieved from www.yesmagazine.org/.

14

Seeking Material Capacity and Embedded Responsiveness

Design and Fabrication of Physically Programmed Architectural Constructs

Achim Menges and Steffen Reichert

This is a compilation arranged from two texts authored by Menges and Reichert; published texts in AD © 2012 and © 2015 John Wiley & Sons Ltd.

Introduction

Most attempts towards climate-responsive architecture heavily rely on elaborate technical equipment superimposed on otherwise inert material constructs. In contrast, natural systems embed all the responsive capacity in the structure of the material itself. In this chapter, Achim Menges and Steffen Reichert present the development of biomimetic responsive material systems that require neither the supply of external energy nor any kind of mechanical or electronic control. They introduce their research on physically programming the humidity-reactive behaviour of these systems and explain the possibilities this opens up for a strikingly simple yet truly ecologically embedded architecture in constant feedback and interaction with its surrounding environment.

Interaction with, rather than protection from, environmental dynamics is increasingly understood as a critical characteristic of performative architecture. Today climate-responsiveness is typically conceived as a technical function enabled by myriad mechanical and electronic sensing, actuating and regulating devices. In contrast to this superimposition of high-tech equipment on otherwise inert material constructs, nature suggests a fundamentally different, no-tech strategy: in various biological systems the responsive capacity is quite literally ingrained in the material itself. Employing similar design strategies of physically programming material systems rather than equipping them with additional technical devices may enable a shift from a mechanical towards a biological paradigm of climate-responsiveness in architecture.

Natural Systems: Ingrained Responsiveness

Nature has evolved a great variety of dynamic systems interacting with climatic influences. For architecture, one particularly interesting way is the moisture-driven movement that can be observed in some plants, different to other plant movements produced by active cell pressure changes, as in the

Figure 14.1 Steffen Reichert, Achim Menges, Responsive Surface Structure II, Department for Form Generation and Materialisation, HFG Offenbach, Offenbach am Main, Germany, 2008. Wood's hygroscopic behaviour is the basis here for simple, moisture-responsive parts that are in one embedded sensor, with no-energy motor or regulating element. They enabled the development of a system that responds to changes of relative humidity by opening or closing the surface. As all the responsive capacity is embedded in the material itself, no additional technical equipment or external energy is needed for the system to react to environmental changes.

Figure 14.2a Conifer cones are biological examples of hygroscopically actuated systems. A spruce cone, for example, reacts to a decrease in moisture content by opening its scales, leading to the release of the seeds. Interestingly, here even the dead tissue is capable of repetitive opening and closing cycles as the humidity responsiveness is ingrained in the material itself.

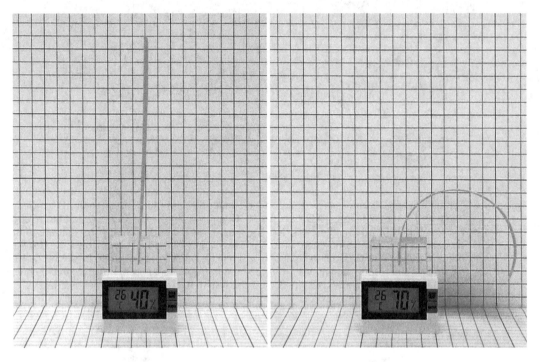

Figure 14.2b Steffen Reichert, Achim Menges and Florian Krampe, Hygroscopic Envelopes, ICD Stuttgart, 2010–11. The humidity-responsive veneer-composite element functions by translating wood's dimensional changes caused by varying moisture content into shape changes. For example, given an increase of relative humidity from 40 to 70 per cent the veneer element changes form a straight to a curved shape. By altering material and manufacturing parameters, the veneer-composite elements can be physically programmed to perform different response figures in various humidity ranges.

well-known example of the Venus flytrap (Volkov, Adesina, Markin, and Jovanov 2008). This movement consists of a passive response to humidity changes. It does not require any sensory system or motor function. It is independent from the metabolism and does not consume any energy. The responsive capacity is ingrained in the material's hygroscopic behaviour and anisotropic characteristics. Anisotropy denotes the directional dependence of a material's characteristics; for example, the different physical properties of wood in relation to grain directionality. Hygroscopicity refers to a substance's ability to take in moisture from the atmosphere when dry and yield moisture to the atmosphere when wet, thereby maintaining a moisture content in equilibrium with the surrounding relative humidity. In this process of adsorption and desorption the material changes physically, as water molecules become bonded to the material molecules.

An interesting example previously encountered as being of particular relevance for architecture is the hygroscopic behaviour of conifer cones enabled by their anisotropic material characteristics (Menges 2008). These cones are organs bearing the reproductive structures of coniferous plants (*Pinophyta*), most commonly known in the form of spruce or pine cones. The seeds contained within the cones are released by opening the scales. At this point the cell tissue of a mature cone is already dead, yet still capable of performing many opening and closing cycles. As this movement is rooted in the material's intrinsic capacity to interact with the external environment, even the no-longer-living tissue still operates. Thus, conifer cones provide an interesting example of how structured tissue can passively respond to environmental stimuli, as the cone scales react to changes in relative humidity.

The cone opening (when dried) and closing (when wetted) is enabled by the bilayered structure of the scales' material. The outer layer, consisting of parallel, long and densely packed thick-walled cells, hygroscopically reacts to an increase or decrease of relative humidity by expanding or contracting, while the inner layer remains relatively stable (Dawson, Vincent, and Rocca 1997). The resultant differential dimensional change of the layers translates into a shape change of the scale, causing the cone's overall opening and closing movement (Reyssat and Mahadevan, 2009). Instrumentalising hygroscopic material behaviour in this way is especially promising in architecture. In contrast to most other modes of actuating material systems, it requires neither supply of external energy nor any kind of mechanical or electronic control. All the responsive capacity is embedded in the structure of the material itself.

Performative Wood: Instrumental Hygroscopicity

The research on humidity-responsive hygroscopically actuated architectural systems at HFG Offenbach and the Institute for Computational Design (ICD) at the University of Stuttgart commenced with the development of reactive bilayered material elements based on the principle of conifer cones. Similar to the cones, the hygroscopicity and anisotropy innate to wooden material was used to achieve this, but in combination with a synthetic composite. Teasing out wood's responsive capacity in this way requires an in-depth understanding of the reciprocities between the anatomy of wood, its behavioural characteristics and its interaction with environmental dynamics. So how is wood hygroscopic?

Wood is a cellular structure. The cell walls, which constitute the actual wood tissue and in most cases enclose an inner cavity called the cell lumen, consist of a natural fibre composite that can be thought of as principally quite similar to the technical composite we all are familiar with, such as glass-fibre-reinforced plastics (Cave 1975). In wood, cellulose, or more specifically cellulosic microfibrils, are attributed the role of the "fibres" that are embedded in a "matrix" of hemicelluloses and lignin (Barnett and Jeronimidis, 2003). Wood is hygroscopic because water can be adsorbed and chemically bonded to the cellulose and hemicelluloses on a molecular level. This water adsorbed within the cell wall is called "bound" water, as opposed to "free" water contained in the cell lumen. The free water has hardly any effect on the dimensional behaviour of wood. In contrast, the removal of bound water (desorption) reduces the distance between the microfibrils in the cell tissue, resulting in both a substantial increase in strength due to interfibrillar bonding and a significant decrease in overall dimension. Interestingly, these changes are fully reversible (Dinwoodie 2000). This is why the pine cone can open and close over and over again, even long after its biological function of releasing the seeds has been fulfilled. It is physically programmed to do so.

The fibre saturation point refers to the state when the cell wall has reached its maximum capacity to hold bound water while there is no free water in the cell cavities. Beyond this point, the cell lumen begins to fill with free water. Generally, the amount of both bound and free water is referred to as the moisture content. It is expressed as the percentage of the water's weight in relation to the weight of the wood substance in which it is contained. Typically, the fibre saturation point is at around 27 to 30 per cent moisture content. Below this point, two fascinating things happen: first, any change to the bound water content within the cell walls will cause a dimensional change of wood; second, the actual amount of bound water content is a function of the relative humidity and, to a much lesser degree, temperature of the surrounding air. The temporal equilibrium condition reached when the wood neither loses nor gains moisture in exchange with the environment is called equilibrium moisture content. As wood always seeks to reach this equilibrium, it continuously responds to changes in the surrounding relative humidity by adjusting the bound water content, resulting in constant dimensional movement.

The anatomy of wood regulates this dimensional movement (Wagenführ 1999). More than three-quarters of a wood cell's wall consists of the middle layer of the secondary wall structure, which has been found to largely determine the dimensional movement of wood (Skaar 1988). As the microfibrils in this dominant wall layer are all oriented at a slight angle to the longitudinal axis of the cell, and as most cells are oriented parallel

Figure 14.3 The veneer-composite element can be used as the basic constituent of a larger humidity-responsive system. As elaborate testing has shown, the material system can be physically programmed to either open (right sample) or close (left sample) in response to an increase in relative humidity.

to the stem axis, the shrinking and swelling of wood is highly anisotropic. Dimensional change along the longitudinal axis (parallel to the grain) of wood is negligible. However, the transverse movement is significant, whereby the dimensional change in the tangential direction (perpendicular to the grain and parallel to the growth rings) is generally greater than in the radial direction (perpendicular to the grain and perpendicular to the growth rings). Depending on grain direction, swelling and shrinking varies from 0.1 per cent (longitudinal) to more than 10 per cent (tangential), an over 100-fold range.

This anisotropic dimensional behaviour was exploited (as part of the research at the ICD Stuttgart and HFG Offenbach) in the development of a humidity-responsive veneer-composite element based on simple quarter-cut maple veneer, chosen because of its relatively high tangential dimensional change in combination with a comparatively low modulus of elasticity. A change in relative humidity, for example from 40 to 70 per cent, leads to a rapid dimensional change of the veneer that is translated into a significant shape change of the element. Given a rapid rise in relative humidity, the element changes from the straight to an acutely curved state within a few minutes or less. The veneer-composite element instrumentalises the material's responsive capacity in one surprisingly simple component that is at the same time embedded sensor, no-energy motor and regulating element. Moreover, all veneer-composite elements respond independently. The resultant decentralised control and collective behaviour at the system level is sensitive to local microclimates and at same time highly robust.

Material Capacity and Responsiveness

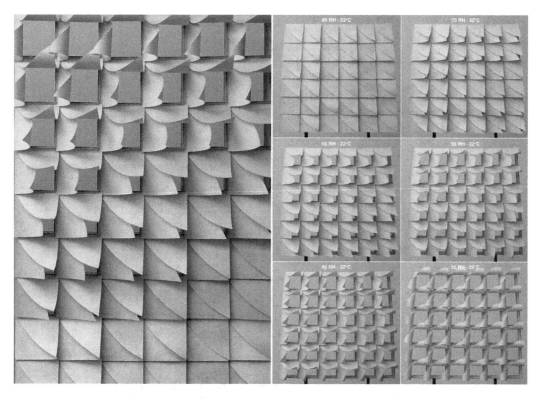

Figure 14. 4 Elaborate laboratory tests in a climate chamber demonstrated the material system's capacity to rapidly respond to changes in relative humidity (right). When the relative humidity increases, the system consistently opens and closes over a large number of cycles. Literally embodying the capacity to sense, actuate and regulate, the surface locally responds to microclimatic variations (left).

Material System: Programmed Responsiveness

The dimensional change of wood is directly proportional to changes in moisture content. Hence, a specific increase in moisture content will always result in the same swelling or shrinking dimensions of a particular piece of wood. However, in combination with another synthetic composite, this linear dependency can be expanded to achieve highly specific yet diverse shape changes. In other words, the veneer-composite elements can be physically programmed as a material system to perform different response figures in various humidity ranges. For example, the ICD's experiments in a climate chamber have shown the following. Using the same veneer as a starting point, two veneer-composite elements can be produced – one entirely straight and the other acutely curved at a humidity level of 40 per cent. When relative humidity rises to 70 per cent, the initially straight element will change to an acutely curved shape as mentioned above, while the other will become straight. Exposed to the very same environmental changes, the two test pieces geometrically respond in exactly the opposite way.

Such substantially different behaviour can be achieved through specific alterations to the production parameters. The composite system elements can be programmed to materially compute different shapes within variable humidity-response ranges by adjusting the following five parameters: (1) fibre directionality, (2) layout of the natural and synthetic composite, (3) length–width–thickness ratio, (4) geometry of the

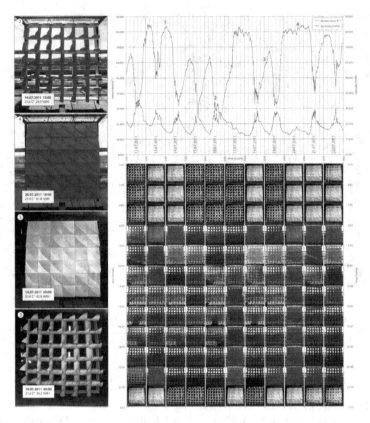

Figure 14.5 The responsive skin system has been long-term tested for half a year in real humidity cycles of the Central European climate. In constant exchange with the surrounding environment it shows consistent and reliable opening and closing cycles in response to changes in ambient relative humidity and temperature.

element, and especially (5) humidity control during the production phase. This enables the development of elements that either open or close when ambient humidity increases, as well as the careful choreography of their response range and behaviour.

The manifold behavioural capacities at the element level open up various possibilities for developments at the system level. So far, two kinds of systems have been investigated by the authors: first, systems that open when the relative humidity level increases (by changes to their surface porosity, these systems have the ability to autonomously ventilate once a defined level of relative humidity is reached) (Menges 2009), and second, systems that operate in an inverse manner, reacting to a rise of relative humidity, for example through approaching rainfall, by closing the structure, thus providing weather-sensitive convertible surfaces. In addition, because relative humidity is temperature dependent, these systems also show a degree of relative thermal responsiveness: given a swift drop in temperature, the surfaces also close. Using functional prototypes, these surface behaviours have been investigated extensively, both as laboratory experiments in a climate chamber with carefully controlled humidity changes and in long-term tests set in the environment and exposed to the real humidity cycles of the Central European climate.

Material Capacity and Responsiveness

Figure 14.6 Steffen Reichert, Achim Menges, Responsive Surface Structure II, Department for Form Generation and Materialisation, HFG Offenbach, Offenbach am Main, Germany, 2008. A responsive system component was developed that can adapt its shape by being based on either a four-, five-, six- or seven-sided polygon. In addition, the component does not require a substructure; the responsive tip is an extension of the thicker structural frame.

System morphology plays an important role in the development of these locally controlled, responsive surface structures, as each region independently senses local humidity concentrations and changes the surface accordingly. The related microclimatic conditions across the surfaces, which are simultaneously affected by and do affect the system's behaviour, are directly influenced by both the local element geometry as well as the system morphology. Accounting for the complex reciprocity of individual elements as well as overall system responsiveness and related macro- and micro-thermodynamic modulations, an integrative computational design process was developed as part of the research presented here in order to derive more specific system morphologies as compared to the relatively simple and regular geometry of the testing prototypes (Reichert and Menges, 2010). In this process, the surface geometry is algorithmically generated and controlled through a number of parameters and constraints based on the material's anatomy, characteristics and behaviour.

The evolution of the system morphology is based on iterative changes to the variables of the algorithmic processes and the evaluation of the generated results. This computational design process allows a relatively simple system consisting only of four-, five-, six- and seven-sided polygonal

Achim Menges and Steffen Reichert

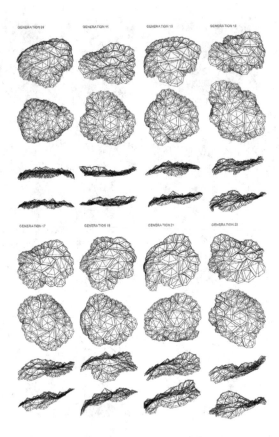

Figure 14.7 Through an evolutionary computational design process a relatively simple system consisting only of four-, five-, six- and seven-sided polygonal elements can specifically adapt its morphological features as, for example, local element density and overall curvature, to structural and contextual requirements.

elements to specifically adapt its morphological features as, for example, local element density and overall curvature, in response to contextual requirements. In addition, this morphology enables the integration of the responsive and structural elements in one system. Through additional lamination with altering grain directionality, the reactive elements gain structural capacity towards the perimeter of each responsive component. In the overall system, this local thickening of the system results in a structural lattice with a responsive surface.

Climactive Architecture: Ecological Embedding

Perceiving wood's innate environmental responsiveness as a versatile behavioural characteristic rather than a difficult to control deficiency allows for teasing out a new performative capacity from one of the oldest and most common construction materials at our disposal. In architecture, this provides an interesting alternative for thinking about responsiveness not as something that is superimposed on inert material constructs by means of high-tech equipment, but rather as a no-tech capacity already fully embedded in the material itself.

Material Capacity and Responsiveness

Figure 14.8 Achim Menges, Steffen Reichert and Scheffler+Partner, FAZ Pavilion, Frankfurt, 2010. The envelope of the pavilion is designed as an integral structural and climate-responsive material system providing for a novel convergence of environmental and spatial experiences. As the responsive capacity is embedded in the material itself, no additional technical equipment or supply of energy is required. When the weather changes from sun (bottom left) to rainfall (bottom right), the related increase in relative ambient humidity automatically triggers an autonomous response and the structure closes to form a weatherproof skin.

The ramifications of releasing this material capacity by employing the aforementioned research in an architectural context may be profound, as the work on the FAZ Summer Pavilion (2010) begins to indicate. Situated on the northern embankment of the River Main in Frankfurt's city centre, the pavilion provides an interior extension of this popular public space. Based on the integral structural and hygroscopic responsive system introduced above, the entire envelope of the summer pavilion reacts to weather changes. On sunny or dry days with relatively low ambient humidity, the surface is fully opened. When the weather changes and rainfall approaches, the related increase in relative ambient humidity automatically triggers an autonomous response and the structure closes to form a weatherproof skin. Once the rain is over, the relative humidity level drops again, causing the pavilion to open. Similarly, the envelope closes at night with considerably lower temperatures than during the day and reopens with the rise of temperature in the morning.

Figure 14.9 Steffen Reichert, Achim Menges, Hygroscopic Envelope Prototype, ICD Stuttgart, 2010–11. A full-scale, functional responsive skin prototype shows how the material's responsive capacity can be explored through a field of surprisingly simple components, all of which are at the same time embedded sensor, no-energy motor and regulating element.

Beyond fulfilling merely the functional requirements of a convertible building skin, the autonomous, passive actuation of the FAZ Pavilion's surface provides for a unique convergence of environmental and spatial experience. The perception of the delicate, locally varied and ever-changing environmental dynamics is intensified through the subtle and silent movement of the responsive envelope. The changing surface literally embodies the capacity to sense, actuate and regulate, all within the material itself. This suggests the possibility of a strikingly simple yet truly ecologically embedded architecture that is in constant feedback and interaction with its environment.

HygroScope: Meteorosensitive Morphology

The HygroScope – Meteorosensitive Morphology installation was commissioned by the Centre Pompidou in Paris for its permanent collection and was first shown in the exhibition "Multiversités Créatives" in 2012. The project provided an opportunity to explore responsive surface structures that are driven by environmental changes and juxtapose them to a context that seeks maximum climate stability. In many ways, the Centre Pompidou embodies the architectural antithesis to the design

Material Capacity and Responsiveness

Figure 14.10 Achim Menges with Steffen Reichert/ICD and Transsolar Climate Engineering, Hygro-Scope – Meteorosensitive Morphology, Centre Pompidou, Paris, 2012. The HygroScope's meteorosensitive morphology responds to changes in the Parisian weather, which is simulated in a display case that serves as a virtual connection between outdoor conditions and the interior of the Centre Pompidou, where it is in the permanent collection.

approach presented before, which seeks to engage the dynamics of the environment. Instead the Pompidou building aims at protecting against them, striving for interior conditions that are as homogeneous as possible. In fact, the technology required for this is celebrated as one of its key architectural features. The purpose of the HygroScope installation was to question this condition by inserting a virtual extension of the exterior climate into the Pompidou's interior, in the form of a large display case in which the fluctuations of the outdoor Parisian climate are reproduced. Situated within the glass case, the meteorosensitive morphology constantly responds to the variations in outside humidity levels by moving its surface elements.

The passive response behaviour, as well as the response range, was physically programmed into the 4,000 geometrically unique surface elements during the fabrication process, which was carried out in-house at the ICD. Two different families of responsive elements form the basis for the articulation of the overall system: cellular apertures based on four- to seven-sided polygons that display a central opening and closing, as well as

Achim Menges and Steffen Reichert

Figure 14.11 The meteorosensitive morphology consists of wood and veneer-composite elements only. The back view of the installation highlights that no additional mechanical or electronic equipment is required, as the performance of sensing, actuating and responding is integrated within the material.

rectangular apertures with side-mounted, flap-like movement. The computational design process generates and adapts these elements based on system-intrinsic constraints and extrinsic data of the heterogeneous humidity distribution within the display case, leading to an overall morphology with cellular aperture clusters that are connected by radial surface-element formations. The responsive surface elements open when there is an increase of relative humidity in the display case, and close again when the humidity level drops. The decentralised system indexes microclimatic zones through locally specific responses, resulting in a cumulative effect of modulating the surface state and appearance, without the need for any additional technical equipment or operational energy supply.

The human sensory system detects minute temperature changes in the sub-degree range. In contrast, relative humidity levels are typically only felt in their extremes. This means that the omnipresent humidity dynamics of our environment are hardly ever consciously perceived by us. The meteorosensitive morphology taps into these ubiquitous yet hidden environmental flows. It harvests the latent energies in these abundant dynamics and employs them to drive an aesthetic performance: The subtle and silent movement of the intricate surface becomes a visual device that provides the visitor with

Material Capacity and Responsiveness

Figure 14.12 The responsive surface elements close with a decrease of relative humidity in the display case (top), and they open again when the humidity level rises (bottom). This surface motion becomes provides the visitor with a unique visual experience of the humidity flux that forms part of our everyday life but usually escapes human perception.

Figure 14.13 Achim Menges with Oliver David Krieg and Steffen Reichert/ICD, HygroSkin – Meteorosensitive Pavilion, FRAC Centre, Orléans, France, 2013. The hygroscopic behaviour of wood is the basis for the pavilion's weather-responsive apertures, which are in one embedded sensor, no-energy motor and regulating element. The pavilion is in the permanent collection at FRAC.

Figure 14.14 Achim Menges with Oliver David Krieg and Steffen Reichert/ICD, HygroSkin – Meteorosensitive Pavilion, FRAC Centre, Orléans, France, 2013. The pavilion features a modular skin with 28 different element shapes, which all originate from the self-forming capacity of elastically bent plywood plates. The centre of each module houses unique meteorosensitive apertures, which embody the capacity to sense, actuate and react, all within the material itself.

a unique experience of the humidity flux that forms part of our everyday life, but usually escapes our perception. It triggers a sense of awareness for a potential new kind of interaction between the built and the natural environment.

HygroSkin: Meteorosensitive Pavilion

The HygroSkin – Meteorosensitive Pavilion project was a first exploration of the architectural implementation of weather-responsive surface structures. Commissioned by the FRAC Centre in Orléans, France, for its permanent collection, this travelling pavilion was first shown in the exhibition "ArchiLab – Naturalizing Architecture" in 2013 (Brayer and Migayrou 2013). The design examines the tension between a deep, undulating skin embedding weather-responsive aperture clusters, and an archetypical architectural volume, the box. In response to the constraints of transport volume for a travelling pavilion, the envelope was developed as a modular system. For this, the project not only furthered the development of the responsive veneer-composite elements employed in the HygroScope installation, but also tapped into several years of design research on elastically self-forming structures (Fleischmann, Knippers, Lienhard, Menges, and Schleicher 2012).

Material Capacity and Responsiveness

Figure 14.15 The deep ecological embedding provides for a unique convergence of environmental and spatial experiences. In response to the outside weather conditions, the pavilion's meteorosensitive architectural skin modulates the interior's degree of enclosure, illumination and interiority.

The 28 skin modules are geometrically unique, but their individual shapes all originate from the self-forming capacity of elastically bent plywood plates. Two fully planar plywood panels are connected by custom joints, which results in the self-forming of a conical surface. Two such surfaces, together with an insulation core, constitute the skins of the sandwich elements, which are robotically trimmed to ensure precision for frequent assembly. Laser scanning revealed that the mean accuracy of the self-forming process is within 0.5 millimetres (0.02 inches), which results in highly consistent panel gaps that accentuate the weather-responsive apertures as the pavilion's most striking architectural features.

The response range of the 1,100 different aperture elements is set between 30 per cent and 90 per cent relative humidity, which corresponds with the humidity fluctuations in a moderate climate zone. In contrast to the HygroScope installation, the HygroSkin pavilion's responsive elements are physically programmed to be open in low-humidity conditions and to close when the humidity increases. As a consequence, the apertures are fully open on a bright sunny day, but once the weather changes and rain approaches, which by nature corresponds with an increase in relative humidity, the skin closes entirely by itself.

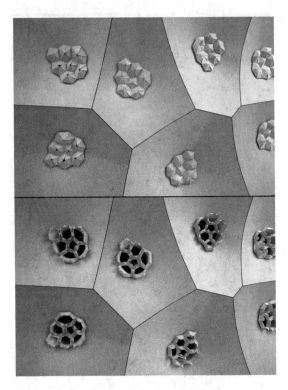

Figure 14.16 The responsive surface elements are physically programmed to close with an increase in relative humidity, and to open again when the humidity level drops. The apertures are therefore fully open on a bright sunny day, but once the weather changes and rain approaches, the skin closes entirely by itself.

The pavilion's architectural performance becomes inseparable from its environment. Its skin continuously adapts to the local microclimate with varying degrees of openness and porosity, leading to a modulation of the envelope's visual permeability and the interior light conditions. In direct feedback with the environmental dynamics, the spatial characteristics of the pavilion continually vary. When closed, the translucent skin and related indirect light in conjunction with the convex undulations of the surfaces, creates a highly introverted space. However, this changes profoundly with the gradual opening of the apertures, as they establish a visual connection to the outside and allow for direct light to enter the interior, which accentuates the transformation with a startling play of shadows. Beyond the functional benefits of an autonomously weather-responsive envelope, the pavilion's deep ecological embedding provides for a unique convergence of environmental and spatial experiences. The fluctuation of varying degrees of enclosure, illumination and interiority in concert with the perception of the locally varied and ever-changing weather dynamics is intensified through the meteorosensitive architectural skin, which embodies the capacity to sense, actuate and react, all within the material itself (Krieg 2014).

Outlook: Ongoing Design Research

The two projects presented here demonstrate the architectural potential of unfolding the inherent performative capacity of wood through advanced design computation and digital fabrication. The

Material Capacity and Responsiveness

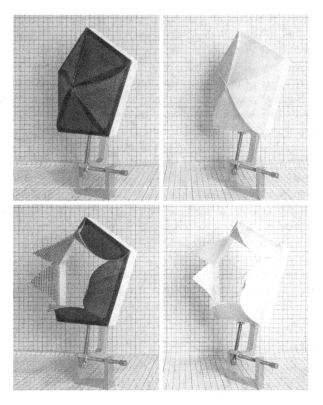

Figure 14.17 David Correa, Steffen Reichert and Achim Menges/ICD, 3D-printed hygroscopic programmable material systems, University of Stuttgart, 2014. Instead of utilising the natural anatomy of wood, advanced additive manufacturing technologies can be employed to design the material structure of weather-responsive elements. The development of custom design tools, machine control and material composition has made possible the production of 3D-printed prototypes (left) that show the same behaviour as the veneer-composite elements (right).

ICD is currently pursuing the further development of this work through two parallel lines of design research. One field of investigation continues to look at the anatomy of wood as a driver in hygroscopically actuated material systems but seeks to explore size and thickness ranges beyond the veneer-composite approach. Ongoing research has successfully demonstrated that element thickness can be increased more than tenfold without compromising the responsive behaviour. In this case, the quarter-cut veneer is replaced with tangentially cut wood plates. While this prolongs the response time, it also adds considerable stability and robustness to the responsive elements, as well as significantly increasing their actuation forces. Log scanning techniques have been integrated into the computational design process, and the design method has been extended with the aim of differentiating grain directionality across larger building parts. This direct interface with the digital fabrication process and elementarisation technique enables the physical programming of more complex movements and sequences, opening up the possibility of designing both substantially larger and more robust responsive elements with sophisticated reversible movements and larger-scale self-forming building parts.

The second line of the ICD's ongoing research extends the work towards designing the material structure itself. As an alternative to utilising the natural anatomy of wood, the aim is to build up the structure of weather-responsive elements through advanced additive manufacturing technologies. The development of custom design tools, machine control and material composition have made possible the production of a first series of prototypes that show the same behaviour as the veneer-composite elements of the HygroScope and HygroSkin projects. An integrative approach to the design computation and 3D printing means form, structure and movement behaviour can be considered from a comprehensive material perspective. The design process directs the composition and organisation of the material structure, enabling the modulation of key material properties at a local level across larger elements. This gives rise to a vast spectrum of additional design opportunities. The ability to tailor the anisotropic characteristics of the material facilitates the physical programming of more complex motions, achieving both multi-directional movements in space and multi-stage responses in time within a single element. The material can also be programmed to respond differently to climatic changes across various areas of the same sample, or across a larger field of many samples. In addition, the 3D printing enables a functional grading from structural to responsive regions within one building part and one fabrication process.

The design research here thus indicates the possible convergence of computationally designing and physically programming the performance of materials that compute form and modulate performance in unison with the environment, and a potential new take on ecologically embedded architecture.

Acknowledgements

HygroScope – Meteorosensitive Morphology, Achim Menges in collaboration with Steffen Reichert, Permanent Collection, Centre Pompidou, Paris, 2012. Project Team: Achim Menges Architect, Frankfurt; Institute for Computational Design, University of Stuttgart; Transsolar Climate Engineering, Stuttgart.

HygroSkin – Meteorosensitive Pavilion, Achim Menges in collaboration with David Oliver Krieg and Steffen Reichert, Permanent Collection, FRAC Centre, Orléans, France. Project Team: Achim Menges Architect, Frankfurt; Institute for Computational Design, University of Stuttgart.

References

Barnett, J. R., & Jeronimidis, G. (Eds.). (2003). *Wood Quality and its Biological Basis*. Oxford: Blackwell CRC Press.
Brayer, A. & Migayrou, F. (2013). *Archilab 2013: Naturalizing Architecture*. Orléans: Editions HYX.
Cave, I. D. (1975). Wood Substance as a Water-Reactive Fibre Reinforced Composite. *Journal of Microscopy*, Vol 104, No 1, pp. 57–62.
Dawson, C., Vincent, J. F. V., & Rocca, A. (1997). How Pine Cones Open. *Nature*, Vol 390, No 18/25, December, p. 668.
Dinwoodie, J. M. (2000). *Timber: Its Nature and Behaviour*. London: E&F Spon Press.
Fleischmann, M., Knippers, J., Lienhard, J., Menges A., & Schleicher, S. (2012). Material Behaviour: Embedding Physical Properties in Computational Design Processes. *AD Material Computation: Higher Integration in Morphogenetic Design*, March/April (no 2), pp. 44–51.
Krieg O. D. (2014). HygroSkin: Meteorosensitive Pavilion, in Fabio Gramazio, F., Kohler, M., & Langenberg, S. (Eds.). *Fabricate: Negotiating Design and Making*, pp. 60–67. Zurich: gta.
Menges, A. (2008). Material Performance – Responsive Surface Structures: Instrumentalising Moisture-Content Activated Dimensional Changes of Timber Components. *AD Versatility and Vicissitude in Morpho-Ecological Design*, Vol 78, No 2, pp. 39–41.
Menges, A. (2009). Performative Wood: Integral Computational Design for Timber Construction, Reform: Building a Better Tomorrow. *Proceeding of the 29th Conference of the Association For Computer Aided Design In Architecture (ACADIA)*, Chicago, 21–25 October, pp. 66–74.

Reichert, S., & Menges, A. (2010). Responsive Surface Structures, Bionik: Patente aus der Natur. *Proceedings of Fifth Bionics Conference, Bionik-Innovations-Centrum (B-I-C)*, Bremen, 22–23 October, pp. 28–35.

Reyssat, E., & Mahadevan, L. (2009). Hygromorphs: From Pine Cones to Biomimetic Bilayers. *Journal of the Royal Society Interface*, Vol 6, 951–957.

Skaar, C. (1988). *Wood-Water Relations*. Berlin: Springer-Verlag.

Volkov, A. G., Adesina, T., Markin, V. S. & Jovanov, E. (2008). Kinetics and Mechanism of Dionaea Muscipula Trap Closing. *Journal of Plant Physiology*, Vol 146, No 2, pp. 694–702.

Wagenführ, R. (1999). *Anatomie des Holzes*. Leinfelden-Echterdingen: Drw Verlag.

15.1
Resiliency in Performativity
A Shared Vision with Sustainability: Preamble

R.K. Stewart

November 2018: Gunman opens fire at bar/restaurant in Thousand Oaks, California USA, killing 13 people and injuring 10+ others. This was the 307th mass shooting in the United States in 311 days. Estimated recovery costs unknown.
September 2018: Three wildfires in California, USA, burn 230,000+ acres, killing 91 people, displace hundreds of thousands of people, destroy 19,000+ structures. Clean-up costs likely to exceed $3 billion; rebuilding costs estimated at $10 to $15 billion.
October 2018: Hurricane Michael makes landfall in Florida, USA. Category 4 storm with 155 mph winds. Flooding and wind damage in Florida/Alabama/Georgia, killing around six people; 1,000,000+ buildings lose electricity. Rebuilding costs estimated at $4.5 to $10 billion.
September 2018: 7.5 magnitude earthquake and tsunami strike Indonesian island of Sulawesi. Tsunami detector buoys fail to warn of 10-foot-high wave that kills 2,000+ people. Around 2.4 million people impacted, 68,000 homes damaged. Rebuilding costs exceed $1 billion.
September 2018: Hurricane Florence makes landfall in South Carolina, USA. Category 1 storm with 90 mph winds moves slowly at 2–3 miles per hour; 40 inches of rain falls in 24 hours, flooding parts of North and South Carolina; 620,000+ people lose electricity; 40+ people killed; rebuilding costs estimated at $20 to $30 billion.
September 2018: Super Typhoon Mangkhut strikes Guam, the Marshall Islands, the Philippines and Southern China. Category 5 storm with 107 mph winds, 3,000,000+ people evacuated, around 70 people killed. Rebuilding costs estimated to exceed $70 billion.
June 2018: Mount Fuego erupts in Guatemala. Pyroclastic flow destroys infrastructure and buildings. More than 2,000,000 people affected, around 110 people killed. Rebuilding costs estimated to exceed $30 million.
May 2018: Dust and wind storm strikes Western and Northern India. High temperatures contribute to storm's high winds and lightning. Houses destroyed, trees uprooted, livestock and 125+ people killed. Estimated recovery costs unknown.
April 2018: Crude oil pipeline spills approximately 407,000 gallons near Amherst, South Dakota, USA. Estimated recovery costs approximately $9.57 million.

February 2018: Earthquake strikes Papua, New Guinea, 7.5 magnitude with 6.5 magnitude aftershock. Thousands impacted by loss of housing and access to food and water, and 160 people are killed. Rebuilding costs exceed $61 million.

February 2018: Gunman opens fire on his classmates at Marjory Stoneman Douglas High School in Florida, USA, killing 17 people and injuring 17 others. Estimated recovery costs unknown.

These are but a few of the "adverse events", natural and man-made disasters, that disrupted the daily lives of people around the globe in 2018. These are the kinds of adverse events anticipated in the 2014 Industry Statement on Resilience signed by more than 24 design and construction industry organizations in the United States. This statement provides a common definition of "resiliency". The definition states that resiliency is "the ability to prepare and plan for, absorb, recover from, and more successfully adapt to adverse events" (Brugger n.d.; American Institute of Architects 2018). The beauty of this definition lies in its simplicity, clearly setting out a specific goal for architects and designers to achieve in our work. Being the creative types we are, we can prepare a design solution that achieves that goal. It is what we do, day in and day out.

It is clearer than ever before that climate change will contribute to creating numerous adverse events that disrupt people's lives. On October 8, 2018, the United Nations Intergovernmental Panel on Climate Change (IPCC) issued a new assessment updating their Sixth Climate Assessment of one year earlier. The IPCC identified the need for "rapid, far-reaching and unprecedented changes in all aspects of society" to limit global temperature rise to 1.5 degrees C in order to ensure a "more sustainable and equitable society" (IPCC 2018). On November 23, 2018, the United States Government released the Fourth National Climate Assessment. The Assessment's Introduction Overview states:

> Climate change, once considered an issue for a distant future, has moved firmly into the present … This National Climate Assessment concludes that the evidence of human-induced climate change continues to strengthen and that impacts are increasing across the country.
>
> *(U.S. Global Change Research Program 2018)*

As the designers of the built environment, architects have an obligation to respond to the implications of these documents and the many others that echo the call to action.

We have seen man-made events become a significant contributor to the adverse events we must address each year. Be it an "active shooter", industrial accident, infrastructure failure, terror attack or similar event, the risk to people's lives and the costs to return them to their "normal" daily routines increase every year. By assessing risk factors related to a specific project, architects and designers can address these risks in the projects they envision.

The challenge inherent in creating resilient communities is massive. Society seeks solutions that mitigate the impacts of these adverse events. Society wants solutions that allow people to quickly return to their normal lives when adverse events occur. Architects, by our training, skills and nature, are not fearful of big challenges. As the profession that envisions a built environment that does not yet exist, architects are uniquely positioned to play a significant role in leading the global response to the impacts of both climate change and man-made events.

We are learning a tremendous amount about how to respond to the risks we face from these adverse events. Architects and designers are bringing their innovative spirit to the task, implementing a broad range of solutions at a variety of scales. As a result we are seeing these solutions tested, and we are finding out what works, and also what needs to be refined and improved. The evidence is mounting that we design buildings and communities to be more resilient. The 2018 *Natural Hazard Mitigation Saves* report issued by the National Institute of Building Sciences updated a previous report on the cost of disaster recovery. The 2018 report found that $1 of governmental funds invested in mitigation returns $6 in reduced recovery costs. It also found that $1 of private industry mitigation investment returns $4 in reduced recovery costs (NIBS 2018). Sharing these lessons with each other is vital at this stage. The more people who bring real-world experiences and understanding to the design community, the quicker we will propel the refinement process, and the sooner we will all be able to live in resilient communities.

The effort to recognize and respond to the challenge of creating resilient communities is in fact a struggle for our survival as a species. In many cases it is a struggle for people's lives. It will always remain a struggle for the quality of life that people will be able to enjoy. We know much about what needs to be done. Each day we are learning more about *how* to get it done. We must be conscious that future generations are watching us to see if we will be thoughtful, intelligent and worthy ancestors. What we do today will determine their conclusion.

References

American Institute of Architects. (2018). *Industry Statement on Resilience*, Retrieved from http://content.aia.org/sites/default/files/2018-04/Resilience_Statement_2018-0410.pdf.

Brugger, L. (n.d.) *AIA Leadership Urges for Increased Community Resilience at White House Conference*, Amerian Institute of Architects. Retrieved from www.aiacontracts.org/articles/12356-aia-leadership-urges-for-increased-community.

Intergovernmental Panel on Climate Change. (2018). *Summary for Policymakers of IPCC Special Report on Global Warming of 1.5°C approved by governments*. Retrieved from www.ipcc.ch/2018/10/08/summary-for-policymakers-of-ipcc-special-report-on-global-warming-of-1-5c-approved-by-governments/.

National Institute of Building Sciences. (2018). *Natural Hazard Mitigation Saves Study*. Retrieved from www.nibs.org/page/mitigationsaves.

U.S. Global Change Research Program. (2018). *Fourth National Climate Assessment Overview*. Retrieved from https://nca2014.globalchange.gov/highlights/overview/overview.

15.2

Resiliency in Performativity
A Shared Vision with Sustainability

Terri Peters

Resiliency is often defined as the ability to become strong, healthy, or successful again after a mishap, or to return to an original shape after being pulled, stretched, pressured, or bent by external forces. Many different disciplines are exploring aspects of resiliency. In ecological systems, resilience relates to the capacity of a system to withstand change (Holling, 1973). In urban studies, resilience is studied in a range of disciplines and studies, such as urban ecological resilience, urban hazards and disaster risk reduction, resilience of urban and regional economies, and promotion of resilience through urban governance and institutions (Leichenko, 2011). In architectural design research and practice, the term is normally used to describe strategies of minimizing environmental impact to achieve better building performance to address climate change and extreme weather (National Institute of Building Sciences, 2018). The term "resilience" could be more focused on making better use of resources we have, maximizing the positive impacts of design, and doing more with less.

The concepts of resilience and sustainability are often used interchangeably in architecture, but this tends to minimize the needs of people and our future needs in considering performance-based design. In the push for new buildings being "green", the human dimensions are often neglected, despite the fact that strategies for designs for human wellbeing and enhanced architectural quality are often compatible with designs for reducing negative environmental impacts (Peters, 2017). The United Nations Environment Programme's new report on global warming states that staying at or below 1.5°C of warming requires slashing global greenhouse gas emissions 45% below 2010 levels by 2030 and reaching net zero by 2050 (UNEP, 2018). Research has shown that overwhelmingly it is the operation of buildings – how, when, in which ways they are used and by whom – that most affects the environmental performance and impacts of buildings (Janda, 2011; Architecture 2030, n.d.). In fact, for typical standards of building construction, the embodied energy used in the construction of a building and its materials is equivalent to only a few years of operating energy. There is a need for studies that investigate the culture around resilient design strategies in buildings to understand resilient design as a process, not an end goal. This means engaging with those that design, use, and maintain buildings in order to understand not only how to make buildings more energy efficient, but also better for people.

There is little doubt that in the future, we will see the impacts of climate change and extreme weather built all around us. In architecture, there is a growing acceptance of the importance of addressing extreme weather, energy use, and climate change but few benchmark built projects that are addressing multiple scales of resilience. There is a rising sentiment in the profession that "resilience is the new green" (Archdaily, 2013), and the building industry is responding to the evidence that buildings in use account for 40% of all greenhouse gas emissions (UNEP, 2018). But the qualities of resilient design are rarely explicitly defined or conceptualized. Typically, resilient design is thought of as related to more established parameters in sustainable design, which focus not only on economic and environmental aspects but also on people and social needs. There is a need for more design offices to explore the qualities of architecture that can develop in the context of resilient design and at scales of the room, building, neighborhood, and city. There is generally a need for a stronger conceptual framing of resilient architecture. For example, what could be made more resilient by redesigning the built environment, the building or the occupant? Our behavior in buildings greatly impacts building performance. Similarly, the qualities of our built environment have been proven to impact our moods, wellbeing, and experiences, and how we behave (McGraw Hill Construction, 2014). Studies show some people are more psychologically resilient than others, and this is in part due to the "protective factors" people have around them that decrease the risks of them being negatively impacted, and "promotive factors" that actively promote their wellbeing to enable them to be more resilient (Patel and Goodman, 2007). Designers believe that our design decisions have the ability to positively impact people's wellbeing, so it would be interesting to know what would be "protective factors" in architecture? Integrating nature and biophilic design are proven to reduce people's stress and promote wellbeing (Kellert, Heerwagen, and Mador, 2013) so perhaps foregrounding these aspects could be effective in assisting people in our adjustment to the realities of a changing climate. The nature-based urban interventions proposed for a number of resilient neighborhoods in Copenhagen are examples of how some design studios are rethinking resilient design to maximize the social impacts of resilient design strategies.

This chapter highlights resilient urban design examples that respond to the Cloudburst Management Plan in Copenhagen. These use nature-based design approaches to better connect people and environmental performance with the goal of resiliency in the face of extreme weather and climate change. This chapter foregrounds how resilient designs can benefit people and our environment, shape our attitudes to the natural world, and amplify our sensory experiences of spaces and places. Research and practice in architectural design is beginning to reframe the focus of resilience as having a shared vision with sustainability, towards a more performance-process-based approach. Three examples are examined: Tåsinge Square by GHB Landscape Architects (completed 2014), Sankt Kjelds Square and Bryggervangen Road by SLA (completed 2019), and Hans Tavsens Park and Korsgade by SLA (starts construction 2019). Each climate-adapted renovation addresses multiple parameters of flooding and extreme weather, by providing socially sustainable environments with new green leisure spaces in the city.

Cloudburst Copenhagen: Performative Design for People

Denmark has a rainy climate, with residents experiencing about 121 days of rain per year. But on 2nd July 2011, more than 150 mm of rain fell in Copenhagen in only two hours, causing serious flooding in basements, roads, and parks, and overwhelming the sewer system. This was a particularly damaging extreme weather event in a series of serious cloudburst storms that impacted the city, causing an estimated €1 billion damage (American Society of Landscape Architects, 2016). This particular event was highly dramatic given the short length of the cloudburst, and it became a catalyst for change, sparking renewed public debate and creating important political and economic support for the development of an ambitious climate adaptation strategy for the city. Later that year, the City of Copenhagen adopted the Climate Adaptation Plan (City of Copenhagen, 2011) which incorporated three levels of climate adaptation based on risk. For example, the Plan requires that if the risk of damage is high, proactive measures like expanding the capacity of sewers and increasing local management of rainwater should be undertaken; if prevention is impossible then the damage must be minimized in various ways, including by adapting areas where rainwater can be redirected and stored; and the lowest-priority measures are those that reduce vulnerability to flooding, such as having pumps ready for use in basements and other clean-up measures. The Climate Adaptation Plan explicitly states (p. 6) that interventions to address the cloudbursts must focus on both the local environment and the aesthetics and benefits to people:

> In Copenhagen we will focus on climate adaptation measures also representing an asset in themselves, regardless of the extent of the expected climate change. In this connection we will work in particular on the use of blue and green elements in the urban space, which will make Copenhagen an even more attractive city.

The Plan also details that Copenhageners should expect to have to deal with a 1-meter sea level rise over the next 100 years (City of Copenhagen, 2011). To begin to address the current and future threats to quality of life, specific urban renovation projects were outlined in the Cloudburst Management Plan (City of Copenhagen, 2012). In the next 10–20 years, 300 small urban design transformations will be implemented around the city, to respond to local needs and current and projected flood events (City of Copenhagen, 2012).

The Danish office TREDJE NATUR was part of the team that designed the 1 sq km neighborhood masterplan for the first Climate Neighborhood in 2012 and this masterplan of Østerbro has informed the climate-adapted renovations, including Tåsinge Square, Sankt Kjelds Square and others (City of Copenhagen Klimakvarter, n.d.). As a key principle the masterplan reclaims 20% of the current road area (50,000 sq m) for pedestrians, bikes, and parks, by optimizing the road infrastructure and parking lots (City of Copenhagen with SLA, n.d.). The masterplan introduces bicycle paths that act as storm water channels, plus water towers, green roofs, urban gardens, greenhouses, and canals that carry water out from the neighborhood to the harbor. These strategies simultaneously give rise to greater biological diversity in the city. TREDJE NATUR are known for their multi-scale approach to resilience, and their ideas extended beyond neighborhood regeneration. They also proposed the concept of using controlled flooding of underground parking structures as temporary water storage, and new materials for sidewalks that cope with rainwater and smaller-scale material and component design. For example, their "Climate Tile" is a rainwater management strategy but also a tactile and modular material system that improves the sidewalks in the city. When sidewalks are demolished for infrastructure works or to widen the sidewalk, then these permeable, modular, sidewalk pavers will be installed in such a way that they drain excess rainwater to street trees and to soil beneath for absorption (TREDJE NATUR, n.d.).

Nature-based Adaptation of Tåsinge Square, Copenhagen, by GHB Landscape Architects

Within this masterplan, the first completed climate-adapted urban renovation in Copenhagen is Tåsinge Square, designed by GHB Landscape Architects in 2014. The project is intended to have an educational value and a focus on community consultation, to set the tone for the more than 300 planned small interventions in the city. A significant emphasis was placed on designers working in close consultation with local residents, to encourage people to be engaged in the process and to support the larger goals of the project. The square is a demonstration project for the rainwater systems: rainwater captured on neighboring roofs is collected into large sculptural collection areas in the square, in containers shaped like giant raindrops. These "raindrops" have a mirror finish, reflecting the sky and inviting people to climb on top and play. People can use handpumps to release some of the water from the raindrops to water the vegetation. Large black tilted umbrella-shaped sculptures mark the new public spaces, providing shelter and directing rainwater. The square's water-themed sculptures are playful and functional.

The new Tåsinge Square is designed to give more space for pedestrians and public space, with enhanced green spaces for recreation, and better street-level quality of life for residents. By narrowing the space for cars and removing on-road parking to reclaim space for pedestrians and public space, the project increases the amount of permeable surface, and so the site can better accommodate heavy rains. By reducing the paved areas, the cars that use the roads around the square are fewer, and moving at lower speeds. The existing local conditions had a sloped site, which is rare for Copenhagen's urban spaces. The sloped site has been redesigned to improve water management, with permeable spaces and slopes in parts of the site to carry the water away from the nearby apartment basements to reduce flooding. The project transforms 1,000 sq m from asphalt to green and garden spaces, lowering surrounding air temperatures, reducing the urban heat island effect, absorbing rainwater, and creating more visually engaging surroundings.

The cloudburst projects can be seen as a benchmark in performance-driven urban design as each embrace both sustainability and resiliency while allowing for flexibility and creativity in balancing competing variables. Each of the cloudburst renovations has a different way of meeting specific goals. This allows for solutions that are attuned to particular conditions, as they vary over time. This strategy of being able to refocus and adjust as needed over time is central to performative architecture.

Renovation of Sankt Kjelds Square and Bryggervangen Road, SLA Architects

SLA's climate-adapted renovation of Sankt Kjelds Square and Bryggervangen Road was completed in early 2019 (Figures 15.2.1–15.2.3). The name of their competition-winning project is "Use Nature in the City" and their project aims to improve the social and ecological functioning of the neighborhood. SLA's design decisions were guided by the aim of making the area more beautiful and useful to residents by integrating trees, plants, walking paths and green space into this streetscape, previously dominated by hard, non-porous surfaces and a very wide circular roundabout (City of Copenhagen Klimakvarter, n.d.). The space devoted to cars was made more efficient and reduced in size, and the area now has a variety of spaces and microclimates. In February 2019 the last stage of the construction, the planting of 586 trees and plants, took place, and the designed network of green rainwater beds became functional. The trees were chosen specifically to be 48 different local tree species, such as willow, oak, and coniferous trees together with selected exotic trees. "Together, the trees, plants and rain beds cover 2/3 of the area's original asphalt, which gives a strong nature injection to the neighborhood," explains Stig L. Andersson, partner and design director in SLA (SLA Architects, n.d.). The project's goal is to encourage residents to spend more time outside and to engage with nature by having areas for outdoor dining, benches between the trees, and large tree trunks that children can play and climb on. During an extreme cloudburst, rainwater will be led to the rain beds, where it will slowly be absorbed and sink down locally or drain further away to the Copenhagen harbor via a cloudburst line. The area now achieves a much higher biodiversity.

There is no doubt that retrofitting Sankt Kjelds Square with so many trees will positively impact the health of residents. Climate change is having numerous negative impacts on human health, and research has found that numerous complex and urgent health research areas relate to climate change, including asthma and respiratory allergies, foodborne diseases and nutrition, and mental-health- and stress-related disorders (Watts et al., 2018). The trees will also likely improve property values in the area, and the studies show urban trees contribute positively to quality of life for residents (Kardan et al., 2015).

Resiliency in Performativity

Figure 15.2.1 Climate adaptation of Sankt Kjelds Square and Bryggervangen Road, SLA Architects, Copenhagen, Denmark, completed 2019. Before and after drawings of Sankt Kjelds Square, which now offers better connected spaces for pedestrians and bikes, and urban nature with new green recreation areas, paths, and trees.
Drawings courtesy SLA

Hans Tavsens Park and Korsgade, SLA Architects

Following on from the success of Sankt Kjelds Square and Bryggervangen Road, the climate-adapted renovation of Hans Tavsens Park and Korsgade (a street) in the Nørrebro district of the city started on site in 2019 (Figures 15.2.4–15.2.6). SLA won the competition with Ramboll (engineers) and the focus is to work in collaboration with local residents to create a blue-green environment that focuses on social and ecological improvement (SLA Architects, n.d.).

SLA called their project "The Soul of Nørrebro" rather than a name that focused more on the locally specific climate goals of the project, which are to filter and purify the rainwater entering the city's lakes and also to use the park's terrain to slow and direct the flow of rainwater during a storm event towards Korsgade, where it will drain into the lakes. The designers aimed to make the ecological functions like water absorption and water purification into practical and beautiful aspects of the neighborhood. Andersson explains that these climate projects can make more of the "extra benefits we get from climate adaptation: The blue, the green, the health, the active and the social. In short: All what makes life in the city worth living" (Peters, 2017). The design of the park and improvement of the street will better connect local residents to nature, using rainwater not only as a force to be controlled, but also as a potential resource as a habitat for plants and animals and as a focus for a series of interconnected public spaces. Hans Tavsens Park will function as a large rainwater catchment basin during storm events, creating a sculptural circular pool. The pool is a striking landmark and symbol for the park and a way of making water a part of the city.

SLA's design improves the spatial qualities and materials of the sidewalks and pedestrian areas along Korsgade. The redesigned street has been narrowed with reduced space for cars and has been

Figure 15.2.2 Climate adaptation of Sankt Kjelds Square and Bryggervangen Road, SLA Architects, Copenhagen, Denmark, completed 2019. The climate adaptation reduces the area of paved roads for cars and provides more permeable areas for absorbing rainwater to reduce flooding.
Photo courtesy SLA. Photographer: Magnus Klitten

redesigned with permeable paving materials and patterns. The street will have vegetation to absorb excess rainwater, and channels of irrigation to focus the water away from the local site to the lake. The planting of grasses and trees to filter and absorb rain also increases biodiversity and improves the experience of the street for residents. With fewer hard impermeable surfaces, the city noise will be dampened, the new greenery will improve biophilia, and birds and pollinators will be attracted to the site. Combined with environmental and ecological benefits, there are a number of social sustainability features that incorporate active design principles, including new bike lanes and multi-functional mini gardens to get people outside playing, tending to nature, and walking along the new streetscape (Peters, 2017).

Multi-functional, Local, and Process-Based Approaches to Resiliency

The encouraging examples of the first climate-adapted urban renovations in Copenhagen share resilient and sustainable aspects. In each case, the focus has been on multi-functional design features that have many functions and that are open to people's customization and residents' input, and can accommodate changes in how people use them, depending on the season or weather. Each project is designed to address specific local conditions, whether that is making the most of a change in slope, or a location

Resiliency in Performativity

Figure 15.2.3 Climate adaptation of Sankt Kjelds Square and Bryggervangen Road, SLA Architects, Copenhagen, Denmark 2019, completed. The climate adaptation by SLA improves people's connection to nature, offering residents new urban nature experiences and health and wellbeing benefits from having nature so conveniently located to home.
Photo courtesy SLA. Photographer: Magnus Klitten

where it makes sense to decrease the amount of parking, or provide shade. In each, the process-based approach has contributed to the overall sustainability of the project. Resilient architecture is a process that is influenced by people's expectations and how people use buildings, not an end goal with clear boundary conditions. The design of resilient environments requires a deep understanding of the specific uses, local needs, and possible stress scenarios, and then devising design strategies that could enable stressed environments to "bounce back". Therefore, resilient design is always locally specific. For example, in these areas of the city, the context of climate change and extreme weather is a focus, but the designers take into account that water imposes varied environmental challenges throughout the year. Not just flash flooding but a number of unusual weather events are impacting Copenhagen, including storm surges, blizzards, and summer dry spells. Resilient buildings and landscapes in this region must plan for all these events, in addition to the day-to-day stresses of significant precipitation or high humidity, or the contrast between high exterior humidity and dry interiors. A strong feature of the urban interventions is that rather than a singular climate change vision for the city, there has been a neighborhood-scale approach that has been carefully planned by TREDJE NATUR, with numerous specific designs by different designers for different needs, in different areas.

The solutions to extreme weather – and to successful resilient design responses generally – are culturally specific in how they are realized by designers. Denmark is a unique context and the

Figure 15.2.4 Hans Tavsens Park and Korsgade, SLA Architects, Copenhagen, Denmark. In progress, started 2019. SLA are considering the ecological functions like water absorption and water purification as practical and beautiful aspects of the neighborhood. The street design also incorporates channels of irrigation (not visible in this rendering) to focus the water away from the local site to the lakes.

Rendering by Beauty and the Bit, courtesy SLA

Figure 15.2.5 Hans Tavsens Park and Korsgade, SLA Architects, Copenhagen, Denmark. In progress, started 2019. Hans Tavsens Park will function as a large rainwater catchment basin for the neighborhood during storm events. The sculptural circular pool is a striking landmark and symbol for the park and a way of making water a part of the city.

Rendering by Beauty and the Bit, courtesy SLA

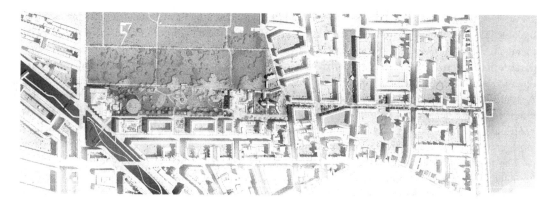

Figure 15.2.6 Hans Tavsens Park and Korsgade, SLA Architects, Copenhagen, Denmark. In progress, started 2019. The renovated park and redesigned streets work together to create an integrated stormwater strategy in the city, moving water along to the lakes while providing urban nature amenities and green surroundings for people.

Drawing courtesy SLA

cloudburst solutions are designed for this particular cultural, political, economic, and ecological setting. For example, the integration of urban nature is made in connection with the mid-rise apartment housing buildings lining the streets that tend to look inward around a central courtyard behind. Increasingly there is a focus on how these buildings can integrate more with the city, and how to make the most use of the fronts of these buildings facing streets. There is a strong cycling culture in Denmark, and a shift towards more active living in the city, and there have been numerous initiatives for narrowing urban roadways in the last few years. The cloudburst renovations respond to a clear desire by residents to reclaim space from cars and create more amenities for residents in front of the buildings. Many urban dwellers have had their basements flooded in storm events, so there is an existing political will for creating stormwater management features in the city. The combination of these specific cultural and political factors has meant that the cloudburst renovations are specific to the needs of residents and are able to be implemented and funded with support from residents and stakeholders. The cloudburst renovations are designed to work with this specific context, and these were not designed to be resilient design strategies that could be replicated around the world in other social or ecological contexts.

Conclusions: A Shared Vision with Sustainability

The challenges of climate adaptation must do more than create buildings that can withstand climate change and extreme weather; the social, political, economic aspects must also be considered. Sustainability is often defined in architecture as the need to manage resources to allow for wellbeing and equity now, and for current and future generations (Brundtland et al., 1987). The current ways of discussing and evaluating the multidisciplinary concept of sustainability in design tends to rely on the three-pillar model of environment, economy, and society. Of these, the social pillar has been largely neglected and remains poorly defined as the wider debate has prioritized environmental concerns (energy use, climate change) and economic considerations (cost savings, speed of construction, short life spans for buildings) (Littig and Griessler, 2005; Davidson, 2009). Still, the concept of sustainability must be interwoven into resilient design through performative solutions.

While current debates around sustainability could be considered to focus more on balancing needs and multiple priorities, resiliency is often defined as the capacity of a system to absorb disturbances and reorganize to sustain the same function, structure, feedback, and identity (Walker et al., 2004). This can be hard to translate into architectural design, which has many performance criteria, often with conflicting goals. Too often in resilient design, the social and human dimensions are ignored and possible synergies are overlooked. A shared concept with both sustainable and resilient design is the notion of time. For example, the cloudburst interventions are designed to be sustainable, long-lasting, and adaptable to change over time. The focus on people and the need to offer tangible benefits to inhabitants as well as, and as part of, the environment, are what sets these projects apart from other green infrastructure projects.

The future of resilient and sustainable environments will likely incorporate a wider definition and connect to concepts beyond architecture and design. Building on theories exploring environment and behavior, resilient design should take into account relationships between the scale of the individual, community, built environment, landscape, neighborhood, city, country, and ecosystem (Stokols, Lejano, and Hipp, 2013). Resilient design strategies must address the tradeoffs between design decisions and consider how buildings can improve people's quality of life. The Cloudburst Copenhagen urban design interventions offer positive examples of resilient design that embody a holistic understanding of sustainable design. If resilient design should better consider building performance and social benefits of proposals, there is an opportunity to consider the direct human health and wellbeing "extra benefits" to constructing more resilient buildings, and foregrounding the social opportunities of creating more resilient and sustainable built environments can be achieved using performance-based strategies for the built environment.

References

American Society of Landscape Architects. (2016). *The Copenhagen Cloudburst Formula: A Strategic Process for Planning and Designing Blue-Green Interventions*, www.asla.org/2016awards/171784.html.

Archdaily. (2013). AIA Puts Resiliency on the Agenda, www.archdaily.com/432802/aia-puts-resiliency-on-the-agenda-resilience-is-the-new-green.

Architecture 2030. (n.d.). *2030 Challenge*, https://architecture2030.org/2030_challenges/2030-challenge/.

Brundtland, G., Khalid, M., Agnelli, S., et al. (1987). *Our Common Future*, World Commission on Environment and Development.

City of Copenhagen. (2011). *Climate Adaptation Plan*, https://en.klimatilpasning.dk/media/568851/copenhagen_adaption_plan.pdf.

City of Copenhagen. (2012). *Cloudburst Management Plan*, https://en.klimatilpasning.dk/media/665626/cph_-_cloudburst_management_plan.pdf.

City of Copenhagen Klimakvarter. (n.d.). *The Climate Resilient Neighbourhood of Osterbro*, http://klimakvarter.dk/en/.

City of Copenhagen with SLA. (n.d.). *Climate Adaptation and Urban Nature Development Catalogue*, https://issuu.com/sla_architects/docs/bynatur_booklet_uk_small.

Davidson, M. (2009). Social Sustainability: A Potential for Politics, *Local Environment* 14: 607–619.

Holling, C. S. (1973). Resilience and Stability of Ecological Systems, *Annual Review of Ecology and Systematics* 4: 1–23.

Janda, K. B. (2011). Buildings Don't Use Energy, People Do, *Architectural Science Review* 54: 15–22.

Kardan, O., Gozdyra, P., Misic, B., et al. (2015). Neighborhood Greenspace and Health in a Large Urban Center, *Nature Scientific Reports* 5: 11610.

Kellert, S. R., Heerwagen, J., Mador, M. (2013). *Biophilic Design: The Theory, Science and Practice of Bringing Buildings to Life*, John Wiley & Sons.

Leichenko, R. (2011). Climate Change and Urban Resilience, *Current Opinion in Environmental Sustainability* 3 (3): 164–168.

Littig, B., Griessler, E. (2005). Social Sustainability: A Catchword between Political Pragmatism and Social Theory, *International Journal of Sustainable Development* 8: 65–79.

McGraw Hill Construction. (2014). *The Drive Toward Healthier Buildings: The Market Drivers and Impact of Building Design and Construction on Occupant Health, Well-Being and Productivity*, www.worldgbc.org/sites/default/files/Drive_Toward_Healthier_Buildings_SMR_2014.pdf.

National Institute of Building Sciences. (2018). *Whole Building Design Guide* "Resilience," Washington, DC, www.wbdg.org.

Patel, V., Goodman, A. (2007). Researching Protective and Promotive Factors in Mental Health, *International Journal of Epidemiology* 36 (4): 703–707.

Peters, T. (2017). Superarchitecture: Building Better Health, *Architectural Design* (March/April): 24–31.

SLA Architects. (n.d.). *Hans Tavsens Park and Korsgade*, https://sla.dk/files/2914/9449/3217/SLA_Ramboll_HansTavsensPark_UK.pdf.

Stokols, D., Perez Lejano, R., & Hipp, J. (2013). Enhancing the Resilience of Human-Environment Systems: A Social Ecological Perspective. *Ecology and Society*, 18 (1): 7. https://doi.org/10.5751/ES-05301-180107.

TREDJE NATUR. (n.d.). *Green Climate Adaptation*, www.tredjenatur.dk/en/portfolio/green-climate-adaption/.

UNEP (United Nations Environment Programme). (2018). *Emissions Gap Report 2018*, www.unenvironment.org/emissionsgap.

Walker, B. H., Holling, C. S., Carpenter, S. R. et al. (2004). Resilience, adaptability and transformability in social–ecological systems, *Ecology and Society* 9 (2): 5.

Watts, N., Amann, M., Arnell, N., et al. (2018). The 2018 Report of the Lancet Countdown on Health and Climate Change: Shaping the Health of Nations for Centuries to Come, *The Lancet* 392 (10163): 2479–2514.

16

Architectonic Design and Computation in Performative Buildings

Brady Peters

Introduction

The genesis of architectural form results from a complex combination of different influences, constraints, and negotiated decisions during the design process. Architects are concerned with building form in regard to its significance and meaning; how spaces are experienced by the senses; and how a building will perform in terms of structure, sound, or sun. The architect's concern for performance is not new; for example, the Code of Hammurabi called for buildings to be structurally stable, concert hall forms have evolved over time to develop preferred acoustic characteristics, and Persian wind towers were developed to encourage natural ventilation. So, while a concern for form and for performance is not new, what is new is the widespread adoption of digital tools in architecture, and this chapter discusses how the nature of the form-giving process of architecture is changing with the adoption of design computation. The adoption of computation is changing the way in which designers think – as Hugh Whitehead writes, "parametrics is more about at attitude of mind than any particular software application" (Whitehead in Woodbury, 2010), and part of this change in thinking relates to the relationship between form and performance. The use of computational tools gives new opportunities for architects to incorporate knowledge from other disciplines. If "architectonic" can be defined as "the science of architecture" (Wikipedia, 2019), then design computation is enabling an expanded *science of architecture* – a system of design tools to develop knowledge about architecture in the form of testable explanations. Computation is enabling new approaches to architectonic design and the creation of performative buildings.

Performative Design

Performance can be defined as "the action or process of carrying out or accomplishing an action, task, or function" (Oxford Dictionary, 2019). As architects, when we talk about performance we are usually referring to how well a building functions in relation to some metric: structural performance, energy performance, acoustic performance, etc. It is inevitable that all buildings "perform" to some degree – after all, all buildings have structure, light, air, and sound; however, these "performances" are not always prioritized in the same way. As a building design emerges out of the complex web of desires, requirements, and constraints, certain features of the design begin to take precedence; a designer may be more concerned with structural efficiency, or acoustic performance, or energy efficiency in a particular design. However, if given the option of a design performing better or worse, designers would almost certainly choose better. And why not – to design well-performing buildings is usually what we are striving for. While shelter is one of our essential needs as humans and one of the primary aims of architecture, most architecture aims to do more than merely shelter, but create space that has cultural meaning and social significance, and has a considered and designed atmospheric experience.

While the concept of performance in architecture has been around for a long time, it is only recently that the concept of performance-based design is gaining importance in the way in which buildings are commissioned, designed, and built. Most building codes dictate a prescriptive approach to architectural design. Greg Foliente states that while "a prescriptive approach describes an acceptable solution … the performance approach is, in essence, the practice of thinking and working in terms of ends rather than means" (Foliente, 2000). It has been shown that a performance-based design approach enables increased innovation as well as cost-optimized construction while at the same time protecting the safety, health, and general welfare of building inhabitants (Foliente, 2000). So, if a performance-based approach is so great, then why do architects not use it? This is likely because performance is project-specific and designs emerge only through a consideration of form, function, and context in a bi-directional design process (Kalay, 1999), and so it is easier to look up regulations in standard codes than re-calculate for each project. This calculation barrier has inhibited performance-based design, but now that architects have access to computational tools more and more architects and engineers are adopting a performance-based design approach.

With the advent of digital design tools architects began to experiment with new architectural forms, and given this new formal freedom that digital technologies enable, architects began to experiment with new drivers for the process of formation. Historian Antoine Picon observed that architects have a "desire to understand form in terms of formation" and turned to building performance as a way to guide the finding of form (Picon, 2010). Branko Kolarevic calls this new kind of architecture "performative architecture," which he explains is not "simply a way of devising a set of practical solutions to a set of largely practical problems" but an architecture that emerges from processes of form generation "that are grounded, on the one end, in intangibilities such as cultural performance and, on the other, in quantifiable and qualifiable performative aspects of building design, such as structure, acoustics, or environmental design" (Kolarevic, 2004) (Figures 16.1 and 16.2).

Tool-user to Tool-maker

Architecture is a practice that is (at least in part) defined by its tools. Historically, architects distinguished themselves from master builders by designing buildings at a remove from their construction (Evans, 1997). The design of buildings requires the use of representational media, and architects have traditionally used drawings and physical models to communicate their designs to those who would build them. It has been argued that it was the invention of drawing – the invention of the pen and drafting board together with isometric projection – that enabled the birth of the architect. The definition of what it means to be an architect is therefore related to the creation of drawings and models (Hill, 2006). In practice today, the architect is paid for drawings sets produced. However, to limit the role of drawings and models merely to instructions for others to follow is to miss a huge part of what the act of drawing brings to the genesis of architecture. Architecture is more than drawing buildings; it is also the conceptualization of what that building is, and drawing and modelling act as generative and explorative devices beyond simply communication tools.

Brady Peters

Figure 16.1 Bloomberg European Headquarters, Foster + Partners, completed 2017, London, UK. The building has a structural sandstone frame, with large bronze fins that shade the floor-to-ceiling glazing. The bronze fins give the building in scale, angle, and density on each façade according to orientation and solar exposure, and are an integral part of the building's natural ventilation system.

Source: Nigel Young/Foster + Partners, 2019

It is one of the central arguments of this chapter is that it is no small matter that the tools of architecture have changed, and are continuing to change. In the last 50 years architects have moved from the drafting board to the computer. Beyond the shift from analog to digital, in the last 20 years there has been a shift in architectural design techniques from the use of software to the development and customization of software. This shift from tool-user to tool-maker is profound. In the early 2000s several architecture practices began to cultivate innovations in digital design approaches through forming internal research and development groups (Whitehead, 2003). The Smartgeometry group was formed at this time with a united goal of developing a new computational platform specifically for architects, and the development of Bentley's Generative Components emerged from these efforts (Peters and Peters, 2013). In 2007 saw the introduction of Grasshopper, a new visual scripting engine for popular CAD software Rhinoceros, where functional components are represented as graphic nodes and are directionally wired together to create an algorithmic logic (McNeel, 2019). Using parametric design tools designers establish the relationships by which parts connect, and build up a design using these relationships, and "this process of relationship creation requires a formal notation and introduces additional concepts that have not previously been considered as part of design thinking" (Woodbury, 2010).

Figure 16.2 Bloomberg European Headquarters, Foster + Partners, completed 2017, London, UK. A distinctive stepped ramp flows through the full height of the building. The bronze-clad ramp is characterized by its smooth continuous three-dimensional loop. It is designed to be a place of meeting and connection, allowing people to hold brief impromptu conversations with colleagues, whilst not impeding the flow of people.
Source: Nigel Young/Foster + Partners, 2019

Specific and Generic Tools

It has been observed that one of the great powers of parametric design is the definition and exploration of design space; that is, the rapid iteration and testing of a range of possible building designs. And while this is a widely discussed and much-used capability, new building projects are demonstrating that this is not the only power of computational design, and may not even be the most significant benefit to parametric design. In a study of several built projects, a key strength of parametric design was in its ability to realize highly specific, differentiated, rule-based designs (Wortmann and Tuncer, 2017). Through computation, architects can automate processes, undertake parametric modelling, and use algorithmic procedures to simulate or analyse data. Computational tools can be used to develop highly specific design systems for particular projects, but also powerful generic tools and frameworks that can be applied to a variety of projects and situations. The development of powerful generic computational tools has resulted in a new "eco-system" of plug-ins that add functionality to the CAD/parametric system (Davis and Peters, 2013). While some of these plug-ins are focused on geometry, there are many that incorporate building performance simulation. This gives architects access to simulation tools that did not exist even a decade ago, and enables architects to now "compute the environment" (Peters and Peters, 2018). Simulation is now accessible within the architect's everyday design environment.

Enter Simulation

Architects are natural simulators, intuitively using different methods of drawing and modelling to predict aspects of tectonics, performance, or experience. While computer modelling and simulation bring new capabilities in terms of the types of performance architects can model, and the level of detail they can study these phenomena at, they also raise potentially problematic issues of representation. The way in which simulation results are visualized plays a crucial role in interpretation and communication, and when drawing for simulation, buildings must be drawn, modelled, and abstracted in different ways; with simulation the epistemological nature of the architectural drawing is changing. Simulation's time-based nature promotes understanding buildings as ever-changing states instead of singular solutions. Architectural designs no longer exist as a static set of two-dimensional drawings, but as a set of live, linked, computational algorithms.

> As architects and engineers navigate this new landscape of data, new potentials for building design emerge as a deeper understanding of architectural environments is exposed through adoption of new techniques of modelling, simulation, and visualization. Architectural representation is changing in the era of computer simulation.
>
> *(Peters, 2018)*

The use of modelling and simulation predicts a future state or behaviour; however, as these are borrowed tools and thinking, there is a risk of errors or inaccuracies through the mis-application or mis-interpretation, and this is a potential argument against the architect's use of simulation. However, architecture has often always borrowed techniques from other disciplines, and to assume architects will not learn or understand does not give architects enough credit, and assumes a static disciplinary state in which change does not occur. Kjell Anderson writes that "while design simulation is often seen as a specialist's tool ... the greatest value for architects is the freedom to play with design ideas and receive timely feedback," and while there are risks in including architects in the simulation process, the risk of excluding them is far greater (Anderson, 2014). To improve simulation for architecture, simulations must be applied more to the early design phases, simulations should be used to analyze alternatives, simulation should be used for more than simply code compliance, simulation should include multiple objectives, and users should be able to combine simulation tools (Hansen and Lamberts, 2011).

Architects are leveraging computational tools and cross-disciplinary expertise to innovate new building designs and building technologies. One such building is the new Bloomberg European Headquarters. Michael R. Bloomberg explains that "from day one, we set out to push the boundaries of sustainable office design – and to create a place that excites and inspires our employees" (BRE, 2019). The building was awarded a BREEAM "Outstanding" environmental rating with a score of 99.1% (BRE, 2019) – the highest sustainability rating for any commercial building in the world. In 2018, the Bloomberg European Headquarters was awarded the Stirling Prize, with the judges calling it a "once-in-a-lifetime" building that has "not just raised the bar for office design and city planning but smashed the ceiling" (Foster + Partners, 2019). Key innovations in the building are: an integrated ceiling panel system, improved water conservation, a breathing façade system, smart airflow that responds to occupancy, and combined on-site heat and power generation (BRE, 2019). Computer performance simulation was used to evaluate options throughout the design phases and so was a key tool for building innovation (Figure 16.3).

Architectonic Design and Computation

Figure 16.3 Solar simulation study. Bloomberg European Headquarters, Foster + Partners, completed 2017, London, UK. Computer performance simulation was used to analyze design options, enabling architects to improve designs that ultimately helped the building achieve a BREEAM "Outstanding" environmental rating.
Source: Foster + Partners, 2019

Interoperability and Beyond

Within contemporary design practices there now exist many pieces of software, and often many of these are used in the same project, which results in a complex web of digital and analogue processes. Interoperability between software systems, and in particular between simulation and design environments, has justifiably received a lot of attention. An increasingly popular way to connect is through run-time interoperable programs – for example, simulation plug-ins for Rhino Grasshopper. These tools enable CAD geometry to run simulation routines natively offering the ability to simulate designs during design. Daniel Knott of Buro Happold feels that it is when "geometry and data are on same page" that design works well; he believes that most of the environmental design work is a balancing act between form and performance (Peters and Peters, 2018). Similarly, Philip Robinson of Foster + Partners' Specialist Modelling Group (SMG) has found that importing geometry from CAD to commercially available acoustic simulation software can be onerous, and that there is a huge advantage to using software that has both design and simulation capabilities (Peters and Peters, 2018). The SMG at Foster + Partners both develops generic digital tools and workflows as well as highly specific design and analysis techniques relating to particular projects. Through the customization of existing software, the use of open-source simulation engines, and the development of new software, the SMG creates tools for geometry generation, front-end solutions that access existing simulation engines, develop new simulation engines, and create customised data visualization. Interoperability is an important part of the workflows it develops. Design teams will use whatever digital design tools are necessary to best accomplish specific tasks. In a recent tower project, the main structure and geometry was designed using CATIA, the interiors used Revit, the façade was done using Dynamo, and Rhino and Grasshopper were the go-to 3D CAD sketching environment. SMG Partner Irene Gallou explains that "you need to use the right tool for the right stage" (Peters and Peters, 2018).

Dr. Michael Wetter from the Lawrence Berkeley National Laboratory predicts that much of the innovation in building science is likely to happen at the interface between different disciplines, and that the need to collaborate more effectively will require new tools, more integrated systems, immersive simulation and visualization, and increased modularization of code which enables users to participate in program development (Wetter, 2011). Just as a key characteristic of parametric and computational design software has been flexibility and customizability, this has also been true in the leading simulation tools available in the building industry, such as TRNSYS, Radiance, and OpenFoam. Xavier DeKestelier has observed that "in the last five years people are using more open source code … not just architecture but also in other industries" (Peters and Peters, 2018).

The larger of Bloomberg's two buildings can utilize natural ventilation. Outside air enters the floor plates through the exterior vertical bronze fins, moves across the floor plates, and rises up and out of the building through a central atrium (*CIBSE Journal*, 2017). Computational fluid dynamic (CFD) simulation was used to evaluate the air movement through the fins. The fins also incorporate acoustically treated vents that open and close to control airflow. Acoustic wave simulation was used to develop custom

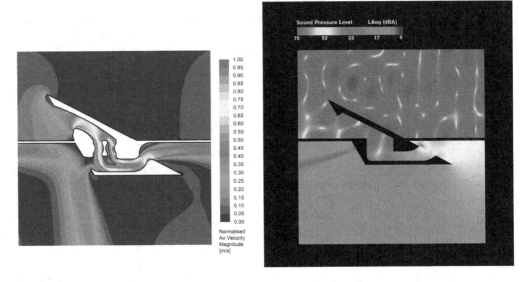

Figure 16.4 Air flow CFD simulation and acoustic simulation of exterior fin. Bloomberg European Headquarters, Foster + Partners, completed 2017, London, UK.

Source: Foster + Partners, 2019

Architectonic Design and Computation

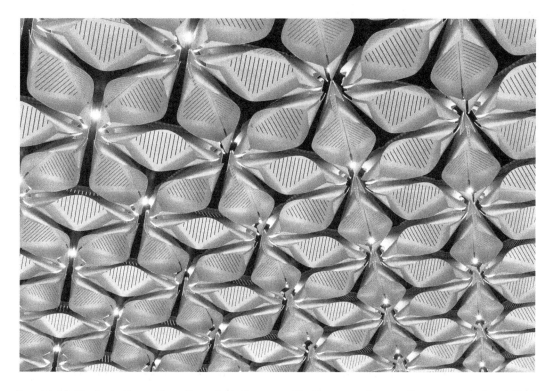

Figure 16.5 Performative ceiling. Bloomberg European Headquarters, Foster + Partners, completed 2017, London, UK.
Source: Nigel Young/Foster + Partners, 2019

baffles within the fins that ensured that while fresh air enters the building, noise from the city will not. The ceiling is another unique and innovative element developed for the Bloomberg building. Inspired by the pressed metal ceilings of New York, the distinctive polished aluminium panels, or "petals," perform multiple roles – ceiling finish, light reflectors, air supply, and acoustic attenuation. The petal design combines various elements of a typical office ceiling into an energy-saving integrated system. The ceiling uses 500,000 LED lights and uses 40% less energy than a standard office lighting solution. The integrated ceiling panel is pushed tight to the underside of the structural steelwork, to maximize the 2.9 m floor-to-ceiling height (Figures 16.4 and 16.5).

Structural Form

Building structure is of prime importance to architecture. The poetics of structural form, material, and connection are celebrated and admired by many architects, engineers, historians, and theorists, and the public. Though the efficiency of structure is not every architect's goal, and the aesthetics of structure can be variously defined, the structural robustness and reliability of building design is of concern to all. With the rise of digital design technology, new modelling techniques have enabled new geometric forms and a new language of doubly curved surfaces in architecture. It has been observed that these expanded formal possibilities enabled by 3D computer modelling and algorithmic techniques have resulted in an explosion of formal explorations – "new and complex shapes can be generated regardless of their structural stability or feasibility" (Block, 2016), and while new digital tools are adept at creating form of seemingly endless complexity, it is becoming "increasingly evident that the state-of-the-art 3D modeling tools are not sufficiently well-suited to solve these challenges ... new tools that integrate shape, design, function, structure, and fabrication have to be developed" (Block, Kilian, and Pottmann, 2015). Computer software such as Karamba, Kangaroo, and RhinoVault now integrates structural simulation directly into the digital design software that architects use. Structural simulation brings real-world forces back to computationally generated geometry. Philippe Block writes that

> thanks to recent innovations in structural engineering, particularly in the development of extremely flexible and fast structurally informed computational design methods, as well as in multi-criteria optimisation techniques, the gap between structural and architectural complex curved geometry is narrowing. The potential of this newly generated knowledge is that it allows for truly holistic designs that find a balance between form and force.
>
> (Block, 2016, p. 70)

With new integrated structural design tools architects are now better equipped to design buildings that incorporate structural performance considerations into the many criteria that influence the creation of form.

Structural analysis was introduced in building construction during the second half of the nineteenth century, and since then all structures have been based on the paradigm of calculability. Computational design provides not only a technical means to automate the calculation of structural performance, but also the opportunity to develop new structural forms that take advantage of progress in the field of computational mechanics and simulation technologies opportunities (Knippers, 2013). The ability to incorporate mathematical logic into the design process and make new design tools has led to the increased incorporation of scientific simulation techniques into building design tools, and the creation of a new design culture at the boundary of architecture and engineering. The recent adoption of computational and simulation techniques is not only changing the range of the technically possible, but also alters the social structures that architects operate within. Jan Knippers notes that "the introduction of computer-aided fabrication methods means more than just the use of new tools: it is the breakup of traditional role models that bears the potential for innovation"; and he believes that the implementation of digital design strategies in practice requires the development of new tools, as existing software is either not available or not satisfactory (Knippers, 2013).

Atmospheric Form

Structural performance is not the only aspect of performance that can be evaluated and integrated into the form-making process. The goal of high-performance buildings must be to improve environmental quality rather than simply meeting minimum standards. Architectural design does not merely sustain, but should enable humans, and the ecosystem in which they live, to flourish. Through light, sound, space, air, temperature, and material, architects choreograph user experience. Juhani Pallasmaa writes that

> every touching experience of architecture is multi-sensory; qualities of space, matter and scale are measured equally by the eye, ear, nose, skin, tongue, skeleton, and muscle ... an architectural work is not experienced as a collection of isolated visual pictures, but in its fully embodied material and spiritual presence.
>
> (Pallasmaa, 2005, p. 41)

Swiss architect and Pritzker Prize winner Peter Zumthor says the characteristic property of buildings to have emotional effect is something that he terms "atmosphere," which is perceived through emotional sensibilities, as opposed to linear thought, and produced as people interact with objects in the real world (Zumthor, 2006).

Contemporary architectural designers attempt to turn these sensory experiences into computable form enabling them to become part of the predictive act of architectural drawing/modelling. There are four primary areas of comfort that should be considered when designing a building: visual, thermal, air quality, and acoustic. To capture the nuances of experience of building is something that currently simulation tools are challenged to predict and communicate. While simulation tools can predict daylight and the acoustic soundscapes of unbuilt projects, these are not experienced in real-time, in 3D, and so are challenged to become a complete experience. Temperature, humidity, and air speed are often not simulated at all in a way that can be experienced and so comfort can only be guessed at through numerical values. So, given these challenges how can architects engage with design at this level? Robin Evans writes that

> the drawing has intrinsic limitations of reference ... not all things architectural ... can be arrived at through drawing. There must also be a penumbra of qualities that might only be seen darkly and with great difficulty through it. If judgement is that these qualities in and around the shadow line are more interesting than those laid forth clearly in drawing, then such drawing should be abandoned, and another way of working instituted .
>
> *(Evans, 1997, p. 159)*

Building designers must look beyond the drawing to design atmosphere – and perhaps digital design and computational performance simulation can offer solutions where drawings cannot.

Air quality and the thermal condition influence both human health and productivity; a well-designed indoor environment helps to increase the mental performance capacity. While there are now established computational workflows for the calculation of "hard metrics" such as solar gain, air temperature, and relative humidity, an emerging trend is to develop simulation routines for more subjective metrics like thermal comfort. Daniel Knott from Buro Happold's Sustainability Group uses the Universal Thermal Climate Index as a way to compute comfort, and Knott's goal is to develop computational techniques to predict "soft metrics" such as productivity, health, and well-being. Knott feels it is these soft metrics that will become increasingly important (Peters and Peters, 2018).

Leading design firms such as Foster + Partners are making progress to develop techniques to predict performance from a user experience perspective, and to use this as a way to influence building form and material. The SMG uses performance simulation to understand the user experience in various ways: light, temperature, the thermal environment, the warming effects of the sun, the light that comes through glass and where it goes, light levels both artificial and natural, glare, and acoustics. SMG Partner Xavier DeKestelier believes that

> the next step is to design buildings based on the user experience, to design buildings that feel great, that are amazing, and that just work. Because the tools are better, we can do what architects did before by intuition and experience, to determine what it is that you want to feel, to design the surfaces around and given the user experience they expect.

Irene Gallou speculates that

> it is similar to when you first study architecture, you don't have any experience when you design, what it is like to be a space. Whereas an experienced architect has an understanding on how

things will perform … simulation give young architects a tool to understand how the environment will work inside the building.

(Peters and Peters, 2018, p. 105)

In the design of Bloomberg European Headquarters in London Norman Foster explains that "the deep plan interior spaces are naturally ventilated through a 'breathing' façade while a top lit atrium edged with a spiralling ramp at the heart of the building ensures a connected, healthy and creative environment" (BRE, 2019). This notion of connectivity and collaboration flows into the design of the furniture systems as well as the open floor plate. Bespoke height-adjustable, radial desks are laid out in clusters and pods for up to six people, allowing for privacy, personalization, well-being, and collaborative working. The Bloomberg European Headquarters can be operated in a natural ventilation mode when weather conditions are temperate; however, this was a challenge as the building is multi-storey and has a deep plan. Fresh air is brought into the building at the perimeter and moves across the floor plates to the atrium, where the air rises up to exit from the roof. CFD simulations were used to predict performance to predict this air flow. Additionally, a physical simulation was of the air flow was carried out – the world's largest water-bath model was built to demonstrate that the natural ventilation system was going to work (*CIBSE Journal*, 2017) (Figures 16.6 and 16.7).

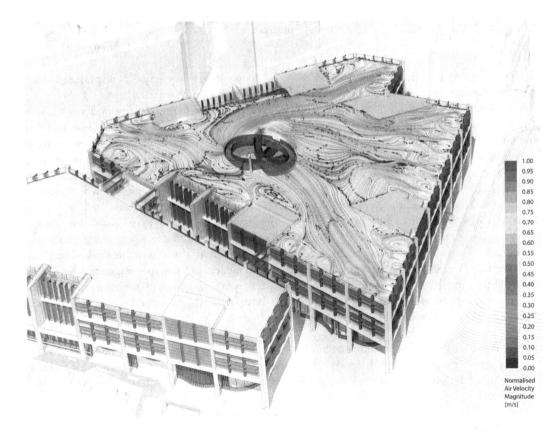

Figure 16.6 CFD air flow model, Bloomberg European Headquarters, Foster + Partners, completed 2017, London, UK.

Source: Foster + Partners, 2019

Architectonic Design and Computation

Figure 16.7 Water flow model simulation model, Bloomberg European Headquarters, Foster + Partners, completed 2017, London, UK. In collaboration with Foster + Partners' model makers, the world's largest water-bath model was constructed to show that the natural ventilation system was going to work.

Source: Foster + Partners, 2019

Towards Architectonic Form

The development and adoption of design computation is changing – and will continue to change – the nature of the form-giving process of architecture. The design of geometry and material is one of the primary concerns of architecture, and architects are concerned with building form in terms of its significance and meaning, and how a design will perform in terms of structure, light, and how it is experienced by the senses. In the last 20 years there has been a shift in architectural design techniques from the use of software, to the development and customization of software. Three ways in which computation is enabling new formal and performative explorations are: parametric tools enable the definition and exploration of design space; computational algorithms enable the design and construction of complex, highly detailed buildings and components; and simulation is exposing new relationships between geometry and space, and physics and atmosphere. Simulation techniques increase structural efficiencies and design creative hybrid systems; this aids the development of complex and creative geometries, and ensures the efficient structural systems. And while structure is a prime concern of architecture, this way of thinking can also be applied to the creation of form from the perspective of atmosphere and experience. Integrated, open-source, and interoperable, computer performance simulation is enabling the exploration of sound, and light, and comfort. The use of computation analysis in form-making is bridging the gap between the sciences and architecture and creating new hybrid cultures and opportunities. The performative approach – to think about ends rather than means – combined with new ways of thinking about parametrics – the establishing of design as a set of relationships – is defining a new architectonic approach to architectural form-making.

References

Anderson, K. (2014). *Design Energy Simulation for Architects: Guide to 3D Graphics*. New York: Routledge.
Block, P. (2016). "Parametricism's structural congeniality," in *Parametricism 2.0: Rethinking Architecture's Agenda for the 21st Century AD Architectural Design*. Vol 86 (2): 68–75.
Block, P., Kilian, A., and Pottmann, H. (2015). "Steering of form – New integrative approaches to architectural design and modeling," in *Computer-Aided Design*. Vol 61 (2015): 1.
BRE Group. (2019). "Bloomberg London: One of the world's highest BREEAM-rated major office buildings." www.breeam.com/case-studies/offices/bloomberg-london/.
CIBSE Journal. (2017). "Designing a natural ventilation strategy for Bloomberg's central London HQ." www.cibsejournal.com/case-studies/designing-a-natural-ventilation-strategy-for-bloombergs-central-london-hq/.
Davis, D., and Peters, B. (2013). "Design eco-systems: Customising the architectural design environment with software plug-ins," in *Computation Works: The Building of Algorithmic Thought AD Architectural Design*. Vol 83 (2): 124–131.
Evans, R. (1997). *Translations from Drawing to Building and Other Essays*. London: Architectural Association.
Foliente, G. (2000). "Developments in performance-based building codes and standards," in *Forest Products Journal*. Vol 50 (7): 12–21.
Foster + Partners. (2019). "Bloomberg." www.fosterandpartners.com/projects/bloomberg/.
Hansen, J., and Lamberts, R. (2011). "Introduction to building performance simulation," in Jan L.M. Hensen and R. Lamberts (Eds.), *Building Performance Simulation for Design and Optimisation*, pp. 1–14. London: Spon.
Hill, J. (2006). *Immaterial Architecture*. London: Routledge.
Kalay, Y. (1999). "Performance-based design," in *Automation in Construction*. Vol 8 (1999): 395–409.
Knippers, J. (2013). "From model thinking to process design," in *Computation Works: The Building of Algorithmic Thought: AD Architectural Design*. Vol 83 (2): 74–81.
Kolarevic, B. (2004). "Back to the future: Performative architecture," in *International Journal of Architectural Computing*. Vol 2 (1): 44–50.
McNeel & Associates. (2019). "Rhinoceros." www.rhino3d.com/.
Oxford Dictionary. (2019). "Performance." https://en.oxforddictionaries.com/definition/performance.
Pallasmaa, J. (2005). *The Eyes of the Skin: Architecture and the Senses*. Chichester: Wiley.
Peters, B. (2018). "Defining environments: Understanding architectural performance through modelling, simulation, and visualisation," in *SU+RE: Sustainable + Resilient Design Systems: AD Architectural Design*. Vol 88 (1): 82–91.
Peters, B., and Peters, T. (2013). *Inside Smartgeometry: Expanding the Architectural Possibilities of Computational Design*. Chichester: Wiley.
Peters, B., and Peters, T. (2018). *Computing the Environment: Digital Design Tools for Simulation and Visualisation of Sustainable Architecture*. Chichester: Wiley.
Picon, A. (2010). *Digital Culture in Architecture*. Basel: Birkhauser.
Wetter, M. (2011). "A view on future building system modeling and simulation," in Jan L.M. Hensen and R. Lamberts (Eds.), *Building Performance Simulation for Design and Optimisation*, pp. 481–504. London: Spon.
Whitehead, H. (2003). "Laws of form," in B. Kolarevic (Ed.), *Architecture in the Digital Age: Design and Manufacturing*, pp. 81–100. London: Spon.
Wikipedia. (2019). "Architectonics." https://en.wikipedia.org/wiki/Architectonics.
Woodbury, R. (2010). *Elements of Parametric Design*. New York: Routledge.
Wortmann, T., and Tuncer, B. (2017). "Differentiating parametric design: Digital workflows in contemporary architecture and construction," in *Design Studies*. Vol 52 (2017): 173–197.
Zumthor, P. (2006). *Atmospheres: Architectural Environments – Surrounding Objects*. Basel: Birkhauser.

17
Simulation Tools for Social Performance
Immersive Building Simulation

Robert R. Neumayr

Until most recently the delineation between the various fields of engineering and architecture has been relying on the clear distinction between the built environment's technical necessities and its social requirements. While the technical necessities include stability, physical integrity, acoustic and thermal performance, tightness or constructability in relation to its users, architecture considers a building's social functions, i.e. its performance as a common spatial framework for communication and interaction, that operates mainly via appearance and legibility for its users within their specific social context.

Within the history of architecture, however, this differentiation is a comparatively recent development. Until the end of the nineteenth century, the high point of Historicism, architects used to have much-more-encompassing responsibilities, being in charge of the concept, the structural design and the form of a building. As Historicism could no longer find adequate answers to the societal problems of that time, new and different theories emerged within the wake of the Modernist project, addressing the same issue but suggesting totally different solutions. This era of contending ideas might be illustrated best by the famous dispute between Josef Hoffmann and Adolf Loos. Matthias Boeckl points out that during this process of conceptual differentiation

> [the] erstwhile comprehensive job description [...] disintegrated into its component parts in the process of modernization, which could also be construed to be a process of specialization; Loos claimed the basic cultural idea, Hoffmann the form – but who was concerned with structural design?
>
> *(Boeckl 2015)*

It was precisely this deconstruction of the architectural ideal into its constituent parts on the one hand, and the modernists' call for establishing close conceptual connections between architecture and industrially assembled products like ships, airplanes or automobiles on the other (in Le Corbusier's programmatic book *Towards A New Architecture*, a whole chapter, "Eyes Which Do Not See" (Corbusier 1982) is dedicated to the description of the aesthetic qualities intrinsic to industrialized products), that gave way to an engineers' approach to the relationship between form, force and material, subsequently developing into the domain of structural engineering. As the complexity and size of building typologies increased over time, other engineering disciplines started to emerge, such as HVAC (heating, ventilation and air conditioning), lighting design and acoustics in the 1950s, when office floors expanded to large-scale spaces, or energy design in the 1970s, when the first the global energy crisis hit the building sector. All of them eventually evolved to form the wide field of different domains of engineering that we know and work in today.

Due to the specialized nature of their expertise, engineers have been traditionally tasked with solving problems and optimizing performance strictly within their respective domain, very much in line with the back-then-dominating modernist design paradigm that postulates a clear separation of different functional systems.

However, our conception of architecture has changed considerably as our linear and binary systems of perception have given way to a more complex and multi-layered understanding of the built environment. Rather than seeing a building as an assembly of independent entities, we have now come to conceptually understand it as a continuous field of connected elements, as a spatial organization that is able to negotiate and interpolate between those elements, which are subjected to the changing forces and currents that guide their use. As Stan Allen remarks, "Field conditions move from the one toward the many, from individuals to collectives, from objects to fields" (Allen 1999).

Recently complex architectural configurations in general and buildings in particular have come to be widely perceived to have an intrinsically networked nature, as they, as I would put it, "are organized primarily around currents and lines of exchange where people, services, and ideas are collected, organized and redistributed in a multitude of directions" (Neumayr and Budig 2009a). A good account of these phenomena is, for example, given by Manuel de Landa in his book *A Thousand Years of Non-Linear History* (De Landa 1997). They consist of a multitude of different layers (some of which are not even architectural), which react and interact with each other, that are influenced by internal and external forces, and that all together form what we observe as our built environment.

In this sense, buildings can be understood as highly integrated complex systems, sub-systems and components, that are interconnected and correlated, complementing each other in order to fulfil architectural, structural, functional, spatial, semiotic and atmospheric criteria. All systems are associative to each other and adaptive to their internal and external conditions, which drive their differentiation. Functions and programmes can also be integrated by systematic differentiation of one pivotal system, which makes one system work on multiple layers, i.e. one series of building components might have structural and atmospheric properties at the same time. As a consequence, it has become impossible to conceive architectural design separated from its related disciplines, such as energy design, material science and structural engineering. Similar to natural systems, these compositions are so deeply integrated that they cannot be easily broken down into their constituent components.

Understanding the built environment as a series of complexly interwoven layers that need to be integrated into the digital design process as seamlessly as possible, this comprehensive approach implies the controlled and simultaneous development of function, form, structure and material, and requires attention on the associative qualities of all single constituents. The act of design is no longer framed by "a singular aesthetic end, but by the multiple constraints and ambitions of each project, as negotiated by the architect" (Rahim and Jamelle 2007).

In the last few years the development of sophisticated computational design and simulation tools – both within architecture and within the engineering disciplines – has opened up the field for more closely-knit interdisciplinary collaboration on multi-layered building configurations. Also, simpler interfaces, common programme platforms and scripting languages make parametric design and engineering technologies alike more tangible for architects, facilitating information interchange and fostering a close collaboration between different disciplines that would have been impossible a few years ago. At the same time, architects are able to develop an immediate and more intuitive understanding of a building's performativity and how design variations might impact a structure's performance or how, vice versa, specific performance criteria might influence their design decisions.

The notion of our environment as a field of continuous but constantly and incrementally changing forces (in which there are no two points where these forces are the same) necessitates the development of digital techniques that are able to simulate and register these dynamic force fields. But it also forces us to find design strategies that allow us to generate digital models whose systems can be differentiated according to the sometimes-minuscule changes of local patterns of internal or external forces. This approach requires the methodical development of a building's systems in a digital model to generate parametrically controllable geometries with high adaptive potentials and connectivity. Variation and continuous differentiation of adaptive elements can then start to reflect the changing and mutually influential forces that influence the different systems in order to eventually articulate complex architectural organizations in an iterative process that repeatedly changes, tests and evaluates a building's configuration in a constant feedback loop according to strictly defined rules and criteria until its performance is optimized.

Architecture is always based on a set of connected design problems that require an architectural solution. Digital simulations and scripted parametric systems, however, always work on architecture's underlying systematics and logics which then guide the generation of project-specific geometries and shapes (Figure 17.1).

This additional architectural layer, that in the end forms the physical framework for its users, needs to be added by the designer as an integral part of the overall design process and will vary according to the designer's capacity and socio-cultural background. Digital tools produce, when applied, a controlled series of possible outcomes and establish a more immediate responsiveness between the designer and his design project. However, they can neither substitute creative potential nor are they capable of producing viable architectural results without the constant intervention of the designer, who in the end still holds responsibility for the project's aesthetic qualities that emerge out of a complex digital design process.

Environmental Simulations

The first and probably most obvious performance criterion that every building design is assessed for is normally its energy balance as environmental concerns and questions of sustainability, ecology and the

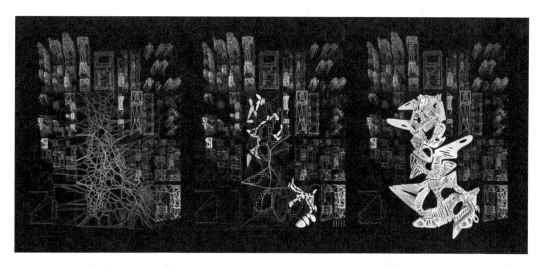

Figure 17.1 Bolojan. Studio Hadid, University of Applied Arts Vienna: Sematectonic Fields. Revealing the underlying information of a data-driven landscape.
Source: Daniel Bolojan. Studio Hadid, University of Applied Arts Vienna

considerate consumption of non-renewable resources have become of great importance over the last decade. Whereas until recently these kinds of comparatively simple simulations had to be done by specialists, new, easily accessible integrated software tools have now enabled architects to run energy simulations themselves. But what at first sounds like a trivial improvement of work flow is – once one comes to think about it – in reality a profound revolution of the design process. While previously a project's work flow was organized in a linear, almost Taylorist fashion with the architect handing over the finished design to the engineer for assessment, integrated simulation tools allow the designer to engage in an continuous iterative design process, where the simulation's results can be seamlessly fed back into the building's altered design, which in turn changes its performance accordingly. The repeated renegotiation of design intention and energy performance, until a global optimum for both is achieved, makes this design strategy a simple yet prototypical example of a multi-layered performance optimization process, all of which is set up in a similar fashion but with varying input parameters and complexity.

Tectonic Articulation

Looking at contemporary fields of complex performance optimization processes, the optimization of a building's structure is arguably the most widespread and prominent one. As discussed before, this interplay between structure and architectural expression has a long tradition within the discipline, and became a major driver for architectural innovation at the beginning of the twentieth century, when the rise of new materials, such as reinforced concrete, started to impact the conceptualization of building structures. Initially imitating the structural logic and appearance of the iron- or steel-framed buildings of that time, engineers and architects alike soon started to see the enormous morphological potential of the new materials, as new, elegant double-curved shell structures started to emerge.

These structures were carefully derived from constructed physical models or based on newly developed mathematical concepts (previously structures were designed in empirical ways, mainly relying on tradition, experience and observation) that helped to explain and understand the flow of forces. That led to an economy of means where structures were optimized according to structural necessities, allowing for an intuitive understanding of the flow of forces through the building.

Felix Candela, Heinz Isler and Eladio Dieste are among the protagonists of this era, as well as Pier Luigi Nervi, whose partly precast yet extremely elegant and delicate rib constructions can be read as the first predecessors of today's differentiated structural articulations. Remo Pedreschi describes this period as being marked by the designers' ambitions to "[incorporate] a strong desire for structural expression and structural efficiency – to make virtue out of economy. Thus they drew together form, force and architecture" (Pedreschi 2008).

In this line of thinking a building's structure, and therefore its optimization, is understood to be only one layer of its multi-layered organization, and as a consequence structural expression cannot be understood as an end in itself but rather as a means to articulate the substantial social function and the complex whole of the space in question.

Neither does the accentuation of structural elements hold any ideological, metaphorical, theoretical, abstract or sensational value in itself (such as one might be able to detect in late Modernist or Structuralist buildings, where the pointed display and over-articulation of structure stems from long-held ideological positions rather than tectonic considerations), nor are buildings materialized solely to the concerns of technical and structural efficiency, which would be the structural engineer's approach. The aim is to negotiate the building's different systems in order to form one coherent spatial organization (Figure 17.2). The design strategy based on this conceptual relationship between a building's technical and articulatory dimensions is known as *Tectonic Articulation*, a term coined by Patrik Schumacher.

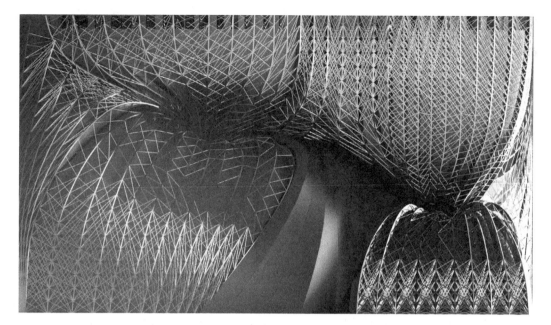

Figure 17.2 Hutz, Park, Urschler. Studio Hadid, University of Applied Arts Vienna: Recursive Statics. Negotiating structure and architectural expression.
Source: Martino Hutz, James Park, Matthias Urschler. Studio Hadid, University of Applied Arts Vienna

> If we define tectonics as the strategic detournement of an element's technically induced morphology in order to address substantial functions in the articulatory dimension, then tectonics can be redeemed and integrated within contemporary notions of handling form-function relationships. We might call this strategy of opportunizing on technical details tectonic articulation.
>
> *(Schumacher 2012)*

The designer's goal is neither to design a structurally optimized building nor to conduct an exercise in creative form finding, but the extension of architecture's formal repertoire through investigation into its morphogenetic potential within a multi-dimensional solution space that is clearly delineated by previous structural research, which sets the limits for the range of possible forms. Tectonic Articulation aims towards the exploitation of its generative capacity rather than merely developing a method of discovering inspiring shapes, contributing to an architectonic code that "is one of several fundamental panhuman sign systems which in concert provide individuals and groups with a multi-nodal and multi stereoscopic template for the creation of humanly meaningful realities" (Preziosi 1979).

However, the resulting formal and spatial articulations always remain tectonic, i.e. they remain structurally or technically motivated. Seen from a structural engineer's point of view on the other hand, these processes might be used to gradually approach "a balance between aesthetic intrigue, innovation and efficiency in new structural forms", as Kristina Shea puts it (Shea 2004).

Social Space as a Generative Tool

All man-made artefacts and objects can be assessed within two distinctive domains. First, there is the domain of practicality, containing all of an object's basic properties which are necessary for it to serve its distinct purpose. And then there is the domain of culture, which talks about the notions that go beyond practicality, such as an object's distinct form, shape and surface articulations. It is the latter domain that anchors an artefact within its specific socio-cultural context.

Traditionally, the façade and its ornamentation has been considered to be a building's only part, whose configuration is shaped – directly or indirectly – by cultural and societal impact. Throughout history, the general ornamental organization of the Italian palazzo (which in turn developed from antique elements that were re-contextualized and arranged according to a set of abstract rules in order to create a complex system of semiological elements enabling contemporaries to unreflectingly understand the building's use and program distribution) remained the dominant model for the composition of all types of representative building typologies. Within that framework the built environment's continuous changes in form and façade treatment were mainly attributed to their constant adaption to the prevailing styles and architectural agendas of a specific time period, closely linking it to its underlying historic background, until Modernism prepared itself to supersede Historicism as the predominant architectural ideology.

It was at that time that architects in general started to question this overly simplistic approach, looking for more intrinsic connections between the built environment and its social parameters. Two researchers, Bill Hillier and Julienne Hanson, proposed to investigate the built environment no longer as a mere collection of buildings or distinct individual spaces, but rather as a system of social relations that needs to be analyzed "at the level of [a] system of spatial relations that constitute the building or settlement" (Hillier and Hanson, 2003) in order to understand the social effects of spatial design, eventually pioneering a set of analytical tools that is today known as Space Syntax. Initially conceived to analyse spatial sequences of small settlements, it was quickly discovered that the very same strategies can be used equally well on the interior of variously scaled buildings.

Seeing the space in question as a network of interconnected spaces, a floor plan's morphological characteristics of spatial configurations and its effects on connectivity, accessibility and visibility can be studied.

For architects, among the increasing number of different notions for analyzing social space that have been developed over the years by different researchers, the concepts of Integration, Space and Depth Distance and Isovists have so far remained among the most influential ones. All of them talk about the integration of a specific location into a given network of spaces; on different levels, however.

Integration measures the number of distinctive iterative steps it takes to get from one space within the networked system to any other, always using the shortest path. The space with the fewest overall number of steps is considered to be the most integrated.

Space and Depth Distance looks at the linear distances of the center point of each space in the network to the center points of all other spaces, adding distances up to an overall distance value for every node in the system in order to find the space with the lowest value and therefore best linear integration.

An Isovist, finally, is the volume of visible space seen from a given point within that space, and measures its visual openness. A convex space, for example, will always be visible in its entirety, whereas any non-convex space (such as a bent or angled room) will from certain positions have non-visible areas.

The results of these analyses are color-based graphs or maps, where color values represent the different levels of integration.

As of today, there are several readily available open-source software programs that can be used to perform spatial network analyses on existing spaces and evaluate their social performativity; however, the use of the principles of Space Syntax within a generative design process still remains challenging. Moving beyond the production of analytical diagrams depicting the connectivity, accessibility and visibility of spaces, exploring the generative potential of Space Syntax allows the designer to question

Simulation Tools for Social Performance

Figure 17.3 Zakharyan. Studio Hadid, University of Applied Arts Vienna: Syntactic Sensations. Spatial distribution of program, optimized according to algorithmic principles based on the social logic of space.
Source: Daniel Zakharyan. Studio Hadid, University of Applied Arts Vienna

traditional methods of spatially organizing complex social, programmatic and contextual relationships. As overall quality of space can hardly be accurately described by the level of spatial integration alone, the existing set of tools needs to be broadened in order to allow for the evaluation of additional relational properties that refine the resulting spatial layout.

Such properties include a space's connectivity to circulation or infrastructural spaces, its adjacency to entrance and ground level, its proximity to local sub-centers or public transport facilities, or the range of required environmental qualities (such as daylight, orientation, or elevation above ground) or the accessibility of various spaces within different search radii, that depend on the social or programmatic value of a space within a certain typological set-up.

In this way the multi-layered relationships between various programs, such as work environments, residential, temporary living, retail, entertainment or culture, within a multi-functional urban structure and the environmental qualities they require can be computationally optimized according to the same set of algorithmic principles; with different integrative values, however, as some relations are prioritized in the process of space allocation that is set up by the designer.

Such an optimization process, that iteratively compares, negotiates and gradually optimizes a multitude of different relational constraints, holds the potential to overcome the traditional semi-spatial layouts that are still common to today's complex programmatically rich urban environments and challenge the vertical discontinuity of a building's typically stacked floor plan layout, thus leading to more seamlessly integrated programmatic spaces (Figure 17.3).

Agent-based Occupancy Simulations

On a smaller scale, the analysis and prediction of spatial occupation patterns in various social spaces, most notably office environments, has also moved more and more into the focus of contemporary design research recently, as a growing percentage of any developed country's economy relies on intellectual capital rather than the means of production. Shifting away from the traditional Taylorist work culture with its long-established linear production logics, where the success of different spatial layouts could be easily measured (for example, by simply counting the number of completed transactions, as routine assignments were handed down from one worker to the next), office tasks have become increasingly complex and knowledge-driven. In Western European countries the knowledge economy at this point represents about a third of all economic activities (Eurostat 2013).

As work procedures became more flexible and spatial occupation patterns more loose and varied, and consequently could no longer be organized and measured according to Taylorist principles, new methods of assessing the performance of spaces need to be developed. Designers, such as the German Quickborner team with their Bürolandschaf concept, started in the 1970s to map the spatial relations between all agents in an office network in two-dimensional matrices in order to find optimized office layouts. However, these design methodologies were still based on the clear assumption that there is a linear relationship between the efficiency of a spatial layout and its successful work output.

In knowledge economies employees increase their respective radius of interaction due to the business's intrinsically networked nature and various new types of knowledge work with their particular needs and mobility patterns emerge (Greene and Myerson, 2011). The exchange of work is less vital than information interchange, communication, and human interaction, and the success of contemporary office environments increasingly relies on continuous formal and informal exchange of information and knowledge between actors in various different configurations. A space's performativity largely depends on its capacity to spatially and semiologically frame the complexly interwoven interactions of its users.

In such a dynamic environment behavioural patterns are no longer linear but rather start to show emergent und unpredictable properties, which are the result of the repeated superimposition of (comparatively simple) interactions of its single constituent components (its agents), which gradually add up to the complex state of the emerging system. The result of such a non-linear process can no longer be predicted. This is also known as a "bottom-up" process, as opposed to a "top-down" process, in which the overall form is determined first. Such emergent systems, however, can be simulated by programming sets of simple agents that continuously interact with each other according to a basic set of rules. This was first achieved in 1987 by Craig Reynolds, who with his simulation program Boids successfully simulated the flocking behaviour of birds. While such Agent-Based Models (ABM) have been commonly used to simulate physical, chemical, biological or sociological processes, architecture has only recently discovered their use for the simulation of life processes. Similar to a flock of birds or a school of fish, human crowds show complex non-linear behaviour that is the result of a single agent's behavioural rules or scripts that in turn are triggered by fellow agents or environmental features. As a consequence, they constitute emergent systems that can be successfully simulated by ABM. While plenty of commercial software programs, such as Cinema4D or Maya, offer readily available tools for crowd simulation, more complex life-like occupancy simulations at this point still require some scripting knowledge and the use of more specialized programs such as NetLogo (an open-source program developed for an academic community) or Unity with its scripting extension (initially developed for the gaming industry).

Agent-based design research is normally directed towards a concrete focal task in the form of a design research brief that acts as an experimental set-up in relation to which empirical and statistical knowledge, conceptual and theoretical resources, simulation methodologies, and design ideas can be systematically brought together and explored.

In order to measure the different qualities and quantities of the agents' interactions with each other, as well as with their environment, research focuses on the location, size, shape, configuration and features of informal office areas, such as communication zones, circulation areas and breakout spaces, where spontaneous communicative encounters and unscheduled opportunities for networking, collaboration and skill exchange most likely occur.

In order to set up a feasible first parametric model, the overall number of input parameters can be initially reduced within the conceptual framework of the simulation, gradually increasing complexity.

The main challenge is the development of a population of agents with plausible, life-like individual behavioural rules that allow for the emergence of an overall plausible, life-like collective event scenario. In order to accomplish this, any agent population needs to display two key properties of "life-process modelling". First of all, variable agent differentiation by status, affiliation, department or position within the social network, implying behavioural difference, and secondly architectural frame-dependency of behaviours, implying local selection from stacks of behaviours dependent on location and spatial architectural qualities.

The first property allows for the integration of client-specific employee structures and hierarchies. The second property facilitates a systematic semiological approach to the design, as it establishes relationships between the agents' behavioural patterns and the furniture elements and features distributed across the space in question.

As the simulations run, systematically emulating various design proposals, relevant measures are recorded and stored to evaluate a scenario's performance in terms of occupational patterns and communicative interaction. Those measures normally include location, frequency, relevancy and range of encounters and interactions as well as communicative histories, circulation patterns and occupancy maps (so-called "heat maps") (Figure 17.4).

Simulations' results can not only be summarized and compared in order to judge the performance of a particular office layout. Once the collected data is statistically analyzed and set in relation to the quantitative parameters, such as position and number of specific reference points and furniture elements, throughout a series of related simulation scenarios (thus parametrically attaching it to the same spatial environmental features with changing locations), it can be used to train prediction algorithms in order to forecast agent behaviour in novel and previously unsimulated scenarios.

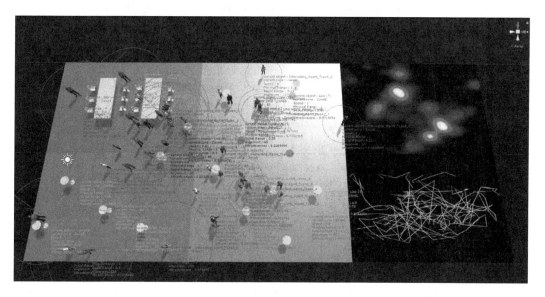

Figure 17.4 Agent-Based Semiology Research Group Vienna, Bolojan. Data read out of an agent-based simulation set-up.

Source: Agent-Based Semiology Research Group Vienna, Daniel Bolojan

Looking at statistical connections between the qualitative, i.e. semiological, parameters of a spatial layout and its features, such as object design, environmental zoning or effective or affective conditions, and the behavioural patterns they generate might eventually lead to understanding the conception of office environments as an explicit design agenda to frame communication with a new and coherent system of architectural signification, rather than an intuitive participation in a historically evolving semiosis of the built environment, in order to develop an approach to architectural design that better engages with the opportunities and challenges of today's networked society.

Evolutionary Design Solving and Genetic Algorithms

In a conventional design process the designer tends to look for viable solutions within a design space whose boundaries are defined by her previous experience and intuition and by historic precedent. Preconceived forms and existing architectural elements that have proven successful in the past are selected and rearranged to fit the new circumstances. This way of working makes it hard to eventually develop unprecedented and innovative design solutions.

It is, however, considered one of the major innovations of contemporary digital design techniques that design space is no longer constrained by the imagination of the designer, as computational power and parametric set-ups allow one to systematically search a much wider field of possible architectural configurations for suitable design solutions. A digital parametric mode, once automated, can be iteratively varied and tested to quickly produce a large number of increasingly performative outcomes.

> As Neumayr and Budig explain in their paper about digital design techniques,
> A parametrically differentiated architectural form can thus not only be seen as the result of coherent relations between geometric conditions [...] but also as a result of a systematic variation of their internal values [...] The scale of variables is subsequently released from its extensive values in order to achieve a wider range of possible outcomes, always driven by the evaluation of its performance criteria.
>
> *(Neumayr and Budig, 2009b)*

Of an initially large number of variations (possible solutions), which are post factum evaluated according to one's performance criteria, only a few will pass the test and become actual proposals to the given architectural design problem. In this line of thought, what Richard Dawkins says about the evolution of animals, that

> [t]he actual animals that have ever lived on Earth are a tiny subset of the theoretical animals that could exists. [...] The vast majority of theoretical trajectories through animal space give rise to impossible monsters. Each real animal is surrounded by a little cluster of neighbours, most of whom have never existed.
>
> *(Dawkins 1986)*

is also true about spatial structures in an architectural design space.

In his book *Darwin's Dangerous Idea*, Daniel Dennet argues that the domains of organisms and biological designs on the one hand and human artefacts such as art, architecture and engineering on the other form part of one single design space (Dennet 1995), and as a consequence the same generative logics apply. And indeed, contemporary digital form-finding strategies as described above can be read as simple evolutionary mechanisms that create new species of architectural or urban configurations. In the same way in which different sets of genomes determine the characteristics of the organisms that

Simulation Tools for Social Performance

surround us, internal parameters, which can be defined and changed, give rise to the qualities and configuration of our built environment.

In simple terms evolutionary theory states that all changes in genomes occur randomly, without purpose or direction. Conventional design effort, however, is normally directed and anything but random. Evolutionary design solvers are therefore used to help us to operationalize the aleatoric potential of digital design processes. They randomize the values of a set of variables previously defined by the designer in order to create a large number of initially arbitrary objects, whose configurations are determined by the variables in question. Manuel de Landa (2003) notes in this context that only if virtual evolution can be used to explore a space rich enough so that all the possibilities cannot be considered in advance by the designer, only if what results shocks or at least surprises, can genetic algorithms be considered useful visualization tools.

In evolution this process is called *random genetic drift* and is merely a lateral motion in design space. It is only when this drift encounters the force of natural selection that successful mutations are identified and selected for further development. This operation is called *lifting*. Lifting occurs in algorithmic design by testing the resulting configurations against a number of success criteria, which must also be determined by the designer. In this process the algorithm selects a subset of the most successful configurations, whose variables are then randomized, only this time locally clustered around previously successful values. This iterative process continues until an optimized configuration emerges, and will typically involve several thousands of iterations.

But a wide distribution of initial genome values is not only important if one wants to arrive at performatively sensible yet typologically surprising and formally fresh results. It becomes essential as soon as one is confronted with design problems that – due to their intrinsic complexity – do not offer an obvious design trajectory. As discussed above, contemporary design briefs often contain two or more possibly contradictory design problems. Furthermore, design proposals often involve more than one building and require balancing functional, urban and environmental necessities. Optimizing a building's or a building cluster's performance according to more than one success criterion always involves negotiating between different local design optima towards a global design optimum, where the overall building performance peaks and often unexpected synergy effects occur. Such outcomes are impossible to predict or conceive manually and therefore require genetic algorithms as a way to methodologically search design space for such performance peaks.

Typical areas of synergy and optimization not only include solving possible contradictions between contextual urban volumetric distribution and solar radiation or energy efficiency, but also spatial distribution with its shared, hybrid, or temporary spaces; circulation and infrastructural spaces; structure; and program distribution (Figure 17.5).

Figure 17.5 Bajcer, Preda, Pop, University of Applied Arts Vienna: editingACHT. Optimizing maximum sun protection against minimal panel structure using genetic algorithms.
Source: Josip Bajcer, Irina Preda, Sergiu Radu Pop. editingACHT, University of Applied Arts Vienna

At the moment "galapagos", a plug-in for Rhino's Grasshopper visual scripting environment, is the most popular and also most versatile evolutionary design solver. However, due to their systematic set-up, genetic algorithms do not scale well with overarching complexity. The subjection of too many variables to mutation quickly leads to an exponential increase in search space size and therefore required computational power. Consequently, it is important to reduce design questions to their simplest form and extract a small but robust set of variables that will determine the desired performance. At this point genetic algorithms typically deal with comparatively simple geometries, building shapes, rays, lines of force distribution, and trajectory splines, but we will see more complex computational set-ups in the near future.

Machine Learning and Digital Design

While digital optimization tools such as genetic algorithms will improve design results in an iterative process that requires the repeated processing of a multitude of differently configured variations in order to gradually build up refinement based on previous successful versions and eventually lead to performatively sensible and optimized design results, they are not per se intelligent in the sense that they can build and store applicable design knowledge by experience and experimentation. The relatively new research fields of artificial intelligence and machine learning have now promised to fill exactly that void.

In their most basic definition, machine learning algorithms are scripts or programs based on statistical models that are used to iteratively improve a specific task based on mathematical interpretation of training data to make predictions for previously unencountered parametrical set-ups.

Within the realm of digital design, artificial intelligence historically can be understood as the latest step in the search for technologies that augment human creativity. Based on ground-breaking discoveries in the field of automation design and its underlying concepts and visions, the desire to scientifically explore and develop tools to assists humans in their creative work and the simultaneous rise of the computer revolution led to the development of a first generation of computer-aided creation programs in the 1980s.

While these first-generation systems were often mimicking traditional analogue tools via digital means (in the same way as the first reinforced concrete structures were designed according to the already-well-known principles of timber-frame constructions) and thus merely facilitating work flow or repetitive tasks, recent research has developed a conceptual framework for artificial intelligence and machine learning in architecture that allows for tools and technologies that are much more directly integrated into the actual design and construction process.

Although artificial intelligence has already been tested and in part successfully implemented in some areas within the wide field of architecture, such as building information modelling for tasks like collision detection, legislation fulfilment, escape route dimensioning or accessibility, or construction processes – for example, by teaching networks of autonomous drones how to collectively assemble a structure from smaller components – machine learning in the field of digital architectural design is still in its infancy.

Machine learning algorithms typically learn by extracting patterns from comparing and connecting relevant information drawn from various databases. However, evolving an artificial intelligence's design sensibilities might alternatively involve some kind of design guidance, where, in the absence of large sets of available data for analyses, the designer helps the machine to identify successful solutions to a design problem. In the context of artificial intelligence this is called *supervised learning*. To have an algorithm design information-rich objects sensibly includes complex computational processes, but in essence it is similar to teaching it how to create, just to take one random example, a simple vase to your particular liking. Your vases come in all kind of sizes and shapes (let us call them *phenotypes*), but they are based on a common set of constituent parameters whose individual values define their actual configurations (the *genotype*). For a simple vase these might be the object's height and the diameters at its top and bottom. If you want to speed up the process, a range of values for each of these parameters can to be set in order to constrain the design space to an area that contains objects with reasonable sizes and proportions. As the algorithm has no previous information to draw upon, it will create a random selection of differently shaped vases, of which you can choose a number of instances that meet your requirements most. These then serve as references for the creation of the next subset of vases, whose shapes and sizes will – iteration after iteration – approach your design optimum, although – due to the heuristic nature of the process – they will never actually reach it. You will therefore need to stop the process at a point when the results are reasonably close to your idea of an ideal vase. This decision-making strategy of "finding satisfactory solutions for a [...] realistic world" (Simon 1979) was first described by Herbert Simon and is generally known as Satisficing.

Such supervised learning algorithms in architectural design, which are still working well within conventional architectural paradigms, are at this time being widely tested in various design environments such as universities or architectural offices, but might only come to full fruition once they can be seamlessly combined with machine learning technologies, which ensure that supervised learning solutions also adhere to algorithmically evolved performance standards, thus making sure that the final designs are both performance-optimized and design-sensible.

However, recent technological progress at the intersection of nature and the artificial has started to also shift the focus of architectural design research towards the emerging notion of hybridization, raising a new set of questions about architectural agency and machine intelligence. In the wake of the last digital turn contemporary digital design strategies were conceived to exploring the new and vast design spaces opened up by the innovative tools and technologies and previously unavailable to architects, in order to expanding architecture's formal repertoire. But as the relationship between architecture and the technologies of the near future will need to be reconsidered, computational design might – sooner rather than later – move beyond form and geometry towards defining an alternate, more interactive model of architecture, where spatial organizations are considered as adaptive environments that actively and anticipatorily engage with their users continuously on a real-time basis.

It is safe to say that machine learning will play an increasingly prominent role in a building culture that finds itself at the intersection of infrastructure, technology, biology and machinic intelligence.

Machine learning algorithms will help us to push architecture further, into the territories of the prediction and optimization of complex social interaction patterns, self-organizing building assemblies, programmable matter and material ecologies and the generation of adaptive emotive urban spaces.

Summary

Architecture, and with it the whole building industry, has witnessed nothing short of a revolution within the last decade. New scientific paradigms, innovative material technologies, novel computational tools and digital design techniques have profoundly shifted our view on the conception and production of architectural and urban space. At the same time, the world around us has changed as well. In an increasingly complex technology-driven society contemporary patterns of use and occupation have become more fast-paced, fluent and interwoven, and global issues of ecology, sustainability and considerate material practice have continuously gained importance.

Present-day design strategies move beyond the conception of conventional static structures that are based on preconceived concepts, traditional shapes and programmatic solutions that have so far dominated global architectural practice under the name of "International Style", towards intelligent design processes that have the capacity to actively engage in the world's current societal, ecological and environmental problems. Within this dynamic design framework new definitions of what constitutes a successful building have emerged and the performance criteria of contemporary buildings and urban structures have shifted accordingly. Buildings are no longer evaluated by their functional design qualities or artistic merits alone, but rather by how well a structure resolves and integrates the numerous design challenges that arise from an increasing multitude of different parameters, necessities and constraints that more often than not are contradictory and seemingly incompatible.

As a consequence, architects also need to reconsider their position within this changing environment. Traditionally architects always assume the role of the generalist, negotiating a design process between the numerous agencies involved in a building process and being responsible for integrating the common design effort in its local or global cultural and environmental context. A role that has become more and more difficult in the last few years as buildings' increasing complexity has put an emphasis on particular expertise that is provided by engineers, who are specialized in a small field of knowledge. However, new software tools and easily accessible computer interfaces have put architects back into a position to be able to assess their projects not only according to their inherent design qualities but also in terms of different performance criteria whose assessments were until recently reserved for engineers. The seamless integration of different software programmes with a simple information interchange allows designers to co-author integrative solutions to contemporary design problems.

However, the performance criteria we as architects develop to measure our designs against must be complex and non-linear, as the design will by definition be the result of a multi-layered optimization process within novel solution spaces that will be defined by material agency, machine learning, self-organizing assemblies and adaptive spatial organizations, challenging the next generation of designers.

References

Allen, S. (1999). *Points + Lines. Diagrams and Projects for the City*. New York: Princeton Architectural Press, p. 92.
Boeckl, M. (2015). Form Follows … ? In C. Thun-Hohenstein, M. Boeckl and C. Witt-Dorring, Boec, (Eds.), *Ways to Modernism: Josef Hoffmann, Adolf Loos and Their Impact*. Vienna: Birkhäuser, p. 123.
Dawkins, R. (1986). *The Blind Watchmaker*. London: Longmans, p. 73.
de Landa, M. (1997). *A Thousand Years of Non-Linear History*. New York: Zone Books.
de Landa, M. (2003). Deleuze and the use of genetic algorithm in architecture. *Architectural Design*. Vol. 72, pp. 9–12.
Dennet, C. (1995). *Darwin's Dangerous Idea*. New York: Simon and Schuster.
Eurostat. (2013). *Science, Technology and Innovation in Europe*. Luxembourg: Publication Office of the European Union, p. 115.
Greene, C., and Myerson, J. (2011). Space for Thought: Designing for Knowledge Workers. *Facilities*. Vol. 29, No. 1/2, pp. 19–30. https://doi.org/10.1108/02632771111101304.
Hillier, B., and Hanson, J. (2003). *The Social Logic of Space*. Cambridge: Cambridge University Press, p. 3.
Le Corbusier (1982). *Ausblick auf eine Architektur*. Braunschweig: Vieweg & Sohn Verlag.
Neumayr, R., and Budig, M. (2009a). Generative Processes: Script-Based Design Research in Contemporary Teaching Practice. In I. Paoletti (Ed.), *Innovative Design and Construction Technologies*. Milano: Maggioli S.p.A., p. 172.
Neumayr, R., and Budig, M. (2009b). Associative Processes: Adaptive Potentials of Script-Based and Generative Design. In C. Gengnagel (Ed.), *Design Modelling Symposium Berlin. Concepts Beyond Geometry*. Berlin: Universität der Künste, p. 271.
Pedreschi, R. (2008). Form, Force and Structure: A Brief History. In M. Hensel and A. Menges (Eds.), *Versatility and Vicissitude. AD 02/2008*. London: Wiley, p. 13.
Preziosi, D. (1979). *Architecture, Language and Meaning: The Origins of the Built World and its Semiotic Organization*. The Hague, Paris and New York: Mouton Publishers.
Rahim, A., and Jamelle, H. (2007). Elegance in the Age of Digital Technique. In A. Rahim and H. Jamelle (Eds.), *Elegance. AD 01/2007*. London: Wiley, p. 7.
Schumacher, P. (2012). *The Autopoiesis of Architecture Vol. II: A New Agenda for Architecture*. Chichester: Wiley & Sons, p. 20.
Shea, K. (2004). Directed Randomness. In N. Leach, D. Turnbull and C. Williams, (Eds.), *digital tectonics*. Chichester: Wiley & Sons, p. 88.
Simon, H. (1979). Rational decision making in business organizations. *American Economic Review*. Vol. 69, No. 4, p. 493.

18
Performative Material Morphologies

Vera Parlac

Introduction

In *Performative Architecture*, Branko Kolarevic and Ali Malkawi summarized an emerging context for performance-based design. In the early 2000s, the emerging digital tools of modeling and simulation integrated design and analysis of buildings into a feedback tool for measuring building performance quantitatively and qualitatively (Kolarevic and Malkawi 2005). What has changed since then? In addition to the use of computational and interactive tools, application and integration of *active* materials in architecture has advanced. Whether they are natural, bioengineered, smart, meta or machinic, or with embedded electronics, what distinguishes these materials from traditional ones are behaviors they exhibit. The principal argument in this chapter is that exploration and inclusion of active matter in design of the built environment is re-orienting architects and designers towards exploring *change* and *agency* that active matter could provide.

The application of technological advancements in material science, digital fabrication and interactive technologies and their inclusion in design and experimental research is offering a possibility of a new kind of (productive) relationship between the built environment and a larger ecology. This relationship is based on materials and material technologies that do not simply exist within the environment but are increasingly imagined and designed as integral contributors to it. For the past few decades, architects have been addressing this question of active materiality. This chapter describes several lines of inquiry triggered by the inclusion of dynamic and active matter into design, prototyping and praxis. The aim is to project possible futures for architecture's relationship to its immediate and its broader environment.

Performativity and Matter

Performativity does not necessarily require a definition of form or meaning – it requires a consideration of effects that take place. The performative in the context of materiality implies certain reflexivity, permeability of boundaries or extension of thresholds through which effects are manifested. Viewed through the lens of performativity any matter has an agency. This is not to say that form is not important in discussion of material morphologies, but that, as D'Arcy Thompson argues, form is a product of forces within the environment (Thompson 1992), and ultimately a product of the performativity of matter.

The perceived inert nature of matter was brought into question in the early twentieth century, but it was through a posthumanist discourse and a shift from representational towards performative understanding of discursive practices (Barad 2003) that matter was granted agency. This shift towards non-human expression centers on material and, as Karen Barad, Professor of Feminist Studies at University of California Santa Cruz, states, it focuses on "matters of practices/doings/actions" as opposed to discourse on "similarity between descriptions and reality" (Barad 2003: 802).

For architects, performativity promotes an ethos that recognizes the role matter can play in an interchange between the built environment and its larger material, social and ecological context. This shift from "what the building is to what it does" (Leatherbarrow 2005: 7) potentially marks a change in attitude from architecture as an object representing an aspiration towards architecture that is an active participant in the material, social and ecological exchanges.

What, then, are performative material morphologies? According to Achim Menges, a professor and a founding director of the Institute for Computational Design and Construction at the University of Stuttgart, performative morphologies have at their core processes of biological becoming rather than processes of technological production (Menges 2013). Natural systems adjust actively to the ever-changing environment that surrounds them. Contrary to that, engineered systems or devices that perform specific tasks under predicable external conditions have their performance goals adjusted immediately if the variation in performance is observed (Holling 1973). This concern with the constancy of performance and a focus on an equilibrium-centered view dominant in the technological realm does not support transition between the internal logic of the constructed (and engineered) and the effects of thermodynamic or indeterminate.

Within the building industry any discussion of performance focuses on accomplishing a task, and is usually measured against some predetermined standards. This is a direct result of the need to specify a problem in order to design an efficient technical solution. As a consequence, buildings become a site for integrating technical solutions, with most of them addressing a particular problem, resulting in complex, bifurcating and oftentimes competing goals. As we increasingly expect buildings to not only house and facilitate various modes of human activity but also to adapt, behave, respond and accommodate the flow of energy and information the goals (problems) are becoming more complex. But the expectation that buildings actively engage with the environment presents an opportunity to recalibrate our attitude towards performance to incorporate not only predetermined standards but effects of indeterminate occurrences. This chapter focuses on materials that can facilitate this active engagement and act as a transition or an interface between buildings and their dynamic environment.

Performative Morphologies

Morphology is the study of form and structure of organisms, while morphogenesis includes forces that play a role in organism's formation; morphogenesis is concerned with the interaction between the forms and environments. Correlating morphogenesis and ecology, Michael Hensel and Achim Menges (Hensel and Menges 2007) formulated a framework for architectural design based on a biological paradigm, and offered a different perspective on the notions of functionality and performance. Traditionally, functionality in architecture relates to the use of a building. The notion of performance, even though widely used in architecture, means different things to different groups. Grounding functionality and performance in the biological paradigm allowed for a search of new kinds of material systems that could align architecture more productively with its broader context. It also permitted the questioning of the boundaries in architecture by embracing environmental dynamics. As Hensel and Menges argue, "the challenge is to formulate a synthesized approach based on a synergetic relation between material thresholds and environmental dynamics" (Hensel and Menges 2007: 18). Michael Weinstock reinforces this argument in his discussion of natural systems by pointing out that material systems based on morphogenetic strategies can modulate and are modulated by environmental conditions. As such, they challenge not only the relationship between formation and materialization in architecture and engineering but also bring into question the emphasis on optimal performance of a single function only (Weinstock 2006).

On a material level, an internal structure (morphology) of matter is of great importance when determining its properties or behaviors. What follows is a discussion of various performative aspects of matter or material systems presented from several perspectives. They include (1) application of embedded technologies, (2) inherent and designed material behaviors, (3) the power of geometry, and (4) use of metabolic processes. These are by no means exhaustive categories but they capture lines of inquiry into active matter, its organization into complex material systems and its application.

Embedded Technologies: Arduino, MEMs and Learning Algorithms

In 2005, an inexpensive open-source microcontroller board called Arduino was released in Italy. It could receive input from a variety of sensors, detecting light, motion, touch, sound, temperature, etc., and it could affect its environment by controlling lights, motors, pumps or other devices and actuators. The platform came with a simple development environment for writing code. Since its release, hundreds of thousands of these inexpensive electronics boards have been sold worldwide, enabling enthusiasts to create all sorts of interactive objects and environments. Arduino boards also found their way into the schools of architecture worldwide, sparking the imagination of students and reigniting the vision of dynamic built environments that could alter their shape, position or orientation. The dynamically changing structures, imagined in science-fiction novels of the 1960s and 1970s, started to emerge as a not-so-distant technological possibility. Ruiz-Geli's *Media-TIC* building in Barcelona features a number of control systems based on over a hundred networked Arduino boards that can sense various changes in the environment and then produce a corresponding reaction not only in shading but also how the building is lit.

As technology is advancing, the micro-electro-mechanical systems (MEMs), made of miniaturized structures, sensors, actuators and microelectronics, are another interesting thread of technological development. Due to their scale these micro machines could be embedded in other materials. For example, Siemens has created micro-sensors for heat changes that could be embedded in glass to measure solar heat gain and trigger the appropriate action, such as darkening the glass by applying electricity to its coating. MEMs can vary in size from below 1 micron to several millimeters and can be relatively simple in structure or have multiple moving elements. Even though very small, these actuators can cause effects at the macro scale. When a MEM is paired with wireless communications the resulting device is called a mote. These incredibly small machines can be designed to sense physical or chemical change within the environment and pass that information along wirelessly. For example, wireless micro-sensors could sense changes in air temperatures, humidity, CO_2 levels and other inputs and transmit that information to the building's management system. The size of only several millimeters, they could eventually be "sprinkled" on building surfaces in their thousands; such dense network sensing holds the promise of turning building envelopes into sensing "skins". Scientists from BAE Systems (a global defense, security and aerospace firm) are developing similar capability for aircraft. This smart skin can monitor variety of factors including temperature, mechanical stress, wind speed or physical movement. The sensory layer would have a high resolution of less-than-1-milimeter-sized motes that together can approximate a nerve density of the human skin. Researchers expect that a layer of motes can be applied to existing and new aircraft as a spray-applied coating (Brownell 2014). There are many different kinds of sensors and data transmitters but what makes motes particularly interesting is their small size, which allows them to be placed almost anywhere; with their wireless connectivity they can form autonomous, dynamic networks (Leavitt 2005) that trigger appropriate responses in real time.

Any information collected by various sensors needs to be sorted, analyzed and used or directed. In organisms, proprioception is an adaptive process that enables the body to vary muscle contraction in response to incoming external information. This is a sensory feedback mechanism that allows the nervous system to keep track of what each part of the body is doing or which part is moving (SPD Australia n.d.). This principle is used in driverless cars with proprioceptive and exteroceptive sensors to sense and respond to the changes in the external environment and to keep track of what each part of the car is doing.

In the *Epiphyte Chamber* project, Philip Beesley, a Canadian educator, architect and artist, uses a distributed proprioreceptive sensor network to integrate interactive "intelligent" components of the system. Combined with the learning algorithms, the previously pre-programmed behaviors are replaced with adaptive ones that include curiosity-based functions. This enables the to acquire novel behaviors over time through interaction with users (Beesley 2016). A two-way relationship between the user and architectural environment has long been a challenge to achieve. The key to attaining that capacity is to exchange information in both directions and engage not only the control and actuation of the motion of the physical structure but also to include human behavior input. In 2009 Cohen de Lara and Hubers used game software to organize the dynamic relations between the input received by the sensors and the output from the behavior of the structure itself (Cohen de Lara and Hubers 2009). With that dynamic feedback, their *Muscle Body* interactive architecture project becomes constantly aware of the movement of the occupants' bodies. At the same time, the occupants perceive that their body movements are shaping the behavior of the space. When this is achieved, an adaptive space could have a transformative effect on participants and on the environment itself. In these scenarios, using learning algorithms promotes an evolving relationship between the user and the environment. The latest projects by Philip Beesley feature an environment that can respond, learn and adapt. His work speculates on and attempts to articulate how tectonic principles meet the dynamics produced by the networks of matter and energy circulation as well as dynamics caused by "environments learning". To some extent his elaborate constructs with interlaying systems that sense and respond (combined with chemical metabolisms) are a simulation of how a sentient inhabitable system might function. They also bring us a step closer towards an inhabitable environment that integrates multiple functions into a multifunctional system suggestive of the workings of biological systems. It is difficult, however, to reproduce the multifunctionality of living systems achieved through organisms' ability to chemically turn on or off certain functions.[1] Such biological sensitivity is what our built environments do not have.

In his seminal book *An Evolutionary Architecture*, John Frazer, an educator and researcher, suggests a new form of designed artifact, one that is interacting and evolving in harmony with natural forces, including those of society (Frazer 1995). To achieve that, architecture depends on information transfer, its relationship to the physical structure and its response to systems that control and activate the intelligence of the physical environment. Application and integration of embedded technologies such as MEMs and motes as well as the use of learning algorithms and proprioceptive sensors are important steps in that direction.

Active Matter: Inherent and Designed Material Behaviors

Prior to the Industrial Revolution, understanding of material properties by builders, architects and craftsmen came from experience and practice. Materials were not standardized. During the Industrial Revolution, when a need for large spaces for transportation and industrial facilities emerged, standardization was a way to ensure uniformity and reliability of new, engineered materials necessary for their erection. Research and exploration of materials was driven by necessity until the second half of the twentieth century. Today, we could say that research in structural materials in particular has reached its maturity. A new frontier for material research is in materials with unusual properties and new functionalities. Whether they are natural, bioengineered, smart, meta or machinic, or with embedded electronics, what distinguishes these materials from traditional ones are behaviors they exhibit. The behaviors can be inherent to the material (as in wood fibers) or designed (as in smart and meta materials). Performativity of these materials lies in their capacity to engage with the surrounding energy fields or chemical environments and contribute to them. This exchange results in a variety of behaviors that render these materials extremely interesting as possible substitutes for complex mechanical components or as smart surfaces that can outperform more traditional materials in capturing heat, regulating humidity, repelling or attracting water, generating movement, etc.

Material-based actuation echoes biological paradigms of kinetic adaptation, which rely on internal (inherent) instead of (external) mechanical actuation. Wood is one of those materials with an intrinsic capacity to produce an actuated response. In his project *HygroScope* (Figure 18.1) Achim Menges employs material instability of wood caused by its moisture content to construct climate responsive material morphology. As Menges (2019) notes, "The material structure itself is the machine."

Joanna Aizenberg at the Wyss Institute at Harvard University is also experimenting with adaptive materials, such as superhydrophic surface materials that can collect rainwater efficiently by switching from a hydrophobic (non-wetting) to hydrophilic (wetting) state. Other adaptive materials explored by

Figure 18.1 *HygroScope* by Achim Menges and his ICD research group at the University of Stuttgart, Germany
Image courtesy of Achim Menges

Aizenberg are light-sensitive materials that can change transparency and harness energy from the environment. Her work reflects deep interest in dynamic and responsive materials as well as multifunctionality of materials still difficult to reproduce. For example, artificial multifunctional materials would be able to change their function if the conditions require that of them and, depending on the conditions, perform mechanical and optical or optical and magnetic functions. Such materials would be able to respond to the changing environment more efficiently by changing their properties (Aizenberg 2016).

Another trajectory in material-based activation is to work with two (or more) materials that react to environmental changes at dimensionally different rates. Doris Sung, an associate professor at the University of Southern California, is experimenting with bimetallic panels in which two laminated sheets of metal expand and contract at different rates when exposed to heat, i.e. direct sunlight. If one end of the laminated sheets is fixed, the different rates of thermal expansion or contraction result in deflection, which can be exploited in different ways, depending on the intended performance of such material assemblies. This method of material activation is well known: the thermally induced bending of bimetallic strips has been used in thermostats for decades to produce an "automatic" electronic contact. What is novel in Sung's work is the scale of application, which has shifted tenfold from millimeters in thermostats to centimeters in the canopy project called *Bloom* she designed, produced and installed in 2012 in Los Angeles (Figure 18.2). The canopy consists of tens of thousands of laser-cut

Figure 18.2 Doris Sung's *Bloom* canopy in Los Angeles is made from thousands of bimetallic components
Image courtesy of Doris Sung

bimetallic components assembled into over 400 hypar-shaped panels that create a self-supporting structure when assembled. When exposed to sunrays, the panels start to open in the morning as the temperature rises and then begin to close in the afternoon as the sun sets and the temperature drops. The bimetallic panels are thermally very sensitive, with almost real-time deflection when exposed to solar heat. Her *InVert Window Shading System* done in collaboration with TBM Designs offers a double-glazed window panel system with a layer of thermo-bimetal sandwiched within two panes of glass. When the interior cavity of the panel is heated, the bimetal curls, constraining light from entering the space. Since the bimetal is heat activated, it does not require additional energy from the electrical grid to move into a shading position, as is the case with most conventional mechanical devices. This system can prevent heat gain and reduce air-conditioning needs and therefore conserve energy.

Smart materials are another example of active materials. Their activation also does not require mechanical support. In contrast to the materials stimulated by ambient energy (wood, bimetals), the behavior of smart materials can be dynamically adjusted by controlled stimuli. Their activation is triggered by chemical, electrical, magnetic or other interactions between the molecular layers of the material. Smart materials are defined in the *Encyclopedia of Chemical Technology* as "objects that sense environmental events, process that sensory information, and then act on the environment" (Kroschwitz 1992, as cited in Addington and Schodek 2005: 9). Michelle Addington stresses that smart materials are not artifacts but technologies of motion, energy and exchange. Their "smartness" is determined by either how it affects a material's internal energy state or whether it changes a material's energy state. When a material's internal energy state is affected, its molecular structure is altered. This results in a property change of the material. On the other hand, the change in energy state results in an exchange of energy from one form to another. So smart materials can either absorb the input energy and undergo a change (as in shape memory alloys, or SMAs) or stay the same while energy undergoes a change (as in piezoelectric materials) (Addington and Schodek 2005: 14).

Smart materials are usually designed for a specific behavior and this presents a limitation in a degree of responsiveness. Hensel and Menges (2007) suggest that smart materials should be able to evolve so that they could respond to varying stimuli and stay active. On the other hand, Joanna Aizenberg describes difficulties in developing multifunctional materials. In biological organisms, change between the optical, electrical or magnetic functions of the tissue happens seamlessly. In artificial materials this change in function requires specific interfaces that are difficult to replicate (Aizenberg 2016). Smart materials have a particular molecular make-up. To respond to varying stimuli, a complex molecular communication, akin to a living cell mechanism, would have to be established. The complex functional relationship that an organism has with its environment is one of the keys to its adaptability. To achieve this in artificial materials would require an interface between technological and biological systems, allowing for complex and dynamic exchange.

Smart materials are radically different from normative building materials. They are designed to dynamically respond to energy fields while building materials are designed to withstand building forces. Even though the scale at which smart materials operate is different from a scale of a building, their capacity for behavior is inspiring architects and designers to explore their application in dynamic material assemblies. For example, SMA or electro-active polymers can act as actuators and produce a motion within or of the materials assembly. Like many other property-changing smart materials, SMA can react to electrical charge with significant material response at the molecular level. This is possible due to a phase change of its internal structure. The high-temperature phase (austenite) and the low-temperature phase (martensite) define the change of its crystalline structure. This enables SMA to recover its initial shape after deformation through a reversible thermo-elastic phase transformation. In other words, SMAs are functional materials that have the ability to change their shape without permanent deformation and to "remember" their original geometry.

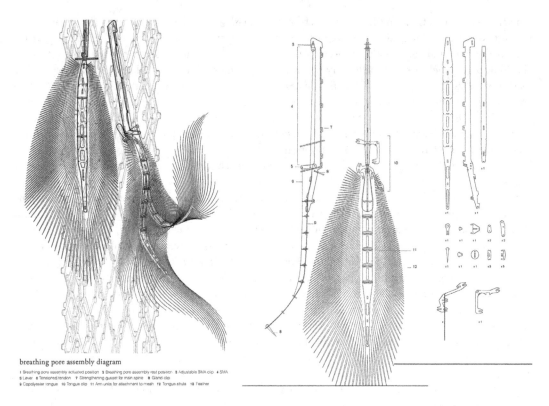

Figure 18.3 Hylozoic Ground project, Breathing Pore assembly drawing diagraming the SMA wire dormant and active position.
Drawing made by Eric Bury and Philip Beesley. Image courtesy of Philip Beesley

Philip Beesley uses SMA's capacity for dimensional change (when electrically stimulated) to generate movement of elements within his responsive environments (Figure 18.3). The environments include several kinds of actuating elements actuated by SMA wires. SMA does not produce a dramatic dimensional change; therefore, most of the dynamic elements in Philip Beesley's projects use a lever or a system of pulleys to amplify the effect of the SMA wire contraction. For example, its capacity to lift weight depends on its diameter, while its length plays an important role in the amplitude of movement. The breathing pores and lashes in the *Hylozoic Ground* project (Figure 18.3) are driven by ten-inch-long Flexinol SMA wire that is only 300 microns in diameter. The contraction of this long wire, amplified by a mechanical lever, translates into a curling motion of the mylar frond. Filters and crickets use shorter lengths of wire in series to provide more subtle kinetic responses (Elsworthy 2010). These elements are relatively light, so that SMA can provide enough force to generate their movement.

Use of SMA in architectural assemblies where weight is of concern has not been sufficiently explored. The *Kinetic Lattice* project (Figure 18.4) developed by Vera Parlac uses strategically positioned SMA springs to further amplify the effect of dimensional change and produce movement in the lattice-structured system. The system's lattice structure and its structural behavior are key to its operation, which relies on the elastic deformation and on connectivity of the constituent members. When SMA springs of this system are activated they introduce tension into the lattice members (intersecting three-layered ribs) and cause a change in the geometry of the lattice cells. This in turn causes tension within

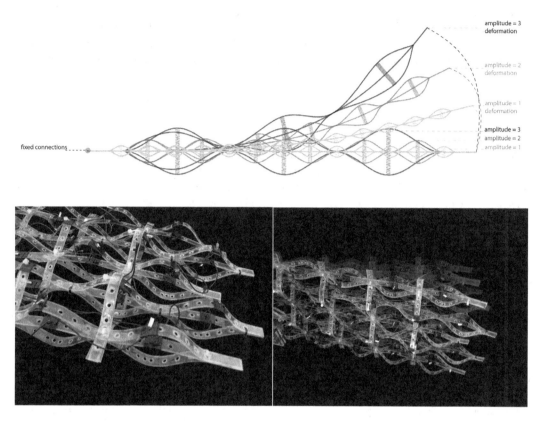

Figure 18.4 The *Kinetic Lattice* project by Vera Parlac is a prototype of the lattice structure actuated by SMA springs
Image courtesy of Vera Parlac

the middle layer of the lattice, which then produces its bending that results in the movement of the entire lattice structure. Strategic placement of the actuators across the lattice produces an accumulated bending effect amplifying the kinetic capacity of the SMA wire (Parlac 2015). Integrated in this way SMA produces robust deformations capable of causing a significant kinetic effect close to the scale of the architectural surface.

Unlike mechanical components, these materials work silently, and their movements often resemble the soft and organic motion of a living organism. This capacity for soft, silent movement of dynamic components can offer a more intimate interface between a dynamic built environment and its inhabitants. Exploration of energetic or chemical exchanges that smart materials can have with their environment can further alter the relationship between the built environment, its inhabitants and the larger ecological context.

None of these examples requires sophisticated sensory, control and actuation systems to produce a dynamic response to changing environmental conditions; instead, they cleverly exploit the intrinsic or designed properties of the materials. Challenges, however, do exist before systems that rely on material-based actuation are fully developed. Most of the prototypes that make use of the designed materials are small-scale; in fact, *scale* remains a principal challenge in developing such smart material-based systems, for the simple reason that materials behave differently at different scales. For many materials, where ambient energy triggers its response, user control is a challenge. Although they could potentially lead to "zero-energy" adaptive elements, actuation of ambient material elements cannot be stopped or regulated. But to fully take advantage of the dynamic capacities of smart materials what is required is a way of thinking that acknowledges the scale at which these materials perform (micro versus macro).

The Geometry of Matter

Geometry is inherent to matter and material organizations and this is evident in biological organisms as well as in inorganic formations. In nature, geometry and patterns of growth or crystallization is how matter gets organized into morphologies and forms. Inherent rules of organization and geometry that govern contingent coagulation of matter determine, to a large extent, its behavior under various exigencies. Manipulation of these rules is what enables material scientists to come up with new materials that might not exist in nature.

Metamaterials are such materials with engineered properties that do not occur naturally. Even though the development of these materials started at the end of the nineteenth century and progressed after the Second World War, it is the current fabrication processes of producing extra-small- and nano-scale elements that have advanced their capabilities. Used mainly in antennas for beam shaping and in stealth technology, these materials are finding new uses in satellite and data processing technology, high-speed fiber-optic telecommunication networks and production of more powerful microscopes or faster electronics.

Metamaterials are not made by manipulating molecular structures but are instead assembled from microscopic plastic or metal elements arranged in recurring patterns. These small elements interact with electromagnetic waves and their shape, geometry, size, orientation and arrangement allows for manipulation of the waves. It is the geometry of the metamaterials' structure and not their material composition that controls their properties, behaviors and effects. Manipulation of these elements determines a metamaterial's electromagnetic properties and can make the electric permittivity and the magnetic permeability simultaneously negative (Wartak, Tsakmakidis and Hess 2011). This is possible because a metamaterial's electromagnetic properties are not determined on the atomic or molecular level (as in conventional materials) but instead depend on the configuration of elements that make up the metamaterial. Therefore, their permittivity and permeability are "tunable" (Metamaterial Technologies 2017). For example, photonic metamaterials are able to produce a negative index of refraction resulting in an optical effect that would shield objects from view – like an invisibility cloak.

Metamaterials with their structures made of regular repeating shapes could also have unusual mechanical properties. Lucas R. Meza, Professor of Mechanical Engineering at the University of Washington, has developed a ceramic metamaterial with unusual elasticity. Samples of these ceramics are strong but ultra-light; they absorb energy and are capable of returning to their original shape after being compressed. Ceramics are strong and stiff but also brittle. The brittleness makes them inadequate structural materials. But the structural logic of metamaterials with an internal structure made of tiny nanotubes that could look somewhat like steel trusses gives ceramics (and other materials) an ability to absorb shocks and dampen vibrations. Although the nanotubes themselves are brittle, their dimensions and overall geometry provide the structure with an unusual ability to spring back after being squeezed (Jacoby 2015). The thickness of the elements that make up the metamaterial's structure is also very important. Unlike the typical large-space engineered structures, the elements made from metamaterials seem to behave differently. The thinner they are, the more resistant to shattering they become. For example, the metamaterial built out of 50-nanometer-thick tubes behaves similarly to ordinary ceramic materials by shattering, while 10 nm nanotubes tolerate compression unusually well even after being compressed to half of their volume (Meza, Das and Greer 2014) (Figure 18.5). They can spring back

Figure 18.5 Ceramic metamaterial by Lucas R. Meza showing a difference between "thin" and "thick" shell ceramic nanolattices
Image courtesy of Lucas R. Meza

into their original shape after removing the pressure. Such capacity is a product of the geometry of the materials structure that enables it to become "squishy" and thereby dissipate energy.

Researchers at Harvard University and the Wyss Institute have developed a kinetic three-dimensional material system using an origami-like structure (based on snapology) that has multiple degrees of freedom. They call this material "mechanical metamaterial," suggesting that, like in all metamaterials, the material's internal structure plays a more important role than its composition. Each unit cell is fabricated using layers of thin polyethylene sheets while the overall structure is formed by connecting the folds of adhesive tape. Small pneumatic pockets are strategically located around specific folds to act as hinges, so when actuated they produce specific motion. The entire system results in a highly flexible mechanical metamaterial that can be folded flat or actuated to perform particular deformations resulting in a specific movement. The geometry of the structure exhibits collective behavior that, depending on a direction of the force, results in different configurations (Overvelde et al. 2016). Chuck Hoberman, one of the project collaborators, noted that this kind of structure could have significant implications for dynamic architecture because it integrates surface and structure (as a dynamic system) instead of relying on standard mechanical components that facilitate movement (Wang 2016).

Metamaterials have a consistent material structure that comes from recurring geometry of its elements. However, variable material structure (with variable density), as found in natural systems, can also be desirable and useful. In 2006, Sean Hanna, an architect and engineer, in collaboration with Timothy Schreiber, a German designer, designed and manufactured the PAN_07 chair inspired by advanced cellular lattices that occur in nature. These lattices, found in wood fiber or bone structures, allow natural structures to stay light by minimizing weight while maximizing resistance to force. In designing the chair material, they used a genetic algorithm to generate the cell topology and machine learning techniques to facilitate a change of shape, size or structure of the cell (depending on where it sits in the body of the chair). This resulted in a material with varying density suited to withstand pressures applied when the chair is used (FoxLin 2011). This logic of material production that emphasizes variability within the continuity of material is very different from the traditional approach in architecture that relies on assembly of standardized parts; it can have broad implications on how we conceptualize materials. In the case of the PAN_07 chair, the scale of fabrication was not at the nano but the millimeter scale. Nevertheless, the approach of "constructing" matter, or more precisely its internal structure, could mean that even at the scale of architecture we could think of materials as

Metabolic Materials

Performative morphologies can partner up with thermodynamic behaviors or metabolic processes to produce active systems that register energetic, thermal or chemical changes in the environment and respond to them. In 1974, Waclaw Szybalski (1974: 404) argued that synthetic biology "would be a field with an unlimited expansion potential and hardly any limitations to building 'new better control circuits' or ... finally other 'synthetic' organisms." In 2017, in an interview with Skylar Tibbits, Arthur Olson, the Anderson Chair Professor in the Department of Integrative Structural and Computational Biology at the Scripps Research Institute, described a transition from descriptive to synthetic science happening in biology, similar to what chemistry underwent in the nineteenth century. With an increasing ability to understand building blocks of living systems, our ability to use them to develop new forms of life or create new material systems that mimic biological processes and principles is growing (Tibbits 2017: 70). What Szybalski foresaw forty years ago is becoming a reality today.

In an article published in 2010, Rachel Armstrong, Professor of Experimental Architecture at the School of Architecture, Planning and Landscape at Newcastle University, discusses a new class of materials, developed with technologies derived from synthetic biology, which are capable of "decision making" by relying on the chemical computational power of their molecules (Armstrong 2010). They are "programmed/designed" to make decisions about their environment and respond to it in complex ways that involve a change in their form, function or appearance. The responsiveness of these materials lies in their capacity for chemical computation. Without the need to rely on traditional computing methods and actuation devices, these materials offer a very different way of imagining an operational capacity of matter (Armstrong 2010).

In 2009 Rachel Armstrong proposed an artificial reef under the city of Venice to prevent continuous erosion. The reef would be built by *protocells* "programmed" to use dissolved carbon dioxide and minerals to build the reef. Armstrong suggests that protocells, guided by a chemical language closely connected to the biological world, may also provide additional benefits, such as improved water quality and rich microenvironments for the marine wildlife (Armstrong 2009). The protocell is an artificially created, relatively primitive cellular system different from any form of life. There are three functionalities that a protocell must possess: a metabolism that harvests energy, genes that control functionalities and a container/membrane that encloses it (Hanczys, Chen and Szostak 2008). The protocells could be produced bottom-up or top-down. A top-down system uses a living cell and removes genes to produce a desired minimal cell. In this way a protocell can be tailored to a specific function.

Leroy Cronin, Regius Chair of Chemistry in the School of Chemistry at the University of Glasgow, is interested in engineering a new kind of building materials using inorganic molecules. These reconfigurable elements would be able to emulate living systems and would be "programed" to modulate environment. According to him they could also be calibrated to generate power, self-repair, change mechanical properties and perhaps even compete with other building "organisms" for resources and information (Cronin 2011). This might mean that the scale of architectural building materials measured in centimeters would have to change to the scale of the building blocks of biology: microns. This new approach to building material suggests that our built environment could share some of the properties of living systems. Joining artificial and natural systems by forming the "metabolic materials" suggests that a built environment can transition from an inert to active matter and, by doing that, form a new kind of relationship to the biosphere.

The *Living Bricks* project, coordinated by Rachel Armstrong, explores this relationship by looking at how to integrate current building technologies with new "living" ones. The Living Bricks or "smart bricks" are part of the *Living Architecture* project. As Ioannis Ieropoulos, a professor at the University of the West of England, would explain, they are standard bricks with imbedded Microbial Fuel Cell (MFC) technology that produces electricity while cleaning/treating wastewater. Fitted in this way the bricks can extract energy from sunlight, air and wastewater and turn it into electricity. The MFCs contain programmable synthetic microorganisms robotically activated and digitally coordinated (Tech Spark 2016). The goal of this research is to construct adaptive structures that interact with their environment though live microbes and establish productive relationships between the structure and its environment.

What is particularly interesting about combining biological and artificial is the possibility to make multifunctional materials that can respond accordingly to a variety of encountered conditions. Markus J. Buehler, McAfee Professor of Engineering at MIT, and research scientist Zhao Qin are doing just that by 3D-printing synthetic protein composite materials that are multifunctional. They are interested in the structure–function relationship many protein materials have. The studies suggest that they have switchable material functions that are triggered by changes in environmental factors such as pH factor, ion concentration, temperature, osmotic pressure or mechanical stresses. This would allow researchers to design and build biological materials with active functions and make them shape-tunable (Qin and Buehler 2017).

Including metabolic materials into the design of the built environment can also happen at a building scale, not only at the scale of material. Arup's engineers developed a photo-bio-reactive façade prototype called *SolarLeaf* that features a layer of microalgae, sandwiched between two sheets of glass that generates biomass and heat as renewable energy resources.[2] The four-story *BIQ House* (2013) in Hamburg has over a hundred of these bioreactor panels installed on its façades, with a total surface area of approximately 200 sq m. Solar thermal heat and algae are harvested in a closed-loop system, in which they are stored and then fermented to generate hot water. *Silk Leaf* by Julian Melchiorri consists of chloroplasts suspended in a matrix made out of silk protein.[3] The synthetic biological leaf absorbs water and carbon dioxide to produce oxygen; it is living and breathing as a leaf. It is very light, with low energy consumption – and biological. Its possible application could be as part of the façade ventilation system.

These low-energy systems that can harvest and transform energy from the environment are, most likely, the future of performative building skins. Their performative capacity is built into the material or in the matter itself, thus eliminating the need for complex mechanical assemblies. With the possibility of manufacturing multifunctional materials, the level of response to the ever-changing and varied conditions of the environment is significantly increased. The materials can be in tune with the environment, allowing the built structures to become more reflexive and more sensitive participants in the biosphere. In these technologies, biology is cajoled into a design material, allowing the boundaries of design to extend into the life itself. For some this is seen as a way to save humanity (from itself), while for others tampering with nature is something dangerous that can lead to ecological catastrophe. Even if we adopt a middle-ground position, it is clear that the impact of synthetic biology is not going to be only economic or scientific, but also cultural, political, ethical and perhaps personal.

Conclusion

Performativity is always focused on processes and their effects. Architects can choose to work towards set criteria that measure buildings' performance in terms of energy, material efficiencies and minimization of waste or they can, together with engineers and scientists, re-think the relationship between the built environment and its dynamic context (climate, information, use) where focus on set criteria might offer only limited success. Addressing dynamics of the environment not only at the scale of a building but also at the scale of material and matter would move performativity from the realm of optimization to the sphere of active/reflexive/affective relationship between a building and its context.

The richness of the performative morphologies arising from the application of new technologies such as embedded systems, innovation in material sciences or synthetic biology is remarkable. An influx of new materials and new technologies in general is transforming the fields of architecture and design; this transformation is at its most potent when current paradigms of thought are disrupted. Research and project examples presented in this chapter are forerunners of what may one day be a more environmentally friendly and energy-efficient way to regulate the climate within a building as well as buildings' relationship to their environment and users.

Michael Hensel, a German architect, educator and researcher, puts forward an argument for a performance-oriented architecture situated within the biological paradigm with an intention to further detach architecture from questions of representation, meaning, form–function dichotomy and post-design optimization (Hensel 2010). The exploration of disciplinary affiliation between architecture and biology can also be found in the works of Frei Otto and his call for the clarification of that relationship due to the problems of the environment emphasizing inaptitude of architectural design to address them (Otto 1971). Analogies to a biological paradigm are in fact present in designs that translate functional principles of biological systems into aspects such as surface effects, thermal regulations or mechanical or interactive solutions to engineering problems or structural proposals. Hensel formulates performance as "active agency" located within a space of dynamic interaction between spatial and material organization, human subject and environment. Formulating performance as an almost self-evolving system seems fitting; it offers an opportunity to understand the built environment as an active agent operating within an equally active context.

More than a decade ago Mark Goulthorpe articulated his attitude of seeing a project as a "distribution of material in space, not as the assemblage of preformed elements," acknowledging that we are "moving from collage to morphology, looking to deploy material as material for its spatial and surface effects" (Goulthorpe 2005: 17). In other words, there is a shift in interest away from material elements and towards material morphology.

Distributing material, and not preformed elements, suggests a different operational scale – that of material intensities. We are starting to incorporate a new series of materials with designed behaviors and inherent dynamic qualities that are beginning to undermine the traditional model of material selection in architecture. Selecting a material for its properties is replaced with choosing a material for its behavior or even designing a material behavior to suit a particular design issue. We see examples of this in medicine where new materials are made (or grown) to address particular medical challenges. Technology transfers from fields such as material science, biomimetics, autonomous robotics, interface design and computation are not only influencing the range of the materials used in architecture but also the very scale at which they are deployed. It is becoming less and less difficult to imbue synthetic matter with the kind of "intelligence" that would recognize changes and adapt to them in an organic way. Introduction and use of these new classes of materials in architecture bring in a level of innovation that is changing the role of a designer. The confluence of information and matter, the rise of interactive surfaces and use of innovative materials ushers "impactful transformation of inert physical materials into connected, information-rich and increasingly lifelike objects" (Brownell 2016). The digital and analog worlds are merging in the built environment, welcoming a new class of materials and an unprecedented scale of innovation that together are changing the role of a designer (Brownell 2016).

The future of dynamic building skins will likely belong to low-energy systems that can harvest the heat from the sun or the kinetic energy of the wind. In many experiments described in this chapter, the "sensing" and "actuating" capacities are built into the material, eliminating the need for complex mechatronic assemblies. Such systems of imbedded intelligence that rely on innate properties of materials are perhaps the most promising direction for developing active building envelopes. At the same time a development and inclusion of new active matter is changing the scale and perspective of architect's engagement. By introducing dynamic relationships with matter, architecture becomes an agent of dynamic exchange between the interior and exterior, structure and skin, user and space – and internal and external ecologies.

If we were to accept change as a fundamental contextual condition, architecture could then begin to truly mediate between the built environment, the people who occupy it and the larger context. As Ed van Hinte notes, "instead of being merely the producer of a unique three-dimensional product, architects should see themselves as programmers of a process of spatial change" (van Hinte et al. 2003: 132). The principal task for architects is to create "a field of change and modification" that would generate possibilities instead of fixed conditions (van Hinte et al. 2003: 132). Through the concept of performative material morphologies design is seen as an ecological agent focused on physical configurations and as a reflexive system engaged in an exchange with the atmospheric systems of flows and processes.

Acknowledgments

This chapter is an excerpt from a manuscript of the book titled *Material Dynamics* that will be published in 2020 by Routledge.

Notes

1 Some progress achieved in synthetic biology where semi-living systems are "programed" through chemical or molecular manipulation to sense and to adapt to specific set of conditions will be mentioned in this chapter in the section on metabolic materials.
2 The project was developed collaboratively by Arup, SSC and Colt International.
3 The project was developed as part of the Royal College of Art's Innovation Design Engineering course in collaboration with Tufts University Silk Lab.

References

Addington, M., and Schodek, D. (2005). *Smart Materials and New Technologies for Architecture and Design Professions*. Burlington: Architectural Press.
Aizenberg, J. (2016). *Interview 2 Biointerfaces International 2016 Conference*. [Online video]. *ETH Zurich*. Available at www.video.ethz.ch/events/2016/biointerfaces/e6ab5e18-6a51-4e88-b813-497fee791ea8.html.
Armstrong, R. (2009). *Future Venice: Growing an Artificial Reef under the City. En Vie – Alive* Available at: http://thisisalive.com/future-venice-growing-an-artificial-reef-under-the-city/.
Armstrong, R. (2010). Systems Architecture: A New Model for Sustainability and the Built Environment using Nanotechnology, Biotechnology, Information Technology, and Cognitive Science with Living Technology. *Artificial Life*, Volume 16 (1), pp. 73–87. DOI: 10.1162/artl.2009.16.1.16101.
Barad, K. (2003). Posthumanist Performativity: Toward an Understanding of How Matter Comes to Matter. *Signs: Journal of Women in Culture and Society*, Volume 28 (3), pp. 801–831. DOI: 10.1086/345321.
Beesley, P. (2016). "Epiphyte Chamber: Responsive Architecture and Dissipative Design". In: Terranova, C. N., and Tromble, M., eds., *The Routledge Companion to Biology in Art and Architecture*. New York: Routledge, pp. 188–196.
Brownell, B. (2014). A Smart Skin for Aircraft Could Make Buildings More Intelligent. *Architect*. Available at: www.architectmagazine.com/technology/a-smart-skin-for-aircraft-could-make-buildings-more-intelligent_o.
Brownell, B. (2016). The Architect as the Orchestrator of Information. *Architect*. Available at: www.architectmagazine.com/technology/the-architect-as-the-orchestrator-of-information_o.
Cohen de Lara, M., and Hubers, H. (2009). "Muscle Body Interactive Architecture". In: Oosterhuis, K., and Xia, X., eds., *iA #2 – Interactive Architecture*. Rotterdam: Episode Publishers, pp. 30–35.
Cronin, L. (2011). Defining New Architectural Design Principles with 'Living' Inorganic Materials. *Architectural Design*, Volume 81 (2), pp. 35–43.

Elsworthy, W. (2010). "Component Design and Actuated Devices an Evolutionary Process". In: Beesley, P., ed., *Hylozoic Ground: Liminal Responsive Architecture*. Cambridge: Riverside Architectural Press, pp. 96–111.

FoxLin. (2011). Sean Hanna and Timothy Schreiber PAN_07 Optimised Cellular Chair. Available at: https://foxlin.com/sean-hanna-and-timothy-schreiber-pan_07-optimised-cellular-chair/.

Frazer, J. (1995). *Evolutionary Architecture*. London: Architectural Association.

Goulthorpe, M. (2005). "Matter". In: Lavin, S., and Furian, H., eds., *Crib Sheets: Notes on Contemporary Architectural Conversation*. New York: Monacelli Press, pp. 16–17.

Hanczys, M. M., Chen, A. I., and Szostak, W. J. (2008). "Steps Towards a Synthetic Protocell". In: Deamer, D., ed., *Protocells: Bridging Nonliving and Living Matter*. Cambridge: MIT Press, pp. 107–124.

Hensel, M. (2010). Performance-oriented Architecture – Towards a Biological Paradigm for Architectural Design and the Built Environment. *FORMakademisk*, Volume 3 (1), pp. 36–56. DOI: 10.7577/formakademisk.138.

Hensel, M., and Menges, A. (2007). *Morpho-Ecologies: Towards Heterogeneous Space in Architecture Design*. London: AA Publications.

Holling, C. S. (1973). Resilience and Stability of Ecological Systems. *Annual Review of Ecology and Systematics*, Volume 4, pp. 1–23. DOI: 10.1146/annurev.es.04.110173.000245.

Jacoby, M. (2015). Metamaterials with Unusual Mechanics. *Chemical & Engineering News*, Volume 93 (14), pp. 28–29. Available at: http://cen.acs.org/articles/93/i14/Metamaterials-Unusual-Mechanics.html.

Kolarevic, B., and Malkawi, A. (2005). *Performative Architecture: Beyond Instrumentality*. New York: Spon Press.

Leatherbarrow, D. (2005). "Architecture's Unscripted Performance". In: Kolarevic, B., and Malkawi, A., eds., *Performance Architecture: Beyond Instrumentality*. New York: Spon Press, pp. 5–19.

Leavitt, W. (2005). Of MEMs and Motes. *FleetOwner* Available at: www.fleetowner.com/information_technology/patentpending/fleet_mems_motes.

Menges, A. (2013). Performative Morphology in Architecture: Integrative Design Research by the Institute for Computational Design. *SAJ (Serbian Architectural Journal)*, Volume 5 (2), pp. 92–105.

Menges, A. (2019). *Morphogenetic Design Experiment*. Available at: www.achimmenges.net/?p=5083.

Metamaterial Technologies. (2017). What are Metamaterials. Available at: http://content.metamaterial.com/blog/what-are-metamaterials.

Meza, R. L., Das, S., and Greer, R. J. (2014). Strong, Lightweight, and Recoverable Three-Dimensional Ceramic Nanolattices. *Science*, Volume 345 (6202), pp. 1322–1326. DOI: 10.1126/science.1255908.

Otto, F. (1971). *IL3 Biology and Building Part 1*. Stuttgart: University of Stuttgart.

Overvelde, T. B. J., de Yong, A. T., Shevchenko, Y., Bacerra, A. S., Whitesides, M. G., Weaver, C. J., Hoberman, C., and Bertoldi, K. (2016). A Three-Dimensional Actuated Origami-Inspired Transformable Metamaterial with Multiple Degrees of Freedom. *Nature Communications*. DOI: 10.1038/ncomms10929.

Parlac, V. (2015). "Material as Mechanism in Agile Spaces". In: Kolarevic, B., and Parlac, V., eds., *Building Dynamics: Exploring Architecture of Change*. London and New York: Routledge, pp. 178–190.

Qin, Z., and Buehler, J. M. (2017). "Multiscale Computational Design of Bioinspired Active Materials for Functionally Diverse Applications". In: Tibbits, S. ed., *Active Matter*. Cambridge: MIT Press, pp. 40–46.

SPD Australia. (n.d.). The Proprioceptive System. Available at: https://spdaustralia.com.au/the-proprioceptive-system/.

Szybalski, W. (1974). "In Vivo and in Vitro Initiation of Transcription". In: Kohn, A., and Shatkay, A., eds., *Control of Gene Expression*. New York: Plenum Press, pp. 404–405.

Tech Spark. (2016). UWE Academics Working on Smart 'Living Bricks'. Available at: https://techspark.co/uwe-academics-working-smart-living-bricks/.

Thompson, D. (1992). *On Growth and Form*. New York: Dover Publications.

Tibbits, S. (2017). *Self-Assembly Lab: Experiments in Programming Matter*. Abingdon and New York: Routledge.

van Hinte, E., Neelen, M., Vink, J., and Vollaard, P. (2003). *Smart Architecture*. Amsterdam: 010 Publishers.

Wang, B. (2016). Harvard Creates Three-Dimensional Actuated Scalable Snapology-Origami-Inspired Transformable Metamaterial. *NextBigFuture* Available at: www.nextbigfuture.com/2016/03/harvard-creates-three-dimensional.html.

Wartak, S. M., Tsakmakidis, L. K., and Hess, O. (2011). Introduction to Metamaterials. *Physics in Canada*, Volume 67 (1), pp. 30–34.

Weinstock, M. (2006). Self-Organisation and Material Constructions. *Architectural Design*, Volume 76 (2), pp. 34–41.

19.1

Dynamic Vocabularies

Technology of Expressive, Communicative and Responsive Surface Architecture and Design of Building Skins and Enclosure Systems in Performative Design Forms

Michael Fox

Introduction

As we continue to embrace a world where the lines between the physical and digital are increasingly blurred, we are beginning to see a maturing vision for performative architecture that actively participates in our lives. This chapter is focused on building skins and enclosure systems that have been designed to respond, adapt, change, and come to life. How architectural design integrates and reconciles the digital lies at the crux of the discussion, and in our contemporary context it is often best defined through reciprocal innovation. Performative building skins and enclosure systems are becoming an inevitable and completely integral part of how we will make our buildings in the future. The platform is ripe to foster unique applications which both affect, and are affected by, developments in digital technology.

As a matter of definition, performative building skins and enclosure systems are built upon the convergence of embedded computation and a physical counterpart that satisfy adaptation within the contextual framework of interaction. The term "interaction" is being used rather inclusively here as a reciprocal influence rather than just a causal effect, and encompassing the often-used terms: "adaptive," "responsive," "intelligent," "dynamic," etc.

In this chapter, three principal factors are examined. First, that "performative" will be thought of as a very inclusive term; second, that the technology has only relatively recently evolved to the extent that we can really explore this area of design; and last, although the futures of such technologically ensnared areas of design are almost impossible to predict, we can rest assured that current development will most certainly serve as an evolving catalyst for what is to come.

Dynamic Vocabularies

For a profession not so long ago dominated by a discourse of styles, we have begun to detect a shift away from questions of representation towards those of processes and behaviors (Farahi, 2013). As a matter of defining dynamic vocabularies in building skins and enclosure systems this appraisal takes a much broader look at the potentials of the systems than a typical definition of performative design might consider.

A number of categorical areas have consequently come to the fore as designers have forged ahead in this area of design. The vocabularies are appropriately organized therefore not technically by how they are constructed or how they look, but rather by how they perform: they *communicate* data or imperceptible phenomenon; they *mediate* the environment and the users, and they *evolve* with both the users and the technological world they inhabit.

The Influence of Technological Advancements

We are now at a time that the economics of obtaining affordable computational hardware and increased aptitude to integrate computational intelligence into our buildings have become accessible to architects. Although the foundations of performative building skins and enclosure systems stretch back to the theoretical work of cyberneticians half a century ago, it was not until the early 1990s when architectural projects began to be initiated in both academia and the professional world that relished the newly available technological advancements of the time. It was a time when wireless networks, embedded computation, and sensor effectors became both technologically and economically feasible to implement. This feasibility fueled experimentation with many of the ideas that had been previously stifled by the technological and economic hurdles of their day. We are now finally seeing an explosion of current exploration due to the influence of feasibility within our technium.

The technium coined by Kevin Kelly (2010) here is used inclusively as a term for the general interconnected system of technology. While there have always been technological advancements, the advancements specific to the tools used in the profession of architecture are relatively recent. Only one generation ago was the first to adopt computers, displacing the analogue tools (and consequently many of the processes) that had been used for centuries. The adoption ensnares a continual advancement in the processes we use to design, visualize, document, incorporate data into, conceptualize, fabricate, and construct architecture. As technology advances, we are finding that the one thing that never changes is that the tools are constantly changing. It is important to understand that the processes and outcomes are tied directly to the tools. As new tools come to the fore, so do new processes, and consequently new capabilities in built form.

The point here is that we should not limit our thinking of performative building skin or enclosure systems as that which can simply perform better than a typical non-computational building skin or enclosure system. We should be thinking about how a building skin and enclosure system can do what was previously not possible to do.

Sensors are readily available today which can sense nearly anything: from complex gestures to CO_2 emissions to the color of your hair. In addition to sensing, an interconnected digital world means that data sets can also be drivers of an interactive building or environment which range from internet usage to traffic patterns to crowd behaviors. Perhaps equally important, the technologies are both economically and technically accessible to designers. In other words, the technologies needed to prototype designs are simple enough that architects who are not experts in computer science or materials and construction are able to conceptualize their ideas in an affordable way to the extent that they can communicate their design intent. It is never to be expected that architects solely execute their futuristic and technologically intensive designs, but it will always be expected that they possess enough of a foundational knowledge to be able to intelligently communicate intent.

Architectural applications with regard to thinking about building skins and enclosure systems are iterative in a technological context. The sensors and robotic components are now both affordable and simple enough for the design community to access; and everything can easily be digitally connected to everything else. Designing performative architecture is not inventing, but understanding what technology exists, and extrapolating it to suit an idea about how architecture ought to perform.

Connected Capacities

It is important to preface a discussion of performative building skins with a brief discussion of the potentials of a connected context. In this respect, architects have learned a great deal from the rapidly developing world of *Tangible Interaction* (Hornecker, 2009), which was developed essentially as an alternate vision for interfacing, in order to bring computing back into the "real world." The "Internet of Things" (IoT) has quite rapidly come to define the technological context of intelligent design inclusively. The context of interaction as defined above exists within this connectedness as one that affects essentially everything, from objects to buildings to cities. The foundations reside in the connected worlds of web, mobile, and spatial interfacing and they are also still evolving.

Perhaps ironically, early theories of computationally connected buildings existed long before mobile devices and web interface technologies changed every aspect of our lives and yet the practical applications were technologically inaccessible. While the first wave of connectivity focused on human-to-human communication, the current focus is on connected things and devices, which extends naturally to buildings, cities, and global environments. It is the goal of the IoT to connect them in a meaningful way (Schneider, 2013). These intelligent things are everywhere in our lives and many of them are already seamlessly embedded into our architecture, ranging from our kitchen appliances to our HVAC (heating, ventilation, and air conditioning) systems to our home entertainment systems, and only now are they beginning to become the external interface via the building skin.

Scott Fisher states,

> The growing number of ubiquitous and embedded computing technologies introduces a new paradigm for how we interact with the built environment ... These technologies are used not only for collecting and providing data, but also as a way to animate and collectively augment the world around us.
>
> *(Stein et al., 2010)*

The interactions are no longer limited to that of people interacting with an object, environment, or building but can be carried out as part of a larger ecosystem of connected objects, environments, and buildings that can autonomously interact with each other.

The connected capabilities of buildings have opened up a wealth of possibilities not only at the scale of the building skin but also the city and beyond. One of the pioneers in this area has been the MIT SENSEable City lab led by architect Carlo Ratti, which has done extensive research into how real-time data generated by sensors, mobile phones, and other ubiquitous technologies can teach us about how buildings are connected, how cities are used, and how new technologies will ultimately redefine the urban landscape. Ratti advocates that urban planning is not just about physical buildings and their context, but about understanding the combination of the physical and the digital. Says Ratti,

> the interesting thing is that now the machine, the computer, is becoming the city. The city has become the interface—to retrieve information, to meet other people, to do all the things happening now with this mixing of bits and atoms.
>
> *(Daly, 2011)*

The Experience of Communication

We do not inhabit architectural buildings simply for shelter; we do so because we desire the experience of space. Our experience of space hinges simultaneously on a great number of architectural factors that include lighting, acoustics, materiality, the people in that space, and the role that the building skin serves in mediating the environment. The implications of the building skin in this respect touch upon simultaneously building performance and aesthetic phenomenology.

As performative buildings begin to do more than respond and become truly interactive in a sense of facilitating "conversations" via reciprocal influence, we are in relatively unknown territory with respect to our behavioral awareness. Furthermore, our buildings are not limited to one-on-one conversations in that they can respond to, convey information about, and interact with groups of users. Such applications simultaneously convey a level of interaction between the individual and groups of individuals. When a building has a true, communicative capability, it can foster a heightened sense of attachment. As Salingaros points out: "Our society tries to understand its own structure, and builds its physical extensions on the earth's surface, guided by the blank slate hypothesis" (2004, n.p.). It is important to recognize that people truly desire space, not style, and to understand the role that computational architectural applications can play in facilitating such desires.

A number of recent building skin systems have been built which exemplify the capability of a performative system to go beyond the pragmatic needs but also to serve as a phenomenological communicator of imperceptible data. In the project entitled "May/September" on the Eskenazi Hospital Parking Structure Façade by Urbana there was the primary goal of creating an exhilarating effect at an urban scale and yet as Rob Ley points out, it also very pragmatically serves as a visual screen for a normal parking structure behind, masking the normal things one might see such as cars, concrete beams, columns, guardrails, etc. It was required that the piece allow for substantial ventilation, which as a requirement naturally worked well with the concept. The intense visual screen was both conceptually and functionally driven by the idea of image creation (Figure 19.1.1).

Translation is also a central theme in the work of Ned Kahn, which hinges on illuminating un-noticed or imperceptible phenomena, where the drivers are not only illuminating and in fact exhilarating but are all the more powerful because they tend to teach us about something that we might not have been aware of or in fact could not see through our senses alone before the translation. In some cases, it involves scaling up the phenomena; in others it simply means adding a field of passive agents that can be manipulated by forces, making it possible for us to understand. The projects rely on a data set of some kind that is sensed and translated back to the participants. Often the case is to visualize complex patterns that exist and translate them to a medium that is simple enough to understand. The works extend beyond simply making us aware of the imperceptible but do so in ways that move us emotionally. Such projects are not so concerned with creating a reality as they are with unveiling the world in ways that we can perceive it (Figure 19.1.2).

Beyond Environmental Mediation

Mediation in this context refers to both people within a building and the exterior environment, which are always in a state of constant flux. The Roman architect Vitruvius in his treatise on architecture, *De Architectura*, asserted that there were three principles of good architecture; these are generally translated to be that of Durability, Utility, and Beauty. Beyond the pragmatic performative concerns, architecture should also delight people and raise their spirits. In each of these three principles lies the inherent necessity to mediate the people within the space and the exterior environment.

The idea of a building façade which can mediate the changing human and environmental conditions is as old as the first hinged window. Interestingly, prior to the curtain wall and air

Figure 19.1.1 Urbana Façade, Rob Ley, Rob Ley Studio.
Source: Serge Hoeltschi, 2014

Figure 19.1.2 Brisbane Airport Car Park Façade, Ned Kahn Studio.
Source: Ned Kahn and UAP, 2012

conditioning (AC), most taller buildings were not wider than 30 to 40 feet and they performed quite well because of their proportions in terms of both daylighting and cross-ventilation. Now, however, the architectural resolution has often been that of completely shutting out the exterior environment and accommodating people by artificial means of lighting and heating or cooling. Inoperable windows coupled with a glass curtain wall would make a tall building literally uninhabitable without AC. It should be noted that operable windows on very tall buildings often do not make practical sense as wind speed increases higher up—a small breeze on the ground is a strong wind at the top of a building. Higher winds combined with moisture can be very troublesome in living units and even worse in an office environment. Furthermore, glass curtain walls are terrible insulators and yet so often buildings are wrapped on all sides with them with complete disregard for the sun and wind.

In the very recent past, however, numerous innovations and experimentations in intelligent building façades have come to fruition. This particular area of performative building skins and enclosure systems has made it into the real world of architecture in a very short time, primarily due to the fact that rethinking the building façade as an intelligent mediator can both save money and make better space. With everything from kinetic panels that breathe to titanium-dioxide-covered walls that scrub the air of pollutants to microalgae used as bio-reactors inside panels, this is clearly the largest single area of innovation in performative building skins. A few pioneering projects exemplify this area.

The KfW WestarkadeTower by Sauerbruch Hutton takes a holistic approach to performance in mediating the environment and the result is like that of an aircraft where the most necessary and appropriate response to all of the forces reconciles itself. The overall form is streamlined to both integrate itself into the context and respond to the prevailing winds in order to exploit them for natural ventilation.

Here we see not just the building skin, but the building as a whole responding to the urban, architectural, environmental, and human conditions. The responsive skin system that breathes like the skin of some organisms, adapting to its immediate environment to act more efficiently. In the KfW tower, sensor-controlled ventilators on the outer skin open and close throughout the day in response to temperature, wind direction, and speed, throwing a ring of positive pressure around the building. That air is drawn into offices through floor vents and windows along an inner façade workers control; then, it is exhausted into the building core. So what you get is a system of natural ventilation that eliminates the need for AC and heat in the fall and spring. In extreme weather, when you need an artificial bump, the pressure balance will not interfere with the heating and cooling systems. The high-technology of the active building skin has a counterpoint in the atmospheric use of color which adds an additional layer of chromatic variation as you move along the street (Figures 19.1.3 and 19.1.4).

Another fantastic example of high performance applied to one of the most high-tech supertall buildings is in the extreme environment of Riyadh. The Capital Market Authority (CMA) Tower is a 385-meter-high skyscraper being built in Saudi Arabia. HOK and Omrania designed the tower with a high-performance solar-control system installed in the tower to moderate light and heat. An external layer of fins, photovoltaics, and perforated fritted panels also provide shade, as well as enhance the thermal efficiency of the triple pane glazing.

Figure 19.1.3 Westarkade Tower detail.
Source: Wicona

Figure 19.1.4 Westarkade Tower.
Source: Wicona (Jan Bitter, 2010)

The triple-glazed façade will be filled with an aerogel to provide thermal insulation. The tower will have an energy-efficient skin to reclaim energy through a photovoltaic array installation on the roof (Figures 19.1.5 and 19.1.6).

The CMA Tower has many layers and many systems superbly integrated into what is inclusively referenced here as an intelligent building skin. Jens Böke, Ulrich Knaack, and Marco Hemmerling (2019) make an interesting point in the way we often reference the building skin in that: "The term skin represents adaptive features and the ability of self-regulation. A descriptive supplement is missing, which emphasizes cognitive abilities. Such a façade must be able to make decisions on the basis of collected information and in the awareness of existing requirements. Against this background, the concept of a thinking façade would be appropriate."

The Biological Paradigm

Technological advancements in manufacturing and fabrication, in particular with respect to materials, have continued to expand the parameters of what is possible in the area of natural adaptation and influence the scale by which we understand and construct our world, resulting in a reinterpretation of the above mechanical paradigm of adaptation. Such advancements have fostered an understanding of adaptation that is much more holistic and operates on a very small internal scale.

A biological paradigm requires more than just understanding pragmatic and performance-based technologies; aesthetic, conceptual, and philosophical issues relating to humans and the global

Figure 19.1.5 CMA Tower from below.
Source: Omrania, 2018

environment must also be taken into consideration. A number of architects and philosophers are beginning to formulate the basis for a physically dynamic architecture which is supported by an improved understanding of biological systems and scale in particular. Arnim von Gleich (2010) and others have identified the main strands of developments in biomimetics as: functional morphology (form and function), biocybernetics, sensor technology and robotics, and nanobiomimetics. The point is that the organic paradigm reinterprets the scale at which designers work and view the world at both ends of the spectrum. In the recent past we have seen innovations in related fields deriving from electronic systems, but now we are beginning to experience an explosion of innovation in manufacturing and fabrication that is heavily influenced by both biology and scale. Until recently, we have seen robots getting smaller and smaller yet still relying on the tiniest of conventional mechanical parts. The possibilities from the vantage point of a materiality make the mechanical paradigm seem dated, ironically before it ever had a chance to fully manifest itself.

Developments in architecture have always been intrinsically tied to developments in materials. As Toshiko Mori points out: "We can theoretically produce materials to meet specific performative criteria; this transformation often takes place at the molecular level, where materiality is rendered invisible" (Weinstock, 2012).

"Intelligent materials" and "smart materials" are general terms for materials that have one or more properties that can be altered. Blaine Brownell (2005) describes transformational materials as those

Figure 19.1.6 CMA Tower detail
Source: Omrania, 2018

materials that undergo a physical metamorphosis triggered by an environmental-stimuli; such change may be either based on the inherent properties of the material or user-driven. Addington and Schodek (2004) divide smart materials and systems into two classes. *Type one* materials undergo changes in one or more of their properties (chemical, electrical, magnetic, mechanical, or thermal) in direct response to a change in external stimuli in the surrounding environment. A *type two* smart material transforms energy from one form to another. This class involves materials with the following types of behavior: photovoltaic, thermoelectric, piezoelectric, photoluminescent, and electrostrictive.

Although not common in architectural scenarios, in many other industries we already see how smart materials can be used as sensors, detectors, transducers, and actuators. As a piezoelectric material is deformed, it gives off a small but measurable electrical discharge. An example of a piezoelectric material is the airbag sensor in your car. The material senses the force of an impact on the car and sends an electric charge to deploy the airbag. Such embedded sensors, composites, and responsive materials are ideal for performative architectural building skin applications. Such an understanding of advancements in both robotics and new materials demonstrates an architectural future whereby adaptation becomes much more holistic and operates on a very small internal scale.

Performative Design as a Catalyst

Philosophically, performative architecture is in a unique position to reposition the role of the designer. The role of the designer should be not so much to create a finished design as to catalyze a design, to ask that it may evolve. In a sense, designing interactive architecture should be an ego-less, emergent endeavor that lies in not designing the future, but designing the platform for the future. Such a position is both noble and profound, for it means the designer must understand people well enough to not only design for them but to design the interfaces and tools for them so that they in turn can become designers. What has made the ubiquitous smartphone so powerful is not that it is a connected device, but that it is a platform for the creation of applications. It has become a catalyst for design and ideas that were never intended.

As the term "adaptive" has increasingly fostered a shift from the paradigm of the mechanical to the biological it has left a gap in the area of control. Robotics helps to fill this gap in the strictly biomimetic approach to architectural design. "Bio-robotic architecture" is a term that defines a biomimetic adaptation that is augmented with robotic control. The project arena defines architecture that goes beyond the mere capacity to interact; it defines a world that repositions the role of the designer as a catalyst of design that can adapt and evolve with the world around it. To preface, let us begin with a bit of clarification in terminology. A cybernetic system is an inclusive one encompassing organism, machine, organization, and the environment.

Cybernetics was defined by Norbert Wiener back in 1948 as "the scientific study of control and communication in the animal and the machine." As a secondary matter of clarification, biomimetics was started by Otto H. Schmitt in 1969 as a scientific approach that studies systems, processes, and models in nature, and then imitates them to solve human problems. *Biocybernetics*, then, is a relatively new term for an abstract science focused on the application of cybernetics in biological science. Lastly, it seems necessary to define *robotics*, which is here interpreted to be a "mechanical agent guided by a program." The point of clarifying such definitions lies in focusing this exploration on how robotics can serve as a means of augmented control for natural biomimetic adaptation.

Early use of pick-and place robotics has primarily employed a system of top-down control when applied to architectural scenarios. Modular application of robotics, on the other hand, relies on decentralized control and although there may be no centralized control structure dictating how individual parts of a system should behave, local interactions between individual modules can lead to the emergence of global behavior. Most architectural applications are neither self-organizing nor do they have higher-level intelligence functions of heuristic and symbolic decision-making abilities. Most applications do, however, exhibit a behavior based on low-level intelligence functions of automatic response and communication. The beauty of such distributed control is that when it is applied to a large system, there is a potential for emergent behavior. An emergent behavior can occur when a number of simple systems operate in an environment that forms more complex behaviors as a collective.

A Question of Control

A number of recent projects have been developed whereby the building skin is quite literally articulated as an interface. In terms of a resolution with respect to the sensing of human factors, recent developments in the area of interface design will eventually play a major role in how we can imagine interaction with architectural spaces and objects.

Interface design is heavily tied to sensor innovation and manufacturing, which has signaled the availability of previously unimaginable means for gathering data and information and non-tangible forms of interaction such as gesture and even brain-wave recognition. It may soon be commonplace to embed architecture with interfaces to allow users to interact with their environments. As architectural scenarios move beyond direct sensing and response conditions we are confronted by the need for more natural and direct means of control. Many in the architectural profession have begun to study and learn from interactive media precedents and usurp the technologies employed for controlling interactive digital environments. Technologies that allow users new means to control and interact with digital information can be broken down into three general categories: touch and multi-touch, gesture, and cognitive control. To date, there are many touch and multi-touch interfaces, gesture interfaces are still in their infancy with regard to architectural applications, and direct cognitive controls reside on the developmental horizon but show fascinating promise.

Gestural language is perhaps the most intriguing means of control in that it enables real physical interactions. Advancements in multi-touch hardware technology are significant to architecture because in many cases the gestures used to control an interface are the most similar to gestures that would be used to replicate these activities in real space with tangible objects. The manipulation of physical building components and physical space itself is more suited to gestural physical manipulation by its users instead of control via device, speech, cognition, or other methods.

"Conventions of Control" by the author and Allyn Polancic (2012) serves as somewhat of an "intervention" to the current profusion of exploration in robotic and interactive architecture from a standpoint of control. As architectural scenarios move beyond direct sensing and response conditions we are confronted by the need for a more direct, yet still natural, means of control. The popular means of interactive control are all too often through either handheld mobile devices or very limited sensing capabilities. The typical disconnect lies in devices being used to control (what should be) an interface. The project demonstrates an interaction with architecture should follow the intuitive nature of gestural language for architecture that is device-free and allows for a variety of input streams. The project demonstrates architecture as an interface which allows users to directly interact with the environments via an adaptive gestural language. Interaction, or "play," with the physical world is crucial to the way humans learn to socialize and understand reality. The evolution of gestural vocabularies to control devices, interfaces, and eventually the entire built environment, should reflect this relationship and ideology (Figure 19.1.7).

Alloplastic Architecture

The important point here is that such systems that are controlled but yet control themselves on another level have the potential to reposition the role of the designer (Figure 19.1.8). Rather than an architecture that literally interprets and responds to human and environmental desires; the architecture is allowed to take a bottom-up role in configuring itself in a malleable way. As Pask states in his foreword to the book *An Evolutionary Architecture*: "The role of the architect here, I think, is not so much to design a building or city as to catalyze them: to act that they may evolve" (Pask, 1969).

In today's computationally interconnected world where communication is paramount, it is ironic to note that although many things in our architectural environments now possess the computational capacity to understand changing conditions, they do not have the appropriate tectonic capacity to appropriately physically respond to it. Currently advancements are being made towards creating a truly ubiquitous computational and kinesthetic material world. Interactive architecture involves both the simultaneous involvement of kinetics and embedded computation. The combination of these kinetic and computation-based systems will allow for an environment to have the ability to reconfigure itself —to automate physical change to respond, react, adapt, and be interactive.

Conclusions

Architectural applications of the performative building skin are iterative in a connected context. The sensors and robotic components are now both affordable and simple enough for the design community to access; and everything can easily be digitally connected to everything else.

While we cannot deny the relevance of performative design in architecture, considering its increasing prevalence in recent years, it is still difficult to determine to what extent it is here to stay. Performative

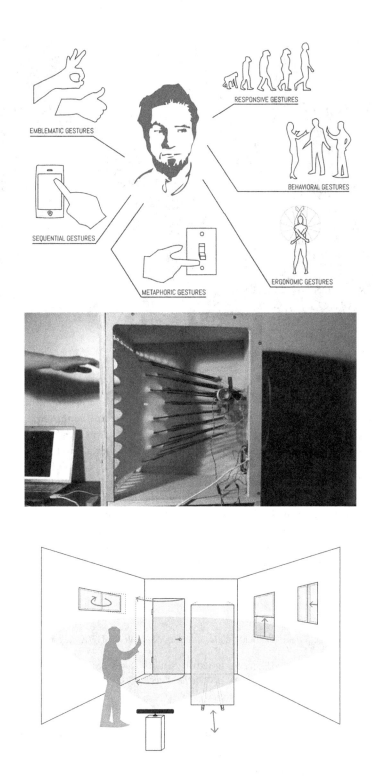

Figure 19.1.7 A vocabulary for gestural control in architecture.
Source: Michael Fox and Allyn Polancic 2012

Figure 19.1.8 Alloplastic architecture.
Source: Behnaz Farahi, 2013

building skins and enclosure systems still have many unanswered questions: Will they be robust enough to withstand failures and gain widespread acceptance? Will they become economically feasible enough to allow for the broad dissemination needed to bring about real change in areas of sustainability and other global issues? Will they make our buildings look different? Will they impact how we actually use our buildings? It is more than likely that performative building skins will accomplish all of the above, and yet fade into the background of our lives, in the same way that users do not think of how an intelligent structural foundation system of a building works to hold the building up against seismic forces, or how an HVAC system works to provide thermal comfort. The way we as users interact with performative building skins will likely become truly seamless. Yet, while we can imagine all buildings integrating various performative systems that are hidden within their fabric, we must also recognize that it is the responsibility of good design to express the performative capacities in the architecture and therefore define its relevance.

References

Addington, Michelle, & Schodek, Daniel. (2004). *Smart Materials and Technologies in Architecture*. London: Architectural Press.

Böke, Jens, Knaack, Ulrich, & Hemmerling, Marco. (2019). State-of-the-Art of Intelligent Building Envelopes in the Context of Intelligent Technical Systems. *Intelligent Buildings International*, 11:1, 27–45. Doi: 10.1080/17508975.2018.1447437.

Brownell, Blaine. (2005). *Transmaterial: A Catalog of Materials that Redefine Our Physical Environment*. New York: Princeton Architectural Press.

Daly, Ian. (2011). Data Cycle: Behind MIT's SENSEable Cities Lab. *Wired*. Retrieved from www.wired.co.uk/article/data-cycle.

Farahi, Behnaz. (2013). Alloplastic Architecture: The Design of an Interactive Tensegrity Structure. In *ACADIA 2013: Adaptive Architecture, Proceedings of the 33rd Annual Conference, Canada*.

Gleich, Arnim Von. (2010). *Potentials and Trends in Biomimetics*. Berlin: Springer.

Hornecker, Eva. (2009). Tangible Interaction. Retrieved from www.interaction-design.org/encyclopedia/tangible_interaction.html.
Kelly, Kevin. (2010). *What Technology Wants*. New York: Viking Press.
Pask, Gordon. (September 1969). Architectural Relevance of Cybernetics. *Architectural Design*, 494–496.
Polancic, Allyn, & Fox, Michael. (2012). Conventions of Control: A Catalogue of Gestures for Remotely Interacting with Dynamic Architectural Space. In *Proceedings to the Association of Computer Aided Design in Architecture Conference*, San Francisco, CA.
Salingaros, Nikos A. (September 2004). Towards a Biological Understanding of Architecture and Urbanism: Lessons from Stephen Pinker. *Katarxis* 3. Retrieved from www.katarxis3.com/Salingaros-Biological_Understanding.htm.
Schneider, Stan (2013). Understanding the Protocols Behind the Internet of Things. Retrieved from http://electronicdesign.com/embedded/understanding-protocols-behind-internet-things.
Stein, Jennifer, Fisher, Scott, & Otto, Greg. (2010). IOT2010 Workshop. University of Southern California, Los Angeles, CA.
Weinstock, Michael. (2012). Material, Form and Force. *Architectural Design*, 82, 104–111.
Wiener, Norbert. (1948). *Cybernetics, or Control and Communication in the Animal and the Machine*. Cambridge: MIT Press.

19.2

Dynamic Vocabularies

Active Façade Tectonics: Sensing and Reacting to the Wicked, Complex Entanglements of Building Envelope Architecting

Douglas E. Noble

Introduction: Approaching Active Façade Tectonics

Active façade technologies are intended to automatically or semi-automatically respond to performance conditions (Schnädelbach 2010). The rapidly advancing technology of the building envelope exceeds individual abilities to design and manage as architects strive to take ownership of the future by naming and defining the offspring. "Performative enclosures" uses lexical semantic reinvention in an attempt to embody the enormously enthusiastic character of an historically optimistic profession. Significant adjustments will be needed to make high-performance building envelopes accepted by designers, owners, and occupants. Performative or high-performance labels are often too narrowly defined. The complexity of performance calls for leadership from the architecture profession and continued adjustments to participants' roles and collaboration. Architects will be called on to bring their unique design skills to address the façades' special place in the built environment. Adjustments will need to be made in architectural research and education. Occupants and the public will need to be engaged in the design, implementation, and operation of the new types of envelopes that will result.

The performance characteristics of high-performance envelopes have traditionally been construed to refer to issues of energy, comfort, and sustainability, but current and future definitions of high-performance will not be circumscribed in this way. The morphology of opportunity for technological systems to sense and react to the environment is proudly pluralistic. Cimmino's observation that "Adaptive architecture must be considered the future of contemporary architectural research because it can decrease the energy balance of buildings by controlling thermal energy, light energy and sound waves" is both accurate and a serious underestimation of the scope of building envelope performance (Cimmino et al. 2016).

Increasing levels of complex technology defy our individual abilities to fully comprehend and rush us towards a potentially improved architectural future involving increased collaboration and an emphasis on the team. This could not have happened at a better time, and it offers the architecture profession an opportunity to escape its regrettable history of domination by paternalistic personality orthodoxy.

Architects intervene in the natural environment to create built settings that they intend will improve lives. Architects bring unique problem-resolving skill-sets along with a fearless and adventurous spirit, but these capabilities are being discounted by the emphasis on STEM (Science, Technology, Engineering, and Math). The building envelope needs to be a product of architects using science, technology, engineering, and math as parts of an arsenal of design methods, or they will face the prospect of the scope of architectural work shrinking.

Professional architecture education is overwhelming. For licensure, a minimum of five years of education is required, followed by years of professional experience and a rich set of exams. The curriculum is dense, and heavily prescribed in the United States by the National Architecture Accreditation Board. Seemingly endless examinations of the curriculum have not identified significant opportunities for reducing content, and thus any attempts to add content can lead to overloaded students. Graduate programs in architecture often also emphasize professional preparation, and research programs in building technology are relatively rare. Doctoral education in building science is poorly funded, extremely limited, and sometimes unrecognized by the profession.

Development of the technology of high-performance building envelopes will need to be accompanied by outreach and engagement with other stakeholders in the design and delivery of the built environment. The small cadre of technology evangelists will likely accept advances with enthusiasm. Acceptance is not the entire goal. Occupants should not simply be the intended victims of technology interventions, but they should help guide it, use it, and provide the feedback to close the loop. Recent developments with self-driving cars may provide a model for improved engagement. Participants in the next generations of high-performance façades will have different expectations for how far they might be willing to "push the envelope" to get to the cutting edge. Architects are well-known, or even notorious, for pursuing "shaving cream" ideas that they perceive as paving the way for the cutting edge that follows. Other collaborators may feel strongly about a more conservative approach.

A preparatory exploration of high-performance building enclosures must examine six interconnected arenas:

1. Concepts of performance
2. Sensoring and reacting
3. Performance metrics
4. Wicked problems
5. Information systems
6. Responsive futures

Concepts of the Performative: Framing an Emergent Discourse

In recent years, architects and especially university academics have begun to use the term "performative" both as a type of shorthand for buildings with higher-performing (and often active) technology characteristics, and as a way of describing design theories, methods, and hypotheses aimed at how buildings engage with their surroundings (Araya 2011). The loose semantic relationship of the word "performative" to optimistic terms like "perform" and "high-performance" has given the architectural use of the term an overwhelmingly positive attribution that belies the borrowed and reinvented original meaning of the term. Over time, architects have taken pleasure in the adoption and redefinition of terms to suit their intentions. The original mis-adoption of the term, and its subsequent widespread use by academics in architecture, have conspired to make the term suspect in many of the same ways that *post-modernism*, *emergent*, and *praxis* once dominated discussions of the built environment. Prior to this new adoptive strategy, *performative* constituted the performance of the specific act by virtue of its utterance, such as the phrase "I now pronounce you man and wife." Just as "greenwashing" became a pejorative for superficial application of the appearance of sustainable technologies, the use of *performative* for buildings that can only boast modest performance risks becoming "performawashing" as a strategy to fool the public (and other architects). Ironically, this chapter is intended for a book that will include "performative" in the title.

Adaptive façades can be transformable, movable, and responsive. They typically react or "pre-act" to conditions of energy, comfort, and sustainability. However, the possible list of adaptations in response to performance has no boundary. There are traditional and less-traditional characteristics of performance, and certainly there will be unforeseen performance issues in the future as new types of man-made problems and opportunities arise.

For example, longevity is a performance issue that sometimes does not get enough attention. There have been proposals for façade longevity involving strategies of systematic replacement and repairability that might allow a façade to last for 1,000 years (Patterson 2017). In another example, real estate brokers can attest to the performance characteristic of view (both into and out of a building). Floor-to-ceiling glass in high-rise Class-A office space went through a period of almost universal demand. In spite of the obvious energy penalties, this is a phase that we have not yet passed through, and the ubiquitous glass façade still reigns. Admittedly, glass façade professionals and architects are getting much better at crafting improved thermal response all-glass façades, and the energy liabilities of all-glass designs from the late twentieth century are quite different from the conditions today.

Pollution mitigation is another arena of façade performance that can be expected to have adaptive features in the coming years. The somewhat over-hyped titanium-dioxide coatings fad of a decade ago will be giving way to systems that can react on concert with energy-sensing systems. Thermal sensors reporting appropriate external temperatures for natural ventilation may need to be over-ridden by sensors detecting unhealthy levels of various types of pollution.

The technology of façades designed for communication or entertainment has long outpaced the ability of local jurisdictions to respond, and the financial performance of active and even interactive billboard or media façades can rival the financial performance of the occupied spaces in the same building.

Adaptive performance for longevity, pollution, and even media façades are just a few of what are certain to be dozens of performance variables that architects and façade designers will face in the near future. The technology to craft adaptive responses for many of these and other performance conditions is likely to be readily available in the near future. Which inputs become more or less important to architects, owners, and society remains to be seen, but the sensor detections and processing of the information towards adaptation will be one of the largest challenges to be faced.

Genetically Modifiable Envelopes: Sensoring and Reacting

Early-twenty-first-century façade sensoring and adapting metrics have been dominated by energy and comfort. However, the boundaries of façade performance will not continue to be essentially framed by these simple and direct building science issues. "Sensors today can discern almost anything, from complex gestures to CO2 emissions to hair color" (Fox 2016). Information systems for adaptive façades can use algorithms to evaluate immediate sensor data in conjunction with long-term data such as local weather and climate, to make decisions about when to activate specific systems. Among the questions we face will include

1. What do we sensor?
2. What new types of sensors will become available?

3. What about sensor malfunctions?
4. What are the privacy issues?
5. How do the algorithms get programmed and checked?

Beginning architecture students can be shown how simple thermal sensors placed both inside and outside a façade can detect timely opportunities for suggesting operating a façade for natural ventilation. In some cases, students build and operate clever systems using simple tools like Arduinos. Typically, these early resolutions detect and analyze one condition and adaptation response involves a limited set of choices, including simple binary choice (open or close the window).

Even in the early technological stages of sensoring, we are already seeing remarkable diversification of the types and amounts of input that can be gathered. Indoor and outdoor temperature sensors are among the most common, as are lighting-level sensors. But these sensor types are already being superseded by sensors that detect additional thermal and lighting conditions. Adding humidity and air-flow rate sensoring capability adds modest complexity to a simple "open or close the window" response decision. Including weather and climate data to the algorithm can allow the response decision to consider reasonable likelihoods of immediate future conditions and factor these into the decision. For example, right now the sensors could indicate if it would be effective to open the windows for improved comfort and energy, but the climate data indicates a high probability of change and so it makes sense to let the comfort performance conditions drift towards the extreme end of the comfort range in anticipation of the changes that will start moving the conditions the other way. In effect, the adaptive system would be saying "I know you are a bit warm, and I could open the windows, but I think I won't do that because I want to hang onto this heat as a cold condition is coming."

As we add more sensors and more types of detection, the decision-making complexity escalates. Detecting for glare, illuminance, noise, pollution, occupancy, and other conditions will give architects additional capability to have the façade adapt. We can also sensor the occupant to try and use individual data. Sensors can observe individuals for body temperature, pupil size, activity level, and more. Knowing that humans generally have temperature preferences in a certain range is one simple type of data. Knowing that there are differences in those ranges based on gender and age, for example, can refine the data. Knowing that this person is sweating, or that person's pupils are dilated (Choi and Yeom, 2017), can provide individualized data to feed the decision-making about operating adaptive façade components.

Using specific human occupants of a space as active (Konis 2017) or passive (Choi and Yeom, 2017) comfort sensors can contribute greatly to the refinement of the façade adaptation decision. This can be done individually or as aggregates of occupants. The potential for significantly improved comfort with direct sensoring of and by current occupants is high. However, this type of sensoring has potential drawbacks. One important issue is that of privacy. It is now common on several social media platforms that posted images containing human faces can be scanned and identified. On a recent post by the author, more than half of a group of 25 students in one scene were identified and labeled. The ability to harvest aggregate and individual data at this level is a serious concern. More than simple identification of individuals, sensors gathering data for apparently benign purposes might be able to be used for less charitable purposes. It is possible to have a sensor that detects the level of pupil dilation of an occupant in order to adjust a façade for improved lighting comfort. As a glare control or lighting-level management tool, this seems potentially powerful. But pupil dilation data has the capability to be surreptitiously used; for example, as a screening tool for illicit drug use.

Sensors also have the capability of malfunction. Recent news about two crashes of the Boeing 737 Max have centered on the flight management software. Key to the analysis of these disasters is that sensors were sending incorrect data (Glanz et al. 2019). Whether the sensors were accidentally or deliberately damaged is important, as is the flight management software's ability to anticipate the possibility of incorrect input. Perhaps the sensor simply failed for unexpected reasons, but if that can happen in a highly technical and carefully considered situation such as one of the most modern aircraft, there are obvious concerns in the lower-stakes and less technical situation of thermal comfort.

The range of future sensor and data input is significant. Sensoring systems can also have the ability to maintain a sort of memory. A sensor can report a thermal data point at 7:55am that falls below the comfort range, and rather than reacting by opening the blinds and letting in more sunshine for heat, the system might remember that for the last week there has been a sudden and dramatic increase of warm human occupancy at 8:00am. Thus, it might be worth waiting to see if that happens again rather than reacting immediately. Sensor system memory might include more than days or weeks of data and might be able to detect diurnal and seasonal patterns, and even learn to anticipate special cases such as office holidays and annual parties.

Adaptive façades can respond to conditions of the building occupants, but they do also have responsibilities to non-occupants and neighbors. An adaptive façade on an overheating building can adjust the façade to reject sunlight. Where is that rejected sunlight going? If one building actively adjusts its solar reflectance index or other façade component, what happens to the neighbors? Conversely, can we expect systems to be actively conversing with the systems of neighboring buildings and "making deals" about the impacts they have on each other? Rejected daylight made headlines when the curvilinear geometries concentrated rejected direct sunlight, creating blinding glare and dangerous heating conditions (Hodge 2010).

Rapidly changing urban form is not a minor consideration. At a recent lecture by the architect of a tall building in China, the speaker mentioned that a detailed wind analysis of the building had unsurprisingly revealed that adjacent buildings had a significant impact on wind speed and direction, and that the structure of the new building had to be adjusted to take into consideration these impacts of neighbors. There were no remarks about whether the owners and occupants of the neighboring buildings ought to have a new wind analysis study for their already completed building. If their building created conditions that impacted a larger new neighbor, could not the larger new neighbor create unexpected and potentially significant impacts on the existing buildings? Do we need to consider urban form sensoring (perhaps by Google Earth) to detect potentially problematic building geometries of neighboring buildings?

The possibilities for sensoring include ground motion sensing (to gain even a few seconds or milliseconds of automated preparation for earthquakes). Wi-Fi and radio detecting might catch smartphone activity spikes such as from the early stages of a local terror attack.

Future adaptive façades will not only be able to act and react, but also pre-act in anticipation of future conditions (Noble et al. 2016; Noble et al. 2018). The array of potential materials, composites, layers, and assemblies of façade fabrication will provide additional depth and nuance to the sets of possible actions. Some systems will need to react at impressive speeds for life-safety conditions, and some systems might use natural rhythms such as growing seasons for long-term passive adaptation.

Complex Entanglements: Establishing Performance Metrics

Adaptive façades responding to individual inputs provides a clear model for teaching about responsive strategies. If it is too bright inside, adjustments to blinds or electrochromic glass can be an obvious response. Some early adaptive façades used just such straightforward schemes. Later systems added more input variables and introduced the problem of conflicting inputs. If it is too bright inside, reduce the amount of sunlight passing through the façade. If it is too cool inside, increase the amount of sunlight passing through the façade. But what happens when it is both too bright and too cool? Which condition is improved at the expense of the other? A vast number of studies in architecture use the phrase "optimization" as if there was a single optimal result. There is not.

Given large numbers of input variables, decisions about what adaptations ought to be made can fall to seemingly trustworthy complex algorithms. But these algorithms ought to be suspect. When it is too cool and too bright, do you value warmth or visual comfort more? How much more? Who decides? If the algorithm decides, who programmed the algorithm?

Imagining that it is possible to somehow craft an algorithm that can decide among the various trade-offs, who is the beneficiary? Should the trade-offs be made to give the most people satisfaction? Many systems are designed just this way, and they can make sense. It is not the case, however, that the plurality or majority should be the target audience for façade adjustments. In a hospital, guests can sometimes outnumber doctors and patients. These three groups have markedly different activity levels and clothing. They have differing levels of adjusting themselves to adapt to out-of-range comfort by, for example, moving to a sunnier spot in the room. Does the algorithm favor the weakest (the patient) or the most numerous (visitors) or the one upon whose skills and comfort the patient is relying (the doctor)?

The algorithm must also take into account that the units of evaluation may not be easily comparable. It is relatively easy to compare saving dollars and British Thermal Units because there are conversion systems, even if those conversion systems are a bit tricky. More difficult is converting "percentage of people satisfied" to dollars. The satisfaction range is also not fixed. Education can expand the comfort range (or at least the tolerance-without-complaining range). Increased income can shrink the comfort range. The comfort range inside can be visually dependent on the multiple sensors and multiple types of sensors; it is possible to obtain conflicting inputs about the same condition. For lighting, is it brightness or illuminance or the direction of the light rays? Perhaps this is dependent on the color of the light and the currently popular circadian rhythm studies. In any event, parsing the data and preparing an automated response system should be incredibly difficult, and we should be highly suspicious of anyone who claims that they can easily solve it.

Seriously Wicked Problems

The concept of "Wicked Problems" was created more than 50 years ago by Horst W.J. Rittel and detailed in print sometime later in a publication by Rittel and Melvyn Webber (1973). For decades, only a few were exposed to this valuable contribution to architecture and planning, but 25 years after Rittel died the phrase "wicked problems" entered mainstream academic and business discourse. With well over 13,000 citations on Google Scholar (admittedly an unscientific sample), the article now might be among the most cited publications ever by an architecture professor. Like any suddenly popular concept, it is now widely misapplied and given meaning that stretches the original intent. Building envelope design is certainly one type of wicked problem. Rittel and Webber enumerated ten characteristics of wicked problems, and they all apply to building envelope design:

Wicked problems have no stopping rule. The design of a building enclosure can typically continue to be improved through added time and effort by the designers. Designers run out of time or money and are forced to conclude the design work in order to get the project built.

There is no immediate or ultimate test of a solution to a wicked problem. The conditions of a building envelope change over time. Improved products and processes appear as the state-of-the-art changes. An apparently successful façade installation can be seen as much less successful in a relatively short time.

Every solution to a wicked problem is a "one-shot operation." Each envelope design will have potentially important differences from previous envelopes, and even small differences will require the design team to adapt to the new conditions.

Every solution to a wicked problem is a "one-shot operation." Each envelope design will have potentially important differences from previous envelopes, and even small differences will require the design team to adapt.

The designer has no right to be wrong. A mistake in the design of a building envelope can endanger lives, as in the case of the John Hancock Tower glass failure in the early 1970s.

Solutions to wicked problems are not true or false, but better or worse. The thermal performance of a façade can be better or worse that the thermal performance of other façades, but there is no one "true" or best façade.

The other key characteristics of wicked problems according to Rittel and Webber include:

There is no definitive formulation of a wicked problem (p. 161).
Wicked problems do not have an enumerable set of potential solutions, nor is there a well-described set of permissible operations that may be incorporated into the plan (p. 164).
Every wicked problem is essentially unique (p. 164).
Every wicked problem can be considered to be a symptom of another problem (p. 165).
The existence of a discrepancy representing a wicked problem can be explained in numerous ways. The choice of explanation determines the nature of the problem's resolution (p. 166).

Supporting: Information Systems

Some architects lament the long-lost days of the "master builder architect" who had considerable knowledge about every aspect of building design and delivery. While there are some building types and scales that continue to allow for this way of working, the breadth and depth of information in modern façade design exceeds the capabilities of even the most extreme polymath. Supporting tools, such as Building Information Modeling, now contain some elements of what will eventually need to be significant information systems incorporating not only the "what and where" of building materials and systems, but also the underlying design reasoning that helped shape the decisions (Kensek 2014). Documenting decision-making is crucial in even moderately complex conditions. Potentially catastrophic results can happen as a result of seemingly innocuous or minor interventions. "There is a reason that we do not paint over that small hole" can be a lost phrase that results in aircraft crashes. Building failures might be less sensational and yet have large negative impacts on many people's lives.

Traditionally, the process of planning and design has been described as a sequence of first understanding the problem, followed by analysis, synthesis, and implementation. This model is not a realistic model of the act of design (Rittel and Webber 1973). An alternative understanding of the reasoning in the design process and the nature of its problems is that designing is more appropriately understood as a process of argumentation. One of the primary reasons is that argumentation tends to help reduce the chances of overlooking some important aspect of the problem at hand. Debate by a heterogeneous group can also help increase the chances of perceiving connections of the current problem with other problems and of comprehending the ramifications of potential courses of action.

The current problem might be treatable in conjunction with a set of other problems, or it can be seen as merely a symptom of a larger problem. The differing participants can see a problem, and its resolution, in dramatically different ways. Argumentation can also take place after a plan, or a set of alternative proposals, has been developed. By inviting debate and criticism, the designer is likely to improve the opportunity to discover and comprehend the ramifications of implementing a plan. Argumentation helps to make the working procedures of design "transparent." *Transparency* here refers to the ability of observers as well as participants to trace the process of design decision-making.

As one type of information system for design, the Issue-Based Information System (IBIS) was developed in 1970 as a method for supporting the decision processes of design through debate and argumentation (Kunz and Rittel 1970). IBIS guides the identification, structuring, and resolving of issues raised by designers, and elicits information pertinent to the discourse. It can be used for decision making or mere problem exploration. The process of developing an IBIS encourages looking at situations from many different points of view. The basic element of the IBIS is the issue. An issue is stated in the form of a controversial question, about which people may have differing points of view. Some examples of issues taken from architecture might be: "What color should this building be?", "Should another skyscraper be built in downtown?" and "What aesthetic style is most appropriate for this building?" Issues can be categorized according to the types of knowledge they pertain to. A person's response to an issue is called a position. In some issues, including all deontic issues (issues of what ought to be), such responses include the two opposing viewpoints: "Yes, that should be" and "No, that should not be." In other issues, predominantly instrumental issues (but also in explanatory, factual, and conceptual issues) there is an open list of positions. The evidence offered to support or oppose a position is known as an argument. One position might have any number of arguments to support or object to it, and some arguments may support more than one position. This "issue, position, argument" information structure is only one example of a possible information system more appropriately designed for architecture and building envelope design.

In Conclusion: Responsive Futures

Widespread implementation of adaptive and responsive façades will require a number of obstacles to be overcome. Public acceptance will be among the first.

Architects and façade designers will need to continue advancing the state of the art through research and education. Research in architecture is notoriously slow and underfunded. Governmental and industry support for this kind of work is quite modest. Programs supporting engineering research and other STEM fields exist at many levels. Even these fields can be described as under-supported in the United States in comparison to some other countries. But architecture research is only the tiniest of fractions of real scientific research.

Without academic and industry research, it is not likely that there will be the kind of significant improvements in the types of sensors, their relative costs, deployment issues, and data analysis. In comparison with the amount of energy being lost through building skins, the respective support levels for research are miserly. There is a need for new materials and advances in making systems smaller.

Any algorithmic tools will need considerable continuous oversight with an active adversarial approach intended to test these systems to their limits.

There will be a widening split between the most technically complex and costly systems and the more widespread low-technology implementations. In a profession and industry that regularly had problems installing double-pane windows upside-down, it will be a challenge to find ways to disseminate technically rich building envelopes. If NASA can make a mistake in converting between metric and SI units (Lloyd 1999), imagine the possibilities for the small architecture office as façades reach NASA levels of technology.

The skills and knowledge of building managers will be pushed. With sophisticated systems, it will no longer be appropriate to simply hire someone's brother-in-law as the building superintendent.

Dynamic façade futures will more likely be designed not by individual architects but by teams of façade designers.

References

Araya, S. (2011) *Performative Architecture*. Ph.D. dissertation, Massachusetts Institute of Technology.
Choi, J., and Yeom, D. (2017) Investigation of the Relationships between Thermal Sensations of Local Body Areas and the Whole Body in an Indoor Built Environment, *Energy and Buildings*, Vol. 149, pp. 204–215.
Cimmino, M., et al. (2016) Composite Solar Façades and Wind Generators with Tensegrity Architecture, *Composites Part B Engineering*, Vol. 115, pp. 275–281.
Fox, M. (2016) *Interactive Architecture: Adaptive World*. Princeton Architectural Press.
Glanz, J., et al. (2019) In Ethiopia Crash, Faulty Sensor on Boeing 737 Max Is Suspected, *New York Times*, March 29.
Hodge, D. (2010) Reflective "Death Ray" Torments Vegas Sunbathers, Reuters, October 1.
Kensek, K. (2014) *Building Information Modeling*. Routledge.
Konis, K. (2017) *Effective Daylighting with High-Performance Facades: Emerging Design Practices (Green Energy and Technology)*. Springer.
Kunz, W., and Rittel, H. (1970) Issues as Elements of Information Systems. Working Paper 131, Institute for Urban and Regional Development, University of California at Berkeley.
Lloyd, R. (1999) Metric Mishap Caused Loss of NASA Orbiter. CNN, September 30.
Noble, D., Kensek K., and Das, S. (2016) *Face Time: The Emergence of the Façade as the Integrative Factor in Holistic Building Design*. Façade Tectonics.
Noble, D., Kensek K., and Elder, M. (2018) *Skins on Campus' Bridging Industry and Academia in Pursuit of Better Buildings and Urban Habitat*. Façade Tectonics.
Patterson, M. (2017) *Skin Fit and Retrofit: Challenging the Sustainability of Curtainwall Practice in Tall Buildings*. Ph.D. dissertation, University of Southern California.
Rittel, H., and Webber, M. (1973) Dilemmas in a General Theory of Planning, *Policy Sciences*, Vol. 4, Issue 2, pp. 155–169.
Schnädelbach, H. (2010) *Adaptive Architecture: A Conceptual Framework*. Media City.

20
Energy-Performative Architecture
Working with the Forces of Nature to Optimize Energy Flows and the Impact on Phenomenology of Architectural Form

Brian Cody

Introduction

Early on in the history of building, an intelligent energy concept, which made efficient use of prevailing natural forces, was of fundamental importance, primarily due to a lack of viable compensation possibilities. This situation more or less endured until the early twentieth century, when in the aftermath of the Industrial Revolution the introduction of fossil-fuel-powered climate control and lighting systems finally "liberated" architecture entirely from the necessity to work with natural forces and began instead to combat them with imported energy. This culminated in the modernist movement and the so-called international style made possible by these technologies (Behling, 2000).

Thus began a period during which it was possible to have architecture which was in many ways unquestionably very good, yet very inefficient in terms of energy use, perhaps exemplified by the international style. And although there has been important work throughout the period since, which has gone against a mainstream of climate-defiant architecture, particularly after the energy crises in the 1970s and at the end of the twentieth century due to concerns about global warming and climate change, this has always been confined to the margins of mainstream architecture. For the most part, the emphasis has been on improving the efficiency of building typologies, which retain in essence the same forms employed by their inefficient fossil-fuel-powered ancestors, albeit improved through increased thermal insulation, more efficient climate control systems and the integration of renewable energy technology.

Building energy performance can be defined as the relationship between the quality of internal environment achieved in a space and the quantity of primary energy required to maintain this internal environment (Cody, 2008). Achieving a high level of energy performance in building design necessitates the use of natural forces. In the context of buildings, these are forces which arise due to natural processes in the buildings environment and which can be harnessed to meet the energy demand required to make a building comfortable or drive processes required for its use and functionality. These forces primarily arise as a result of solar and wind energy but also due to temperature differences between various ambient sources and sinks which allow certain heat flow processes (e.g. ground water or geothermal energy use) to occur.

A building is designed to operate within a natural environment of continuingly changing conditions and provide internal conditions, which diverge significantly from these most of the time. Two approaches can be followed to achieve this goal. The conventional approach is to exclude the external environment as much as possible and employ mechanical systems to provide the desired internal conditions. An alternative approach is to design the building's form, construction and skin to capture and utilize energy flows in the environment, in order to create the desired internal conditions. This second approach, in which the energy of the dominant natural forces, which seem to pose the problem – e.g. wind for a skyscraper, solar radiation in a hot climate, daylight for a museum building – are captured and used in a controlled way to achieve the desired result, is for obvious reasons the more challenging. It also, however, offers greater potential with regard to the efficient use of resources.

Energy design is essentially the use of natural forces and is a fundamentally new way of collaborating on the design of buildings. In the energy design of a building, concepts are developed which minimize building energy demand while optimizing internal environmental conditions in the spaces. Instead of deploying standard solutions, the scientific principles of thermodynamics, heat transfer and fluid mechanics are invoked and applied, in order to develop solutions which use multifunctional building elements and systems to maximize building performance.

Energy strategies in the form-finding process of building design can generate new architectural forms and lead to new aesthetical qualities in architecture and urban design (Cody, 2017). Energy-performative buildings achieve high energy performance due to their architectural concepts and strategies. These are not buildings which merely incorporate technologies to improve energy performance, with no resulting influence on the architecture. The high level of energy performance considered here is achievable only by designing the architecture from the outset with high energy performance in mind.

Architectural form can be influenced and shaped by energy design, both in terms of the appearance of a building in general and the architectural elements and means of expression used to determine this, as well as in terms of its external physical shape. Energy design strategies also impact on the phenomenology of the architectural form, the way architecture is experienced or perceived by all the senses in a real physical interaction between a person and a building – arguably the way all architecture should finally be evaluated. This refers to both the experience of someone inside a space as well as of someone outside the building – normally at street level. These are the ways a building ultimately impacts on people in an immediate physical sense and I would argue that the process of designing a building entails approaching the design simultaneously from both of these perspectives, i.e. from within and without.

In considering the impact on phenomenology of form, we should be less concerned with the appearance of the form and more with how it is experienced. The focus of architectural discourse, education and of course practice has long been heavily focused on visual aspects. Of course, architecture can be treated as art, to be visually appraised and enjoyed. Of course, our visual perception is also the most important sense for collecting information. However, architecture needs to be more than this. Architecture is about how we experience the spaces with all our senses, both within buildings and in the spaces between buildings in our cities. It is the quality of this total experience, which determines the true value and quality of our built environment.

The environmental aspects of buildings account for a large part of our experience in buildings. A space feels too warm or too cold. We perceive the air to be stale or fresh or possibly we feel uncomfortable due to high air speeds in the form of drafts. The odors, the noise level and spatial acoustic characteristics (e.g. reverberation time) are pleasant or otherwise. The systems to control the internal environmental conditions also often account for a large part of our interactions with a space and therefore our experience of the space. An experience many of us are familiar with is the first night

Energy-Performative Architecture

in an unfamiliar hotel room, especially if you arrive late. The interactions with the lights, windows, shading and HVAC (heating, ventilation and air conditioning) systems provide for multifarious experiences, not all of them of the pleasant variety.

One of the primary tasks of a building design is to create comfortable spaces. And this is easier said than done. The result of good energy design is a good internal environment, not the systems to achieve it. The energy design approach uses building form, skin and construction to modify the sea of ever-changing conditions the external climate of a particular location offers up and bring it as close as possible to the desired internal environmental condition, thus minimizing the energy demand of the climate control systems. In energy design, the focus and aim of the design is a building with an optimal internal climate, minimized energy demand and a high spatial quality. The materials, technical systems, etc., used to achieve these goals are merely elements of the solution and not aims in themselves.

Case Studies from Contemporary Practice and Recent Research

In order to explore the relationships between energy, architectural form and its phenomenology, I will use case studies from recent research and contemporary practice, in which I have been involved in over the course of the last 30 years.

In the early 1990s, shortly after the Berlin Wall came down, one of the first of a new generation of ultra-low-energy buildings was to be constructed in former East Berlin; the pioneering Low Energy Apartment Building in the Marzahn district (Assmann Salomon & Scheidt architects). At the outset of the design process, I convinced the client to make a radical departure from the conventional design process in which an architectural design concept is prepared and subsequently optimized in terms of energy performance, and instead, as an initial step, carry out studies to find the optimal form to incorporate the required building program in terms of energy performance, the results of which were then used to generate the architectural design (Hawkes, 2002). The final form has a large curved south-facing façade with a high proportion of glass while the area and glazed proportion of the north façade are minimized (Figure 20.1).

The building is structured in three thermal zones: the living rooms on the south side, an unheated buffer zone on the north side, in which the staircases and lifts are located, and the rooms requiring the highest internal temperatures, the mechanically ventilated bathrooms, in the middle. The projecting balconies on the south side provide effective shading in summer but allow the lower winter solar radiation to penetrate into the apartments. Sliding doors in the walls separating the rooms on the south side enable the sun to reach deeper into the spaces and also allow a more flexible use of the spaces (Figure 20.2).

For the Braun headquarters building near Frankfurt in Germany (schneider + schumacher architects), built in 2000, a high-performance double-skin façade was developed, which gives the external appearance of a smooth glass façade while improving the thermal and energy performance of the skin to a level which enabled the mechanical systems required in the building to be significantly reduced, allowing mechanical ventilation and conventional heating systems to be dispensed with (Figure 20.3).

A network of capillary tubing integrated into a thin plaster layer on the underside of the concrete slab, which is fed with warm water in cold weather and cool water in warm weather, is the only system needed to provide comfortable internal conditions in the offices (Figure 20.4).

The building skin comprises two layers with a separating membrane provided in the façade cavity at each floor level and for each façade planning module. Each module has an external window, which is automatically controlled, and a narrow vertically aligned opaque element in the inside skin which is manually operated for ventilation. The shading device is located in the cavity. In the middle of the U-formed building plan, a central atrium is formed with a polytetrafluoroethylene (PTFE) foil cushion roof construction which provides the second skin for the office façades facing into the atrium, which is

343

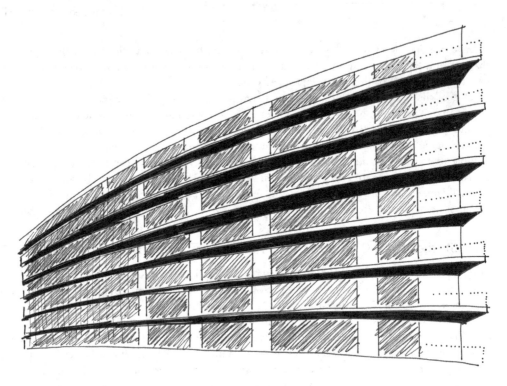

Figure 20.1 Low Energy Apartment Building, Berlin, south view.
Source: Brian Cody

Figure 20.2 Low Energy Apartment Building, Berlin, apartment.
Source: Brian Cody

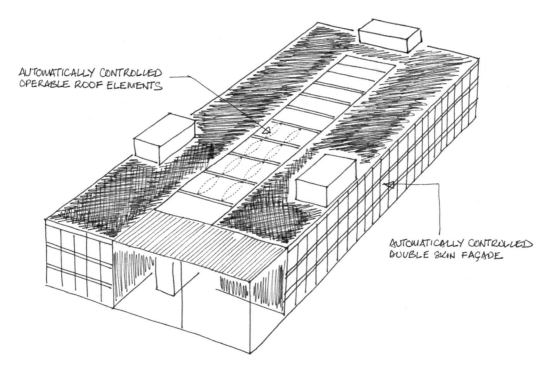

Figure 20.3 Braun HQ Germany, double-skin concept.
Source: Brian Cody

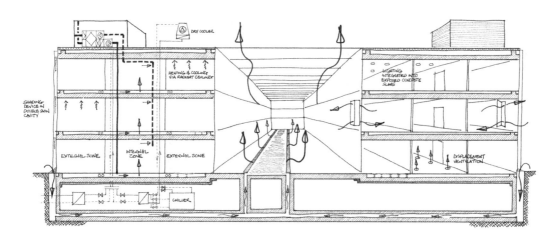

Figure 20.4 Braun HQ Germany, energy concept.
Source: Brian Cody

an unheated buffer zone. The outer skin of the building is automatically controlled via the building management system. Inspired by the example provided by human skin, the façade reacts to ambient outside conditions, the outer layer opening and closing in response to external air temperature and user behavior, while the shading device in the façade cavity is controlled in response to incident solar radiation. The sensory environment provided by the radiant heavyweight ceiling slabs, the opaque vertically aligned elements for natural ventilation, the fully glazed but effectively shaded façades and the automatic control system of the smart skin also provided a unique spatial experience for its occupants when completed at the start of the twenty-first century (Figure 20.5).

For the Duales System Pavilion at the EXPO 2000 in Hanover, the building owner, a provider of take-back packaging systems, wanted a pavilion which avoided overheating without recourse to conventional air conditioning in line with their corporate philosophy of a closed ecological loop. The anticipated large number of visitors in the summer months and the high internal loads due to exhibition lighting and equipment, together with the wish that the pavilion could be dismantled after the EXPO and rebuilt somewhere else, provided a substantial challenge. Conventional thermal mass in the form of a heavyweight building structure was obviously not an option. The design, developed with Atelier Brückner in Stuttgart, responds to this challenge with the provision of thermal mass which can be easily transported (Figure 20.6).

Water tanks, which can be emptied and re-filled after moving to a new location, were integrated into the spiraling lightweight steel construction exhibition ramp. Spray nozzles incorporated into the façade allowed water to be sprayed from the façade at night and thus cooled by evaporation (Figure 20.7).

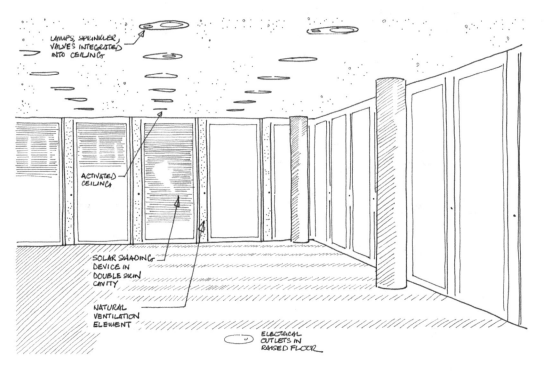

Figure 20.5 Braun HQ Germany, office interior.
Source: Brian Cody

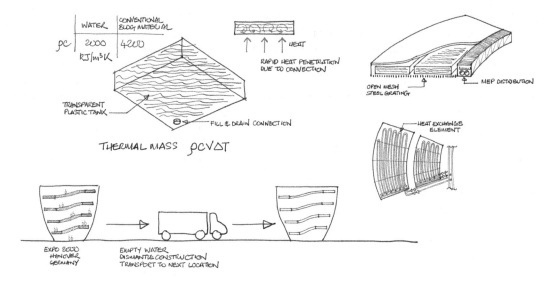

Figure 20.6 DSD Pavilion, EXPO 2000, approach.
Source: Brian Cody

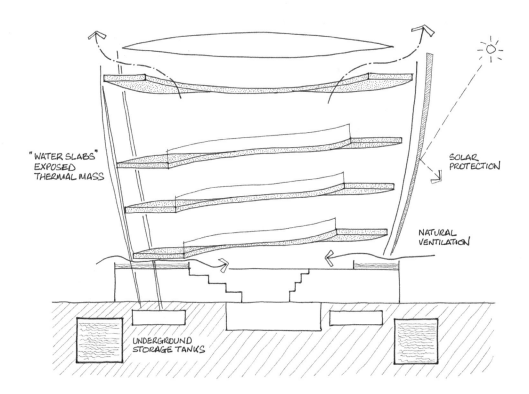

Figure 20.7 DSD Pavilion, EXPO 2000, concept.
Source: Brian Cody

This water was circulated in a secondary circuit coupled to the water tanks by means of heat exchanging tubing. The thermal mass could thus be activated and cooling energy regenerated. Similar to the way humans and some animals perspire to lose heat in warm conditions, the building "sweats". In the case of the pavilion, this does not occur as a direct response to overheating as in the natural world, but at nighttime when it is cooler, in order to regenerate itself for the anticipated hot day ahead. The concept of an ecological closed loop embodied in the concept of the Pavilion matched the corporate philosophy of the building owner so well that it was decided to include it in the exhibition. The energy design concepts became part of the exhibition, including monitors with touch screens which allowed visitors to interact with the building and its systems and take part in a virtual simulation of the building's energy systems, whereby the effect of changing parameters such as the nighttime evaporative cooling system operation could be experienced, or data on the real-time operation of the systems viewed. The influence of the energy design strategies did not stop at the architecture of the building containing the exhibition but became a part of the exhibition experience itself.

The OEVAG bank headquarters building in Vienna city with Carsten Roth Architects, completed in 2010, brought forth a completely new typological solution for an office atrium building (Figure 20.8).

Cellular offices, providing space for concentrated working, form an external ring facing the surrounding streets in a perimeter block formation, while communication spaces and circulation elements form independent structures, which are inserted into a large interstitial atrium space within the office ring. This spatial structure ensures equal quality for all working spaces and creates a dynamic vertical atrium space, which encourages and supports informal communication and incorporates circulation elements and shared areas (meeting rooms, etc.). The special areas requiring a more intensive building services infrastructure are grouped together and thus more efficiently served. In terms of energy demand, the solar load for the special areas is significantly reduced and the compact design reduces the transmission heat losses of the building considerably. In this case, the influence of energy performance strategies on

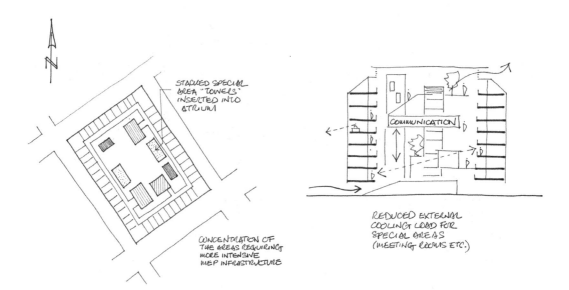

Figure 20.8 OEVAG bank HQ, Vienna, conceptual approach.
Source: Brian Cody

form is not visible in the outer building form or in the façade composition but is evident in a subtler way – in the configuration of the building, in its floor plan and section. The very specific building form also offers a unique spatial experience.

The form of the new headquarters building for the European Central Bank in Frankfurt (Coop Himmelb(l)au architects), completed in 2014, was strongly influenced by considerations to maximize building energy performance and employ wind and thermal buoyancy to provide controlled natural ventilation of the offices (Figure 20.9).

A double skin was wrapped around the two towers to create a central atrium and double-skin façades on the external sides of the towers. The atrium was horizontally divided up into three sections with a height of approximately 60 meters each, in order to keep the pressure differences between floors manageable. Functional areas (meeting rooms, recreation zones, communication bridges, lifts, etc.) were moved out of the office towers and into the atrium, allowing more efficient spatial organization of the office towers. The dynamically formed atrium connects the two towers and improves communication within the building complex. The façade incorporates selective glazing, effective quasi-external automatically controlled movable solar shading and specially designed operable elements, which allow natural ventilation during a large part of the year. The naturally ventilated atrium is a buffer zone with minimal thermal conditioning, offering spatial and communication potential in the form of a vibrant vertical city. The office workers arrive and leave their working spaces every day by passing through this remarkable space with magnificent views of the city of Frankfurt but also with a sense of connection to the whole spatial volume containing the institution: the element of vertical connectivity often missing in high-rise office buildings. The use of the specially designed natural ventilation elements in the

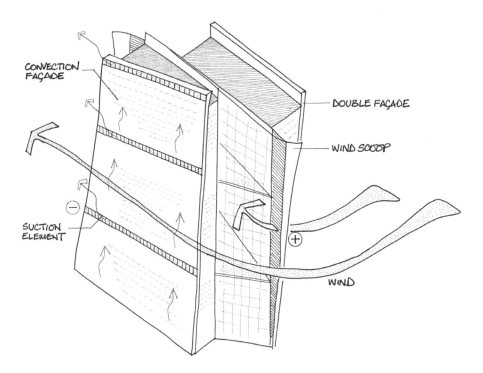

Figure 20.9 European Central Bank HQ, Frankfurt.
Source: Brian Cody

façade provides a direct relationship with the ambient environment, allowing the passage of fresh air from outside but also olfactory and auditory aspects of the surroundings to permeate and color the perceived experience indoors, in a fundamentally different way to conventional concepts employed in high-rise office towers, which tend to eschew this connection with the outside through the use of sealed building envelopes.

In the design of the NRW archive building in Duisburg, Germany with Ortner + Ortner architects, one of the most important design decisions was taken at the start of the design process during the competition phase. The program was archive space for the storage of important government papers, together with the necessary office working space. Due to the hygroscopic nature of paper, constant internal environmental conditions must be maintained, in order to prevent damage to the documents (especially harmful are rapid fluctuations in relative humidity) and thus this type of building is usually fully air conditioned. An old corn storage building was located on the site and was to be preserved. Very early on in the design process, we adopted a radical solution, in which the two functions of document storage and office working were completely separated, thus altering the conventional operational structure of the organization (Figure 20.10).

The existing windows in the corn storage building were closed up and this building was extended and used for the archive spaces, while the working spaces for the employees were provided in a new office building alongside. By removing the external thermal loads via the windows and the internal thermal loads by providing no working spaces in the archive facility itself (people enter via air locks to collect or return the documents), it was possible to maintain the necessary stable environmental conditions in the archive with help of the exposed thermal mass of the structure and with minimal technical systems

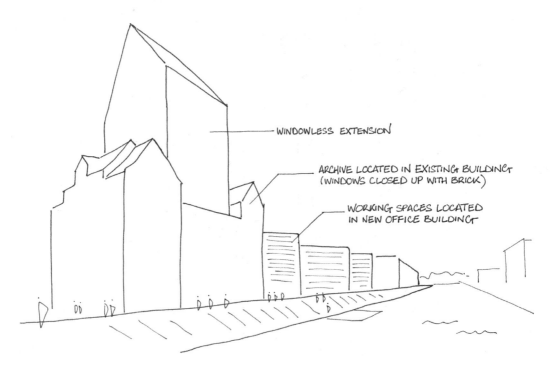

Figure 20.10 NRW state archive building, Duisburg, Germany.
Source: Brian Cody

and energy input. By configuring the program such that the office spaces and the archive are separated and housed in structures with very different characteristics, the necessary thermal conditioning of the archive building, which was completed in 2014, can be largely achieved by passive measures and the existing historical structure could be used to maximum effect.

With OMA architects we developed a new university campus building typology for the École Centrale Paris building, completed in 2017, which achieves high energy performance by utilizing synergetic interactions between the various uses while creating a new form of campus space under a "climate envelope". The building comprises teaching spaces, laboratories and offices for an engineering school, all enclosed within this climate envelope, so that the in-between spaces form an indoor campus. Placing the envelope around the whole campus volume instead of around individual buildings reduces the amount of heat transfer area to outside and creates a unique spatial environment between the program of offices, laboratories and teaching spaces (Figure 20.11).

Within the climate envelope, composed of a PTFE foil roof and glass façades, a macroclimate is created, which is not as closely controlled as the internal environments within the laboratories and the offices. This transitional space between the internal and external environments supports and enhances the campus atmosphere and informal communication. The specific typological approach works to enhance both communication between people and synergetic energy flows between the many diversified uses under its roof, transferring surplus heat from the laboratories to spaces which require heat, such as the offices (Figure 20.12).

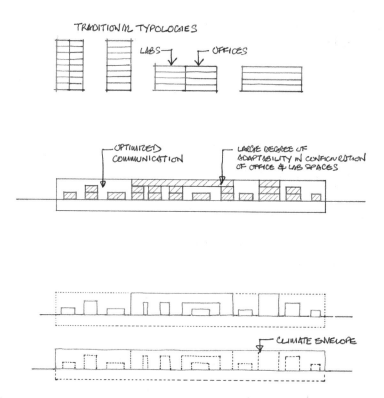

Figure 20.11 École Centrale Paris, typology considerations.
Source: Brian Cody

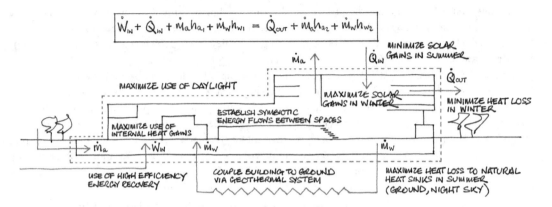

Figure 20.12 École Central Paris, energy concept.
Source: Brian Cody

The user experience of space at both the university campus level and within the teaching and research spaces themselves is unique and differs substantially from the experience in conventional typologies.

In the first-prize-winning design in the competition for the new Adidas office building in Herzogenaurach, Germany in 2014, in collaboration with the architects DMAA, we developed a very-deep-plan building form in defiance of the prevailing conventional wisdom in Germany

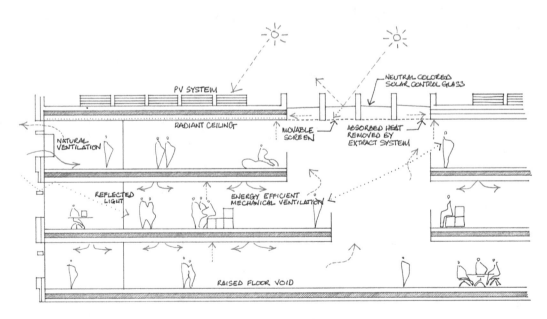

Figure 20.13 Adidas Office Building, energy concept.
Source: Brian Cody

that an energy-efficient office building should have a shallow floor plan for natural light and ventilation. Instead, the design comprises office platforms within a large volumetric enclosure offering a unique three-dimensional working environment (Figure 20.13).

Strategically placed voids introduce and distribute natural light and the entire roof is used for solar electricity production. The reduced grey energy due to the compact form and much-reduced façade area together with the increased energy production of the large roof surface more than compensates for the increased artificial lighting demand in the internal zone of the building, so that the proposed design not only offers a new and unique spatial environment, which meets the special needs of the company, but also achieves enhanced energy performance.

In 2016 we completed a study for the real estate developer ARE (Austrian Real Estate), in which the task was to develop concepts for a radically different approach to the construction of apartment buildings and subsequently monitor their implementation in pilot projects across Austria. The point of departure was a five-year development program for privately funded housing. A small group of interdisciplinary experts was formed, and working closely with Cino Zucchi in Milan and Elsa Prochazka in Vienna, I proposed an energy concept employing a layered-skin construction, which incorporates strategies to provide energy-efficient ventilation and maximize energy performance, while at the same time offering an extension of inhabitable space depending on external conditions. Two important aspects to be addressed by the project were the increasingly strict requirements for building ventilation (user-independent ventilation to prevent building damage caused by high internal humidity and the provision of operable windows for natural ventilation at locations with high external noise levels) and the rapidly rising increase in nationwide electrical energy demand, in part caused by measures introduced to increase energy efficiency of the building stock. The developed concepts allow the creation of different thermal zones leading to new spatial qualities. The double-skin "smart façade" reacts to changes in external and internal conditions, providing tempering of the incoming supply air, maximizing passive solar energy use in winter and providing effective solar protection in summer, and is to be constructed using timber module construction. Large radiators constitute a fast-reacting heating system which can provide a response that is temporally and spatially aligned to the actual demand, so that the spaces are only conditioned when required. They also provide cooling and some dehumidification in summer.

In effect, the complex multilayered external walls and the ubiquitous mechanical ventilation systems used in present-day construction methods are replaced with inhabitable space (Figure 20.14).

Options were explored in which the second skin is extended over the roof with shared space provided at the ground floor and top floor levels, so that not only are conventional walls eliminated but also conventional roof and ground floor constructions. The approach leads to a very different experience of space in many ways. During a large part of the year, particularly during the so-called changeover seasons, the living space is extended by opening up the inner façade completely by sliding the glass panels to the side. Operable elements in the façade open and close automatically in order to maintain the required air quality, based on measured CO_2 concentration and relative humidity levels (Figure 20.15).

The use of "radiators" – traditionally used for hydronic heating systems – for cooling and dehumidification leads to visible condensation of the moisture-laden air in summer on the radiator surface, thus impacting on both the visual and thermal experience.

The strategies employed emphasize the use of natural forces, especially the sun, to achieve high performance instead of the more conventional approach of protection against the external environment with very high levels of insulation and airtight construction. To study the effect of unfavourable user behaviour on the performance of the concept, we studied this aspect in both the proposed and conventional concepts. Interestingly, the proposed concepts showed clear advantages when compared with conventional low-energy concepts such as the "passive house" concept, as the sensitivity to occupant behaviour was shown to be much less pronounced.

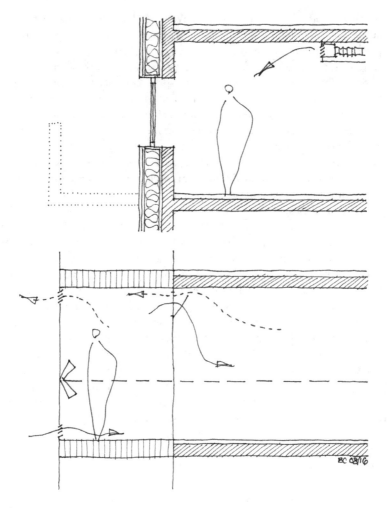

Figure 20.14 Façade concept, ARE study.
Source: Brian Cody

In a study carried out at an urban design scale for a large expansion of the university campus in Heidelberg, Germany, the objective was to investigate ways of arranging the given program of research facilities within the constraints of the 10-hectare site and find the most promising configurations in terms of energy performance. The study was carried out in advance of the competition process for the masterplan and the results, including guidelines with regard to optimal orientation, configuration, typology, etc., were made available to the teams partaking in the competition. Eight typological masterplan configurations were developed and their total energy performance – including potential building-integrated renewable energy production – was investigated in a dynamic simulation environment. Embodied energy demand and aspects such as the potential for creating effective spaces to facilitate informal communication and the effect on the local microclimate in the surrounding areas and on the existing campus were also considered. The goal of the study was to develop energy design parameters to guide and inform the subsequent masterplan design process. Among the typologies studied was a configuration employing atria both as communication spaces and as an energy design strategy. Using an optimized floor plan

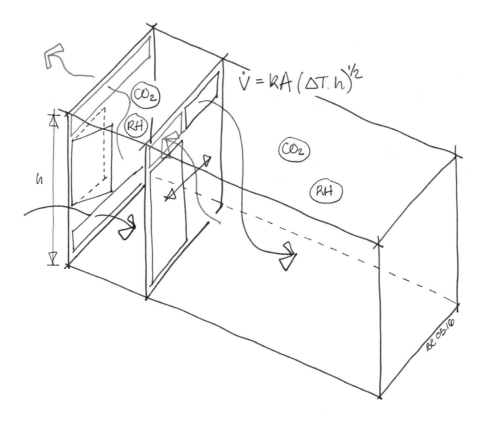

Figure 20.15 Natural ventilation concept, ARE study.
Source: Brian Cody

configuration, waste heat from the laboratories can be used passively (i.e. without the use of any active systems) to temper the unconditioned atrium and reduce the heat losses from the offices in winter (Figure 20.16).

The study showed that, based on the given site parameters, low-rise perimeter block-type configurations – with or without atria – had the highest performance, largely due to the increased solar energy production potential of the larger roof areas. A major concern of the study was related to the microclimate generated between the buildings and thus the experience of outdoor campus life the various typological approaches would foster.

In recent research at my institute we have been investigating "smart skins": façades which maximize energy performance by varying their properties to adapt to changing external and internal conditions. By continually selecting, mediating and modulating between inside and outside, such dynamic building skins can perform as a filter and play an important role in achieving desirable internal conditions within the sea of ever-changing conditions existing in the external climate. The proposed smart-skin concept incorporates and uses forecast data relating to future weather and likely user behavior (based on past experience and using an embedded artificial intelligence approach) as well as present-time data to decide the optimal configuration of physical properties and thus optimize performance (Figure 20.17).

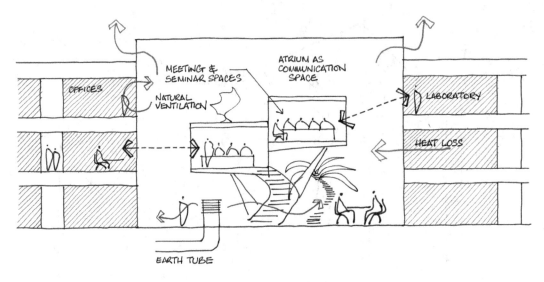

Figure 20.16 Atrium building typology, Heidelberg University Campus.
Source: Brian Cody

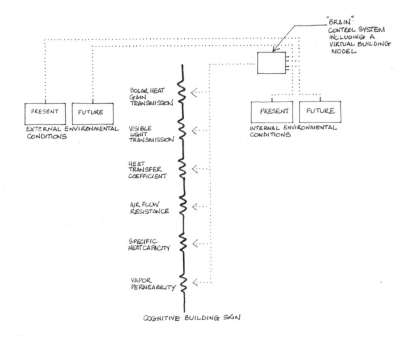

Figure 20.17 Smart façade concept.
Source: Brian Cody

Energy-Performative Architecture

The research carried out essentially involves the development of mathematical models which allow the potential energy performance to be simulated, and the optimal spectrum within which the building physics characteristics of the façade need to be varied to be determined, thus forming an important scientific basis for the development of a completely new approach to façade design. The models are complex, as a myriad of options for each parameter needs to be determined and compared for each time step. Then, as the simulation advances in time, the so-called "thermal history" associated with the processes needs to be recorded and integrated into the next time step (Cody et al., 2016). Presently we are investigating the incorporation of knowledge about the predicted short-term future into the model. Using weather forecasts and artificial intelligence algorithms, future external and internal conditions can be predicted. A by-no-means-trivial question the work throws up is the following: if we could accurately predict the short-term future in this way, would we be able to use that information to optimize the performance of façades in a significant manner? In any case, it does not take much imagination to imagine how such cognitive, sentient "smart skin" façades would impact on the sensory experience and phenomenology of the building spaces behind them.

Another research project at my institute is concerned with the energy aspects of "vertical farming" concepts. In the present-day food production system, food is grown on agricultural land outside the city and fossil fuels are used to manufacture the fertilizers and pesticides required to achieve the desired crop yields and to power the necessary agricultural machinery. After harvesting, the food stuffs are transported to facilities at other locations, where processing and packaging takes place, and are then distributed, finally arriving at retail outlets in towns and cities. For all of these processes, further energy use is required, today largely derived from fossil fuels. In the vertical farming concept, food production

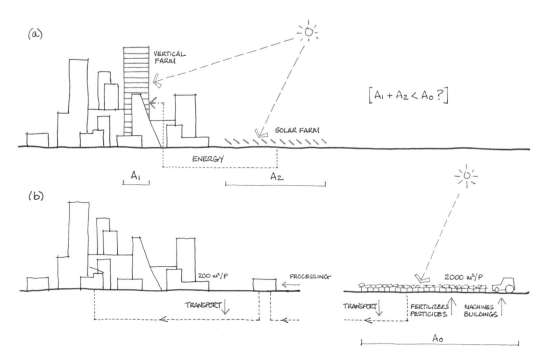

Figure 20.18 Vertical farming concept.
Source: Brian Cody

takes place in buildings with stacked levels on compact urban plots, significantly reducing land use for farming compared to the conventional system (Despommier, 2010). The energy demand, on the other hand, particularly for artificial lighting, is significantly larger and assuming that in the future this energy demand will have to be met by renewable sources, the land use for this becomes very significant owing to the low energy density of the sources. Therefore, the concept becomes viable if the total land area required, including the land required for the energy supply systems, is less than that required for conventional farming (Figure 20.18).

The potential of vertical farming thus depends strongly on the energy design strategies, and herein lies the focus of our research (Balasch et al., 2018; Podmirseg, 2016). A critical question is the impact on urban design and city life should this new typology be introduced on a large scale. This building type is essentially an industrial production facility with sparse human occupation and while these types of buildings have traditionally been located in the peripheral regions of cities, the whole premise of vertical farming is to locate the buildings in central urban areas, close to the human population, in order to reduce transportation energy demand. In addition to the obvious spatial implications for city planning and urban design, the implications for the working environment of the people employed in this radically new type of building will need to be considered.

The Virtual Dimension

The decision to employ movable walls on the low-energy building in Berlin described above, in order to allow solar energy to penetrate deeper into the apartments, obviously altered the spatial experience of the rooms too, allowing larger and smaller spaces to be created as needed. However, the users' experience of the building spaces was probably even more fundamentally affected by another energy design strategy. To foster a heightened awareness of the residents with regard to the effects of their behavior on the thermal behavior of the building and in order to strengthen their relationship with the building, a direct feedback loop in the form of a small visual display screen was included in each apartment, which provides information on the status of the various systems and the resulting energy consumption in real time. Measured data, collected during a monitoring period of two years after occupation, confirmed the effectiveness of this feedback loop on building performance (Senatsverwaltung, 2006). It should be noted that this was back in the 1990s before the widespread use of smart phones, etc. The information and communication technology available at the time was generally a lot more limited than at the present time. Today, there exists a vast – largely untapped – potential for the use of widely available technology to optimize communication between buildings and users and thus optimize energy performance. Considering all we have learned from fields such as behavioral economics in recent years, the possibilities for using a supplementary virtual environment to augment the physical one and contribute to increased performance via suitable interactions with the building's users is surely immense (Thaler, 2008). Of course, this digital/virtual environment also adds an additional dimension to the sensory experience.

Research work at my institute suggests that real progress in sustainable development cannot be achieved without a radical restructuring of the physical infrastructure of society. In the past twenty years we have created a new virtual environment with digital infrastructure, which, at least in theory, gives many working people unprecedented freedom with regard to the physical location where they carry out their work, basically allowing them to work almost anywhere. Today many people avail themselves of the possibilities offered up by these systems, in order to be more independent in both spatial and temporal terms. Nevertheless, we continue to design, construct and expand our cities and urban environments in essentially the same manner as was done a hundred years ago. In an interdisciplinary research project, we investigated the possibility of using this new virtual world to allow us to reconfigure our physical environment and infrastructure and in essence "rethink the city" (Figure 20.19).

Energy-Performative Architecture

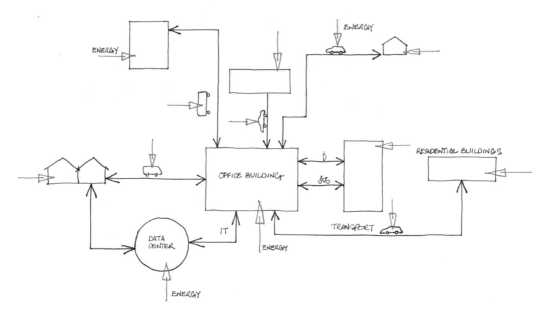

Figure 20.19 Rethinking the city.
Source: Brian Cody

By modelling the energetic structures of typical corporation and company structures, we showed that there is enormous potential to use new information and communication technologies to allow the generation of radically new forms of both building and transport systems, with the aim of increasing total energy efficiency. The results suggest an urban model with much smaller commercial office buildings than those we know today. These would become centers of face-to-face communication, while residential buildings would be configured to allow effective office work at home.

Building on these results, in further research work we studied more generally the consequences of more effective use of building space and the use of synergies between physical and virtual infrastructure, living and working spaces, teleworking, etc. In the search for strategies for spatial, temporal and virtual densification, a new typology, incorporating all the necessary infrastructural elements of society, including even industrial and agricultural uses, food production, energy generation, etc., was developed. In the cell-like structure of this so-called Hyper-Building-City model, each cell has the ability to work independently and function in a self-sufficient manner. However, when linked together, they mutually assist each other so that the whole is more than the sum of the parts (Figure 20.20).

The Hyper Building itself is a structure which allows a population density roughly equal to that of Manhattan, needs no external energy supply and no external water supply, produces no waste, emits no CO_2 emissions and needs little or no external food supply. Vertically distributed spaces for residential, office and industrial use are provided alongside parks and areas for agriculture, biomass and energy production. Linked together, they form a three-dimensional urban structure, combining urbanity and nature, density and diversity. A central feature of the conceptual approach is the synergetic integration of the different systems and the exploitation of symbiotic relationships between nature, man and technology. Plants supply oxygen for humans. Humans supply CO_2 for plants. Biological waste is used as fertilizer. Waste heat is reused, and water recycled. The implications for the spatial experience of buildings and cities – should these concepts, which are largely driven by energy design considerations, be even partly

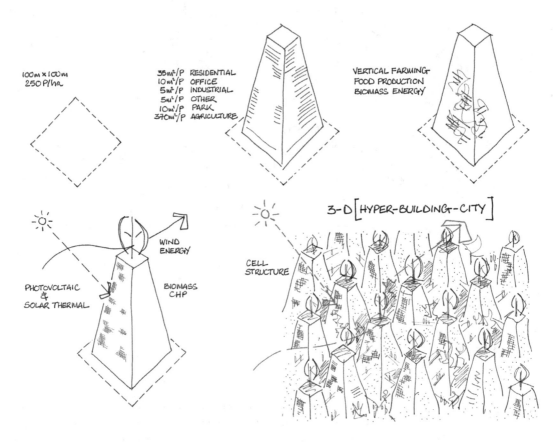

Figure 20.20 Hyper-Building-City.
Source: Brian Cody

implemented – are clearly enormous. In any event, it seems evident that the solution to one of the most central problems of our time, namely that of energy supply in a world with limited resources, will inevitably affect the form of the built environment and its phenomenology in a significant manner

Bibliography

Ampenberger, A., Cody, B., Löschnig, W., Petriu, E A., Podmirseg, D., Sommer, B., & Traxler, H. (2011). *UTE – Telearbeit und Energieeffizienz*. Graz: Österreichische Forschungsförderungsgesellschaft mbH (FFG).

Balasch, J., Cody, B., Diwold, K., Keutgen, A., Keutgen, N., Podmirseg, D., & Sautter, S. (2018). *Vertical Farming. Ermittlung der Anforderungsbedingungen zur Entwicklung eines Vertical Farm - Prototyps zur Kulturpflanzenproduktion*. Graz: Bundesministerium für Verkehr, Innovation und Technologie.

Banham, R. (1969). *The architecture of the well-tempered environment*. Chicago: University of Chicago Press.

Behling, S. S. (2000). *Solar power*. Munich: Prestel.

Cody, B. (2008). Building Energy and Environmental Performance tool BEEP, Entwicklung einer Methode zum Vergleich der tatsaechlichen Energieeffizienz von Gebaeuden. In: H. Bliesener (Ed.), *HLH Fachzeitschrift*. Duesseldorf: Verein Deutscher Ingenieure, Springer-VDI-Verlag.

Cody, B. (2014). The Role of Technology in Sustainable Architecture. In: *Wolkenkuckucksheim, Internationale Zeitschrift zur Theorie der Architektur*. Jg. 19, Heft 33. Retrieved from www.cloud-cuckoo.net/fileadmin/hefte_de/heft_33/artikel_cody.pdf.

Cody, B. (2017). *Form follows energy*. Basel: Birkhäuser.

Cody, B., Sautter, S., Tepavcevic, A., & Wermke, C. (2016). *Smart façade - Energetische potentiale von adaptiven fassadensystemen*. Vienna: Nachhaltig wirtschaften. Retrieved from https://nachhaltigwirtschaften.at/de/sdz/projekte/smart-facade-energetische-potentiale-von-adaptiven-fassadensystemen.php.

Despommier, D. (2010). *The vertical farm*. New York: St. Martin's Press.

Hawkes, D., & Forster, W. (2002). *Architecture, engineering and environment*. London: Laurence King.

Lloyd Jones, D. (1998). *Architecture and the environment*. London: Laurence King.

Podmirseg, D. (2016). *Up! Contribution of vertical farms to increase the overall energy efficiency of cities*. PhD. thesis. Graz: Graz University of Technology.

Senatsverwaltung für Stadtentwicklung. (2005). Niedrigenergiehaus Marzahn - Ergebnisse. Retrieved from www.stadtentwicklung.berlin.de/bauen/oekologisches_bauen/de/modellvorhaben/niedrigenergie/niemegker/ergebnisse.shtml.

Senatsverwaltung für Stadtentwicklung. (2006). *Energieeffizientes Planen und Bauen in Berlin, Evaluierung von Projekten aus dem Landesprogramm Stadtökologische Modellvorhaben*. Berlin: Senatsverwaltung für Stadtentwicklung.

Thaler, R. H., & Sunstein, C. R. (2008). *Nudge: Improving decisions about health, wealth, and happiness*. New Haven: Yale University Press.

21

Adaptation
Bio-Receptive Materials with a New Outlook on Performativity and Sustainability

David Benjamin

In the fall of 2018, the United Nations Intergovernmental Panel on Climate Change released a report that was both familiar and unfamiliar. It built on facts we already knew about climate change: carbon emissions cause warming, which causes sea-level rise and extreme weather and loss of biodiversity, which in turn causes disease and hunger and migration and death. But it also reached a new conclusion: the world has only 12 years to radically reduce carbon emissions and avoid the most catastrophic global effects. The warming target of 1.5 degrees Celsius (rather than 2.0 degrees) is required, not optional. The difference of half a degree dramatically improves our odds of preserving any coral reefs, avoiding the collapse of insect life, escaping the trigger of irreversible planetary transformation, and minimizing drought, floods, extreme heat, and poverty for hundreds of millions of people. Urgent and unprecedented action is required. Not eventually. Now.

Architecture makes up 30–40% of global carbon emissions. And 15 of the 20 largest cities in 2050 have yet to be built. Most of the contemporary focus in sustainability in architecture aims to reduce *operational energy* and *operational carbon*—the energy and carbon emissions involved in heating, cooling, and lighting. Yet over the past 50 years, there has been a dramatic increase in *embodied energy* and *embodied carbon*—the energy and carbon emissions involved in extracting, transporting, manufacturing, and assembling materials into buildings. There is growing awareness that embodied energy and carbon are crucial. We must not only reduce the amount of carbon emissions for operating a building; we must also reduce the amount of carbon emissions in the process of making a building in the first place. In fact, with only 12 years to achieve unprecedented change, embodied carbon becomes even more significant. The traditional calculation says it may be worth it to add carbon now (in embodied carbon during a year of construction) if you can save carbon later (in operational carbon over the 80-year lifespan of a building). But the new context of urgency means that it matters *when* the carbon is emitted. Adding carbon now may cause us to miss our only chance of avoiding catastrophe.

In this context, it is hard to imagine a more important aspect of building performance than carbon emissions. But the carbon emissions of architecture are not simple to calculate or easy to design with. And they do not "perform" independently from social, cultural, and aesthetic factors. While achieving low-carbon performance is critical, it must be addressed holistically and in a fair and equitable way.

This will require applying specific materials and mechanical systems, but it will also require designing new ways of life and developing new definitions of buildings.

I believe buildings are living organisms. They breathe and pulse. They inhabit complex ecosystems of species, technologies, and culture. And understanding buildings requires understanding these vital signs and these ecosystems.

Furthermore, buildings are not static, solitary objects dug into a single site. They are dynamic systems connecting many different places. They talk with their natural and urban contexts. They join together and cooperate with each other. They involve a longer duration and a wider geography than we typically consider. They actually begin with matter extracted from the earth and end with matter sitting in a landfill. They involve energy, labor, and resources from around the globe.

And just as *buildings* might be broader and more multi-dimensional than the traditional definition, the *design ecosystems* that architects create for themselves might be broader and more multi-dimensional.

Along these lines, the design ecosystem of my studio, The Living, includes a variety of interconnected forces, and involves a hybrid of familiar and new, ancient and cutting-edge, technical and social, tangible and atmospheric, practical and critical.

The output of our work involves research, books, and buildings. The topic of our work often involves climate change and carbon emissions, both directly and indirectly. And our approach often involves new possibilities at the intersection of biology, computation, and design.

For me, a big part of the story of computation in architecture dates back to 1906 when an Italian economist named Vilfredo Pareto published a thick book called *Manual of Political Economy*. It was filled with small hand-drawn graphs and with hundreds of equations, the algorithms of this era. One of the concepts advanced in the book was called Pareto efficiency. This referred to a society where nobody can be made better off without somebody else being made worse off. As an example, Pareto imagined a society with a fixed amount of resources for producing bread and wine. One option would be to make a large amount of bread and a small amount of wine. Another option would be the other way around. For each option, if production was efficient, then this version of society would become a point on the Pareto Frontier. And since all of the points on the Pareto Frontier were mathematically equivalent, this frontier could be used to study trade-offs between different options for distributing resources.

While the principle of Pareto efficiency was developed to describe economics and the design of societies, in recent years architects have used a similar framework with aspects of building design—such as the design of a structural frame for a tall building, with weight of material on the x-axis (instead of bread) and horizontal displacement on the y-axis (instead of wine).

In this sense, whether or not architects realize it, Pareto's theory has provided a foundation for the current obsession with performance and optimization in architectural design.

Many architects today—like many economists—are enchanted by efficient and optimal designs because they are so clear and unambiguous.

But as Pareto noted a century ago, efficiency is very narrow. An *efficient* distribution of resources does not necessarily equal a *socially desirable* distribution of resources. An *optimal design* does not necessarily equal a *good design*.

At about the same time Pareto was working on efficiency, biologist D'Arcy Wentworth Thompson was sketching the patterns and body structures of plants and animals for what would become his famous book, *On Growth and Form*.

Thompson set out to explain natural phenomena in terms of physical laws. He developed an approach that was mathematical and algorithmic, which was unusual for biologists at the time.

Thompson developed an ingenious method for graphing the geometric transformation from one organism to another, such as the way the Scarus fish becomes the Pomacanthus fish when its orthogonal grid becomes a grid of coaxial circles. Thompson's equations were elegant, original, and compelling.

And his approach has influenced not only biologists, but also architects—and even features of architectural software.

Yet Thompson, like the early Pareto, was so committed to his own novel approach that he neglected important genetic and chemical evidence. In other words, he had a huge blindspot.

Pareto and Thompson are not heroes to me. In fact, both are problematic in their own ways. Pareto, in particular, advanced theories that may have increased inequality and oppression at the time, as they dismissed democracy and encouraged Italian fascism.

So I am describing these figures not as inspirations, but in order to argue that all influential theories and technologies have blindspots. And my hypothesis is that one way to deal with these blindspots is to cultivate a diversity of approaches.

Pareto chose the quantitative over the qualitative. Thompson chose the mathematical over the chemical. But in both cases, it may be more helpful to understand the two forces interacting *together* rather than choose just one.

And when we turn to architecture, we might start by acknowledging that our own design approaches and design theories and design technologies all involve assumptions and potential blindspots.

My hypothesis is that as an antidote, we might work to cultivate multiple perspectives, multiple tools, and a design ecosystem with sufficient biodiversity. We might also replace the paradigm of the individual genius with a more collaborative, distributed, and open paradigm.

And in understanding the past context of Pareto and Thompson—and the future that extends well beyond them—I think it is important to note that both computation and biology have changed radically in the past 10 years.

While architects and designers have been fascinated by nature and biology for hundreds of years, biology of today is different. It is now possible to grow a cell alone on a glass slide instead of inside an organism. It is now possible to visualize neurons firing inside of a live animal in real time (Figure 21.1). It is even possible to cut and paste DNA and bring to life creatures that never before existed, such as yeast that produces anti-malaria medicine. And as of just a few years ago, with the demonstration of CRISPR and gene drives, it is now possible to redesign, or even eliminate, an entire species very quickly, essentially molding evolution itself.

In addition, it is now possible to apply the latest techniques of computation—such as computer vision and machine learning—to processes such as biological growth. Biological functions involve hundreds of dimensions, but if they can be simulated in a computer model, then they become a more actionable part of the design process.

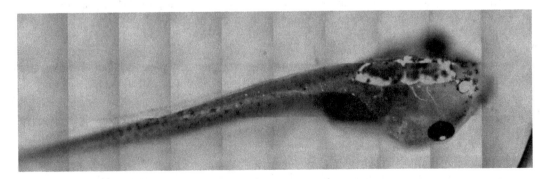

Figure 21.1 New research and technologies by the Ali Brivanlou Lab at Rockefeller University enable the visualization of neurons inside a live tadpole.

Source: Courtesy of the Ali Brivanlou Lab

Yet the more you learn about biology, the more you see how complex biology is and how much we still have to learn about it. In this sense, design with biology may involve design with a black box, design with forces beyond our complete control, and design with uncertainty. Design with biology might offer an alternative to the framework of efficiency that dominates computation and that tends to condition work on architectural performance. A biological outlook for design might aim for diversity and robustness of the population rather than perfection of the individual. And this new biological outlook calls for a new method of design.

One of our recent projects brings together biology and cities. It involves new ideas about ecosystems and public health. It is an experiment with an updated definition of building performance. And it has the potential to offer new strategies for reducing carbon emissions.

Subculture: Microbial Metrics and the Multi-Species City—a project by Kevin Slavin, Elizabeth Henaff, and The Living—started with the hypothesis that just as we are increasingly aware of the bacteria in our own bodies and the way a *gut microbiome* contributes to individual health, we might start paying attention to the bacteria in our cities and the way an *urban microbiome* contributes to collective health.

In other words, microbes are all around us, even though they are invisible. They are in the air, on our food, and on our architecture. And contrary to the twentieth-century thinking about the dangers of disease and the corresponding benefits of sterile environments, we now know that most microbes are beneficial to us. While a few species of microbes can cause us harm, 99% of microbes actually help keep us alive.

In other words, our built environment has always been influenced by our ideas about performance. When we believed that microbes were a human enemy, our definition of building performance included sterility—and in corresponding fashion our materials were smooth and synthetic, and our architecture was uniform and universal. Now that we know microbes are a human friend, our definition of building performance might evolve to include cultivating microbial life and biodiversity. Our materials might become textured and organic. Our architecture might become non-uniform and diverse.

In this context, for an installation at Storefront for Art and Architecture in New York City, we set out to explore two things: maps and models. For maps, we measured the microbiome at the gallery in Soho and compared it to the microbiome of places like the Brooklyn Navy Yard.

For models, we explored design scenarios for architecture that promotes microbial life. In terms of performance, we are thinking about whether in the future we might establish "microbial metrics" in the same way we have standards for measuring structural integrity, thermal conductivity, and ergonomics. And we are thinking about whether "probiotic architecture" might improve public health.

As part of our test, we developed a "bio-receptive" material to catch and host microbes. This bio-receptive material is the opposite of materials that aim to kill microbes, such as anti-microbial sheetrock or high-pH concrete. Instead, it is a material calibrated to select for diverse and beneficial microorganisms. And the material we started with is wood. Wood is well-suited for hosting microbial life based on its molecular composition and its micro and macro shapes.

At Storefront's gallery space, the panels of the facade were transformed with wood tiles cut from standard lumber, deliberately eroded through sandblasting at various depths to create diverse microclimates. Each microclimate had distinct grain and knots that created different pockets of shade and moisture (Figures 21.2–21.4). This allowed us to see that even the most common and humble building material—a cheap 4x4 post of Douglas fir—has a material story to be uncovered that may offer a range of visible and invisible effects. And with a building envelope of bio-receptive wood, architecture becomes a sensor for the urban microbiome.

As a second component of the project, we set up a biology lab in order to sequence DNA on-site. The first step was to swap sand-basted wood tiles from each test location in the city in order to collect surface microbes. The next step was to place the swab in a liquid solution, using agitation, separation, and marker beads to produce a pure DNA solution. Then we loaded the DNA solution into a flow cell to be processed by a portable DNA sequencer. To complete the process, we derived sequence

Figure 21.2 When wood is sand-blasted, the process erodes the soft areas and preserves the hard areas, creating complex three-dimensional forms.
Source: Courtesy of The Living

Figure 21.3 Even a standard piece of lumber, such as a 4x4 post of Douglas fir, has unique grain and knots which tell a unique story of its development.
Source: Courtesy of The Living

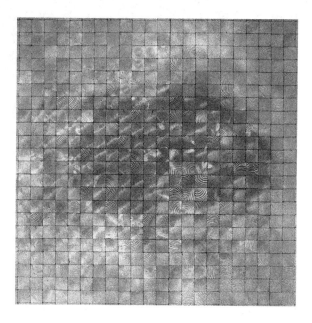

Figure 21.4 Wood can be designed as a bio-receptive material, with diverse microclimates for microbes that offer a new kind of performance for architectural envelopes.
Source: Courtesy of Rafael Gamo

data (the famous A, T, C, and G of DNA) as the sequencer monitored electrical charge of the DNA strands.

Finally, after we sequenced the DNA from each location, we designed a system to automatically draw the output as an early and rough map to an uncharted territory (Figure 21.5).

This map is raw and it is at a coarse resolution—like our understanding of urban metagenomics—but it has already allowed us to see some interesting things. For example, in the Brooklyn Navy Yard we saw microbial DNA that performs the function of breaking down heavy metals, which indicates that the Navy Yard has specific pollutants not found in Soho.

In the end, we are using a gallery installation as an active, living experiment. We are exploring a new architectural envelope and a new way of seeing some of the important matter and organisms that keep us alive. We are reframing buildings as stewards for the urban microbiome. And we are proposing that performance extend beyond local human occupation to non-human animals and microbes, and ultimately back to global human health (Figures 21.6 and 21.7).

While this project does not aim to directly reduce carbon emissions, it opens up design frameworks and definitions of building performance that may do so in the future. As we understand more about the urban microbiome and specific microbes living on and in our architecture, it may be possible to design materials that cultivate species of microorganisms that capture carbon. Certain microbes (including some of the bacteria in soil) are known to remove carbon from the air as part of their normal metabolisms. What if our buildings could be designed to host massive communities of these kinds of bacteria—microbial cities within human cities—that actively sequester carbon? What if creating more housing and more cities and more infrastructure actually had a carbon-reducing impact rather than a carbon-polluting impact?

Of course, this is an unproven hypothesis, and it should not be used to generate false optimism, or to suggest that a single engineered solution should be pursued without understanding its other

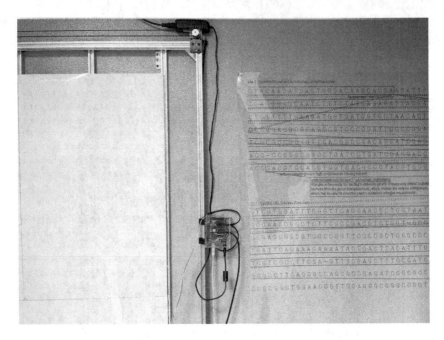

Figure 21.5 With the building envelope as an open-ended experiment, the microbiome of multiple locations is mapped and compared.

Source: Courtesy of The Living

Figure 21.6 This prototype suggests a new type of aesthetic performance as well as a new type of technical performance.

Source: Courtesy of The Living

Figure 21.7 In the future, "probiotic architecture" may be designed to improve public health.
Source: Courtesy of Rafael Gamo

consequences, or to support the belief that technology will save us. But it represents the kind of possibility that might be opened up by integrating biology, computation, and design. It might suggest a new framework for adapting our concepts of architecture, performance, and climate change. And it might even give a whole new meaning to the future of life on earth.

Portions of this essay are adapted from the introduction to *Now We See Now: Architecture and Research by The Living* (Monacelli Press, 2018) and from the installation text for "Subculture: Microbial Metrics and the Multi-Species City," by Kevin Slavin, Elizabeth Henaff, and David Benjamin.

22

Phenomenology of Interactivity
Patterns of Human Interaction with Urban Built Environments and the Impact of Computer Automation

Mitra Kanaani

Introduction

This chapter focuses on the multiple meanings of phenomenology of human interactions and the impact of computer automation on human interactivity in current urban environments.

> The definition of phenomenology is the study of structures of experience, or consciousness. Literally, phenomenology is the study of 'phenomena': appearances of things, or things as they appear in our experience, or the ways we experience things, thus the meanings things have in our experience. Phenomenology studies conscious experience as experienced from the subjective or first person's point of view.
>
> *(Stanford Encyclopedia of Philosophy, 2013)*

Also, *interactivity* by definition is the extent to which something is *interactive*. By definition, it is the process of two people or things working together and influencing each other. However, in modern times the concept of *interactivity* is also referred to "the involvement of users in the exchange of information with computers and the degree to which this happens" (Cambridge Dictionary, n.d.).

The concept of human interaction with built environments is as old as civilization. However, in our media- and technology-driven age, urban settings have evolved to integrate spatial dynamics and people within the context of built environments. This has augmented the manners in which and reasons why citizens interact with each other and their urban settings. The exploration of the phenomena of human interaction with their built urban environments includes a survey on the current ways computers and technology have augmented and enhanced these interactions to higher levels of sophistication.

Computers can now assist physically challenged users, develop sensory stimulants and increase environmental cognizance. This chapter not only surveys the origin and multiple facets of interactivity, but also enquires into the impacts and psychological effects of human and computer interaction with built environments.

For the purpose of understanding the meaning of this promulgating concept in the design of contemporary built environments, it would be helpful to analyze various types of human interactivities as explored throughout the history of built environments. Major elements, such as population density, have significant implications for interactivity with and within built settings, before and after application of computational automation.

The Origins of Human Interaction Patterns in the Built Environment

In order to synthesize phenomenology and the knowledge of how humans interact with their built environment, analysis must revolve around the social, cultural and psychological dimensions that shape these interactions. Patterns of interaction are governed by three main sub-patterns that predefine and ultimately shape human interactions with urban settings:

1. Geometrical patterns with respect to the emergence of a combined pattern of built and natural environments
2. Density patterns
3. Mobility patterns

The interaction of these patterns ultimately contributes to three urban characteristics that define human relationships with urban settings. These characteristics are: *Urban Legibility*, *Urban Identity* and *Urban Affinity*.

Geometrical Patterns, Mental Mapping and Urban Legibility

In his book *Image of the City*, Kevin Lynch investigates the wider context of the city, and identifies five urban elements that contribute to the development of urban legibility through point-of-view of perceptions, known as mental maps.

These five elements are:

1. *Paths* that allow mobility and access for occupants and facilitate interactions within urban settings
2. *Edges* that while limiting interactivity develop and define boundaries and the scope of interactions, contributing to the legibility of urban settings
3. *Districts* that as areas share common identifiable points and characteristics, and contribute to mental mapping of the urban elements, while defining the scope and boundaries of interaction
4. *Nodes,* such as squares, plazas and junctions, which create their own unique characteristics, and develop mental maps for people developing points of references within built environments, while assisting with wayfinding
5. *Landmarks,* which contribute to a sense of legibility, as well as orientation and visibility within the urban fabric, contributing to the development of clear mental maps (Lynch, 1996, p. 47)

For urban inhabitants and users of architectural environments, a clear mental map of the built fabric is a means to develop not only a sense of orientation and wayfinding, but also a sense of belonging and security. Inhabitants who for any reason have not situated themselves within a perceived contextual map tend to be insecure and depressed within their urban settings. Similar feelings are applicable to many large-scope building types, such as airport terminals, convention centers and sport facilities. This is one of the reasons why newcomers to urban environments often feel insecure, agitated, disoriented and even depressed until they have developed a clear mental map of the area. Additional social, environmental, economic and political factors contribute to emotional responses to city environments, complicating analysis of this relationship.

Urban Density Patterns, Networks, Textures and Human Interactivity Patterns

The concept of *density*, or the number of people per unit area, is considered highly important in the fields of urban planning and architecture (Rapoport, 1975). However, when discussing interaction, other demographic factors such as cultural background and socioeconomic status affect the manner in which groups engage with each other and each element of the built environment. Twentieth-century studies conducted by prominent sociologists such as Simmel (1903/1976), and Wirth (1938) emphasized population size as conducive to the density of human aggregates' interaction. Within these aggregates, various patterns and models of interaction have been identified. In particular, the relationship between urban density and crime, and the study of size and communication in macrostructures, speak to the "transitionary" and "superficiality" nature of urban social interactions (Davidson & Martin, 2014, p. 209).

Wirth suggests "urbanism" is a way of life and argues that factors such as population size, density and heterogeneity contribute to the development of certain urban conditions, or "urbanism." Similar to Simmel, Wirth believed in the superficiality of human interaction in urban environments. In his article "Urbanism as a Way of Life," he notes:

> Characteristically, urbanites meet one another in highly segmental roles. This is essentially what is meant by saying that the city is characterized by secondary rather than primary contacts. The contacts of the city may indeed be face to face, but they are nevertheless impersonal, superficial, transitory and segmental.
>
> *(Wirth, 1938, p. 12)*

In the past fifty years there have been two polar opposite models of urban growth. On the one hand, the explosion of urban sprawl and suburbs offer compensation for a compromised urban quality of life. On the other, the transformation of traditional urban neighborhoods has seen a "return to the City," as discussed by Kevin Lynch in *Good City Form* (1984). Urban specialists have studied the various effects and impacts of each on its occupants and on a multitude of ecological and environmental factors (Duany et al., 2001, p. 3).

The immediate implication of sprawl is a difference in density, which should not be confused with size.

> This has a direct relationship with preferences for the size of social neighborhood based on the enjoyment of nature, a liking for a clean and quiet environment, a desire to control one's own home – with the security, satisfaction, and cash savings that come with that – and a perception of low-density residence as a good place for rearing children.
>
> *(Lynch, 1984, p. 261)*

On the other hand, the desire to live near others is a strong draw to communities throughout the world and across cultures. Culture is a major determinant which can lead to segregation and various social pathologies, particularly when coupled with political economy. Density texture in all its multitude forms is a complex issue with explicit spatial features and relates directly to the way elements of a settlement mix. Objectives and intentions may serve to segregate, integrate, cluster, diversify or purify land use. For many social thinkers, identifying a compromise between private space and the desire to live in proximity to others has become an important goal. Many urban geographers seek to create a world in which people's work, residence and leisure are fully integrated (Lynch, 1984, pp. 261–9).

Mobility Patterns, Access and Human Interactivity Patterns

Mobility patterns study the movement of people within or between distinct urban settings. An individual's movements are related to access systems, timing of activities and modes of travel.

Combined with density, these factors contribute to the performance of urban settings. The time–cost trade-off has impacts on choices and preferences of travel (Ewing & Cervero, 2010). Particularly strong cultural attachments to personal vehicles, combined with residing outside of employment or leisure areas, increases time spent travelling and reduces human interactions. This results in further social inequalities. Lack of regulations to promote use of convenient safe alternate modes of transport, such as biking, walking or public transport, also reduces opportunities for interaction. Today, professionals using transit systems to commute between work and residence typically demand comfort, internet access, ease of entry and exit, space and safety. In general, cities with more clustering of density around transit hubs are considered more sustainable and friendly.

For public encounters such as using transportation systems, maintaining boundaries is one of the major factors controlling interactivity between people. According to Hall (1966), all cultures have varying concepts for intimate, personal, social and public distances. For some cultures, these distances may be inappropriate or even forbidden. This issue increases concerns for safety and security, triggering preferences for using certain choices of public transit systems over personal vehicles. Interactivity with public built environments is thus limited by choice. However, in general, technology and digital media are blurring these constraints and offering new ways for humans and built environments to interact, while acting as a medium between the spatial built setting and the subject, meaning the user.

Urban Identity and Human Interactive Patterns

One of the components of environmental imageability is the recognition of urban elements, which contribute to the meaning of "urban identity." Imageability is defined as the ease with which a word gives rise to a sensory mental image, and was originally used by Paivio, Yuille and Madigan (1968). However, in this case it is used for the purpose of identifying and developing a sensory mental image of urban elements. Urban identity leads to imageability, legibility and visibility, and promotes interactivity by way of contributing to the development of mental mapping, supporting navigating within urban contexts. Urban identity is based on a two-way process between urban elements and perception. The tools of urban identity include the shapes, colors and geometrical arrangements of architecture. In modern architecture identification of building types and its honest expression is a key component of programming and design and one of the tools for setting the ground for its interactivity. Distinctions between residential, office, hospital or restaurant typologies not only contribute to recognition as distinct entities, but also promote patterns of relation and interactivity with observers and users.

Through development of the built form and application of advanced construction techniques, modern architecture has provided the means to create appropriate vocabularies befitting ease of identification of various architectural types. Throughout history, the legibility of building façades and urban settings has been considered by designers and master builders. Providing interactive built environments has been a way of thinking in architecture and urban planning.

Cities are gravitational force fields and networks of communication that are formed and sustained by interactions between people. Settlements with higher levels of interaction are more likely to flourish. According to Lynch:

> Since it is not just spatial patterns, but also technology, institutional patterns, and the human cognitive structure which impose limits on the flow of information, then one is led to propose the use of space-transcending communications, institutional reforms, and various technical intensifiers of human cognition.

(Lynch, 1984, pp. 334–5)

With its manmade identifiable elements, the city becomes a container for and a symbol for the complex dynamic entity which we call "society." Delange, in his review of Lynch's *Image of the City*, refers to Lynch's argument that an environmental image has three components: *identity*, which is the recognition of urban elements as separate entities; *structure*, which is the network of relationships of urban elements to other objects and to observers; and *meaning*, which provides practical and emotional value to observers (Delange, 2009). These elements have overlapping representations and objectives, allowing urban inhabitants to create their own interpretations and plan their own interactive agendas. The last component referred to as, *meaning*, results in what is termed "urban affinity."

Urban Affinity

Urban identity can transform to "affinity" in day-to-day life in the city. When an individual arrives at a sense of security and peace and begins to enjoy the urban setting, they have reached urban affinity. This is particularly true when the three poles or selected zones of *work*, *home* and *leisure* are intertwined, creating in their totality, a sense of *home*. The combination of these three poles within an individual's urban network provides a sense of stabilization and allows for mental and cultural balance and satisfaction in the face of multi-local forms and societal challenges. Inevitably and naturally, urban affinity creates spontaneous interaction and a drive toward identification and experimentation, corresponding to further affinity to urban built elements. In a self-perpetuating cycle, interaction and communication between the individual and the urban setting warrants further affinity.

Urban affinity corresponds to compartmentalized operational structures that have deep roots in mental, social and cultural being, and even more so in "wellbeing." This is by way of a network of productive and amicable spaces for daily life creating a wider sense of "home." When an individual develops a spontaneous or natural liking, attraction, or even attachment to the environment and its related urban setting a *meaningful* relationship is constructed. By way of *meaning*, the city conveys to the individual a combined practical and emotional value.

In recent decades amidst dissemination of technological advancements and their diffusion into day-to-day urban life, the scope and manner of interactions, and thus the quality of practical and emotional values, has undoubtedly been transformed.

Architectural Elements Used as Interactive Mediums

The history of architecture and urban design includes many examples of built forms as direct means for coherent communication between people and their built settings.

The graffitists of Pompeii combined words and images to produce appealing and striking representations of familiar identities and activities, while conveying various sentiments through the architecture of their city. These drawings on alleys, signs, building interiors and exterior façades reveal the importance of messages intended for public dissemination, as well as the high level of interactivity within the urban setting. In Pompeii, there are uncovered evidences that reveal architecture was used as an interactive medium to communicate with citizens and for sharing news, feelings and messages. These messages decorated a variety of typologies including religious buildings, amphitheaters, theater precincts, entrance halls, domestic residences, gladiators' quarters and the private areas of slave residences. They covered a variety of messages and announcements, including games, shows and major public gatherings. When Pompeii was rediscovered in the eighteenth century, the uncovered graffiti relayed the sentiments of city occupants. Graffiti indicated how, for instance, the local population felt about certain shows or games. The painted images, drawings and love poetry reveal the social class and life of the artists, and provide details about interactions of the people with each other and their urban setting.

Phenomenology of Interactivity

Architecture throughout the ages has repeatedly reinforced the usage of architectural elements as interactions between built environments and urban citizens. The Egyptian Papyrus Columns of the Hypostyle Great Temple of Amun, depicting the daily ritual and processional scenes are another ancient example. Images on the columns include Pharaoh bringing offerings to the Gods (1390–1224 BCE) (Figure 22.1).

The carving of Persepolis palace in Pasargadae Iran, dating from 518 BCE, also tells stories of rituals (Figure 22.2).

They carved on the stone façades and the double-headed forms of bulls and lions on the columns' stone capitals, as well as the relief sculptures of the monumental stairs, which represented delegations from twenty-three nations bringing tribute to the sovereign. The stone figures of this magnificent palace depict the pageantry and banquets which were taking place in the palace. Stonehenge in Salisbury, England provides another example (2900–1400 BCE). Perhaps the most famous prehistoric monument, Stonehenge exemplifies the ability of early civilizations to create such evocative spaces using stone material (Figure 22.3).

The most interesting aspect of the henges is the opportunity for occupants and citizens to interactively engage with their ecosystem by developing a structure that acts as an observatory and almanac for establishing an annual calendar allowing prediction of solar and lunar eclipses (Moffitt et al., 2004, pp. 12–37). The city of Yazd in Iran, with its naturally air-conditioned architecture of residences, using wind and water to climatize the interior spaces, is a perfect example of the interactivity of natural elements with the built environment and the building occupants (Figure 22.4).

The modern example of this interactivity in architecture is the Eden Project by Grimshaw in Cornwall, England (Figure 22.5).

In general, the designs in ancient built forms were focused on the concepts for performative links permitting interaction between humans, the environment and the celestial realm.

Figure 22.1 Great Temple of Ramesses II, Abu Simbel, 1285–1255 BCE.
Sketch credit: Nasim Rowshan

Figure 22.2 Persepolis palace in Pasargadae Iran, dating from 518 BCE.
Sketch credit: Nasim Rowshan

Figure 22.3 Stonehenge in Salisbury, England, 2900–1400 BCE.
Sketch credit: Nasim Rowshan

Phenomenology of Interactivity with Respect to Performativity in Architecture

According to the Merriam-Webster Dictionary, phenomenology is the study of the development of human consciousness and self-awareness. It is "the interpretive study of human experience with the goal to study and elucidate human situations, events, meanings, and experience as they occur" (Von Eckartsberg, 1998). On the other hand, *interactivity*, by definition, is the process of two people or things working together and influencing each other. Also, it is the ability of a computer to respond to a user's input.

Figure 22.4 Wind tower of the city of Yazd in Iran.
Sketch credit: Nasim Rowshan

Figure 22.5 The Eden Project by Grimshaw in Cornwall, England.
Sketch credit: Nasim Rowshan

In the contemporary architecture, the concept of "performativity" offers valuable theoretical tools and a framework for understanding and development of interactivity and the creative/productive aspects of the *design* within various architectural typologies.

The term "interactivity" can best address the different modes of users' "participation," while recognizing the agency of both a building's spatial requirements and users in the process of constructing the realities of the building's type. The recognition that every building construct, based on the programmatic requirements of its architectural type, always performs particular interpretations of reality and events, shaping practices that construct and position social subjects, has led to new narrative and interpretative techniques in the design of various typologies. In the contemporary smart construct of various building typologies this has led to a consideration for performativity with a keen eye on the interactivity of "live" and "passive" users, as well as other types of means for "animating" the building's spatial objects and contents. The focus of building types and urban installations on the subjective or even affective responses is increasingly becoming one of the most important aspects of programming phase of the design process. Additionally, there is an increasing concern about the quality of "multi-sensorial experiences" of the participating users and their interactive engagement and comfort in the design of spatial entities.

As the building type and construct takes on its role as an active agency in providing opportunities for users' interactive experiences, the building's performative agenda should provide opportunities and mechanism for adjustability as well. This means the performative design agenda allows for provision of practical and analytical tools that will allow the built form to consciously shape and evaluate its activities and interactivities.

The Concept of Interactive Architecture and the Impact of Technology

Today *interactive architecture* is defined by a multitude of terminologies, including *Intelligent*, *Smart*, *Responsive* and *Flexible Architecture*. These characteristics become associated with contemporary performance-based architecture, through integrating technology and computers into urban and architectural constructs. This architecture contextualizes the advancement of new emerging technologies and is inherently integrative with tectonics of the built forms. It facilitates a framework for human interactivity with the environment from both a natural and built perspective. Interactive architecture highlights design concepts that address the changing demands of occupants and their social and environmental needs. This trend, while in its infancy, offers multiple approaches which, rather than becoming distinct or outdated, will undoubtedly evolve based on constantly progressing technologies.

As the creation of manmade environments shifts toward flexible building types with dynamic spatial requirements and evolving functions, architecture becomes increasingly integrated with and dependent on computation. Interactive architecture is a constantly changing vision based on the demands of sophisticated and technologically savvy future users. By the same token, the demand for architecture based on user type becomes what is called *Smart* or *Intelligent Architecture*. This is a transitional phenomenon adopted from advancements in mechanical, computational and biological realms of sciences. According to Marcos Novak, when considering users as a design factor, the term should be modified to *Transactive Intelligent Architecture*, a level of architectural dynamism that allows for transformativity of both itself and its users (Marcos Novak interview 2001; see Silva, 2005).

According to Michael Fox and Miles Kemp,

> The driving force behind the renewed interest in adaptable architecture is the technologically influenced and changing patterns of human interaction with the built environment. Today's intensification of social and urban change, coupled with concern for issues of sustainability, amplifies the demand for interactive architectural solutions … Technology transfer from similarly integrated interactive developments in other fields, will continue to predicate, impact and evolve with interactive architecture.

(2009, pp. 18–19)

The adopted technologies are, for the most part, transferred from fields of science and engineering, including aerospace, automotive, electromechanical, biological, computational and interface design, digital media, and all innovations related to manufacturing and fabrications. Adaptation of these paradigms, particularly biological, in architectural design with the goal of interactivity by no means rejects the need for aesthetics and philosophical considerations in design. Rather, they provide an additional layer of analysis.

Means of Technological Interactive Approaches in the Built Form

Intelligent architectural and urban environments are constructed systems allowing for various methods of mobility, movement, flexibility and adaptability within contextual and geometrical forms and entities. The ultimate design objectives are ease of use, human comfort and augmented spatial qualities to improve built environments, and define relationships to natural elements. These architectural and urban environments are charged to meet anticipated occupant uses through proper execution of activities within spaces, as well as provision of opportunities for generating new ways for interaction. Based on these design objectives, indoor or outdoor architectural typologies are integrated with technological strategies and systems that are inherently adaptable to various functions and expected contingencies.

The main objective when designing interactive spaces is to provide methods to control the space. This can vary from full direct control to application of a system with the capacity to be fully adaptable. There are various approaches for promoting interactivity. However, it is primarily through *Kinetics* and *Embedded Computation*. A kinetic approach becomes functional not only by way of its own technical mechanics, but also by computational automation systems.

"Kinetics ... will be defined generally as either transformable objects that dynamically occupy predefined physical space or moving physical objects that can share a common physical space to create adaptable spatial configurations" (Fox & Kemp, 2009, p. 27).

Contemporary built environments are expected to possess overlapping functions, and flexible performative qualities allowing for spatial optimization. Examples include a café that becomes a reading room, library and computer lounge; or a meeting hub that is also an extension of a house. Kinetics provides opportunities for dynamically flexible and adaptable forms, which meet various social needs and individual demands. However, multi-functionality of design is distinct from spatial optimization. Kinetic systems allow for a multiplicity of optimized spaces that have the potential to change function and use of physical resources at any given time. Most current typologies, such as convention centers, sport centers, gymnasiums, arenas, theaters, cultural centers, museums and recreational centers, or hospitals demand inherent design flexibility, multi-functionality and ease of reconfiguration.

An additional demand is the capacity to segregate public and private functions, while properly connecting occupants with each other and with visual and acoustical systems. Multi-functionality has become a highlight of the design of electronic devices to the design of the indoor and outdoor spaces within architectural and urban environments. Inevitably such designs integrate kinetic approaches, providing for interactive responses. Kinetic approaches also provide dynamic interactivity between buildings and surrounding environments, with respect to seasonal changes for the comfort of occupants. This is particularly beneficial when buildings are sited in extreme climates. Buildings with integrated kinetic systems have the capacity to transform physical shape and façade appearance in response to climatic nuances, and thus provide more suitable indoor climates.

Transportability is another opportunity provided by kinetic approaches. Transportability, or design for mobility, is a type of adaptive change utilized throughout the centuries by groups with nomadic lifestyles across the globe. In the last century, transportable structures for large-scope non-permanent uses, such as for holding musical concerts, exhibitions, expositions, sport games, and circuses have become more economically viable and practical.

Kinetic architecture has also been used by contemporary architects for design innovation. Santiago Calatrava, in his Milwaukee Art Museum, utilized an enormous moveable wing to provide different environments based on the time of day and weather conditions. This pragmatic representation and execution is a symbolic design concept that emulates natural manifestations (Figure 22.6).

Achieving design concepts through dynamic kinetic components provides possibilities for movement, and conveys an inherent message of the built form design objective. Today's kinetic approaches combined with computation-based systems provide interactive opportunities in design with potential for change and reconfiguration.

Embedded Computation, in the context of interactive design for built environments, "is a system that is literally embedded into the building and that has the ability to gather information, process it, and use it to control the behavior of the actual physical architecture" (Fox & Kemp, 2009, p. 58). In physical manifestation, these systems consist of sensors as information collectors, processors and interpreters. Effective systems sense climatic and environmental changes, and arrive at responses to control changes. Change is central to interactive architectural design solutions of built environments. Computer-based networks are charged to understand the physical conditions of a given space through active control research, and respond to gathered data in an appropriate interactive manner. Active control research was originally developed for monitoring and modifying the structural behavior of buildings through the application of sensors attached to corners of the building for detection and measurement of external forces. This has been specifically used for measuring seismic performance of structures, and mitigating forces which are unleashed on a building's structural armature during catastrophic events such as

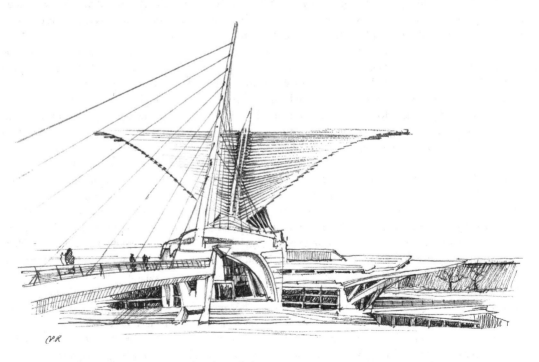

Figure 22.6 Milwaukee Art Museum, Santiago Calatrava.
Sketch credit: Nasim Rowshan

earthquakes or hurricanes. Computers enter the process and activate necessary types of resistance to mitigate external energy impacting structural systems through strong winds or seismic activity. This technology has been implemented in large-scope structures and high-rises through the application of energy-dissipating devices, passive mass dampers and seismic base-isolation systems for spaces housing sensitive substances and documents, or lifesaving activities that must not be interrupted. Adaptive control of such systems can effectively interact with a variety building systems, including fire safety, security and environmental control, as well as considerations for energy conservation, improving comfort and safety for occupants and efficiency in building operations.

Control of built spaces has also been expanded to *home automation*, which has the capacity to adapt to changes in human actions and behavior, including notifying occupants by email or text about dangerous situations such as system failures, overheating, freezing or leaks, before these incidents become problematic or uncontrollable. Interactive systems are charged with the capability to operate buildings, neighborhoods and regional devices from remote locations, and are manufactured in various easy-install kits that can be personized based on user desires and required level of sophistication.

Embedded computer-based systems also provide greater interactive opportunities for controlling remote indoor and outdoor urban spaces for large crowds. Audiences can observe or even participate in major events from remote locations in real time. The level of control of computer-based systems varies with the desired level of *intelligence* planned for the space. It can be fully or partially interactive, which Fox and Kemp call "reactive." In the simplest system a one-to-one relationship is established in real time via an on–off system, which is in the user's control of the space. An example is the basic thermostat controlling temperature through a low-tech approach with no computer involvement. The use of adaptive control and methods of actuation can apply to every element and system of a building to the level of intended interactive dynamism and intelligence, as well as interdisciplinary needs planned for the building. (Fox & Kemp, 2009, pp. 58–94).

Currently, the combination of physical kinetics and embedded computation-based methods satisfies many levels of interactive sophistication between humans and built environments. Levels can also be influenced through application of smart materials, sensors, interface designs and robotics. The highest goal for intelligent buildings is to integrate systems of sensors that assess the conditions of indoor/outdoor environments and status of systematic elements to achieve efficient operational performance for comfort of the occupants. This is an objective for interactivity where a building is inherently active and interactive in becoming a medium or a biosphere between occupants and the surrounding climatic and ecological elements.

> The success of humanity as a species is dependent on our ability to act and react – to recognize and analyze situations and respond to them in an appropriate manner … As technology has improved and had a greater impact on our lives, more and more energy has been devoted to the development of automatic systems that make things happen faster and with greater efficiency. Automation can take two forms: an action that is carried out to a predetermined, unchangeable pattern; and an action that is carried out toward predetermined result though the process may be changed along the way. The second form can be described as intelligent automation, the key difference being that it has a built-in, reactive quality. In architecture, the inclusion of some form of intelligent building system is becoming more and more common.
>
> *(Kronenburg, 2007, p. 209)*

Mediated Environments for Physically Challenged Users

Technology and computer automation have intervened and provided new solutions to mediate lifestyle challenges, particularly for the elderly and people with physical disabilities. This includes the most common device for vertical circulation, the elevator, which can be programmed to stay inactive on the first floor, or any other floor as programmed. Other systems such as fire doors, smoke sensors that activate closing mechanisms or interactive visual and sound alarms for the sight- or hearing-impaired significantly reduce fire-related danger. Stairways, chairs and walking ramps are examples of other unique mediating designs that can assist occupants with limited mobility to reach a safe destination in emergency situations. These are developing in response to specific uses of indoor and outdoor environments; for example, users of sophisticated automated wheelchairs designed to support various levels of disability. The realm of Universal Design is focused on adopting further interactivity between physically challenged individuals with their built environment, including adjustable height, reach and access, as well as maneuverability, safe movement and comfort, with the ultimate goal of improving independence and self-sufficiency.

Psychological and Sociological Impacts of Interactively-Based Built Environments on Human

"Human beings are most satisfied in environments where they feel a connection between what they see and who they see and who they are" (Kopec, 2006).

According to the *Theory of Interactionism*, people and environments are separate but interacting entities. By the same token, *Interactional Territories* are spaces controlled by a group of interacting individuals.

"To a certain extent, our behaviors are nothing but learned intuitions growing out of our experiences of the world" (Fox & Kemp, 2009, p. 142).

As users of built environments, we operate intuitively. However, when a built architectural setting has the capacity to react to our actions through integrated interactive and intelligent means, it stimulates another mode of awareness, and changes behavioral patterns. The more sophisticated the interactivity, the greater the need for cognitive awareness and skills to interact intelligently with the built environment. The potential for architectural environments to inform and reflect occupants is increased the more interactive they are and the more effective their impact is on behavior.

Computer-controlled built environments are undoubtedly influencing occupants differently than one-on-one interactions. These developments have positive consequences, but they also have side effects. These influences can span to far distances. The dynamism and flexibility of spaces, and capacity offered by various computer- and kinetic-based approaches, allow for expansion of the scope of the reach and influence of the space beyond its physical boundaries. Influences can now be at regional, national and global levels. Inevitably this transforms occupant behaviors, expectations, and perceptions of space, and ultimately the manner in which they utilize spatial entities. This is just the beginning of a novel lifestyle for users of the built environments of all kinds and scopes, with respect to what the meaning of *interactivity* provides for them.

In recent decades, common lifestyle transformations have been endorsed by major companies, educational institutions and public entities through the application of advanced technologies, such as telecommuting, as well as the pursuit of on-line education. Virtual reality and on-line shopping, working, teaching and receiving education, as well as banking have reduced physical and face-to-face interactions, and transformed the concept of interactivity. This has transformed organizational and programmatic set-up of many professional fields, including high-tech scientific entities, educational institutions and many service-based industries, such as mail delivery. Reduced direct interaction has also affected social life. For many, activities such as dating and socializing are now carried out on-line from the comfort of home or other private locations. This is a major transformation in day-to-day life, resulting in remote interactive conditions and individualized busy lifestyles for those engaged as professionals, customers, educators, students and home makers, being interactive in real time and on-line in their private surroundings.

The remote interactive lifestyle has brought about a degree of comfort, convenience and economic advantage for families, particularly working mothers. However, it demands a high level of self-organization and discipline to maintain an efficient, balanced and productive lifestyle. This new interactivity in educational and work environments is a remote social interaction that has its own psychological and sociological ramifications.

With respect to some of the negative side effects of this phenomenon, there are concerns about the effects of *computer automation* in various fields of employment. Questions are raised about current and future needs of many specialties and services, and the replacement of workers and knowledge-based jobs by automated systems, particularly when they are replaced by robots. This issue has been subject to many debates and unresolved discussions throughout the past decade or so.

Behavioral Interactivity through Kinetic and Computer-Based Strategies

Human sensory perception of space and cognitive levels can be influenced drastically by the presence and impact of computers, and the level of interactivity provided for occupants within and beyond spatial boundaries of the space. Architecture has the power to teach users to adapt to new ways of living. This is a great tool for designers, particularly when augmented through the interactive possibilities provided by kinetics and embedded computation. Technological advancements allow buildings to convey information and messages, respond to our needs and interact with users. Some interactive strategies are more cognitive than intuitive and require knowledgeable users and timely activation for full effectiveness. Design strategies which engage occupants with space in natural and built environments are always the most useful, since by default they become part of an intuitive interactive space. This pattern can be adopted and learned by repetition. Additionally, an interactive environment can be a device – such as an ATM, or an entity with systems and devices that promote certain behavioral patterns between users and spaces, while promoting lifestyle awareness. Lavatory faucets programmed to run for short periods control water use and lighting fixtures with integrated motion sensors to turn lights on or off as is needed are examples that increase user awareness about water and energy consumption in buildings.

Since the beginning of the twenty-first century, robot technology is becoming increasingly a part of our daily lives, acting on humans' behalf. The design and usage of robots as drones, care or cooperating industrial robots, intelligent algorithms or exoskeletons are creating the link to the new paradigm of interaction between mankind and machines. With the intent to improve the world and make it a more convenient and safer place for living, the designers of robots have been focusing on the creation of humanoids and autonomous cars, as well as various interfaces of adaptive computer programs and intelligent homes' or work environments' functioning based on touch pads. While robotics is increasingly becoming accessible and personal, the question as to how and to what extent they will interactively and effectively perform on behalf of humans as a medium with the surrounding manmade and natural environment is not a known agenda, yet.

There are various experimental works, such as Philip Beesley's "Living and Metabolic Architecture," that allow architecture as animated entities and living systems to become interchangeable and interactive with its users, as well as his immersive installations that use touch and motion-tracking sensors to react and adapt to the movements of people. Also, Greg Lynn's vision of future habitats and rotating residential units with full performativity offering automatic rotational and movement flexibility of space with robot-controlled lounge chairs are a few examples manifesting the visionary designers' views of the new ways of interactivity of humans with their manmade and natural environments using advanced technology as a medium (Kries et al., 2017).

Mitra Kanaani

Architectural Vocabulary as an Interactive Tool for Dialogue between Users and the Environment

This is the era in which building façades transcend beyond simple enclosure systems or weather barriers, and begin taking on artistic roles to convey messages and raise awareness. The skin of a building can share information about architectural type, use and activities inside the space. As part of the concept of interactivity, the architecture of public urban and community developments is designed to establish identity, act as a communication tool and be a hub for interior and exterior users of the built environment. Such buildings are planned with the concept and program as meeting and assembly places for large events, which not only allow interactivity of large groups, but also stimulate interactivity among the wider audience and spectators outside the community as well (for example, the AT&T Global Olympic Village, Atlanta, 1996, by FTL Design Engineering Studio).

Today, many buildings are designed to have an interactive impact on their neighborhood and the wider city. One example is Sendai Mediatheque, in Sendai, Japan. Designed by Toyo Ito and completed in 2000, the structure is an iconic expression that has attracted both local and outside users and visitors and has stimulated interactivity through the development of business opportunities. The building layout and open-planned interior spaces with integrated functions stimulate and generate opportunities for individualized choreographed interactivities between the built setting and with other users (Figure 22.7).

Sustainability is another area in which interactivity has flourished. Contemporary considerations regarding climate awareness and energy efficiency have resulted in the design of building biospheres with façade skins and enclosure systems that interact with regional natural conditions. Nicholas Grimshaw's British Pavilion at Expo 92 in Seville, Spain offers an early example, in which solar panels powered

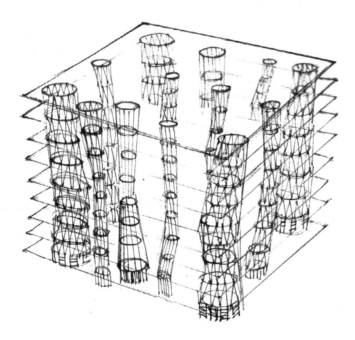

Figure 22.7 Sendai Mediatheque, Sendai, Japan. Toyo Ito, completed in 2000.
Sketch credit: Nasim Rowshan

Phenomenology of Interactivity

a cooling water wall on one side, while a translucent fabric enclosure system featured on the other. This design speaks of an architecture that is in direct dialogue with climatic elements within its ecosystem (Figure 22.8).

In recent decades, the concept of transformability has become a design goal and one approach to integration of the meaning of interactivity in architectural environments. Transformability goes hand in hand with interaction, and considers the meaning of change without necessarily including possibilities of physical movement. This is about possibilities of transformation in the surface image of the architecture, combined with electronic communication devices such as light-emitting diode (LED) screens. In such designs, the entire façade, or a section of the enclosure system's skin, becomes a programmable screen, displaying video, images or texts that are controlled from remote distances.

For instance, structural membrane systems on building façades can act as computer-controlled projector screens to display events happening inside the structure. By offering informational messages, media technology transforms the dynamics of urban complexions, and activates curiosity, attracting further interaction. In many cases, expression is abstract and an artistic message to stimulate a level of intellectual interactivity between observers and the built environment.

One example of architecture integrated with transformable interactivity through LED technology is Herzog and De Meuron's Allianza Arena, in Munich, Germany. The interactive building skin consists of LED and ethylene tetrafluoroethylene (ETFE) cushions as cladding elements that are set in place by a rubber clamping system, which allows for expansion and contraction due to the fluctuation of temperature (Figure 22.9).

Figure 22.8 British Pavilion at Expo 92 in Seville, Spain, Nicholas Grimshaw.
Sketch credit: Nasim Rowshan

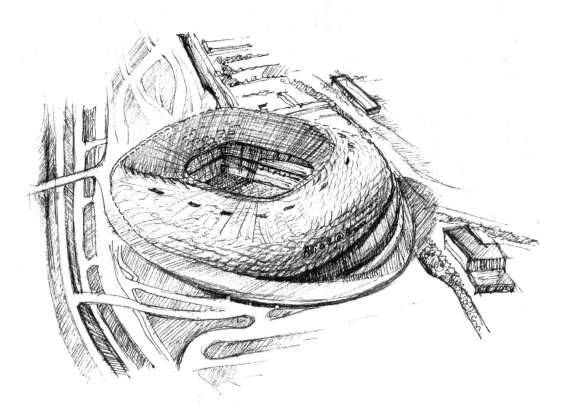

Figure 22.9 Allianza Arena, Munich, Germany, Herzog De Meuron.
Sketch credit: Nasim Rowshan

Design goals for transformability can work toward augmenting building efficiency, functionality and productivity for intended activities and interactivities. This can occur by connecting interactive outdoor/indoor relationships. According to Robert Kronenburg, transformability provides opportunities for human engagement in important ways:

> Firstly, by creating an environment or an object that is not static, it brings life to what is normally considered an inanimate art. Secondly ... it creates a more democratic form of architecture ... Buildings that can significantly alter their shape over a limited time period establish a different sense of identity to wholly static ones, and people respond in a very different way to an environment that is motive than to one that is static. This is because their involvement with the building becomes an interaction rather than a simple action.
>
> *(2007, p. 171)*

Flexible Architecture for Creating a Sense of Place and Interaction

Flexibility and interactivity are related in the design of architectural environments, mainly with respect to function and siting. In these cases, the main design objectives are to create spatial entities that will be adopted by all user types and possess the potential to adapt to their needs while stimulating a distinct sense of place. This can be achieved by developing spatial design solutions that are clear, legible and offer direct views and sightlines from occupants to functions. There are at least four ways in which design augmented by computational automation promotes interactivity:

- Transformable spaces and elements that have the potential to adopt or convert to other types of use. This not only applies to geometrical two-dimensional forms and three-dimensional volumes of the space, but also to the positioning of elements.
- Use of space, adaptable in a multi-functional way through continuity of the layout and fluidity of the volumes, which is not locked into a specific function.
- Careful planning and an inviting layout, along with integration of design ideas that encourages freedom of movement and interactivity within spaces. This can be careful planning of *functional* spaces within circulation patterns, while simultaneously encouraging ease of accessibility, along with direct sightlines and views to primary spaces.
- Kinetic means and intelligent computational automation techniques for identification of activities and appropriate responsive actions, toward even more complex arrangements. This can augment spatial functionality and interactive qualities.

Contemporary communities demand greater creativity in interactive architectural environments that conveys a sense of place relative to their own unique cultural societies, and is recognized by all stakeholders. Measures of achievement for such goals are dependent on lessons learned from the application and execution of interactive design methods and experimentation of their outcomes. The potential for success lies in integrative design thinking processes.

Interactivity: Interaction Design

The topic of "human to human" and "human to the built form" interaction is an ongoing discussion, particularly since the expansion of the field of urbanism in the twentieth century. However, as computer involvement in every aspect of our lives becomes more dominant, the topic of *Human–Computer Interaction* is increasingly becoming a known and interesting field of research by thinkers from various disciplines. There are four factors affecting these interactive relationships: Humans, Computers, Task Environments, and Machine Environments. In essence all relate to human experience. It is through performing a task or using an object that the state of "interactivity" is substantiated.

In recent decades, the practice of *Interaction Design*, focusing on interactive environments, systems, services and digital products, is for the most part related to user interactions. Considering that interactivity is about physical states, mental states and behavioral responses to manipulation, the question is: can computer automation contribute to more enriching human life experiences? In summary, the story has just begun.

References

Clark, J.M., & Paivio, A. (2004). Extensions of the Paivio, Yuille, and Madigan (1968) Norms. *Behavior Research Methods, Instruments, & Computers*, Volume 36, Issue 3, pp. 371–383. doi: 10.3758/BF03195584.
Cambridge Dictionary. (n.d.). Interactivity. http://dictionary.cambridge.org/dictionary/english/interactivity.
Davidson, M., & Martin, D. (2014). *Urban Politics: Critical Approaches*. London: Sage.
Delange, M., (2009). Review: Kevin Lynch – *Image of the City: Mobile Media and Urban Design*. http://themobilecity.nl/2009/05/08/review-kevin-lynch-the-image-of-the-city/.
Duany, A., et al. (2001). *Suburban Nation: The Rise of Sprawl and Decline of the American Dream*. New York: North Point Press.

Ewing, R., & Cervero, R. (2010). Travel and the Built Environment: A Meta-Analysis. *Journal of the American Planning Association*, Volume 76, Issue 3, pp. 265–94. www.tandfonline.com/doi/abs/10.1080/01944361003766766.

Fox, M., & Kemp, M. (2009). *Interactive Architecture*. New York: Princeton Architectural Press.

Hall, E. (1966). *The Hidden Dimension*. New York: Doubleday.

Kopec, D. (2006). *Environmental Psychology for Design*. New York: Fairchild.

Kries, M., Hohenstein, T., & Klein, M. (2017). *Hello Robot: Design between Human and Machine*. Berlin: Vitra Design Museum and the MAK.

Kronenburg, R. (2007). *Flexible Architecture that Responds to Change*. London: Lawrence King.

Lynch, K. (1984). *Good City Form*. Cambridge, MA: MIT Press.

Lynch, K. (1996). *The Image of the City*. Cambridge, MA: MIT Press.

Moffitt, M., Fazio, M., & Wodehouse, L. (2004). *A World History of Architecture*. United States: New York: McGraw-Hill.

Rapoport, A. (1975). Environment & Behavior, Toward a Redefinition of Density. *Sage Journal*, Volume 7, Issue 2, pp. 133–158.

Silva, C. (May 2005). *Liquid Architectures: Marcus Novak's Territory of Information*. Master thesis submitted to LSU, Agricultural and Mechanical College. Interview of Marcus Novak (Spring 2001) by Allesandro Ludovico, Neural. http://etd.lsu.edu/docs/available/etd-01202005-102411/unrestricted/Silva_thesis.pdf.

Simmel, G. (1903/1976). *The Metropolis and Mental Life: The Sociology of Georg Simmel*. New York: Free Press.

Stanford Encyclopedia of Philosophy. (2013). Phenomenology. https://plato.stanford.edu/entries/phenomenology/#WhatPhen.

Von Eckartsberg, R. (1998). Introducing Existential-Phenomenological Psychology. In R. Valle (Ed.), *Phenomenological Inquiry in Psychology: Existential and Transpersonal Dimensions*, pp. 227–246. New York: Plenum Press.

Wirth, L. (1938). Urbanism as a Way of Life. *American Journal of Sociology*, Volume 44, Issue 1, pp. 1–24. www.uc.edu/cdc/urban_database/fall03-readings/urbanism_as_a_way.pdf.

23
The Cybernetics of Cybernetics
A Performative Idiom

Theodore Spyropoulos

Austrian radical architect Hans Hollein (1968) proclaimed "*Alles ist Architektur*" (Everything is architecture). Published originally as a manifesto that appeared in the journal *Bau*, this provocation reflected a heightened awareness of the limitations of traditional definitions of architecture in favour of an understanding of design as an experimental vehicle for the construction of new forms of communication. Beyond building, Hollein stated,

> A true architecture of our time will have to redefine itself and expand its means. Many areas outside of traditional building will enter the realm of architecture, as architecture and 'architects' will have to enter new fields. All are architects. Everything is architecture.
>
> *(p. 2)*

Architecture in an expanded field of experimentation resonates with great magnitude today as we live in an age where science fiction has become fact. Our contemporary age is as radical as ever with change, latency and uncertainty being the new norm. The once comfortable and understood historical models of the past have proven limited in their capacity to engage and address the complexities of the contemporary condition. As we live in ever-evolving information-rich environments, the question is not why but how architecture can actively participate.

Hollein's proclamation, like others during this period of the late 1960s, looked outside of traditional architectural discourse and practice of the time in an attempt to radically rethink what architecture could be. Experimentation extended from pure speculative design to novel research in ephemeral structures, material computation and systems thinking. Beyond technological optimism a cultural project emerged that questioned how we live and the environments that we live within. This open interrogation and plurality of approaches created a culture of design that was socially aware and forward-thinking. Within the context of this research attention has been given to a strand of experiments and research initiatives that focused on the role of cybernetics, communication, art and technology from the mid-1960s until 1970. Experiments for Art and Technology/EAT (1966), MIT's Architecture Machine Group (1967) and Centre for Advanced Visual Studies (1967), along with landmark exhibitions such as Reichardt's *Cybernetic Serendipity* (1968) and Burnham's *Software: Information Technology: Its New Meaning for Art* (1970) all pointed to a diverse terrain of approaches within the artistic, scientific and technological fields that were converging in exciting and yet-to-be-understood ways. The attempts

Figure 23.1 Minimaforms (Theodore and Stephen Spyropoulos), Emotive House, Sci-Arc Close Up Exhibition, Los Angeles, United States, 2016.

Source: Minimaforms

within these experiments were to speculate and correlate relationships, construct understandings through experimentation. Through thought experiments and scenario speculation this short but seminal period brought about a motivated design synergy which, it will be argued, can offer new perspectives for some of the challenges that we face in contemporary design.

In September 1969 a landmark issue of *Architectural Design*, guest edited by Roy Landau, brought issues of interaction and digital computation into the mainstream architectural media. Alongside articles by Negroponte, Price and Brodey, the issue featured an essay by the cybernetician Gordon Pask (1969), who introduced the idea that "architects are first and foremost system designers who have been forced to take an increasing interest in the organizational systems properties of development, communication and control" (p. 494). Architecture, Pask (1969) argued, had no theory to cope with the pressing contemporary complexities of the time, and it was only through a cybernetic understanding of systemic processes that the discipline could evolve (Figure 23.2).

Central to Pask's argument was an understanding of the world through the pursuit of "communication and control" and the elucidation of what he termed "aesthetically potent environments": external spaces designed to foster pleasurable interactions. These interactions were to be framed through a commitment to novelty. "Man," he wrote, "is prone to seek novelty in his environment and, having found a novel situation, to learn how to control it." The pioneering cybernetic issue of *AD* was in many ways anticipated (with an obvious sense of dread) when Read (1964) published *A Concise History of Modern Sculpture*. Writing about what he saw as the "tortuous dematerialisation of post-war

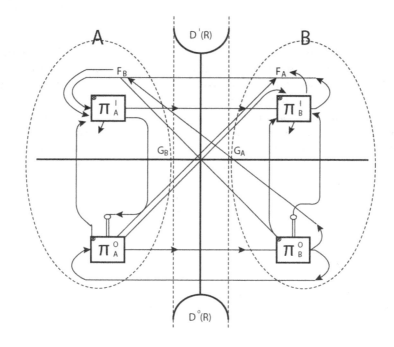

Figure 23.2 Gordon Pask's diagram illustrating Conversation Theory.
Source: Minimaforms

Figure 23.3 Minimaforms (Theodore and Stephen Spyropoulos), Memory Cloud Detroit, Detroit Institute of Art, Detroit, Michigan, United States, 2011.
Source: Minimaforms

sculpture," with more recent works resembling merely "scribbles in the air," Read argued that sculpture's only hope for salvation lay in the pursuit of stability, "an art of solid form" (Burnham 1968, p. 1). In his own book, *Beyond Modern Sculpture*, the US art historian Burnham (1968) responded to Read's broadside by suggesting that the survival of sculpture would depend on its ability to offer a "transition from object to system." In a spirit very similar to Pask's call to architectural arms, Burnham argued for the importance of systemic innovation, pursued specifically through kinetic installations, light sculptures and cybernetic art. As a main feature of this research operative installations and prototypes serve to expand this systemic approach towards a model that is participatory and behavioural in practice.

English psychiatrist William Ross Ashby (1956) in his landmark book *An Introduction to Cybernetics* articulates its early conceptual framework when he states,

> Cybernetics ... is a 'theory of machines' but treats, not things but ways of behaving. It does not ask 'what is this thing?' but 'what does it do?' ... It takes as its subject matter the domain of 'all possible machines,' and is only secondarily interested if informed that some of them have not yet been made, either by Man or by Nature. What cybernetics offers is the framework on which all individual machines may be ordered, related and understood.
>
> *(Johnston 2008, p. 11)*

Behaviour as subject in early cybernetic discourse made little to no distinction between objects, organisms or machines, and only considered agency as a product of an entity's capacity to produce change in an environment. This served as a fundamental driver for the behavioural classification proposed in the seminal paper *Behavior, Purpose, and Teleology* (Rosenblueth, Wiener & Bigelow 1943) which influenced some of the core conversations at the cybernetics conferences held between 1946 and 1953 at the Josiah Macy, Jr. Foundation.[1] Furthering Ashby's questioning of what things do, Pickering (1995) in his book *The Mangle of Practice: Time, Agency and Science* makes an important distinction with what he sees in second-order cybernetics as a shift from "the representational idiom" to what he states as "the performative idiom." The representational idiom maps the world and describes it as it is, while the performative idiom is concerned with agency and influencing this world through action. Pickering sees this as "the emergent interplay of human and material agency" (p. 46). Within the context of this chapter I have described it as interplay between human and non-human agency.

The convergence of cybernetics, anthropology, conceptual art and complexity sciences brought about thought experiments that reconceptualized our "understanding of understanding," as Heinz Von Foerster would say. A conceptual framework that would acknowledge the observer as not something outside of the system but within a system challenged the orthodoxies of scientific method and the finite results that were ascribed to them. Von Foerster articulated this distinction between "observed systems" and "observing systems" as a foundational development in what became known as second-order cybernetics or the cybernetics of cybernetics. This conception of understanding within this research has been of great importance as it has offered a new perspective for how one could conceive of design systems within a shared environment. Observing systems that could engage other systems in a manner that privileges communication, learning and experience. Von Foerster (1979) spoke to this in a presentation at the University of Illinois, Urbana Champaign titled "Cybernetics of Cybernetics," where he reminded the audience of biologists and theoreticians of Humberto Maturana's famed proposition, "Anything said is said by an observer," which he followed up with a request to expand this by adding, "Anything said is said to an observer."

The thesis expands this observer function towards implications that second-order cybernetician Gordon Pask articulates and pushes further in his conversation theory. His concept of conversation as a model of interaction enables a framework that is both open and informal but contingent on

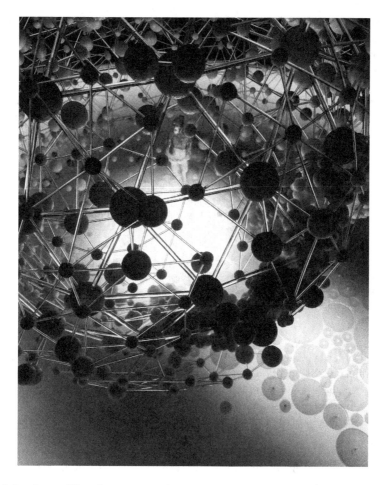

Figure 23.4 Minimaforms (Theodore and Stephen Spyropoulos), Of and in the World, Somerset House Courtyard, London, England, 2018 to current.
Source: Minimaforms

communication and engagement. Conversations can start from anywhere, but are between participants, and they can last as long as that engagement is necessitated and agreed between participants. The rules of interaction are formed through the engagement and the content or subject of discussion can migrate and evolve as parties see appropriate. A conversation as understood by Pask is circular and can be conducted with a human, a machine or with oneself.

Of and in the World: A Second-Order Approach

Second-order cybernetics within the framework sets the core theoretical component. Evolving from first-order cybernetic command-and-control practices, second-order cybernetics made an obvious yet profound inclusion of the observer within the observing system. Known as the "cybernetics of cybernetics," the observer is actively engaging and relationally evolving understandings with the observed. This inclusion expanded the complex set of circular relationships that every observer engages with when they attempt to understand the processes and knowledge extracted from their observations. Fundamentally this brought into question deterministic and finite understandings of how we conceptualize, perceive, represent and communicate. Second-order cybernetician Ranulph Glanville (2003) explains that

> the observer is no longer neutral and detached ... The aim of attaining traditional objectivity is either abandoned/passed over, or what objectivity is and how we might obtain (and value) it is reconsidered. In this sense, every observation is autobiographical.

What Glanville and other second-order cyberneticists foreground is the presence of an observed agency that through interaction, engagement or experience connects and directly situates their observations within a behavioural framework that is truly theirs. This is stated throughout the literature of second-order cybernetics and within the philosophical discourses of the radical constructivists. Radical constructivist Bernhard Poerksen (2004) states

> the observer is the point of fixation for all divergent interests; the observer, by general consent, plays the central role in any cognitive process. Despite all the differences, such a common research interest is in itself of great consequence, of course, because it entails the need to re-assess the investigative efforts of one's own in relation to those of others.
>
> *(p. x)*

Within second-order cybernetics and constructivists' discourse, questions of difference, distinction and change all influence the attention and possibilities that could be ascertained through observation. This sets up a conceptually beautiful problem, in acknowledging that each observer's observations are their own and are inherently inaccessible to others in pure form.

Ranulph Glanville (2003) implies a behavioural understanding of this paradox when stating,

> while we all observe and know differently, we behave as if we were observing the same thing. What structure might support this? One supporting the essential difference while retaining the possibility of communication: when the basic assumption is that we are all different, we all see and understand differently.

Communication and the interface of our interaction with each other, our environment or with non-human agents therefore cannot be assumed. Sociologist Andrew Pickering (2010) argues that

> Cybernetics stages for us a vision not of a world characterized by graspable causes, but rather of one in which reality is always 'in the making,' to borrow a phrase from William James. We could say, then that the ontology of cybernetics was non-modern in two ways: in its refusal of a dualist split between people and things, and in an evolutionary, rather than casual and calculable grasp of temporal process.
>
> *(pp. 309–371)*

Pickering expresses these primary cybernetic qualities that have played a vital role in my revisiting this approach to observation and understanding as the critical framework to enable curiosity, conversation and adaptation within practice. The situated complexity of observers, the environment of this observation, and the potential to draw out communication and shared experience motivates the underlying premise argued as a behavioural framework for design within this thesis. The role of this framework to engage in real time with the complexities of communication within a collective is hypothesized through a model for interaction as conversation. Enter design.

The strength of second-order cybernetic discourse could be argued resides in its plurality of method for breaking disciplinary orthodoxies. Gregory Bateson (anthropologist, social scientist and biologist), W. Ross Ashby (psychiatrist), William Grey Walter (neurophysiologist) and Ranulph Glanville (architect and educator) shared a complex second-order framework that enabled them to consider how observers (human and non-human agents) constructed through participation an understanding of their world. Through this plurality and individuated observer understandings, the need to examine frameworks that explore new forms of communication that are collective and shared motivates much of the design research that has been developed as authored experiments. This behavioural framework developed within this thesis is argued as participatory and conversational, allowing for potential exchanges that offer the possibility for what Bateson (1977) would say "is a difference which makes a difference" (p. 459). Bateson saw the capacity of observers to actively engage with differences especially within their environment through what he spoke of as "ecology of mind." This conceptual apparatus of Bateson was not predicated on bounded singularities but rather defied holistic understanding; he states, "The mental world—the mind—the world of information processing—is not limited by skin" (p. 460). Beyond skin for Bateson (or any form of materialism) is the desire to see thoughts as having agency they further transform from the thing itself into an ecology of ideas that may find form he speculated in art. Bateson went further to express the fundamental human aspect of observation and understanding. He said, "it is the attempt to separate intellect from emotion that is monstrous, and I suggest that it is equally monstrous—and dangerous—to attempt to separate the external mind from the internal" (p. 470). The emotive aspect of the observer offers a window into the human complexities within an observer's construction and the need to conceptualize a framework to allow for this to be shared. Bateson followed by suggesting that

> there are bridges between one sort of thought and the other, and it seems to me that the artists and poets are specifically concerned with these bridges. It is not that art is the expression of the unconscious, but rather that it is concerned with the relation between levels of mental process.
>
> *(p. 470)*

In considering Bateson's cybernetic considerations it is noteworthy to see some parallels developed with experimental art practice during this period.

Like Bateson, performance artist Allan Kaprow (2003) shared an interest in the environment. Kaprow pioneered a movement of performance art that he described as "Happenings" and "Environment" art. If Bateson and other cyberneticists believed in active observer principals, Kaprow would describe these principals as experience. He stated that he wanted to understand

> art not separate from experience ... what is an authentic experience? ... environment is a process of interaction ... even a crude experience, if authentically an experience, is more fit to give a clue to the intrinsic nature of aesthetic experience than is an object already set apart from any other mode experience.
>
> *(p. xi)*

This gives a window into why Kaprow believed that there should be no distinctions between art and life. He believed in what he described as "performing life." Kaprow like Gordon Pask believed that art had constraints. Kaprow stated that "A work of art, like an experience, has its limits; the questions are, what kind of limits and do they model themselves after those in other art or in life?" (p. xvii). What is central in this intellectual enquiry is that this thought experiment is relational and by actively engaging in this the observer is influenced by and influences their environment through this enquiry. Pask would describe this environment as an "aesthetically potent environment" which would foster "pleasurable" forms of interaction. What constitutes an observer in this environment is agency, and through novelty Pask believed human curiosity would exhibit the desire to control it. In contrast this would challenge some tenets of second-order approaches such as cyberneticist Ross Ashby's belief that "Cybernetics deals with all forms of behavior in so far as they are regular, or determinate, or reproducible. The materiality is irrelevant, and so is the holding or not of the ordinary laws of physics" (1956, p. 1). Beyond thought the thesis is concerned with constructing frameworks that are operational and have the capacity to observe, respond and act in the world. I would argue it is this performativity in constructing cybernetic machines/frameworks that enables design to expand and offer new knowledge through experiments that serve as proof of evolving concepts. The thesis within this understanding is greatly influenced by Pask's concepts of conversation theory that evolved through his making of machines that learned, his interests in the dramatic arts and architecture and his desire to explore a form of humanity in humans or machines. In discussing Pask's work in his book a *The Cybernetic Brain: Sketches of Another Future,* Pickering (2010) says his

> interest in conversation, understood very generally as any form of reciprocally productive and open-ended exchange between two or more parties (which might be humans or machines or humans and machines) was, in fact, the defining topic of all of Pask's work.
>
> *(pp. 322–323).*

This attention to environment and performance within second-order cybernetics and the deeper circular relations that are understood through interaction and experience set the stage for this thesis and the active role the design experiments play in constructing participatory environments (Figure 23.5).

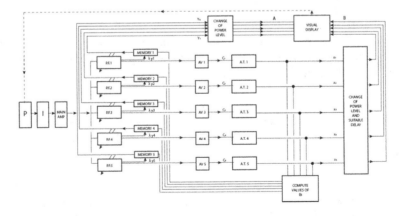

Figure 23.5 Gordon Pask's diagram illustrating his Musicolour Logic.
Source: Minimaforms

Participants as Performers

Spatial environments as ecologies of interaction serve as a stimulus for participation. Participatory models offer dynamic and intuitive relationships between the environment, observers and performers within the system. It is through this participatory model for interaction that one sees that architecture can serve as a host to enable scenario-based exchanges that amplify space as an interface for communication. This communication in principle can be human or non-human. The architecture argued for is active, anticipatory and adaptive through continuous exchanges that are real-time and behavior-based. Architecture is understood to have agency; to sense, to learn, to stimulate, to understand and to get bored.

Through direct experience participants evolve their novel relations into enquiry and constructive understanding. This dialogue between things that emerges through curiosity and play can exhibit collective tendencies that can be experienced as intelligent. Intelligence Glanville (2001) reminds us "is experienced by us." He continues,

> from individual instances we have observed: that is, we observe, we generalize (find pattern) and we create the concept of intelligence, which we then both modify as we go, and allow to determine whether various acts and behaviors we observe are intelligent or not.
>
> *(p. 2)*

Figure 23.6 Minimaforms (Theodore and Stephen Spyropoulos), Petting Zoo, FRAC Centre, Orleans, France, 2011-current.
Source: Minimaforms

The move towards a spatial and conversational model of interaction pursues a definition of an intelligent architecture in the spirit that Glanville has defined. "Intelligence depends on the interface of our interaction" (p. 8). The challenge posed is to construct environments that are shared between participants and allow for complex interactions to arise through human agency and the observed agency of these interactions. The concept of intelligence explored within this chapter is not attributed to things as a property but something arising between things, a product of interface and interaction.

This was summarized by Pask (1970) when he stated,

> When learning to control or to solve problems man necessarily conceptualizes and abstracts. Because of this, the human environment is interpreted at various levels in a hierarchy of abstraction. These propensities are at the root of curiosity and assimilation of knowledge. They impel man to explore, discover and explain his inanimate surroundings. Addressed to the social environment of other men, they lead him into social communication, conversation and other modes of partially co-operative interaction.
>
> (p. 76)

Behaviour as Performance: Constructing Frameworks to Experiment

Over the last decade cybernetics as a discourse and practice has reemerged within our contemporary technological landscape. Today cybernetics-related issues are discussed in mainstream media with accelerated forms of automation, artificial intelligence, advanced manufacturing and adaptive systems impacting society. Many of the early conversations and thought experiments are being rediscovered precisely for their problematizing of similar conditions that we see present today. Beyond design this has included cultural and political theorists, architectural historians and technologists who see cybernetics from one of two prevailing perspectives. The first perspective sees cybernetics as a science that has been evolving into new territories. Some have described this as a possible third order while shaping specialized discourses of today such as the study of artificial intelligence, robotics and complexity theory. This group would include cyberneticists such as Glanville and Ascott whose interests examine cybernetics' qualities in design, education, intelligence and interface. Glanville believed that it remained an all-pervasive system of relations that has become ubiquitous. For cybernetics to be "reborn" he, like other cyberneticists, looks to design and art with the recognition that the act of design was circular and cybernetic embodying conversational forms of interaction.

In considering their positions with respect to design, behavior and space, it is important to take a moment and reiterate the seminal relationships that observers can have with the world and the methods that can be deployed to understand them. This understanding today means something particular. Glanville makes a correlation with our current cultural landscape in a profound manner as he relates second-order cybernetics to the primary framework of communication and exchange, the Internet. This example highlights the capacity to construct complex relationships in a conceptual apparatus that allows for this complexity to be scaled. The power of second-order cybernetic perspectives afforded experiments within this thesis to explore human and machine interactions at multiple scales and with varying orders of magnitude. The capacity to move beyond styles or orthodox methods was liberating for a designer to understand that the sensibility of the relations between the things themselves are evolving and changing, as are the internal relations within themselves. The role of design then was to capture these relations momentarily, allowing the observer to situate themselves relative to this understanding within other relations. These evolving relationships embody this concept of the dance that von Forester and Glanville described as a metaphor for second-order cybernetics.

The Cybernetics of Cybernetics

Figure 23.7 Minimaforms (Theodore and Stephen Spyropoulos), Emotive City, Nesta Innovation Department Commission, London, England, 2015.
Source: Minimaforms

Another key cybernetic concept was that of the Black Box, a conceptual tool that allows observes to construct thought experiments without fully understanding the world within which the black box has been situated.

Ashby reminds us in *An Introduction to Cybernetics* of the cybernetic concept of the black box. He says, "What is being suggested now is not that black boxes behave somewhat like real objects but that real objects are in fact all black boxes, and that we have in fact been operating with black boxes all our lives" (p. 110). This spirited relationship with the world evolves the revolutionary discourses of second-order thinking to expand and examine forms of practice as participation. It should come to no surprise that many of the cyberneticists operating from this perspective are involved in education and have influenced this cybernetic community and the field of contemporary art, architecture and technological practices that have come from this position.

The second perspective, it can be argued, takes a critical approach towards cybernetic thinking from a historical perspective of its implementation and speculation. Architectural historian and theorist Felicity Scott (2010) reminds us of many of the challenges of cybernetics that rendered it to many a "dead" science. Scott points out historically to narratives that were overly optimistic in their technological futures. She uses as an example the architectural historian and theoretician Reyner Banham, who published *Theory and Design in the First Machine Age* (1960). She writes that

> While mega-structures and other experimental practices of the 1960s embraced the period's libertarian sentiments and the 'belief in the permissive and the open-ended, in the future 'alternative scenarios,' [*sic*] it had soon become apparent (not only to Banham, but also to architects) that the work harboured a paradoxical call to order, an atavistic alliance with modernist dreams of a totalizing environmental control. The urge to impose a simple and architectonic order on the layout of human society and its equipment

was "auto-destructive," Banham concluded; it contained an "inner contradiction that could not be resolved" (p. 1). Publications such as Scott's *Architecture or Techno-utopia*, Heim's *Rise of the Machines: A Cybernetic History* and Pickering's *The Cybernetic Brain: Sketches of Another Future* have served to contextualize some of the crises associated with cybernetic thinking. Beyond the polarity of these positions the thesis operates in-between where complexity and uncertainty become part of the means to conceptualize an evolving conversational dialogue with things.

Through development of project-based experiments, key concepts of behavior, enabling, interfaces and performance are demonstrated through the co-construction of cybernetic machines. This chapter extracts key cybernetic concepts from my PhD in an attempt to offer a behavioural approach for constructing a framework for architecture today (Spyropoulos 2017). In the words of Bateson (2000),

Figure 23.8 Minimaforms (Theodore and Stephen Spyropoulos), Petting Zoo, FRAC Centre, Orleans, France, 2011 to current.

Source: Minimaforms

> It follows, of course, that we must change our whole way of thinking about mental and communicational process. The ordinary analogies ... which people borrow from the hard sciences to provide a conceptual frame upon which they try to build theories about psychology and behaviour ... is non-sense. It is in error.
>
> *(p. 459)*

Glanville (2001) articulates this from his desire to consider a framework for an intelligent architecture. He states,

> The attribution is to the shared behavior (in this space between) to which each contributes. Intelligence is not in the (behavioral) action, or even the consequent reaction, but in the actions/reactions shared between the participants, and takes form as their interactive behavior. Intelligence is shared: recognition of it may be single, or mutual.
>
> *(pp. 12–24)*

Architecture makes demands. To explore architecture today is to see in it the possibility to construct new conceptions of space. Architecture within a performative idiom is durational. Space our medium. In constructing the fundamental relationships of how we live and understand our world we need to examine methods that fundamentally see making and acting in the world as intellectual enquires. How then do we explore and speculate on architecture today? How can we conceptualize our world and see architecture as an interface that enables us and helps us to engage. Architecture is a social act in its creation and in its agency to interface. To consider architecture today we must move from the singular towards a conception of collective participation and co-construction that sees to experiment with space in all of its manifestations. What new architectures will evolve and push design into the future of future present? The answers are in the experiment.

Note

1. The Macy Conferences brought together a diverse group of cross-disciplinary scholars that included mathematician and computing pioneer John von Neumann, founder of cybernetics Norbert Wiener, social scientist Gregory Bateson, cultural anthropologist Margaret Mead, biophysicist Heinz von Foerster, father of information theory Claude Shannon, amongst others. The meetings were foundational in the development of cybernetics and systems theory.

References

Ashby, W. R. (1956). *An Introduction to Cybernetics*. New York: John Wiley & Sons.
Bateson, G. (1977). *Steps to an Ecology of Mind*. New edition. Northvale: Jason Aronson.
Bateson, G. (2000). Form, Substance, and Difference. In: *Steps to an Ecology of Mind: Collected Essays in Anthropology, Psychiatry, Evolution, and Epistemology*, pp. 454–471. New edition. Chicago: University of Chicago Press.
Burnham, J. (1968). *Beyond Modern Sculpture: The Effects of Science and Technology on the Sculpture of this Century*. New York: George Braziller.
Glanville, R. (June 2001). An Intelligent Architecture Convergence. *International Journal of Research into New Media Technologies*. 7: 2.
Glanville R. (2003). Second-Order Cybernetics. In: Parra-Luna F. (Ed.). *Systems Science and Cybernetics, Encyclopedia of Life Support Systems*, n.p. Oxford: EoLSS Publishers. Retrieved from: https://cepa.info/2326.
Hollein, H. (1968). Alles ist Architektur. *Bau: Magazine for Architecture and Town Planning*. Retrieved from: www.ica.org.uk/sites/default/files/Press%20Release%20Everything%20is%20Architecture.pdf.
Johnston, J. (2008). *The Allure of Machinic Life: Cybernetics, Artificial Life, and the New AI*. Harvard: MIT Press.
Kaprow, A. (2003). *Essays on the Blurring of Art and Life*. Expanded edition. Berkeley: University of California Press.
Pask, G. (1969). The Architectural Relevance of Cybernetics. *Architectural Design*, September No 7/6, pp. 494–496. Chichester: John Wiley & Sons.

Pask, G. (1970). A Comment, a Case History and a Plan. In: Reichardt J. Rapp & Carroll. (Eds.). *Cybernetic Serendipity*, reprinted in J. Reichardt (Ed.), *Cybernetics, Art, and Ideas*. London: Studio Vista.

Pickering, A. (1995). *The Mangle of Practice: Time, Agency, and Science*. Chicago: University of Chicago Press.

Pickering, A. (2010). *The Cybernetic Brain: Sketches of Another Future*. Chicago: University of Chicago Press.

Poerksen, B. (2004). *Certainty of Uncertainty: Dialogues Introducing Constructivism*. Exeter: Imprint Academic.

Read, H. (1964). *A Concise History of Modern Sculpture*. New York: Holt, Rinehart & Winston.

Rosenblueth, A., Wiener, N., & Bigelow, J. (1943). Behavior, Purpose and Teleology. *Philosophy of Science*. 10 (1): 21.

Scott, F. D. (2010). *Architecture or Techno-utopia*. Reprint edition. Cambridge, MA: MIT Press.

Spyropoulos, T. (2017). *Constructing Participatory Environments: A Behavioural Model for Design*. Doctoral thesis. London: University College London.

von Foerster, H. (1979). *Cybernetics of Cybernetics*. Biological Computer Laboratory. University of Illinois at Champaign-Urbana.

24
Performative Design Strategies
The Synthesis Process of a Woven Complexity

Pieter de Wilde and Clarice Bleil de Souza

Introduction

The design of buildings that perform well is a challenging task, which combines the careful blending of architectural form-finding with technical considerations of structural behaviour, building science aspects, economic considerations and other requirements. It involves the specification of a product that meets a wide range of performance requirements. At the same time, buildings are complex, and by their nature positioned at a specific location and context. Most buildings are unique, bespoke products with a custom-designed geometry, and consist of many parts and (sub)systems, which broadly can be categorized as building structure, façade, infill and building services. The needs of the client are typically formulated in a design brief or architectural programme that varies from project to project. Mostly client needs are only general statements and need to be developed into more formal technical performance requirements. For instance, a client may ask for an office environment without glare. A technical performance requirement would express the lighting conditions in the office in terms of a Daylight Glare Index (DGI) and stipulate under what sky conditions this DGI needs to be studied; the requirement will also define exactly what level of DGI is still acceptable for this client, where a DGI of 16 is just perceptible, 20 just acceptable, 22 the borderline between comfort and discomfort, 24 uncomfortable and 28 intolerable. Obviously, the definition of such technical performance requirements needs to be based on in-depth expertise in the subject. The design process then needs to create building proposals that meet the requirements; in the specific example this will be the spatial definition of office space, complete with window openings, artificial lighting systems, daylighting and shading systems, and definition of the properties of all surfaces inside the space. Building design thus is a highly unique process which needs to be customized to the specific conditions of each individual case.

In the design stage, there is no actual building yet that can be studied in order to observe or measure performance; therefore, the only way to predict performance is to employ computational tools or to rely on extrapolation of previous experiences of the design team. As many tools relate to specific performance aspects such as thermal, lighting or acoustic performance, approaches have been developed that allow the sharing of information between tools; this ability of tools to share data is named interoperability. An initial framework for sharing data was the use of a common "product model" for the storage of building information, with interfaces to specific performance analysis tools.

Over the years this has grown into a wider, all-encompassing digital approach which is commonly known as building information modelling (BIM). In current practice, BIM tools such as Revit are now the mainstream technology used to define and capture building geometry and properties such as the cost of building elements, material properties and order of construction. However, in the field of building performance prediction, many challenges remain. For instance, while thermal analysis is arguably one of the most developed fields of building performance simulation, there often is a significant discrepancy between predicted performance and measurement results once a building has been constructed and occupied.

Various actors may be involved in a design project, from a single designer/architect to a large design team that involves structural engineers, building science consultants, building services engineers, fire safety experts and others. Design teams may comprise different companies and may be globally dispersed, especially for large and prestigious projects. Within teams, there may be different organisational structures; for instance, Negendahl (2015) discerns between situations where an architect is assisted by an engineer, where architect and engineer are partners, and situations where a hybrid practitioner emerges that blends the disciplines of architecture and engineering.

Architects are still following apprenticeship models when learning about design and in a way digital design tools do not really change this paradigm. Despite being focused on functionality, engineering design processes did get updated in relation to design thinking because of manufacturing processes and mass production demands. On one hand, one can argue that architects do not have to respond to these types of pressure, but on the other hand, the level of requirements imposed in relation to the various aspects of building performance and behaviour cannot be addressed anymore through the use of Renaissance design methods.

While design thinking has been somehow discussed in relation to manufacturing processes through digital fabrication and BIM, the decision-making process related to considerations of the different and interwoven aspects related to building performance still needs further thinking. Functionality was condemned by the post-modernism movement but building technology and the sustainability movement made legislation and client and user requirements evolve in the opposite direction. Designers now have to be reconciled with the fact that they have to produce buildings that work, and in the future even behave according to predictions. Design thinking and design processes need to be prepared to cope with this or they will be subject to embracing engineering design methods or deterministic decision support systems to quantify behaviour taking design control out of the hands of the architects.

This chapter invites designers to reflect on how they work, particularly exploring different types of design decision-making models available, which could be used in the different stages of the design process to better cope with addressing technological and sustainability requirements related to building performance. It critiques and situates the appropriateness of the different types of decision-making methods within the different design stages and highlights gaps to invite the community to further reflect upon.

Building Performance: Definition and Tools

Building performance is a concept that is used by many authors, yet also one that often remains undefined. It has been noted that often "technical articles of research tend to use the term 'performance' but rarely define its meaning" (Rahim, 2005: 179); this tends to apply to the building discipline but also to many other fields that use performance, such as the automotive, engineering, medical and sport sectors.

However, there is a body of work that defines system performance as an attribute that measures how well a system is able to meet intended system functions. Taking this definition further, one may look at building performance in three categories: performance of building as an object/system, performance of building as a construction process, and aesthetic performance. For each of these categories, a number of performance categories may be defined. For buildings as an object, building performance can then be defined as quality, resource saving, workload capacity, timeliness or readiness. Examples in each of these categories would be thermal comfort (quality), efficient use of water (resource saving), number of passengers an airport can process per hour (workload capacity), ensuring heating/cooling schedules meet room use (timeliness) or reaction time of a lift system (readiness). For building as a process, typical categories will be cost, time, quality, safety, waste reduction and customer satisfaction. Building performance in terms of aesthetics is a category that needs further work, but typically relates to attributes such as creativity, interpretation and enchantment (de Wilde, 2018a: 111). The building design process has to cater for all of these dimensions of performance (Figure 24.1).

Building Performance Simulation

A key prerequisite for the design of buildings that perform well is the ability to predict future building performance. Instruments to do this are provided in the form of building performance simulation tools. In principle, these are computer programs that carry out advanced engineering calculations which in turn represent physical processes. These tools emerged in the 1960s and 1970s with the introduction of personal computing, and in response to concerted efforts in the field of building energy efficiency since the first energy crisis. General overviews of the development of the field are provided by Clarke (2001) and Augenbroe (2003); a genealogy of more specific thermal simulation tools is provided by Oh and Haberl (2016). These overviews show that simulation tools have evolved over the years and are often the subject of continuous development rather than step changes. Some of the original engines like TRNSYS are still around today; others like DOE-2 and BLAST have morphed into the EnergyPlus simulation engine. More recent developments focus on the development of "shells" around simulation engines, which make it easier for the tool user to enter geometry details and help modelling efforts through extensive defaults; examples of these are DesignBuilder, IES, OpenStudio and Safaira. More fundamental work looks at the Modelica programming language, and the reuse of building system models on the component level. Overall it can be observed that building simulation tool development is a rather slow process, mostly consisting of gradual improvement rather than step changes, and that the driving force is evolution rather than clean-slate design based on specific software development requirements (de Wilde, 2018b).

The science and application of building performance simulation is advanced and promoted by the International Building Performance Simulation Association (IBPSA). Similarly, the symposium series on Simulation for Architecture and Urban Design (SimAUD), an offshoot of the Society for Modelling and Simulation International, promotes the use of simulation amongst architecture researchers. Some of the other organisations that influence the development and application of simulation are the Chartered Institution of Building Services Engineers (CIBSE) and the Royal Institute of British Architects (RIBA) in the UK, and the American Society of Heating, Refrigerating, and Air-Conditioning Engineers (ASHRAE).

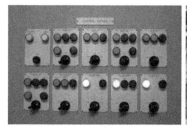

Figure 24.1 Three views of building performance (object, process and aesthetics).

Building Information Modelling and Interoperability

BIM is the process or activity of generating and managing digital representations of buildings, including their geometry and physical and functional characteristics. From a buzzword around ten years ago (Eastman et al., 2011), this has now become a leading principle in the construction industry; in, for instance, the USA, the UK, Singapore, Sweden and Finland the use of BIM is mandatory for all public sector projects. The underlying technology has grown from early efforts in building product models and building process models, where the product models describe the properties of the building as an object, whereas the process models describe the activities that are carried out with those objects. BIM fuses product and process models together in a joined-up digital environment. Early seminal work on this area is Eastman (1999). Typically, one will employ different applications within a design process, thus leading to a need for data exchange between these applications; the capability to do this is named *interoperability*.

Typical BIM authoring software (tools that support the digital design of buildings) are Autodesk Revit, Graphisoft ArchiCAD and Bentley Architecture. The data exchange with building simulation software, mostly building energy modelling or BEM tools, typically takes place via an intermediate format named gbXML. The name gbXML stands for *green building XML* and this is an industry-supported schema for sharing building information.

While BIM is clearly changing the way industry works, with many tasks now carried out in a digital environment, BIM also is subject to an element of hype. Ideas like intelligent BIM, where there is seamless collaboration between actors and tools within one environment, have significant hurdles to overcome and existing systems fall short of being able to deliver these ideas in practice, especially where building performance analysis is at stake.

In other disciplines, such as economics, the "performativity thesis" is the concept that models and theory cannot only explain reality, but that their use also may shape and form that reality (Santos and Rodrigues, 2009; Vosselman, 2014). Translated to buildings, *performative building design* then becomes a building design process where one expects that the focus on building performance and the use of building simulation tools will lead to buildings that perform better. This idea of performative building design has a long tradition in the world of building research; see, for instance, Markus et al. (1972) or Clarke (2001). However, the collection of hard evidence for the impact of building performance theory and tools on resulting building performance is extremely difficult, as this would require the comparison of measured building performance data from a set of buildings designed with such theory and tools with similar data from a control group that did not have this intervention. While this type of data is very hard to obtain in the first place, further complexity arises from the potential noise in such an experiment: improvements attributed to theory and tools may also stem from other influences, such as financial incentives, building regulations or attitudinal shifts amongst various actors.

Performative Design

There is a significant number of efforts that aim to contribute to performative building design. These efforts are mostly embedded in a wide range of approaches such as green building design, eco-house design and sustainable buildings, although many of these remain relatively open-ended. Other approaches that are more specific on the role of performance, tools and building science knowledge are Passivhaus design (Feist, 1996), performance-based building (Bakens et al., 2005; Jusuja, 2005), performance-based building design (Becker, 2008) and high-performance building design as per ASHRAE certification. Another work emphasizes the need to consider a wide range of performance aspects, typically by bringing together actors with different contributing expertise early in the design process; this is often advocated under the term "integral" or "integrated design"; see, for instance, Glicksman (2008) or Pelken et al. (2013).

A wider discussion of design for performance takes place in the adjacent fields of product and systems engineering (Gilb, 2005; INCOSE, 2015). However, translation of ideas and concepts of those areas to that of building design needs extreme care: there are fundamental differences between these other fields and buildings in terms of product series, system longevity, upgrade/renovation, product transportability and fabrication conditions. Some developments such as the use of robots in construction (Bock, 2015) or automated additive manufacturing (Labonnote et al., 2016) may be reducing some of these differences but change of the construction industry typically is a slow process.

In performative building design strategies, a crucial issue is the framing of the interaction between design process with theory and tools (Bleil de Souza, 2013; de Wilde, 2018a). There are three main interpretations of this framing:

1. The view that design takes place by a number of design experiments (exploration of different design options) with special characteristics distinct from scientific experiments (systematic variation of independent parameters)
2. The view that design is essentially a process of finding solutions to design problems
3. The view that design can be seen as a series of decisions which depend on the type of problem and the knowledge of the decision maker

Interestingly, this issue seems to be under-explored by most of the existing literature on performance-based building design (from aesthetic to building physics), with most work emphasizing a range of performance aspects that need to be considered and then moving straight into claims about design support and optimization. As a consequence, the literature on the subject seems rather biased towards normative decision making for design, where authors describe how design ought to take place. This fits well with the knowledge base on decision making (Jordaan, 2005) and approaches such that of Utility Theory and Multi-Criteria Decision Making. In contrast, there is a very limited literature on design observations, with the work of Struck et al. (2009), Harries et al. (2013) or Zapata-Lancaster and Tweed (2016) being some of the exceptions. There seems to be little reflection on the theory of naturalistic decision making (Klein et al., 1993), which focuses on a series of decisions as made by experts and where context awareness is crucial issue; yet it may be argued that this maps well to what actually happens in building design processes.

Design Experiments

Under this view, each piece of design is treated as a "universe of one" and problem and solution co-evolve through the "conversation" the designer develops with the materials of the situation (Schön, 1983/1991). Designers engage in a process of testing and developing ideas (Coyne and Snodgrass, 1991) through a cycle of move – appreciation – move, either using paper-based sketches or by manipulating form and exploring parametric changes using 3D digital models (Figure 24.2).

"In order to formulate a design problem to be solved, the designer must frame a problematic design situation: set its boundaries, select particular things and relations for attention and impose on the situation a coherence that guides subsequent moves" (Schön, 1988). "To frame a problem, you have to begin with a 'what if' situation to be evaluated" (Schön, 1983/1991). These "What if" situations are actually experiments which according to Schön (1983/1991) can be of three different types:

1. *Exploratory experiments (open-ended "what ifs")*, experiments of an exploratory nature in which actions/moves are undertaken without specific predictions or expectations associated to them but

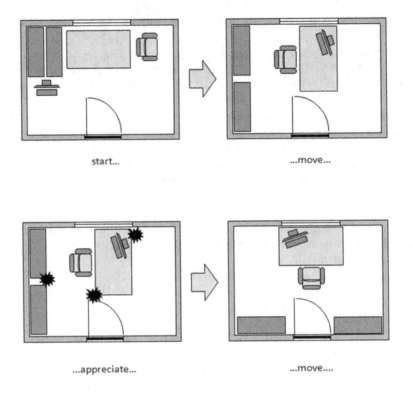

Figure 24.2 Design experiments.

simply used to explore new options in terms of their outcomes. They are important types of experiments for designers to acquire new knowledge, build up repertoire and gain insights.

2. *Move-testing experiments (simplified "what ifs")*, experiments undertaken with an end in mind with consequences judged in terms of achieving or not achieving this end. They are normally used for designers to affirm or negate moves in relation to the type of changes they produce.

Moves that get intended consequences are affirmed, whereas moves that do not get intended consequences are negated. At the same time, the practitioner appreciates the value of the situation, judging if (s)he likes what (s)he gets from the action undertaken in terms of local and global consequences.

(Bleil de Souza and Tucker, 2014)

3. *Hypothesis-testing experiments (quasi-scientific "what ifs")*, experiments used to confirm or disconfirm a hypothesis proposed by designers.

The best alternative is defined based on confirmations of the consequences of a given hypothesis together with predictions derived from alternative hypothesis that conflicted with observations. In hypothesis-testing experiments designers are constantly reframing the problem through a new hypothesis to be tested.

(Bleil de Souza and Tucker, 2014)

However, contrarily to scientific experiments, designers "seek to exert influence in such a way as to confirm not refute their hypothesis" (Schön, 1983/1991).

Notably, design experiments have a particular characteristic: they are always related to "transforming the situation from what it is to something [the designer] likes better" (Schön, 1983/1991). Contrarily to scientific experiments which aim to add to the body of knowledge in a field by producing reliable and reproducible results and therefore provide evidence for technological or knowledge development, design experiments are assessed in terms of how desirable are their outcomes in relation to design intentions as well as how much they conform to or violate implications set up by earlier moves and how these moves fit into the designer's appreciation of the new problem created.

This dictates how the design process proceeds as "the perceived changes produced by earlier moves determine the need for and the direction appropriate to reflection in action" (Schön, 1983/1991). "The process is stopped when changes in the whole are satisfactory or when new features which give the situation new meanings and affect the nature of questions to be explored are discovered" (Bleil de Souza and Tucker, 2014). Objectivity and distance are not mandatory, the results are biased and the progress is defined and controlled by designers while creating a large part of what they are trying to understand.

Design Problems

Heavily based on the works of Simon (1973/1996) and Rittel and Webber (1973), this view proposes design is essentially a process of finding solutions to design problems either through simply pairing problems with solutions (Alexander, Ishikawa and Silverstein, 1977) or through the co-evolution of problem and solution (Cross, 2001) (Figure 24.3).

The design process can be seen as a collection of sub-processes in which the type of problem definition evolves gradually from ill-defined or wicked to well-defined (Cross, 2001, Goldschmidt, 2001; Harfield, 2007; Jones, 1981, to cite a few). To rationalists, the concept-generation stage can be seen as ill-defined as the problem is open to constant redefinition, and can have loose criteria and boundary conditions, and no clear aims, making it impossible to define the means to achieve them.

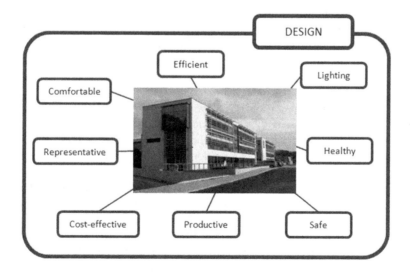

Figure 24.3 Sub-problems within the design process.

A more comprehensive view (Buchanan, 1995; Coyne, 2005; Zimring and Craig, 2001, to cite a few) considers the concept-generation stage as actually "wicked", expanding the concept of ill-defined problem to acknowledge the social forces involved in shaping any kind of problem structure. Contrarily to Simon (1973/1996), who proposes that ill-defined problems can be decomposed into self-contained parts to become well-defined problems, with clear solution criteria and desired states to be achieved through potentially scientific means, wicked problems will "depend on the abilities and priorities of a problem solver not necessarily by a problem given" (Zimring and Craig, 2001) to become well-defined, i.e. they would depend on a designer's decisions about shifting the whole problem framing from constant problem restructuring to only discrete restructuring.

Thinking in terms of generic types of problems is useful because well-defined problems can be rewritten consciously into known structures, are likely to have specific constraints and can be set to follow predefined rules. They can be mapped into a familiar structure, previously defined by the design community, and the problem-solving activity is subsumed to a search through a solution space with clearly defined boundaries. The problem structure tends not to be questioned and the whole design activity becomes mainly a matter of optimization. For wicked problems, the interpretation of the problem is up to the designer to handle, which implies the discovery of a strategy to invent an appropriate problem structure to be used when formulating a design hypothesis. The problem space is explored from a particular perspective "in order to frame the problem in a way that stimulates and pre-structures the emergence of design concepts" (Cross, 2004). Designers impose their views, positions and preferences in seeing the brief and in constructing the problems to be solved, defining and limiting the solution possibilities available to them (Harfield, 2007).

> Designers formulate a partial structuring of the problem space and then transfer that partial structure into the solution space, and so develop both problem and solution in parallel [...] or [they] first identify a partial structure in the solution space, such as a preferred shape or form, and then use that to structure the problem space.
>
> *(Kruger and Cross, 2006)*

Thus, the conceptual design stage can be seen a stage in which problem and solution tend to co-evolve, i.e. the designer tries to understand the problem by attempting to solve it and solves the problem by attempting to understand it (Cross, 2001), whereas the detailed design stage can be seen as well defined, meaning goals can be clearly set together with an action plan to achieve them.

Design Decision-Making

The predominant work in this view is concerned with normative theory which prescribes how design ought to take place, and how to select the best solution from a set; see, for instance, Becker (2008). The design process emphasizes another avenue of thought stemming from the work of Simon (1973/1996: 118): that where design is in essence a process of making "rational choices among given alternatives". This view goes back to the early theory of performative building design, with Markus et al. (1972) already dedicating a full chapter of their seminal book to "design as a special kind of decision making" (pp. 13–28). The concept of rational decision making is well-established in engineering and supported by mathematics (Hazelrigg, 2012). It leads to a significant attention on the use of optimization techniques as exemplified by Machairas et al. (2014) or Nguyen et al. (2014). Yet Simon (1973/1996: 27) already noted that one may opt to decide on an alternative that is "good enough" rather than "best" and introduced the verb "satisficing" to indicate this type of decision making. The aforementioned theory of naturalistic decision making again emphasizes decisions but takes a longitudinal view where there are chains of decisions rather than single choices, and where expertise and situational awareness play important roles (Klein, 1993).

The way decisions are made in itself is the subject of debate. Kahnman (2011) distinguishes between two systems, and intuitive and an analytical one, which help humans making decisions in different contexts. Hammond (1988) contends that these two systems are ends of a continuous system in which analysis and intuition alternate in cycles depending on changes to task characteristics over time. In his earlier work, Hammond (1980, 1987; see also Hammond, 2015) relates the decision-making process to the type of problem interwoven with the knowledge of the decision maker. Dynamic decision making is examined based on a theory of task characteristics and task conditions in which the following well-established types of judgement and cognitive activities are applied (Figure 24.4):

- Intuition vs. analysis, opposite types of judgement
- Patterns and functional relationship seeking, cognitive activities not mutually exclusive

When exploring task conditions in relation to the type of cognitive activity they induce, Hammond (1988) notes that pattern seeking is predominantly used with information prone to high degrees of conceptual organisation requiring coherent explanations. Patterns are commonly associated with visual image formation, and pattern seeking implies data matching with a template acquired by training and/or experience. Functional relationship seeking is predominantly used with information which requires description and prediction, with no easy formation of visual images associated to them. Seeking also implies data matching with a template acquired through training and/or experience.

Both cognitive activities can match arbitrary, non-arbitrary or both types of templates. Arbitrary templates are mainly empirical (empirical patterns or empirically justified functional relations), normally lacking theoretical basis. Non-arbitrary templates are usually derived from theory, forming a coherent whole with elements inter-related by causal explanations (patterns) or containing rules which fit within a network of laws not necessarily empirically justified (functional relationships). Templates which are both (arbitrary and non-arbitrary), theoretically and empirically justified are normally considered the ones providing the soundest basis for decision making.

Interestingly, Hammond notices that seeking patterns and functional relations can be pursued either through intuition or analysis, depending on a set of 11 task characteristics mainly related to task cues (number, metrics, distribution, redundancy and display) and their relationships in the model, the nature of the task (prone to decomposition or not, prone to imposition of organising principle or not, degree of uncertainty) and the time period allowed for the task to be completed. Most of task characteristics listed in this model do resemble Simon's classification of well-defined vs. ill-defined problems. However, Simon missed details in relation to availability or not of organising principles, display of cues and time

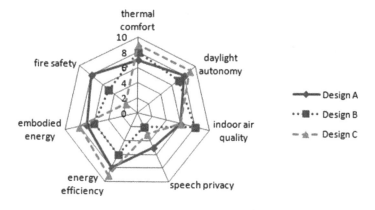

Figure 24.4 Design decisions.

available for the task to be completed; details which are well taken on board by Schön in his model of the practitioner conversing with the materials of the situation.

Hammond finishes his report on the use of judgement and decision making in dynamic tasks by relating intuition and analysis with a set of properties which have to do not only with the task but also with the decision maker's knowledge and understanding of the situation. He connects analysis with expert knowledge, cognitive control, awareness and a high level of confidence in the method, and intuition with commonsense knowledge, low cognitive control and low confidence in the method but high confidence in the answer.

> Intuition […] is generally considered to be an unconscious, implicit, automatic, holistic, fast process, with great capacity, requiring little cognitive effort. By contrast, analysis […] is generally characterised as conscious, explicit, controlled, deliberative, slow process that has limited capacity and is cognitively demanding […] the key wisdom lies in being able to match modes of cognition to properties of the task.
>
> (Dhami and Mumpower, 2018)

Challenges and Complexity

Exploring the "fit" between the three main views of the design process and existing building performance simulation tools and digital support environments, we can make the following observations:

Computational Support for Doing Design Experiments

Digital representations of buildings are an excellent tool for undertaking design experiments once the building is already defined. They allow designers to explore and manipulate building representations in a simulated environment and study their consequences without having to invest in changes to an actual building, i.e. consequences of design experiments for building performance can be predicted. However, there is one important caveat: the analysis tools need to have the capacity to simulate the relevant systems and changes. This is a non-trivial issue; most models are simplifications of reality within one or two domains (e.g. thermal reality, lighting reality), meaning changes outside the simulated domain will not show an effect as manipulations may introduce systems or features that the analysis tool cannot handle, either because these tools normally have a series of limitations or because the changes produce effects outside the domain they deal with. Think of adding triangular geometries to a tool that is designed to only handle rectangular geometries or adding acoustic panels to thermal simulations – the thermal effect will be assessed but the acoustic one will not.

Hypothesis-testing is arguably one of the main drivers for commercial building performance analysis; this is essential for ensuring that a design meets performance standards as mandated by building regulations or required to get certain certification levels in schemes like LEED and BREEAM. However, similar caveats arise: hypothesis-testing will be limited by the domain being investigated and the assumptions and capabilities that are inherent in the analysis tool that is being used.

Computational Support for Solving Design Problems

The notion of problem solving is more challenging in terms of computational support. Tools cannot cope with wicked or ill-defined problems as they are normally domain-specific and rely on a series of input parameters specified by designers, so rules and equations can be applied to compute the effect of changes. The essence of simulation tools is based on modelling already-well-defined problems, decomposed by the user into a series of known domain-specific templates that can be solved by using existing programmable solutions and then recombined into a large system to assess its response to a series of domain-specific criteria. Tools like TRNSYS and EnergyPlus include predefined models for a series of these templates which can be toggled on or off according to user needs. However, these predefined models severely limit the solution space. An alternative is the use of Modelica to combine templates, with full access to model equations and interlinkage, imposing higher levels of computer literacy on the users.

The idea of well-defined problems can also be extended to parametric design, where the computer generates design solutions by running many permutations of design parameters, capitalizing on the ability of the computer to handle large amounts of data; however, such approaches are limited to the predefined parameter range and hence "think inside the box", even though they may outperform human creativity. To a certain extent, this idea also fits with BIM when seen as strictly a "product modelling". If seen as a "process modelling", BIM can potentially open up other avenues where software may indeed support "out of the box" thinking and where the ability of computers to handle countless building alternatives in parallel may yield surprising results.

Computational Support to Design Decision Making

Simulation tools fit well with analytical judgement and are suitable to be applied to tasks after functional relations to assess performance are identified. They provide lists of domain-specific templates for either theoretically and/or empirically justified relationships (e.g. fluid flow, thermodynamics) bringing computational support to expert knowledge through well-accepted methods promoting controlled environments for domain-specific experiments to be undertaken. By contrast, they are normally unsuitable to intuitive judgement, lacking "the big picture" by being domain-specific, forcing the explicit declaration of variables and demanding high cognitive effort to be operated.

However, this should not exclude them from assisting in pattern seeking, an under-explored field which could bring benefits to certain domains as well as to non-expert users. Simple algorithms for template matching could be embedded in simulation tools to support pattern seeking in performance queries and performance assessment (Bleil de Souza and Tucker, 2015). Machine learning techniques could be used to implement knowledge management schemes for design decision making by aiding designers to abstract real problems into domain-specific templates facilitating modelling activities, supporting simulation settings and the application of analysis processes to assess performance as well as the understanding of limitation and uncertainties associated with results, facilitating knowledge transfer and knowledge sharing (Tucker and Bleil de Souza, 2016).

Conclusions

Considering that none of the interpretations of framing interactions between the design process with theories and tools are mutually exclusive, this opens a wider discussion in terms of the roles of analysis and creativity in design.

Performative design requires both creativity and analysis. Many efforts in the field fail to span the wide area that needs addressing, and take very simplified views of that is needed on the other side, ignoring some of the deep complexity that needs to be taken into account:

- Architects who do not want to do analysis, architects who cannot do analysis because they do not have enough knowledge, architects who think relying on consultants is enough, architects who do want to do analysis, architects who are full of intentions but cannot at all transform their ideas into practice, etc.
- Engineers who focus on analysis and optimization, investing a lot of time and energy to explore a specific problem/issue while the overall design process may move on and render all efforts redundant, and who may show a lack of creativity and tendency to stick with known solutions

However, in designing buildings that meet the performance requirements of the client, both creativity and analysis are needed. This limits the prospects of cookbook recipes that fail to allow for innovation and iteration. The need to combine creativity and analysis leads to a need for deep subject knowledge in areas such as building science; without mastering of the basics this is hard to implement. Unfortunately, the typical design curriculum and the amount of technical knowledge that it contains falls short of what is needed. At the same time engineering is overly based on scientific analysis, and needs more constructivist teaching, teaching of using fundamentals in design, and student engagement with experimentation in loose and creative ways.

Existing analysis tools are typically not designed to support building design; they are suitable for checking whether designs meet regulatory targets but should be redeveloped to allow designers to learn and experiment. Data transfer as inherent in interoperability approached and deeply embedded in current BIM technology is useful but does not solve deeper issues that are related to the role that tools play in design. Schön's experiments may be a good starting point for revisiting the tools used in the industry. These experiments are powerful generic descriptors for how decisions are made regardless of a decision-making classification system; they encompass normative as well as naturalistic decision-making processes all in one in terms of the rationale and types of actions proposed.

References

Augenbroe, G., 2003. Trends in building simulation. In: A. Malkawi and G. Augenbroe (eds), *Advanced building simulation*, pp. 4–24. New York: Spon Press.
Alexander, C., S. Ishikawa and M. Silverstein, 1977. *A pattern language: towns, buildings, construction*. Oxford: Oxford University Press.
Bakens, W., G. Foliente and M. Jasuja, 2005. Engaging stakeholders in performance-based building: lessons from the Performance-Based Building (PeBBu) Network. *Building Research & Information*, 33 (2), 149–158.
Becker, R., 2008. Fundamentals of performance-based building design. *Building Simulation*, 1 (4), 356–371.
Bleil de Souza, C., 2013. Studies into the use of building thermal physics to inform design decision making. *Automation in Construction*, 30, 81–93.
Bleil de Souza, C., and S. Tucker, 2014. Thermal simulation software outputs: a framework to produce meaningful information for design decision-making. *Journal of Building Performance Simulation*, 8 (2), 57–78.
Bleil de Souza, C., and S. Tucker, 2015. Thermal simulation software outputs: a conceptual data model of information presentation for building design decision making. *Journal of Building Performance Simulation*, 9 (3), 227–254.
Bock, T., 2015. The future of construction automation: technological disruption and the upcoming ubiquity of robotics. *Automation in Construction*, 59, 113–121.
Buchanan, R., 1995. Wicked problems in design thinking. In: V. Margolin and R. Buchanan (eds), *The idea of design: a design issues reader*, pp. 3–20. Cambridge, MA: MIT Press.
Clarke, J., 2001. *Energy simulation in building design*, 2nd ed. Oxford: Butterworth-Heinemann.
Coyne, R., 2005. Wicked problems revisited. *Design Studies*, 26 (1), 5–17.
Coyne, R.D, and A. Snodgrass, 1991. Is designing mysterious? Challenging the dual knowledge thesis. *Design Studies*, 12 (3), 124–131.
Cross, N., 2001. Designerly ways of knowing: design discipline versus design science. *Design Issues*, 17 (3), 49–55.
Cross, N., 2004. Expertise in design: an overview. *Design Studies*, 25 (5), 427–441.
de Wilde, P., 2018a. *Building performance analysis*. Chichester: Wiley Blackwell.
de Wilde, P., 2018b. Intelligent computing for building performance analysis. In: I. Smith and B. Domer (eds), *Lecture notes in computer science: advanced computing strategies for engineering*, pp. 457–471. Cham: Springer.
Dhami, M., and J. Mumpower, 2018. Kenneth R. Hammond's contributions to the study of judgment and decision making. *Judgment and Decision Making*, 13 (1), 1–22.
Eastman, C., 1999. *Building product models: computer environments supporting design and construction*. Boca Raton: CRC Press.
Eastman, C., P. Teicholz, R. Sacks and K. Liston, 2011. *BIM Handbook: a guide to building information modelling*. Hoboken: Wiley.
Feist, W., 1996. *Grundlagen der Gestaltung von Passivhäusern*. Darmstadt: Verlag Das Beispiel.
Gilb, T., 2005. *Competitive engineering: a handbook for systems engineering, requirements engineering, and software engineering using planguage*. Oxford: Butterworth-Heinemann.
Glicksman, L., 2008. Energy efficiency in the built environment. *Physics Today*, 61 (7), 35–40.
Goldschmidt, G., 2001. Visual analogy: a strategy for design reasoning and learning. In: C. Eastman, M. McCracken and W. Newstetter (eds), *Design knowing and learning: cognition in design education*, pp. 199–219. New York: Elsevier.

Hammond, K., 1988. Judgement and decision making in dynamic tasks. *Information and Decision Technologies*, 14, 3–14.

Hammond, K., 2015. Causality vs generality: judgement and decision making struggles to become a scientific discipline. *Journal of Applied Research in Memory and Cognition*, 4, 176–179.

Hammond, K., R. Hamm, J. Grassia and T. Pearson, 1987. Direct comparison of the efficacy of intuitive and analytical cognition in expert judgement. *IEEE Transactions on Systems, Man and Cybernetics SMC*, 12 (5), 753–770.

Hammond, K., G. McClelland and J. Mumpower, 1980. *Human judgement and decision making: theories, methods and procedures*. New York: Praeger.

Harfield, S. (2007). On design "problematization": theorising differences in designed outcomes. *Design Studies*, 28 (2), 159–173.

Harries, A., G. Brunelli and I. Rizos, 2013. London 2012 Velodrome: integrating advanced simulation into the design process. *Journal of Building Performance Simulation*, 6 (6), 401–419.

Hazelrigg, G.A., 2012. *Fundamentals of decision making: for engineering design and systems engineering*. Available from www.engineeringdecisionmaking.com/.

INCOSE, 2015. *Systems engineering handbook: a guide for system life cycle processes and activities*. San Diego: Wiley.

Jasuja, M. (ed), 2005. *PeBBU final report: Performance-based building thematic network 2001–2005*. Rotterdam: CIB.

Jones, J.C., 1981. *Design methods*. Chichester: John Wiley & Sons.

Jordaan, I., 2005. *Decisions under uncertainty: probabilistic analysis for engineering decisions*. Cambridge: Cambridge University Press.

Kahnman, D., 2011. *Thinking, fast and slow*. London: Penguin Books.

Klein, G., J. Orasanu, R. Calderwood and C. Zsambok (eds), 1993. *Decision making in action: models and methods*. Norwood: Ablex.

Kruger, C., and N. Cross, 2006. Solution-driven versus problem-driven design: strategies and outcomes. *Design Studies*, 27 (5), 527–548.

Labonnote, N., A. Rønnquist, B. Manum and P. Rüther, 2016. Additive construction: state-of-the-art, challenges and opportunities. *Automation in Construction*, 72, 347–366.

Machairas, V., A. Tsangrassoulis and K. Axarli, 2014. Algorithms for optimization of building design: a review. *Renewable and Sustainable Energy Reviews*, 31, 101–112.

Markus, T., P. Whyman, J. Morgan, D. Whitton, T. Maver, D. Canter and J. Fleming, 1972. *Building performance*. London: Applied Science Publishers.

Negendahl, K., 2015. Building performance in the early design stage: an introduction to integrated dynamic models. *Automation in Construction*, 54, 39–53.

Nguyen, A., S. Reiter and P. Rigo, 2014. A review on simulation-based optimization methods applied to building performance analysis. *Applied Energy*, 113, 1043–1058.

Oh, S., and J. Haberl, 2016. Origins of analysis methods used to design high-performance commercial buildings: whole-building energy simulation. *Science and Technology for the Built Environment*, 22 (1), 118–137.

Pelken, P., J. Zhang, Y. Chen, D. Rice, Z. Meng, S. Semahegn, L. Gu, H. Henderson, W. Fing and F. Ling, 2013. Virtual Design Studio: Part 1 – interdisciplinary design processes. *Building Simulation*, 6 (3), 235–251.

Rahim, A., 2005. Performativity: beyond efficiency and optimization in architecture. In: B. Kolarevic and A. Malkawi (eds), *Performative architecture: beyond instrumentality*, pp. 177–192. New York: Spon Press.

Rittel, H., and M. Webber, 1973. Dilemmas in a general theory of planning. *Policy Science*, 4 (2), 155–169.

Santos, A., and J. Rodrigues, 2009. Economics as social engineering? Questioning the performativity thesis. *Cambridge Journal of Economics*, 33, 985–1000.

Schön, D., 1983/1991. *The reflective practitioner: how professionals think in action*. New York: Basic Books.

Schön, D.A., 1988. Designing: rules, types and worlds. *Design Studies*, 9 (3), 181–190.

Simon, H.A., 1973/1996. *The sciences of the artificial*, 3rd ed. Cambridge, MA: MIT Press.

Struck, C., P. de Wilde, C. Hopfe and J. Hensen, 2009. An investigation of the option space in conceptual building design for advanced building simulation. *Advanced Engineering Informatics*, 23 (4), 386–395.

Tucker, S., and C. Bleil de Souza, 2016. Thermal simulation outputs: exploring the concept of patterns in design decision-making. *Journal of Building Performance Simulation*, 9 (1), 30–49.

Vosselman, E., 2014. The "performativity thesis" and its critics: towards a relational ontology of management accounting. *Accounting and Business Research*, 44 (2), 181–203.

Zapata-Lancaster, G., and C. Tweed, 2016. Tools for low-energy building design: an exploratory study of the design process in action. *Architectural Engineering and Design Management*, 12 (4), 279–295.

Zimring, C., and D.L. Craig, 2001. Defining design between domains: an argument for design research á la carte. In: C. Eastman, M. McCracken and W. Newstetter (eds), *Design knowing and learning: cognition in design education*, pp. 125–146. New York: Elsevier.

25

Design Sensibilities: Intangible and Qualitative Design Factors in Performative Design

Enactive Experience in the (Neuro)science of Form

Kristine Mun

What emanates from the body and what emanates from architectural surrounds intermixes.
(*Madeline Gins and Shusaku Arakawa,*
Architectural Body, *2002)*

Introduction

When we think about the term "intangible" it immediately brings to mind ephemeral qualities such as air and light, something we cannot "touch" or "grab" but is mostly "felt". It is this *felt* sense that can be understood as the performative measure of design by how people feel in the space they inhabit. We perceive our world through the senses afforded in our body and all its organs, most importantly the brain. According to Arakawa Gins, as alluded to in the quote above, our body as a whole sensory-motor mechanism is a system responsible for how we perceive, interpret and are affected by our environment. Research in neuroscience shows that while we give primacy to vision as the dominant way to gain information around us, the subtler way this is occurring is through the body, and in particular, through movement. This chapter discusses how sense and sense-perception are actuated by and created in *movement* and most importantly that *perception comes from action*. If one considers the experience of the user obtained through the felt sense, the performativity dimension could then be heightened when we incite movement as an intentional factor in architecture. To do this, we turn to *form* as the vehicle that motivates movement and structures the intangible qualities of experience that are emotive and are felt by raising a sense of delight, pleasure, exhilaration, tranquility, contemplation and many other descriptions of feelings. When action and perception are understood as experience through movement, the terrestrial ground is *affective*. Meaning, *Experience Follows Form*. The triadic formation of *action–percept–affect* that produces experience is described here through the works of Arakawa Gins, NOX/Lars Spuybroek and principles of perception discussed in the field of neuroscience.

Body + Architecture, an Integrated Whole

Architecture is a discipline of many layers of discourse in histories, theories and cultures of human behavior, cognition and actions that provide meaningful and intentional procedures to produce a *form*. Although through history this term has been debated, argued, promoted and even demoted, we can conclude that all *forms* produce an affect when our bodies are in engagement with them. We often take into account the physical dimensions of the human body and bodies (e.g. load, height) when designing spaces. However, the standards of the physical limits of the body only describe a fraction of the real dimensions that the body affords in its relationship to architecture and the built form. The information that is explicitly left out is the interiority of the body, which relates to our feelings, cognition and other natures of being human that produce comfort, motivation and habitation. Should this information be part of the *Standards* of architecture that we need to consider for performativity and comfort? One could argue that such information in this age of great scientific advancements in the twenty-first century may be the imperative difference that ultimately puts human at the center of producing architecture.

One of the most unique visionary artists/architects of the twentieth century depicting our body as an extraordinary correlate of architecture was Shusaku Arakawa (b. 1936) and Madeline Gins (b. 1941): a Japanese artist who was a protégé of Duchamp, and a visionary American poet. Starting with radical expressions of art in the 1960s, they soon turned to architecture as a means of expressing their formidable philosophy on human nature. Their profound radicalizations of architectural elements, compositions, angles and forms were agents for not only defining ourselves but re-imagining ourselves in the experiential dimension of perception. To them, perception was embedded in body movement.

Their partnership and work are exemplary as an inter- and trans-disciplinary approach towards architectural procedures and the production of meaning. Their approach encompassed ideas and thoughts from neuroscience, cognitive science, developmental biology, biophysics, consciousness, experimental psychology, autopoiesis and dynamic systems theory, as well as theories in aesthetic experience, affectivity, performativity and the philosophies of Deleuze and Heidegger (Jondi, 2013). Arakawa strongly felt that to be an artist one must first be a scientist and to know what it really means to be human, that is, to know what this body is about and how it operates to live (Yamaoka, 2012). The most important aspect to consider in all this is that for Arakawa Gins, the "all-encompassing" theories and philosophies combined produce the necessary means to create the condition to observe the "transformation of embodied and distributed cognition" (Jondi, 2013).

Many of their unbuilt works in the form of illustrations, paintings and computer renderings fuel ideas about how architecture and the built environment influence the lives of citizens and, in a way, life itself. Arakawa Gins "launch a complex re-arrangement of knowledge that is capable of taking in technological advances that have marked our new century. [...] Their revisionist re-definition of man in this post-human(istic) state is tantamount to launching a scientific revolution, if not a revolution *tout court*" (Rabaté, 2003). *Sensorium City*, their first-prize entry for the Tokyo Bay competition in 1994, depicting a large-scale utopian park and living quarters, presents layers of artificial terrains that bring complex orders of movement through variegated field of forms. The confluence of parks, residences and other potential programming comes from the layer complexities of forms that produce "life events" on one terrestrial ground.

In that same year, the Nagi Museum of Contemporary Art commissioned their first permanent architectural work, entitled *Ubiquitous Site · Nagi's Ryoanji · Architectural Body* (Figure 25.1). Here, Arakawa Gins describe how this space can be embodied:

Figure 25.1 Ubiquitous Site · Nagi's Ryoanji · Architectural Body 1994, Estate of Madeline Gins. Reproduced with permission of the Estate of Madeline Gins. Photo courtesy: Nagi, MOCA

the small entrance room, the stairway and the cylindrical room present an exercise in perception and physical experience. The balance between self-consciousness and the perception of one's body is broken down, the 'axis' shifts, consciousness leans out, is 'doubled' and 'something' emerges. This 'something' existed in the perceptions of a newborn child. We have forgotten it in growing up.

(Reversible Destiny Foundation, n.d.)

Their most well-known series of projects, under the name *Reversible Destiny* (Figure 25.3), sends a provocative message that "death is immoral" and that we can reverse our destiny. One clearly cannot take this literally, but the message is that if we as artists/architects are serious about the role of producing "life conditions" we must re-examine our understanding of it. Their famous statement "we have decided not to die" is really a statement about learning how to live, and to them, architecture can save lives. Their purposeful play of formal relationships was meant to challenge the body to move through architectural spaces and environments, sometimes in very difficult ways where the users themselves may lose their balance or fall. In fact, the floor itself as a surface is not subjected to the hegemony of a horizontal ground but rather pushes the condition of a floor to wrap around, curve upwards and modulate its surface where bodies must contend with its new condition, such as the interior floors of the *Bioscleave House*, the *Lifespan Expanding Villa* (Figure 25.2). Their intent to drastically shift normative conditions by manipulating a single ground surface into manifolds of surfaces formulates a new nature that supports and sustains life through movement – not to struggle but to be challenged. Arakawa Gins

Design Sensibilities

Figure 25.2 Biocleave House – Lifespan Expanding Villa 2008, Estate of Madeline Gins. Reproduced with permission of the Estate of Madeline Gins. Photo by Dimitris Yeros

promoted the notion that changes in the positioning of the body bring awareness (they use the term "consciousness") and alter one's perception.

David Leatherbarrow explains, "the building is its *effects*, and is known primarily through them, through its actions or performances" (Kolarevic, 2005). Architecture produces an effect in the users by the nature of its form, structure, material and composition of spaces, causing one to move in certain directions, interpret the use of spaces and build a protocol around habit/habitation to necessitate good living. The building's performative qualities, such as atmospheric lighting and ephemeral qualities of materials such as reflection and transparency, are the deliberations of the architect. However, the effect of the form also produces an *affect* in the user that influences their emotions and feelings. In this view, performativity of form that is understood through the sensory-motoric mechanism, the *sensible body*, is an *embodied experience* that is found in the correlation of *action*, *percept* and *affect*. It is important to stress that both effect and affect are critical to the performativity of architecture and that the performative dimension of the user is *felt* through experience.

Intensive Science of the Sensible Body

Qualitative intensities are bound in this triad of *action–percept–affect*. These intensities all around us come as subtle *energies* through the complex system of the body that then registers these *forces* in our body (and brain) and constructs our perception. Interestingly, as Mallgrave points out, "the word 'aesthetics' indeed comes from the Greek word *aisthētikos*, which simply means 'sense perception' or 'to perceive'" (Mallgrave, 2015). Aesthetics then is not merely an image of something but rather, as perception is action, the co-evolution and

Figure 25.3 Site of *Reversible Destiny* (1995), 195,000 sq ft Public Park in Yoro-Park, Gifu Prefecture, Japan 2008, Estate of Madeline Gins.
Reproduced with permission of the Estate of Madeline Gins. Photo by Kunio Miyagawa

co-exchange of action-events between the object and subject. American psychologist William James purports that "pure experience" is the primal stuff which everything is composed of, and his radical empiricism did away with the split between subject/object and fundamentally brought the *real* only as "pure" experience of the unified subject/object (Taylor, 1996). Thus, knowing things comes does not come by way of identifying and classifying terms like a list of meanings in a dictionary, which separates the intrinsic interiority from the thing described; knowing is really only done through experience. Aesthetics as sense-experience are formal registers that accompany our body. Experience and aesthetics depicts an intensive science of the sensible body referencing which I reference here to Manual DeLanda's "reconstruction" (DeLanda, 2005; Protevi, 2003) of Deleuze's principles regarding complexity theory in the procedures of an (architectural) process, mainly addressing the emergence of novel events (formal, aesthetic, or experiential) arising from the networked relationship of information (actual or virtual) coming into form. Let us look at this another way in terms of geometry.

A circle is only a circle in an ideal state. *Round*, however, is a material geometry, a vital geometry as reflected in free abstract lines. A significant idea expanding on these notions of geometry was presented by Edmund Husserl with phenomenological empiricism. In the *Origin of Geometry* Husserl positions geometry as an ideality that transversally cuts through all culture and history. "The ideal mathematical object is Husserl's privileged example; it has already reduced any empiricity to phenomenal sense" (Derrida, 1989). He argues that the "origin of geometry is an inquiry into the sense-history of geometrical truths, into the origin and transmission of geometrical ideal objectives or objects, an inquiry that can only be a sense-investigation" (Derrida, 1989). Distinguishing between fixed, intelligible forms (i.e. a circle) and sensible, perceived forms (i.e. roundness), Husserl says

> that there are nonetheless essences (that are) intermediate ... these are morphological essences. ... Every morphological determination works according to the qualitative gradations of sensible intuition: more or less, smooth surfaces, sides, lines, or more less rough angles and so on ... and that before exactitude emerges, proceeding from the factual, an essential form becomes recognizable through a method of variation. ... By variation, we can obtain inexact but pure morphological types: 'roundness' under which is constructed the geometrical ideality of the circle.
>
> *(Derrida, 1989)*

Upon these notions, geometry does not hold the privileged position of the abstract rule that guides over the material formation, but rather, material organization gives implication to geometry itself. Husserl's sense-investigation is exactly that which occurs before the eidetic forms have been constructed. In other words, in order to conceive the circle, we must understand the round. Roundness is strictly a result of material condition.

One of the most renowned philosophers on aesthetics in the twentieth century is Gilles Deleuze. His scholarly work in cinema was a significant step in the understanding of image tied to movement. To Deleuze, art is an affirmation of the "self-movement" of the communicative characteristics. He believed that the vital issue in painting, art and music is to formulate images that will capture the mind as opposed to reproducing the images (Deleuze, 2003). In his book *The Logic of Sense*, Deleuze creates an ontological unity based on systems, relations and folding as the principle by which objects and subjects appear or are being actualized from a *virtual plane* into reality. This virtual plane, what he calls the "plane of *immanence*", relates to the process of "coming into being" (*becoming*) occurring through individuation. We can consider this similar to the concept of *emergence* – that is, something that self-generates and arises from complex orders of intensive and intangible forces that drive action.

The significance of this emphasizes the performative dimensions of *becoming*, rather than being itself; that is, *process* (and hence action) is the substance of the *thing* itself. The point to focus on here is that the *logic of sense* as perception, affection and material individuation comes together in a single *process of becoming* that is fully situated in a milieu of intensive forces. For Deleuze sense and sensation are in *intensities* and *differences* and it is *intensity* and *difference* themselves that are the key factor for genesis. This intense, central motivating force of emergence cannot be embraced through empirical modes of knowing but instead must be understood through a sense encounter. For instance, heat would be detected upon touch and this is bound with a sort of universal applicability of the senses. "Intensity", Deleuze argues, "is the form of difference in so far as it is the reason of the sensible" (Deleuze and Guattari, 1994).

The Affect of Experience

"There is no structured information on the outside – it becomes only information by forming it through the body, by transforming the body, which is called action" (Varela, 1992).

Deleuze embraced another figure in the philosophy of science from the turn of the twentieth century: Henri Bergson. Bergson brought forth the idea that there is a vital force, *elan vital*, in things that causes them to become. In particular he links cognition and affect, defining affect as "that part or aspect of the inside of our bodies which mix with the image of external bodies" (Bergson, 1990). This is produced by any perception and therefore, for Bergson, "there is no perception without affection" (Bergson, 1990). All human activity produces and is produced by *affect*.

In 1990 Wolfgang Prinz, a cognitive scientist and director of the Max Planck Institute for Human Cognitive and Brain Sciences, first proposed that perception and action are coded in a common representational domain and are therefore linked by shared neural resources. In the event of *observing* an action, the internal mental awareness of the *"approaching state"*, a mental perceptual act, is actually felt in the body as if the body is experiencing the action itself. In neuroscience a system called the "mirror neuron system", discovered in the late 1980s by Giacomo Rizzolatti and his team, explains that mirror neurons play a performative role in our perception when we *observe* the action of another. "Mirror neurons represent a distinctive class of neurons that discharge both when an individual executes a motor act and when he observes another individual performing the same or a similar motor act" (Acharya and Shukla, 2012). A *motor act* is not movement itself but refers to an abstract organization of movements towards an object that becomes the purpose.

Rizzolatti's experiment with a pair of macaque monkeys demonstrated an internal correlation between the representations of perceptual and motor functionalities. When one monkey is observing the action of the other – for example, grabbing an object – the non-active monkey's premotor cortex lit up, in the similar region in the brain of the monkey doing the action. Rizzolatti explains that we have two ways of understanding others: by logic or by the mirror neural system, which implies that comprehension does not necessarily imply cognitive reasoning but rather comes from a combination of motor and perceptual act. This demonstrates that when we observe actions of others, it can trigger the same neural responses in our brain and *simulate* in our bodies a linked signal of the observed action to our self. This was their understanding of *empathy*. In their account, this simulation via neural responses re-fired in our brain as the senses felt in the body emphasize that perception is not an act of merely seeing but an engagement of motor resonance between subjects.

What is not fully distinguished by Rizzolatti is defining the difference between seeing an event and seeing the image of the event. Gallagher notes that Rizzolatti fails to clearly distinguish what is happening in the role of *simulation* (Gallagher, 2017). However, this is interesting when we begin to think about the simulation in the mind as the "approach state" that precedes the action itself. Another explanation from neuroscience tells us that action creates perception through our somatosensory system that responds to pain, temperature and touch, and proprioception, which is the sensation of body position and movement, i.e. self-produced movement (Tuthill, 2018). The proprioceptive stimuli, which is the "internal forces that are generated by the position or movement of a body", gives us implicit knowledge of our body (Dougherty, 1997). This allows us, for example, to drink coffee without spilling it because we know how to bring the cup to where our mouth is without having to consciously calculate the spatial coordinates of it. "Self-perception involves integrating changes in visual, tactile, and proprioceptive stimulation from self-motion and discriminating these changes from those of other objects" (Bahrick, 2013). What is even more interesting, however, is that as action creates perception, there is also an anticipatory part of expectation that produces action (Friston et al., 2010). For example, in the case of observing a hill that presents an expectation of moving upwards, our body will propel to move up the hill (cf. Spuybroek, 2004, project: *H20-Expo*). This implies that as form in architecture affects the way we move through space it also affects the way we experience the space. Emphasizing the constructed mental states between our body and our environment through action, the floor then becomes *enactive* to anyone walking on it via their action or even their expected action which affects his or her perception. Alva Noë writes in his book *Action in Perception* that "Perception is not something that happens to us, or in us … It is something we do" (Noë, 2004).

Expanding this idea that perception and action are inextricably tied, Chilean biologist Francesco Varela describes an *enactive* approach to understand perception

> emphasiz(ing) the growing conviction that cognition is not the representation of a pre-given world by a pre-given mind but is rather the enactment of a world and a mind on the basis of a history of actions that a being in the world performs.
>
> *(Varela, Evan and Eleanor, 1992)*

Such interface is composed by three layers which dynamically participate in the architectural experience:

1. the constitutive relatedness describes the living-lived body relationship between cognitive activity and experience (such as the relationship between perception, action, and emotion);
2. the embodied action defines cognition as bodily interaction with the environment through sensorimotor coupling of perception and action;
3. the sense-making represents cognitive beings as self-individuating and sense-producing systems thanks to their bodily organization.

(Jelic, 2016)

As Arakawa Gins were so astutely aware that movement creates perception, their site was a site of *potential* dynamic forces embodied in form. Form is a "landing site" as Gins would say (Gins and Arakawa, 1997). To clarify, the "landing sites" for Gins are everywhere and anything that produces life-generating opportunities, but here we focus on form, specifically form which becomes a site for an *event*. Once again, Deleuze's aesthetics are found in this sense reality, presented through the affect–event singularity. Embodied within the limits of material capacity, the intensive forces are also preserved and hence become part of style. Further, as procedural methods are laid out, the precept operates as a means of considering the different forms of the senses. For Deleuze, the affect operates in conjunction with the precept as a crucial element of his perspective on sensation. Together they form the intensity of the *sensation*.

Continuity of Form, Inform, Perform

As Lars Spuybroek stated with his keen observation:

Technology mixed with architecture in a very particular way in the 20th century. There were basically two trends, one Corbusian, plastic and formal, expressed through a technology of concrete, the other programmatic and structural, Miesian, expressed through a technology of steel. Mies equated freedom – or flexibility – with neutralism, by a programmatic indeterminacy, an architecture that refrained from determining human behavior in advance.

(source not found)

One could state that the universal organizing form that pervades modern architecture would have to the grid. It is widely accepted in our practice to justify Euclidean geometry as sufficient enough to the practical making of architecture because deeply embedded in history are the ideal Platonic forms as the stable forms and that in its symbolic argumentation supports all aesthetic reasoning as well. This is quite adequate for the physical world since Euclid's axioms are quite true in both theoretical and practical models. However, with our awareness of non-Euclidean geometry, it would be a grave mistake to limit our instruments of architecture, one being geometry, to the strict understanding to one ideology of spatial form.

In architecture, the mid-twentieth century's formal order that provided organizational configuration as well as formal articulation was the Cartesian grid. As Lars Spuybroek states in the quote above, Mies employed a technology of the grid that regulated space and flexibility in an open plan. The mathematicians and scientists of this time, however, contrasted this starkly, particularly because computers and their computational ability were proving new constructs of reality. In 1959, the Macy Conference, the first cybernetics convention held in Chicago, brought together many scientists, mathematicians and theoretical biologists, and the newly emerging computer scientists, to discuss a new paradigm that deflected the pre-deterministic orders. Soon afterwards, a theory called the *complexity theory* opened up a whole different way to understand the world. Scientists and physicists grew away from the mechanistic view of the world posed by Newton – that all phenomena can be reduced to atoms and particles and we observe movement that follows a deterministic plan. With *complexity* we understand that organization in nature cannot be described by a teleological point of view but that there is a phenomenon of a spontaneous appearance of novel structure or the autonomous adaptation to a changing environment. This *event* represents the transcendental recognition of immanence and the emergence of difference contains the varying degrees of intensity, contributing to *variation* as a central quality of aesthetics.

Surfacing for Enaction

In the way that Arakawa Gins uses form to give agency to human experience, the work of NOX/Lars Spuybroek structures experience by designing continuity in form such that the *intense differences* are co-evolving with the user and formed as experience. Spuybroek breaks down the typical distinction in architecture that the surface of action is on the floor and the surface of perception is on the wall. Instead, similar to Arakawa Gins, Spuybroek trades discreet elements with continuity. The intertwined relationship of action–perception is depicted in the *wetGRID* where the explicit (re)positioning of the body when viewing the installed paintings has influence on how the information is received and perceived (Figure 25.4).

Figure 25.4 Sketch of Conrad Waddington's Epigenetic Landscape redrawn by Irene Lok (2019).

Design Sensibilities

Spuybroek's earliest built work *Fresh Htwo0 Expo* (1993–1997) is an exhibition hall describing fresh water in the Netherlands (Figure 25.5). It was built with varying geometry that as a whole produced formal and experiential continuity that unfolds as one walks through the space. One of the first fully electronically interactive building, the interior is outfitted with a variety of responsive electronic sensors that people fully engage with their bodies, such as digital puddles that ripple when people stomp on them and a spine of light that is actuated by the mass of bodies moving through space. However, it is in *form* where the ground becomes enactive that we want to draw our attention to here. There is a bifurcating moment half-way through the building where the floor bends and becomes a pocket-like space that emerges from the split geometry, like blistering. The emerged form is now *vague*, embracing a "both-and" position of being a floor and a wall. A new typology of a wall-ground continuous surface that is sloped like a hill induces in our mind the *potential* of the plane to be climbed on or, if one has enough momentum, to run "on the wall" to the upper level, instantly taking a different route then the architecturally planned circulation path. This is the "approaching state" that is in the mind that happens before the action takes place enough to *call-to-action* by the user what the building provides. Moreover, interactivity does not

Figure 25. 5 wetGRID, 1999–2000, Nantes, France (NOX).
Image from *Machining Architecture* (2004) with permission from Canadian Centre for Architecture. AP173 Lars Spuybroek fonds, Canadian Centre for Architecture, Gift of NOX/Lars Spuybroek

solely exist in the electronic devices throughout the building but the *form* of the architecture itself is interactively engaged with the user. Experience in form is truly human-motivated that involves complexity arising from *differences*.

Spuybroek states:

> It's not so easy to take the elements out of architecture, because they are not given. The only thing that is given in architecture is the working on certain problems, like in philosophy or painting we have a history on dealing with certain built-in problems. Architecture has a life. A material, physical approach to architecture and the experiencing body becomes necessary. We have a moment of experience and this constructivism (productive generation) running simultaneously, not one after another. So one should mobilize everything before it becomes an idea, or else you are just materializing an idea and communicating that with language, which is reading and mind, and therefore not experience.
>
> *(source not found)*

This central concept in Spuybroek's work is worked through in material state to produce complex articulations of *form* that is *informed* by material state and *performs* at the experiential level. Surfaces are continuous, multi-directional with manifolds of latent forces for potential action in every crevice of the surface. Conrad Waddington, a theoretical biologist and one of the members of the Macy Conference, described this best in his diagram of the *epigenetic landscape* where latent forces below the surface of a mountain co-operates with action that is taking place above (Figure 25.6). This interchange of forces performs, co-evolves and interrelates the subject/object relationship into a single continuum. In other words, the subject and its environment are unified in action and, more specifically, the surface of action *is* the surface of perception.

Unity in action but not uniformity in form (DeLanda, 1991) is the systemic design process that Spuybroek lays out as *Form, Inform and Perform*. Regularity and universality as central concepts of the

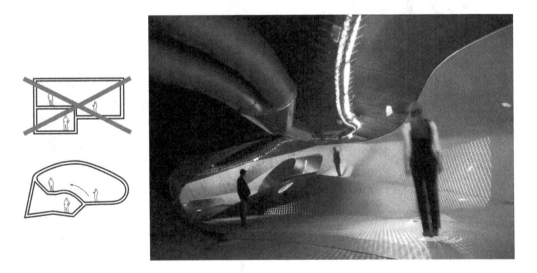

Figure 25.6 Fresh HtwoO Expo, the Netherlands, Water Pavilion 1993–1997 (NOX).
Image from *Machining Architecture* (2004) with permission from Canadian Centre for Architecture AP173 Lars Spuybroek fonds, Canadian Centre for Architecture, Gift of NOX/Lars Spuybroek

twentieth century left out orders of complexity, intensity and life, producing differences. Instead, to achieve a form that emerges from a complex order of intensive forces, both analog and digital processes are set up as a *machinic* system. These *machinic* assemblages, referencing Deleuzian *abstract machines*, self-generate and self-form by the affordances that are latent in their own internal systems rather than imposing external orders such as a *grid* that predetermines orders over matter. Akin to Frei Otto's experiments and the infamous string model of Gaudi, whom Spuybroek would consider as the first computing architect, the projects at NOX were made of rubber tubes and lacquer, wool thread and water for SoftOfficeUK and oWTC, amongst many other projects (Figure 25.7).

Affective performativity through *formal articulation* and event *becomings* are the intangible sensibilities that arise from autopoiesis and cognitive science combined (Rosenberg, 2003). The self-generated material computing model that begins in a flexible and adaptive state hardens into a rigid form but maintains its flexible open-ended programming in the final building. The central idea is that the abstract diagram *machines* structure + program + aesthetics are all one encompassing process of design. That is, form, inform and perform all happen in one continuum of design.

Enactive Topology as Lifeform Typology

Turning to Corbusier's plastic and formal expression of technology of concrete in the quote above, there is an essential moment in his work that specifically distinguishes the condition of the discreet and continuous. Clearly represented in Villa Savoye, the difference is found in the stair and the ramp. While both is a movement in the vertical direction, the discreet action of the stairs is a Cartesian set-up, going from point A to point B. More importantly, as Corbusier states "A stair separates one story from another; a ramp connects" (Le Corbusier, 1946). The diagonal ramp that connects the two floors is part of the space that creates an unfolding of continuous perception of space that activated by and in movement. The other purveyor of concrete architecture where the diagonal condition is made explicit was Paul Virilio with architect Claude Parent and artists Michel Carrade and Morice Lipsi. They formed a multi-disciplinary

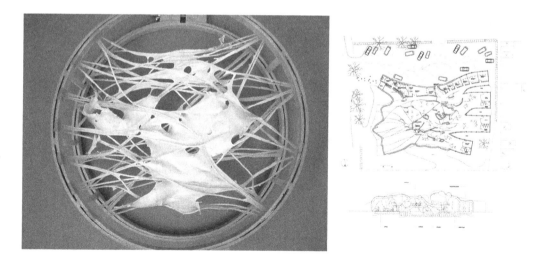

Figure 25.7 Form-finding analog computing model for SoftOfficeUK (2003).
Image from *Machining Architecture* (2004) with permission from Canadian Centre for Architecture AP173 Lars Spuybroek fonds, Canadian Centre for Architecture, Gift of NOX/Lars Spuybroek

group named Architecture Principe in 1963 (Virilio, 1997). Keenly understanding the dynamic movement of a plane, they traded the orthogonal conditions for diagonal slopes in their discourse on "The Function of the Oblique" (Figure 25.8).

In the oblique therein lie the potential energy movements onto the body as it moves through the incline. The potential movement expressed as a diagram eventually led to the critique of *speed* in the new age of technological fever. Years later, when Virilio moved from typology to dromology, he left behind one kind of body in space for another kind of body in cyberspace and became anesthetized. "Virilio's work is shown to be plagued by a consistent aestheticizing impulse, which acts as a form of anaesthesia and 'numbs' the concern for the political" (Leach, 1999).

Today, the pervasive typological form of vertical glass towers stacking the same flat floors on top of one another does very little to the experience of the body. The Cartesian set-up of an elevator core that brings us from one level to another displaced horizontal surface on a different level homogenizes the experience of the architecture that is flattened almost immediately. Previous paradigms aimed for efficiency determined by the manufacturing mindset of the Industrial Revolution should re-thought. If we redefine minimalism and efficiency such as in the work of Frei Otto, which embraces differences and complexity as part of an "optimized" model (Otto, 1996), we can bring back a multi-varied architecture that brings beauty and delight together with structure that will harness experience in form. To reiterate, the body is affected by form and how we shape our architecture in formal terms is central to how we experience it.

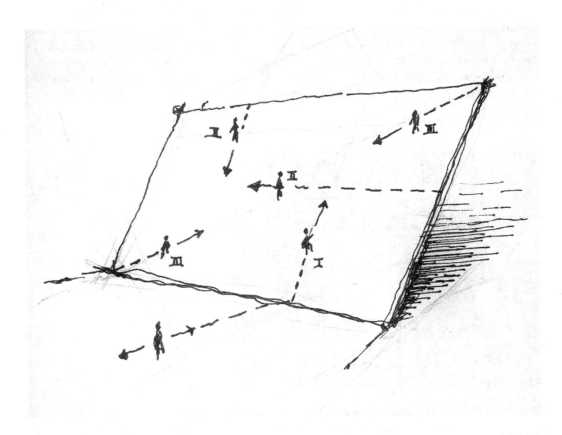

Figure 25.8 Sketch of Claude Parent and Paul Virilio's Function of the Oblique redrawn by Irene Lok (2019).

In conclusion, the topological condition of Arakawa Gins and Spuybroek gives us "landing sites" of new possibilities, and the rethinking of form is necessary. The human body and brain are constantly in need of stimulation to keep them alive. Human perception in action is the aesthetic experience that is propelled by systems of variation, change and differences. To be performative to the human condition, a different approach is needed, and we must embrace the enactive condition of the body to the architecture as a unified whole. We are seeing new forms emerging and they must not be dismissed as *just another form*. Form has weight, and play must come back to the body through form. These are the intangible sensibilities that bring aesthetics to the foreground in *action*, *percept* and *affect* as an important triad of performativity.

References

Acharya, S., and Shukla, S. (2012). Mirror neurons: enigma of the metaphysical modular brain. *Journal of Natural Science, Biology, and Medicine, 3* (2), 118–124.

Allen, M. (2015). Compelled by the diagram: thinking through C. H. Waddington's epigenetic landscape. *Contemporaneity: Historical Presence in Visual Culture*, 4, 119–142, 199. DOI: 10.5195/contemp.2015.143.

Bahrick, L. E. (2013). Body perception: intersensory origins of self and other perception in newborns. *Current Biology*, 23 (23), PR1030–R1041. 10.1016/j.cub.2013.10.060.

Bergson, H. (1990). *Matter and Memory*. New York: Zone Books.

Bergson, H. (1998). *Creative Evolution*. New York: Dover Publications (first printed in 1911).

Casile, A., Caggiano, V., and Ferrari, P. F. (2011). The mirror neuron system: a fresh view. *Neuroscientist, 17* (5), 524–538.

DeLanda, M. (1991). "Uniformity and Variability: An Essay in the Philosophy of Matter". www.t0.or.at/delanda/matterdl.htm.

DeLanda, M. (2002). *Intensive Science and Virtual Philosophy*. New York: Continuum.

DeLanda, M. (2004). Materiality: Anexact and Intense. In L. Spuybroek (Ed.), *NOX: Machining Architecture*, pp. 370–377. London: Thames & Hudson.

DeLanda, M. (2005). *Intensive Science and Virtual Philosophy*. London and New York: Bloomsbury Academic.

Deleuze, G. (1990). *The Logic of Sense*. Trans. Constantin V. Boundas. New York: Columbia University Press.

Deleuze, G. (2003). *Francis Bacon: The Logic of Sensation*. Trans. Daniel W. Smith. Minneapolis: University of Minnesota Press.

Deleuze, G. (2005). *Pure Immanence: Essays on A Life*. New York: Zone Books.

Deleuze, G., and F. Guattari. (1994). *Difference and Repetition*. Trans. Paul Patton. New York: Columbia University Press.

Deleuze, G., and F. Guattari. (2004). *A Thousand Plateaus*. Trans. Brian Massumi. London and New York: Continuum.

Derrida, J. (1989). *Edmund Husserl's Origin of Geometry: An Introduction*. Trans. John P. Leavey, Jr. London: University of Nebraska Press.

Di Dio, C., Macaluso, E., and Rizzolatti, G. (2007). The golden beauty: brain response to classical and renaissance sculptures. *PLOS ONE, 2* (11), e1201. 10.1371/journal.pone.0001201.

Dougherty, P. (1997). Somatosensory systems. Neuroscience Online, University of Texas. https://nba.uth.tmc.edu/neuroscience/m/s2/chapter02.html.

Reversible Destiny Foundation. (n.d.). Home page. www.reversibledestiny.org.

Friston, K., Daunizeau, J., Kilner, J., and Kiebel, S. (2010). Action and behavior: a free-energy formulation. *Biological Cybernetics*, 102, 227–260. 10.1007/s00422-010-0364-z.

Gallagher, S. (2017). *Enactivist Interventions: Rethinking the Mind*. Oxford: Oxford University Press.

Gins, M., and Arakawa, S. (1997). *Reversible Destiny: Arakawa Gins (We Have Decided Not to Die)*. New York: Harry N. Abrams.

Gins, M., and Arakawa, S. (2002). *Architectural Body*. Tuscaloosa: University of Alabama Press.

Goard, M. J., Pho, G., Woodson, J., and Sur, M. (2016). Distinct roles of visual, parietal, and frontal motor cortices in memory-guided sensorimotor decisions. *eLife*, 5, 10.7554/eLife.13764.

Jelic, A., Tieri, G., De Matteis, F., Babiloni, F., and Vecchiato, G. (2016). The enactive approach to architectural experience: a neurophysiological perspective on embodiment, motivation, and affordances. *Frontiers in Psychology*, 7:481. DOI: 10.3389/fpsyg.2016.00481.

Keane, J. (n.d.). AG3 Conference. www.architectural-body.com/?page_id=4035&lang=en

Keane J., and Glazebrook, T. (2013). Here Where It Lives … Bioscleave. *Inflexions* 6, "Arakawa and Gins" (January), 1–21. www.inflexions.org.

Kolarevic, B., and Malkawi, A. M. (2005). *Performative Architecture: Beyond Performativity*. New York: Spon Press.

Lakoff, G. (1997). Testing the limits of brain plasticity or, why is there a wall down the middle of the tub? In Gins, M., and Arakawa, S. *Reversible Destiny*. New York: Harry N. Abrams.

Leach, Neil. (1999). Virilio and architecture. *Theory, Culture & Society*, 16 (5–6), 71–84.

Le Corbusier (1946). *Jeanneret: Ouerve Complete de 1929-1934*. Toulouse: Les éditions d'architecture.

Maldiney, H. (1973). *Regard parole espace*. Lausanne: Éditions L'Âge d'Homme.

Mallgrave, H. F. (2015). Know thyself: or what designers can learn from the contemporary biological sciences. In S.SS Robinson and J. Pallasmaa (Eds.), *Mind in Architecture: Neuroscience, Embodiment, and the Future of Design*, pp. 9–32. Cambridge, MA: MIT Press.

Massumi, B. (1998). Sensing the virtual, building the insensible. In S. Perrella (E d.), *Hypersurface Architecture*: *Architectural Design* (Profile 133), 68 (5–6), 16–24.

Maturana, H. R., and Varela, F. J. (1992). The nervous system and cognition. In *The Tree of Knowledge*. Boston: Shambala.

Mertins, D. (2004). Bioconstructivisms. In L. Spuybroek (Ed.), *NOX: Machining Architecture*, pp. 360–369. London: Thames & Hudson, 2004.

Noë, A. (2004). *Action in Perception*. Cambridge, MA: MIT Press.

Otto, F., and Racsh, B. *Finding Form*. Fellbach: Edition Axel Menges.

Protevi, J. (2003). "Intensive Science & Virtual Philosophy" by Manuel DeLanda [Book Review]. *Journal of the British Society for Phenomenology*, 34 (3), 330–333, DOI: 10.1080/00071773.2003.11007415.

Rabaté, J.-M. (2003). Introduction. *Interfaces: Image Texte Language*, 21/22 (I), 5–11.

Rees, E. (2008). Tropological turns in *Peer Gynt*. *Ibsen Studies*, 8 (2), 150–172.

Rizzolatti, G., and Sinigaglia, C. (2007). *Mirrors in the Brain: How Our Minds Share Actions and Emotions*. Oxford: Oxford University Press.

Rosenberg, M. E. (2003). Constructing autopoiesis: the architectural body in light of contemporary cognitive science. *Interfaces: Image Texte Language*, 21/22 (I), 163–186.

ScienceDaily. (2016). Neuroscience: Linking perception to action. 8 September. www.sciencedaily.com/releases/2016/09/160908131001.htm.

Spuybroek, L. (2004). *Machining Architecture*. London: Thames and Hudson.

Spuybroek, L. (2009). *The Architecture of Continuity: Essays and Conversations*. Rotterdam: nai010.

Taylor, E. I., and Wozniak, R. H. (1996). Introduction. In *Pure Experience: The Response to William James*, pp. ix–xxxii. Bristol: Thoemmes Press.

Terada, R. (1999). Imaginary seductions: Derrida and emotion theory. *Comparative Literature*, 51 (3), 193–216.

Tuthill, J. C., and Azim, E. (2018). Current biology. Proprioception, 28 (5), R194–R203. 10.1016/j.cub.2018.01.064.

Varela, F., Thompson, E., and Rosch, E. (1992). *The Embodied Mind: Cognitive Science and Human Experience*. Cambridge, MA: MIT Press.

Virilio, P., and Parent, C. (1997). *Architecture Principe 1966 et 1996*. Besançon: Les Editions de l'Imprimeur.

Waddington, C. H. (Ed.). (1968). *Towards a Theoretical Biology, Vol 1: Prolegomena*. Edinburgh: Edinburgh University Press.

Yamaoka, N. [Director]. (2012). *Children Who Won't Die* [Documentary, Biography]. Germany.

26

Health and Wellbeing

Performance-Based Design Concepts for a Healthful Built Environment and Human Equilibrium

Dak Kopec

The notion of health and wellbeing as applied to the designed environment is a reemerging trend toward the inclusion of specializations within design education. Sustainable practices, and health and wellbeing are two focus areas that are well positioned to be expanded upon to form specializations beyond the first professional degree. The application of health and wellbeing as part of the built environment is best understood through Sir Isaac Newton's three laws of motion (Hall, 2015):

1. *Every object persists in a state of rest or uniform motion in a straight line unless it is compelled to change that state by forces impressed upon it.* The fundamental ideas pertaining to design have remained the same for centuries. Recent social and technological changes are forces pressuring many professions, including design, to evolve.
2. *Force is equal to change in momentum per change in time. For a constant mass, force equals mass times acceleration.* Professions, and the way things are done, are like a mass moving throughout time. Medicine, engineering, and law have been accumulating mass by adding to their areas of specialization. Mass provides greater strength and greater inertia for propulsion into the future.
3. *For every action there is an opposite and equal reaction.* Change always brings about a reaction and temporary imbalances. Much the same as a pendulum that swings back and forth, it slows and eventually finds center. In biological terms, finding center means homeostasis. Without change, settlement and decay become the action.

Each of Newton's laws can be used to understand the current state of design within the bigger context of social and technological advances. These advances have a direct effect on the occupants of designed buildings. The lack of balance results from our current limitations in replicating all of the beneficial factors and elements found in the natural environment. The results have negative outcomes for our health and wellbeing. For example, the increased use of the pharmaceutical class of medications called SSRIs (selective serotonin reuptake inhibitors) positively correlates to the social shift of humans spending more time indoors. Regardless of the amount of natural light entering a building, humans require unfiltered full-spectrum sunlight for serotonin regulation (Aries, Aarts, van Hoof, Ing, 2013). A fundamental premise of performative architecture is the ability to negotiate between the intended and unintended consequences in order to bring about equilibrium for the inhabitants the architecture was designed to serve.

Intended and Unintended Outcomes

Today, health and wellbeing are social concerns that have answers and conundrums based in technology. Smart building technology has the ability to alter lighting patterns based on the movement and positioning of the sun in the sky. The stabilization of optimal lighting inside of a building has the ability to maximize human productivity; however, the unintended consequence is insomnia. Human needs are not segmented or regimented within a linear context. Basic human patterns related to temperature, hunger, and sleep are based on graduating increments. Once we have reached a level that necessitates an action, we are then able to satiate the need. In other words, all of us can tolerate being inside of a walk-in freezer for a given duration of time. However, there will be a point where we will need to get out, or perish from the experience. For many who suffer from insomnia, the continuation of optimal lighting inhibits the body's gradual build-up of melatonin. We rely on melatonin for sleep and the regulation of our circadian rhythms (Touitou, Reinberg, and Touitou, 2017).

When technology is used to echo the human condition, as opposed to enhancing performance, the unintended consequences can range from mild to devastating. As part of performativity, the use of technology to facilitate the increase and decrease of interior lighting levels throughout the course of 12 hours can assist with the sleep–wake cycle, thus decreasing the need for sleep aids. Within the United States, poor sleep patterns are estimated to result in annual losses of more than 100 billion USD. These losses come from long-term reductions in productivity, accidents, comorbid health conditions, and other unintended consequences (Wickwire, Shaya, and Scharf, 2016).

Reliability and Replicability as Foundations

Trends and concerns related to health and wellbeing in relation to human occupation of buildings has provided unique opportunities for design professions. These opportunities are as diverse as the buildings themselves and provide many avenues for research. The holy grail of research is to identify outcomes that are reliable and replicable. However, diversities within the human condition bring about many confounding variables that effect levels of reliability within highly replicable buildings. Building type, materials, layouts, and other static elements are easily measured and applied elsewhere with similar results. However, the people, their beliefs, and worldviews affect interpretation and internalizations related to quality, value, and their responses. Therefore, we can hypothesize that interventions based on typology are high in replicability, but low in reliability. Person-centered healthcare interventions are low in replicability but high in reliability. Consider these concepts in terms of a headache. Person A might require a large bathtub, because this person has found that hot baths help to alleviate the headache. The use of a bathtub for hot baths as a means to thwart headaches is a reliable intervention, but only for people similar to person A. Because this intervention does not work for everyone, it is probable but not reliable. Relaxing in a cooler dark room to thwart the headache is an intervention with positive outcomes for most people. This method can be replicated to most everyone as a remedy; if it works for the vast majority of all populations, it ranks high on a reliability scale.

When attempting to achieve health and wellbeing within the designed environment the focus must be on health, wellbeing, and design as ideas, elements, and attributes that compliment, compete, and intersect. A shift in design methods based on replicability to methods based on reliability lacks popularity because of confounding factors like regionalism and place attachment. These ideas limit the replication of designs. Likewise, baseline standards currently used by third-party credentialing bodies such as

WELL, Fitwel, and even JCAHO (Joint Commission on Accreditation of Healthcare Organizations) would come under greater scrutiny because of the loss of reliability for select groups of people.

When designing for health and wellbeing, it is important to understand the relationship between reliability and replicability. Basic biological health and building materials can be replicable, but mental, social, behavioral, and personal factors cannot. This fundamental concept is pivotal to health and wellbeing, especially if the definition is based on the World Health Organization (WHO; 1946) as being *complete mental and social health and not merely the absence of disease or infirmity.*

Intersections of Reliability and Replicability

The idea of overgeneralizations, as applied to health and wellbeing, are ideas based in replicability and used to substantiate reliability. For example, the trend toward less segmentation and greater openness for visual access is fraught with logic-based and conceptual errors. The benefit of open plans is the enhanced visual access and increased personal control through perceptual information. Visual access does have the unintended consequence of visual and auditory overstimulation and loss of privacy. Stimulation levels beyond one's coping capacity increase levels of stress.

Stress is categorized as acute and chronic. An emergency room that uses an open floor plan can lead to acute stress for the person needing care. This form of stress will result in the release of cortisol, which impedes memory performance and disrupts higher-level cognition (Hood, Pulvers, Spady, Kliebenstein, Bachand, 2015). This translates to poor communication between the client, their family member, or the healthcare provider.

The employee who works in an open-plan emergency room is subjected to increased stimulation on a regular bases, which can lead to chronic stress. The persistent stress can result in physiological changes in the brain's neural circuitry. The effects include poor decision-making, higher levels of anxiety, and mood disorders that effect behaviors (McEwen, 2017). This translates to higher employee turnover, a probable need for pharmaceuticals, and increased costs to the overall healthcare system.

Performativity in architecture should be based on a multifactorial approach that includes reliability and replicability. This approach would thus reduce replicability probabilities but increase reliably probabilities. Put another way, buildings would be unique from region to region, but fundamentals such HVAC (heating, ventilation, and air conditioning) would be the same. In this case, Cedars-Sinai (Los Angeles), the Mayo Clinic (Rochester), and Brigham and Women's (Boston) would look and feel very different within multiple areas while infection control and ventilation systems would be similar.

The Indoor Phenomena

Recent decades of social and technological evolution have resulted in changes to our lifestyle. For millennia humans spent the majority of their lives outdoors surrounded by the natural environment. They were exposed to other life forms that evolved and thrived within the natural environment. For young people, access to a diverse array of stimulation for all levels of sensory detection fostered the growth of neural connections, thereby allowing for greater discernment between competing stimuli. Sight and sound, for example, are senses developed during infancy and early childhood. As we observe different stimuli, we form neural connections that allow us to assign meaning to variations, and to discern the best behavioral response. For example, a person who was raised in the wilderness learned to interpret select environmental sounds as a threat and thus behaved accordingly. The neural connections required for this skill allowed that same person to be in a conversation with another person while concurrently remaining vigilant to detect a potential danger.

Lessons taught through visual and auditory observations of animals, birds, insects, and rustling leaves were essential for survival. Within the natural environment, many action–reaction situations informed behaviors. Light and shadow, cloud formation, and color saturation of the sky all served as visual stimuli and cues that informed behaviors and served as predictors. The level of acuity we developed through neural connections translated to a greater probability for survival.

Our relatively recent shift to an indoor environment has resulted in the need to produce replicas of natural stimuli. Where birds, butterflies, falling leaves, et cetera, helped to develop visual tracking for infants, we replaced that stimuli with mobiles that contain items that drift in a circular pattern. However, a deeper look into the effects of movement from birds, butterflies, and falling leaves within the natural environment reveals that the visual stimulation is accompanied by a variety of other stimuli. The mobile thus provides visual sensory stimulation based only on vision. Neural connections based on sensory integration are stronger and more resilient to the effects of age-related atrophy.

Recent social evolution patterns documented by the Environmental Protection Agency suggests that the average citizen of the United States spends roughly 90% of a 24-hour cycle inside of the built environment (Zhou et al., 2017) where the air can be up to five times more polluted than outside (EPA, 2017). The effects of spending so much time indoors increase our exposure to high levels of contaminated air. Indoor air pollutants can affect neural development and processing, respiratory- and immune-system functioning, and mood and psychological disorders. These affects can precede or be amplified or accompanied by the multileveled effects common to the interior environment. These include:

- Increased spatial confinement
- Increased sensory amplification
- Decreased distance perception
- Decreased inspiration (inhalation) demands
- Decreased energy demands resulting in decreased caloric expenditure

Most interior environments lack the ability for people to reach sensory perception thresholds. A sensory threshold can include: how far in the distance a person can detect the flicker of a flame? What is the width of peripheral vision for a person to detect stimuli from the side, up, or down? How low, and from what direction, can a person detect the ticking from a clock placed far away? These thresholds are developed and refined through significant exposures to the vast expanses common to the exterior environment. When we remain or spend the majority of our time indoors, exposure to diversity and intensity of stimuli can be insufficient for acuity development. Colin Turnbull demonstrated this supposition in his book *The Forest People*, where he discovered that native tribes living deep in the dense jungle lacked cognitive understanding of depth perception, and this perception lacked visual refinement (Turnbull, 1987). Granted, Turnbull's subjects did live outdoors, but the greater point is the loss in cognitive processing of visual stimulation. Turnbull's discovery was based on social learning and experience; the people had the mechanical ability to see in the distance, but not the cognitive capacity to understand what they detected.

Unlike Turnbull's subjects, the ability to see in the distance does have a basis in biology. Access and exposure to full-spectrum sunlight results in the activation of specific cells in the retina that help prevent myopia (Mani and Schwartz, 2017). Because a child's eye is not fully formed until age eight (Kopec, 2018), insufficient visual stimulation and too much time inside and behind UV-filtered windows can result in compromised distance vision (the eye) and development of visual acuity (neural connections).

Full-spectrum sunlight, which is not available within the interior environment at sufficient levels, is important for many biological functions. The Office of the Surgeon General (2004) has stated that access to full-spectrum sunlight is necessary for the development of bone strength, which will help to keep bones healthier during the natural aging process. Vitamin D associated with full-spectrum sunlight is also needed for optimal neuromuscular- and immune-system functioning (Mead, 2008); the production of serotonin, which is needed for mood stabilization (Lambert, Reid, Kaye, Jennings, Esler, 2002); and the regulation of melatonin secretion and absorption (Blatt, Khaiboullin, Lombardi, Rizvanov, Khaiboullina, 2016), which is required for optimal circadian rhythms. Seasonal Affective Disorder is an example where insufficient full-spectrum sunlight has a negative effect on people. This causes decreased levels of serotonin in the blood stream and limits the production and uptake of melatonin, thus affecting our circadian rhythms and causing mood fluctuations.

Necrophilia, Biophobia, and Biodominance

Discussions about performative design and its relation to health and wellbeing cannot occur without a discussion of nature. Erich Fromm coined the term "biophilia" in 1973 to mean "love of life." As the counter-balance to this concept, he used the term "necrophilia": "love of death." It is true that the term "necrophilia" has been narrowed and popularized to mean "sexual intercourse with the dead." However, Fromm intended the term to be more broad and less pedestrian. Taxidermy, animal-pelt wall or floor coverings, butterfly or insect collections, and dried flowers are all examples of death that many adore. In terms of wellbeing, necrophilia can occur when we memorialize death. The chained-off locations where students were shot by the Ohio National Guard on the Kent State University campus in the early 1970s, and the 9/11 memorial museum in New York City are memorials to death that we deem important. From this perspective, necrophilia is an important part of wellbeing and the healing process.

Fromm was not the only person to assign an opposite to the concept of biophilia. Ulrich (1993) described "biophobia" as "the fear of nature." He suggested that humans have a desire to avoid the natural environment. Many people in tropical zones avoid natural environments because of fear. Malaria, dengue fever, and Zika virus carried by mosquitos are common within tropical zones. Fear also comes from the bite of a snake or spider, and the multitude of other life-threatening possibilities. Both Fromm and Ulrich suggested a push–pull relationship between biophilia and its opposite.

Kopec (2018) states that we have a fascination with death, we enjoy life, and we love nature as long as we can control it. He argues that biophilia is limited to *biodominance*. He uses the example of mud in the third edition of *Environmental Psychology for Design*. He says, when we are going to work or a dinner party we want to avoid mud for fear of getting dirty. Health spas, on the other hand, use mud as wraps, or in vats that we can sit in. These desirable uses are an important aspect of wellbeing.

Biophilic measures through biodominance are an important aspect of performative design and are seen in the uses of healing gardens, parks, and other planned "green" spaces. These spaces are found outdoors, and within many buildings. These contrived environments have tremendous value in enhancing air quality, evoking calmness and contemplation, and providing multilayered levels of stimuli. They are, however, sanitized. One is not likely to encounter a poisonous snake; nor is there a potential of contracting poison ivy, oak, or sumac; nor is one likely to slip on mud, wet leaves, et cetera, and fall.

Spatial Qualities

Spatial confinement common to the interior environment also means increased concentrations of interior pollutants. The average adult who works at a desk inhales roughly 7–8 liters of air per minute (Glynn, 2017). Within those 7–8 liters are a mixture of oxygen, carbon dioxide, and particulates such as dust, dander, et cetera, and chemicals derived from office equipment and off-gassing (collectively known as ozone and volatile organic compounds). The smaller and more confined the space equates to increased percentages of gasses inhaled as part of those 7–8 liters per minute.

In 2017 the Cleveland Clinic listed over 50 chemicals, some of which are heavy metals found in a typical residential environment (Cleveland Clinic, 2017). The numbers of chemicals are thought to double within public buildings. This is because 1,500 new synthetic chemicals are introduced into the market place each year (Akovali, 2012), and according to Greenguard Certification (n.d.), who cite the United States Environmental Protection agency as claiming that 72% of all chemicals we encounter are within interior environments. Plastics, inks, glues, et cetera, are commonplace within commercial buildings. Plastics, for example, are more durable, easily cleaned, and relatively inexpensive. However, they off-gas and add particulates to the air as part of their natural decay. Our exposures to these chemicals result from one or more of the four pathways of entry into the human body:

1. Inhalation – what we breathe
2. Ingestion – what we put in our mouth and swallow, such as a paint chip or tiny particles that land on our food
3. Injection – what enters our body through a puncture from a carpet tack, nail, or any other sharp item
4. Absorption – agents absorbed through the skin, or through mucus membranes (eyes, nose, or across the placenta)

Epigenetics

The exposure levels now common within interior environments can have negative effects on developing brains and nervous systems. Lead and mercury, for example, are heavy metals known to impair intellectual growth (Sigelman and Rider, 2017). According to the National Institute of Mental Health (n.d.), epigenetics is the relationship between environmental factors and the triggering of select genes to turn on or off. Scientist believe that epigenetics is a cause for many of the mental disorders that we see as commonplace in today's society. While gene mutations cause mental and physical disorders, mutations are not inherited; only the gene with the potential of being activated can be inherited.

Currently, there are many different types of chemicals found within the built environment; 17,000 of them are petroleum-based (called petrochemicals). Unfortunately, only 30% of those petrochemicals have been tested for their effects on health and the environment (Fried, 2015). Plastics, for example, are petroleum-based, and plastics are prolific within the built environment. It is true that plastic will never go away, but plastics will break down into microplastics. Some of the softer plastics that require bending and twisting also contain phthalates. Within the built environment these soft plastics can be found in vinyl flooring, packaging, and many other materials used for the construction of the built environment. The effects of phthalates on the human body are numerous. For example, López-Carrillo et al. (2010) demonstrated a connection between phthalates and the onset of breast cancer. Other conditions traced back to phthalates include diseases of the liver and kidneys.

Indoor Air Quality

A couple of important concepts about air quality are the relationship between air and space, and air movement within a space. As spaces become smaller due to increased numbers of people (higher social densities) and objects occupying that space (decreased spatial volume), and overall decline in square footage as a cost-saving initiative increases carbon dioxide and volatile organic compounds (VOCs), and viral or bacterial agents will occur. A single cough, for example, can produce 3,000 droplets. Now imagine those droplets are in the confined space of a 6 x 7 foot (or 1.8 x 2.1 meter) elevator cab. Now imagine those same 3,000 droplets in a 20 x 20 foot (or 6.1 x 6.1 meter) room. Imagining the dispersion of 3,000 droplets within each environment demonstrates the effects of increased densities on health and wellbeing. As we continue to look at reduced square footage as a cost-saving measure, we will need to balance this action with increased ventilation, thereby decreasing energy efficiency.

The breathing zone that we occupy is a significant determinant of the quality of air we bring into our bodies. Each person's breathing zone is within a 10-inch radius of the person's nose and mouth (Ojima, 2012). While total air volume is important, another factor pertains to vertical versus horizontal air spaces. The majority of viruses have a mass that causes them to linger closer to the ground. When horizontal volume is diminished, the viruses can be found at higher elevations within the vertical space. The most-contaminated air is between 0–2 feet (or 0–61 cm) from the ground, and the least-contaminated air can be found at about 5 ft 7 in (or 1.75 meters) from the floor (Kopec, 2008; EPA, 2017). Children, little people, and those who sit in confined environments for extended periods are generally exposed to the poorest levels of air quality. It is not the height of the person that determines primary breathing zones, but rather the height of the nose and mouth from the ground.

Movement and circulation significantly influence air and air pollutants within a given space. Routine movements within a space stir up air pollutants that cause the pollutants to be at higher elevations by the end of the day. When little to no movement occurs during the night, pollution settles down to the average of 0–2 feet (or 0–61 cm) from the ground (Kopec, 2008; EPA, 2017). Mechanical engineers carefully study all public interior spaces to determine the placement of intakes and vents for the HVAC systems. The idea is to place intake vents where the air is most polluted. The contaminated air is filtered and then vented back into space through ducts, usually located closer to the ceiling.

When assessing a building for performativity it is best to calculate the peak of day movements and the effect of movement and air circulation on the distribution patterns of contaminated air. Additionally, stronger HVAC systems that allow higher MERV-rated (Minimum Efficiency Reporting Value) filters mean more and smaller particles can be captured.

Health Effects of Increased Urbanization

The United Nations (2015) states that 9.7 billion people will inhabit the planet by 2050. According to the United Nations Department of Economic and Social Affairs Population Division (2014), roughly 54% of the world's population live in urban areas, which is a 14% increase from 1950. The urban population is expected to grow another 12% by 2050. This means that 66% of the world's population will reside in one of the planet's cities.

Petroleum-based combustion engines used for leaf blowers, lawn mowers, chain saws, boats, all-terrain vehicles, motor vehicles, et cetera, are the greatest source of outdoor pollutants. Gasoline engines produce secondary organic aerosols, which are tiny particles that make up 40–60% of the aerosol mass in urban environments (American Geophysical Union, 2012). These particles penetrate deeper into the lungs and can result in heart and respiratory complications. Diesel engines common to trucks are another form of combustion engine that cause pollution. Reşitoğlu, Altinişik, and Keskin (2015) state engines that use diesel fuel are one of the largest contributors of carbon monoxide, hydrocarbons, particulate matter, and nitrogen oxides. The urban environment has a great deal of hardscaping, which prevents harmful particles from permeating into the soil. Because these particulates land on hard surfaces (concrete, asphalt, and stone), they are blown around by the wind and tracked into buildings by people. Hence, particulates infiltrate buildings and are present in higher levels within our everyday air currents.

Increased social densities and objects can impede air movement or redirect air circulation within an interior space, thus diminishing the efforts of the ventilation system. This situation often occurs because calculations are based on static factors such as walls, and rarely consider the probable human interactions (i.e. more people entering and exiting a building) and interventions such as propping a door open. The use of positive pressure to prevent outdoor air from infiltrating the building is a method used to inhibit exterior pollutants from entering a building.

Globalism and Population

The number of people over the age of 60 will be over 2 billion by 2050. These numbers will place significant burdens on our healthcare systems (WHO, 2018). A person born in the United States today can expect to live to roughly 78.8 years of age (Centers for Disease Control and Prevention, 2017), and the office of the Assistant Secretary of Health states that more than 75 million Americans already live with a chronic health condition. Not only are humans living longer (Parekh, 2016), we are doing so with greater financial resources being dedicated to a chronic illness.

Increased globalism is another factor that needs to be considered in tandem to age. Bacteria and viruses can travel from one part of the globe to another in hours. Many have questioned when globalism will reach its zenith (Lane, Maznevski, Mendenhall, McNett, 2009), and what the implications will be on human health. The greatest risks from bacterial and viral agents are airports, airplanes, convention centers, resorts, and nightclubs. These enclosed designed environments are the congregating points for multiple people who may be affected by a bacterial or viral infection that can easily infect another person. Closed environments often translate to more people in closer proximity to each other. Droplets from a cough or sneeze can travel roughly 19–92 feet or 6–28 meters per second at peak thrust (Wei and Li, 2017). Hence, a single person walking through an airport can contaminate hundreds of people.

Increased social density means that bacteria and viruses are able to spread from person to person more rapidly, affect more people, and mutate/evolve faster. Darwin's evolutionary theory, which is based on natural selection, states that the weaker will die off and the stronger continue to proliferate. Darwin spoke of species, but the concept helps to explain why virulent strains of bacteria (Beceiro, Tomás, Bou, 2013) and viruses (Tscherne and García-Sastre, 2011) have become omnipresent in recent decades.

USAID (U.S. Agency for International Development; 2016) states that "75 percent of new human diseases are caused by microbes that originate in different species." Microbes jump species because high social densities place us closer to livestock. The natural evolution of microbes is significantly faster. Faster evolution combined with closer proximities to our food sources is the causal factor behind the recent bird and swine flu epidemics. This means that air circulation and decontamination are important performativity measures for indoor environmental quality.

John Beard, Director of the Department of Ageing and Life Course at the WHO, states in relation to the health issues affecting a growing senior population:

> Deep and fundamental reforms of health and social care systems will be required [...] But we must be careful that these reforms do not reinforce the inequities that drive much of the poor health and functional limitation we see in older age.
>
> *(WHO, 2014)*

In other words, those without financial abilities should not be relegated to inferior services.

Aging in the Interior Environment

Occupying confined spaces has the unintended consequence of decreasing the body's full range of motion, caloric expenditure, lung capacity, muscle and bone strength, muscle and joint flexibility, and balance and coordination. When we are young, our bodies develop in response to our activities (running, jumping, and swimming). All of these activities require deeper inspirations and more forceful expirations, which demand stronger respiratory muscles and larger alveoli sacs (the point where air [O_2] and carbon dioxide [CO_2] are exchanged). The increased surface area of the alveoli allows for more gas exchanges; hence increased lung volume. Without opportunities to bring about prolonged and deeper inspirations, the alveoli will not grow to full potential, thereby limiting lung capacity into adulthood.

Running, jumping, and swimming put needed pressure on the epiphyseal (the growth plate located at the end of bones), which causes bones to grow and strengthen. Muscles support our bones, and the growth or atrophy of muscles has a direct relationship with the demand we place upon them. Strong muscles help to support joints and provide a greater baseline of strength. The outcomes here are two-fold: less joint damage, and fewer muscle-related mobility problems in old age.

A person who has been active throughout their growth and development is more likely to remain active into their older years. Greater activity translates to increased caloric expenditure. Too much time spent inside means less activity and decreased caloric expenditure. When we consume more calories than we expend, the excess calories are converted to fat and stored for later use. By 2030, it is estimated that 38% of the world will be overweight and 20% will be considered obese (Hruby and Hu, 2015).

Our recent social evolution suggests that we prefer to be indoors. This requires designers to include opportunities that promote bone, muscle, and joint strength while concurrently fostering balance and coordination. Transitions from one level to another might add to existing methods by including ladders, climbing walls, or ropes. However, would people be inclined to use them?

Conceptualizing Health and Wellbeing

Western society has evolved to see the topics of health and wellbeing pertaining to design following two trajectories. The first is societal conceptualizations of disease and the remedy. The second is wellness and to what degree is wellness a benefit versus a luxury. These two concepts are sources for much discourse. Neither health nor wellbeing has a definitive operational definition, which is the identification of one or more specific events or conditions that can be measured or tested (Grinnell 2016). As mentioned above, in 1946 the WHO attempted to define health with the definition *a state of complete physical, mental, and social wellbeing and not merely the absence of disease or infirmity*. In recent years this definition has come under scrutiny because of the rise in chronic illness, age-related limitations, and long-term disabilities that arise from assorted body insults (accidents, violence, and repetitive injuries). The use of the word "complete" presupposes that anything outside of the norm indicates a lack of health. The alteration of the definition to state the *individual norms* for physical, mental, and social wellbeing would thus consider sociocultural differences and labeling practices.

Most people within society look to clinical medicine as the all-knowing authority and magic bullet for our ills. The "magic bullet theory" is an idea coined by physician and scientist Paul Ehrlich, who suggests a singular intervention (in this case a pharmaceutical) will yield the desired outcome (Kopec, 2012). For many within clinical health professions, the idea of health, and the profession's ability to provide cures, move far beyond the magic bullet to incorporate a multipronged approach.

Wellbeing lacks agreed-upon operational definitions. Some regard the attainment of wellbeing as the professional assistance from a counselor or therapist, while others define it as the personal pampering at a spa, or the incorporation of New Age spiritualism within their lifestyle. None of these definitions are wrong, but when we go to operationalize wellness the idea and concept is difficult to define and it is even more difficult to develop outcome measures. This, however, is not to say that designers should not be striving to achieve wellness within the design process. The choice whether to sit or stand at a computer, the ability to eat one's lunch in a garden or traditional-dining-room atmosphere, or opting to climb a ladder to get to the second floor while using a staircase to get to the third floor are personal decisions that afford self-determination and personal empowerment; significant attributes of wellbeing.

Evolving Design Education Paradigms

Educational training leading to a specialization allows the practitioner to advance his or her skill and knowledge set, thus fomenting the development of experts with deeper knowledge. However, incorporating specializations into design practice without a strong subject area foundation can result in overgeneralizations, and the loss of professional credibility.

In the early 2000s the United States Green Building Council (USGBC) inspired the development of design concentrations and specializations at the college and university level in the area of sustainability. Arguably, this was among the first codified design specialization. In 2014 the USGBC partnered with Delios International to help tackle a phenomenon called "Sick Building Syndrome" (Environmental Illness Resource, 2016). Joshi (2008) explains the six primary categories of it:

1. Chemical and biological contaminants
2. Ventilation
3. Electromagnetic radiation
4. Psychological factors
5. Lighting, ergonomics, and acoustics
6. Temperature and humidity

Academic programs specializing in health and wellbeing, as concepts, are appearing within many graduate schools of design. Likewise, the USGBC and Delios are promoting building certifications that offer outside testament of a building's capacity to promote health and wellbeing. A problem that has arisen within the design professions is the lack of unified operational definitions. Currently many academic programs have specializations carrying the title "healthcare", but these specializations run the gamete of typology (hospitals), person-centered (conditions) and community-based (social justice). All of these programs address health and wellbeing, but do so from different viewpoints. This can lead to confusion pertaining to expertise and contributions within the practice of design.

In order for a profession to develop a specialization, the content of the specialization must be clear and concise with operational definitions. A question that must come with the advent of any claim being made is, "Do the professionals have the prerequisite knowledge to support the knowledge being promoted?" As already mentioned, health and wellbeing are conditions that can be defined independently and as an aggregated whole. However, the definitions are not ubiquitous. The word "health" has definitions based on temporal factors, such as *prevention*, *curative*, and *rehabilitative*. Health can also refer to the physical body, state of mind, or quality of social interactions. Wellbeing has similar diversities within its definition, albeit emotion is a common denominator.

Each of the current health and wellbeing programs offers beneficial information. To codify this information into a generally understandable outcome that has meaning to practice, consideration must be given to the integration of psycho-neural-biology. This direction provides a clear body of knowledge from which the individual can steer him or herself into areas of interest.

Conclusion

Inertia brought about through specializations from other professions has placed force upon the design professions to examine their practice in terms of future relevance, or risk a reduction in scope of practice, or potential obsolescence. Design education has added post-professional degrees and robust concentrations in the area of healthcare and wellbeing. Paradigms that have supported the advanced generalist have been challenged to support specialization. Like other professions (i.e. law, medicine, and psychology), the use of a first professional degree is merely a foundation that is built upon. As design professions evolve to form specializations, greater depth of practice will follow.

Collaborations between disciplines will also allow for a more holistic vision of causality and intervention. Adding design professions to the healthcare process assumes experts from social and design sciences will become equal partners within the healthcare continuum.

Sir Isaac's Newton's second law, "force equals mass times acceleration," is important. Identifying and promoting qualified healthcare designers requires critical mass within the design professions to ensure continued acceleration toward professional specialization. This specialization adds to the overall enhancement of the human condition within performative design. Without a unified agreement of what a specialization entails, Newton's third law of every action having an opposite and equal reaction will likely ensue in a direction contrary to the positive evolution of design professions. If we are going to put ourselves out as experts, we must be the experts. These phenomena contribute to Newton's first law, which states our profession will remain stagnate unless outside pressures force change. The bigger question now is whether the design professions will respond to the outside pressures, or will they deflect the pressures, thereby reducing our overall scope and relevance.

References

Akovali, G. (2012). Plastic materials: Polyvinyl chloride (PVC). In F. Pacheco-Torgal, S. Jalali, and A. Fucic (Eds.). *Toxicity of Building Materials*. Cambridge: Woodhead Publishing, p. 43.

American Geophysical Union. (2012, March 2). Gasoline worse than diesel when it comes to some types of air pollution. ScienceDaily. Retrieved from: www.sciencedaily.com/releases/2012/03/120302193928.htm.

Aries, M.B.C., Aarts, M.P.J., van Hoof, J., and Ing, E. (2013). Daylight and health: A review of the evidence and consequences for the built environment. *Lighting Research & Technology*, 47, 1, 6–27.

Beceiro, A., Tomás, M., and Bou, G. (2013). Antimicrobial resistance and virulence: A successful or deleterious association in the bacterial world? *Clinical Microbiology Reviews*, 26, 2, 185–230.

Blatt, N.L., Khaiboullin, T.I., Lombardi, V.C., Rizvanov, A.A., and Khaiboullina, S.F. (2016). The skin–brain connection hypothesis, bringing together ccl27-mediated t-cell activation in the skin and neural cell damage in the adult brain. *Frontiers in Immunology*, 7, 683, 1–6. Retrieved from: www.ncbi.nlm.nih.gov/pmc/articles/PMC5237636/.

Centers for Disease Control and Prevention. (Last updated March 17, 2017). Life expectancy. CDC/National Center for Health Statistics. Retrieved from: www.cdc.gov/nchs/fastats/life-expectancy.htm.

Cleveland Clinic. (2017, May 2). Household chemicals chart: What's in my house. Retrieved from: https://my.clevelandclinic.org/health/articles/household-chemicals-chart-whats-in-my-house?view=print.

Environmental Illness Resource. (Last updated May, 2016). Sick building syndrome (SBS). Retrieved from www.ei-resource.org/illness-information/related-conditions/sick-building-syndrome/.

Environmental Protection Agency. (2017, January 17). Why indoor air quality is important to schools. Retrieved from: www.epa.gov/iaq-schools/why-indoor-air-quality-important-schools.

Fried, G. (2015). *Managing Sport Facilities*, 3rd ed. Champaign, IL: Human Kinetics.

Glynn, K. (2017). *Gasping for Air: How Breathing Is Killing Us and What We Can Do about It*. Lanham, MD: Rowman & Littlefield.

Greenguard Certification. (n.d.). Indoor air quality. Retrieved from: http://greenguard.org/en/consumers/consumers_iaq.aspx.

Grinnell, R. (2016). Operational definition. PsychCentral. Retrieved from: https://psychcentral.com/encyclopedia/operational-definition/.

Hall, N. (Ed.). (Last updated May 5, 2015). Newton's laws of motion. National Aeronautics and Space Administration. Retrieved from: www.grc.nasa.gov/www/k-12/airplane/newton.html.

Hood, A., Pulvers, K., Spady, T.J., Kliebenstein, A., and Bachand, J. (2015). Anxiety mediates the effect of acute stress on working memory performance when cortisol levels are high: A moderated mediation analysis. *Anxiety, Stress & Coping, 28*, 5, 545–562.

Hruby, A., and Hu, F.B. (2015). The epidemiology of obesity: A big picture. *Pharmacoeconomics, 33*, 7, 673–689.

Joshi, S.M. (2008). The sick building syndrome. *Indian Journal of Occupational and Environmental Medicine, 12*, 2, 61–64.

Kopec, D. (2008). Health Sustainability and The Built Environment. New York, NY: Fairchild Books.

Kopec, D. (2012). *Environmental Psychology for Design*, 2nd ed. New York, NY: Fairchild Books.

Kopec, D. (2018). *Environmental Psychology for Design*, 3rd ed. New York, NY: Bloomsbury Press.

Lambert, G.W., Reid, C., Kaye, D.M., Jennings, G.L., and Esler, M.D. (2002). Effect of sunlight and season on serotonin turnover in the brain. *Lancet, 360*, 9348, 1840–1842.

Lane, H.W., Maznevski, M.L., Mendenhall, M.E., and McNett, J. (2009). *The Blackwell Handbook of Global Management: A Guide to Managing Complexity*. Chichester: Wiley Blackwell.

López-Carrillo, L., Hernández-Ramírez, R.U., Calafat, A.M., Torres-Sánchez, L., Galván-Portillo, M., Needham, L.L., Ruiz-Ramos, R., and Cebrián, M.E. (2010). Exposure to phthalates and breast cancer risk in northern Mexico. *Environmental Health Perspectives, 118*, 4, 539–544.

Mani, A., and Schwartz, G.W. (2017). Circuit mechanisms of a retinal ganglion cell with stimulus-dependent response latency and activation beyond its dendrites. *Current Biology, 27*, 4, P471-4482.

McEwen, B.S. (2017). Neurobiological and systemic effects of chronic stress. *Chronic Stress*, 1, n.p. doi: 10.1177/2470547017692328.

Mead, M.N. (2008). Benefits of sunlight: A bright spot for human health. *Environmental Health Perspectives, 116*, 4, A160–A167.

National Institute of Mental Health. (n.d.). Brain basics. Retrieved from: www.nimh.nih.gov/health/educational-resources/brain-basics/brain-basics.shtml.

Office of the Surgeon General. (2004). *Bone Health and Osteoporosis: A Report of the Surgeon General*. Rockville, MD: Government Printing Office.

Ojima, J. (2012). Gaseous contaminant distribution in the breathing zone. *Industrial Health, 50*, 3, 236–238.

Parekh, A.K. (Last reviewed March 22, 2016). Living with not one, but six chronic conditions. Retrieved from: www.hhs.gov/ash/about-ash/multiple-chronic-conditions/about-mcc/living-with-not-one-but-six-chronic-conditions/index.html.

Reşitoğlu, İ.A., Altınışık, K., and Keskin, A. (2015). The pollutant emissions from diesel-engine vehicles and exhaust aftertreatment systems. *Clean Technologies and Environmental Policy, 17*, 1, 15–27.

Sigelman, C.K., and Rider, E.A. (2017). *Life-Span Human Development*, 9th ed. Boston, MA: Cengage Learning.

Touitou, Y., Reinberg, A., and Touitou, D. (2017). Association between light at night, melatonin secretion, sleep deprivation, and the internal clock: Health impacts and mechanisms of circadian disruption. *Life Sciences, 173*, 94–106.

Tscherne, D.M., and García-Sastre, A. (2011). Virulence determinants of pandemic influenza viruses. *Journal of Clinical Investigation, 121*, 1, 6–13.

Turnbull, C. (1987). *The Forest People*, reissued ed. New York, NY: Touchstone.

Ulrich, R.S. (1993). Biophilia, biophobia and natural landscapes. In S.R. Kellert and E.O. Wilson (Eds.). *The Biophilia Hypothesis*. Washington, DC: Island Press.

United Nations. (29 July, 2015). World population projected to reach 9.7 billion by 2050. Retrieved from: www.un.org/en/development/desa/news/population/2015-report.html.

United Nations, Department of Economic and Social Affairs, Population Division. (2014). *World Urbanization Prospects: The 2014 Revision, Highlights*. New York, NY: United Nations.

USAID. (Last updated: October 21, 2016). Emerging pandemic threats. Retrieved from: www.usaid.gov/what-we-do/global-health/pandemic-influenza-and-other-emerging-threats.

Wei, J., and Li, Y. (2017). Human cough as a two-stage jet and its role in particle transport. *PLOS ONE, 12*, 1, 1–15.

Wickwire, E.M., Shaya, F.T., and Scharf, S.M. (2016). Health economics of insomnia treatments: The return on investment for a good night's sleep. *Sleep Medicine Reviews, 30*, 72–82.

World Health Organization. (1946). Preamble to the Constitution of the World Health Organization as adopted by the International Health Conference, New York, 19–22 June, 1946, chaired by Thomas Parran.

World Health Organization. (2014). "Ageing well" must be a global priority. Retrieved from: www.who.int/mediacentre/news/releases/2014/lancet-ageing-series/en/.

World Health Organization. (2018, February 5). Aging and health. Retrieved from: www.who.int/news-room/fact-sheets/detail/ageing-and-health.

Zhou, C., Zhan, Y., Chen, S., Xia, M., Ronda, C., Sun, M., Chen, H., and Shen, X. (2017). Combined effects of temperature and humidity on indoor VOCs pollution: Intercity comparison. *Building and Environment, 121*, 15, 26–34.

27

Reciprocal Relationships of Materiality and Human Engagement

Expanding the Role of Material Systems towards Sensorial Socio-Spatial Agency

Sean Ahlquist

The field of computation in architectural design focuses sharply on synchronizing techniques of advanced manufacturing with a material's performative qualities. The proficiency of fabrication evolves, in kind, with technical specificity of the vast material hierarchies that define the assembly, form and responsivity of an architecture. The term "material system" is often used to encapsulate moments where the performative effects of an architecture operate at the behest of specific material constructions, often of minimal material use, that respond to contextual forces and energies.

What if we begin to expand the scope of the myriad energies that shape and inflect upon the material media of an architecture? The promise of the material system is, through the mechanisms of design methodology and means of bespoke production of material differentiation, to elicit a highly tailored architecture. As a part of perfecting the calibration between design and fabrication, the exhaustive efforts of trial and error give way to the inevitable desire to celebrate the elaborate material-driven process and the resulting finely articulated material system. Yet, this largely self-referential validation truncates the latent capacities of such intricate material systems to explore beyond the closed-loop relationship with *site* and adventure into the open-ended reciprocations with *human experience*.

Architecture is undoubtedly a *system*, physical and environmental constructs that operate in dynamic exchange with social, political, economic, and cultural apparatuses that both map and are mapped by architecture's expansive domain. If we expect the material system to assume the entirety of this role, then it requires the embrace of the *extra*-systemic. A form of external agency that is not explicitly bound to the processes of material design or the concerns of making. Particularly, this chapter explores human interposition as an inexorable agent mediating material and environment. This poses a significant conceptual shift from enabling the designer to instrumentalize a material architecture to endowing human behavior with authority to transform and ultimately define the parameters, meaning and efficacy of an architecture.

Design agency is often construed as design-*er* agency – the effectiveness of a knowledge set and tableau of technological and material procedures to devise, explore and ultimately specify the material construction, in some cases, operation, of an architecture. Seeking to invoke human agency, the material-centric paradigm is forced to accept manners of non-architectural expertise and their means to impose upon and re-form environment, which in this instance is the material entity. Examining *physical imposition* as a form of agency, the somatosensory system becomes both a mechanism of highly individualized expertise for knowledge acquisition and design intervention. In viewing architecture as dependent on bespoke material performance, the tactual sense fits as a well-aligned sensory modality. Subsequently, design encompasses physiological sensorimotor scales. Certain mechanisms *absorb* stimuli of object, surface, substance and event, while more complex *filters* process and discriminate across all sensory modalities to construct a response. David Katz, a German psychologist in the era of the Gestalt movement who researched visual and tactual perception, states:

> The tactual properties of our surroundings do not chatter at us like their colors, they remain mute until we make them speak.
>
> *(Katz, 2016)*

Introduction

For the Great Exhibition of the Works of Industry of All Nations, the first World's Fair in 1851 in London, England, Gottfried Semper offered various schemes by which the wares of the industrial exhibition could be experienced. Through his own self-critique of these schemes emerged the argument to privilege products of the applied arts, as they best depicted artifacts "from the need for nourishment, shelter, protection, the measurement of space and time, and ... should serve as the first and most essential items of consideration" (Semper, 1989). By contrast, a more literal progression, from raw materials and machinery to manufactures and ultimately to fine art seemed backwards. It prioritized form and classified purely by material, in a manner that struck Semper as a "guidebook" that eschewed any underlying motivations.

> Architecture, like its great teacher, nature, should choose and apply its material according to the laws conditioned by nature, yet should it not also make the form and character of its creations dependent on the ideas embodied in them, and not on the material?
>
> *(Semper, 1989)*

Contemporary conversations around the topics of architectures born of novel means of fabrication are commonly demarcated by their material composition and machinic processes, rather than any contextual, cultural or educational factors that may propel them. Their ubiquity of material and fabrication techniques in research, education and practice are ripe for a shift from scrutiny centered on *how?* to a critical imposition of *why?* As it reaches maturity, a critical territory opens for questioning the material system's experiential ramifications. One can impose a gauge based on Semper's off-hand rejection of the *guidebook* approach. To what end does the discussion narrate a series of material procedures, or portray the interrelationships of extra-systemic motives and consequences of particular material outcomes?

The Conventional Im/material System

In its broadest definition, the *material system*, as exemplified in Figure 27.1, marks a territory of architectural research and practice where geometric, structural, spatial and environmental effects are inextricably interconnected and born of generative rules of material production and sequences of assembly, abstaining from standardized material formats or construction logics (Menges, 2008). Often the evolution and operation of natural systems has served as the foil for the *immaterial* component of the material system – conceiving architecture as an equilibrium between material self-organization *and environment*. Von Goethe's *Morphology* captures "character and function" as a multitude of geometric

Reciprocal Relationships of Materiality

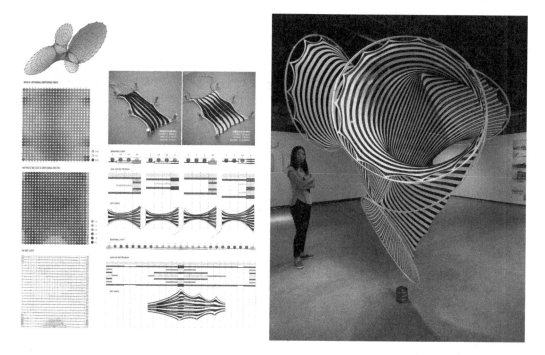

Figure 27.1 Mobius Rib-knit Textile-hybrid Prototype (University of Michigan, Sean Ahlquist) – a material-centric exemplar showcasing articulation of a multi-material tensile surface through computer numerical control (CNC) industrial knitting technology – Taubman College of Architecture and Urban Planning, Ann Arbor, 2014.
Diagrams and photo by Sean Ahlquist

states emerging through internal growth mechanisms and stimulation to and from external forces, where never does a moment of "permanence, repose or termination" exist (1989). Von Bertalanffy contributed *General System Theory* to understand growth, stability and decay through examining *relationships*, as opposed to discrete parts – understanding that equilibrium is notational whereby any particular state is a moment in non-equilibrium (Hammond, 2003).

D'Arcy Thompson uses mathematics as a relational mechanism to capture the inscriptions of environment unto form. His morphometric mappings "pass quickly and easily from the mathematical concept of form in its statistical aspect to form in its dynamical relations" (Thompson, 1961). What Thompson called *homologies*, DeLanda calls *transformational limits*. These are the boundaries of what is possible based upon a discrete set of mathematical functions and variables, assuming the "mathematical model of a physical process can be given a spatial form" (DeLanda, 2007). In linking mathematical models to a material reality, DeLanda distinguishes *properties* – the material relationships that define a physical entity, and *capacities* – the transformational potential for such properties to affect and be affected by external forces.

Equally, from these theoretical foundations for a material system emerges a valuable contribution in thinking beyond the material-centric: *interaction*. The mathematical definition of relations defines the extent of *virtual* possibilities. But it is *interaction* that triggers relations of a particular magnitude and elicits an *actual* reality. When exploring the material–material and the material–atmosphere interface, the contemporary material-centric view holds its systematic nature at the "collapse of material properties and material formation … a representative view of architecture [being] dismissed in favor of form as an explicit expression of material processes" (Ahlquist and Menges, 2011). Design is an effort to choose a path among the *n* number of virtual possibilities that describe the states across the matrix of material and atmospheric interactions.

Yet, if a system only *tends* towards but never achieves equilibrium – according to von Bertalanffy – then *when* do we define the status of an architecture when its underlying character is constructed of processes in constant transformation? One facet of this answer is in blurring the agents of design – from design-er agency to a paradigm of *n*-design agency – and the forms of agency from the pursuit of *virtual relations* to the realization of *interactional instances*.

Conceiving the Extra-systemic

> Context acts as an operator to assign meaning to the metaphorical signals we receive from the world, but it is not found in those signals. It is found, rather, in the consequences of our response to those meanings in that environment.
>
> *(Johnson, 1971)*

Frei Otto, the German architect and engineer, provided key learnings in the inextricable relation of structure, form and design process in, among his extensive explorations catalogued in the *IL* series of books, the study of the behavior of soap film (Otto, IL 18 Forming Bubbles). The array of studies serves as part of a series of translational steps to understand the production of particular geometries shaped by the equilibrium of forces with only the thinnest of membranes. The soap film's moment of equilibrium defines the snapshot of a geometry, which subsequently becomes the seed to Otto's exploration in similar structurally-efficient geometries of architectural-scale membrane materials and constructional logics – such as textiles, cable-nets and pneumatics. When immersed within Otto's experimental design process, this exemplar is a *virtual* exercise, a study of computing form and force by which the material is an abstraction. Yet, these exemplars can be assessed for their immaterial and extra-systemic nature through their visual capacities and atmospheric interactions. For instance, its iridescent reflections and refractions, though in constant flux due to the purity of force equilibrium, are properties of both. They are mappings locked inextricably between the observer's orientation to the material system and relationship to the surrounding surfaces, color and lighting conditions.

What we do not see in the previous example is the condition where observer becomes an instrument of the material system. To disturb the perfection of the soap film, then the interaction to form, deform and destroy defines the totality of the architectural system in its temporal, spatial, visual and tactile transformations. David Katz, through experimental work in the early 1900s, provides a foundation for tactual perception. He relates the physiology of capturing cutaneous, kinesthetic and thermal stimuli to tactual experience as the processing of stimuli when interacting with media, objects and events (Loomis, 1991). While a counterpoint to the precision of the soap film study, Katz offers an analysis of a matchbox encased in cotton fibers. Through visual observation, the boundary of the matchbox is only roughly perceptible beyond the cotton's film-like quality. Yet, to invade the volume of the cotton mass tactually is to render that material invisible as the shape of the immersed matchbox becomes more prominent and known. Initially, the event is constructed through visual cues yet shifts from approximate to null when the matchbox is masked by the outer sheathing of cotton. The tactile feedback shifts from vagueness of the cotton to more distinct pressure as the surfaces of the matchbox are contacted. In Katz's term this exemplar defines *volume touch* – the shifting computation of form through varying levels of resistance in tactile stimuli.

In aligning the interdisciplinary concepts that help define art as a performative medium, Simon Penny poignantly states "interaction confers agency" (2017). James J. Gibson, an American psychologist, offers the term "affordance", as part of ecological psychology, seeking to place the organism, "as eyes on the head of the shoulders of the body", as a living *and acting* being in exchange with the world (Gibson, 2015). Though oft argued, the concept of affordances, in this context, best offers a more granular view of interaction:

> a three-way relationship between the environment, the organism and an activity, ... an improvised and ad-hoc accomplishment, a moment-by-moment response to immediate needs and the setting in which it takes place. The organization of action emerges within the frame of the action itself.
>
> *(Dourish, 2001)*

This subsequently positions social agents within the bounds of the extra-systemic material system where the sensory system is the form of design agency as receptor of stimulation and driver of action (Figure 27.2). As components of *interaction*, one can only pursue the design of stability or homeostasis in this system of systems view if it is a temporal, dynamical one. Alain Berthoz, an expert across the discipline of biomechanics, psychology and neurophysiology, points out "stable does not mean motionless" (2000). This places feedback as a material and human agent – as a manner of interaction that *is* the reality of an architectural system, not the function that simply transitions from one observable state to another. The balance, grip and motion of a glass, the liquids it contains, the weight of both and shifting center of gravity are registered through the multi-scalar stimuli to and from cutaneous, kinesthetic and thermal receptors. "In the absence of this feedback logic, we are clumsy" (Jones, 2018).

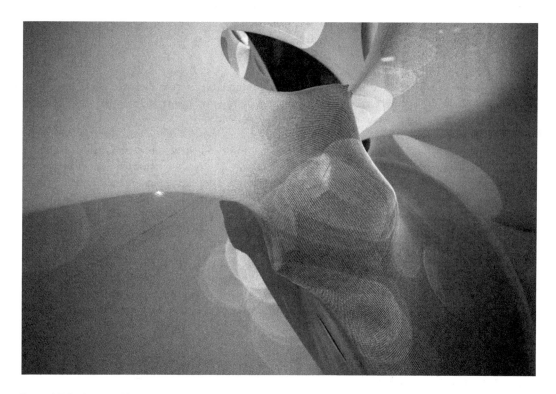

Figure 27.2 SensoryPlayscape Prototype (University of Michigan, Sean Ahlquist) – showcasing sensori-motor-driven design interaction upon the interactive tactile *material system* – Taubman College of Architecture and Urban Planning, Ann Arbor, 2018.

Photo by Sean Ahlquist

Sean Ahlquist

Extending the Temporal Scale of a Material System

> The design goal is nearly always underspecified and the 'controller' is no longer the authoritarian apparatus which this purely technical name commonly brings to mind. In contrast the controller is an odd mixture of catalyst, crutch, memory and arbiter. These, I believe, are the dispositions a designer should bring to bear upon his work (when he professionally plays the part of a controller) and these are the qualities he should embed in the systems (control systems) which he designs.
>
> *(Pask, 1969)*

The architectural practitioner and theorist Christopher Alexander, in his essay "Systems Generating Systems", speaks of the necessity to parse the architectural design process from the operation of the architecture itself (1968). These two distinct efforts are necessary to shift, in his view, from architecture as object to architecture as an environmental system. First, discerning and constructing a *generating system* – the "kit of parts and combinatory rules" that when enacted creates a series of emergent effects. Second, observational measures of properties – distinctive of the rules of the generating system – emanating from the *generated system*. Alexander provides the analogy of the flame to depict the unknowing-ness of the parts, which requires the observational view of the outcome, in order to define the system's properties.

> The 'parts' are flows of vapourised wax, oxygen and burnt gases – the processes of combustion and diffusion give the interaction between these flows – and these interactions show us at what size and shape the flame will be approximately stable.
>
> *(Alexander, 1968)*

The components of the candle – the wax, the wick, the liquids that coat the wick – are inert and in themselves contain no energy for heat or illumination. Only during the state of combustion do the properties of the flame itself become observable and measurable.

Distinguishing the generating system from the observational view of the whole is critical, yet there is a problematic ego in taking a designer's vantage point of the system-level properties. In the example of the flame, the temporal condition of its flickering behavior becomes the permanent, singular narrative for this environmental scenario. There has been a terminus to the design process, notably at the equilibrium state by where the prescribed level of observational detail has become perceivable. But what of other perturbations that can minutely affect, drastically alter or completely nullify certain system-level features? Particularly, what of human presence – the absorption of the flame's heat and interference with the pathways of light – and intervention – the flame's ignition, dousing and re-ignition – as it affects and introduces new levels of detail, transformations and observable features of this environmental situation? Are these not agents that are active within the system? Interestingly, this proposition does not require a reconstitution of the *generating system*. Those physical components and relationships remain present and active. But it does suggest a premature truncation of design process when we consider the acquisition of observable traits via *multiple* vantage points, of design or other intentions, as encompassed *within* not subsequent to design process.

Other than Control and Equilibrium

> [I]n a sense, [the architect's] brief was quite narrow. The problems could all be solved by the judicious application of pure architectural rules. ... Pure architecture was descriptive (a taxonomy

of buildings and methods) and prescriptive (as in the preparation of plans) but it did little to predict or explain.

(Pask, 1969)

Gordon Pask, a British cybertician, helped to advance Norbert Weiner's cybernetic theory through its application in art, theatre and architecture. He developed, in the 1950s, an exemplar for embracing such other-ly intentions, within the generating system, through a device called Musicolour. The adaptive cybernetic device transformed sonic frequencies, of a musical performance, into electrical signals that drive dynamic lighting displays. The compelling aspect of this device was its ability to get "bored". As the same sonic pattern would repeat during a current or prior event, the threshold to act upon its consequent electrical signal would rise, to a point where the corresponding lighting effect is nullified.

The machine would thus provoke the musician to invent while also acting as inquisitor of emergent patterns. In this entirely temporal scenario, it is difficult to discuss the concept of equilibrium. It is far too simple to say equilibrium is the continual activation of *any* lighting scheme. At best, it is a temporal synesthetic effect, but this is only assessable from an individual station-point – an audience member, musician or conductor, for instance.

Pask saw the intent of the Musicolour system primarily to *explain*. He is the designer of how signals travel from *this* to *that*. The musician is the orchestrator of the disruptions and shifts that formulate an environment in continual transition. Pask sees the device not by itself a learning machine, but rather coupled with the musician as part of a prolonged dialogue on learning. As Andrew Pickering states "in performance the performer learned (performatively rather than cognitively) about the machine (and vice versa), and Pask therefore regarded Musicolour as a machine in which one could learn – scientifically, in a conventional sense – about learning" (2010). *Design*, in this instance, takes place in the presence of the audience – an alternate timescale to the narrow brief confined by the architect's *pure architectural rules*.

> An aesthetically potent environment should … respond to a man, engage him in conversation and adapt its characteristics to the prevailing mode of discourse.
>
> *(Pask, 1971)*

Through Musicolour, there is also an important reimagining of *control*, a critical term in von Bertalanffy's General System Theory as well as cybernetics. Whether cycles of growth and degradation in natural systems or a mechanistic view of the same, an open system exists through hierarchies of control mechanisms that respond to varied external inputs. Pask loosens the term "control", posing the possibility for a system to *problem solve* or *come to terms with*, while "exploring the relationship to human adaptive behavior, not attempting to build a machine that could mimic it" (Pickering, 2010).

> We first diverge as we consider a number of inquiry boundaries, a number of major design options, and sets of core values and core ideas. Then we converge, as we make choices and create an image of the future system. The same type of divergence-convergence operates in the design solution space.
>
> *(Banathy, 1996)*

Applied to Alexander's design paradigm, *convergence* encapsulates the construction, articulation and relation between components of the generating system – the conscious effort to define the "inquiry boundaries". Divergence occurs as the generating system is deployed and the effort shifts towards one of observation – perceiving and metering the outward emergent effects of the system while it is in operation. Alexander and Banathy, alike, position this as the path by which the designer travels. But it is Pask's "learning scenario" that moves us beyond the designer being the *sole auteur* and *observer* of the larger system. As opposed to *divergence*, which implies a measurable vector, *departure* more aptly speaks towards a wider possibility of deviations and redirections, by author of alternative motivations. This suits both the extra-systemic of human agency and its being entrenched within an extended scope and lifespan of design process.

Design Process as Homeostat Array

> One can start from the idea that the world is filled not, in the first instance, with facts and observations, but with agency. The world, I want to say, is continually doing things, things that bear upon us not as observation statements upon disembodied intellects but as forces upon material beings.
>
> *(Pickering, 1995)*

> The would-be model maker is now in the extremely common situation of facing some incompletely defined 'system,' that he proposes to study through a study of its variables. Then comes the problem: of the infinity of variables available in this universe, which subset shall he take? What methods can he use for selecting them?
>
> *(Ashby, 1972)*

The homeostat, of which Musicolour is an example, defines the principles for a mechanism of adaptive behavior, learning to respond and continually re-stabilize against external disturbances. The work of Ross Ashby, a psychiatrist and one of the pioneers of cybernetics, laid the foundation for the homeostat, which led to Pask's applications in the arts and architecture. The logic of the homeostat positions the performance of a design as the expression of a design *in process*. It presents a conceptual framework for the performative design process to emanate from and actively operate upon an *ill-defined* notion for its objective and the *unknowingness* of its means to achieve that objective (Cariani, 2009). Extracting again from the Musicolour scenario, the objective – a synesthetic environment of light and sound – is not known until the human actor engages the system. The means for creating a certain synesthetic involves a process of learning, the musician's effort to understand the correlations between patterns of sound and light, which via the machine's adaptive nature to prevent from becoming "bored" is being continually recalibrated.

For Ashby's homeostat, the device utilized electrical current as both input and output, where the output was altered as the current moved through various media – a magnetic coil, a rotating vane and a charged volume of water. What sparks the discussion of *machinic agency* is Ashby's assembly of multiples of these homeostats, where the output of each was input to the others, with a goal to maintain a stable current across the entire system.

Ashby's setup is trying, for itself, to design the controller, through its "coming to terms with" the electrical signals being received from all other controllers. He invoked notions of creativity by allowing the homeostat to randomly reconfigure its internal media in response to an input that did not meet the specific measure of being stable. The *agency* that this scenario portrays is that "it did things in the world that sprang, as it were, from inside itself, rather than having to be fully specified" (Pickering, 2002). In this form of agency, as Pickering calls the "dance of agency", the homeostat and the designer can both be ignorant of the details of the endeavor. This requires recognizing that the endeavor is *not* to find equilibrium across the system, but rather for the controller to discover its best configuration (Cariani, 2009). In shifting the focus from system equilibrium to celebrating the "dance of agency" as the primary, edification – the traverse of agents through countless disruptions, states and reconfigurations – blankets process, mechanism and the design itself. Any perturbation is an *action of design* sparking an array of observational effects, and the choice of a particular station-point – a motivation – to observe and meter specific effects in preparation for a response.

Pickering defines this, in the context of constructing scientific knowledge, as a shift from the retrospective to the performative. The first is an "activity of representation; scientific knowledge is thus supposed to create a mirror image or a map of how the world is, while people and objects are just spectators in the process", and the second more appropriate "performative idiom ... is all about doing: points of view are decentered, action is set in an environment and material and human agencies are entwined together" (Fazi, 2011). The homeostat array, from its very genesis to its operation, exhibits an open-ended design process at which the "scientist-homeostat could be seen as open-endedly searching through spaces of the material performativity of its environment, which itself open-endedly and unpredictably unfolds" (Pickering, 2002).

Parameters of Intra- and Inter-active Design Agents

> Culture evolved out of natural opportunities. The cultural environment, however, is often divided into two parts, 'material' culture and 'non-material' culture. This is a seriously misleading distinction, for it seems to imply that language, tradition, art, music, law and religion are immaterial, insubstantial, or intangible, whereas tools, shelters, clothing, vehicles and books are not. ... There have to be modes of stimulation, or ways of conveying information, for any individual to perceive anything, however abstract.
> *(Gibson, 1966)*

In arguing for the extra-systemic material system, design – both the task of *designing* and *the* design – is being repositioned as a situational acquisition of knowledge involving a form of human agency that is simultaneously observant of and inflective upon the discovery of that very knowledge. Building upon Alexander, this knowledge acquisition is parsed into two modes of design agency: (1) evolution of the generating system, and (2) perturbation and observation of the integrated whole.

Pickering provides an analogy for the former in conceptualizing Pask's Musicolour and Ashby's homeostat as part of a scientific *culture* that prioritized the "real-time understanding of *practice* ... to be contrasted with retrospective approaches that look backward from some terminus". He states

> the intentional character of human agency has a further aspect of temporal emergence, being reconfigured itself in the real time of practice, as well as a further aspect of intertwining with material agency, being reciprocally redefined with the contours of material agency in tuning.
> *(1995)*

This necessitates rejecting the notion of a terminus in the design process, and supports a naiveté on the part of the creator and the creation. Pask must be capable of building the circuitry in order to deploy Musicolour, though need not be thoroughly cognizant of its actual outcomes. This leverages authority to any observer and their particular knowledge set through which outcomes of the system are ascertained. What is essential to this proposition is the ability to embrace otherly expertise, what ultimately defines extra-systemic agency, without requiring its capture, encoding or embedding while enabling its integrality to the evolution – learning – of outwardly effects from the system in operation.

Von Bertalanffy defines the primary components of a homeostatic feedback-dependent system as count, species and association (1969). Through Pickering, human agency is inserted as a critical participant in the construction, operation and reconstruction of these terms (1995). He offers the concepts of modelling, bridging and filling, and transcription to articulate this form of agency. *Modelling* is the action of developing the exemplars, which could be of explicit machines, or of conceptual frameworks. In either case, this terminology represents an open-ended sequence which extends upon the *model of* a prior condition. What we previously referred to as a design pathway through continual points of convergence and departure is what Pickering captures in the activity of *modelling*. Departure from a previous exemplar is termed *bridging*, which "tentatively fixes a vector of cultural extension to be explored" (Pickering, 1995). *Transcription* denotes the transference of previous methods and operations to the space loosely demarcated by this new vector. *Filling* marks the new terms instituted in order to initiate guidance along this new vector. The combination of these efforts explains Pickering's *dance of agency*, where bridging and filling are the unencumbered moves – the ill-defined ones as a repercussion of having ventured into a new domain of modelling. Whereas transcription is a "forced move", an implementation of fixed, established operators and expertise.

Sensorial Nature of Human Agency

> [E]very organism is in one sense continuous with its environment across the boundary of its skin, exchanging matter and energy. But in a very important sense it is discontinuous with the environment. It is highly selective in what it will take in, and of that, what it will assimilate. ... In modern terms, it is [what makes] a homeostatic system.
>
> *(Gibson, 1966)*

As we have discussed, the observation of a system's both intrinsic and extra-systemic relationships is more of an *active query* – forming knowledge through invoking disturbances as being a part of the system, in contrast to the passive observation of an external spectator. Gibson's ecological psychology provides an examination of the human agent's experiential and perceptual capacities – its internal logics for absorbing, organizing and acting upon the external stimuli of the environment in which they are situated. In particular, seeking to place the individual as a learned agent of disturbance and stabilization, among other material agents, accesses Gibson's framing of "action-produced stimulation [that] is *obtained* – not imposed – that is *by* the individual not imposed *on* him" (1966).

Stimuli are events. Only at the moment when a stimulus reaches the threshold as to pique the observer's receptor does it actually register as a stimulus. "A stimulus may specify its source, but it is clearly not the same thing as its source" (Gibson, 1966). Nor is a single stimulus the complete description. Though from the same *station-point*, an alternate construction of an object within an environment will be construed if built through either visual stimuli, tactile stimuli or both. Such discrimination is also important when understanding that stimuli themselves are "patterns and transformations of energy" taking place both at the point of the receptor and as part of a temporal sequence. This pattern, of what Gibson also refers to as "form", defines borders, durations, magnitudes and transitions of stimuli through, in the least, computing fluctuations.

Gibson further distinguishes the manners in which stimuli are obtained, while prioritizing "*seeing* [sensing] and *acting* [response]" as deeply intertwined (Dourish, 2001). The acquisition of knowledge, discernment of and intervention with environment rests on degree of "stimulus energies", level of sensitivity to them, and mobility for orientation to and from them. Gibson poses two modes through which stimulation is acquired and made purposeful: "by moving the organs of the body that are called 'motor' and by moving the organs of the body that are called 'sensory'" (Gibson, 1966). The former – of the body, where Gibson uses the term "proprioception" – requires stimulation as part of executing a particular motoric action, leading to what is conventionally termed *behavior*. The latter, which Gibson classifies as *perception*, seeks stimulation as a means to build information of and response to the environment in which one is situated.

> To kick a stone is no better guarantee of its presence than to see it, actually, for both depend on the energizing of receptors whether in the toe or the eye. Mechanical impact is one thing and photochemical reaction is another, but either one can be an informative stimulus.
>
> *(Gibson, 1966)*

Both of these work on a scale from *imposed* to *obtained*, discriminating between passively or actively gaining such sensorial information, of the body and of the environment. Summed up in terms of the visual *system*, it is the "hierarchy of organs and functions, the retina and its neurons, the eye with its muscles and adjustments, the dual eyes that move in the head, the head that turns on the shoulders, and *the body that moves around the habitat*" (Gibson, 2015). Gibson refers to this as *obtained perception* – "the active orientation and adjustment of the body to explore and obtain information of the environment" (Goldstein, 1981). In forming perception, the gathering of sensorial information and response to sensation occurs more dynamically with environment. We "cognize and calibrate further action, based on the perception of our actions in the world" (Penny, 2017) (Figure 27.3).

> [T]he sequential organization of action is not formulaic outcome of abstract planning, but rather is an improvised, ad hoc accomplishment, a moment-by-moment response to immediate needs and the setting in which it takes place. The organization of action emerges within the frame of the action itself.
>
> *(Dourish, 2001)*

While conceptually we may want to position human agency as another homeostat in an array of material machines, we have to recognize that it is one which does not uniformly follow the same operational scheme. Using Gibson's framework, Pask's conductor situated in the Musicolour environment is an example of the complex balance of the matrices for knowledge acquisition through variants of imposed and

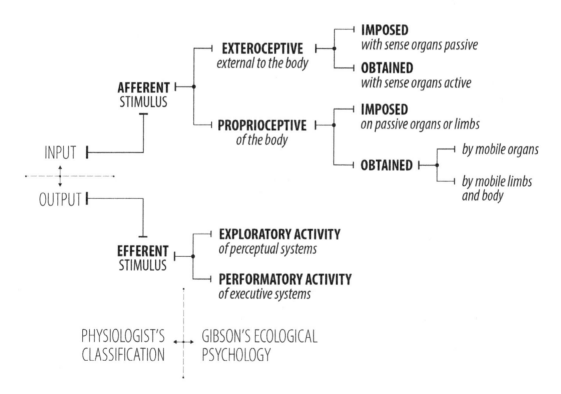

Figure 27.3 Diagram of stimuli related to input and output of the nervous system, based on Gibson's ecological psychology (1966).
Redrawn by Sean Ahlquist

obtained – perception and proprioception. An imposed perception of sound and visual effects is actively augmented with the obtained perception of their emergent patterns. As frequency and pattern require duration, there is an obtained proprioception in the movement of the body and limbs to, at once, orient attention and receptors towards the effects at play, but more importantly to confirm the precise motion of the conductor's baton as to orchestrate the sounds from the musicians and their instruments – they themselves embedded agents in the Musicolour scenario. Berthoz packages the framework for agency of man and machine, as exemplified by Musicolour, into three basic elements – *regularity*, *chance* and *movement* – properties which equally encompass the structure of nature and of human perception (2002).

Forming an Eco-Social Material System

> Development can only be understood as the multiple, mutual, and continuous interaction of all the levels of the developing system, from the molecular to the cultural.
>
> *(Thelen & Smith, 1998)*

This approach for embedding extra-systemic agents within the material system can be exemplified, in more specific architectural terms, through on-going research in positioning architecture as a key discipline in exploring the relationship of environment, behavior and social function, particularly for children with the neurobehavioral condition of autism, as shown in Figure 27.4 (Ahlquist, 2016). The common traits of autism spectrum disorder include impairments in communication, social interaction and behavioral regulation (Baio, Wiggins, Christensen, et al., 2018). The linkages between social function and the sensory domain poses architectural concerns. High degrees of sensitivity are commonplace, from hyper- to hypo-sensitivity and across multiple sensory domains – typically tactile and auditory, likely to produce poorly modulated behavioral responses, and in social settings lead to stigmatization and isolation (Baranek, 2005).

A lack of adaptability to stressful conditions inhibits participation in the "daily occupations that provide … means to learn skills, develop relationships, and meet biological needs that support health and well-being" (Chang et al., 2012). Conversely, such heightened sensitivities to negative stimuli will carry similar enhanced sensitivity to *positive* stimuli which brings the potential for enhanced and sustained developmental effects (Ellis et al., 2011). Such hyperawareness to external stimuli provides a test-bed to explore Gibson's description of the inextricable three-way relationship between environment, organism and activity.

> We are embodied in the world, but also that the world is the site and setting of all activity. It shapes and is shaped by the activities of embodied agents.
>
> *(Dourish, 2001)*

This poses the need for an architecture that balances the *imposition* of detrimental stimuli, to recall Gibson's term of *imposed perception*, with the *obtained perception* of beneficial stimuli – the training of one's orientation towards beneficial stimuli to create an equilibrium between behavior and environment. This exposes a critical un-knowingness in defining the boundary between these two states. If one takes seriously the adage *when you have met one individual with autism, then you've met one individual with autism*, then agency over the factors that define a social, environmental situation would only logically have to be ceded to *sensorimotor expertise* of that *one individual*.

> Every organism is in one sense continuous with its environment across the boundary of its skin, exchanging matter and energy. But in a very important sense it is discontinuous with the environment. It is highly selective in what it will take in, and, of that, what it will assimilate.
>
> *(Gibson, 1966)*

Reciprocal Relationships of Materiality

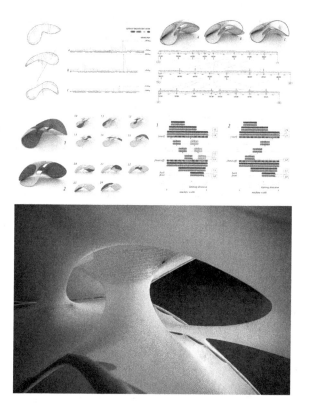

Figure 27.4 SensoryPlayscape Textile-hybrid Prototype (University of Michigan, Sean Ahlquist) – self-forming structural material system integrating bending-active laminated glass-fiber-reinforced polymer beams and form-active (tensioned) textiles manufactured via computer numerically controlled knitted machines – Southern Illinois University, Carbondale, 2016.
Diagrams and photo by Sean Ahlquist

Design no longer functions through the discussion of an *instant* – but rather *scenarios*. To isolate a sensory condition and track its singular associated trigger would be to create such an experimental setup as to imply an "artificial consciousness" (Katz, 2016). *Interaction* is then considered an *act of design*. In the context of generating agency for individuals with autism, the question is of *magnitude*. To what degree is the action allowed to reshape the material and social nature of the environment, and to what degree is it innately responsive or overtly manipulated? In the context of creating a system where the line between detrimental and beneficial can be discovered, this would mean that agency is as vast as possible.

Requisite Variety of Scenarios

> The larger the variety of actions available to a control system, the larger the variety of perturbations it is able to compensate.
>
> *(Ashby, 1956)*

If heterogeneity is a desired trait, the formation has to occur at the micro-scale of materialization. The component is more abstractly defined at levels such as chemical bonds and fibrous orientations.

> The material system is now truly founded upon processes, which span all scales, noticing that the component is defined in the realm of actions, needing to be bonded or be oriented. Material properties are no longer discreet factors but are now capacities in and of themselves. To be oriented means orientation in comparison to another.
>
> *(Ahlquist & Menges, 2011)*

The design *model*, most readily analogous to the *weather model*, is best described as a compilation of processes, rather than a static geometric representation (Ahlquist & Menges, 2011). A *design space* or *solution space* is constructed by the variables and constraints within these particular processes, shown with the "platform" framework in Figure 27.5. Exploration of variants within the bounded design space would, in simple terms, be considered the act of designing. The most effective version of the design model for a *material system* would be one that contains the processes of *making* across the extents of all material scales – "actively incorporate[ing] the 'design' of processes and protocols from which material form emerges" (Ahlquist & Menges, 2011). The array of material hierarchies captured parallels the degree of articulation possible in the technical operation of the material system itself.

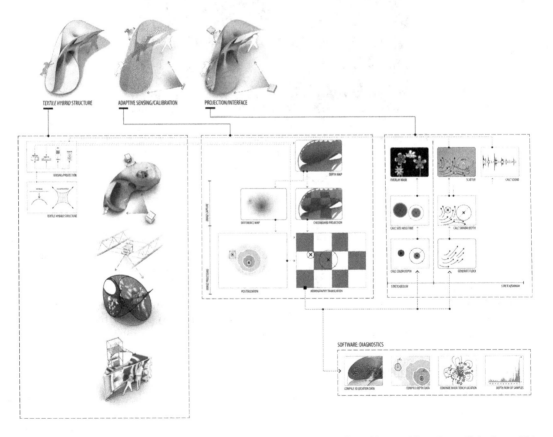

Figure 27.5 Modular platform for SensoryPlayscapes (University of Michigan, Oliver Popadich, Sean Ahlquist) – interchangeable platform between textile environment, sensing and projective, graphical interface.
Diagram by Sean Ahlquist

Reciprocal Relationships of Materiality

The concept of a design space can be traced to the *homologies* of D'Arcy Thompson, expressed in his analogy with the glass blower: "all possibilities of glass forming are [captured in] the transformations of the simple tube through the external influence of unequal heating and cooling" (Ahlquist & Menges, 2011). Yet, this reflects the troublesome binary condition between design process and artifact. Instead of comparing iterations, tracing the steps of particular guidebooks, as an a priori design exercise, it is necessary to employ *observation-as-interaction* as the nature of the design space. The binary between design-ing and design-ed becomes temporal, if not so temporal as to be blurred. Design-ed no longer represents the summation of the conventional designer-led design process – activating just one of the paths through the design space. *The action of design, as an inquiry or perturbation upon the material system, is the design itself.*

The homeostats of Ashby, described earlier, were some of the earliest examples of systems adaptive to their own agency. Pertinent to this discussion, they showcased that both machine and designer could be indeterminate towards their own performance (Cariani, 2009). In large part, this was reliant upon Ashby's Law of Requisite Variety – defining the robustness of the system through its possession of a certain number of ill-defined alternative states (Ashby, 1956). In Ashby's study of the process of *regulation*, it is shown that the controller must house as many states as to respond to varied and unknown external stimuli. It is only through traversing these alternate states, realizing the *situational* iterations within the design space, through which "information gain" and "uncertainty reduction" is achieved. The statistician George E. P. Box defines this as an iterative conveyance from *data getting* to

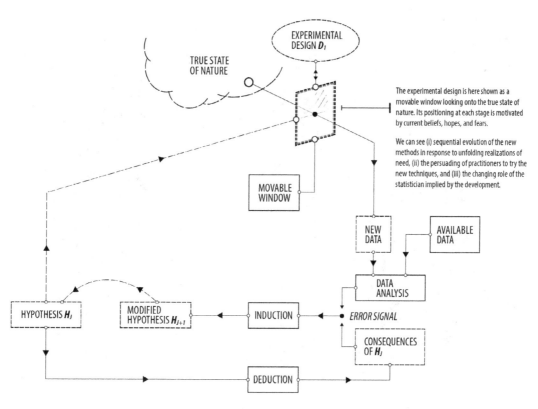

Figure 27.6 Diagram capturing the on-going reciprocation between speculation and learning across modes of scientific practice as defined by statistician G. E. P. Box (1976).
Redrawn by Sean Ahlquist

data analysis (Box, 1976). In his concept of the *tentative theory*, discrepancies from an initial exploration formulate a new iteration, and so the cycle of "unfolding new realizations" goes (Figure 27.6).

State-switching of the Situated Material System

> The environment consists of opportunities for perception, of available information, of potential stimuli. Not all opportunities are grasped, … not all stimuli excite receptors. But what the environment affords an individual in the way of discrimination is enormous.
>
> *(Gibson, 1966)*

> (Men) People of uncommon abilities generally fall into eccentricities when their sphere of life is not adequate to their (powers) abilities.
>
> *(Goethe; see Wood, 1893)*

Ashby's homeostat utilized a series of "switchings between alternative sets" to internally modify its state as a randomized attempt to regain stability across the entire system. The enumeration of the state-switching option defines, in its simplest terms, the requisite variety. As we shift from inputs of electrical signals to

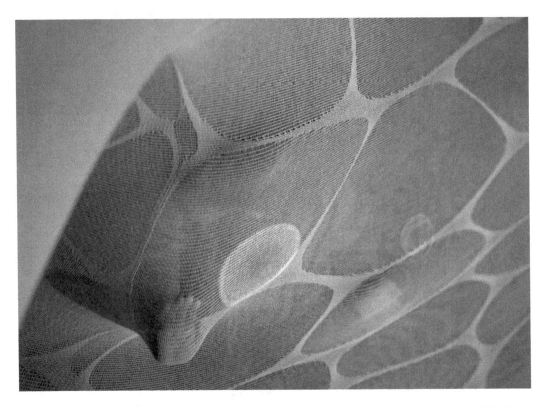

Figure 27.7 Field study for SensoryPlayscape Prototype (University of Michigan, Sean Ahlquist) – engaging gradations of tactile stimuli largely upon combined yarn structure and stitch pattern – Pediatric Therapy Center, Columbus (Indiana), 2019.

Photo by Sean Ahlquist

interactions of human agency, then *state* can be reframed ultimately as *function*. Not in the conventional sense; rather, functionality is a form of *tentative use*, iterated upon to explore and specify a temporal ideal effectiveness. As ill-defined and temporal are the *switchings* of human and non-human agency, so *unknown* are the potential *state-functions* outside of the individual interaction.

In the adaptive environments designed for children with autism, the balance between materiality and state-function is explored through textiles and interactive projections as the media that encompasses the *state-space* of sensorimotor functions (Figure 27.7). Intending to capture the ability to explore, learn and master new movement behaviors, the core functionality is in expanding social opportunities through a buffered sensorially-responsive environment (Ahlquist et al., 2017). While building new sequences of movement through varying sensory stimuli, the sustained interest and variability of such movement patterns is critical to allow for generalization of the skill beyond the specific site in which it was mastered (Ketcheson et al., 2017) (Figure 27.8).

The composition of the textile interface becomes an exemplar for the relationship between material hierarchy and degrees of functional operation when viewed through the linkages to kinesthetic learning. Yarn – as a winding of fibers – is formed into stitches – as an interlocking of loops – which constructs a surface – as a manifold 3D geometry – and forms an interface – as a tensile surface. At each scale is an operative function of elasticity: (1) elastic filaments and the ability to straighten coiled inelastic fibers, (2) the conformable nature of a stitch allowing bi-directional elongation of the initially looped geometry, and (3) 3D geometry through which differential surface tensions emerge. To present variable elasticity as one of the primary *selectors* to switch between requires the activation of *successive stimulation*.

Figure 27.8 Field study for SensoryPlayscape Prototype (University of Michigan, Sean Ahlquist) – activating proprioceptive sensorimotor behavior in choreography with the form-active geometries of the material system – Haisley Elementary School, Ann Arbor, 2017.

Photo by Sean Ahlquist

> [A]ll impressions on the hard-soft dimension owe their existence to successive stimulation. Resting the touch organ really motionless on an object precludes any sure judgement as to whether it is hard or soft ... where the spatial-temporal pattern of excitation of the pressure and muscle sense organs is crucial for the development of the experience of elasticity.
>
> *(Katz, 2016)*

There is a switching, or more appropriately a *grading*, between sensorimotor states. In the tactile scale, pressure at the skin receptors transmits to the deeper receptors in the joints and muscles as the degree of engagement – pressure upon – the elastic textile increases. To be enveloped within the tensile geometry shifts to a proprioceptive action. Through the expanse of tactile engagement with the body, an enhanced notion of movement is proffered. Pressure to the core and resistance to the limbs better enables registration of their position and orientation in space. A vestibular state-function is generated in the maintenance of balance and spatial orientation as part of moving across the shifting doubly-curved surfaces (Figure 27.9).

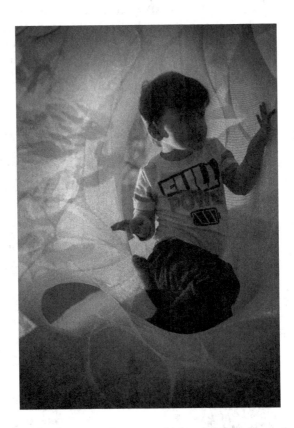

Figure 27.9 Field study for SensoryPlayscape Prototype (University of Michigan, Sean Ahlquist) – triggering vestibular interaction across multiple hierarchies of the material system from fiber elasticity to spatial organization – Pediatric Therapy Center, Columbus (Indiana), 2019.

Photo by Sean Ahlquist

Each of these kinesthetic scenarios can occur in any physical location within the material system. It, therefore, can be said that the human agency is not only in the spatial transformation of the material agent, but it is in that temporal moment that the state-function bounces between and across scales of tactile, proprioceptive and vestibular action. The child's intervening is an act of design, where there has been no a priori function assignment.

Conclusion

[M]an is prone to seek novelty in his environment and, having found a novel situation, to learn how to control it. … In slightly different words, man is always aiming to achieve some goal and he is always looking for new goals. … My contention is that man enjoys performing these jointly innovative and cohesive operations. Together, they represent an essentially human and inherently pleasurable activity.

(Pask, 1976)

To engage in human behavior as a part of the discipline of architecture, outside of philosophy and conjecture, reaches beyond the curriculum of the discipline. Thinking of the sensorimotor mechanisms, that drive behavior, as inquisitors and perturbations of the materiality of architecture, these are parameters

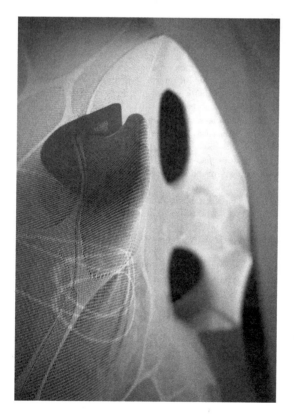

Figure 27.10 Field study for SensoryPlayscape Prototype (University of Michigan, Sean Ahlquist) – Pediatric Therapy Center, Columbus (Indiana), 2019.
Photo by Sean Ahlquist

outside of the descriptive and prescriptive pure architectural rules. The material system is but one homeostat, where its narrative only emerges once placed in the context of adjacent human and non-human homeostats. Where design agency is sensorimotor, one can only define both the material architecture and its extra-systemic realities while it is in motion. Motion through the human agent's methods of acquiring reciprocal knowledge of environment, or in deploying, flaunting or muting the learned capacities (Figure 27.10). A design – as an exemplification of the design process itself – is not trying to impart another's knowledge, or a pre-scripted narrative upon the individual, but enable the individual to discover their own knowledge and pathway, from a divergent, un-knowing but functional station-point.

References

Ahlquist, S. (2016). Sensory material architectures: Concepts and methodologies for spatial tectonics and tactile responsivity in knitted textile hybrid structures. *International Journal of Architectural Computing*, 14 (1), 63–82.

Ahlquist, S., Ketcheson, L., & Colombi, C. (2017). Multisensory architecture: The dynamic interplay of environment, movement and social function. *Architectural Design*, 87 (2), 90–99.

Ahlquist, S., & Menges, A. (2011). Materiality and computational design: Emerging material systems and the role of design computation and digital fabrication. In M. Kanaani & D. Kopec (Eds.). *The Routledge companion for architecture design and practice: Established and emerging trends*. New York, NY: Routledge. 149–168.

Alexander, C. (1968). *Systems generating systems: Architectural design theory*. London: John Wiley & Sons.

Ashby, W. R. (1956). *An introduction to cybernetics*. New York, NY: John Wiley & Sons.

Ashby, W. R. (1972). Analysis of the system to be modeled. In R. M. Stogdill (Ed.). *The process of model-building in the behavioral sciences*. New York, NY: W. W. Norton. 78–97.

Baio, J., Wiggins, L., Christensen, D. L., et al. (2018). Prevalence of Autism Spectrum Disorder among children aged 8 years – Autism and Developmental Disabilities Monitoring Network, 11 sites, United States, 2014. *MMWR Surveill Summ* 2018; 67 (No. SS-6):1–23.

Banathy, B. H. (1996). *Designing social systems in a changing world*. New York, NY: Plenum.

Baranek, G. (2005). Sensory and motor features in autism: Assessment and intervention. In F. R. Volkmar, R. Paul, A. Klin, & D. Cohen (Eds.). *Handbook of autism and pervasive developmental disorders*, 3rd ed. Hoboken, NJ: John Wiley & Sons. 831–857.

Berthoz, A. (2000). *The brain's sense of movement*. Cambridge, MA: Harvard University Press.

Berthoz, A. (2002). *The brain's sense of movement: Perspectives in cognitive neuroscience* (G. Weiss, Trans.). Cambridge, MA: Harvard University Press.

Box, G. E. P. (1976). Science and statistics. *Journal of the American Statistical Association*, 71 (356), 791–799.

Cariani, P. A. (2009). The homeostat as embodiment of adaptive control. *International Journal of General Systems*, 38 (2), 139–154.

Chang, M. C., Parham, L. D., Blanche, E. I., Schell, A., Chou, C. P., Dawson, M., & Clark, F. (2012). Autonomic and behavioral responses of children with autism to auditory stimuli. *American Journal of Occupational Therapy*, 66 (5), 567–576.

DeLanda, M. (2007). Real virtualities. In A. Menges & S. Ahlquist (Eds.). *Computational design thinking*. London: John Wiley & Sons. 142–148.

Dourish, P. (2001). *Where the action is*. Cambridge, MA: MIT Press.

Ellis, B. J., Boyce, W. T., Belsky, J., Bakermans-Kranenburg, M. J., and Van IJzendoorn, M. H. (2011). Differential susceptibility to the environment: An evolutionary–neurodevelopmental theory. *Development and Psychopathology*, 23 (1), 7–28.

Fazi, M. B. (2011). Cybernetics in action. [Review] Andrew Pickering (2010) *The cybernetic brain: Sketches of another future*. *Computational Culture*, 1, n.p.

Gibson, J. J. (1966). *The senses considered as perceptual systems*. Boston, MA: Houghton Mifflin.

Gibson, J. J. (2015). *The ecological approach to visual perception*. New York, NY: Taylor & Francis.

Goldstein, E. B. (1981). The ecology of J. J. Gibson's perception. *Leonardo*, 14 (3), 191–195.

Hammond, D. (2003). *The science of synthesis: Exploring the social implications of general systems theory*. Boulder, CO: University Press of Colorado.

Johnson, A. R. (1971). The Three Little Pigs revisited. In P. Batchelor & J. Pearce (Eds.). *Collaborative design in community development: Eleven views*. Raleigh, NC: North Carolina State University. 173–186.

Jones, L. A. (2018). *Haptics*. Cambridge: MIT Press.

Katz, D. (2016). *The world of touch*. (Lester E. Krueger, Trans.). New York, NY: Routledge. (Original work published 1989).

Ketcheson, L., Hauck, J., & Ulrich, D. (2017). The effects of an early motor skill intervention on motor skills, levels of physical activity, and socialization in young children with autism spectrum disorder: A pilot study. *Autism*, 21 (4), 481–492.

Loomis, J. M. (1991). Reviewed work(s): *The world of touch* by David Katz and Lester E. Krueger. *American Journal of Psychology*, 104 (1), 147–150.

Menges, A. (2008). Integral formation and materialisation: Computational form and material gestalt. In B. Kolarevic & K. Klinger (Eds.). *Manufacturing material effects: Rethinking design and making in architecture*. New York, NY: Routledge. 195–210.

Pask, G. (1969). The architectural relevance of cybernetics. *Architectural Design*, 39 (9), 494–496.

Pask, G. (1971). A comment, a case history and a plan. In J. Reichardt (Ed.). *Cybernetics, art and ideas*. London: Studio Vista, 76–99.

Pask, G. (1976). *Conversation theory: Applications in education and epistemology*. Amsterdam: Elsevier.

Penny, S. (2017). *Making sense: Cognition, computing, art, and embodiment*. Cambridge, MA: MIT Press.

Pickering, A. (1995). *The mangle of practice: Time, agency, and science*. Chicago, IL: University of Chicago Press.

Pickering, A. (2002). Cybernetics and the mangle: Ashby, Beer and Pask. *Social Studies of Science*, 32 (3), 413–437.

Pickering, A. (2010). *The cybernetic brain: Sketches of another future*. Chicago, IL: University of Chicago Press.

Semper, G. (1989). *The four elements of architecture and other writings* (H. F. Mallgrave & W. Herrmann, Trans.). Cambridge: Cambridge University Press.

Thelen, E., & Smith, L. B. (1998). Dynamic systems theories. In W. Damon (Ed.). *Handbook of child psychology*. New York, NY: John Wiley & Sons, 258–312.

Thompson, D. W. (1961). *On growth and form*, abridged ed. Cambridge: Cambridge University Press.

von Bertalanffy, L. (1969). *General system theory: Foundations, development, applications* New York, NY: George Braziller.

von Goethe, J. W. (1989). Formation and transformation (B. Mueller, Trans.). Woodbridge, CT: Ox Bow Press.

Wood, R. J. (1893). *Dictionary of quotations from ancient and modern English and foreign sources: Including phrases, mottoes, maxims, proverbs, definitions, aphorisms, and sayings of wise men, in their bearing on life, literature, speculation, science, art, religion, and morals especially in the modern aspects of them*. London and New York, NY: Warne.

28

Computing Performativity

The Role of Coding Within BIM for the Execution of Performative Design Concepts

Karen Kensek

Concepts

This chapter expands on available practical approaches to performative design thinking toward the achievement of performance-based building. It focuses on coding using a building information modeling (BIM) approach and explores its potential for performative design. BIM goes beyond 3D modeling by storing and then supplying data that can be exported to simulation tools for supporting architecture design, engineering, construction, and operation (AECO) of buildings. It relies strongly on interoperability, the ability to exchange data between applications, to do this. Performative design methodologies often use BIM's ability to share data among the team members in a design project. In essence, a building information model represents the building as an integrated database of coordinated information. Theoretically, it enables an overall 3D depiction of a building and its characteristics by including everything in a single source model. Architects and consultants can use this model with simulation tools for predicting the future behavior of a building and informing decisions they make while the building is still being designed.

This ideal of BIM as a single database that describes the building from conception to operation has been a touchstone for BIM evangelists. In addition to graphically depicting the design, the building information model can hold key pieces of data about the building that can be used to analyze building performance. This data could be input by the designers, consultants, or even manufacturers, and then used in analysis software. The key to achieving this is interoperability between the model and the analysis software. As an example, BIM can support sustainable design in several ways with different levels of interoperability:

- The BIM software can have built-in simulation capabilities; hence there is no necessity to transfer the model to a different software program. For example, because the software includes the project's location, the 3D geometry can be used for shadow casting. The designer can use this information for preliminary layout of the building design and shading devices and for placement of solar panels based on solar radiation. Initial daylighting studies can also be performed.
- The 3D model's geometry alone can be exported to more sophisticated simulation software that can balance daylighting, advanced interior lighting design, and lighting control systems to save energy.

- The model with associated data, e.g. the types of windows and the wall construction, can be sent to an energy modeling software program to determine energy consumption for heating and cooling. This informs the overall design of the building and the selection of the HVAC (heating, ventilation, and air conditioning) system.
- With the appropriate software, it is also possible to use the model for showing compliance with sections of green building certification programs such as LEED (Leadership in Energy and Environmental Design).

However, although complete interoperability is a worthy visionary goal, it often fails when put to practical use, and pragmatic workarounds have been developed by architects, engineers, and other consultants to minimize the inevitable problems. The interchange of information from the building information model to and from analysis software is far from perfect – data is sometimes lost, the model can be misinterpreted (e.g. a shading device becomes a roof element that is treated differently in the calculations), and it is difficult to go back from the simulation software to the BIM software. This is a hindrance to iterative design. These problems are known by the designers and consultants who work with the software. They have developed in-house tricks and techniques to improve their own workflow, much of which is based on the expertise of the user and knowing exactly where the interoperability fails.

Other methodologies are also being used that instead rely upon the ability of the designer to use scripting or coding to improve the functionality of the software and to develop plug-ins that can achieve some of the goals of simulation, especially in the early stages of design. Some designers are using coding to extend 3D modeling and BIM functionality for form generation, analysis, and practical task-solving in an office.

Terms

In order to understand how BIM and simulation are being used together in the building industry, it is important to understand some terms that are commonly used and know about a few common software programs (there are many others!). The terms have been grouped into four categories: modeling (3D model and BIM), analysis software, best-performance scenarios and optimization, and coding.

Modeling

A 3D model is a geometric description of a building. For early design studies, this can be a very simple massing study that describes the walls, roofs, floors, and perhaps windows' placements. For construction, complex models are created that show architecture details, structure (sometimes even to the extent of showing rebar and stirrups for the structural model), MEP (mechanical, electrical, plumbing) and other important systems, and fabrication details such as node connectors, beam/column steel plates, specialized handrails, complex façade joints, and others specific to the building. Depending on the software, the internal data of a 3D model is usually based on surface modeling or solid modeling. Point clouds are also 3D models, but typically they do not work with simulation software. Examples of software include AutoCAD (when used in 3D), Sketchup, Rhino, 3DS Max, and many others. A building information model is also a 3D model. However, it is substantially different in that it is composed of parametric components such as doors, walls, ducts, pipes, furniture, etc., that have data attached to them. For example, a window might have associated with it its 3D geometry, cost, R-value, manufacturer, material, glass type, and other characteristics. A building information model can be stripped down to just a 3D model by discarding the data and parametric features. Revit, Tekla, ArchiCAD, and Digital Project are a few examples of BIM software.

Analysis Software

Analysis software is used to make predictions of the future performance of buildings so that architects and engineers can make informed decisions during the design stage. Common applications include daylighting potential, shadows, thermal comfort, energy consumption, seismic, wind, cost, clash detection, and hundreds of others. Often overlooked, form generation is also a kind of analysis as the designer creates, tests, and evaluates the shape of a building. Analysis software often uses a 3D model for the basis of the simulation. Hence interoperability between 3D modeling and simulation software can increase efficiency and improve accuracy as the model does not need to be recreated. Many file formats (beyond what are listed) exist to achieve this workflow, including dwg and dxf for 3D model description, IFC for BIM, and inp and gbXML for energy software. Although many formats exist, problems can appear when they are used to transfer data between programs, including missing objects, disappearance of data, and assignment of components to a wrong category (for example, sun shades becoming roofs) that make interoperability a skill to master. In addition, in almost all cases there is no "round tripping;" changes made in analysis software cannot be exported back to the 3D modeling or BIM software.

Best-Performance Scenarios and Optimization

Traditional simulation software is good for evaluating "best-performance scenarios." Many case studies can be run in the software with different parameters, results visualized, and information provided to the designer as to the relationship between the specified parameters and output. For example, different sizes of windows can be compared versus their daylight potential and thermal consequences in a climate zone. Simulation software programs often can run hundreds, even thousands, of cases, sometimes automatically. Trade-offs can be studied, and semi automatic optimization (or at least "better performance") is becoming more common. In some software, scripting or other programming tools allow the user to batch-run thousands of simulations and show the results in a way to allow the designer to choose what solution best fits her constraints (Figure 28.1).

As with the best-case scenarios, designers are generally using their experience and software applications for graphing and visualizing multiple options to "optimize" or find the best solution for one variable or competing objectives. "Optimization" algorithms have also been developed that can be used to determine better solutions for a set of results. Some of these are built into a specific simulation software; others are available as plug-ins for use in many kinds of applications. Solving for an optimal solution for one variable can be as simple as running the software multiple times until an acceptable value is reached. This might not necessarily be the "optimal" value, but it is often good enough. However, when there are multiple trade-offs between variables, it can be difficult to do. For example, a designer might want to balance glare, amount of daylighting, allowable WWR, and summer solar radiation contributing to cooling loads. Multi-variable optimization algorithms can offer potential solutions for well-defined questions. In some cases, these are built directly into the software – for example, cost optimization for site grading; and mechanical system design for energy efficiency, air flow distribution, and thermal comfort considerations; and energy consumption versus WWRs. Genetic algorithms and evolutionary systems provide a framework whereby locally optimal solutions can be searched for within a nearly infinite generative field of variation. Graphs can be made to show the better solutions along the Pareto front (Figures 28.2 and 28.3).

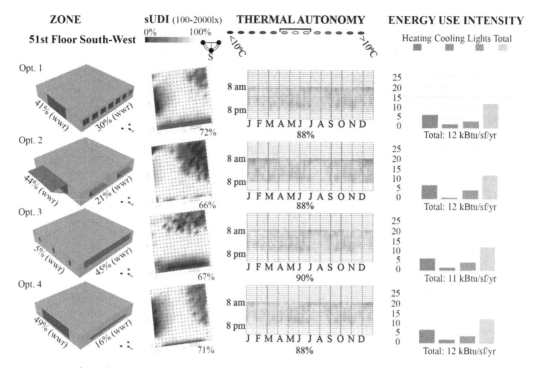

- Very similar outcomes despite having shading devices or not
- Similar results from design solutions that seem to be contradictory

Figure 28.1 Four options are shown for the windows and shading of the 51st floor of a building (left column). The parameters are window-to-wall ratio (WWR), distribution of glass, and inclusion of shading devices. The results are then compared for their daylight (sUDI), thermal autonomy, and energy use intensity (EUI) to determine which solution would be best. Rhino and Grasshopper were used to create this custom tool.

Courtesy of Alejandro Gamas

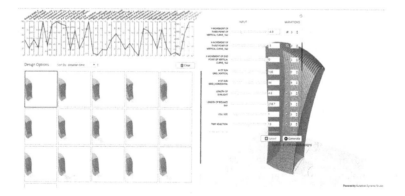

Figure 28.2 Design options of the south façade surface and their corresponding solar glare distribution are compared using Autodesk Fractal to determine potential glare due to the convex shape of the south façade. Multiple shape constraints are shown on the graph; the sliders on the right are used to control simulation settings. The next generation of this tool, Autodesk Refinery (beta), not only generates options, but also does optimization.

Courtesy of Tian Chen, Kunyu Luo, and Yijin Yuan

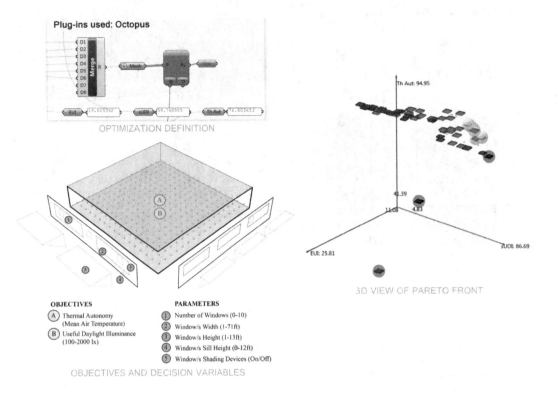

Figure 28.3 Octopus is an optimization module for use in Grasshopper. In this case, the parameters were the number of windows and their width, height, sill height, and whether or not they have shading devices. The 3D graph shows the solution set for daylight (sUDI), thermal autonomy, and EUI for all of the case studies generated based on these parameters.
Courtesy of Alejandro Gamas

Coding

Coding/scripting/programming used in this context is a method of extending a software program's functionality through a series of instructions for the computer to execute. A script can allow access to the software program's "internal guts" through an Application Program Interface (API) in several ways. One method is to categorize the types of programming into text-based and visual programming, also called graphical algorithm editing. Text-based is the traditional method of computer programming using lines of code in languages such as C# and Python or even languages such as AutoLISP or RhinoScript that are used directly in the software (Figures 28.4–28.6).

In visual programming, users interact with graphic program elements instead of typing lines of text code. Nodes (the boxes) are created; they can be numbers, sliders for adjusting values, operators and functions, list manipulation tools, graphic creators for geometry, notes, calculation, customizable nodes, and other types depending on the tool. They are virtually wired together, and the program is resolved from left to right (Figures 28.7 and 28.8).

Mathworks' Simulink is an example of a graphical programming environment often used for engineering applications for modeling, simulating, and analyzing multidomain dynamical systems. Grasshopper is a graphical algorithm editor tightly integrated with Rhino's 3D modeling tools; Dynamo is used within Revit, and additionally Dynamo Studio is a stand-alone environment; and Marionette for

Computing Performativity

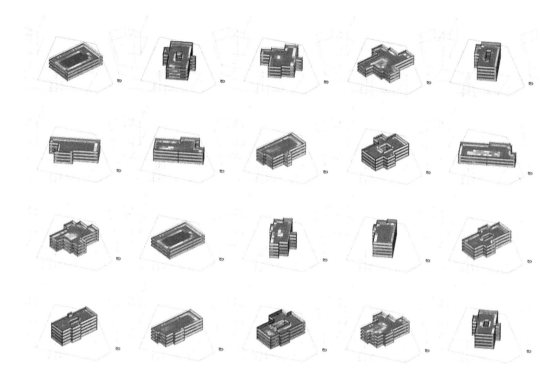

Figure 28.4 A passive performance optimization framework was developed in Grasshopper to improve the performance of daylighting, solar control, and natural ventilation strategies in the early stage of design. It uses a code-compliant reference building in four different climate zones and urban locations (Los Angeles, Helsinki, Mexico City, and New York City) to demonstrate its ability to generate design solutions and optimize results based on daylighting performance (sUDI) and EUI. The image shows 20 iterations of an optimization run.
Courtesy of Alejandro Gamas

Vectorworks is their algorithmic method to create design forms. All of these enable designers to create forms, run some types of simulation, and automate tasks. Some also include optimization modules (Figures 28.9–28.11).

Analyzing a Building: Different Workflows

There are many workflows that designers and consultants use for analyzing their design intent; it is important to note that almost always a 3D model has been created beforehand. One option is to only use the simulation software without any additional software. The user can create the necessary 3D model, add data, and get results without worrying about interoperability problems. However, the benefits accrued by already having a 3D model are negated – efficiency is lost by having to create a new model, and accuracy between the design version and simulation version of the 3D model could be a problem. A second workflow uses the 3D model initially created, and then it is imported into the analysis software. Because only geometry and not data is transferred, this process usually works properly. There are more potential problems when both data and the 3D geometry initially created is imported into analysis software. As previously mentioned, numerous glitches can occur when

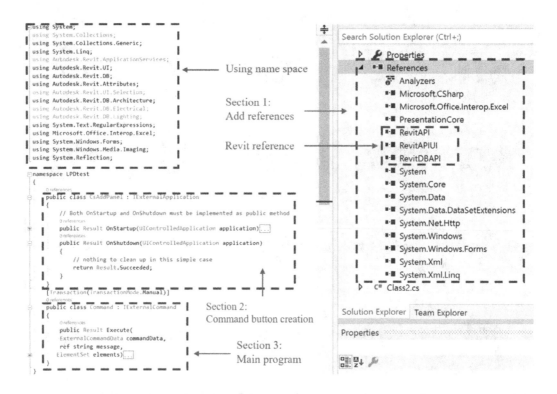

Figure 28.5 This is part of the program to calculate lighting power density in each space. The program is divided into three parts: add references, command button creation, and main program.
Courtesy of Lu Huang

Figure 28.6 Exterior building "shades" on a high-rise building are generated using RhinoScript.
Courtesy of Alice Hovsepian

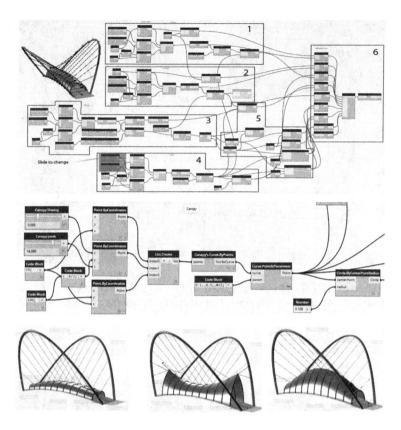

Figure 28.7 The top image shows the structure of the Dynamo code. The middle image zooms into the control nodes for the canopy's swing and peak, which are controlled by slider bars. The third row shows three results of simple parametric changes to the bridge's canopy using these slider bars.

Courtesy of Rustem Ilyassov and Yerbol Tazbibayev

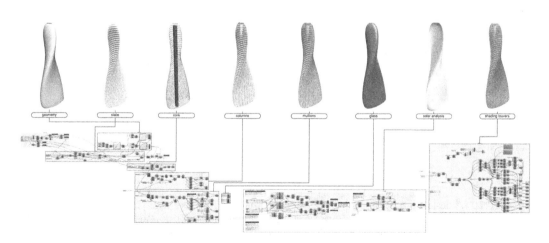

Figure 28.8 Each part of the Dynamo code adds parameters to the twisted building form: slabs, core, columns, mullions, glass, solar analysis, and shading louvers. These are updated automatically if the original geometry (far left) is changed.

Courtesy of Jeffrey Vaglio

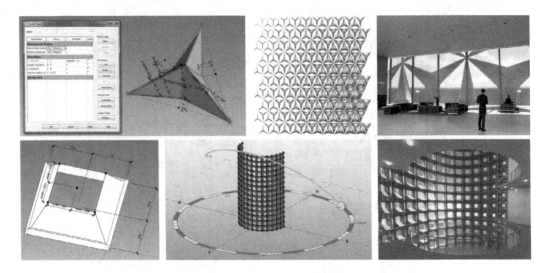

Figure 28.9 Revit adaptive components are used in Dynamo as interactive solar façade components. When the sun's position changes, the façade components change the size of the openings.

Courtesy of Ilaria Toldo and Dennis Chow (top); Rustem Ilyassov and Yerbol Tazbibayev (bottom)

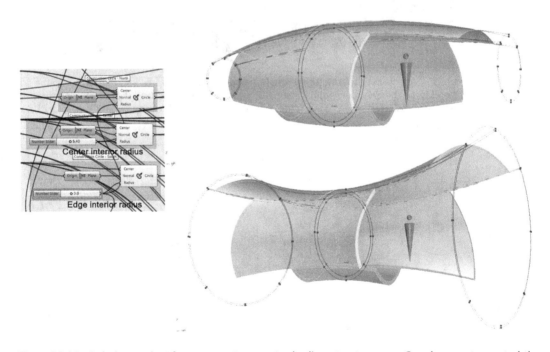

Figure 28.10 A design project for a pre-cast concrete shading structure uses Grasshopper to control the shape of the panels. One of several parameter sliders (edge interior radius) is shown that modifies the carapace design, updates the form, and verifies that the concrete panels match on the edges.

Courtesy of Ivan Monsreal

Figure 28.11 The carapace design team uses Rhino and Grasshopper to evaluate variations of form in the early stages of design.
Courtesy of Michael Gonzalez, Rebecca Kosar, and Hugo Ortego

importing data that make interoperability a challenge. Conceptually, this workflow from BIM to simulation is excellent if these types of problems can be overcome. Another variation is to include a plug-in/app in the modeling software that more seamlessly connects it to the simulation software with only a few clicks of the mouse. Or the analysis software can be entirely built into the 3D model or BIM software; for example, shadow casting and sometimes lighting illuminance can be done this way. More complex simulations are usually not directly part of the modeling software.

Another workflow is to program additional functionality into the 3D modeling or BIM software by using existing modules or creating new ones through scripting or coding that is text-based or through visual programming. This is an incredibly important workflow that is having an impact in the AEC industry and will continue to do so, especially because it empowers users to create new features and incorporate often freely available apps created by others. There are many examples where this workflow and the one that supplies a plug-in to link to an advanced simulation software package are used together to create a custom workflow for the user. Examples are given in four categories:

- Create new functionality or links to simulation software in a 3D modeling software program
- Create new functionality in BIM software
- Create new functionality in BIM software: Dynamo
- Create new functionality in BIM software: Internet of Things

Create New Functionality or Links to Simulation Software in a 3D Modeling Software Program

The use of RhinoScript and Grasshopper are excellent examples of coding within a 3D modeling environment that includes making custom commands, generating forms, automating repetitive tasks, creating new plug-ins, allowing interaction with cloud applications, and many other uses. RhinoScript is based on Microsoft's VBScript (Visual Basic Scripting Edition) language. Python is also available in Rhino and in Grasshopper. Both RhinoScript and Python are text-based. Grasshopper has become incredibly popular since its release in 2007 (then called Explicit History) and has been offered directly within Rhino since Rhino 6.0. As a visual programming environment, its interface generally makes it easier for beginners to get started with, but it also offers advanced features and the ability to link in modules that others have written.

There are hundreds of apps available (www.food4rhino.com) for Rhino and Grasshopper, including some that link them to other software programs for the actual simulation. A variety of examples are listed below (for both Rhino and Grasshopper) that are illustrative of the range available within the analysis, architecture, and environmental design categories; other apps exist for BIM, manufacturing and fabrication, civil engineering, robots, naval efficiency, and even jewelry design (Figures 28.12 and 28.13).

- Archsim Energy Modeling connects in the EnergyPlus simulation engine
- DIVA-for-Rhino runs thermal, daylight, solar radiation, and glare analysis
- Ladybug and Honeybee are used with weather data files and connect Grasshopper to building energy and light simulation engines (EnergyPlus, Radiance, Daysim, and OpenStudio)
- PanelingTools helps designers explore paneling concepts and rationalize complex geometry for analysis and fabrication
- Salamander allows structural nodes and elements within Rhino so that they can be exported to a finite element software program (e.g. Robot, GSA and ETABS) for analysis
- Sunflower Solar Analysis provides insolation analysis of buildings and sites
- Toro generates stadium designs and analyzing views from the seats

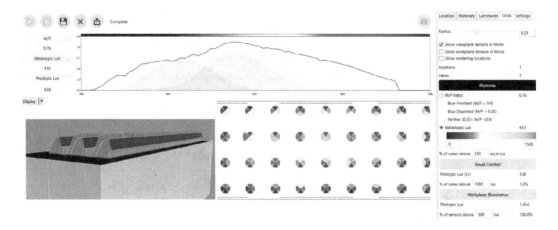

Figure 28.12 Rhino is shown being used with the ALFA software program to study clerestory alternatives for maximizing EML (Equivalent Melanopic Lux) for circadian lighting and minimizing glare. ALFA comes with an enhanced user interface that is embedded in Rhino.

Courtesy of Tannaz Tahmassebi

Computing Performativity

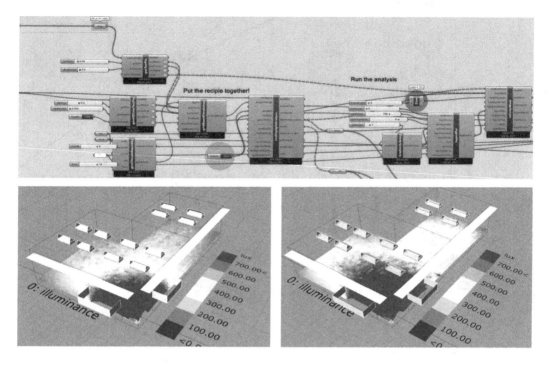

Figure 28.13 A Grasshopper script is used for daylighting simulation of a building with kinetic skylights (top). The simulation results are shown with skylight louvers closed to 0 degrees (bottom – left) and opened to 90 degrees (bottom – right).
Courtesy of Kunyu Luo

- TRNLizard enables thermal and daylight building simulation with TRNSYS 18
- Xylinus generates G code directly and has tools for 3D printers
- Custom nodes and apps can be written by oneself

Create New Functionality in BIM Software

New features can be created in BIM software by creating macros through coding, generally in C#, or with the use of a visual programming language using Dynamo. Visual Studio can be used with the Revit API; it is a .NET API allowing the use of any .NET compliant programming language (C#, VB.NET, etc.) to develop a macro that can be run directly from Revit. The Revit API is extensive; Dynamo allows access to much of it in a structure that for some designers is easier to use. Similar to Grasshopper, there are many modules or packages that can be freely downloaded, and custom nodes can be developed using Python. Excel xlsx or csv format files can be used for input of data and storage of output values. In many ways Excel has become an important mode of interoperability between software programs, especially for storing large data sets or results of calculations and allowing them to be easily transferred between software programs (Figures 28.14–28.18).

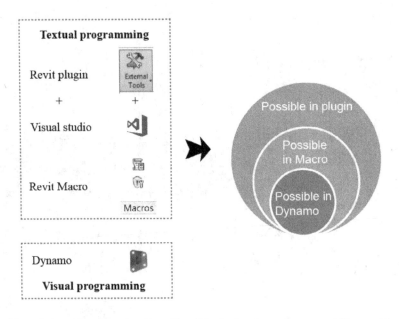

Figure 28.14 The relationship of the functionality of Revit plug-ins, macros, and Dynamo is shown.
Courtesy of Lu Huang

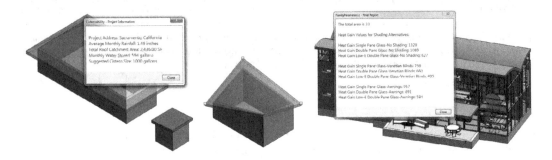

Figure 28.15 Simple Revit plug-ins were written in C# for potential water collection off of roofs (left) and heat gain of windows (right).
Courtesy of Barley, Shui, and Tucker (left); Daubert, Harrison, and Reego (right)

Collecting spatial elements	`//collect all rooms` `FilteredElementCollector a = new FilteredElementCollector(doc).OfClass(typeof(SpatialElement));`

Scanning elements	`//Check each room`
	`foreach (SpatialElement e in a)`
	`{`

Getting room's name	`    Room room = e as Room;`
	`    //Get letters in room.name`
	`    string roomname = Regex.Replace(room.Name, @"\d", "");`
	`    //Get room serial number`
	`    int roomserial = Convert.ToInt16(Regex.Match(room.Name, @"\d+").Value);`

Getting room's area	`    // Get room area and name` `    double roomarea = room.Area;`

Figure 28.16 This partial code snippet shows the process of querying a Revit drawing to find the areas of each of the rooms.
Courtesy of Lu Huang

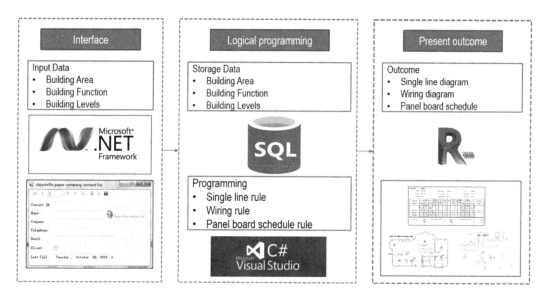

Figure 28.17 The MM Electrical Tool was created as a plug-in for Revit for creating single line electrical diagrams. This methodology diagram explains the development of the tool including its three main components: input interface, calculations, and output.

Image courtesy of Mingming Zhou

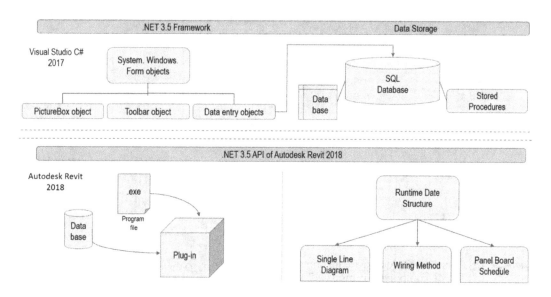

Figure 28.18 The MM Electrical Tool's detail methodology diagram, from the viewpoint of a programmer, shows the relationship between the .NET framework, SQL database, and Revit API.

Image courtesy of Mingming Zhou

Create New Functionality in BIM Software: Dynamo

As with 3D modeling software, one can create new functionality in BIM software such as Revit. BIM has the advantage over 3D modeling in that the components can have data associated with them that aids in the analysis process (Figures 28.19–28.22). A few professional examples are:

- Stadium design: sight line analysis; canopy design, drain flow, and heat map analysis
- Code compliance: automatic creation of escape routes; and room area code compliance
- Structural applications: automatically generate rebar; visualize loads and capacity; improve the efficiency of the structural modeling process; create complex structural shapes in Revit; and structural optimization
- MEP: design data calculations for space heating; electrical single line diagrams; and placement of equipment, such as sprinklers, air terminals, lighting, and associated data based on the room-type specifications
- Office workflow: automating the generation of sections and elevations; changing text from lower case to upper case; creating worksets; and renaming sheets automatically

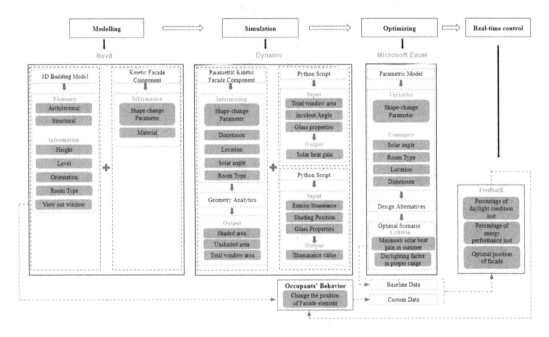

Figure 28.19 The methodology diagram shows the use of BIM + Dynamo + Python + Excel. A kinetic façade component is modeled, simulations calculate solar heat gain and illuminance, and changes to the component are made to optimize the results. Figures 28.20–28.22 are of this same project.

Courtesy of Kunyu Luo

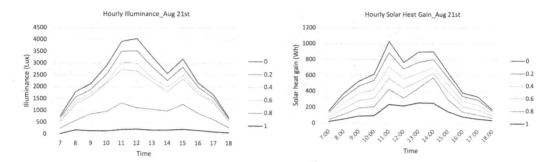

Figure 28.20 The hourly illuminance (left) and solar heat gain (right) were calculated for six versions of a kinetic façade component. These six versions are for shading devices completely open to completely closed. The lines on the two graphs show the results during the day for the six versions (0 is open; 1 is closed).

Courtesy of Kunyu Luo

```
#illuminance distribution of clear sky
#input: beta --- Angstrom's turbidity coefficient
#       w --- amount of precipitable moisture in the atmosphere (cm)
def ClearSkyLumDist(skyAzimuth,skyAltitude,sunAzimuth,sunAltitude):
        #calculate the angle between sky element and sun
        cosGamma = math.sin(math.radians(skyAltitude))*math.sin(math.radians(sunAltitude)) +
math.cos(math.radians(skyAltitude))*math.cos(math.radians(sunAltitude))*math.cos(math.radians(sky
Azimuth-sunAzimuth))
        gamma_R = math.acos(cosGamma)
        gamma = math.degrees(gamma_R)

        #calculate zenith luminance Lz (unit: kcd/m2)
        if sunAltitude<=60:
                if T_turbidity>3:
                        Lz = (1.34*T_turbidity-3.46)*math.tan(math.radians(sunAltitude)) +
0.1*T_turbidity + 0.9
                if T_turbidity<=3:
                        Lz = 0.56*math.tan(math.radians(sunAltitude)) + 1.2
        if sunAltitude>60:
                if T_turbidity>3:
                        Lz_60 = (1.34*T_turbidity-3.46)*math.tan(math.radians(60)) +
0.1*T_turbidity + 0.9
                        Lz = (3.25*Lz_60*math.sin(math.radians(sunAltitude)))/((3.25-
0.1050*(sunAltitude-60) + 0.001*math.pow((sunAltitude-60),2))*math.sin(math.radians(60)))
                if T_turbidity<=3:
                        Lz_60 = 0.56*math.tan(math.radians(60)) + 1.2
                        Lz = (3.25*Lz_60*math.sin(math.radians(sunAltitude)))/(   (3.25 -
0.1050*(sunAltitude-60) + 0.001*math.pow((sunAltitude-60),2))*math.sin(math.radians(60)))
```

Figure 28.21 Eight custom Python nodes were created in Dynamo. This partial Python script was for a luminance distribution calculator.

Courtesy of Kunyo Luo

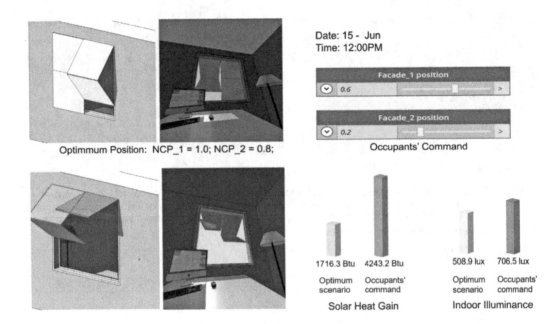

Figure 28.22 The final simulations determined the "optimal" position of a kinetic shade for different times of the day. Occupants could move the shade (for example, to get a better view outside), and this prototype dashboard would show how that decision impacted solar heat gain and indoor illuminance.

Courtesy of Kunyu Luo

Create New Functionality in BIM Software: Internet of Things

Combinations of the aforementioned tools can also be used. 3D modeling, BIM, coding and/or visual programming can be used with the Internet of Things (IoT) or with existing systems like those used for facilities management to interface between the digital and real worlds (Figures 28.23–28.25).

Summary

Building analysis, whether for aesthetics or performance metrics such as those used for sustainable design, can be made more efficient and accurate using existing 3D models that are initially developed for design studies. Building information models that contain appropriate data can also be used with simulation software. A 3D model is a subset of a building information model. A building information model not only contains the 3D geometry of a building, but it also has the potential to store within itself data necessary to explain non-graphic information like material characteristics (R-values, glass transmissivity, density, reflectivity, etc.). This allows for a potentially more streamlined method of interoperability with analysis software programs, which enhances their usability to provide predictions of building performance while the architect is still making design decisions.

Computing Performativity

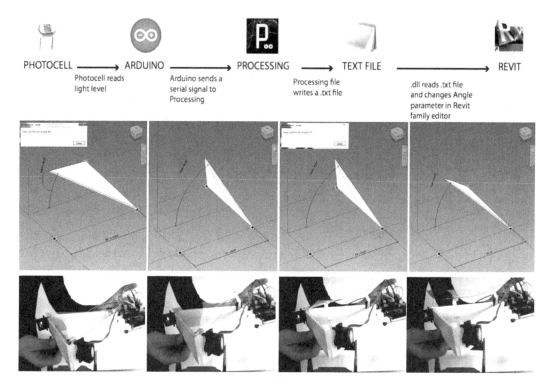

Figures 28.23 A photocell senses the light level in the real world. Using an Arduino microcomputer and the Processing programming language, a text file sends information to Revit (top row), and a digital model rotates (middle row). In other studies, this digital model became a series of shading devices on a building. The photocell's input also controls a physical model (bottom row).
Courtesy of Winston Kahn

Interoperability is becoming easier to achieve between a digital model and simulation software, and the software to create the model is currently improving. Simulation software programs are providing more types of visualization to aid the designers. Performative design thinking is being used increasingly by architects and engineers collaborating on design projects.

Several general workflows (including coding) have been described that use either a 3D model or a building information model as the basis and then create links to simulation software and provide new functionality. Best-performance scenarios (e.g. providing more daylight to office spaces) can be produced not only through numerous iterations of the software but also by genetic algorithms and other sophisticated optimization modules. Trade-offs can also be more easily studied. For example, a designer might want to increase the number of windows to provide more daylighting, but she would then also have to consider how to mitigate the increased heat gain during summer months. The designer controls the variables and evaluates the multiple outcomes. Coding, whether through text-based programs or through visual programming, is an important component of the toolset

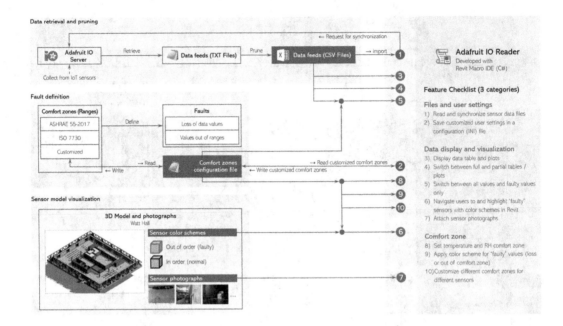

Figure 28.24 A BIM-based visualization tool, Adafruit IO Reader, was developed to interface real-time IoT sensor data information with Revit for facilities management. Sensors in the real world send temperature and humidity data to the cloud. Adafruit IO Reader downloads the data and checks it for faults, e.g. lost or incomplete data. In the Revit 3D model, the list of faults is examined, and the malfunctioning sensor's location can easily be determined.

Image courtesy of Gelin Su

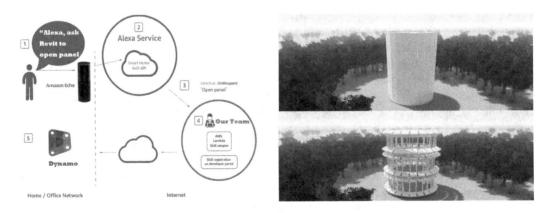

Figure 28.25 A program was written to control Revit with voice commands using Alexa and Dynamo; in this example, the shades are verbally told to "open."

Courtesy of Yanlong Li, Xiao Hu, Qianwei Zhou

available to designers to incorporate building analysis into the workflow of their firms by allowing them to add features or a new process to aid performative thinking. Numerous variations exist within firms on how to incorporate this.

Both 3D modeling and BIM are mainstays in academia and the building industry. Students are graduating with the necessary skills to create them and are improving their expertise within professional firms. They are also well versed in the problems and potentials of interoperability as they have encountered these issues and others while navigating the growing ecosystem of software tools available to the AECO industry. In addition, scripting, whether used for creating complex forms or achieving new functionality, has become increasingly pervasive in many schools of architecture.

It is significant that many members of the next generation of designers will be more fluid and comfortable with coding; even now programming is being taught in some elementary schools, and architecture students are experimenting with its use in studios. As one small piece of evidence, examine the examples in this paper – all of them were made by architecture or building science students, current or recently graduated.

Acknowledgements

Students (see individual figure captions)
Faculty (of student work shown): Karen Kensek, Kyle Konis, Nathan Miller, Douglas E. Noble

Resources

A few website and papers are listed here if you would like to learn more about this topic.
To learn more about Dynamo (Autodesk Revit):
   Description: http://dynamobim.org/
   Primer: http://dynamoprimer.com/
   Tutorials: https://dynamobim.org/learn/
   Packages: https://dynamopackages.com/
To learn more about Grasshopper (McNeel Rhino):
   Description: www.grasshopper3d.com/
   Tutorials: www.grasshopper3d.com/page/tutorials-1
   Apps: www.food4rhino.com/
To learn about Marionette (Vectorworks):
   Description: http://developer.vectorworks.net/index.php/Marionette_Basics
   Tutorials: www.vectorworks.net/training/marionette
To learn more about Simulink (MathWorks):
   Description: www.mathworks.com/products/simulink.html
   Getting started: www.mathworks.com/help/simulink/index.html

Further Reading

Kensek, Karen. *Technical Design Series: Building Information Modeling* (Routledge 2014, 312).
Kensek, Karen. "Teaching Visual Scripting in BIM: A Case Study Using a Panel Controlled by Solar Angles," *Journal of Green Building 13* (Winter 2018), No. 1: pp. 113–138.

Kensek, Karen. "'Integration of Environmental Sensors with BIM: Case Studies Using Arduino, Dynamo, and the Revit API,' 'Integración de sensores medioambientales con BIM: casos de estudio usando Arduino, Dynamo, y Revit API'." *Informes de la Construcción 66*, 536, e044 octubre-diciembre 2014 ISSN-L: 0020-0883: pp. 31–39. doi: http://dx.doi.org/10.3989/ic.13.151.

Konis, Kyle; Gamas, Alejandro; and Kensek, Karen. "Passive Performance and Building Form: An Optimization Framework for Early-Stage Design Support," *Solar Energy 125* (2016): pp. 161–179.

29

Professional Practice and the Performative Delivery of Architecture

Precision, Prediction, Value

Phil Bernstein

Introduction

In setting out the remit for this volume, Mitra Kanaani defines "performativity in architecture" as that which

> postulates the condition and the level of expected engagement of human users with the spatial qualities of the constructs and the environments created within them. In performative architecture, the designer *establishes a function or a continuum of dynamic relationship between a subject (user) and an object (spatial formal entity)*.
>
> *(Kanaani & Kopec, 2016, p. 100; emphasis added)*

As is our tendency, architects prefer to refract the opportunities of emergent technology—in this case, the ability to shape and manipulate space and its perception through digital controls and informational display—as a compositional, aesthetic, or otherwise ineffable possibility of design. I shall leave that investigation to other contributors here, concede to them the Vitruvian obligation for delight, and suggest that "performative architecture" might have an entirely different but equally important definition for firmness and commodity: predictable outcomes of the design and construction process. What does "performativity" in architecture mean in the context of the systems of delivery, the agency of architects in those systems, and the relationship of architects to their collaborators upon whom they are dependent to achieve their design?

The application of the theory of performativity to architecture is, in some ways, reductive. The philosopher John L. Austin posited the concept of "performative language, which does something in the world" as opposed to what he called "constative language," or that which describes things in the world that are either true or false (Cavanaugh, 2015). Making a promise is an example of performative language: doing so is not simply declaring facts but rather changing the obligations and responsibility of the *promisor* while setting the expectations of the *promisee*. Architecture certainly "does things" ranging from the simple fulfillment of function to the expression of aesthetic ideas. "Performative architecture" in this sense goes beyond how the building may "perform" in response to a user's experience and interaction with its systems, but rather embraces the larger phenomenon of how the building itself is formulated, executed, and operated in the world. We will call this "performative delivery" to draw the distinction going forward.

The architect is the primary conceptualizer of those things that must be done by her architecture, and her activities in some sense involve a series of promises: to the builder to provide clear directions to translate her vision to physical form; to the client, to fulfill the aspirations of the project; to the public to provide a suitable environment while protecting their health and safety. These obligations circumscribe the broad responsibilities of the architect as the agent of the client to translate, coordinate, and ultimately manifest a building, driven by a fundamental principle of the architect–client relationship: the architect asserts that by virtue of the design and construction process, certain things will "happen": that there will be an effective relationship between the architect, her collaborators, and the builder; that resources (including the owner's money) will be stewarded responsibly; that the building will operate as advertised; and that the client can use the building toward the ends that inspired its construction.

As the digital age slowly transforms the building industry, the information age is expanding the capabilities of designers and builders who are no longer dependent on age-old means of transmitting the complexities of the construction enterprise with low-fidelity drawings, charts, and text.[1] The convergence of several such technologies promises to dramatically expand the depictive potential of this enterprise, including:

Building information modeling (BIM)—a platform for the high-resolution, three-dimensional representation of a building including geometry, parameters, and descriptive meta-data.
Computational/generative design tools—the use of algorithms, programs, and/or scripts to generate, organize, and optimize design alternatives.
Analysis and simulation engines—software to evaluate, analyze, and predict the characteristics and behavior of a design or process prior to its physical actualization.
Big data—the collection, organization, and manipulation of large quantities of digitized data to support and document the design, construction, and operation of a building.
Machine learning—the application of artificial intelligence to enable computers to support design, construction, and building operations.
Industrialized construction processes—the application of manufacturing protocols such as mass production, robotics, automated assembly, and informational supply chain management to the construction process which has been traditionally heavily reliant on on-site, localized procedures.

These technologies in concert create two related opportunities for performative delivery as described here. First, the physical and behavioral aspects of building design can be depicted with much greater precision and accuracy than was possible during the era of mere drawing, which relied exclusively on methods of abstraction and scale, combined with correlated text descriptions, all of which were largely exchanged between collaborators on paper. Digital models that describe physical and analytical characteristics of a design are projections of the design constructed virtually before physically. Abstraction through the tools of orthographic projection like plans, sections, or elevations gives way to an interactive, robust digital projection of the proposed future state of the building. Clarity and accuracy of process and result improve accordingly.

BIM, at the vanguard of these innovations, has already yielded a practical if prosaic result that demonstrates this change in the level of precision. Prior to the widespread implementation of BIM, projects were widely subject to errors of coordination in the field, as elements designed and documented in two dimensions would clash in actual three-dimensional space, either directly (hard clashes) or with tight clearance (soft clashes). The implementation of BIM, particularly on complex projects, broadly improved the coordination of complex construction projects with the virtual elimination of such conflicts and enhanced planning of the construction process itself (Jones & Laquidara-Carr, 2015).

BIM creates a data taxonomy that forms the basis of the second opportunity of technology-enabled performative delivery: prediction. As design, construction, operation, and use of buildings becomes more reliant on data (BIM, big data), computational procedures replace manual processes like alternative generation and evaluation (generative design, machine learning), and construction operations transition to automation (industrialized construction), the delivery of a physical building will be preceded by its virtual creation. That virtual environment is a testing ground—and experimental platform—where numerous ideas can be understood, explored, tested, and evaluated. The representation of the built artifact, the procedures by which it will be built and operated, and evidence of other project performance combine to create the potential to define and assert not just the physical results of design but the outcomes it alleges to produce.[2] The promises the architect makes in providing her services are not simply the enforcement of design intent in her drawings, but rather commitments to the specific efficacy of the building's performance. The predictive power of simulative, digital, data-rich environments that are the future of design and construction instrumentalizes the denizens of performative delivery to create outcomes, rather than artifacts.

The contrast of this approach with the current operating principles of design-to-construction is stark. The struggle to resolve the ambiguous relationship between the acts of design and construction has plagued architects since the turn of the twentieth century, as the profession wrestled to define itself as somehow apart from, but reliant upon, the building trades (Woods, 1999). The resulting systems of project delivery—the business structures within which clients, designers, and builders configure themselves to produce projects—rely on transactional, commoditized exchanges of obligation, risk, and value. Lacking any other agreed-upon means by which to measure the success of such systems, these models are driven by lowest first-cost: lowest design fees, lowest contractor bid, lowest supplier costs, etc. The attendant risks of the construction enterprise are ambiguously distributed, unequally born, and the resulting confrontations are often resolved not in the studio or jobsite but in the courtroom. As buildings become increasingly complex and their briefs more demanding—including the emergent demands of the original definition of "performative architecture" described elsewhere in this text—a paradigmatic shift in the relationships between owner, designer, and builder are not just long overdue, but demanded.

Over a century of tinkering with delivery models has yielded scant improvement despite hundreds of thousands of iterations and resulting buildings. From the earliest days of "complex construction" where architects played the role of both designer and coordinator of subcontractors, through the dominance of design/bid/build approaches where the builder is brought after design and chosen based on price alone, to the emergence of "construction managers" and various flavors combining (or subsuming) design within construction ("design/build"), owners remain largely unsatisfied with the results (Bernstein, 2014; Construction Management Association of America, 2015). Each variation defined a new role or relationship between the various players but maintained the transactional nature of exchanges of information, obligation, risk, and value; same race cars, different engines, same track.

Performative delivery, however, derails the essences of these transactions and therefore the relationship of the players in the process by replacing the traditional media of transaction—drawings, specification, bids, submittals, shop drawings—with the promise of specific results and outcomes. This new delivery model transforms the output of delivery structures from "things" (buildings) to "outcomes" (buildings that do things).

This shift, made possible by the predictive potential of digital design and construction, reframes the roles, relationships, and expectations of the primary players (architect, builder, client, and users), the processes of building design, construction, and use, and the measures of success of their efforts and interactions with architecture. Delivery today is a maelstrom of implicit and explicit promises to make things happen: the architect "promises" competent instructions and information to the builder, but the accuracy and completeness of that information is typically questionable. The builder "promises" to deliver a building within targets of time, quality, and budget but has a multitude of escape hatches (requests for information, change orders, declarations of the architect's incompetence, guaranteed maximum prices). Owners convert those promises into expectations of project performance and quality, and, eventually, efficacy of result, but lack an understanding of the instruments of design or the processes of construction. Ultimately, they do not build just to meet schedules or budgets, but rather to achieve social ends: educate (schools), heal (hospitals), sell (retail), or work (offices).

These end goals, however, are a pretty high hurdle to ask designers and builders (even those properly armed with technology) to jump. A progression of potential performative states and accompanying objectives is a roadmap by which the industry can build the capabilities of performative delivery, fully wrought. One such progression is summarized in the following table:

Table 29.1 Objectives and Resulting Performance States of the Stages of Delivery of a Building

Project Stage	Design !	Construction !	Operation !	Use
Objective	**Aspirational:** *What does the building intend to be and do? Can the design be built and operated within constraints?*	**Executional:** *What is the best process for realizing the physical result?*	**Operational:** *How should the building operate as a system (quality, durability, energy use)?*	**Social:** *Does the finished project achieve the strategic objectives of the owner and the public?*
Performative State	**Predictable:** *The projected state meets practical, physical and social objectives.*	**Practical:** *The building is constructed within resource constraints (time, money, materials)*	**Physical:** *The building systems serve as specified.*	**Useful:** *The project delivers the highest objective of its design.*

Achieving project "performance" becomes more challenging (and the results more profound) as its focus moves from left to right on this continuum. Designers can begin by anticipating ultimate use and operation while setting up projects to be properly constructed; builders, working with design collaborators, can optimize construction process to meet the basics of schedule, budget, and quality. The resulting artifact can operate in accordance with the brief specified. Ultimately, the project provides the social good defined by its originator, the client, and manifest by its users and the public at large.

An immediate opportunity for a performative delivery strategy can be found in the rapid emergence of "offsite construction," where manufacturing techniques like automation, prefabrication, and assembly augment traditional on-site, "stick-built" construction. Construction clients, always looking to improve faltering productivity and uncertainty in projects, increasingly believe the time has come for industrialized construction methods (Facilities Management Institute, 2018). Many of these processes, however, must be anticipated early by the architect and her engineers and instantiated into the fundamentals of the design itself; the decision to use a prefabricated enclosure system that is integrated into the building structure cannot be made after the construction documents are complete. Understanding and analyzing the potential use and performance of such industrialized construction systems therefore demands the early collaboration of designers and builders, understanding and sharing of the procedural implications of the approach, and a shared obligation for the risk and the reward of success. Predictive analysis of the performance of such systems is at the heart of these refactored relationships.

Of course, much of what is described here comprises a particularly hellish vision for those who manage and allocate risk in the systems of delivery: insurance providers and bonding agencies, who write the checks in the face of various systemic failures of design and building. "Promising" to obtain a specific outcome flies in the face of fundamental principles of professionalism: to use best judgment and due care without guaranteeing an outcome, where competency is measured by the illusive "standard of care."[3] If competent designers and builders can, over time, increase their ability to predict the outcomes of their work along the continuum described above, the traditional scramble to assign, disabuse, and then relent to risk in the building process will disappear, replaced with new exchanges of value between the constituents. Rather than optimize value exchange (and related payments) for lowest possible cost, the exchange of information and related decisions will be based upon outcomes predicted *a priori* by a combination of sophisticated representational and analytical systems and the collective wisdom of experienced architects, engineers, and builders.[4] Inasmuch as digital systems can represent a more complete and dynamic history of past experience (via big data and machine learning) these judgments (and measures of their professional competence) harken back to the standard of care itself.

There are early signs in the marketplace of the emergence of "performative delivery" in the form of what is now becoming known as "integrated project delivery" (IPD). In this model, designers, builders, and their clients work in concert toward agreed project goals, and profit is correlated to the successful achievement of those goals. The characteristics of IPD delivery are rapidly evolving and are not as institutionalized as, say, design/bid/build or even design/build models, but the central concepts of projects touting "integration" of any sort are collaboration and risk/reward sharing. In its purest form, a project delivered via IPD is based on a single, collaborative contract signed by the primary players (client, designers, builders) that stipulates that decisions are made collaboratively, rewards are based on measured project benefits that directly result in profit, and that risk is a shared burden of the entire team that agrees that they will not sue each other. "Integration" is the central characteristic of the operating model, starting with the single contract, spanning across the sharing of (usually BIM-based) information and decision-making, and resulting in new value creation from shared profits that are connected to specific project outcomes. Performativity in IPD means defining and then achieving these outcomes as the central basis of the design and construction process.

While IPD delivery models emerged in concert with the concept of BIM, its adoption (at least in the United States) has lagged far behind the technology, due in large part to the concerns about liability and risk articulated above. Delivery innovation is retarded in the building industry by a variety of pathologies: the disaggregated market, slow project timelines, and low profit margins. But behind the primary hesitation to adopt new models in the face of obvious failures of delivery is the nagging question of responsibility, risk, and reward.

The transformational changes required to reach performative delivery—a "superset" of IPD—demand a new definition of professional competence and risk that breaks from the tradition of the standard of care, which is by definition backward-looking and therefore an inhibitor to innovation.[5] And until this "risk conundrum" is broken, it is unlikely that the industry will move toward performative delivery, no matter how compelling the catalyzing technology that inspires it. A mature performative delivery model brings the design/build team closer to the business objectives of the client, suggesting that an alternative risk measurement model might be at hand, espoused in the corporate governance model called "the business judgment rule."[6] Corporate leaders, who are expected to exercise business judgment in support of their company goals, are protected by this concept, which states:

> Shareholders challenging the wisdom of a business decision taken by management must overcome the business judgment rule … For efficiency reasons, corporate decision makers should be permitted to act decisively and with relative freedom from a judge's or jury's subsequent second questioning. It is desirable to encourage directors and officers to enter new markets, develop new products, innovate, and take other business risks.
>
> *(American Law Institute, 1994, p. 174)*

Early versions of IPD implementation[7] proposed the creation of a "special purpose entity" (SPE), a temporary corporation formed by the architect, builder, and client for the express purpose of supporting the design and construction of the owner's project (American Institute of Architects, 2013). Not yet a holistic solution, but rather as a first attempt to break the risk logjam, a performative delivery model, operating under the contractual aegis of an SPE, might cite the business judgment rule to define and allocate the associated risks of delivering a project based on outcomes and not fixed prices.

If solving the risk bind is the gateway to more integrated and coherent strategies for delivery based on principles of performativity, new models of value exchange are the accelerant. Technology enables methodological improvements, but real change in delivery requires associated evolution of the business propositions of design and construction, particularly fees and compensation. Risk and reward are strongly correlated in every market save construction, and performative delivery offers an opportunity to repair this misalignment. Providing accurate construction documents, meeting construction cost estimates, deploying systems that consume reasonable amounts of resources while limiting carbon emissions, or creating buildings that achieve productive ends are all very valuable—and in many cases, measurable—results that can be correlated to financial rewards. IPD models today are experimenting with the idea that outcomes and profit are intertwined, and one begets the other. Over time, as designers, builders, and most importantly clients understand the potential of the potent combination of technology-driven precision and prediction with experienced professionals, performative delivery may be the real route to a better architecture.

Notes

1 The industry itself is desperately in need of improvement and is behind most others in both digitization and the productivity growth technology has catalyzed in other sectors of the economy; see McKinsey Global Institute (2017).
2 For a more detailed exploration of the evolution of design intent in the digital era, see Bernstein (2018).
3 The standard of care measures adequacy of performance by comparing the acts of a professional to what a competent practitioner in similar circumstances might have done. For a more detailed exploration of this question, see Bernstein (2018, Chapter 2.3).
4 In early studies of the interaction of expert computational systems and professional judgment, weather prediction was found to be more accurate when digital models were "tweaked" by experienced meteorologists; see Silver (2012).
5 Since the standard of care is comparative to other practice, it can only be demonstrated by historical example and is therefore regressive rather than progressive.
6 This concept was introduced to the author by attorney Leslie P. King, who often defends architects in construction-related matters; see King and Cantor (2018).
7 Forms of IPD have been extant for over a decade. For a complete description of the model and its implementation, see Fischer et al. (2017).

References

American Institute of Architects. (2013). C199 – 2010 Standard Form of Agreement between Single Purpose Entity and Contractor for Integrated Project Delivery. Retrieved from www.aiacontracts.org.
American Law Institute. (1994). *Principles of Corporate Governance: Analysis and Recommendations*. St. Paul, MN: American Law Institute Publishers.
Bernstein, H. M. (2014). Managing Uncertainty and Expectations in Building Design and Construction. In *McGraw Hill Smart Market Reports*, edited by H. M. Bernstein, 64. New York, NY: McGraw Hill Construction Analytics.
Bernstein, P. (2018). *Architecture, Design, Data: Practice Competency in the Era of Computation*. Basel: Birkhauser.
Cavanaugh, J. R. (2015 March 10). Performativity. In *The Oxford Bibliography*. Retrieved from www.oxfordbibliographies.com.
Construction Management Association of America. (2015). *2015 Owners Survey Report*. Retrieved from www.cmaanet.org.

Facilities Management Institute. (2018). "New Day, New Mindset: Rethinking Offsite Construction." In *FMI Owner Survey*, 41. Raleigh, NC: Author Raleign.

Fischer, M., Khanzode, A., Reed, D. P., & Ashcraft, H. W. (2017). *Integrating Project Delivery*. Hoboken, NJ: John Wiley & Sons.

Jones, S., & Laquidara-Carr, D. (2015). Smart Market Report: Measuring the Impact of BIM on Complex Buildings. In *Smart Market Reports*. New York, NY: Dodge Data and Analytics.

Kanaani, M., & Kopec, D. (2016). *The Routledge Companion for Architecture Design and Practice*. New York, NY: Routledge.

King, L. P., & Cantor, D. (2018). *Innovation and the Standard of Care: Can They Co-Exist?* (Lecture at Yale School of Architecture). New Haven.

McKinsey Global Institute. (2017). *Reinventing Construction: A Route to Higher Productivity*. Retrieved from www.mckinsey.com/industries/capital-projects-and-infrastructure/our-insights/reinventing-construction-through-a-productivity-revolution. New York, NY: McKinsey & Company.

Silver, N. (2012). *The Signal and the Noise: Why Most Predictions Fail – but Some Don't*. New York, NY: Penguin.

Woods, M. N. (1999). *From Craft to Profession: The Practice of Architecture in Nineteenth-Century America*. Berkeley, CA: University of California Press.

30
Performing Architecture
A Reflection on the Rituals and Procedures of Practice

Kyle Miller

Although we have a record of ritualistic events in religion and broader cultural activities taking place thousands of years ago, performance only emerged as a definitive medium in the arts in the early twentieth century. Ranging from action painting to unconventional poetry readings to new forms of theatre to endurance demonstrations, many artists turned to performance art to expand the boundaries of their native disciplines—be it painting, sculpture, or film; traditional disciplines whose boundaries were more strictly defined during the preceding 300-year period. Throughout the twentieth century, performance art established itself as a weapon against the praxis of orthodox art. When a movement reached an impasse, artists turned to performance art to swiftly indicate new directions (Goldberg, 2011). For example, Surrealist art gains popularity in the mid-1920s with "exquisite corpse" drawing games at parlors and is said to have begun in 1917 with *Les Mamelles de Tiresias*, a play written by Guillaume Apollinaire. Apollinaire believed that theatre should be a metaphysical experience entangling the unconscious minds of the performers and the spectators. Using performance as a medium, Surrealism—among other achievements—resolves the contradictory nature of Cubism's abstraction of reality while opening up new conceptual territory for the hyper-real. Not only in Surrealism but also in other movements within the fine arts, it is the combination of the convergence of artist and audience with advancement and production of disciplinary knowledge and techniques where the impact of performance as a medium is articulated.

It should not be surprising that such abrupt changes in direction from one art movement to the next take place. As the conceptual and speculative become quotidian and commonplace through codification and replication, tactical reworkings of previously dominant conceptual trajectories take the form of new theoretically oriented directions for the arts that employ performance as medium to develop and deliver content. For example, and in addition to the aforementioned use of performance in Surrealism, the early-twentieth-century Futurists combined performance and painting to challenge a ubiquitous public fascination with dated and regressive political and artistic traditions. To disrupt a complacent public, artists used performance as a device to become both *creators* of new forms of theatre and *art objects* in and of themselves as they cared little to distinguish efforts of the poet, painter, and performer (Goldberg, 2011). Of critical importance is the acknowledgement that these new trajectories do not correspond to the dominant conceptual support structures established by previous generations, nor do they tend to the demands on artistic production imposed by broader cultural contexts and the marketplace—thus operating freely and in a manner that attempts to move discourse forward through projection and speculation rather than backward through analysis and critique.

In contemporary architecture—in a time when emerging designers are inventing and defining new conceptual support structures for their work—performance pieces are used to sponsor new conceptual movements. Whereas previously dominant models of experimental architecture emphasized algorithmic and data-driven design validated through quantitative performance, these new movements scrutinize the procedural aspects of professional practice and emphasize intellectual narratives and the aesthetic qualities of the results. Perhaps the arrival of these new conceptual support structures is quite timely given the proclamation that there is no longer a singular discipline of architecture as a result of the fragmentation of shared mediums and value systems among emerging practitioners (Meredith, 2013). However, what is unique is the attention paid to medium—as opposed to technique or subject matter—as the primary means of establishing a position in the ever-expanding discipline of architecture.

The topic of medium in architecture has been of interest and under intense scrutiny during the last decade. Beginning with Michael Meredith's proclamation in 2013 that there is no more architecture, only architectures, the fracturing and genrefication of the discipline of architecture has been continuous and persistent. Contemporary architecture is no longer limited to *Form*, *Space*, and *Order* as its primary and only mediums to manipulate. Claiming *Bodies*, *Lines*, *Plans*, *Profiles*, and *Rocks*, among other abstract supports, more nuanced territory has been carved out by emerging designers who maintain an interest in *Form*, *Space*, and *Order*, but desire to operate more surgically within the domain of more fundamental mediums (Bair et al., 2018). Through continuous proclamations from not only Meredith, but also from Robin Evans (and even as far back as Leon Batista Alberti), architecture must be understood as being projected and understood through representation, rather than the building itself. It was Evans who first stated that, "Architects do not make buildings; they make drawings of buildings" (Blau, 1989). This distinction is a critical one for it opens up the possibility for a multitude of traditional mediums and technical supports to take the place of the building—the medium of the builder. Beyond working conceptually on *Form*, *Space*, and *Order*, the act of writing about architecture, conceiving an idea, preparing specifications, corresponding with clients, outsourcing production, signing contracts, producing renderings, and drawing details can all serve as conceptual arenas for contemporary architects.

Just as artists turned to performance as a medium to sponsor the cultivation of new creative directions, a small group of emerging architects have used the performance to initiate inventive ways to scrutinize and mine the creative potential of the aforementioned rituals and procedures of professional practice. Turning away from the dominant trajectories of experimentally minded architects active in the 1990s and 2000s—formal morphology, animation, surface articulation, affect and sensation, data-driven design, and technological positivism, to name a few—the newest generation of so-called avant-garde designers are developing new architectural knowledge and generating new cultural activity without the burden of limitations imposed by an existing, previously dominant conceptual support structures. Topics deemed vapid and unimaginative by previous generations of architects are featured as departure points for this new group of architects who are using architecture as the subject matter of performance pieces. These architects are engaging conventional modes of construction, utilizing off-the-shelf products, and participating in the procedural aspects of document production within the architectural design process. Events such as drawing enclosure details, specifying paint, and crowd-sourcing design criticism are positioned as new conceptual territories for contemporary architecture. Rather that diminish the significance of these acts through relegation to the periphery, these procedures are highlighted as core conceptual territories and are featured as both the subject matter and output of works from emerging architects.

Projects from four newly established creative practices best demonstrate the use of performance as a new medium for architecture. In these projects, the architects are *performing* architecture in that they elevate the status of intermediate conventional procedures to resultant acts and artifacts with unprecedented and unexpected intellectual and aesthetic value. These architects—Andrew

Atwood and Anna Neimark (First Office), David Eskanazi (D.ESK), Curtis Roth and Erin Besler and Ian Besler (Besler & Sons)—have produced art and architecture that use the ritualistic aspects of producing architecture as the subject matter and recurring conceptual support for their design research.

> Without [a prefatorial statement] this becomes a sort of installation, an installation without the proper authorization, an alien without the proper papers. In fact, only when it's prefaced is it worthy of bearing that name: Installation.
>
> *(Atwood and Neimark, 2013)*

Preface (2013) and *Possible Table* (2014) are two projects from Andrew Atwood and Anna Neimark (First Office) that demonstrate the manner in which the architect may operate as a conceptual artist using architecture as the subject matter of their critical investigations. Collectively, these two projects can be understood as performance pieces enacted by First Office.

Preface was installed at SCI-Arc in 2013 and made of not only the physical objects exhibited in the SCI-Arc gallery, but also all of the supporting materials—the exhibition poster, promotional video, prefatorial statement, and exhibitor's agreement. Each of these peripheral materials and documents, which are oftentimes blindly produced or agreed to automatically, were mined for their latent conceptual potential. In doing so, First Office elevated the status of these lesser-known acts and artifacts by featuring them alongside the "final" piece as having equal significance and weight with respect to the act of producing an installation within an educational institution. To an unsuspecting spectator, the box fans, remnants of painter's tape, fire alarms, and electrical outlets have very little to do with the exquisitely crafted pedestals that are featured within and fill the gallery, but they are just as significant. Just as the Futurists did, First Office attempts to "disrupt a complacent public" to encourage prolonged attention to every aspect of both the creative act and also the contractual and legal responsibilities of installing work within SCI-Arc (Figure 30.1).

Possible Table was installed at the Taubman College Liberty Research Annex in 2014. Like *Preface*, *Possible Table* is not only comprised of physical objects—here, white-painted 3/4-inch plywood, two gray-painted

Figure 30.1 *Preface*, First Office, 2013.
Courtesy of First Office

Performing Architecture

trestles from IKEA, and a Master Giant Foot Rubber Door Stop from Staples—but also the act of the curators receiving and unpacking the materials, discovering a document that specified the assembly of these materials, and following the vaguely defined instructions to compose the materials to match the associated drawing set (Figure 30.2). An excerpt from the specifications set reads as follows:

1. 1.1 RELATED DOCUMENTS

   A. Enclosed construction drawings might apply to this section.

2. 1.2 SUMMARY

   A. Section Includes:

      1. Table Alignment
      2. Shim Placement

   B. Related Requirements:

      1. Section 000002 "Projector Setup"
      2. Section 000003 "Drawing Placement"

3. 1.3 TABLE ALIGNMENT

   A. Align the table using what appears to be its longest edge, as shown in drawings.
   B. Set this apparent longest edge roughly parallel to the board, at a distance of about 3'-0" from the board.
   C. Align the center of the longest edge by eye to the center of the board.

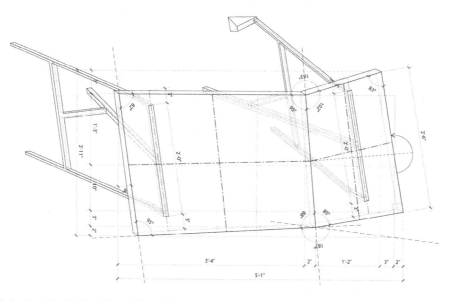

Figure 30.2 Possible Table, First Office, 2014.
Courtesy of First Office

4. 1.4 SHIM PLACEMENT
   A. The table may contact the ground with three of its four outer legs.
   B. Use the Staples Giant Doorstop enclosed between the fourth outer leg and the ground, to provide a fourth point of contact.

END OF SECTION 000001

(Atwood and Neimark, 2014)

Preface and *Possible Table* reveal the broader ambitions of First Office to use the notion of performing architecture as a way to generate architectural content and alter the manner in which that content is consumed. By using the procedural aspects of architecture as fodder for their conceptual endeavors, First Office enlivens the most quotidian aspects of practicing architecture.

> *Training Wheels* is an oblique reference to the development of an architectural practice. Its title [...] suggests that the work is a contextual installation scaled to fit all the normal aspects of architectural practice.
>
> (Eskanazi, 2015)

Training Wheels is a project by David Eskanazi that was installed in 2015 in the Banvard Gallery at the Ohio State University's Knowlton School of Architecture. Serving as a critical reflection on the size of an object normally affiliated with the term "installation," *Training Wheels* challenges the assumption that big things are more serious than small things.

Comprised of 20 oversized and crudely constructed cardboard wheels that confuse the distinction between scaled models and full-scale constructions, *Training Wheels* is an exercise in playfully linking the virtual and the physical and the representational to the real. Similar to First Office's *Preface*, *Training Wheels* reflects upon on the very nature of being asked to make an installation, allowing its intellectual value to transcend the visual and physical properties accessible in the Banvard Gallery.

By calling into question the value, validity, and significance of installation as a medium for architecture, Eskanazi is using performance to simultaneously contribute to architecture discourse through critical reflections on scale and spatial experience that provoke physical engagement through the projective associations of making (Figures 30.3 and 30.4).

While the projects above from First Office and D.ESK provide *critical* commentary on the inner workings—the black box—of the discipline and practice of architecture, the following projects from Curtis Roth and Besler & Sons reveal, in a *projective* manner, the performance of architecture to a broader audience through engagement and participation. Here, *critical* implies an act that operates in-between and outside of dominant paradigms of form and culture and is ideological, dogmatic, indexical, and hot (Hays, 1984). *Projective* is an act that works with and convenes dominant paradigms of form and culture and is compliant, participatory, engaged, and cool (Somol and Whiting, 2002).

> The *work* of architecture is a *work* of architecture. That is: that today our instruments manufacture ad hoc spatial constructions through eclectic distribution of design's labor.
>
> (Roth, 2017)

Some Dark Products is a book from Curtis Roth that collects adventures in outsourcing and crowd-sourcing many forms of architectural labor—design, detailing, visualization, and criticism, to name a few. In scrutinizing the acts that comprise a primary deliverable of the professional practice of architecture—a building—Roth unveils the complex network of both sanctioned and

Figures 30.3 and 30.4 Training Wheels, David Eskanazi, 2015.
Courtesy of David Eskanazi

illicit behaviors that more accurately describe the extents of the architect's efforts. *Some Dark Products* amounts to a "travelogue of nine instruments for architecture." Two instruments in particular, "Instrument I: The Detail" and "Instrument V: The Text," reveal the clever processes Roth conceives of to perform acts of and associated with architecture through manipulating conventional labor and production streams.

"Instrument I: The Detail" begins with Roth commissioning eight building drainage details—from weep-holes to scuppers—from an Ahmedabad-based corporation called Silicon Valley Infomedia, a subsidiary of Shadowmine Systems, that, in turn, outsources detailing to drafting technicians working in the Rason Special Economic Zone in North Korea. Roth provided Silicon Valley Infomedia with AutoCAD template files within which a leak was to be drawn. Roth rendered the commissioned drawings with a fluid simulator and removed the detail, producing an "after-image" of the drawings' journey from Columbus to India to China to a USB-drive that was smuggled across a highly militarized North Korean border and back (Figures 30.5–30.7).

"Instrument V: The Text" suggests that criticism can be outsourced to the masses. Drawing a parallel to crowd-sourced military intelligence—the locating of targets of state-sponsored violence through crowd-based media surveillance—Roth concocts a method of architectural criticism that links the "ever-present backdrop of everyday social media platforms" to the transformation of IP addresses into laborers. The result of asking Internet laborers to analyze the interior architecture of a backdrop of an uploaded webcam image yields some wonderful acts of criticism. One worker writes, "The tiling in the kitchen walls gives the room a very welcoming vibe. It shows that the owner of the room is outgoing and fun" (Roth, 2017). "Instrument V: The Text" updates the accepted means of establishing broad cultural preferences of décor and challenges the established method of consuming trends delivered in lifestyle magazines.

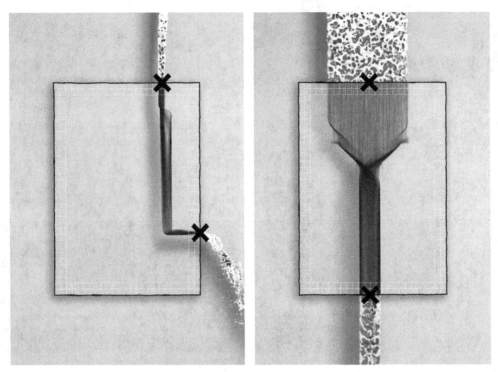
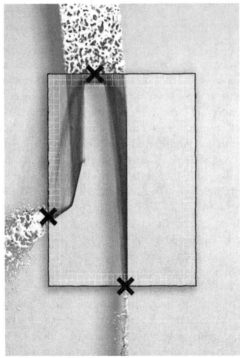

Figures 30.5–30.7 The Detail, Curtis Roth, 2017.
Courtesy of Curtis Roth

Roth's nine instruments for architecture present an unexpected and refreshing re-positioning of what it means to perform architecture while simultaneously exposing the economic and political infrastructures of traditional performance venues, namely professional practices. The results reconstruct the boundaries of time and space typically associated with the design, construction, occupancy, and evaluation of architecture.

> The project examines the kinds of problems that arise when the networks of building construction, digital management software, material distribution, and circulation are forced to confront conceptual issues.
>
> *(Besler and Besler, 2014)*

The Entire Situation is a project by Erin Besler and Ian Besler (Besler & Sons) installed at the MAK-Mackey Gallery in Los Angeles in 2014 and at the Chicago Cultural Center on the occasion of the 2015 Chicago Architecture Biennial, where it was exhibited alongside custom software developed together with Satoru Sugihara/ATLV, called *StudFindr*.

The Entire Situation combines the historical theoretical inquiry into the building's corner—famously identified as "the corner problem"—with the technical aspects associated with detailing, building information modeling, and construction. The installation is made of freestanding walls constructed of metal studs and white-painted gypsum board that comes together at unique angles. The physical convergence of walls becomes a site of intense scrutiny, not only for the resolution of molding that must meet at an irregular angle, but also for the conceptual resolution of the corner, an endeavor that first begins with efforts put forth by Bramante, Brunelleschi, and other Renaissance architects as they grapple with how architectural elements and embellishments turn the corner and retain both formal order and visual integrity (Figures 30.8 and 30.9).

As a bespoke software platform, *StudFindr* presents these technical and conceptual problems to the general public. At the 2015 Chicago Architecture Biennial, *StudFindr* was available for the general public to use—to propose custom compositions of walls and view an immediate technical resolution of their proposal. *StudFindr* translates quick digital scribbles into fully detailed and refined virtual constructions.

In making the act of design more accessible, *The Entire Situation* and *StudFindr* enable the broader public to perform architecture and unknowing participate in the theoretical resolution of architecture's corner problem.

These particular projects from Andrew Atwood and Anna Neimark, David Eskanzi, Curtis Roth, and Ian Besler and Erin Besler exemplify the manner in which architects (and the broader public in some instances) can act as conceptual artists performing architecture. The performances exaggerate the ongoing break and drift away from previously dominant conceptual, aesthetic, and formal paradigms while establishing new trajectories for contemporary architecture—paired with a disposition that one might describe as clever or whimsical: terms that would not necessarily be used to describe the previous generation of digital form virtuosos and advocates of technological salvation.

What comes of these generational performance pieces, with overtones of either defiance and resistance or optimism and participation, is yet to be seen, but the opportunity to open up new trajectories and value sets for contemporary architecture—just as has been the case in the fine arts throughout the twentieth century—is made possible by the theatricality of performing architecture. For this new generation of experimentally minded architects, performing architecture produces fresh intellectual and physical outputs that leverage the internal workings of architectural practice for novel means of social, cultural, experiential, and technological interaction.

Figures 30.8 and 30.9 The Entire Situation, Besler and Sons, 2014).
Photographs by Joshua White, JWPictures.com

References

Atwood, Andrew, and Anna Neimark. (2013) "Preface." Retrieved November 21, 2018. http://firstoff.net/projects/Preface/.

Atwood, Andrew, and Anna Neimark. (2014). "Possible Table." Retrieved November 23, 2018. http://firstoff.net/projects/Possible_Table/.

Bair, Kelly, Kristy Balliet, Adam Fure, and Kyle Miller. (2018). *Possible Mediums*. Barcelona: Actar.

Besler, Erin, and Ian Besler. (2014). "The Entire Situation." Retrieved November 21, 2018. www.beslerandsons.com/projects/the-entire-situation/.

Blau, Eve. (1989). "Architectural Projection," in *Architecture and its Image: Four Centuries of Architectural Representation*. Montreal: Canadian Centre for Architecture, p. 369.

Eskanazi, David. (2015). "Training Wheels." Retrieved November 21, 2018. www.d-esk.net.

Goldberg, Rose Lee. (2011). *Performance Art: From Futurism to the Present*. London: Thames & Hudson.

Hays, K. Michael. (1984). "Critical Architecture: In Between Culture and Form," in *Perspecta* Vol 21, pp. 14–29.

Meredith, Michael. (2013). "P.M.S.A. (Post-Mediums-Specific-Architecture)," in *Everything All at Once*. New York: Princeton Architectural Press, p. 20.

Roth, Curtis. (2017). *Some Dark Products*. Stuttgart: Akademie Schloss Solitude.

Somol, Robert, and Sarah Whiting. (2002). "Notes around the Doppler Effect and other Moods of Modernism," in *Perspecta* Vol 33, pp. 72–77.

31
Educating Accountable Architects
The Future Performers

Ted Landsmark

The Design Profession and Architecture, Engineering, and Construction Businesses

What Designers Do, and for Whom

Architecture is the art and practice of designing and constructing buildings. The design profession defines the physical environments within which we live, work, recreate, heal, relax, and achieve spiritual sustenance. Architects create ethical strategies and physical spaces for solving client needs, and services that create experiences within these spaces. Design for its own sake may produce aesthetically satisfying sculpture, while architecture incorporates patterns of interactions across buildings, landscapes, and interiors. Designing for these patterns of utilitarian human interaction engages public health, safety, and general welfare. Architects are accountable for contributing to community health and well-being.

Twenty-first-century trends are reshaping what designers do, and for whom (Ramirez 2019). Just as construction managers and engineers employ innovative tools to shape designs, architects are redefining their roles in the built environment. The design professions have historically depended on commercial, health care, hospitality, and institutional clients, and twenty-first-century design trends focus on energy efficiency; sustainable design; resilience; green urban planning; accessibility; flexible and individualizable spaces; designs for underserved populations, including refugees; preservation; and re-cycling. The tools, materials, and methods of twenty-first-century design rely on digital innovation, artificial intelligence, automation and robotics, off-site manufacturing, and creativity from more gender, cultural, and ethnically diverse design professionals. These trends substantially modify the expectations placed on design educators.

The Emergent Tools Shaping Performative Digital Design

Architects design spaces that establish and reinforce ordered patterns of social behavior. The architect's core design competency provides a measure of anticipatory control over the social performance of designed spaces (Schumacher, Chapter 2). Predictable outcomes of the design and construction process are an expected outcome of performance-based design, transforming the output of architectural design processes from *things* (objects, artifacts, or environments), to *outcomes* (buildings and spaces that achieve predicted experiences and quantifiable results).

Digital architectural design was initially welcomed as a cost-effective tool for rendering evolving design iterations, and has become a generative tool for form-making. Computationally-based performative design enables rapid prototyping of ideas into innovative physical forms unique to the twenty-first century's availability of previously unknown materials. Digitized visualizing and prototyping make performative design a methodology for designing dynamically, and for assessing predicted quantifiable outcomes that enable clients to expect building performance within identifiable parameters.

Technologically proficient students, and advanced practitioners interested in energy modeling and the testing of new biomorphic materials, embraced digital tools more for their creative possibilities than for their utility in reducing legal liabilities. Innovative technical proficiency came to be expected of architecture school graduates, and younger design aspirants teamed with experienced practitioners to share their expertise. This collaborative process produced a quarter-century of virtual imaging technology, innovative engineering simulations, and comparative research into the efficacy of increased sustainability, new materials, and accelerated construction.

Commercial and residential buildings are now managed remotely, changing the dynamics of initially-projected design outcomes and actual building energy use and performance. Predictive analytics are the basis of metrics that assess building performance during post-occupancy analyses. Digital design platforms anticipate cost efficiencies and reduce legal exposures for errors and omissions in drawings. The predictive capabilities of rapidly evolving software encouraged knowledgeable private clients and government agencies to mandate digital design approaches.

Performative design practices and human-centered post-occupancy analyses have implications for design education pedagogies. Robert Neumayr (Chapter 17) describes how simulation algorithms have become tools for projecting building performance in regard to lighting, acoustics, thermal energy, and environmental flows. Architects have employed automotive thermodynamic engineers to project how buildings can be designed to reduce heat energy transfers in built environments. Acoustical engineers use simulation algorithms to tune spaces for sound transmission. Light engineers employ simulation algorithms to project seasonal shadow patterns of buildings on landscapes, and to adjust combinations of light in work spaces designed to increase productivity while reducing energy costs. Building production costs can be managed more rigorously as digital tools have enabled the growth of an off-site industry of printed and manufactured components and entire buildings.

Architecture as a Business

Professional spatial design fields are sensitive to corporate, industrial, and residential supply and demand business cycles. After the Great Recession of 2008, for example, 40% of architects in some markets were laid off, and national publications railed that architecture was one of the worst fields an aspiring professional might enter.[1] Yet within a few years, the corporate and institutional investment increased, and major firms achieved their highest-ever revenues. Throughout these business cycles, professional designers have needed to exhibit skills in spatial design, technical proficiency and accountability, expeditious and predictable project delivery, adherence to the law and ethics, socio-cultural awareness, and budget and personnel management skills. Design enterprises can now better predict their business outcomes with greater refinement than ever before. Yale design educator Phillip Bernstein and Syracuse designer educator Kyle James Miller cite the convergence of digitized manufacturing processes, re-imagined labor deployment, and computer-based building construction practices, to project new approaches to management based on the growing awareness of design performativity.

Digital design enables firms to bring together specialists working concurrently on the development of schematic drawings, from different parts of the world, in real time. Architectural educators Marvin Malecha and Joon-Ho Choi argue (Chapters 9.1 and 9.2) that successful performative design processes rely on well-communicated feedback among design team members, facilitating interdisciplinary collaboration that enhances design and cost efficacy. Professional architectural practices now incorporate elements of interior architecture, landscape design, urban planning, industrial design, planning, and environmental stewardship. The work involves resiliency, designing for diverse individuals, families and children, health and wellness, approaches to climate change, and energy and resource sustainability.

An era of global cross-disciplinary firms has emerged, with specialized sub-practices embedded within enterprises that support consolidated research, personnel, and financial functions, and shared engineering and visualization infrastructures. Research and professional practice have become increasingly intertwined, as predicted design outcomes need to be evaluated through collaborative, integrative, data-driven practices that inculcate diverse perspectives into the design process. Computerized tools such as Integrated Project Delivery have become the norm in design production, and are central to professional development within firms.[2] The multi-disciplinary approach to design development is central to the integrated design thinking that acquires and processes knowledge and understanding through thought, diverse experiences, and the senses, supplanting formerly intuitive approaches to design. Some architecture schools have responded by discarding their traditional hand-drawing pedagogies in deference to broadly educating students to work in the digital environments that enable graduates to be immediately employable.

Visionary architect Reiner de Graaf posits that architecture now learns from what it applies within an environment, and applies what it learns toward improving its quantifiable outcomes (De Graaf 2017). Buildings, interiors, and environments will be valued for their embedded self-improving artificial intelligence, software, and ease of use, just as advanced technological products have come to be valued. The success or failure of a self-learning and self-healing building or environment is partly dependent on the cybernetics and information flows within that setting, all of which can be programmed by talented digital designers. As data and information flows facilitate design decision making, the values of the designers of the information have become increasingly important.

Artificial intelligence enables human designers to develop autonomic designs with embedded intelligence that enables buildings and environments to learn from post-construction conditions and to improve use conditions for their users over time. Building users have long modified initial designs to create higher levels of performance – artificial intelligence and machine learning algorithms can now automatically adjust building responses to environmental and usage conditions and make dynamic physical compensations for shortfalls in building performance. Coupled with remote building management tools, these predictive design tools enable the development of buildings and environments that can be resilient to changing conditions and can help heal themselves and their users.

Performative architecture has been scaled up beyond individual buildings and their immediate environments to influence the development of "smart cities" where quantitative data informs policy decisions that influence daily operations in dense urban environments. Concepts of concentration, interconnection, and resilience; mixed modalities of housing, recreation, production, education and recreation; and urbanity have focused urban planners on the development of neighborhoods, cities, and regions that better modulate or control energy consumption, transportation flows, employment access, social relations, mobility, place-making for cultural purposes, or maintenance planning.[3] Such planning enables real estate developers to better predict the quantifiable outcomes of their projects in the near and long term, enhancing the value of financial modeling tools.

Smart Cities that increase the quality of life for individuals and communities while reducing patterns of unnecessary resource consumption are beginning to emerge. Performative design enables city planners to assess the actual impacts of interventions that make cities "smart" by measuring how varying interventions may improve or degrade the quality of life and efficacy of design and planning interventions. This work assesses urban mobility and public transportation patterns, real estate investment outcomes, resilience and environmental quality in neighborhoods and for individual properties, housing patterns, noise and light impacts, energy use, and a range of social, architectonic, and planning metrics.[4]

Predictive simulations have been a key tool for projecting the impacts of climate change on buildings and environments. LEED certification grew in part because replicable data sets could test the efficacy of design interventions intended to reduce energy use in individual buildings and in building interactions in communities. Algorithms for predictive urban analytics shape design outcomes for individual buildings, building and material system interactions, and regional climate impacts on construction and zoning, affecting private real estate development and public policies toward uses of the built environment.

An emerging shared global vision of long-term sustainability (the ability to manage resources in order to retain utility over extended time periods) and resilience (the ability to recover after a mishap or disaster) has been informed by predictive analytics, and the emergence of designers' ability to consider regenerative designs that return energy to environments has been enhanced by performative analytics (Kolarevic, Chapter 4). New building materials, production techniques, and long-term performance parameters are developed and assessed through predictive digital tools, and are increasingly subjects to be addressed by designers (Fox, Chapter 19.1).

The obligation to enhance sustainability is codified in Canon VI of the *Code of Ethics and Professional Conduct* of the American Institute of Architects, under "Obligation to the Environment," providing that architects should promote sustainable design and development principles. Architectural practitioners and educators carry the responsibility of enhancing well-being through their work, and this responsibility ultimately holds architects accountable to their clients and to the general public. The material and symbolic artifacts created by designers and builders are representations of how a civilization adapted to its environment.

Defining the Accountable Architect: The Promise of a Just City

What Designers Ought to Be

The emergent accountable architects must have skills above and beyond traditional design *per se* – they must be managers within a team that can predict utilitarian outcomes of the consequences of the designs produced. The predictability of specific performance outcomes will be increasingly important as the costs of resources, and the need for sustainability and resilience, become paramount. Building owners, and communities within which buildings are developed, abhor any waste of valuable time and capital resources. The architect is the manager and allocator of scarce design resources, and that management carries within it the assumption of risk for the project's failure, and the rewards of being held accountable for achieving successful design outcomes.

An architecture based on the performance of designed spaces demarcates the design disciplines from the fine arts. Architects, beyond employing such digitized morphogenetic flow and performative analyses of spatial design (often performed by engineers and data analysts), incorporate into the design process an understanding of social psychology, anthropology, and human interactions. Setting quantifiable performance expectations assists in overcoming a Renaissance approach to design, of designing and building bespoke, custom buildings and environments that may fail to meet expectations of longevity, or public health and safety requirements. As architects are accountable to the public for the consequences of their work, performative design enhances the likelihood of a team achieving lower liability and higher public accountability for the work produced. Performativity addresses an architecture of dynamic process both in design methods and in outcomes (see Fisher, Chapter 6).

Systems of signification are embedded in designs that can be modeled for their utility, and also imbued with social meanings that transcend functionality. Aesthetic and poetic considerations carry significance for differing cultural groups, and can also be taught in design programs (Ibañez and Arbib, Chapters 7.1 and 7.2). Understanding these dovetailed concepts of the design of safe and functional spaces, and designing humanistic spaces with symbolic meanings, re-establishes the architect as a competent professional with training and skills that acknowledge both outcomes. Predicting the performance of buildings and spaces thus combines both quantifiable and qualitative data to sustain the utility and quality of buildings into the future.

The efficacy of designs is based on achieving predicted outcomes over extended times, and the ability to predict outcomes is embedded in how buildings and environments are formulated, executed, and operated once occupied. The performative architect designs and fabricates humanistic buildings and environments that meet the needs of currently known inhabitants, and unknown future users including children, the disabled, elderly, and, more broadly, changing environments. Predicting the longer-term integrity of a designed work is a key element in building trust and accountability between the designer, the client, and the public at large (National Architectural Accrediting Board 2019).

What should accountable design values include? I believe that the designer's work ought to be tied to values that improve the human condition and the environments within which we live, and that humanistic values ought to be integrated into design education.

Predictive analytics imbue the designer with a power over processes and outcomes that can re-assert the architect's hegemony in the design process. The ultimate as-built solution brings together new research, prior knowledge, wisdom drawn from experience, and collaborative management skill in a process of *design thinking* that has been applied in numerous professional fields beyond traditional architecture. An architect's agency is ultimately determined by whether their work performs as predicted, and endures over time. Architectural agency has increased as the scope of scientific and technological knowledge has enabled the design profession to be more quantifiably accountable for design outcomes. Thus, trusted architects gain clients' and public respect as the designers reduce design and building legal liabilities by projecting and addressing potential failures,[5] and by projecting the potential successful quantifiable outcomes of their design interventions. These basic principles establish goals to be attained by accountable architects in their pursuit of predicting and improving their design outcomes.

Values Inherent in an Accountable Architects' Designing within a Just City

No software or artificial intelligence system is value-free. On the contrary, data mining, predictive analytics, and artificial intelligence have been employed with negative consequences, including the manipulation of elections, financial markets, and consumer purchasing patterns. Micro-targeting of individuals has been used by propogandists and retailers to affect groups' social behaviors. Discrimination and inherent biases are intrinsic in algorithms, necessitating that designers be clear in articulating their values and their presumed outcomes at the outset of a design process. The ability to design for what is known, what should be known, and what can be reasonably predicted into the future is the essence of what enables architects to be held accountable for the integrity of their work.

Conceptual work by Harvard professors Fainstein (2010) and Griffin (2017) defined a rubric for a Just City, and seeks to redirect the goals and resources of development within disadvantaged communities away from economic growth per se, and toward the development of wider social benefits including equity and material well-being combined with principles of diversity and inclusive participation in designing improved environments. The two core principles of a Just City are:

A) Acceptance:

Belonging – individuals feel accepted and comfortable in a setting despite their age, gender, race, sexuality, or income

Caring – communities support individuals within a community, materially, for healthy well-being, and spiritually

Empathy – individuals are comfortable exercising the ability to recognize and understand the feelings and points of view of another person

Inclusion – individuals accept differences in personal identity, and act positively on the intention to involve diverse opinions, attitudes, and behaviors in shared decision making

Reconciliation – individuals and entities within a community embrace a process of finding a way to make two different ideas, facts, or points of view coexist or be true at the same time

Respect – there is within a community a mutually earned and shared honoring of different voices, opinions, behaviors, and cultural expressions

Tolerance – an acceptance of differences among individuals

Trust – a willingness to promote a confidence earned through the demonstration of fulfilling commitments and promises made among people and institutions within and between communities

B) Resilience:

Adaptability – an acceptance of responsibility by individuals or collective groups to contribute fairly to the creation and maintenance of just conditions for all

Durability – an ability of all social and spatial systems to remain strong and in good condition over long periods of time

Sustainability – Just Cities maintain the quality of not being harmful to the social or spatial well-being of others, or depleting non-renewable resources, and thereby ethically supporting a long-term social and spatial balance between resources and patterns of use of those resources

What Must the Accountable Architect Be Able to Show?

From a long-term business perspective, the architect should be required to understand the evolving trends in design firm management and practice.

The architect must demonstrate the ability to work effectively in multi-disciplinary environments, particularly where matters of sustainability, resiliency, and planning are to be addressed.

Multi-disciplinary practice management includes the oversight of complex processes indicating an awareness that:

- Design is but one element of architecture.
- Team dynamics, personnel practices, and finance are essential to project success.
- Employing more women and people of color enhances interpersonal skills in work environments.
- Business and personnel management practices are essential to designer success.
- Architects must be able to effectively transmit ideas and processes to clients and ensuing generations of design users, in written and visual formats.
- Imaging, representation, adaptation of visual data, and translation of ideas into coherent visual forms are essential components to design presentations.
- Marketing is essential to design firm survival.
- Ethics are a key element of the design process.
- Diversity, inclusion, and cultural competence are integral to the design process and to how architects present themselves and their work to clients and to the public.
- Compassion for others and care for environmental conditions should be demonstrated by designers, to overcome public perceptions of designer hubris, and to transform the culture of design away from hierarchical business models.

- Modeling of physical and conceptual outcomes of both the artifact created, and the longer-term environmental impacts and outcomes of that artifact, are a key predictive part of the design process.
- There is a need for the application of sustainable design protocols involving immersive building simulation and rapid prototyping to test design assumptions and impacts.
- Performative designers of the future should be able to demonstrate with strong predictive models that their architectural work is intended to be long-lasting and consistent with evolving trends toward resilience and sustainability.
- Performative designers should build into their engagements with clients a commitment to two- and five-year post-occupancy evaluations of their work.
- Advocacy for the environment and public service for those in need are important values embedded within professional practice, as is expected in other professions such as law and medicine.
- Project management focused on the allocation of risk and risk mitigation is essential for client satisfaction and public accountability.
- Some form of investment in and financial ownership of the designer's idea, model, and product are essential to provide the designer with a long-term stake in the outcome of the project, deriving a potential annuity based on the success of the designer's work.
- Architects are fundamentally committed to and have the ability to bring beauty, poetry, and grace to the utilitarian elements of the design algorithms they work with to produce predictable design outcomes.

Education for the Accountable Architect

Accreditation: Professional Design Education Designed and Regulated

As architects have evolved from being artisans designing single, craft-based structures for known clients into multi-talented professionals using digital tools to design complexly-interacting spatial environments, the educational expectations of the profession have become more layered and demanding. Accreditation standards determine the shape and direction of architectural education.

The National Architectural Accrediting Board (NAAB) was established in 1940 to develop and oversee standards for architectural education. The NAAB accredits professional architecture degrees offered by higher education institutions with U.S. regional accreditation, and promulgates Student Performance Criteria and procedures for architectural education. These standards are developed collaboratively by educators, licensed practitioners, regulators, and students. The National Conference of Architectural Registration Boards (NCARB) requires a degree from an NAAB-accredited professional degree program to satisfy the education requirement for certification, and most state registration boards require an NAAB-accredited degree as a prerequisite for licensure. Those seeking registration must meet local jurisdictional requirements for professional experience.

The NAAB has recognized three types of professional degrees: the Bachelor of Architecture, the Master of Architecture, and the Doctor of Architecture (a non-professional, academic degree that does not qualify the holder to sit for licensure). A program may be granted an eight-year or shorter term of accreditation, depending on the extent of its conformance with the NAAB's educational standards. The NAAB is a signatory to multilateral international accreditation agreements, and its standards are consistent with U.S. regional accreditors.

The NAAB seeks to operate in an open, transparent manner in keeping with best accreditation practices nationally. It periodically evaluates individual architecture programs to ensure that graduates have the technical and critical thinking skills required to pursue a competent career in the profession.

The minimum standards that all NAAB-accredited programs must meet are described in the NAAB Conditions for Accreditation, and in the NAAB Procedures for Accreditation (2019). The organization's intention to maintain organizational transparency extends to periodic self-evaluative processes for reviewing the Conditions for Accreditation, the publication of visiting team reports, and to requirements that accredited programs make information available to the public. The 2019 Accreditation Review Forum sought to strengthen programs' learning and teaching culture, and reaffirmed the NAAB's intention of "establish[ing] productive pathways for advancing the discipline of architecture as a significant contributor to the enrichment of human culture and society" (NAAB, 2019).

Skills sought by accreditors have fallen broadly into five categories:

- Architectural education and the *academic community* around it
- Architectural education and *students* engaged therein
- Architectural education and the *regulatory environment*
- Architectural education and the *profession* graduates would enter
- Architectural education and the *public good*

Taken together, these realms parallel the expectations of the component members constituting the NAAB: the Association of Collegiate Schools of Architecture representing the academy, the AIAS representing students, the NCARB representing state licensing agencies, the American Institute of Architects representing the profession, and a public member of the NAAB Board representing the broader public good.

The NAAB Conditions for Accreditation call specifically for professional architectural education programs to demonstrate that they have met broad standards for:

- Positive learning cultures and respectful learning environments
- Culturally rich, diverse and inclusive educational environments
- Programmatic and personal self-assessment and reflection
- Student performance criteria manifesting a graduating student's awareness and ability to demonstrate:
  - *Critical thinking and representation skills*, including professional communication, design thinking, investigative, architectural design, systems ordering, historical precedent use, global culture, and cultural diversity skills
  - *Building practices, and technical knowledge skills*, including the ability to create building designs with well-integrated systems, constructability through accurate technical information legibility, showing principles of environmental stewardship and exhibiting minimum standards of skill in pre-design work, site design, codes and regulations, technical documentation, structural and environmental systems, building envelope systems and assemblies, building materials and assemblies, building service systems, and financial considerations
  - *Integrated architectural solutions* involving research, evaluating decision-making processes, and integrative design
  - *Professional practice* involving the comprehension of the business of architecture and construction, an understanding of the roles played by key actors in the building process, and an understanding of professional codes of ethics. These awareness expectations include knowledge of the roles of stakeholders, the responsibilities of project management, sound business practices, legal responsibilities, and an understanding of the parameters of professional conduct.

The 2014 Accreditation Review Conference committed to enabling individual institutions to define their resources for themselves (including physical, financial, information, and human) as long as they were consistent with their mission statements and the NAAB's principles. Program quality assessments evolved away from "box checking" to asking programs to define themselves and verify how they had met the Conditions.[6] The 2019 Accreditation Review Forum considered further changes and agreed on clarifying principles:

- Multi-disciplinary practice is an essential competence.
- Systems thinking and integrated design are core to the discipline.
- The profession's goals are increasingly diverse.
- Some subjects and practices cannot and should not be learned in school, so design firms must play a role in professional education.

For many years, visiting teams assessed programs against the NAAB's prescribed *structural* or *input* standards: what mattered to the assessors was how many and what kinds of volumes were held by a program's library, whether a campus was fully accessible or had an on-site shop space, the numbers of computers readily available to students, the amount of dedicated desk space allocated to each fully enrolled student, the presence of certain explicitly stated guidelines within course curricula, or the credentials held by teaching faculty. Such input factors have largely evaporated as measures of a program's quality. As the predictability of design outcomes has come to dominate professional practice, evidence of learning outcomes has come to dominate accreditation reviews.

Evolving Pedagogical Expectations

To meet the NAAB's core standards, accredited programs largely adopted a nineteenth-century, Beaux-Arts-based, atelier teaching method, augmented by work in materials and building laboratories or digital fabrication labs. The pedagogy was based on an "intuitive creative," studio-based teaching approach divorced from quantitative and performance-based professional practice concerns. The Beaux-Arts system itself reflected its particular era, as Jean-Nicolas-Louis Durand's Neoclassical system of compositional gridding was a strategy for managing unprecedented and newly complex building programs (Durand 1799). Viollet-le-Duc's structural rationalism[7] responded to new materials and evolving trade practices, and governmental patronage led to conforming aesthetic expectations.[8]

The atelier approach to design education has prevailed in most architecture schools well into the twenty-first century. Pedagogies often start with a blank slate, for an unnamed client, on an inchoate landscape, and conclude with objects of utility and beauty. Lectures have addressed liberal arts, historical, and technical subjects; few courses were offered on-line or off-site, and there was little hands-on experiential learning from actual building projects. Studios have been scheduled largely in time blocks that preclude learning from other disciplines such as economics, health, business management, engineering, political science, law, sociology, or psychology. Case studies of professional practices, predicted outcomes, or of the causes of design failures were a small part of this pedagogy, creating a divide between what many faculty, administrators, and some accreditors have favored as an intuitive, clean-sheet, studio-based teaching method, and what professional practitioners said they needed to see in new graduates in order to add immediate value to firms' day-to-day work. Many aspects of architectural practice remained unexplored. Little accreditor attention was directed toward assessing users' comfort or well-being, client expectations, the regeneration or sustainability of non-renewable resources, or the magic of aesthetic pleasure derived from experiencing a well-designed facility. Change in architectural education has been slow to come.

The Carnegie Foundation-funded *Boyer Report* (1996) criticized architectural education for being out-of-touch with professional design practice, and remote from other academic and professional disciplines on university campuses. Architectural education has been repeatedly criticized by staff at large firms, state licensing boards, and national accrediting bodies, as too academic and unengaged from real world design and building; too removed from the needs of the economically disadvantaged, disabled, people of color, and women; abusive to students; and too hierarchical and insular in pedagogy. Design school graduates demanded more teaching of the tools of sustainability, and the values of social justice for the underserved.

Architecture school graduates now enter diverse careers – real estate, health design and physical therapy, film animation, construction, software design, gaming, product development, and digital fabrication of archaeological artifacts. Accreditors recognized that large urban and small rural schools, and both artisanal and theoretical programs, have utilized the NAAB's technically-oriented Student Performance Criteria to shape curricula that prepared graduates to think pragmatically and innovatively. These criteria have provided a framework for teaching design thinking that effectively translates ideas into material forms.

The understanding of how design thinking could be taught began to shift curricula away from *tabula rasa* approaches to pedagogy, toward research-oriented and hands-on teaching. Quantitative research, digital design and presentation skills, and three-dimensional modeling skills and fabrication have become increasingly integrated into curricula. On-line design exploration, changes in the more advanced digital skillsets of newly arrived students, and changes in what professional firms needed from graduates shifted accreditation criteria away from input metrics toward evaluations based on performative outcomes of graduates. Input criteria for assessing program strengths, such as whether programs had invested in particular capital improvements or curricular innovations, were superseded by *outcome* measurements; i.e., whether graduating students could actually demonstrate, through their manifested work, the ability to show they had learned the skills expected to be shown by a competent architectural school graduate.

Graduates of accredited schools must now meet expectations of technological proficiency, and show knowledge of client expectations of design and production speed, expectations of project management expertise, resiliency expectations, changes in fabrication, and global capital flows. The knowledge and skills that graduates can actually demonstrate has taken precedence over how much money a school may have spent on new technologies. Demonstrable learning outcomes have supplanted structural teaching inputs as the standard for determining what an architectural graduate has actually learned. In this way, diverse and independent schools in rural desert settings can be accredited as equitably as large programs within major urban universities.

In considering these emerging trends, Deamer and Bernstein (2011) proposed substantial changes in the structure of architectural education. Deamer's approach would provide for a three-year, professional graduate studio sequence of learning with a first year focused on the formal attributes of two-dimensional design; the second year on building in three dimensions, including program, site, structure, and mechanical systems; and the third year on four-dimensional design including time-based procurement, construction, occupation, and maintenance. Throughout, the creation of experiences of space, and the historical, economic, cultural, economic, ecological, labor-oriented, political, technological, and representational dimensions of design would be considered.

Performative design utilizing predictive data-based models of design outcomes inevitably changes what designers, clients, and the public can expect of an architectural design. This paradigmatic professional design change leads inexorably to changes in design education. A profession based on predictable outcomes must educate entrants into that profession on the responsibilities inherent in being held accountable for those outcomes. Understanding that inherent accountability requires knowledge of technical fields beyond design, and of the humanities.

Tools of a Values-Based Design Education

Architects are environmental and procedural problem-solvers for their clients and the public. These professionals combine *tabula rasa* conceptualization, design, project management across multiple disciplines, financial and personnel management, awareness of physical contexts, knowledge of new and old materials and assembly techniques, analysis of engineering analysis, social psychology and human patterns of use, awareness of the health impacts of built environments, and, ultimately, the transmogrification of ideas into physical, material forms that are utilitarian, cost-effective, and delightful. The term "design" includes originating, extrapolating, or assembling elements of a solution to solve a problem in a way that can be made manifest, whether in the development of an idea into an object, transforming a concept into a plan, or the creation of a strategy that can be implemented. Studying to be a designer is a process of developing humanistic problem-solving skills that may be useful to others, without regard to the discipline within which such design thinking may be applied.

Tom Fisher argues, from his experience as an influential large-university design school dean, that architecture is a field with multilateral boundaries with the arts, science, humanities, and sociology, and that the scope of its realm and the domain of its influence are not constant. At the University of Minnesota, Fisher oversaw studies in landscape, fashion, and industrial design as well as architecture. He asserts that architectural education has had to consider the insufficiencies of intuitive creative approaches to teaching design thinking, and that a more "cognitive" approach to teaching, incorporating more predictable and quantitative data, is radically redefining the divisions that have emerged between architectural education and professional design practices. Increasing attention to building performance has contributed to a new understanding of the ways in which buildings are *perceived, made, and experienced*, and this change is reshaping architectural education.

The twenty-first-century architectural educator transcends the mere teaching of design skills, to include the technical skills and values necessary to work responsibly and accountably with the support of other professionals. An architectural education premised on predictive design pedagogies would supplement technical and utilitarian expectations to enable graduating students to demonstrate evidence of and exposure to:

Design, Technical, and Managerial Expertise

These skills are the same as those mandated by the NAAB since its inception.

Case-based and Evidence-based Learning

Work by educator Laura Lee (2018), and architectural educator/lawyer Carl Sapers, has emphasized experiential and case-based approaches as key components of design education, and as positive supplements to studio-based learning.

Experientiality

The roots of analyses for human interaction with urban settings and environments can be traced back several centuries, and performative design has brought a new sophistication to these explorations. Designers can now use digital tools to assess the impacts of interactivity with environments on human behavior as never before, and can apply findings to improving those interactions for the elderly, children, the disabled, and others previously marginally considered in designing buildings and environments (see Kanaani, Chapter 22).

Commitment to Life-long Learning

Studying design in an architecture school is only the beginning of a life-long process of updating professional skills and knowledge.

Resiliency, Collaborative Ecological Sensitivity, Recovery, and Engaged Social Responsibility

Urban resilience is the capacity of individuals, communities, institutions, businesses, buildings, environments, and systems within a city to survive, adapt, and grow no matter what kinds of chronic stresses and acute shocks they experience (Rockefeller Foundation 2019).

Engaging with Clients and Users

Few architecture schools teach the value of marketing and client engagement. Design schools generally teach presentation skills, often without including writing. Practitioners must persuade clients and the public of the value of many challenging concepts – sustainability, historic preservation, resilience, and diversity of design. Designers must be clear, intentional, and persuasive in presenting design solutions that are accountable, verifiable, quantifiable where possible, and predictable, in order to enhance the long-term credibility of the profession.

Health and Well-being

Environmental design requires that interdisciplinary design thinkers address Vitruvius's concept of *utilitas*, or the accommodation of buildings and environments to the body (ergonomics) and its activities (space planning). Human comfort and the health needs of inhabitants are well addressed through the data and visualization tools of performance-based design. Environmental design assists in expanding the promotion of human capacities of users, including healing and learning abilities. Performative architecture places the satisfaction of human equilibrium at the center of its purpose, including predictive theories of healthful environments that synthesize multiple facets of health, well-being, and spatial design and performance (see Kopec, Chapter 26).

Human Comfort

A study of structures designed prior to the advent of air conditioning provides some understanding of how bioclimatic design adapts to regional climate to maximize building performance (Rudofsky & Fathy, 1965). This approach to design, combined with evolving understandings of neuroscience-based human interactions within environments, and visually digitized human ergonomics, can lead to the design of predictable sequential spatial narratives that are both useful and experientially intriguing.

Data use and digitized visualization do not exclude intuitive and emotive concepts of beauty and poetics in design. Buildings and environments project and encompass intangible and qualitative aspects of the performative design process. Buildings incorporate perceptions and sensibilities that evoke historic, spiritual, and symbolic experiences that are the essence of perceived beauty. Performative design can anticipate some of these experiences from a neuroscientific perspective (see Mun, Chapter 25). Talented designers imbue spaces and artifacts with the sinuous poetry and aesthetics that transform cubes and flats into places that inspire one to visit again, work better, and seek to replicate and share those sensibilities with others.

Education Ahead: Specific Areas of Study to Educate Accountable Architects

Vitruvius (c.90–c.20 BCE) set forth three primary attributes of good architecture: *firmatis* (durability), *utilitas* (utility for the users), and *venusas* (joy in the aesthetics of the building). The NAAB in turn set forth four broad attributes needed in graduates of contemporary architecture programs: *critical thinking and representation skills*, *knowledge of building practices and technical knowledge*, the ability to *integrate disciplines to achieve solutions* to design problems, and knowledge of *professional practice*. Performative design permits the consolidation of these expectations (utility, durability, and technical knowledge can now be combined through artificial intelligence in creative new ways), while the concept of who the client is has expanded beyond the known entity that pays for the work, to the broader public seeking resiliency.

Four broad realms of education remain paramount: *technical expertise*, *managerial awareness*, *service to clients and the public*, and *aesthetics* created by the designer. Performative design enables experimentation, prototyping, integration of concepts, delivery of the artifact, and post-occupancy analysis of the outcome. Design educators can approach professional education based on these broad realms, while preparing graduates to design in small or large firms, virtually anywhere in the world, for diverse client needs. Performative design transforms education to become innovatively outcomes-based beyond the classroom, yet rooted in the best design traditions.

The accreditation standards that govern architectural education evolve incrementally because they must be applied within more than 100 public and private, large and small institutions with widely varying resources. Consensus on implementing radical new standards is difficult to achieve. Nonetheless, trends in the twenty-first century have centered on making the standards more transparent, based in critical thinking and problem-solving, and focused on students' abilities to present evidence of outcomes-based learning. In this regard, the following pedagogical recommendations deserve further discussion:

1   *Academic and formal:*

   Maintain and periodically update the 2014 NAAB *Student Performance Criteria* to adjust to technological and construction innovations and findings based on post-occupancy evaluations within the built environment.

   Assure that design school graduates are capable of designing on multiple scales (micro to environmental), *in situ* and remotely, and fabricating, in diverse media with traditional and innovative materials, objects for human consumption that are safe, healthy, ergonomically sound for diverse users, efficient for their intended purposes, energy-efficient, and resilient.

   Eliminate the five-year B.Arch. and require students entering a professional degree program to hold an undergraduate liberal arts and sciences degree, or to have completed at least two years of liberal studies prior to entering a professional design program.

   Move universally to three-year Master's program with an intensive 1.5-year required core curriculum, and 1.5 years focused on specialization; provide Continuing Education credits for five-year NCARB re-certification.

   Combine in-studio design and jury critique with case studies, on-line performance-based digital learning, and in-field experiential learning in a concurrent three-year professional Master's degree program.

   The concept of "design professionalism" should parallel the professional and ethical standards of other licensed professions such as law, medicine, and accounting, where vetted critiques of professional trends and failures are published transparently by independent reviewers.

   Stress a commitment to life-long learning.

   The profession must delineate the values that differentiate doctoral (research-focused) vs. professional education as a path to professional practice.

   Architecture should include the focus of interior design's body of knowledge on design outcomes and performance, and on health, comfort, and well-being. Architectural education should also develop specializations, minors, and two-year certificates:

   - Computer-aided design
   - Health design, ergonomics, comfort, well-being, and environmental health
   - Housing
   - Communications design, immersive video, and three-dimensional media

- New materials development
- Sustainability, resilience, and climate change
- Environmental graphic design
- Interior architecture
- Landscape architecture
- Urban informatics
- Predicting economic and ecological performance of built environments
- Light and color
- Hospitality

2 *Technical:*

- Inclusivity in personnel management
- Anthropology, sociology, human factors engineering
- Representational and presentation skills
- Digital skills

3 *Managerial:*

- Construction management
- Law and regulation of design
- Post-occupancy analysis
- Design firm management

The Fundamental Outcomes of a Performance-based Design Education

Performative design reshapes education away from the measurement of input factors in assessing the quality of a pedagogy, to one that emphasizes *learning outcomes*, as well as meeting the requirements of professional licensure. Continuing questions to be asked of accreditors, educators, and the profession include:

- How well are educational programs addressing inter-disciplinarity and systems thinking?
- How replicable are the attributes that add value and quality to a designed artifact?
- Are schools teaching students to meet client expectations?
- How can performativity encourage designing fixed spatial artifacts and environments that have characteristics of mobile technological devices, i.e., flexibility, adaptability, resiliency, the capacity to learn from experience, and the ability to meet known performance standards?
- Is architectural education sensitive to preservation, resiliency, regeneration, evolving cultural and use perspectives, and time in the creation of objects that survive?
- Can performative design increase the sharing with clients of the concepts and examples of what is resilient, and of what fails to meet evolving standards of environmental sensitivity? (Leve & Salvadori 1992)
- How well is education meeting the evolving expectations of inclusivity and cultural sensitivity?
- How can schools address a renewed architecture of well-being?
- How can performative design enhance dynamic aesthetics that are derived from and consistent with quantifiable outcomes?
- What is the value of schools' and architects' service to the public?

Architects are not the heroic, autonomous "master builders" portrayed in *The Fountainhead* (Rand 1943). They are team members, facilitators, and collaborative leaders who undertake research into precedents and innovations in spatial design, and synthesize such data to predictably manage design processes and outcomes. Evidence-based research, predictive information, and comparative analysis inform the process of designing, and the architect's understanding of the design and building process, in order to iteratively formulate options that meet the client's needs (Lee 2018).

Predictive analytics and performative design translate values into material accomplishments in the built environment that provide health, safety, resilience, and well-being benefits to the general public. Professional design practices, based on achieving predictable outcomes, require educated practitioners who are well-versed in rigorous design principles and in the realities of accountable social relations and management. Design educators are challenged to provide graduates who are capable of meeting this standard of performance.

Notes

1 Vanessa Quirk, "After the Meltdown: Where Does Architecture Go From Here?" Huffington Post, December 6, 2017; Catherine Rampell, "Want a Job? Go to College, and Don't Major in Architecture," *New York Times*, January 5, 2012.
2 Krisstoffer Negendahl, "Building Performance Simulation in the Early Design Stage: An Introduction to Integrated Dynamic Models," in *Automation in Construction 54*, 2015.
3 See, for example, the work of Yona Friedman, Eckhard Schultz-Fielitz, Kenzo Tange, and Kisho Kurokawa cited by Michael Stepner and Alejandro Zaera-Polo in Chapter 13.
4 Dan O'Brien, "Confronting Inequality and Economic Mobility: Data-Driven Lessons from Boston, For Boston." Boston Area Research Initiative Spring Conference, 2018.
5 See NCARB Professional Development Program texts preparing emerging architects for licensure examinations.
6 Interview with Andrea Rutledge, NAAB Executive Director who oversaw the 2014 Accreditation Review Conference, April 1, 2019.
7 Le-Duc, the Beaux-Arts system of design education.
8 Peggy Deamer, "Black Box: Articulating Architecture's Core in the Post-Digital Era," ACSA 107th Annual Meeting, Pittsburgh, PA, March 28, 2019.

References

Boyer, E., & Mitgang, L. (1996). *Building community*. Princeton, NJ: Carnegie Foundation for the Advancement of Teaching.
De Graaf, R. (2017). *Four walls and a roof: the complex nature of a simple profession*. Cambridge: Harvard University Press.
Deamer, P., & Bernstein, P. (2011). *BIM in academia*. New Haven, CT: Yale School of Architecture.
Durand, J. N. L. (1799). *Recueil et parallele des edifices de tour genre, anciens et moderns*. Paris: De Avanzo et Cie.
Fainstein, S. F. (2010). *The Just City*. Ithaca, NY: Cornell University.
Griffin, T. L. (2017). *The Just City Lab: The Just City Index*. Cambridge, MA: Harvard Graduate School of Design, Just City Lab for Black in Design.
Lee, L. (2018) *Architecture from 1% to 10 billion: mapping the missing middle*. Unpublished presentation to Design Futures Council Rome Forum, October 2018.
Leve, M., & Salvadori, M. (1992). *Why buildings fall down: how structures fail*. New York, NY: W. W. Norton.
National Architectural Accrediting Board (2019). *National Architectural Accrediting Board conditions for accreditation*. Retrieved from: www.naab.org/accreditation/.
Ramirez, S. (March 8, 2019). The 11 most influential trends of 2019. Dwell. Retrieved from: www.dwell.com/article/architecture-trends-2019-cf7f9ecf.
Rand, A. (1943). *The fountainhead*. Indianapolis, IN: Bobbs-Merrill.
Rockefeller Foundation. (2019). *100 resilient cities, 2013–2016*. Retrieved from: 100resilientcities.org.
Rudofsky, B., & Fathy, H. (1965). *Architecture without architects*. New York, NY: Museum of Modern Art.

Epilogue
Towards Responsibly Anticipatory Evolvable Architecture for the Anthropocene

Jim Dator

I was very pleased when Mitra Kanaani asked me to write the Epilogue for this collection of essays on performative architecture. It is a topic I have long had interest in—well before the term was used, or at least widely used.

The first teaching job I accepted as a fresh PhD was in the College of Law and Politics at Rikkyo University in Tokyo, Japan (1960–66). As Branko Kolarevic notes in this volume, traditional Japanese dwellings are fascinating to westerners in part because they are so profoundly performative, with open, flexible interior spaces, often embracing a microscopic garden outside, inviting many uses, and uncluttered by permanent furniture. The *tokonoma* within each house displays objects that evoke feelings of vastness, tranquility, and humility. I was transfixed by the plain beauty (*shibui*) and flexibility of it all—though I also noted that the homes of most ordinary Tokyoites were anything but "uncluttered". At the time, most Japanese said they lived in tiny "rabbit hutches" cheek by jowl with their neighbors whose activities they had learned not to notice or hear, in a forest of ugly medium-rise apartment buildings called, without irony, "mansions".

When my family and I reluctantly returned to the United States, it was to Virginia Tech, in the remote mountains of Blacksburg, Virginia where a newly-coed military academy was becoming a university with a political science department that was expanding in directions that attracted me. By one of the many extraordinary strokes of fate that have characterized my life, our duplex housemates were David and Jane Greene, he of Archigram fame and she an associate of Mary Quant on Carnaby Street. Michael Webb, another member of the Archigram Group, lived nearby. They were visiting scholars in the School of Architecture, and my wife and I tagged along with them on many learning adventures, not all entirely academic.

David Greene and Michael Webb revealed to me the mysteries of their Living Cities, Walking City, Plug-in-City, Instant City, and other projects. They also convinced me of the virtue of erecting buildings that would collapse at the end of ten years in order to make room for new, more appropriate structures—or for none. It was their cushicles and suitaloons that most interested me, then and now: Raze all existing structures and clear the land of everything but electrical plugs and water-supplying and waste-removing infrastructure so that individuals and groups can hook up, open up, and join their cushicles for group shelter and privacy, conduct some business, then unjoin the cushicles, fold them back up, tidy up the grounds, and move on—this all seemed supremely desirable to me.

I spent considerable time, not only with David and Mike, in the Virginia Tech School of Architecture while it was a hotbed of innovation. Indeed, I patterned my futures classes after the way I saw architecture being taught at Virginia Polytechnic Institute then, and still believe that futures studies and architecture are twin-sister disciplines. On the basis of my three years at Virginia Tech, I was convinced that architects were the grooviest people on the planet, leading humanity to bright and dynamic futures. However, when the chance came to go to the University of Hawaii, thus getting closer to the sun and to vibrant Asian/Pacific cultures, I fled from the dark and narrow hollows of Appalachia without hesitation.

Several authors in this book (Kolarevic, Whalley, and Pasquero and Poletto) mentioned the importance of Archigram in the development of performative architecture.

Simon Sadler subtitled his book about Archigram as "Architecture without Architecture", and I think that gets it right (Sadler, 2005).

David and Jane Greene (and their two boys) also spent some time in the Art School of the University of Hawaii, and John and Magda McHale by another quirk of fate were visiting Fellows for a while at the East-West Center on the university campus as well, greatly influencing my views of the futures and of architecture especially, and so I continued to be an architecture wannabe during my forty-plus years as head of the Hawaii Research Center for Futures Studies in the Political Science Department of the University of Hawaii at Manoa. During the last decade or two, I was formally an adjunct professor in Architecture, and both co-taught courses with their excellent faculty and served on many DArch committees.

Architects and Futures

Because of this history, Mitra asked to write an epilogue based on the contributions to an earlier book of hers (Dator, 2016). My opening sentence was

> In contrast to many people who call themselves "futurists," architects are truly effective in creating the futures—what they design and build often persists for a very long time, shaping, thwarting, and facilitating behavior for generations to come, long after the mortgages have been paid and they themselves are dead and gone.

However, when I reflected on what I saw most architects were taught, and how they practiced it, I did not see any clear recognition by architects of an obligation to think about the impact of their work on future generations. I made a comprehensive review of the architectural literature and did encounter a few books or articles that could fairly be called "futures-oriented". I reviewed all of the D. Arch theses submitted to the Hawaii School of Architecture, but few of them were futures-oriented at all. More distressingly, my review of the essays written for Mitra's book about architecture design and practice, with a subtitle about "emerging trends", showed they overwhelmingly ignored the future, or when they did infer or actually mention it, everything was pretty much the same as the present except maybe bigger, more, or better. This is an image of the futures that I call "Grow", or "Continued Growth". Since the mid-nineteenth century, this has been the official image of the future of all major institutions in every part of the world, especially the so-called "Developed World". The entire purpose of education from K through PhD is to create people who can invent, use, and buy products and services that keep the economy growing. It is very, very difficult to find courses that suggest that other images of the futures, such as Collapse/New Beginnings, Discipline, or Transformation, are plausible (perhaps desirable) even though such images do exist in the minds and inform the actions of many people on Earth. Few of the possibilities that most futurists are concerned about —exhaustion of energy and other natural resources, climate change, sea level rise, severe shortages of food and water, continued global population growth (and local population decline), economic and political collapse and the like, on the one hand, and automation, robots, artificial intelligence, space research, biotechnologies, nanotechnologies, smart materials, and their potential for full unemployment, on the other—make their way into most curricula. Thus, they were wholly invisible to most authors of Mitra's book. There were notable exceptions to be sure, which I highlighted and discussed, but for the most part, time and the futures was a dimension that did not seem to be fundamental to most architects.

When Mitra asked me to take a look at the chapters in this book, I approached my task with some hesitation and much anticipation. Anything about "performative architecture" certainly would be time-aware and futures-oriented, I presumed. In my judgment, some of the essays are, some are not, and there are several truly spectacular exceptions—a great improvement from a few years ago.

Some Evolutionary Features of Architecture from the Holocene to the Anthropocene

For most of our brief existence on this planet since our emergence during the Holocene Epoch approximately 12,000 years ago, we *Homo sapiens sapiens* have lived in small, mobile, homogenous groups within natural environments of what is called "subsistence affluence" (Sahlins, 1972). While some caves were apparently inhabited for thousands of years, their tenants changed frequently, and most human shelters were flexible, mobile, and easily disposable. It was only much more recently—a few thousand years ago—with the growth of human population and the necessity of horticulture and then agriculture that some humans began to settle down, property and its defense became important, and eventually civilizations—that is to say, life centered on cities—emerged in several parts of the world. During this later period, some structures were made of stone, initially megaliths such as Stonehenge, later increasingly elaborate pyramids, temples, and palaces. Permanence—or at least persistence—became possible and highly prized. However, in some parts of the world—China, Korea, and Japan, for example—for thousands of years, until modern times, buildings large or small were made mainly of wood, with little or no stone or brick, thus requiring constant repair or re-construction, often on exactly the same pattern. Stunning examples of this are the wooden Ise Shrines in Japan from the seventh century CE, that even to this day are precisely rebuilt in alternating adjacent plots of land every twenty years by craftsmen who pass the construction knowledge down from generation to generation, making sure it is never lost. The Ise Shrines are made permanent by being regularly, totally, and precisely rebuilt (Teeuwen and Breen, 2017).

Since the establishment of agriculture four to five thousand years ago, most people have lived in shelters of their own creation that they themselves could adapt, repair, rebuild, or re-imagine as they wished and their cultures allowed. Sometimes, stone edifices were appropriated by ordinary folks into habitats for themselves as the structures and cultures of their creators crumbled to dust.

In this volume, Brady Peters, citing Kolarevic, notes that architects are highly dependent on the tools they have. New tools change thought and practice. The computer is given as a current example. One of the fundamental technologies that was powerfully instrumental in shaping the evolution of humans and human settlements from the mobility and adaptability of our long period of hunting and gathering to that of sedentary agriculture and urban areas was the slow evolution of writing. While hunting and gathering societies had ways of passing on memories from person to person across time as well as space, these methods provoked more of a *feeling* of permanence and accuracy than the fact of either. In spite of many mnemonics aimed at keeping the story straight, communication beyond the immediate face-to-face was essentially a game of "telephone" where what was received and passed on progressively deteriorated. Humans thus have actually lived most of our lives "fact free", constantly reinterpreting and adapting past and present beliefs and practices to fit current needs and sentiments of whoever gets to tell the stories.

All this changed with writing and civilization. Now the dead hand of the past had an active role in governing everywhere, not only in far-flung regions of the present but also, with the creation of institutions and bureaucracies devoted to preservation and transmission, far into the future right down to the present day. All modern institutions are still guided in major ways by ideas and formulas from thousands of years ago—something impossible without a recording system like writing, and institutions designed to transmit the written words securely and accurately (Dator et al., 2014).

So, for most of our existence, we lived in an eternal present. Past, present, and future seemed to be exactly the same for everyone generation after generation except when some catastrophe, natural or human-inflicted, destroyed the material and cultural basis of a way of life—and a new, linear, predictable normal was established.

We are biologically and psychologically predisposed to view the future as flat and unchanged from the present and past.

The main two exceptions to this were the cyclical daily and seasonal rhythms of nature, which evoked a sense of continual repetitive sequences, on the one hand, and the terrifying uncertainties of death, and imagined life after death, that promoted spiritual and religious beliefs, practices, ceremonies, and edifices, on the other.

Thus, the early days of the creation of civilizations should be viewed less as unique periods of sudden rapid discontinuity and change, and more as typical periods of abrupt change followed by stasis and stagnation that slowly became a new normal. If your mores, your language, your customs, your spiritual and intellectual beliefs and practices did not get written down and preserved, and someone else's did, then your culture and your previous identity was gone, often along with your life, while those of the people lucky enough to have theirs written down, and not subsequently lost or destroyed, could have their cultural identities preserved forever and ever.

As several authors of this book have pointed out, while there were architects and self-conscious architecture at least from the agricultural/civilizational era onward, architects' duties and the performativity of their buildings were restricted pretty much to the three principles of Vitruvius plus a law of Hammurabi: their buildings should exhibit *firmitas*, *utilitas* and *venustas* (stability, utility, and beauty/delight), and not fall down. As many authors in this book point out, this is in fact to say that the buildings should be performative; that the concept of performativity is nothing new, per se.

Of Vitruvius' three principles, *firmitas* is of the most consequence for my discussion here since in fact most habitats of humanity did not exhibit it. People were more interested in having their habitats be easy to build, flexible, adaptable, repairable, and perhaps portable. Of course, they should not blow away with the first gust of wind, or allow rain and snow to enter freely, but permanence was not itself a prime desideratum.

Unsurprisingly, for the rich and famous it was another story. Their monuments were meant not only to be useful and beautiful, but also to last for all time, and so architects, whose loyalty and labor typically has always been in the service of the rich and powerful and not of ordinary folks, did their best to please their patrons. For their buildings to persist as functioning structures of awe-inspiring beauty and obedience-inducing power was a prime consideration for architect and patron alike, down to the present time.

Architecture and Modern Times

As several authors in this book have also pointed out, this preference for permanence was challenged, but by no means eliminated, by the scientific-industrial revolution that was in full force in Europe by the eighteenth century and spread globally during the nineteenth and twentieth centuries to the present whose ID is "progress" and Password is "development". Suddenly everything old that still existed was bad and should be replaced by something new that quickly itself became old, crying out for a newer new that was often just an old new forgotten and then rediscovered and idolized by new generations for whom indeed it was new. Favored architects wracked their brains, libraries, and other cultures and earlier times to come up with ideas for buildings that still expressed the Big Four, but did so in appealing new forms.

In many ways, that is where we are now: even though buildings are sometimes demolished to make way for new buildings before their paint is dry or their mortgage paid off, there is still a pretense between architects and clients that *their* building will last and function well and beautifully forever. True, the creation of new materials (steel and concrete), new energy sources (first coal, then oil), electricity and incandescent lighting, elevators and related developments in the late nineteenth and early twentieth centuries encouraged architects and architecture to take off into truly new dimensions—up, up, and away out. But except for a few spectacular improvements in glass and warm/cool air circulation; the creation of academic departments of architecture; and a huge increase in the demand for new buildings spurred by the explosive growth of global population from two billion to approaching eight billion people, there really were no major breakthroughs in performativity for a long time. Unlike many other aspects of life, even World War II did not provoke much truly new in building materials or design, except for plastics.

But since the 1960s, a revolution has been brewing, finally threatening the predominance of *firmitas*, as evidenced in many essays in this volume. One driver of this revolution is the rapid rise of quantitative techniques made ever easier by advances in the hardware, software, and orgware of computers that allows flexibility and virtuality in the consideration of alternatives in *utilitas* and *venustas* well beyond what was ever possible before. The second is the slow but steady emergence of new materials that mimic, rival, and perhaps will exceed not only anything that is possible in wood, brick, steel, and concrete, but also by organic nature itself.

These two developments are well recognized by several authors in his book. An early sentence in Chapter 14 by Achim Menges and Steffen Reichert says that "Interaction with, rather than protection from, environmental dynamics is increasingly understood as a critical characteristic of performative architecture." They add:

> [I]n various biological systems the responsive capacity is quite literally ingrained in the material itself. Employing similar design strategies of physically programming material systems rather than equipping them with additional technical devices may enable a shift from a mechanical towards a biological paradigm of climate-responsiveness in architecture.

Similarly, Michael Fox (Chapter 19.1) observes that

> As Michael Weinstock poetically states, 'Material is no longer subservient to a form imposed upon it but is instead the very genesis of the form itself.' [...] Toshiko Mori points out: 'We can theoretically produce materials to meet specific performative criteria; this transformation often takes place at the molecular level, where materiality is rendered invisible.'

Brian Cody (Chapter 20) states that through "research at my institute we have been investigating 'smart skins': façades which maximize energy performance by varying their properties to adapt to changing external and internal conditions."

Vera Parlac (Chapter 18) summarizes these observations as evidencing

> a change in attitude from architecture as an object representing an aspiration towards architecture that is an active participant in the material, social and ecological exchanges [...] Selecting a material for its properties is replaced with choosing a material for its behavior or even designing a material behavior to suit a particular design issue.

Most of these essays focus on the possibility of increasing interactivity between the inhabitants and their building. Some emphasize the need for architecture to design with nature, and especially to build so as to achieve environmental sustainability. There is a long tradition in architecture going all the way back to the beginning that declares that buildings should consciously and specifically relate to the dynamic forces of the physical environment in which they are located. Braham (Chapter 11) stresses that wind direction and velocity, temperature, differences due to varying altitudes and seasons, sunlight and cloud cover, rain, snow, flooding, drought, and the like should all be basic considerations in design and construction. However, with the new sources of energy and materials and other technologies of the past 100 years, most buildings have been designed and built specifically to ignore any features of the surrounding environment, as Brian Cody makes clear.

One of my favorites examples of this is the concrete structure housing the School of Business at the University of Hawaii at Manoa, which looks like a suped-up castle fit for medieval Europe, complete with narrow slots that seemed intended to allow archers to launch arrows at invading hordes—except they are filled with glass. There are no openable windows in the entire structure. While its overall performativity was horrible from the beginning in numerous ways (one entire wing had to be taken down almost immediately before it collapsed), it nonetheless won some kind of an architectural prize for what some judges somewhere must have thought was *venustas*. A second example is the building created about the same time to house the departments of the various social sciences at the University of Hawaii. I happened to be the representative for the political science department on an advisory committee and strongly objected when the building was also designed to be totally dependent on air conditioning with no windows that could be opened. Even though the university overseers complained about the additional cost, they finally did allow some offices to have small, openable, windows. I worked in that building for over 40 years and almost never needed to close the window, or to turn on the air conditioning, because of the steady, gentle, cooling, trade winds that wafted down Manoa Valley. Similarly, my home in Waikiki has needed neither artificial heating nor cooling since it receives wind and sun that keep the temperature and humidity balanced perfectly.

Until recently. Presumably because of global climate change, there are more and more days when the trade winds stop and humidity rises to very uncomfortable levels. Sea level rise is clearly evident in Hawaii. Waikiki—the economic engine of tourism—is built on land drained by the Ala Wai Canal that was once a swamp and eagerly seeks to become a swamp—or worse—again. Huge hotels and other buildings, situated irresponsibly close to the rising seas, are experiencing storm surges that promise soon to be shorelines of a new normal.

Everything seems to be changing, but to what and for how long and how dramatically different no one knows for sure. Only a diminishing (but politically very important) number of Deniers reject the fact of significant human-induced climate change, but while no one can be certain of the consequences and the duration of any single change or set of changes, it is a crime against future generations that so few people and institutions have turned serious attention to preparing for a world of opportunity and challenges quite different from the present or any past. Each passing day brings more scientific evidence of the abrupt discontinuities climate change might bring in all areas of life (Intergovernmental Panel on Climate Change, 2019; McKibben, 2019).

Architecture in the Early Anthropocene

From my point of view, this is a new and imminent responsibility that architects must embrace, but with a few notable exceptions, even though several authors mention climate change, most fail to treat it with the urgency I believe it requires. Notions of *firmitas* still rule—both for buildings and for the environment of buildings.

Epilogue

Futures studies has long insisted that it is no longer possible to "predict" "*THE* future" (Gidley, 2017). The best we can do, and must do, is to continuously forecast a range of alternative futures that enable us individually and collectively to anticipate and adapt to whatever changes and continuities present themselves, and also to act so that our increasingly artificial world is suitable for humans and other forms of life—and/or that humans and other life forms are modified to be evolvable in the artificial environments humans have unwittingly created.

I am among many people who are convinced that "nature is dead"—"nature" in the sense of processes and places uninfluenced by human activities. Everywhere we look there are signs of increasing human presence: "There is no place on [or under or above] Earth where the hand of man has not set foot." We need to understand that ideas of "sustainability", "preserving nature", and the like are now dangerously passé. Humans must take "responsibility for our rose". It is we who transformed a natural self-organizing wilderness into an artificial garden requiring our diligent care—and perhaps, soon, into a precarious Iron Lung demanding our total attention (Dator, 2004).

I said earlier that we *Homo sapiens sapiens* emerged in what geologists call the Holocene Epoch about 12,000 years ago. Many geologists and other scientists now say that humans have become a new, major geological force that has pushed Earth and all on it into a new epoch, the Anthropocene, as several authors in this book well understand. Claudia Pasquero and Marco Poletto (Chapter 10) observe that "In the Anthropocene Age [...] we have built [an] Urbansphere" out of

> synthetic biology, biotechnology [and] artificial intelligence, [that] opens scenarios where the boundaries between natural and artificial, landscape and city, human and non-human realms are blurred ... [This symbiosis] forces us to redefine the modern and mechanical understanding of cause–effect by re-describing the boundaries of an object within its environment and by taking into account the multiple interlocking feedback loops.

Zaera-Polo (Chapter 13.1) says that "In the Anthropocene, humans have become capable of modifying natural ecosystems, geological structures, even the climate; we have become so powerful that it is increasingly difficult to delimit the natural from the artificial." As a consequence architects should be

> primarily driven by concerns that, for the first time in history, transcend human societies and threaten the very survival of the planet [...] Rising sea levels are expected to have a massive impact on cities around the world in the coming decades, and their impact is already felt through natural disasters and plummeting real estate values.

Whalley (Chapter 5), under the heading "Architecture and the Anthropocene", declares emphatically:

> This in my mind is humankind's greatest challenge. It is both a crisis and an opportunity to restructure future development, with probably one of biggest influences on this rapid change being our built environment. *The role of the architect is instrumental in forging a long-term viable future.* A performative design approach that searches for optimized solutions is the critical and only way forward.

I put that sentence in italics because it points towards my understanding of the role of architects and architecture from now on. I would expand the word "forging" to mean *helping people and communities envision, design, build, and move towards* long-term viable futures, *on a continuing basis*. And rather than merely being "instrumental" I would say that architects must see themselves and act as pivotal in this task.

One of the most stimulating essays in this regard comes from David Benjamin (Chapter 21), who reminds us that

> When we believed that microbes were a human enemy, our definition of building performance included sterility—and in corresponding fashion our materials were smooth and synthetic, and our architecture was uniform and universal. Now that we know microbes are a human friend, our definition of building performance might evolve to include cultivating microbial life and biodiversity [...] We are reframing buildings as stewards for the urban microbiome. And we are proposing that performance extend beyond local human occupation to non-human animals and microbes, and ultimately back to global human health.

"I believe buildings are living organisms", Benjamin concludes.

> They breathe and pulse [...] buildings are not static, solitary objects dug into a single site. They are dynamic systems connecting many different places. They talk with their natural and urban contexts. They join together and cooperate with each other. They involve a longer duration and a wider geography than we typically consider.

I believe some other authors of this book would agree.

At the same time, we must act here with profound humility and care. Douglas E. Noble's contribution (Chapter 19.2) makes it very clear that, simply in the area of "active façades" alone, there are a myriad ways things can go wrong, and almost as many ways in which they might be made right while Dak Kopec (Chapter 26) reminds us of the enormous dangers to human health and wellbeing that our hermetic environments wreak now, and that Anthropocene artificiality may exacerbate even more profoundly. The ultimate failure of the Biosphere 2 Project as designed (Nelson, 2018) exemplifies how very far away we are from being able to mimic the many essential processes of Biosphere 1 (i.e., Earth) successfully. It might have been better if we had postponed the invention of agriculture so as not to interrupt natural processes (Diamond, 1992) until we understood much better how nature works. But that is futile advice now. It is like telling a teenager she should postpone puberty until she is more mature and can calmly cope with the changes she is experiencing. It is now our ethical and professional responsibility, for better or worse, ready or not, "to govern evolution" (Anderson, 1987).

Fortunately, this enormous and perhaps ultimately-impossible challenge might be able to be met because of another feature that was mentioned in several chapters in this volume, but whose implications for the future were not discussed as fully as they must be, in my view: the rapid rise of mobile, autopoietic artificial intelligence (AI) for decision-making and action-taking purposes that may ultimately surpass that of humans in many if not all cases. Many people who are aware of such "strong AI" consider it a threat to humanity. It might be, if not properly understood, directed and/or responded to (Brockman, 2019). But it also means that we have more intelligence than just what puny humans possess in order to achieve usefully "Anticipatory Architecture".

Mariana Ibañez (Chapter 7.1) exhibits an excellent understanding of how AI might change everything, referring here to drama and not to architecture:

> When nonhuman actors are not humanoid in form or are able to move at rates of speed or with agility that is beyond human [or animal] capacity, a dissonant break may form in audience communication [...] Ultimately, the question that will arise will be not of acceptance of nonhuman agents ... but of the rise of nonhuman audience members.

The monopoly on sapience that *Homo sapiens sapiens* presume to have on Earth may soon be broken as we are joined, once again, by other sapiential (and emotional) entities, this time of our own creation, who, like all children, are no longer entirely under our control or even understanding.

Ibañez mentions a poem by Richard Brautigan as capturing early on the essence of this image of the future: "All Watched Over by Machines of Loving Grace". I have used it many, many times to express what I call a "Transformational" image of the future. Brautigan imagines a world in which electronics and biology are in perfect harmony. The third and final verse envisions a future

> where we are free of our labors
> and joined back to nature,
> returned to our mammal
> brothers and sisters,
> and all watched over
> by machines of loving grace
>
> *(Brautigan, 1969)*

Will architects rise to this challenge? Can they? While the overall discussion of "educating the accountable architect" by Ted Landsmark is impressive, I regret that he does not include futures studies among the subject matter that all schools of architecture should teach, and that questions about the futures beyond "grow", or "sustainability" or even "resilience" should be included in official accrediting exams for architects. Until that happens, I doubt that most architects will feel they are obliged to fulfill their performative obligations in the Anthropocene towards their clients, the broader community, and future generations.

While at the outset I credited my baptism into the cult of performativity to David Greene and Michael Webb of the Archigram Group, several authors in this book properly put them into a broader context, citing work by Gordon Pask, Norbert Wiener, William Ross Ashby, Warren Brodey, Jack Burnham, Gregory Bateson, Nicholas Negroponte, Charles Eastman, Andrew Rabeneck, Cedric Price, Reyner Banham, John Frazer, and others (I would add from my experience Buckminster Fuller, Marshall McLuhan, John and Magda (Cordell) McHale, and Yona Friedman). Terms used by these people to describe their ideas, such as "intelligent architecture", "anticipatory architecture", "evolutionary architecture", "living architecture", "adaptive-conditional architecture", "responsive architecture", and the like should now become descriptive of almost everything architects do.

However, unlike for these pioneers, the point of performativity now should not primarily be esthetic, fanciful, "utopian", or responsive to historical patterns of nature. I believe anticipatory, adaptive, continual performativity is essential if humans are to survive and thrive in futures very different from any that humans have ever experienced. Once upon a time for a building to exhibit *firmitas* meant for it to stand its ground on *terra firma*. Now *firmitas* means that buildings must be able to co-evolve within rapidly evolving environments.

Our uncertain futures demand that all buildings be permanent only in being permanently flexible, adaptive, intelligent, anticipatory, and evolvable. Fortunately, we have or can create tools, techniques, theories, and ethical actions to make that so. Indeed, this might well be the new maxim: "Responsibly Anticipatory Evolvable Architecture", ready for whatever changes the futures bring; continuously adaptive in anticipation of perpetual change.

References

Anderson, W. T. (1987). *To Govern Evolution*. New York: Houghton Mifflin Harcourt.

Brautigan, R. (1969). Machines of Loving Grace. In *The Pill versus the Springhill Mine Disaster*. Hendersonville: Four Seasons Foundation.

Brockman, J., ed. (2019). *Possible Minds: 25 Ways of Looking at AI*. New York: Penguin.
Dator, J. (2004). Assuming "Responsibility for Your Rose". In Paavola, J., and Lowe, I. (Eds.), *Environmental Values in a Globalising World: Nature, Justice and Governance*. London: Routledge, pp. 215–235.
Dator, J. (2016). Alternative Futures in Architecture. In Kanaani, K., and Kopec, D. (Eds.), *The Routledge Companion for Architecture Design and Practice: Established and Emerging Trends*. New York: Routledge, pp. 549–564.
Dator, J., Sweeney, J., and Yee, A. (2014). *Mutative Media: Communication Technologies and Power Relations in the Past, Present, and Futures*. New York: Springer.
Diamond, J. (1992). *The Third Chimpanzee*. New York: HarperCollins.
Gidley, J. M. (2017). *The Future: A Very Short Introduction*. Oxford: Oxford University Press.
Intergovernmental Panel on Climate Change. (2019). Global Warming of 1.5 Degrees C. www.ipcc.ch/site/assets/uploads/sites/2/2018/07/SR15_SPM_version_stand_alone_LR.pdf.
McKibben, B. (2019). *Falter: Has the Human Game Begun to Play Itself Out?* New York: Henry Holt and Company.
Nelson, M. (2018). *Pushing Our Limits*. Tucson: University of Arizona Press.
Sadler, S. (2005). *Archigram: Architecture without Architecture*. Cambridge: MIT Press.
Sahlins, M. (1972). *Stone Age Economics*. Chicago: Aldine-Atherton.
Teeuwen, M., and Breen, J. (2017). *A Social History of the Ise Shrines: Divine Capital*. New York: Bloomsbury Publishing.

Index

Aarhus University 235
Abu Dhabi 48–49
Acconci, Vito 56, 59
accountable architects 505–508; education for 508–516
accreditation *see* education, for architects
Action in Perception 422
action-perception cycles 108; *see also* sense-perception
active glass walls 201–202
actor-network theory 2
adaptive architecture 46–47, 61; building envelopes 47–50; dynamic structures 50–54; interactive and reactive 58–60; lo-tech and hi-tech designs 56–58; open building 55–56; psychotropic and emotive houses 54–55
Adaptive Architecture conference (2011) 53
Addington, Michelle 214, 307, 326
Adidas office building, Herzogenaurach 352–353
aesthetics, intelligent *see* artificial intelligence (AI)
affordances 111, 213
after-action review process 155–156
agent-based occupancy simulations 293–296
agent-based parametric semiology 20–30, 295–296
Ahlquist, Sean 443–462
AHR 48–49, 50
air conditioning systems 77, 200; *see also* HVAC systems
air quality 436–437
Aizenberg, Joanna 305–306, 307
Al-Bahr Towers 48–49, 50
Albert Kahn Associates 66
Albright, Thomas 110
Alexander, Christopher 2, 448
Ali Brivanlou Lab, Rockefeller University 364
All Watched Over by Machines of Loving Grace 100
Allen, Stan 34, 288
Allianz Arena 121, 385–386
Altinişik, K. 437
Amateur Architecture Studio 90
American Institute of Architects 156, 193, 235, 505, 509
American Law Institute 489
American Society of Heating Ventilating and Air-Conditioning Engineers (ASHVE) 198

analysis software 466
Andersen, Kurt 86
Anderson, Kjell 278
Angius, Pierandrea 22, 31
Animate Form 33–34
animation 34
Anthony Hunt Associates 70, 75
Anthropocene Island Project 176
anti-architectural theories 17–18
Apollinaire, Guillaume 492
Arakawa, Shusaku 416, 417–419, 423
Araújo, Miguel B. 192
Arbib, Michael A. 103–112
Archigram 46, 66, 180
Architectural Association School of Architecture, London 22, 32–33, 33
Architectural Design 390
Architectural Engineering Collaborative 37
architectural history *see* history, architectural
Architecture and Energy 200
Architecture Machine Group 389
Architecture of the Well-Tempered Environment, The 199
Architecture or Techno-utopia 400
Architecture Principe 428
Arduino 303
ARE (Austrian Real Estate) 353
Aristotle 88, 89, 90
Armstrong, Rachel 312–313
artificial intelligence (AI) 94–95, 298, 504; architecture and environments 98–101; augmented tectonics 95–97; contracts in subsystems 107–108; and performing arts 97–98
Arup 78, 79, 106, 313
ASHRAE (American Society of Heating, Refrigerating and Air-Conditioning Engineers) 140, 406
Association of Collegiate Schools of Architecture 509
Astana, Kazakhstan 38, 182–183, 184
AT&T Global Olympic Village 384
Atelier Brückner 346
Athens Charter, The 219
Atwood, Andrew 493–494

527

Index

augmentation 94–95; architecture and environments 98–101; and performing arts 97–98; and tectonics 95–97
Austin, John L. 485
Autodesk Fractal 467
Autopoiesis of Architecture, The 20

Bachelard, Gaston 109
Ballard, James Graham 46, 54–55
Ban, Shigeru 56, 58
Banathy, B.H. 449
Banham, Reyner 199, 201–202, 400
Banvard Gallery, Ohio State University 496
Barad, Karen 302
Barlow, William Henry 66
Barnett, Jonathan 150
Bataille, George 15, 17
Bateson, Gregory 395, 400–401
Batty, M. 229
Bauhaus movement 121
Beard, John 438
Bechthold, Martin 11
Beesley, Philip 59, 60, 304, 308, 383
Bejan, Adrian 117–118
Belanger, Pierre 226
Benjamin, David 362–369
Bentley Systems' Generative Components 276
Bergerman, Schlaich 79
Bergson, Henri 421
Bernstein, Phillip 485–490, 503, 511
Bertalanffy, Ludwig von 445, 449, 451
Berthoz, Alain 447, 454
Besler & Sons 494, 499
best-performance scenarios 466, 467
'Better Places for People' 78
Beyond Modern Sculpture 392
bioclimatics 189–190, 206–207; applications to design 192–198; buildings and power hybrids 199–202; comfort criterion 202–206; law of 190–192
biological design 364–369
biological functionalism 210–217
biomimetics 327
Biomorphic Future Vision 123
BioNinja 175
Biophilia 78
bio-receptive materials 365–367
Bioscleave House 418–419
Bio.Tech Hut 182–183, 184
biotechnical forms 174–188
BIQ House 313
black box concept 399
Black Mirror 237
Bleil de Souza, Clarice 403–414
Block, Phillipe 282
Bloom canopy 306–307

Bloomberg European Headquarters 276, 277, 278–279, 280–281, 284–285
Boeckl, Matthias 287
Böke, Jens 324
Bordeaux Law Courts Projects 126
Bosco Verticale 232
botanical gardens 74–76
bound spaces 22, 23–30
Box, George E.P. 457–458
Boyer Report 510–511
Bozikovic, Alex 236
Braham, William W. 189–207
Brain Landscape: The Coexistence of Neuroscience and Architecture 108
Braithwaite, Hunter 153
Brand, Stewart 109
Braun HQ 343–346
Brautigan, Richard 100, 101
Breuer, Marcel 198
Brisbane Airport Car Park 322
British Pavilion 72–74, 384–385
Brooklyn Navy Yard 365, 367
Brooks, David 235
Brown, Scott 211
Brownell, Blaine 325
Brunel, Isambard Kingdom 66
Brunelleschi, Filippo 146–147
Buchanan, Richard 158
Budig, M. 296
Buehler, Markus J. 313
Building Centre, London 53
building envelopes 317–318, 332–333; and concepts of performance 333–334; connection and communication 319–320; energy performance 343–346, 349–350, 355–357; human and environmental mediation 320–324; and information systems 338–339; interaction and control 327–328; problems and complexities with 336–338; sensors 334–336; technological advancements 47–50, 56, 318–319, 324–326
building information modelling (BIM) 404, 406, 413, 464–465, 473, 486–487; software for custom workflows 475–480
building skins *see* building envelopes
Burbuja Lamp 42
Burdett, Richard 236
Burnham, Jack 392
Burnham, Sophy 116
business, of architecture 503–505
business spaces 22–30
Byggervangen Road, Copenhagen 266–267, 268, 269

Calatrava, Santiago 380
Campbell, Lucy 228–238
Candela, Felix 34
Capital Market Authority (CMA) Tower 323–324, 325, 326

carbon emissions 362–363, 367
Carnegie Mellon University (CMU) 135–136, 137
Carpenter, Jamie 79
Carpo, Mario 95
Carrier, Willis 197
Carsten Roth Architects 348
Cartesian grid 423
Caudill, William 151
Center for Building Performance and Diagnostics (CBPD) 135–136, 137
Centre Pompidou *see* Pompidou Centre
Chance, Robert 66
change, architectural 46–47, 61; building envelopes 47–50; dynamic structures 50–54; interactive and reactive 58–60; lo-tech and hi-tech designs 56–58; open building 55–56; psychotropic and emotive houses 54–55
Charmaz, Kathy 128
Chartered Institution of Building Services Engineers (CIBSE) 168
Chatsworth House 63
China 230, 237
Choi, Joon-Ho 132–144, 162–172
Cimmino, M. 332
Citicorp Center 150–151, 152, 159
cities *see* urban settings
City Hall, London 123
Civilization and Climate 203
Clément, Gilles 180
Cleveland Clinic 436
Climate Adaptation Plan, Copengagen 264–265
climate change 221–222, 263–264, 266, 341, 362
climate modulation 5, 8–10, 72–73; *see also* bioclimatics
Climate Near the Ground 192
climate-responsive systems *see* responsive material systems
Cloud 9 Architects 49, 50
Cloudbusrt Management Plan, Copenhagen 264–271
CMA Tower 323–324, 325, 326
Code of Hammurabi 229, 274
coding 468–469
Cody, Brian 341–360
cognitive thinking 108, 116–120, 129
Cole, Henry 64
collaboration 485–490
Colloquy of Mobiles 182
colouration 41
Commerzbank, Frankfurt 201
communication networks 224
computation 274, 363; atmospheric form 282–285; changing tools of architecture 275–277; emergence of 70–71; morphogenesis 34–35; simulation tools 278–279; software for custom workflows 473–480; structural form 281–282; terms used in 465–469; workflow variations 469–473; *see also* building information modelling; interoperability; machine learning algorithms; simulation tools
concave vs convex spaces 22–30
Concise History of Modern Sculpture, A 390–392
Confluence Park 37
Conquergood, Dwight 91
constructivist research philosophy 127–129
controlled environment agriculture (CEA) 231–232
Conversation Theory 47, 94
convex vs concave spaces 22–30
Cook, Peter 180
Coop Himmelb(l)au 349
Copenhagen 264–271
corals 175–178
Corbusier 66, 99, 103, 106–107, 108, 118, 154, 199, 200, 202, 219, 427
corporate space planning 21
creative cognition 115–117
critical thinking 117
Cronin, Leroy 312
Cross, N. 410
Crotty, Michael 126, 127
crowd modelling 20–21
Crystal Palace 64–66, 67
Cuvier, Georges 210, 211
cyber-gardens 182–184
Cybernetic Brain, The 396, 400
cybernetics 47, 327, 389–393; frameworks for experimentation 398–401; participants as performers 397–398; second-order approach 181–182, 393–396

da Vinci, Leonardo 119
Darwin, Charles 211, 212, 217, 438
Darwin's Dangerous Idea 296
data collection 132–140, 235
Data Moiré 40–41
Dator, Jim 517–525
Davis, M. 230
Dawkins, Richard 296
De Architectura 119, 320
Deamer, P. 511
Death and Life of Great American Cities, The 229–230
decision-making theory 410–412, 413
deep dive approach 157–158
deep learning 109
DeKetselier, Xavier 280, 283
DeLanda, Manuel 297, 420, 445
Deleuze, Gilles 175, 417, 420, 421, 423
Delios International 440
delivery strategies 485–490
Demetrios, Eames 158
Dennett, Daniel 15, 16, 296
depreciation 85–86

Index

design strategies 403–404; computational tools 405–406, 412–413; theories on 406–412
Design with Climate 189, 192, 193, 196, 198, 205
D.ESK 496
Dickie, G. 210
diffuse heritage 7–9
digital craft 41–44
digital morphogenesis *see* morphogenesis
digital tectonics 38–39
DiMaggio, Paul 92
Diploma Unit 11 33
discrete architecture 3
DMAA 352–353
Dome of the Rock 65
Dourish, P. 447, 453
dRMM 51, 52
drones 233–234, 236
dry-stone walls 8
DS+R 99
Duales System Pavilion 346–348
Dubai 51, 80, 81
Dublin Castle 186
Durotaxis Chair 42
Dykers, Craig 154
Dymaxion House 214
dynamic façades 47–50, 56
dynamic structures 50–54
Dynamo software 468, 471–472, 475–476, 478–480

Eames, Charles 158
Eames, Ray 158
Eastman, C. 47
Eberhard, John 108
École Centrale Paris 351–352
Ecological Approach to Perception 213
ecoLogicStudio 174–175
Eden Project 64, 74–76, 122, 375, 377
education, for architects 508–516
Ehrlich, Paul 439
emancipation *see* freedom, of action
Embedded Architecture 9–10
embedded architectures 2, 3, 4
embedded computation 380–381, 383
Embryological Houses 212
Emergence and Design Group 32–33
Emotive City 390, 399
E-motive House 55
enclosure systems *see* building envelopes
Encyclopaedia of Chemical Technology 307
endosymbiosis 175–177
energy consumption 71–72, 162–163
Energy Innovation Center, Pittsburgh (EIC) 231
energy performance 341–343; case studies 343–353; research 353–358; virtual environments 358–360
Entire Situation, The 499, 500

envelopes *see* building envelopes
Environmental Protection Agency 434, 436
Environmental Psychology for Design 435
Epigenetic Landscape 424, 426
epigenetics 436
Epiphyte Chamber 304
Eskanazi, David 494, 496
Eskenazi Hospital Parking Structure 320
ETFE (ethylene tetrafluoroethylene) 48, 49, 50, 75
Euclid 423
European Central Bank HQ 349–350
Evans, Robin 34, 283, 493
Evolutionary Architecture, An 33, 304, 328
evolutionary design solving 296–298
Experiments in Art and Technology (EAT) 389
experiments theory 407–409, 412

fabrication 32, 33, 34, 35, 38, 42
façades 140–143; *see also* building envelopes; dynamic façades
Fainstein, S.F. 506
Fanger, P.O. 203
Farbstein, Jay 154
Fathy, Hassan 5
FAZ Summer Pavilion 249–250
Fernández-Galiano, Luis 198, 200
First Office 494–496
Fisher, Scott 319
Fisher, Thomas 83–93, 512
flexible architecture *see* adaptive architecture
Flexible: Architecture that Responds to Change 52
Florence, University of 9
Florence Duomo 146–147
Focke, John 151
Foerster, Heinz Von 392
Foliente, Greg 275
Ford Motor Company 66
Forest People, The 434
Formalhaut 51, 53
form-finding 35–37, 63
Forty, Adrian 210
fossil fuels 222, 231, 341
Foster, Norman 68, 90, 123, 284
Foster + Partners 236, 276, 277, 279–281, 283, 284–285
Foundation for Critical Thinking 117
Fox, Michael 59, 317–330, 334, 378, 382
FRAC Centre 253–254, 397, 400
Frascari, Mario 217
Frazer, John 33, 304
Free to Learn 153
freedom, of action 15–17
Fresh Htwo0 Expo 425–426
Fromm, Erich 435
Frost Science, Miami 77–78, 79
FTL Design Engineering Studio 384
Fukuoka, Japan 56, 57

Fuller, Buckminster 66, 214
Fulton Center, New York 78–80
Fun Palace 47, 181
Function of the Oblique 428
functionalism 121, 210–217

Gagge, A.P. 203
Gallagher, S. 422
Gallese, Vittorio 110
Gallou, Irene 280, 283–284
Gattara, Alessandro 110
Gaudi, Antonio 34
Geddes, Robert 106
Gehry, Frank 84
Geiger, Rudolf 192, 204
Generator 47, 181
genetic algorithms 296–298
geodesic shells 75
Geoffroy, Étienne Saint-Hilaire 210
gestural language 328, 329
GHB Landscape Architects 265–266
Gibson, James J. 206, 212–213, 446–447, 451, 452, 454, 458
Gibson, L. 153–154
Gins, Madeline 416, 417–419, 423
Giorgio, Francesco di 94
Glanville, Ranulph 182, 394, 395, 397–398, 401
glazing 70–71
Gleich, Arnim von 325
global population 71, 438
global warming 72, 221–222, 263, 341, 362
Globe and Mail 236
Goethe, Johann Wolfgang von 444–445, 458
golden ratio 117–118
Goldschmidt, Richard 215–217
Good City Form 229, 230, 372
Google Sidewalk Lab, Toronto 236
Gould, Stephen Jay 216–217
Goulthorpe, Mark 314
Government Serices Center, Boston 86
Graaf, Reiner de 504
Grasshopper software *see* Rhino Grasshopper software
Graves, Michael 92
Gray, Peter 153
Great Exhibition (1851) 64, 444
Great Hypostyle Hall, Temple of Amun 375
Great Pyramids of Egypt 118
Great Stove 63, 64
Great Temple of Ramesses II 375
Greene, David 46
greenhouse gas emissions 263, 264
Griffin, T.L. 506
Grimshaw, Nicholas 68, 73–74, 375, 384–385
Grimshaw Studio 82
Grospoli terraced vineyard, Lamole 9

grounded theory 128
Guattari, Felix 175, 184–185
Guazzelli, Alex 111

Hadid, Zaha 99
Hall, E. 373
Halprin, Lawrence 157
Hammond, K. 411–412
Hanna, Sean 311
Hans Tavsens Park, Copenhagen 267–268, 270–271
Hanson, Julienne 292
Happold, Buro 80
Haque, Usman 60
Harrison, Wallace K. 66
Harvard University 311
Hayek, Friedrich 14
health factors *see* wellbeing, promotion of
Hegel, Georg Wilhelm Friedrich 15
Heidegger, Martin 417
Heidelberg University 354–355, 356
heliothermic planning 197–198
Hemmerling, Marco 324
Henaff, Elizabeth 365
Hensel, Michael 1–11, 32–33, 130, 302, 307, 314
Herman Miller factory, Bath 68
Herron, Ron 46, 70–71
Hertzberger, Herman 90
Herzog, Thomas 121, 385
HFG Offenbach 241, 243, 247
Highland Park, Michigan 66
Hillier, Bill 292
Hinged Space Housing 57
Hinte, Ed van 55–56, 60–61, 315
history, architectural 7–9, 63–69, 119–126
Hoberman, Chuck 311
Hoekstra, A.G. 177–178
Hoffman, Josef 287
HOK 323
Holl, Steven 56, 57, 59
Hollander, J.B. 117
Hollein, Hans 389
homeostats 450–451, 457, 458
Hoof, J. Van 203
Hopkins, Andrew D. 189, 190–192
Hopkins, Gerard Manley 104
Hopkins, Michael 68
HORTUS 177, 178, 179–180, 182–184
Housing and Home Finance Agency, USA 193
How Buildings Learn 109
Huang, Alvin 32–45
human interaction patterns *see* interactive architecture
human perception *see* sense-perception
human physiological data 164–172
human progress 14–15
Human-Building Integration Lab, USC 135–137
Huntington, Ellsworth 203
Husserl, Edmund 420–421

Index

HVAC systems 189, 199, 202, 203, 206, 437
HygroScope 250–254, 305
hygroscopicity 241–245
HygroSkin 253–256
Hylozoic Ground 308
Hyper Building 359–360

I, Worker 97
Ibanez, Mariana 94–102
IBM Watson Experience Centre, San Francisco 40–41
IDEO 157
IEQ (indoor environmental quality) 134–140, 162–172
Igus factory, Cologne 69
Illuminating Engineering Society of North America (IES) 168
Image of the City, The 111, 371, 374
Industry Statement on Resilience 261
Ingels, Bjarke 236, 237
Instant City 180
Institut du Monde Arabe 47, 48, 124, 213
Institute for Computational Design, Stuttgart (ICD) 242, 243, 245, 250, 257–258
Institute of Contemporary Arts, London (ICA) 182
interactive architecture 58–60, 182, 320, 370–371; human interaction patterns 371–374; impact of technology 327–328, 378–381, 383–387; interactive mediums 374–376; phenomenology of 376–378; and physically challenged users 381–382; psychological and sociological impacts 382–383
Interactive Architecture 59
interdisciplinarity 146–148, 150–154, 417; case studies 162–172; defining strategies 154–159; innovation through play 148–150; reflective practice 159–161
integrated project delivery (IPD) 489–490, 504
International Building Performance Simulation Association (IBPSA) 405
International Congress of Modern Architecture 219
International Energy Agency 72
Internet of Things 480
interoperability 279–281, 403–404, 406, 464–465, 473–480
Introduction to Cybernetics, An 392, 399
Intuition as the Basis for Creativity 116
intuitive thinking 116–117, 119–120, 129
Irata, Oriza 97
Ishiguro, Hiroshi 97
Isler, Heinz 34
Issue-Based Information System (IBIS) 339
Italian palazzo styles 292
Italian terraces 8–9
Ito, Toyo 384
Itsuko Hasegawa Architects 125

Jackson, Richard 238
Jackson Architecture 76
Jacobs, Jane 229–230, 237
James, William 420
James B. Hunt Library, North Carolina State University 154, 155, 156
James Carpenter Design Associates 80
Japanese houses 56
J.B. Pierce Laboratory of Hygiene, Yale University 203
Jenny Sabin Studio 42–44
Jensen, O.B. 228, 236
Johnson, A.R. 446
Johnson, Philip 199
just city 506–507

Kaandorp, J.A. 177–178
Kahn, Lou 148–149, 151–153
Kahn, Ned 320, 322
Kahnmann, D. 411
Kanaani, Mitra 115–130, 228–238, 370–387, 485
Kaprow, Allan 395–396
Katz, David 444, 446, 460
Kawagoe, Japan 56, 58
Kazakhstan 38
Kelly, Kevin 318
Kemp, Miles 59, 378, 382
Kensek, Karen 464–483
Keskin, A. 437
KfW Westarkade Tower 322–324
Kibble Palace 63, 65
Kinetic Lattice 308–309
kinetic systems 379–380, 383
Klein, Naomi 220, 221
Knaack, Ulrich 324
Knippers, Jan 282
Knott, Daniel 279, 283
Kolarevic, Branko 46–62, 275, 301
Koolhaas, Rem 211
Kopec, Dak 431–441
Köppen, Wladimir 191–192
Korsgade, Copenhagen 267–268, 270–271
Kronenburg, Robert 52, 381, 386
Kruger, C. 410
Kuma, Kengo 3
Kwinter, Sanford 3, 215

Lake|Flato Architects 37
Lamarck, Jean-Baptiste 211
Lambert, Kelly 235
Lambert, Léopold 17–18
Landau, Roy 390
Landsmark, Ted 502–516
Lang, Jon 126
Larkin Building, Buffalo 200
learning algorithms 304
Leatherbarrow, David 109, 419
Leçons d'Anatomie Comparée 211

Lee, Laura 512
LEED certification 505
LeMessurier, William 150–151, 159
levelling terrain 10
Lever House 200
Ley, Rob 320, 321
life, reflection of 88–90
lifespan architecture 108–109
lighting quality 163, 165, 166–168, 432
linear movement 51
Living Bricks 312–313
Living Room House 51, 53
Lloyds of London 90
LOF 199
Logic of Sense, The 421
London Illustrated News 66
London Zoo Aviary 181
Long Island Duck 211
longevity 84–85, 87, 334
Loos, Adolf 88–89, 287
Low Energy Apartment Building, Berlin 343, 344, 358
Luebkeman, Chris 130
Lumen 42–44
Lynch, Kevin 229, 230, 371, 372, 373–374
Lynn, Greg 33–34, 212, 214, 383

Macagno, Eduardo 109
machine learning algorithms 298–299, 413
Machining Architecture 427
Maison Bordeaux 51
Malecha, Marvin J. 146–161
Malkawi, Ali 301
Mallgrave, Harry Francis 110, 419
Mamelles de Tiresias, Les 492
Mangle of Practice: Time, Agency and Science 392
Manual of Political Economy 363
Martin, Leslie 1
Martins, Pim 2
Marx, Karl 14, 17
mashrabiyas 5, 47
Mason, Paul 220
material and spatial organisation complex *see* spatial and material organisation complex
Material Basis of Evolution, The 217
material systems 33, 36, 42, 301–303, 313–315, 443–446; conceiving the extra-systemic 446–447; and digital craft 41–44; eco-social forms 454–461; embedded technologies 303–304; geometry of matter 310–312; inherent and designed behaviour 304–310; metabolic materials 312–313; *see also* responsive material systems
MATONT 6–7
Matsys Design 37
May/September 320, 321
Mazria, Ed 195

McCosh, J. 210
McLuhan, Marshall 223
media façades 334
Media-TIC 49, 50, 303
meeting spaces 22–30
Melchiorri, Julian 313
Memory Cloud Detroit 391
MEMS (micro-electro-mechanical systems) 303–304
Menara Mesiniaga 125
Menges, Achim 32–33, 240–258, 302, 305, 307, 456
Meredith, Michael 493
Merks, R.M. 177–178
Merleau-Ponty, M. 100–101
Mesiniaga Tower 125
Messiah score 146, 147
metabolic materials 312–313
Meta-Folly 181
metamaterials 310–312
Meuron, Pierre de 385
Meza, Lucas R. 310, 311
Microbe Wiki 176
microbes 365–367
microclimates 9, 192–197, 204, 205
micro-electro-mechanical systems (MEMS) 303–304
Mies (van der Rohe) 66, 423
Milam, San Antonio 200
Millennium Commission 74
Miller, Kyle James 492–500, 503
Milne, A.A. 159
Milwaukee Art Museum 380
Mind in Architecture: Neuroscience Embodiment, and the Future of Design 110
Minimaforms 390, 391, 393, 397, 399, 400
minimalism 90
Minima/Maxima 38–39
Mises, Ludwig von 14
MIT (Massachusetts Institute of Technology) 193, 319, 389
modelling tools 278, 281–282, 404, 406, 413, 465; software for custom workflows 473–480; workflow variations 469–473; *see also* building information modelling (BIM)
Molinaire, Elaine 154
Mollerup, Per 107
MoMA PS1, New York 42–44
Moore, Charles 157
Mori, Toshiko 325
morphogenesis 32–34, 177–178; and digital tectonics 38–39; expanded definitions 34–35; form and performance 35–38, 302–303; material systems and digital craft 41–44; performativity expanded 44–45; polymorphism and patterns 39–41
Morphosis 99
Moses, Robert 237
MTA Public Arts Program 79
Muller House 89
Mulligan, C.E. 228, 235

Index

multidisciplinary practice 165, 168, 169–170, 504, 507–508; *see also* interdisciplinarity
Mun, Kristine 416–429
Muscle 55
Muscle Body 304
Museum of Fruit, Tokyo 125
Musicolour 94, 396, 449, 450, 451, 453–454

Nagi Museum of Contemporary Art 417
Naked House 56, 58
National Architectural Accrediting Board (NAAB) 508–510, 513
National Conference of Architectural Registration Boards (NCARB) 508, 509
National Institute of Building Services 261–262
National Institute of Mental Health 436
Negendahl, K. 404
Negroponte, Nicholas 47, 58, 94
Neimark, Anna 494
Nervi, Pier Luigi 290
Nested Catenaries 5–7
nesting spaces 24, 25
Neumayr, Robert 287–300, 503
neuroscience 103, 108–112, 422
New Bodies, New Architecture 97
New York 42–44, 56, 59, 66, 78
New York Times 149, 235
Newton, Isaac 431, 441
Nextoffice 51, 52
Niche Tactics: Generative Relationships between Architecture and Site 214
Nichols, Tom 153
Noble, Douglas E. 332–339
Noë, Alva 422
non-discrete architecture *see* embedded architectures
non-human theatre 97–98
Norwegian Outdoor Recreation Act 10
Notre-Dame Cathedral 118
Nouvel, Jean 47, 48, 124, 213
Novak, Marcos 378
NOX 424–427
NRW archive building 350–351
Nutter, Susan 154

OCEAN | SEA (Sustainable Environmental Association) 4, 8
OCEAN Architecture | Environment 10, 11
O'Donnell, Caroline 210–217
OEVAG Bank HQ 348–349
Office of the Surgeon General, USA 434–435
Oldfield, Philip 199, 201
Olgyay, Aladar 193, 195, 197–198, 200
Olgyay, Victor 189, 192, 193–196, 197–198, 200, 203
Olson, Arthur 312
Olsson, M. 228, 235

OMA 51, 351
Omrania 323
On Growth and Form 34, 363
Oosterhuis, Kas 55
open building 55–56
open plan designs 56
optimisation algorithms 466–468, 469
Origin of Geometry 420
originality 83–84
Orkney Islands 63, 64
Orpheus and Eurydice 95, 98
Ortner & Ortner 350
Oslo Fjord, Norway 10
Osterbro 265
Otto, Frei 3, 34, 36, 37, 314, 428, 446

Paddington Station, London 66
Pallasmaa, Juhani 109, 282
PAN_07 chair 311
paradoxes, in performativity 83–88, 92–93; performance as a form of making 90–91; performance as a mirror 88–90; performance as a way of moving 91–92
parametric semiology 20–30, 295–296
parametricism 18, 20–21, 22, 39, 277
Pareto, Vilfredo 363, 364
Paris Agreement (United Nations) 72
Park, J. 136
Parlac, Vera 301–315
Parthenon 118
participation 90–91, 397–398; *see also* interactive architecture
Pask, Gordon 46–47, 60, 94, 181, 182, 328, 390, 391, 392–393, 396, 398, 448, 449, 451, 453–454, 461
Pasquero, Claudia 174–188
passive house standards 202
patterns 39–41
Paxton, Joseph 63, 64–66, 67
Pedreschi, Remo 290
Peña, William 151
Peñalosa, Enrique 235–236
Penny, Simon 446
Perez Art Museum, Miami 78
Performance Architecture: Beyond Instrumentality 107, 301
performing arts 88–90, 97–100, 492–493
peripheral settings 9–11
Persepolis Palace, Iran 375, 376
Peters, Brady 274–286
Peters, Terri 263–272
Peterson, Andrew Townsend 192
Philip and Patricia Frost Museum of Science, Miami 77–78, 79
Photo.Synth.Etica 186
physical barriers 18
Piano, Renzo 90, 122, 160–161
Pickering, Andrew 392, 394, 396, 449, 450–452

Picon, Antoine 95–96, 275
pigeon towers 7, 8
Pilkington company 70
play, in projects 148–150, 151–153
Poems and Prose (G.M. Hopkins) 104
Poerksen, Bernhard 394
poetics, of architectural form 94, 100–101, 103–104, 109–112
Poetics of Space, The 109
Polancic, Allyn 328
Poletto, Marco 174–188
pollution 221, 222, 225, 231, 334
polymorphism 39–41
Pompeii 374
Pompidou Centre 90–91, 177, 179–180, 183, 250–251
poor performance 83, 85–87
population density 372, 438
Possible Tale 494–496
post-occupancy evaluation (POE) 135–140
Prague Castle Lobkowicz Palace Museum 146, 147
Pre-Architectural Programming for a Juvenile Services Center 154
Preface 494, 496
Preziosi, D. 291
Price, Cedric 47, 181
Printworks Building, Dublin Castle 186
Prinz, Wolfgang 422
private vs public sectors 87–88
problem seeking 151, 159
problems, with buildings 83, 85–87, 132, 133–134
problems/solutions theory 409–410, 412–413
procedures, of practice 493–500
Prochazka, Elsa 353
productive landscapes 8
productivity gains 14
professional practice: accountable architects defined 505–508; delivery strategies 485–490; design and business 502–505, 509; education for accountable architects 508–516
programming *see* coding
project delivery 485–490
project scaling 148
PSFS, Philadelphia 200
psychotropic houses 54–55
public vs private sectors 87–88
Pure Tension Pavilion 36–37
Python software 474, 475, 478, 479

Qin, Zhao 313
qualifications *see* education, for architects
Quickborner 294

Radiolaria 75
Ratti, Carlo 319
Ravindran, K.T. 229

reactive architecture 58–60
Read, Herbert 390–392
recycling 225–226
Reference Technology Scenario 72
reflective practice 159–160
Reflective Practitioner, The 160
Reichert, Steffen 240–258
Renaissance 19
research 115–116, 132–135; cognitive thinking 116–119; constructivist philosophy 127–129; historical overview 119–126; post-occupancy evaluation (POE) 135–140; research-by-design tools 129–130; role and types of 126–127; simulation modelling 140–144; virtual reality 144
resiliency: Cloudbusrt Management Plan, Copenhagen 264–271; definition and overview 260–262, 263–264; and sustainability 271–272, 507
Reşitoğlu, I.A. 437
responsive architecture *see* adaptive architecture
Responsive Architectures: Subtle Technologies 59
responsive material systems: ecological embedding 248–250; *HygroScope* installation 250–254; *HygroSkin* pavilion 254–256; instrumental hygroscopicity 243–245; natural systems 240–243; ongoing design research 256–258; programmed responsiveness 245–248
Reversible Destiny 418, 420
Revit software 468, 472, 475–477, 481, 482
Reynolds, Craig 294
Rhino Grasshopper software 276, 279, 280, 298, 467, 468, 469, 472–475
RhinoScript software 470, 473–475
Rialto Studio 37
Rietveld, Gerrit 56
Rifkin, Jeremy 220
Rise of the Machines: A Cybernetic History 400
Rittel, Horst W.J. 337–338, 409
rituals, of practice *see* procedures, of practice
Rizzolatti, Giacomo 422
Robinson, Philip 279
robotics 327, 383
Rogers, Richard 68, 90, 121–124, 126
Ross Ashby, William 392, 395, 396, 399, 450, 457
Rossi, Aldo 109
rotation 51
Roth, Curtis 494, 496–499
Rudolph, Paul 86
Ruiz-Geli, Enric 49, 303
rural settings 9–11

Salingaros, Nikos 320
Salk, Jonas 148–149, 151–153
Salk Institute 149
Salvation Army building, Paris 199
San Antonio River, Colorado 37
San Jose, California 234
Sankt Kjelds Square, Copenhagen 266–267, 268, 269

Index

Sanoff, Henry 157
Sapers, Carl 512
Sauerbruch Hutton 322
Saussure, Ferdinand de 22
Sayonara 97
scale ranges 11
Scandinavian Everyman's Right 10
schema theory 108
Schmitt, Otto H. 327
Schnier, Jorg 120
Schodek, Daniel 326
Schön, Donald 160, 409, 412
Schreiber, Timothy 311
Schroder House 56
Schumacher, Patrik 13–31, 39, 290–291
SCI-Arc 494
Science per Forms 97–98, 99
scientific cognition *see* cognitive science
Scott, Felicity 399–400
scripting *see* coding
Seagram Building 66
second-order cybernetics 393–396
Sejong, Korea 99–100
self-organisation 35–36, 44
Selimiye Mosque 65
semiology, parametric *see* parametric semiology
Semper, Gottfried 444
Sendai Mediatheque 384
SENSEable City (MIT) 319
sense-perception: affective experience 421–423; enactive topology 427–428; human body and architecture 417–419; science of the sensible body 419–421, 452–454; Spuybroeck's theory and works 423–427
Sensorium City 417
sensors 223–224, 334–336
SensoryPlayscape 447, 455, 456, 458, 459, 460, 461
Seville Biennale of Architecture (2008) 182
shading systems 47, 48
Shakespeare, William 89
shape-memory alloys (SMA) 307–309
Sharifi-ha House 51, 52
signification *see* parametric semiology
Silicon Valley Infomedia 497
Silk Leaf 313
Simmel, Georg 372
Simon, Herbert 299, 409, 410, 411–412
Simulation for Architecture and Urban Design (SimAUD) 405
simulation tools 130, 140–144, 278–279, 288–289, 405; agent-based occupancy simulations 293–296; and building information modelling 464; environmental simulations 289–290; evolutionary design solving 296–298; machine learning algorithms 298–299; social space 291–293; tectonic articulation 290–291
Skara Brae 63, 64

skins *see* building envelopes
Sky Reflector Net 79, 80
SLA Architects 266–268
Slavin, Kevin 365
Sliding House 51, 52
Sloot, P.M. 177–178
Smart Architecture 55, 60
smart cities 228–238, 504–505
smart materials 307–310, 325–326
SmartGeometry Group 276
Smith, Adam 14
Snohetta 154
SOA Architects 232
Socci, Paolo 9
social order 14–18
social performativity 291–293; agent-based parametric semiology 20–30; built environment as societal information progress 18–20; coordination and control 15; as demarcation criterion 13–14; freedom and emancipation 15–17; human progress via societal progress 14–15; spatio-visual semiological systems 21–30
societal information processes 18–20
Society of Building Science Educators (SBSE) 195
Socrates 228
software *see* modelling tools, simulation tools
Soho, New York 365, 367
solar control 193–195
Solar Control and Shading Devices 198, 205
Solar Energy Fund (MIT) 193
SolarLeaf 313
Some Dark Products 496–499
South Korea 230
Southern Cross Station, Melbourne 76–78
space syntax 292–293
spatial and material organisation complex 4–5
spatial confinement 435–436
spatial order 14–15, 20, 293–296
spatio-morphological signification 18–19
spatio-visual semiological systems 21–30
Spencer, Herbert 213
Spuybroeck, Lars 416, 423, 424–426
Spyropoulos, Theodore 389–401
St. Pancras Station, London 66
Stacey, Michael 53
Stanford Encyclopedia of Philosophy 370
Stein, Richard 200
Stember, Marilyn 159
StemCloud 2.0 182
Stephens-Davidowitz, S. 235
Stepner, Michael 228–238
Sterk, Tristan d'Estree 55, 59, 60
Stewart, R.K. 260–262
Stonehenge 119, 375, 376
Storefront for Art and Architecture 56, 59, 365
structural stripes 38
Stubbins, Hugh 150–151, 159

StudFindr 499
Studio Hadid, Vienna 289, 291, 293
Studio Integrate 8
Sullivan, Louis 121, 211
Sullivan, Patrick 154
Sung, Doris 306–307
Sunguroğlu Hensel, Defne 1–11
sunk costs 85–86
SuperTree 185
Sussman, A. 117
sustainability 2, 8, 263, 271–272, 362–363, 384–385, 505; *see also* resiliency
Sustainability Pavilion 80–82
Sydney Opera House 104–106
Synthesis Design + Architecture 36, 40, 42
synthetic intelligence *see* artificial intelligence (AI)
system morphology 247–248
Szybalski, Waclaw 312

Taghaboni, Alireza 51
Tangible Interaction 319
Tasinge Square, Copenhagen 265–266
Tatsuno, S. 231, 236
Taubman College Liberty Research Annex 494
teamwork *see* multidisciplinary practice
tectonics 38–39, 95–97, 290–291
Telkes, Maria 193, 204
terraces 8–9
The Living 363, 365
theatre 88–90, 97–100
Theory and Design in the First Machine Age 400
thermal comfort 202–206
thermal sensation 164, 165–166, 167
Therme at Vals 111–112
TheVeryMany 38–39, 41
Thompson, D'Arcy Wentworth 34, 212, 213, 214, 301, 363–364, 445, 457
Titchener, Edward B. 110
Tokyo-Montana Express, The 100
tools 275–277; *see also* modelling tools; simulation tools
Tour Vivante 232
Townsend, A.M. 228–229, 236
Training Wheels 496, 497
transdisciplinarity 146–148, 150–154, 417; case studies 162–172; defining strategies 154–159; innovation through play 148–150; reflective practice 159–161
transformability 385–386
transformative architecture *see* adaptive architecture
Translations from Drawings to Building 34
transportation 372–373
TREDJE NATUR 265, 269
Tsui, Eugene 123
Tucker, Simon 408, 409
Turnbull, Colin 434
Turner, Victor 90
Typical Forms and Special Ends in Creation 210

Ubiquitous Site/Nagi's Ryoanji/Architectural Body 417–418
UCL, London 187
Ulrich, R.S. 435
UN (United Nations) *see* United Nations (UN)
unbound spaces 22, 23–30
Understanding Media 223
Unité d'habitation 200
United Nations Secretariat Building 66
United Nations (UN) 201, 221, 437; Environment Programme 263; global population 71–72, 230; Intergovernmental Panel on Climate Change (IPCC) 261, 362
United States Department of Agriculture 190, 191
United States Department of Energy 78
United States Green Building Council (USGBC) 440
United States National Climate Assessment 261
University of Southern California (USC) 135–137
Urban Designs as Public Policy 150
urban farming schemes 9
urban settings 9–11, 71–72; health effects 437–438; human relationships with 371–374; of the near future 219–226; smart cities 228–238, 504–505
Urbana Studio 320, 321
US Agency for International Development (USAID) 438
Uzton, Jorn 105–106

Varela, Francesco 422
Vaudoyer, Léon 211
Vaulted Willow 41
ventilation systems 47, 77, 78
Venturi, Robert 211
Vers Une Architecture 106–107
vertical farming 357–358
Villa Savoye 427
Virilio, Paul 427–428
virtual environments 358–360
virtual reality 144
Vitruvian criteria 13
Vitruvian Man 119
Vitruvius 119, 120, 215, 320, 513
Vogel, Craig 158

Waddington, Conrad 424, 426
Walking City 46
Walter, William Grey 395
Wang, Lei 22, 31
water management 221–222, 232–233, 346–348
Waterloo Terminal, London 70–71
Webber, Melvyn 337–338, 409
Weber, Max 17
Weiner, Norbert 449
Weinstock, Michael 32–33, 302–303
wellbeing, promotion of 264, 271, 431–432, 439–441; indoor lifestyles 433–435, 435, 439; interior pollutants 435–437; nature's benefits 435;

537

Index

reliability and replicability 432–433; urbanisation and globalism 437–438
Wells Cathedral 65
wetGRID 424, 425
Wetter, Michael 280
Whalley, Andrew 63–82
When Brains Meet Buildings 108
Whitehead, Hugh 274
wicked problems 337–338, 410
Wiener, Norbert 327
Wilde, Pieter de 403–414
Wilson, E.O. 78
wind power 76–78
windcatchers 5
Windhover, The 104
Winnie-the-Pooh 159
Wirth, Louis 372
wood 243–244, 365–367
Woolf, Carla 116
work spaces 22–30
World Expo (1992) 72, 73, 384–385
World Expo (2000) 346
World Expo (2020) 80, 81
World Graph model 111
World Green Building Council 72, 78
World Health Organization 221, 433, 438, 439
World Urbanization Prospects (United Nations) 71
Wright, Frank Lloyd 90, 92, 199
Wriston, Walter B. 150–151
Wu, Yihui 22, 31
Wyss Institute 311

XenoDerma 187
Xu, Yanling 22, 31

Yazd, Iran 375, 377
Yeang, Ken 125

Zaera-Polo, Alejandro 219–226
Zaroukis, E. 187
Zheng, Lei 22
Zucchi, Cino 353
Zumthor, Peter 111–112, 283